Building Cycles

For Kerstin, Anna and Christina,
who have been very patient.

Building Cycles
Growth & Instability

Richard Barras

Property Market Analysis
London

(W)WILEY-BLACKWELL

A John Wiley & Sons, Ltd., Publication

Library of Congress Cataloging-in-Publication Data

Barras, Richard.
Building cycles : growth and instability / Richard Barras.
    p. cm. — (Real estate issues)
  Includes bibliographical references and index.
  ISBN 978-1-4051-3001-1 (pbk. : alk. paper) 1. Cities and towns—Growth.
2. Community development, Urban. 3. Business cycles. 4. Construction industry.
5. Real property—Valuation. I. Title.
  HT153.B3435 2009
  307.76—dc22
                                                                      2009011834
A catalogue record for this book is available from the British Library.

Set in 9/12pt Trump Mediaeval by Macmillan Publishing Solutions, Chennai, India
Printed and bound in Malaysia by Vivar Printing Sdn Bhd

1 2009

The Royal Institution of Chartered Surveyors is the mark of property professionalism worldwide, promoting best practice, regulation and consumer protection for business and the community. It is the home of property related knowledge and is an impartial advisor to governments and global organisations. It is committed to the promotion of research in support of the efficient and effective operation of land and property markets worldwide.

Real Estate Issues

Series Managing Editors

Stephen Brown   Head of Research, Royal Institution of Chartered Surveyors
John Henneberry   Department of Town & Regional Planning, University of Sheffield
K.W. Chau   Chair Professor, Department of Real Estate and Construction, The University of Hong Kong
Elaine Worzala   Professor, Director of the Centre for Real Estate Development, Clemson University.

Real Estate Issues is an international book series presenting the latest thinking into how real estate markets operate. The books have a strong theoretical basis – providing the underpinning for the development of new ideas.

The books are inclusive in nature, drawing both upon established techniques for real estate market analysis and on those from other academic disciplines as appropriate. The series embraces a comparative approach, allowing theory and practice to be put forward and tested for their applicability and relevance to the understanding of new situations. It does not seek to impose solutions, but rather provides a more effective means by which solutions can be found. It will not make any presumptions as to the importance of real estate markets but will uncover and present, through the clarity of the thinking, the real significance of the operation of real estate markets.

Books in the series

Greenfields, Brownfields & Housing Development
Adams & Watkins
978 0 632 0063871

Planning, Public Policy & Property Markets
Edited by Adams, Watkins & White
9781405124300

Housing & Welfare in Southern Europe
Allen, Barlow, Léal, Maloutas & Padovani
9781405103077

Markets and Institutions in Real Estate & Construction
Ball
978140510990

Neighbourhood Renewal and Housing Markets
Edited by Beider
9781405134101

Mortgage Markets Worldwide
Ben-Shahar, Leung & Ong
9781405132107

The Cost of Land Use Decisions
Buitelaar
9781405151238

Urban Regeneration in Europe
Couch, Fraser & Percy
9780632058412

Urban Sprawl
Couch, Leontidou & Petschel-Held
9781405151238

Real Estate & the New Economy
Dixon, McAllister, Marston & Snow
9781405117784

Economics & Land Use Planning
Evans
9781405118613

Economics, Real Estate & the Supply of Land
Evans
9781405118620

Development & Developers
Guy & Henneberry
9780632058426

The Right to Buy
Jones & Murie
9781405131971

Mass Appraisal Methods
Kauko & d'Amato
9781405180979

Economics of the Mortgage Market
Leece
9781405114615

Housing Economics & Public Policy
O'Sullivan & Gibb
9780632064618

Mortgage Markets Worldwide
Ben-Shahar, Ong & Leung
9781405132107

International Real Estate
Seabrooke, Kent & How
9781405103084

British Housebuilders
Wellings
9781405149181

Forthcoming

Transforming the Private Landlord
Crook & Kemp
9781405184151

Housing Markets & Planning Policy
Jones & Watkins
9781405175203

Towers of Capital: office markets & International financial services
Lizieri
9781405156721

Affordable Housing & the Property Market
Monk & Whitehead
9781405147149

Property Investment & Finance
Newell & Sieracki
9781405151283

Housing Stock Transfer
Taylor
9781405170321

Real Estate Finance in the New Economic World
Tiwari & White
9781405158718

Contents

Preface

Most economists of the nineteenth and early twentieth centuries believed that an understanding of economic processes was enhanced by examining real historical events. They also believed in talking to real businessmen and studying the fortunes of actual companies. Many modern economists do neither. Economic theory today is far more mathematically elegant than it was a century ago, but that advance has been achieved at the cost of some loss of realism. Its practitioners sometimes seem to forget that economics remains a social science, as they develop theories which represent a world that they believe should exist, rather than one that they observe does exist. Economic cycles are an area of study in which theory is especially prone to drift apart from reality.

As far as possible, I have sought to ground this study of building cycles within their historical context. I have also drawn on 25 years of experience acting as a consultant to the property industry, first in Britain, then in Europe and, most recently, worldwide. As American pioneers of building cycle research such as Homer Hoyt and Clarence Long discovered, working with property investors and developers provides invaluable insights into the problems faced by an industry in which each product is unique, in which the lead times are the longest of any capital goods sector, and in which there is extreme uncertainty attached to each investment decision. Such insights have strongly influenced the approach adopted in this book.

In the Introduction to his landmark study of *Building Cycles and Britain's Growth*, the economist J. Parry Lewis offered his view on how to undertake a proper study of building cycles:

'I have been forced to conclude that the building cycle presents a problem of method as well as of theory, and that if it is to be properly studied either a mathematically minded economist must turn to history, or an economic historian must invoke some mathematics' (Parry Lewis, 1965: 1).

This is valuable advice which I have attempted to follow in writing my book some 40 years later. The adopted approach is unashamedly eclectic, mixing the qualitative with the quantitative, economic history with econometric analysis. Such eclecticism is, I believe, in tune with a new spirit of enquiry which is beginning to permeate economic theory. Some economists are now experimenting with ideas about the indeterminacy of outcomes in complex non-linear systems, ideas which have originated in theoretical physics and have come to influence other fields of study such as biological evolution. When multiple outcomes are possible, the path of economic development is historically dependent: it cannot be predicted without the knowledge of the sequence of historical events that have shaped it. In other words, history matters – and this is nowhere more apparent than in the study of building cycles. Though the processes which cause these cycles may be broadly invariant through time, each occurs in a unique historical context, and each contributes differently to the trajectory of economic growth and urban development.

A further question arises as to the best way to combine historical analysis with economic theory. Over the past 40 years there has been a fierce debate about the validity of the 'new economic history' school which emerged at the end of the 1950s. The devotees of this school champion a positivist approach to the quantification of economic history through the construction of econometric models, aiming to explain historical processes through causal relationships derived from neoclassical theory. The limitation of the method is that it can dispense with too much of the concrete reality of economic development in order to accommodate the formal requirements of the model structure: the complexity of history is subordinated to the simplification of econometrics. The distinguished economic historian David Landes highlights why the abstractions of the new economic history school are inadequate to explain major phenomena such as the Industrial Revolution:

'Here let me state a golden rule of historical analysis: *big processes call for big causes*...I am convinced that the very complexity of large systemic changes requires complex explanation: multiple causes of shifting relative importance...' (Landes, 1994: 653)

In this spirit, an eclectic approach in which econometric models are used to illustrate a textured qualitative argument, not subsume it within a parsimonious causal structure, may be intellectually less satisfying but is almost certainly better able to capture the historical reality.

The book aims to examine the role that building cycles play in both economic growth and urban development, acting simultaneously to generate growth and propagate instability. For investment in buildings contributes not only to the productive capacity of the economy but also to the fabric and infrastructure of our towns and cities. Just as building cycles are the source of the greatest volatility in economic growth, so they act both to propel and destabilize urban development. Each cycle creates a new vintage of buildings of distinctive specification, style and location; each vintage makes a unique contribution to the capital stock and urban fabric of an economy, while at the same time hastening the obsolescence of previous vintages. New buildings are designed to meet the economic and social needs of their time, while existing buildings, designed for earlier times, must be adapted as best they can to accommodate changing occupier requirements. This tension between slowly changing urban forms and rapidly changing urban functions is what ties urbanization and economic development together through the medium of building investment. For this reason, it forms the unifying theme of the following narrative.

Work on the book was started long before the American housing market crash which precipitated the global economic crisis of 2008, with ramifications potentially as profound as those which followed the Wall Street Crash of 1929 and the Great Depression of the early 1930s. Without stretching the patience of my publisher to breaking point, no conclusive analysis of these events can be offered here. That must await the efforts of future commentators. However, what I have endeavoured to do is indicate how this latest crisis offers a particularly spectacular example of a phenomenon which has been observed at fairly regular intervals during the past 300 years and more. Property markets are particularly prone to generate speculative booms in which over-building and price bubbles go hand in hand, and when such booms go bust the effects are likely to be transmitted to the wider economy with devastating results. In the boom years building investment is viewed as a generator of growth; during the slump attention switches to the building cycle as a propagator of instability. In the spirit of the great Austrian economist Joseph Schumpeter, my main message is that these are but alternative manifestations of the same process of capitalist development: the price of growth is instability.

I would like to acknowledge the help and support received from people I have worked with in two separate but interwoven strands of my professional life. My interest in building cycles was first aroused when I was undertaking research at the Centre for Environmental Studies (CES) in London during the 1970s. The dramatic boom–bust cycle of the early 1970s caused me to wonder why such events occurred, how universal they were and what were their wider effects. The CES was a very creative intellectual environment in which to work, and I am grateful to Andrew Broadbent, Doreen Massey, Alejandrina Catalano and Dieneke Ferguson in particular for the discussions and collaboration which helped me to formulate my early ideas.

During the 1980s, I became interested in the impact of technical change on economic and urban development, working first at the Technical Change Centre in London, under Sir Bruce Williams, and then as a visiting research fellow at the Science Policy Research Unit (SPRU), University of Sussex, under Professor Christopher Freeman. The work of Chris Freeman and his team at SPRU was inspirational, because it has revived interest in the long-term cyclical interaction of technical change and economic growth, drawing particularly on ideas first advanced by Schumpeter. These ideas have informed much of my historical analysis of the building cycle.

In 1981, David Cadman and I founded Property Market Analysis (PMA), a research consultancy designed to provide objective analysis and forecasts of property market conditions for the international community of investors and developers, initially confined to the United Kingdom but then broadening out to cover European and, more recently, global markets. Because of my involvement with PMA since the beginning of the 1980s, the majority of my professional life has been spent working in private consultancy rather than academia. Nevertheless, for the reasons outlined above, consultancy has provided a fruitful environment in which to further my understanding of the building cycle. Indeed, partnership with David Cadman has proved to be the most creative and rewarding relationship of my working life. For the intellectual stimulus of our professional collaboration and the warmth of his personal friendship, I offer David heartfelt thanks.

Soon after PMA was established, we were joined by Carol Wright, and it was the three of us who together built the practice over the next 20 years. Carol's contribution was equally vital to the success of the business, both in terms of the development of our consultancy skills and the management of our clients. I owe her a considerable debt of gratitude, in further acknowledgement of my good fortune in choosing two business partners who also became personal friends – not something that is always easy to achieve in the world of consultancy.

In recent years, the management and direction of PMA has passed to a new generation of Partners, and I would like to thank all of them for their support and help during the writing of this book. They are Paul Clark, Stephen Waterman, Marc Espinet, Martin Kemp, Raimund Noss, Nicholas Price, Ian Wells, Lorna Fraser, Melanie Hare and Catherine Kervennic. In addition I would like to thank those PMA Associates who have provided particular assistance with parts of the analysis: Christina Burbanks, Philip Hammond, Christopher Jessop, Kelly Whitman and Edward Whittall. To all the clients, too numerous to mention, with whom PMA has worked over the years, acknowledgements are due for revealing the challenges they face in confronting the risks and opportunities inherent in that most turbulent of markets, the property market.

Special thanks are due to my publisher, Madeleine Metcalfe, for her tolerance and understanding in the face of my repeated delays in delivering a manuscript somewhat larger, and considerably later, than had originally been anticipated.

Finally, and most importantly, I want to thank my wife Kerstin without whose advice and support I would not have become an economist, nor embarked upon a career in property research, nor undertaken the writing of this book. By reading and commenting upon the draft text, she has offered invaluable suggestions for improving the structure and presentation of the argument; the shortcomings which remain, I willingly acknowledge to be entirely my responsibility.

Abbreviations used in the text

BEA	Bureau of Economic Analysis (US Department of Commerce)
BLS	Bureau of Labor Statistics (US Department of Labor)
DCLG	Department for Communities and Local Government (United Kingdom)
DfT	Department for Transport (United Kingdom)
FHWA	Federal Highway Administration (US Department of Transportation)
FRB	Federal Reserve Board (United States)
GLA	Greater London Authority
HSUS	Historical Statistics of the United States
IPD	Investment Property Databank
NBER	National Bureau of Economic Research (United States)
NCREIF	National Council of Real Estate Investment Fiduciaries (United States)
ONS	Office for National Statistics (United Kingdom)
PMA	Property Market Analysis
USCB	US Census Bureau

1

Introduction: A Historical Approach

The idea of cyclical growth

The idea that the world is subject to a continuous cycle of flux and change originated with the early Greek philosophers. As their ideas developed and spread during the sixth century BC, there emerged two opposing views as to the nature of the physical world. For the South Italian school, as personified by Parmenides of Elea 'Study of matter gave way to the study of form' which led to 'an unqualified denial of physical movement and change' (Guthrie, 1962: 4–5). In contrast, Heraclitus of Ephesus, schooled in the Ionian tradition, believed in a law of cyclic change such that 'Rest, not movement, was the impossibility. Any apparent stability was only the result of a temporary deadlock between the opposite tensions which were ceaselessly at work' (Guthrie, 1962: 5). Heraclitus's world view is summarized by the famous statement attributed to him by Plato: 'you cannot step into the same river twice', which Plato interpreted to mean that 'everything moves on and nothing is at rest' (Guthrie, 1962: 450).

It is not perhaps too fanciful to observe some similarities between the world view of Heraclitus and that of the nineteenth century classical economists, who sought to describe the historical, non-equilibrium processes by which an economy develops, and twentieth century economists such as Schumpeter, who were concerned with the cyclical motion of economies under the impact of technological innovation and institutional change. In contrast, echoes of Parmenides can perhaps be heard among the neoclassical economists of the twentieth century, with their ahistorical emphasis on the behaviour of economies that are either in a static state of general equilibrium or moving smoothly between a succession of such states along an equilibrium growth path (Schabas, 1995).

The built environment offers perhaps the most extreme example of the dichotomy between these opposing world views. At any point in time, the physical fabric of our towns and cities appears to be the most permanent and fixed aspect of the material world in which we live. Yet these built forms are the product of dynamic processes of economic growth and urban development that are subject to just that cyclical flux and change to which Heraclites alluded. The longer the time frame within which buildings are viewed, the more impermanent they seem: less as solid forms and more as transient manifestations of human activity.

The City of London offers a useful illustration of this paradox. Though the City today appears to be the quintessential central business district of a modern metropolis, densely packed with office buildings, it contains within it echoes of a building history stretching back over two thousand years. Roman walls, the Norman Tower, the medieval Guildhall and classical St. Paul's Cathedral are among the most prominent surviving monuments of that building history. They are the standing survivors of what Schumpeter evocatively described as the 'gale of creative destruction' (Schumpeter, 1943: 84). And the gale blows ever more fiercely today. Offices have been the main focus of construction activity in the City since the mid-nineteenth century, proceeding through a succession of development cycles, each of which has produced a distinct vintage of building stock. Yet most of the office buildings from earlier vintages have been 'blown away', demolished to make way for larger, higher-quality and technically more advanced replacements. Furthermore, the pace of obsolescence and redevelopment is accelerating, as the flux of investor and occupier demand intensifies: the City's office stock may look permanent today, but much of it will be gone tomorrow.

A historical perspective

The aim of this book is to explore the cyclical forces which drive economic growth and urban development, as manifested through investment in the buildings that make up the physical fabric of cities. The basic argument is that the key determinants of urban investment can be encapsulated in two interrelated processes – of innovation and accumulation – and that these are subject to cyclical forces that propel urban development along its secular growth path. In order to understand how these forces change the form and function of cities, there are attractions in adopting a holistic 'processual' approach of the type that has become increasingly popular in the social sciences. Historians and archaeologists have been in the forefront of developing such methods; they have sought to articulate cultural and material change over long periods of time by examining the interaction of different spheres of human activity – economic, technological, demographic, social, institutional, political and cognitive. In so doing, they have borrowed rather eclectically from a range of disciplines and theoretical approaches (Renfrew and Bahn, 1991: 405–34). What characterizes the approach is a focus on the dynamic, non-equilibrium behaviour of social systems as they evolve within their particular historical context.

The classic application of historical analysis to urban development remains *The City in History* by Lewis Mumford (1966). He deploys an impressive range of themes to trace the evolution of cities from the first urban settlements of Mesopotamia to the modern metropolii of Europe and North America; en route he covers architecture and crafts, religion and philosophy, and politics and sociology, just as much as technology and economics. The work of the French historian Fernand Braudel offers a more formal example of the processual approach.

He distinguishes three levels of historical analysis: the surface phenomena of specific events (*les événements*), the rhythms of cyclical change underlying superficial events (*les conjonctures*) and the secular trend of long-term evolutionary development (*la longue durée*). Each of these levels of analysis operates over very different timescales (Braudel, 1980: 74–6). A recent example is provided by Fischer (1996), who has analysed price records from Western Europe and the United States going back to the twelfth century, and identified four great waves of inflation that have marked the 'rhythm of history' as it has progressed through nearly a millennium of economic, social, political and cultural change.

A brief return to our London example illustrates how the processual approach might be applied. The construction, bankruptcy and resurrection of the Canary Wharf project in Docklands was the crowning event of the late 1980s/early 1990s office building boom in London. In turn, this boom was a particularly spectacular example of the pronounced cyclical tendency in London office development that has been apparent since the mid-nineteenth century. And, more fundamental still, this office building cycle is but a recent irregularity superimposed on the long-term evolution of London from a provincial city on the edge of the Roman Empire to one of the three most important nodes in the global financial economy. Here it should be noticed that moving through the layers of explanation increases both the level of generality and the timescale over which the explanation is applied.

By adopting a historical analysis of the cyclical forces which drive economic growth and urban development, four propositions run through the book:

1 In economies at different stages of development, endogenous propagation processes combine with irregular exogenous shocks to create a cyclical tendency for building activity to progress through alternating phases of boom and slump.
2 As the most volatile member of the family of investment cycles, building cycles help to propel the trajectory of economic growth as it develops through the accumulation of productive capital and the embodiment of technical progress.
3 Successive cycles produce distinct vintages of building stock embodying innovations that are a crucial component of the process of urban development, whereby evolving urban functions both adapt to and shape urban forms.
4 The volatility of property markets affects the flows of investment into buildings as a store of wealth as well as a component of productive capital, creating fluctuations in asset values that echo and intensify the cyclical accumulation of physical stock.

Growth and cycles are two aspects of a single process of economic development: rather than viewing cycles as mere deviations around a long-run equilibrium growth path, they should be seen as providing the very dynamic which propels an economy to progressively higher levels of activity. Surges of investment provide the impetus for economic growth by delivering successive vintages of capital stock that expand productive capacity, install new technologies and introduce new products. Lags in construction and market adjustment create an endogenous tendency for investment to fluctuate between overshoot and correction, a tendency that is accentuated by the impulse of historical events. Since buildings are the most durable component of capital stock, and have the longest construction lags, building cycles tend to be the most volatile and prolonged of any economic cycles. The unstable nature of building investment impacts upon the trajectory of economic growth, the flows of financial investment and the profile of urban development.

It is important to recognize that the motion of each building cycle differs from the last in terms of its timing, duration and severity, because each is the result of a unique combination of market conditions and external events. Similarly, each cycle produces a unique vintage of buildings distinguished by the prevailing technologies and occupier requirements which shaped it. Herein lies the danger of adopting too deterministic an approach to describing the processes of cycle propagation. Building cycles, like other economic cycles, are historically dependent; their behaviour evolves in response to changing economic, technological and institutional conditions. The most satisfactory approach to their study is therefore to combine a theoretical framework which explains the cyclical behaviour of building investment with a long-run historical perspective that describes how observed sequences of cycles have moved through time.

Historical examples

Building booms have been recorded throughout history. Two examples are offered here to illustrate how particular combinations of historical events can create such booms, even when the market processes that make such booms a persistent phenomenon in modern capitalist economies are absent or under-developed. Picking up on the central theme, these historical examples also demonstrate how building booms act as drivers of economic growth, wealth creation and urbanization.

Imperial Rome

During the rule of the Emperor Hadrian (117–138 AD), there was a major construction boom in Rome and its harbour city of Ostia that was qualitatively as well as quantitatively different from the building activity that had gone before. This wave of construction can be attributed to a combination of factors:

- Population and economic output had grown strongly during the previous 50 years, as conquest expanded the Roman Empire to its maximum extent; one result was that the commercial and administrative demands of this vast Empire were creating a rapidly growing middle class enjoying an era of growing prosperity (Scheidel et al., 2007: 592–618).
- There had been a technological revolution in construction methods brought about by the adoption of brick-faced concrete as the main building material; this favoured larger-scale, industrialized structures and a simpler architectural style than that which had prevailed previously (Bowman et al., 2000: 764–5).
- A reduction in the price of the new building techniques and materials had been achieved through the reorganization of the brickyards in Rome under Trajan and Hadrian, making it economically viable to build on a mass-produced scale to meet the growing demands of the middle class (Ward-Perkins, 1981: 146).

The result was the standardized construction of multi-storey apartment blocks, shops, workshops and warehouses on a much more intensive scale than previously:

> 'Pressures of population and the rise in land values made for tighter, more economical planning, the most conspicuous manifestation of which was a tendency to build upwards all those types of building that lent themselves to such a development. Shops with apartments over them, apartment-houses of three, perhaps in places even four or five, storeys, commercial buildings of two and sometimes three storeys became the regular rule' (Ward-Perkins, 1981: 151).

In Ostia, the Hadrianic building boom created the infrastructure required to accommodate the growth in trade passing through Rome's main harbour. Building investment thus sustained the commercial development on which the health and wealth of the Empire was so dependent, maintaining Rome's unique position as a 'city of wonders at the heart of a mobile world' (Bowman et al., 2000: 405). After the building boom ended, there is evidence of a slump in brick production and the bankruptcy of smaller producers. Building output did not recover until Septimus Severus (193–211 AD) initiated a new programme of public works at the start of the next century (Ward-Perkins, 1981: 135).

Here we can observe that same combination of economic, technological and institutional factors which translate rising occupier demand into more intensive patterns of development in the modern city. Furthermore, the response of the building industry to economic growth appears to have been no more measured and proportionate in Ancient Rome than it is in the modern world; rather it proceeded through those alternating phases of boom and slump that are so familiar today.

Tudor and Stuart London

Around 1550, the Tudor city of London was still contained within the walls built more than 1300 years earlier by the Roman founders of the city. In other words, the city and City of London were still synonymous. Its population at that time has been estimated at some 75,000, probably less than the city contained at the peak of the Roman occupation, and much less than Europe's leading cities of the day – Naples, Venice and Paris (Boulton, 2000: 316). During the mid-sixteenth century, the combination of expanding international trade and commerce, population growth and religious reform generated the first real estate boom in London's modern history. The dissolution of the monasteries during the Reformation created the institutional trigger for this boom, as the Crown sold off or gifted prime City sites to courtiers and officials, creating a new class of rentier landlords. As Porter (1994: 37) puts it:

> 'A hectic property market followed, encouraging opportunistic redevelopment comparable perhaps to the speculative fever following the Second World War. And this real estate boom occurred just when population was soaring and the economy was hotting up. With the buyers' market in land and property created by the Dissolution promoting new workshops and housing, the Reformation fuelled London's economic expansion'.

In other words, this building boom both fed off and reinforced London's accelerating growth. Not only was there widespread rebuilding within the old City, but the first major wave of suburban expansion rolled out beyond its boundaries. By 1600, the population of London had reached 200,000; it had become the third largest city in Europe and was rapidly catching up with Paris.

Despite periodic government attempts at containment, the suburban expansion of London gathered pace during the seventeenth century, as the resident population of the City decentralized to cheaper locations and more profitable and intensive commercial uses occupied the central area. At the time of the Great Fire in 1666, only a quarter of London's population remained within the old City boundaries. Though the Fire destroyed most of the medieval City, piecemeal but regulated rebuilding by individual property owners was favoured by the City Corporation over expensive, large-scale master planning, both in recognition of the realities of fragmented land ownership and as the way to hasten economic revival. The result was that within less than ten years, most private houses were re-occupied, major commercial buildings had been rebuilt and trade was flourishing again (Reddaway, 1940). Once more, a major building boom in London had provided a catalyst for a new surge of growth.

During the development bonanza that followed the Fire, important institutional innovations occurred which would have a crucial bearing upon the future development of London. One of the key figures of the period was Nicholas Barbon, often identified as London's first speculative developer (Jenkins, 1975: 41). He perfected the technique of acquiring dilapidated properties at prices below their redevelopment value and then profitably rebuilding on credit at a higher density, using standardized designs and construction methods that allowed for tight cost control. Equally important were the building leases pioneered by the Earl of Southampton in the 1660s; these long leases were issued to house-builders at low ground rent on the conditions that the properties were built to a specified standard and their ownership eventually reverted to the landowner. By this arrangement, the landowner obtained a regular income for little capital outlay yet kept long-term control of his estate, while the speculative builder used bank borrowings to underwrite his development profit. 'Here we have the beginning of that system of speculation by hereditary landlords which brought half London into being' (Summerson, 1978: 40).

An illustrative building cycle: London (1714–1900)

By the start of the eighteenth century, London's dominance of domestic and overseas trade had fuelled its growth to such an extent that it had become the largest city in Europe, with a population of some 575,000. During the next two centuries, Britain became the first nation to undergo an Industrial Revolution and to establish the institutions of a modern capitalist economy. The development of London was integral to this national economic transformation: there evolved within the metropolis a uniquely diversified economy embracing manufacturing, commerce and finance that was the dynamo of Britain's national and international expansion.

During the eighteenth century, the City of London consolidated its role as the nation's centre of trade and commerce, and began its transformation into an international financial centre, while in the West End the seat of government at Westminster acted as the nucleus for the development of elegant residential estates to house the nation's rich and powerful. During the nineteenth century, progressive waves of suburban expansion swallowed up surrounding villages and rural areas to accommodate the city's new industries and house its burgeoning middle and working classes. Each major wave of expansion was facilitated by a burst of infrastructure investment – firstly in roads and then in railways (Rasmussen, 1982: 134–9 and Olsen, 1976: 308–19). The cumulative result was that by the middle of the nineteenth century London was propelled into first place among world cities, with a population that grew at an accelerating pace from 1.12 million in 1801 to 2.68 million by 1851 and 6.59 million by 1901 (Mitchell, 1988: 25). So dominant was London at its apogee in 1875 that it was almost twice as large as Paris and four times the size of Berlin (Chandler and Fox, 1974: 371).

A remarkable data series captures the trajectory of London's building during these two centuries. It is based on the records of a public registry of deeds relating to land and building transactions, predominantly for house-building, in the County of Middlesex, which covered virtually all of London north of the River Thames excluding the City itself. The full series runs from 1709 to 1914, but the period of most consistent reporting falls in the range 1714 to 1900 (Sheppard et al., 1979). The total annual number of registered deeds is illustrated in Figure 1.1 in logarithmic form, along with a smooth but variable trend that has been fitted to the series. What Figure 1.1 shows is a strong and increasing growth trend in London building during the eighteenth and nineteenth centuries, paralleling the accelerating growth of the British economy during the Industrial Revolution. As a result, there was up to 50 times as much building activity recorded at the end of the period as at the beginning. This yields a long-term average rate of growth in London building of around 1.8% per annum between 1714 and 1900, but this average conceals a secular rise from an average growth rate of around 1.2% per annum before 1750 up to around 2.4% per annum after 1850, under the growing impact of industrialization.

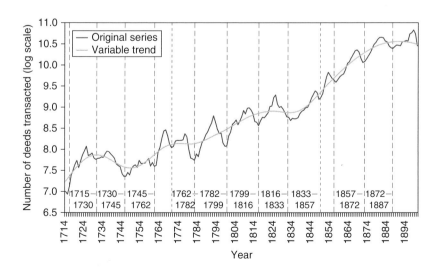

Figure 1.1   Trend in London building 1714–1900.
Source: Sheppard et al. (1979).

It is also clear that the pace of London's development was not smooth, but rather proceeded in the classic pattern of alternating booms and slumps, creating the sequence of building cycles delineated in Figure 1.1. Again quoting Porter (1994: 208): 'London was periodically overbuilt, and within the ceaseless trade cycles of boom and bust there were often more plots and properties than purchasers.' It was as a response to accelerating population growth that the supply of housing regularly moved from shortage to glut, each time unleashing a new wave of suburban development fuelled by the speculative investments of landowners, transport operators, builders and financial institutions. The processes of speculative building that drove the development of London in the nineteenth century are described in Dyos (1968: 63), who points out that 'The supply of capital for house-building certainly ebbed and flowed but there is...rather more evidence of over-building in periods of easy money than of under-building when money was tight.'

As illustrated in Figure 1.1, the period of the London building cycle during the eighteenth and nineteenth centuries is estimated to have averaged between 15 and 17 years. External triggers for the cycle included changes in population growth, wars, financial crises, variable credit supply, government policy and infrastructure investment. Crucially, the period covered spans '...the transition from a pre-industrial 18th century situation of erratic fluctuations dominated by harvests and wars to a post-Napoleonic wars position of a regular cycle, with fixed capital formation at the heart of it but influenced somewhat by innovation and financial crises' (Crafts et al., 1989: 45). These words refer to the genesis of the business cycle in the British economy, but they are equally applicable to the contemporaneous building cycle in London. The cyclical fluctuation in London building during the eighteenth century was strongly influenced by the exogenous impacts of wars and harvests, while during the nineteenth century endogenous market mechanisms reinforced the cycle, as a capitalist economy became firmly established in Britain.

The structure of the book

This brief discussion of the London building cycle in the eighteenth and nineteenth centuries illustrates the approach to be taken in the book, both in terms of understanding the historical context and describing the characteristics of the cycle. In order to describe how the cycle operates, and how it contributes to the processes of economic growth and urban development, we need to develop a theoretical framework to aid understanding and a methodological framework to assist description.

To develop a suitable theoretical framework, we must start by examining what economic theory has to say about the sources of growth and the causes of cycles. Chapter 2 reviews the development of economic growth and business cycle theory over the past two centuries. The reason for combining cycle theory with growth theory within the review stems from one of the underlying premises of the book: that they are two aspects of the same phenomenon. There have been periods when economic thought has recognized their interconnectedness and times when it has not. At present, growth theory and business cycle theory tend to be treated as separate topics, and so it is valuable to delve back in time to periods when the two strands of theory were better integrated.

Chapter 3 focuses down on the specific theoretical and empirical studies of the building cycle that have been undertaken. Again a historical approach is adopted, following the development of ideas from the first building cycle studies of the 1930s through to present day research on the cyclical behaviour of all aspects of real estate markets. The review distinguishes between those studies which have offered a primarily empirical description of cycle behaviour and those which have sought to provide a theoretical explanation for that behaviour. To conclude the chapter, the main ideas about cycle behaviour are drawn together in a conceptual model of how the classic building cycle operates, articulating the links between the real economy, the property market and the money economy as the cycle proceeds through the four phases of recovery, prosperity, recession and depression.

The following Chapters 4 to 6 analyse the historical relationship between building investment, economic growth and urban development. The methodological framework adopted for the historical analysis is presented in Appendix A. This provides a discussion of the technical issues involved in separating an economic time series into a secular growth trend and the cyclical fluctuations around it, using the London building series illustrated in Figure 1.1 as an example. Alternative methods of cycle identification are reviewed, and the outcome is a preferred method of trend and cycle decomposition that is applied to the other building series employed in the book.

In Chapter 4, building investment is treated as a driver of economic growth, adding to productive capacity and embodying technical progress, with the building cycle acting as a key source of propulsion in the growth process. The trends and cycles in residential and non-residential building investment in the United Kingdom and United States are compared using UK data from the mid-nineteenth century and US data from the start of the twentieth century, with the US data allowing non-residential building to be broken down into its industrial, commercial and office components. A model of economic growth is presented in which investment is split into the two complementary components of productive capital, buildings and equipment, in order to isolate the contribution to UK growth made by building investment over the past century and a half.

The role of building investment in urban development is the subject of Chapter 5. Recent theories of urban development stress the interrelationship between the economies of agglomeration which cause cities to form, and the endogenous processes of knowledge formation that drive economic growth. Revolutions in building and transport technology provide a powerful impetus to urban growth, operating through an urban development cycle that fuels both innovation in urban activities and the accumulation of urban capital. The manner in which technical change, population growth and industrialization interact within the urban development cycle at national level is illustrated with UK data from the late eighteenth century and US data from the early nineteenth century. The operation of the cycle at urban level is then described, with a particular focus on the chronology of building cycles in London over the past three centuries.

A case study of the office development cycle in the City of London is presented in Chapter 6. Having discussed the evolution of the City economy from a self-contained medieval city into a global financial centre, the course of the office building cycle since the mid-nineteenth century is charted. The cycle chronology provides a framework for identifying successive vintages within the existing office stock, which are then analysed in terms of their location, building size, rent level, occupier profile and rate of redevelopment. The distinctive characteristics and market performance of each vintage allow conclusions to be drawn about the manner in which technical change, economies of scale and obsolescence operate through the development cycle.

A simulation model of the building cycle is presented in Chapter 7, with its mathematical formulation set out in Appendix B. Its purpose is to show how building cycles are generated and sustained along an economic growth path. The model incorporates an endogenous cycle propagation mechanism to ensure that fluctuations around the growth path are persistent, and allows for exogenous impulse shocks that set off the self-sustaining cycle. The model relationships are formulated as a system of difference equations; simplified linear versions of the model can be solved analytically, while more complex non-linear forms require a simulation approach to demonstrate model behaviour under more realistic conditions. To test the validity of the model, it is calibrated using data for the City of London, and its performance compared with the observed behaviour of the office building cycle as presented in the previous chapter.

In Chapter 8 we move the historical analysis from the long term to the near term. The post-war period has seen the rapid growth of investment demand for property, both from households owning their own dwellings and from financial institutions including property within their multi-asset portfolios. Investment demand can in part operate autonomously from occupier demand, and the tensions between the two have been heightened by the integration and globalization of real estate and capital markets. As a result, the instability of the property cycle has increased, and its impact on the wider economy has intensified – as dramatically illustrated by the crash of 2008. Three examples of the operation of property cycles in global investment markets are presented. The first is a comparative analysis of post-war growth and cycles in the UK and US residential and commercial markets; the second charts the globalization of the office market cycle across a range of world cities during the past 25 years; the third demonstrates how successive waves of development have driven the global diffusion of two iconic building forms, skyscrapers and shopping centres.

The concluding Chapter 9 synthesizes the main strands of the preceding analysis into a theoretical framework formulated to aid understanding of the building cycle. Five themes are highlighted: building cycles and economic growth; propagation of the building cycle; building cycles and urban development; integration of real estate and capital markets; globalization of the building cycle. The themes are intended not only to explain the motion of the cycle itself, but also to show how it relates to the broader processes of economic growth and urban development. By understanding the past we will be in a better position to anticipate the future.

2

Growth and Cycles: The Economic Debate

The underlying theme

'The recurring periods of prosperity of the cyclical movement are the form progress takes in capitalistic society'

(Schumpeter, 1927: 295).

Schumpeter's often-quoted statement summarizes the essence of this chapter, and indeed this whole book. Cyclical fluctuations have been, and continue to be, an intrinsic characteristic of economic growth in capitalist societies. Furthermore, as we saw in the last chapter, they appear to have been a feature of pre-capitalist economies as well. There is a powerful argument that these fluctuations are not merely temporary deviations around a long-run growth path, but rather cycles are a manifestation of the very dynamic that propels an economy forwards, a dynamic in which growth and instability are inextricably intertwined.

Economic growth results from the continuous interplay of equilibrating and disequilibrating forces, and cyclical fluctuations are a consequence of that interplay. These fluctuations are not regular in length or severity because the economy is neither an oscillating machine nor a pulsating organism; rather it is a complex of interconnected human activities that develop historically under the influence of technological, social, political and cultural processes. At times the equilibrating forces seem unchallenged, as economic growth proceeds smoothly, while at other times disequilibrium causes the sort of turmoil experienced in market crashes or economic depressions. As a general rule it can be said that equilibrating forces predominate in the long run: the growth trajectory of capitalism over more than two centuries has been impressive, and on a global scale shows no sign of slackening. However, it is equally true that the fluctuations caused by disequilibrating forces have never disappeared, and almost certainly never will. Indeed, to put it at its most extreme, it can be argued that without the dynamic interplay between the equilibrating and the disequilibrating, there would be no forward motion at all.

If this view of the interplay between economic growth and cycles is accepted, then they should be studied as two aspects of the same phenomenon, not two separate phenomena. There has been a vigorous debate about growth and cycles since the very emergence of capitalism, and over these two centuries or more the emphasis given to one aspect or the other, and to their interrelatedness, has fluctuated as markedly as the economic system itself. Indeed, it is often observed that nothing is more cyclical than the literature on economic cycles (Zarnowitz, 1992: 20). In the aftermath of each severe recession, there is a flurry of commentary and research that is the genesis of new theories to explain what has happened. Such it was during the 1930s, when the Great Depression inspired Keynes to publish his General Theory (1936), launching the Keynesian Revolution that transformed the foundations of economic theory and policy formation. The success of post-war Keynesian demand management policies in stabilizing economies led many commentators to herald the 'end of the business cycle' (Bronfenbrenner, 1969). However, the onset of the global recession of 1973–5 shattered this complacency and spawned a whole new corpus of modern business cycle theory.

'The most important lesson from this experience is that an historical perspective is essential if we are to understand how business cycles are generated and evolve' (Solomou, 1998: 1). The point is that cycle behaviour changes over time; each cycle is uniquely defined by its historical context and its relationship to the trajectory of economic growth. This is a central theme in the history of economic thought produced by Rostow (1990), which provides a helpful guide to the development of ideas about growth and cycles. In developing his history, Rostow stresses the need to '...demonstrate the intimate linkage between growth and cyclical fluctuations of different periodicity with major innovations...accounted as endogenous to the system'. He goes on to offer this summary of how a satisfactory theory should characterize the dynamics of economic growth:

'The system that emerges does incorporate the notion of a dynamic, moving equilibrium although...the system inherently lurches through time, overshooting and undershooting its optimum sectoral (and therefore aggregate) paths. It is also a non-linear (or chaos) system marked by irreversible change where stable equilibrium is ruled out and disequilibrium drives the sectors toward equilibrium paths passed through but never sustained' (Rostow, 1990: 7).

We shall now review how ideas on growth and cycles have evolved since the late eighteenth century as the precursor to offering a plausible theoretical framework for the study of building cycles. In addition to Rostow (1990), earlier sources on the development of theories of growth and cycles up to the Second World War are Haberler (1937) and Hansen (1951), while these themes are covered to a more limited extent within general histories of economic thought such as Roll (1992) and Vaggi and Groenewegen (2003). For more radical critiques of mainstream growth and cycle theory, see Sherman (1991) and Taylor (2004a).

The growth story

The classical economists

It has become accepted wisdom that the discipline of economics as a social science was founded by Adam Smith, with his publication of *The Wealth of Nations* in

1776, at the outset of the Industrial Revolution in Britain. This treatise launched the classical tradition in political economy, with its emphases on the sources of growth and its periodic crises. Smith pointed to the division of labour as the key source of growth. Specialization leads to incremental technical improvements and productivity growth, while productive employment generates an economic surplus in the form of capitalists' profits that can be saved and invested in the accumulation of capital, thereby facilitating technical progress, expanding productive capacity, widening the market and driving the growth process. Smith did not comment directly on the propensity of the growth process to be subject to cyclical fluctuations, which is perhaps understandable given that the fluctuations in trade, manufacturing and building in Britain during the eighteenth century appeared largely to be the product of the random impacts of the success or failure of harvests and the timing of wars (Rostow, 1990: 41–2).

If Smith's prognosis of the prospects for long-term growth was broadly optimistic, the political and economic turbulence of the Napoleonic Wars caused the views of his successors, Malthus and Ricardo, to be distinctly gloomier. They were concerned about the limits to growth imposed by a tendency towards diminishing returns in production. In *The Principles of Political Economy and Taxation* (1817), Ricardo argued that as population grows, the margin of cultivation must extend to ever poorer quality land, reducing the marginal net return to agriculture and therefore the general rate of profit across the economy as a whole, leading to a declining rate of economic growth. To offset this tendency, he recognized that economic growth means capital accumulation, which in turn means productivity growth and rising real wages. This encourages employers to substitute fixed capital for labour, reducing the costs of production and the price of commodities, thereby boosting wages and profits and sustaining the rate of growth. However, in the third edition of *Principles* (1821), Ricardo expressed the fear that while investment in machinery can sustain the rate of economic growth through embodied technical progress, it can also create technological unemployment, as the demand for labour grows more slowly than the volume of capital (Roll, 1992: 170–2).

The inflationary and then deflationary impacts of the Napoleonic Wars generated explicit discussion of the causes of economic crises, with particular attention being focused on the question of whether or not generalized over-production/under-consumption crises could occur in capitalist economies. In his *Traité d'Economie Politique* (1803), the French economist Jean-Baptiste Say argued that there can be no such generalized crises due to insufficient purchasing power in the economy. According to his much-quoted law, supply creates its own demand in a self-adjusting economy because commodities exchange at market-clearing equilibrium prices determined by the interaction of supply and demand. The counter-argument was proposed by Sismondi, in *Nouveaux Principes d'Economie Politique* (1819), who asserted that gluts are both possible and likely in an economic system in which wide disparities in income mean that labour may command insufficient purchasing power to consume all that is produced, particularly in the face of technological unemployment. In a forerunner to subsequent debates about investment risk and uncertainty, he also pointed to the problems faced by producers trying to formulate market-clearing strategies when they have only partial information about market conditions and competitor decisions (Vaggi and Groenewegen, 2003: 121–3).

Sismondi foreshadowed Marx. By the time he started writing the first volume of *Capital* (1867), industrial capitalism had become firmly established in Western Europe and North America, and so had the business cycle. Economists therefore began to pay more attention to the sources of instability in economic growth. Indeed, instability and crisis were central to Marx's analysis of the capitalist mode of production. The surplus value extracted from labour employed in production is invested by capitalists in machinery that boosts productivity, cheapens the value of products and increases the size of the surplus. Furthermore, each round of investment in labour-saving machinery creates technological unemployment, swelling the ranks of the 'industrial reserve army' and maintaining downward pressure on real wages. Like Sismondi, Marx believed that over-production crises were an inevitable result of the contradiction between the competitive pressure to increase surplus value through investment and the need to realize that value through the creation of sufficient effective demand to consume the products of the economy. He also pointed to a periodic tendency towards over-investment which expands the demand for labour and increases wages, leading to a fall in the rate of profit and an interruption to accumulation (Rostow, 1990: 140–1).

The neoclassical revolution

A contemporary of Marx, but with a reformist rather than revolutionary political perspective, John Stuart Mill is now placed in a transitional position between the classical and neoclassical traditions. In his *Principles of Political Economy* (1848), he moved away from the labour theory of value that had been central to classical theory, instead offering the outlines of an early supply and demand theory of price formation. On the other hand, he accepted the classical belief that there is an inherent tendency for the rate of profit to fall and for growth to slow as capitalist economies develop. Influenced by the sharp business cycle fluctuations of the early nineteenth century, he pointed to the growing risk of boom–bust instability associated with a falling profit rate, which impels some entrepreneurs to seek higher returns in more risky investments, generating speculative bubbles that subsequently burst. He thus pioneered ideas about the destabilizing impact on growth of investor expectations, particularly when there is a significant delay between an investment outlay and its return (Rostow, 1990: 109–12).

During the second half of the nineteenth century, the experience of industrial expansion and rising prosperity in Western economies brought about a fundamental shift in the focus of economic enquiry. Though business cycles persisted, classical concerns about the long-term sustainability of growth appeared to have been answered satisfactorily, and there was widespread belief in the benign effects of scientific, technological and economic progress. In this climate of optimism, the emerging neoclassical school turned its attention to the efficiency of resource allocation within an established market economy, and the necessary conditions for the maintenance of a market-clearing general equilibrium. The neoclassicists were concerned to investigate how the individual decisions of firms and households, operating with fixed production technologies and consumer tastes under conditions of diminishing marginal returns, translate into an optimal allocation of society's productive resources between competing uses. Their ahistorical focus on the microeconomics of short-run price formation was in sharp contrast to the classical concern with the macroeconomics of long-run development. Consequently, much less was heard about the dynamics of growth and cycles.

One exception is provided by Alfred Marshall in his key work *Principles of Economics* (1890). Though firmly located in the neoclassical tradition, he did address issues of relevance to growth and cycles by recognizing the limitations of a general equilibrium analysis of supply and demand in a theoretical stationary state: '...economic problems are imperfectly presented when they are treated as problems of statical equilibrium, and not of organic growth' (Marshall, 1920: 461). Instead, he adopted a partial equilibrium framework for analyzing adjustments to supply and demand over different time periods. In particular, Marshall's theory of production allows firms to expand their capacity in the long run by investing in new technologies and organizational structures with the potential to reduce average costs through increasing returns to scale. In the same vein as Mill, he attributed the occurrence of business cycles to switches in the psychology of the business community through successive phases of the cycle. When optimism prevails, strong demand for loan capital boosts investment and output, but as the boom proceeds, speculative investors seek out increasingly risky ventures; when some of these fail, lending is cut back, pessimism takes over and investment and output slump (Rostow, 1990: 173–5).

Technology and growth

Though the neoclassical revolution switched the attention of most economists away from the classical concern with growth and cycles, some heretics persisted in exploring these issues during the early twentieth century. One particular focus of interest was the role of technological progress, both in driving long-run growth and causing fluctuations in investment.

Amongst the most virulent critics of the dominant neoclassical orthodoxy was the highly idiosyncratic American political economist Thorstein Veblen. During an era of huge structural transformation in the US economy, the prevailing focus on economies in a stationary state of general equilibrium struck him as perverse. In *The Theory of Business Enterprise* (1904), he attempted to construct a theory of the modern business enterprise as a social institution forever adapting to the relentless march of technological progress. He made a distinction between 'industrial capital', as the physical means of production employed by a firm, and 'business capital', as the monetary value attached to those assets. This distinction underlies his explanation of the business cycle: 'this fund of money values...bears but a remote and fluctuating relation to...the old-fashioned concept of industrial capital' (Veblen, 1904: 136). The producer interest is to invest in reorganization and new technology, which tends to reduce the earning capacity of existing physical assets through economic obsolescence, whereas the investor interest is to maintain or enhance the monetary values of these assets. The result of this contradiction is a tendency for the value of assets as business capital to increase above their value as industrial capital during boom periods, necessitating a periodic writing-down of monetary values that may overshoot in the opposite direction during phases of liquidation and depression (Roll, 1992: 410–4).

In a more mainstream tradition, Joseph Schumpeter attempted to bridge the gap between the neoclassical economics of general equilibrium and the classical economics of growth and cycles (Vaggi and Groenewegen, 2003: 265–9). In *The Theory of Economic Development*, first published in German in 1911, he pointed to the limitations of static equilibrium analysis, believing that a proper study of the development of capitalist economies must focus on the impact of technical progress and the role of the innovating entrepreneur in creating a continuous flux in economic activity. Furthermore, the emphasis should be on the discontinuous and irreversible impact of major innovations, rather than on continuous, incremental changes in technology along a theoretical balanced growth path. Schumpeter adopted a broad definition of innovations to include new products, new inputs to production, new methods of production, new forms of industrial organization and new markets. Creative entrepreneurs raise credit to invest in new combinations of these innovations, disturbing the existing equilibrium both by providing a new impetus to growth and by accelerating the obsolescence of established methods. The reason for growth proceeding through 'a wave-like movement of alternating periods of prosperity and depression' is that innovations do not appear in a smooth and continuous sequence, but rather 'discontinuously in groups or swarms' (Schumpeter, 1934: 223). Swarming occurs because the success of a few pioneering entrepreneurs encourages the emergence of clusters of imitators eager to exploit the newly revealed possibilities.

Schumpeter started his theory of economic cycles in the boom phase: a wave of primary innovation occurs in specific industries, its impacts then spread in secondary waves throughout the economy and the entrepreneurial profits made by successful innovators are ploughed back in a circular flow of capital accumulation that drives the whole process. The instability created by the boom causes the economy to move into a compensating phase of depression that is attributable to three circumstances. First, high boom-time demand from innovators for means of production (especially new plant and equipment) drives up their prices, which imposes extra costs on existing enterprises; second, when the new products appear on the market, they drive down the prices and receipts of the existing producers already suffering cost increases; third, once their new products are launched, the successful entrepreneurs pay off their debts, inducing a credit deflation (Schumpeter, 1934: 231–6). Investment in entrepreneurial activity is cut back, stagnation hits the capital goods industries, and decreased demand and deflation permeate the whole economy, as it struggles towards a new equilibrium – but an equilibrium that represents a more advanced stage of development than that which obtained at the start of the cycle. The duration of the cycle is a function of the gestation period of the innovations and the adjustment period of the wider economy to their introduction.

Keynes

Despite the heretics, neoclassical theory held sway through the early part of the twentieth century, until the onset of extreme economic turbulence after the First World War, with a severe recession in 1920–1 followed by the Great Depression of 1929–32. Persistent deflation with high unemployment and surplus capacity called the neoclassical model into question, highlighting the need for a fresh economic perspective – and along came John Maynard Keynes, with his ground-breaking *General Theory of Employment, Interest and Money* (1936).

What Keynes sought to do was identify where the self-adjusting properties of a market economy might break down, so that a return to full employment equilibrium after a shock is not assured. He started with the determination of effective demand. At any point in time, the intersection of an economy's aggregate demand and supply functions uniquely determines the level of effective demand at which entrepreneurs' profit expectations are maximized. This may set output and employment below their full-capacity levels, whereas in the classical system based on Say's Law, demand always adjusts to fit supply. Effective demand consists of three components – consumption, investment and government expenditure. Consumption is an increasing function of total income, determined by a marginal propensity to consume of less than one, such that the share of consumption in total income decreases with increasing income. Savings are not, therefore, a function of interest rates, as in the classical system, but rather they are determined as the residual part of income after consumption is deducted. It is the propensity to consume and the planned levels of investment and government expenditure that determine the equilibrium level of output and employment, such that savings and investment are brought into balance. Adjustments to this equilibrium are determined by the 'multiplier' derived from the marginal propensity to consume: a shift in investment expenditure requires a matching shift in savings, which induces an amplified adjustment to income because of the scaling effects of the multiplier.

It is through the determinants of the planned level of investment that Keynes directly addressed the causes of economic instability. He asserted that the volume of investment is governed by the market balance between two factors – the cost of capital and the expected rate of return. His concept of the expected rate of return on an investment, which he termed the 'marginal efficiency of capital', was based on investor expectations about the prospective yield over the whole life of the asset. He pointed to the considerable problems of formulating such long-term expectations:

'Our knowledge of the factors which will govern the yield of an investment some years hence is usually very slight and often negligible. If we speak frankly, we have to admit that our basis of knowledge for estimating the yield ten years hence of a railway, a copper mine, a textile factory, the goodwill of a patent medicine, an Atlantic liner, a building in the City of London amounts to little and sometimes to nothing; or even five years hence' (Keynes, 1936: 149–50).

However sophisticated the approach they take to forming long-term expectations, Keynes believed that investors must also employ a large measure of subjective judgement and hope for a fair share of luck. Moreover, an optimistic mind-set is essential if they are to make the necessary commitment to major projects in the face of myriad uncertainties – a desirable characteristic that prompted Keynes's famous remarks about the need for long-term investors to indulge their 'animal spirits' through '…a spontaneous urge to action rather than inaction, and not as the outcome of a weighted average of quantitative benefits multiplied by quantitative probabilities' (Keynes, 1936: 161–2).

Keynes was also concerned that as society grows richer its average propensity to consume will fall, so that there is a proportionate growth in the volume of savings which requires a proportionately greater level of investment in order to maintain full employment. Under these conditions, the full employment level of savings may exceed planned investment, because the two are not automatically brought into balance by the interest rate. Furthermore, the larger the capital stock, the less attractive may be the marginal returns from additional investment unless there is a compensating reduction in the rate of interest. But here we encounter another problem – the 'liquidity trap'. If the money supply is increased in order to lower the interest rate, the speculative demand for money increases since people become more inclined to hoard cash as a store of value. This places a floor on how far interest rates can fall, and the additional funds are directed into hoarding rather than investment.

In the tradition of Mill and Marshall, Keynes stressed the influence of psychological factors on the fluctuations in investment that are at the heart of the business cycle. The later stages of a boom are characterized by optimistic expectations about the future returns from capital assets that are sufficiently strong to offset their growing abundance, their increasing costs of production and the adverse effect of rising interest rates. However, it is in the nature of investment markets that when disillusion sets in it does so '...with sudden and even catastrophic force...the essence of the situation is to be found...in the collapse in the marginal efficiency of capital' (Keynes, 1936: 315–6). Keynes suggested that the period of delay before there is a recovery in confidence, and therefore in the marginal efficiency of capital, is determined by two factors. The first is the average durability of existing capital assets, which determines their rate of obsolescence and therefore the length of time before significant replacement demand is created. The second is the carrying cost of the surplus stocks of goods produced during the boom, which determines the rate of price decrease necessary for these surpluses to be absorbed so that inventory investment can resume.

The neoclassical growth model

Keynes did not develop a theory of long-run growth; in his model, adjustments occur over months not years. Thus, he considered the impact of investment on income via the multiplier, but not its role in the accumulation of productive assets via the accelerator, which relates the level of investment demand to the rate of growth in output (see the next section). This omission was rectified by two of his disciples, Harrod (1939) in the United Kingdom and Domar (1946) in the United States, who independently developed Keynesian growth models with similar properties. Their concern was to identify the conditions under which a full employment growth path can be sustained with investment fulfilling its dual role of income generator on the demand side and capacity augmenter on the supply side. They showed that for a balance to be maintained between planned savings and investment, the equilibrium or 'warranted' rate of full employment growth must equal the savings rate divided by the capital–output ratio. Furthermore, there is a separate 'natural' rate of growth for an economy which is the maximum growth rate it can sustain in the long run, defined by the sum of the rate of labour force growth and the rate of labour-augmenting technical progress. If the warranted rate is above the natural rate, there will be a build-up of excess productive capacity; if it is below the natural rate, there will be growing unemployment.

The full employment growth path defined by the Harrod–Domar model runs along a 'knife edge' of instability, dependent upon four fixed parameters being maintained in their equilibrating proportions (the savings rate, capital–output ratio, labour force growth rate and the rate of technical progress). Furthermore, any deviation from the path tends to increase in a cumulative fashion, implying a degree of instability that does not accord with observed reality. Subsequent developments of the growth model explored how a degree of flexibility could be introduced, so that deviations from equilibrium do not become self-reinforcing, but rather generate self-correcting fluctuations around the growth path that are more typical of the business cycle. To introduce such flexibility, at least one of the model parameters must be allowed to vary, thereby adjusting the warranted or natural rates of growth in a manner which counters the disequilibrium tendency.

The neoclassical critique of the model, initiated by Solow (1956) and Swan (1956), focused on its restrictive assumption of fixed proportions of production as embodied in a constant capital–output ratio. Their argument was that this failed to allow for factor substitution between capital and labour as their relative availability, and therefore relative prices, change. Thus, if the warranted rate of full employment growth exceeds the natural rate, labour shortages lead to an increase in real wages and a substitution towards more capital-intensive methods of production, which raises the capital–output ratio and reduces the warranted growth rate. There may be cyclical instability in the short-term, while techniques of production adjust to a change in relative factor prices, but the assumptions which underlie the neoclassical aggregate production function, of factor price flexibility and factor substitutability allied to constant returns to scale, ensure that the equilibrium growth path is self-regulating in the medium term.

Though alternative theoretical approaches have been suggested, the neoclassical model has remained the cornerstone of growth theory for the last 50 years (Sorensen and Whitta-Jacobsen, 2005). However, as has been acknowledged by its most eminent proponent, the focus on steady-state growth has led to a divorce between growth and cycle theory: '...a theory of equilibrium growth badly needed – and still needs – a theory of deviations from the equilibrium growth path...The problem of combining long-run and short-run macroeconomics has still not been solved' (Solow, 2000: xiv). Furthermore, there remains considerable dispute about the scope and limitations of the model.

A continuing area of debate concerns the nature and sources of technical progress, widely accepted to be the main engine of growth in total factor productivity (assuming technical progress is assigned to both capital and labour as factors of production). In the original neoclassical model, it was assumed to be 'manna from heaven', a disembodied, exogenous factor that increases productivity incrementally and is neutral in its impact on the balance between capital and labour within the aggregate production function (Solow, 1957). This led to a stream of empirical 'growth accounting' studies, pioneered by Denison (1967), which aimed to explain productivity growth in terms of factors such as advances in knowledge and improved resource allocation between industries. Subsequent versions of the model examined the effects of a labour-saving or capital-saving bias in new technology and explored alternative ways of embodying technical progress within the growth process by linking it to capital accumulation (Kennedy and Thirlwall, 1972).

The question as to whether technical progress is disembodied or embodied within the capital stock became a matter of considerable debate (Hercowitz, 1998).

Solow himself followed his original model with a version in which technical progress is embodied in successive vintages of investment, each of which consists of capital stock utilizing the latest productive techniques (Solow, 1962). The assumption of ex-post factor substitutability is still maintained so that, as each vintage ages, progressively less labour is assigned to it in order to maintain the same marginal productivity of labour across the vintages. Under this assumption, successive vintages of physical capital can be aggregated into a quality-adjusted measure of 'equivalent capital' in which the later, more technologically advanced vintages have greater weight. In an alternative version of the vintage model, capital is no longer malleable once installed, and each vintage operates with a fixed technology throughout its life. The older the vintage, the lower the productivity of labour working with it; consequently, as real wages rise, there comes a point at which the oldest surviving vintage is no longer profitable to operate, and so economic obsolescence causes it to be scrapped. Furthermore, the higher the savings and investment rate, the higher the average level of labour productivity and therefore the shorter the economic life of capital goods. Consequently, an increase in the investment rate leads to accelerated obsolescence as well as an increase in the rate of embodied technical progress (Salter, 1966; Solow et al., 1966).

In a more recent development, the Solow model has been augmented by expanding the aggregate production function to include human capital as an input alongside physical capital and labour. Human capital embodies the stock of knowledge which determines the skills and quality of the labour force and thereby contributes to the level of labour productivity. In the augmented Solow model, human capital accumulation through education and training thus reinforces the impact of physical capital accumulation as a driver of labour productivity growth (Mankiw et al., 1992).

Modern growth theory

The accumulation of knowledge, and therefore technical progress, remains an unexplained exogenous factor in the augmented Solow model. However, a crucial strand of modern growth theory has focused on technical change as an endogenous process generating increasing returns to scale in production through the externality benefits derived from 'knowledge spillovers'. Human capital is accumulated through learning and the sharing of knowledge, and this knowledge is applied to implement innovations in the sphere of production. Early versions of the theory linked the accumulation of knowledge to the accumulation of physical capital: knowledge grows with learning, and learning is the product of experience in using the improved techniques embodied in new capital equipment. Thus, Kaldor (1957) defined a 'technical progress function' in which the rate of increase in labour productivity is a function of the rate of growth of capital stock per worker. In his famous 'learning by doing' paper, Arrow (1962) offered an alternative formulation in which learning is a function of the cumulative sum of past investments, and output increases more than proportionately to scale increases in labour and capital because of the learning effect.

A seminal paper by Romer (1986) set the benchmark for modern endogenous growth theory. He defined new knowledge to be the product of investment in research and development (R&D), which adds to the stock of knowledge available to all producers, thereby generating increasing returns in production. Lucas (1988) developed a similar model that explicitly incorporates the accumulation of human capital through a process of 'learning by studying' rather than learning by doing. The population can choose to divide its time between working and studying, and it is the amount of study time combined with the existing stock of human capital which determines the rate of accumulation of new human capital. A subsequent model by Romer (1990) assigned a portion of human capital to the invention and production of new varieties of capital goods. The greater the quantity of human capital devoted to R&D, the greater the increase in the store of knowledge, the more rapid the increase in new types of physical capital, and therefore the faster the rate of endogenously generated technical progress. In an alternative version by Grossman and Helpman (1991), innovation and imitation occur through investment in research designed to improve the quality of a fixed set of consumer goods that climb stochastically up 'quality ladders'. Young (1993) proposed that the two endogenous growth traditions, based on learning and invention, should be integrated in a hybrid model of 'bounded learning' in which learning by doing can only be sustained by a flow of inventions emanating from R&D. For a survey of this family of endogenous growth models in the neoclassical tradition, see Verspagen (1992); for a critique of their prediction that an increase in the resources devoted to R&D increases the rate of economic growth, see Jones (1995).

An alternative strand of endogenous growth theory has eschewed the neoclassical model in favour of a neo-Schumpeterian approach. This school stresses the importance of concrete social institutions rather than abstract economic agents when analyzing the growth process, and is biased in favour of applied studies at the industry rather than aggregate level (for recent summaries of the main ideas, see Nelson, 2005 and Dosi et al., 2005). The aim is to look inside the 'black box' into which technology has been pushed by mainstream neoclassical theory (Rosenberg, 1982), seeking out the sources of the basic inventions and innovations which become embodied in new production processes and lead to the establishment of new products and industries (Schmookler, 1966). Attention is focused on how innovations originate through R&D, how they are subsequently diffused through commercial application and how their application involves a process of continuous technical improvement allied to workforce learning and institutional change. Using a terminology adopted by Mokyr (1990: 13), the fundamental 'macroinventions' which emerge out of R&D lead to a subsequent stream of 'microinventions' which arise as the new technologies are improved, adapted and diffused.

The processes by which innovations originate and permeate through an economy have been extensively measured and modelled (see Grübler, 1990, for a review). The classic study of the diffusion of innovations by Rogers, first published in 1962, describes a process in which the first innovators launch the new product or process; the innovation is then taken up by a cohort of 'early adopters' whose experience of its benefits encourages an accelerating take-off in adoption by an 'early majority' and then 'late majority' of users; finally, as the market for the innovation nears saturation, the rate of adoption decelerates as the 'laggards' finally join the established body of users (Rogers, 2003: 272–85). The transfer of knowledge and experience is vital to the diffusion process, as the early adopters learn from the innovators, and the majority learns from the early adopters. Empirical evidence suggests that the rate of adoption follows a symmetric bell-shaped distribution which can be represented by an S-shaped logistic growth curve. Formal modelling of the diffusion process started with Mansfield (1961), who developed a simple model to explain the rate at which firms imitate an innovator in terms of the profitability and costs of installing the new technology and the proportion of firms that have already installed it (the 'bandwagon effect'). Subsequent diffusion models set the adoption process within a dynamic framework which allows the technology to improve and productive capacity to grow through time (Metcalfe, 1981).

More recently, the neo-Schumpeterian school of innovation studies has endeavoured to model the disequilibrium nature of the growth process by drawing analogies between biological evolution and economic competition (e.g., see Dosi et al., 1988; Foray and Freeman, 1993). The evolutionary theory proposed by Nelson and Winter (1982) characterizes economic growth as a stochastic process of business development in which firms apply decision rules that replicate the operation of dynamic competition through innovation and imitation. Silverberg et al. (1988) and Chiaromonte and Dosi (1993) have developed 'self-organization' models of innovation, whereby technical progress is embodied in capital equipment, the competitiveness of individual firms evolves through cumulative learning, and their investment decisions are made stochastically in the face of uncertainty about future demand, relative competitiveness and the technical opportunities available to them. Metcalfe (1998) presents a version of the evolutionary model of economic development designed to demonstrate how it can be related back to the mainstream of neoclassical growth theory.

Indeed, Schumpeterian ideas are filtering back into the neoclassical mainstream. A new body of theory is founded on the importance of 'general purpose technologies', which become engines of growth because their universal applicability facilitates complementary innovations across every aspect of economic life (Bresnahan and Trajtenberg, 1995; Helpman, 1998). In this vein, a version of the endogenous growth model developed by Aghion and Howitt (1992) assumes that innovation is a stochastic process, and that the rate of successful innovation is proportional to the share of the skilled labour force assigned to R&D. Each successful innovation establishes a new and more efficient production technology that renders previous technologies obsolete, thus introducing a Schumpeterian process of creative destruction through innovation. Model solutions allow cyclical fluctuations to be generated because expectations of a future increase in research investment discourage current research by threatening the profitability of the innovations it may generate. For an elaboration of this neoclassical Schumpeterian model, see Aghion and Howitt (1998).

Historical dependence

One of the most influential ideas to have emerged from endogenous growth theory is that of 'path dependence' (Arthur, 1989, 1994). The more a complex technology is adopted, the greater is the experience gained in its use. This learning by doing creates a positive feedback effect, generating increasing returns in production and encouraging further improvements in the technology. Specific historical events may determine which of several competing technologies is initially selected, but once adopted these positive feedback effects mean that the technology in use improves more than its competitors, thereby 'locking-in' the economy to a particular trajectory of development. Path dependence thus results from the operation of increasing returns once historical events have determined the initial adoption of one technology rather than another. Among the consequences of path dependence are the non-predictability, inflexibility and potential inefficiency of economic outcomes. Random events may influence technical progress in an unpredictable fashion, while increasing returns can lock the economy into a dominant technology that may have inferior long-run potential compared to its less successful competitors. Furthermore, lock-in may be reinforced by 'inter-relatedness', an idea first put forward by Frankel (1955): the more complex the matrix of interconnections between components of the production process, the more difficult and costly it is to switch from one technological regime to another.

An important implication of path dependence is 'non-ergodicity' – the impact of short-term historical events upon economic development may be permanent not temporary. 'Under increasing returns... 'History' becomes important' (Arthur, 1989: 128). Ergodic theory originated in theoretical physics: ergodic systems are a class of dynamical systems that 'forget' their initial state as they evolve through time, while non-ergodicity characterizes non-linear systems under conditions of positive feedback (see Strogatz, 1994, for an introduction to the dynamics of non-linear systems). As well as its application to economic growth theory, the concept of non-ergodicity finds biological parallels in the evolutionary theory of punctuated equilibrium (Arthur, 1994: 11). The implication of non-ergodicity in economic systems is that a major event such as the oil price shock of the 1970s may not be cancelled out by the negative feedback effect of diminishing returns which, under the assumptions of the neoclassical model, inevitably direct the economy back on to its uniquely determined equilibrium growth path. With increasing returns, multiple equilibria are possible, outcomes are indeterminate and the chosen adjustment path is historically dependent.

As far back as the 1930s, Nicholas Kaldor questioned the determinateness of economic equilibrium when considering the dynamic adjustment of an economy towards an equilibrium state. He pointed out that, unless equilibrium is achieved instantly or assumed to be independent of the adjustment path, 'It is not possible...to determine the position of equilibrium from a given system of data, since every successive step taken in order to reach equilibrium will alter the conditions of equilibrium' (Kaldor, 1934: 124). He subsequently returned to this theme, asserting the 'irrelevance of equilibrium economics' because of its premise that an economic system will converge to a unique steady-state growth trajectory irrespective of its starting point and its subsequent adjustment path. Instead, drawing on a ground-breaking but neglected paper by Young (1928), he proposed that economies enjoying increasing returns to scale develop endogenously according to a process of 'cumulative causation', such that '...the actual state of the economy during any one "period" cannot be predicted except as a result of the sequence of events in previous periods that led up to it' (Kaldor, 1972: 1244). Theories of economic growth incorporating increasing returns and cumulative causation are attracting renewed interest (see, for example, Skott and Auerbach, 1995).

Kaldor's insights have inspired a group of economists to employ the idea of hysteresis in order to introduce historical time into the theory of economic growth. Also drawn from theoretical physics, hysteresis is a concept closely related to non-ergodicity. A system with hysteresis may be in a number of different states, independent of the current inputs to the system; such a system exhibits path dependence, such that its outputs cannot be predicted without examining the history of its inputs. Growth models have been developed to incorporate hysteresis by expressing the current endogenous state of an economic system as a function of a set of apparently exogenous variables that are themselves in part a function of past values of the endogenous variables, as well as a current set of genuinely exogenous variables. Furthermore, the parameters which define the model relationships are themselves allowed to vary endogenously through time, so as to capture changes in the technological and institutional regimes which determine the supply-side structure of the economy (Setterfield, 1997). With such models, the current state of the economy depends on its own sequence of past states (its adjustment path), and it does not forget the exogenous shocks to which it has been subjected. In a refinement of the approach as applied to non-linear systems, the economy can be shown to have a selective rather than complete memory, in that only the most extreme past shocks influence its current state (Cross, 1993).

The crucial importance of introducing historical dependence into growth models is the recognition that the growth trajectory of an economy evolves through time under the influence of endogenously generated changes in technology, output composition and institutional structures. Furthermore, it creates the possibility of re-uniting growth and cycles in a modern theoretical framework that echoes the approach taken by the classical economists more than a century ago. Cycles are not simply the result of random exogenous shocks disturbing a steady-state growth path, but rather they are endogenously generated fluctuations integral to the growth process, with each cycle different from the last and each contributing to the cumulative historical development of the economy. Thus, during an economic boom, expenditure on R&D will tend to increase, shifting the economy on to a higher growth path; conversely, a slump can lead to accelerated liquidation of capital stock embodying obsolete technologies, freeing resources for more productive uses. That brings us to the dynamics of the business cycle.

Historical perspectives on business cycles

Pioneering studies

By the middle of the nineteenth century, the business cycle, or trade cycle, was widely recognized as a recurrent feature of economic growth. The first comprehensive study entirely devoted to the phenomenon was *Des Crises Commerciales* by Clement Juglar, first published in 1860 and updated in 1889, in which he combined theoretical, historical and statistical analyses of cycle behaviour. Juglar marshalled data series for France, Britain and the United States from 1800, mainly on price and monetary variables, to date crises and compare their incidence between countries, focusing in particular on cycles with a duration of between 5 and 10 years.

Following Juglar, a large number of business cycle studies were published in the later nineteenth and early twentieth centuries. They proposed a variety of causes for the phenomenon, most of which have been covered in the previous section on the development of growth theory. Haberler (1937) and Hansen (1951) provided a thorough summary of these early cycle theories, which they grouped into several categories, such as over-investment, under-consumption, monetary and psychological theories, making a particular distinction between endogenous and exogenous causes. Haberler stressed that the different theories were not mutually exclusive, often differing in emphasis rather than substance. Nevertheless, it is apparent that over-investment theories predominated in his survey, with many writers seeking to explain the principal causes of the periodic investment booms and slumps that are a persistent and dominant feature of the business cycle. Among the proponents of this approach, there was a strong Anglo-Saxon tradition, in the studies by Mitchell, Clark, Robertson and Pigou, which was influenced by the work of Tugan-Baranowsky in Russia, Spiethoff in Germany, Cassel in Sweden and Aftalion in France (Haberler 1937: 68).

The publication of *Business Cycles* by Wesley Mitchell in 1913 launched the modern study of economic cycles. While earlier writers had tended to describe disturbances to economic growth as 'crises' or 'fluctuations', Mitchell was the first to apply the more regular concept of 'cycles' to the phenomenon and introduce formal statistical methods for measuring cycle periodicity and amplitude. He assembled a vast array of physical and monetary data series for the United States, England, France and Germany, covering the period 1890–1911, and undertook a historical analysis of their movements through time. On the basis of this analysis, he developed a conceptual model in which he attempted to integrate several of the processes that other writers had identified as causal factors in the formation of cycles. Influenced by Veblen's institutionalist approach, he placed particular emphasis on factors influencing the profitability of business enterprises. In a key passage on 'How prosperity breeds a crisis', he described the way in which rising costs and interest rates encroach on profits during periods of economic expansion, thereby reducing the rate of output growth, creating over-capacity and a cutback in investment that reverses the boom into a depression, with an accompanying liquidation of debt. When he moved on to consider 'How depression breeds prosperity', there is a hint of Schumpeter: 'the longer the period during which new construction is checked by business depression the greater becomes the accumulation of technical improvements of which new plants can take advantage, and therefore the greater becomes the inducement to invest in new equipment' (Mitchell, 1913: 567).

While Mitchell was reluctant to identify a primary cause for the business cycle, Clark (1917) proposed that it is the formation of demand for investment goods via the 'accelerator' which constitutes the crucial, endogenous factor sustaining fluctuations in a growing economy. His argument was based on the distinction between replacement investment, to cover worn out or obsolete capital stock, and induced investment, generated by an increased level of output. The demand for replacement investment is proportional to the size of the existing capital stock, which in turn is proportional to the current level of output. In contrast, what drives the demand for induced investment is the growth in output, which is far more volatile. Clark used an analogy with the laws of motion: 'If demand be treated as a rate of speed at which goods are taken off the market, maintenance varies roughly with the speed, but new construction depends upon the acceleration' (Clark, 1917: 220). Modest variations in total economic activity are amplified by the accelerator to create far greater fluctuations in induced investment demand. In particular, if the growth in total output slows down, this deceleration can create an absolute contraction in the demand for investment goods, while a contraction in total output can cause a severe recession in capital goods industries. Different investment goods have varying economic lives and therefore generate varying rates of replacement demand; the more durable the capital good, the lower the necessary level of replacement investment, which means that there is a smaller stabilizing component of investment demand and a more volatile investment cycle.

In *A Study of Industrial Fluctuation* (1915), Robertson also sought to link growth and cycles through a technical aspect of the investment process: in his case, the gestation period and lumpiness of capital goods investment, which create a periodic tendency for investment to overshoot. A rise in product prices or fall in production costs induces increased investment, but investor expectations of future returns tend to be determined by current market conditions, without adequate allowance for the additional supply of capital goods coming on stream from competitors during the gestation period of the investment. The result of this miscalculation is over-investment, exacerbated by the lumpiness of individual investments, which is inevitably followed by a compensating cutback that induces an economic downswing. This cyclical tendency is reinforced by the need to replace capital goods at the end of their economic life: a surge in investment in one cycle is echoed by a surge of replacement investment in a subsequent cycle. The severity and duration of each cycle reflect the lumpiness, the economic life and the gestation period of the capital goods employed in the leading sectors of the economy: 'the longer therefore this period of gestation, the longer will the period of high prices continue, the greater will be the over-investment, and the more severe the subsequent depression' (Robertson, 1915: 14). While exogenous factors such as a new invention may trigger an economic upswing, and monetary factors such as credit supply may aggravate the fluctuations, it is the intrinsic characteristics of investment goods that maintain the cyclical momentum of the growth trajectory.

The long tradition, going back through Keynes and Marshall to Mill, of attributing the business cycle to fluctuations in investor expectations about future returns, formed the centrepiece of Pigou's *Industrial Fluctuations* (1927). Optimistic expectations lead to more borrowing to fund an investment boom and an expansion of output; excess production and over-investment then generate falling profits and a switch to pessimistic expectations, leading to a phase of economic contraction. Expectations result from both real and psychological causes. Pigou listed exogenous factors such as harvest yields, wars, technical inventions and the discovery of new sources of raw materials among the real causes of changes in investor expectations. Among psychological causes, he focused on 'errors of forecast' in those sectors in which goods are produced in advance of final demand, allowing expectations to be affected by undue optimism or pessimism to an extent that is influenced by the quality of available market information. Again the point was made that the longer the production delays, the greater the likely range of forecast error, and therefore the more severe the resultant fluctuations, which means that sectors producing plant and buildings are likely to be the most volatile in the economy.

Measuring trend and cycle

In a follow-up study to his seminal 1913 work, Mitchell (1927) emphasized the need to integrate the study of growth and cycles by exploring the relationship between secular trends and the fluctuations around them. He considered how demography, resource endowment and technology drive secular trends, and examined methods for identifying variable trends and isolating cyclical fluctuations, using curve fitting or moving averages. For the cyclical component of an individual data series, he proposed measures of amplitude, based on standard deviations around the fitted trend, and duration, based on the identification of peak and trough turning points. He suggested how the relationships between different time series can be investigated by comparing turning points and applying correlation analysis, and explored the ways in which different series can be combined into general indices of the business cycle through the unweighted or weighted average of the deviations around their secular trends. In conclusion, he stressed the need to move beyond the statistical abstraction of his methodology in order to recognize the distinctive character of each identified cycle within its historical context: 'Just as a review of theories of business cycles made us see the need of statistics, so our review of statistics makes us see the need of economic history' (Mitchell, 1927: 359).

The emphasis on cycle measurement in Mitchell's work led to the foundation of the National Bureau of Economic Research (NBER) in 1920. Since its inception, the NBER has sponsored a stream of empirical studies that have informed much of the subsequent work on economic cycles, particularly in the United States. Outstanding among its early publications were those of Kuznets (1930), and Burns (1934), both of whom followed Mitchell's lead in examining the relationship between cyclical fluctuations and secular trends, and both of whom pursued disaggregated analyses at the industry level. They fitted 'primary trends' to output data for different industries, in order to investigate how average growth rates varied through time and between sectors, then isolated the 'secondary movement' of growth rates around each primary trend. These secondary movements of accelerating and decelerating growth, termed 'swings' by Kuznets and 'trend-cycles' by Burns, emerged as a consistent phenomenon across different sectors and exhibited a longer-term rhythm than the business cycle fluctuations superimposed upon them.

The study by Kuznets of *Secular Movements in Production and Prices* (1930) has been particularly influential in subsequent research on business cycles in general, and building cycles in particular. He identified uneven technical progress as the most important factor explaining the relative advance and retardation of different industries through their life cycle, as output growth and price reduction first accelerate and then decelerate under the impact of revolutionary innovations in production techniques. He fitted curves to output and price data for different American and European industries in order to establish their long-run primary trends, and around these trends he used moving average smoothing to isolate the fluctuating secondary movements which he termed swings. From the turning points and deviations in the secondary movements of output and prices, he argued that the long swing has an average period of around 22 years, it has greater amplitude in capital compared to consumer goods industries and its amplitude tends to increase as the rate of growth in the primary trend increases. By informal observation, he identified a tendency for secondary movements in prices to lead secondary movements in output and proposed a causal mechanism to explain the relationship. A period of rising prices tends to boost profits, stimulating investment in new capital goods which, after a gestation period, provide the capacity for a more rapid expansion of output and employment; however, this expansion of employment leads to declining marginal productivity and a fall in profitability that then sends the long swing into reverse.

Empirical studies, which derived secular trends from time series data using curve fitting or moving averages and then extracted the residual deviations as cyclical fluctuations, began to come under critical attack during the 1930s. Frickey (1934) applied 23 different curve fitting methods and six different moving averages to a series on US pig iron production between 1877 and 1914, producing cycles that ranged in period from 3.2 to 45 years; he concluded that the properties of the derived cycle were dependent on the method used to detrend the data. In a different vein, Slutzky (1937) offered a mathematical demonstration that apparently quite regular cycles observed in a time series could result from the additive impact of random causes, rather than from some periodic cycle-generating process.

Despite these sceptical views, the flow of empirical studies of the business cycle continued unabated. A major step forward was taken by Tinbergen (1939), who pioneered the use of econometric models to measure the causal relationships thought to underlie business cycles. He worked with three investment variables that showed strong fluctuations – iron and steel consumption, railway rolling stock orders and residential construction – using data series for the United States and four European countries. Regression analysis was employed to explore the lagged relationships between these investment variables and possible causal variables such as profits, interest rates, input costs and rents (for house-building). Tinbergen's work provoked a long-running debate about the validity of using econometrics to test economic theories, a debate sparked by a famous critical review from Keynes (1939) and the response from Tinbergen (1940). Keynes queried the applicability of statistical methods to the analysis of a phenomenon as complex as the business cycle; nevertheless, the subsequent widespread adoption of econometric modelling in cycle studies suggests that, in this instance, Keynes was swimming against the tide.

The next step was made by Burns and Mitchell who, with their publication of *Measuring Business Cycles* in 1946, provided the foundations for post-war empirical research on economic cycles and devised measurement techniques that remain in use today (Gordon, 1986; Zarnowitz, 1992). Mitchell's 1927 study was their point of departure, and their main innovation was the derivation of 'reference cycles' to represent the general business cycle, against which the motion of 'specific cycles' in individual economic variables could be measured. They analysed monthly data series for a wide variety of economic variables, in order to locate the peak and trough reference dates that were chosen to define the reference cycle. Over the span of each reference cycle, the values of a specific series were averaged so that its individual observations could be expressed as 'reference-cycle relatives'; a similar set of 'specific-cycle relatives' was derived in the same manner over the span of the specific cycle. By this means, the inter-cycle secular trend was removed for the purposes of cycle identification, although it could be captured by the change in intra-cycle means between successive cycles. Having derived the monthly relatives, they were smoothed at the turning points using a 3-month average in order to estimate peak-to-trough amplitudes. The timing, duration and amplitude of each specific cycle could then be compared to those of its corresponding reference cycle, and by averaging across a set of consecutive cycles, the cyclical behaviour of a series was summarized as a unique trough–peak–trough profile that captured both its timing and amplitude.

As with Tinbergen's earlier econometric study, the work of Burns and Mitchell generated another controversial debate, this time triggered by a critical review from Koopmans (1947) that echoed some elements of the earlier Keynes critique. He attacked the attempt to measure economic cycles without reference to any underlying theory, which he believed led to an analysis that was one dimensional, mechanical and ahistorical. Koopmans thereby initiated the 'measurement without theory' debate that remains alive today. This debate is relevant not only to cycle measurement but also to the separation of cycles from growth trends, a methodological issue that continues to feature heavily in the business cycle literature. These questions are considered in detail in Appendix A.

As the measurement of trend and cycle has proceeded during the post-war period, a set of 'stylized facts' of business cycle behaviour has been proposed as broadly true for different countries and time periods. The main facts can be summarized as follows (Lucas, 1981: 217–8; Zarnowitz, 1992: 22–30; Dore, 1993: 19–28):

- Cyclical fluctuations occur around a long-run growth trend, so that successive peaks and troughs tend to occur at progressively higher levels.
- Fluctuations are persistent and recurrent, but not strictly periodic.
- Investment fluctuates more strongly than consumption or aggregate output.
- Output fluctuations across broadly defined sectors move together; i.e. they exhibit a high degree of conformity.
- There is a pro-cyclical relationship between labour productivity and output.
- Business profits are pro-cyclical and highly volatile.
- Price and wage inflation are generally pro-cyclical; unemployment is counter-cyclical.
- Short-term interest rates are pro-cyclical; long-term rates are less so.

A family of cycles

So far we have been discussing economic fluctuations around a growth path in terms of the general concept of a 'business cycle'. However, during the first part of the twentieth century, up to four types of economic cycles were described, each with a distinctly different duration: minor cycles (3–5 years), major cycles (7–11 years), long swings (15–25 years) and long waves (45–60 years). The generic business cycle that had been described by Juglar was typically associated with fluctuations having a period of up to 10 years. Kitchen (1923) termed these 'major cycles', and provided evidence for the existence of a separate 'minor cycle' of around 40 months, such that two to three minor cycles aggregate to form a major cycle. Beyond the major cycle, we have seen that Kuznets (1930) identified long swings in economic growth, with a duration of around 20 years, while the Russian economist Kondratieff (1935) proposed the existence of long waves in the development of capitalist economies that last for 50 years or more and are manifested particularly through prices.

The extent to which this family of cycles actually exists and the degree to which the different cycles might interact remain the subject of considerable debate. One view is that the generic business cycle can take either a mild or severe form, and that the build-up of financial conditions during a sequence of mild cycles creates the conditions for an occasional severe cycle, the spacing of which creates the impression of a longer cycle. A succession of mild cycles marks the expansion phase of a long swing, during which inflating asset prices provide the security for rising debt–income ratios. Eventually, a shortage of liquidity bursts the speculative bubble, triggering a financial panic and setting off a deflationary spiral in which asset values and debt fall sharply, multiplier effects reduce aggregate demand and the economy plunges into severe depression (Minsky, 1964).

An alternative argument is that each cycle is essentially an investment cycle associated with capital goods of differing durability, lumpiness and gestation period. On this basis, minor cycles are associated with inventories, major cycles with plant and machinery, long swings with building construction and long waves with major infrastructure works (see the schema set out in Table 2.1). Scepticism has been expressed about the apparently rational relationships between the proposed cycle periods, such that one Kondratieff long wave appears to contain three Kuznets cycles, each of which in turn contains two Juglar cycles, each in turn containing two to three Kitchen cycles. However, Mosekilde et al. (1992) use the modern theory of dynamic non-linear systems to demonstrate that the phenomenon of 'mode-locking' observed in physical and biological systems might explain how interacting economic cycles could adjust to one another so as to attain a rational ratio between their periods within a composite cycle of variable amplitude.

The most controversial member of this family of cycles is the long wave. In his famous paper, first published in Russian in 1925, Kondratieff analysed the longest data series he could assemble on industrial output, overseas trade, commodity prices, wages and interest rates, mostly from Britain, France and the United States, covering the period from the late eighteenth to the early twentieth century. Where necessary he normalized the series with respect to population size, fitted a secular trend using least squares, then smoothed the deviations from the trend by a 9-year moving average in order to eliminate short and major cycles. He argued that for most of the chosen series, particularly the price series, the resultant smoothed deviations exhibited long-wave fluctuations lasting between 50 and 60 years, and identified three long waves in the historical data: a First Wave (late 1780s/early 1790s until 1844–51), a Second Wave (1844–51 to 1890–6) and an incomplete Third Wave (starting 1890–6). It was his belief that long waves affect the motion

Table 2.1 A business cycle schema.

Cycle	Originator	Length (years)	Investment driver
Minor	Kitchen	3–5	Inventories
Major	Juglar	7–11	Plant and machinery
Long swing	Kuznets	15–25	Building
Long wave	Kondratieff	45–60	Infrastructure

Source: van Duijn (1983: 6–7).

of shorter business cycles, so that during the upswing of the long wave, periods of prosperity are more numerous, whereas years of depression predominate during the downswing. He did not propose a theory to explain long waves, but did suggest that a Schumpeterian innovation process is closely bound up with their movement: 'During the recession of the long waves, an especially large number of important discoveries and inventions in the technique of production and communication are made, which, however, are usually applied on a large scale only at the beginning of the next long upswing' (Kondratieff, 1935: 111).

Schumpeter himself was influenced by Kondratieff. His *Business Cycles* (1939) is a more detailed elaboration of the ideas set out in *The Theory of Economic Development*. He extended his two-phase cycle (prosperity–depression) into a four-phase cycle (prosperity–recession–depression–recovery) by making the recessionary downswing and recovery upswing explicit (Schumpeter, 1939: 149). His main theoretical development was to identify waves of innovation operating over different timescales as the origin of economic cycles of different duration: '…if innovations are at the root of cyclical fluctuations, these cannot be expected to form a single wavelike movement, because the periods of gestation and of absorption of effects by the economic system will not, in general, be equal for all the innovations that are undertaken at any time' (Schumpeter, 1939: 166–7). He adopted a stylized three-cycle schema incorporating minor cycles, major cycles and long waves, with the different cycles interacting to form a composite cycle in which their fluctuations are periodically reinforced when in phase and dampened when out of phase (Schumpeter, 1939: 212–9). Schumpeter attempted to validate the schema through an ambitious historical analysis of output, employment, price, wage and interest rate data for Germany, Britain and the United States over the three long-wave periods identified by Kondratieff. In this historical analysis, he argued that the start of each long wave was marked by concentrated swarms of basic innovations in leading industrial sectors – as in the 1780s/90s (cotton textiles, iron smelting, the steam engine), the 1830s/40s (railways, followed by steel in the 1860s/70s) and the 1890s/1900s (electricity, chemicals, motor vehicles).

Long waves

Mensch (1979) was the forerunner of a second generation of long-wave studies. He developed the Schumpeterian theory of long waves into what he termed a 'metamorphosis model' of industrial evolution, in which the idea of innovation clusters was combined with that of the product life cycle. During a period of prosperity, established technologies and products mature while innovation becomes more incremental, demand stagnates and markets saturate; the result is that productivity growth slackens and profitability falls, eventually leading the economy into depression. During the depression, reduced profits and spare capacity offer greater inducement to translate inventions into basic innovations, which accelerates their gestation process and causes a cluster of innovations to appear together; this innovation cluster then propels the economy into its next long-wave upswing through the creation of new industries, new products and new markets.

Freeman et al. (1982) offered an alternative innovation-based explanation for the generation of long waves through the emergence of 'new technology systems'.

These are composed of groups of interrelated innovations which establish new leading sectors of industry that can develop rapidly because of a bandwagon effect whereby swarms of follow-up innovations continue to improve the products and expand their markets. Van Duijn (1983) suggested that the infrastructure investment accompanying such a technological revolution provides a propagation mechanism for long waves. Perez (1983) broadened the theory to represent the long wave as a succession of modes of development, driven by the interplay between the emergence of a new 'techno-economic paradigm' and the necessary restructuring of the whole 'socio-institutional framework' in order that the new technologies can flourish. In a more recent contribution, she has explored how finance capital funds successive technological revolutions, creating a tendency towards over-investment which culminates in speculative bubbles and financial crises (Perez, 2002). An alternative Marxist interpretation of long waves has been proposed by Mandel (1995). Technological revolutions are triggered by periodic increases in the rate of profit, due to shocks such as war or social upheaval; increased profitability generates a surge of investment in new technologies which boosts labour productivity; however, as the new technologies mature, the rate of profit declines and growth slackens once more.

As has already been indicated, the very existence of long waves remains a matter of dispute. Early critics of Kondratieff and Schumpeter asked why major innovations should bunch together to generate an upswing, whether there really are investment gestation lags of sufficient length to propagate long waves, how long waves can be separated out from the shorter period fluctuations caused by long swings and major cycles and whether the waves are in fact no more than statistical artifacts created by the detrending methodology (Kuznets, 1940; Garvy, 1943). More recently, in response to the second generation of long-wave studies, Rosenberg and Frischtak (1983) expressed the view that innovation-based theories have so far failed to explain the causes of long waves when evaluated against four criteria: causality, timing, economy-wide repercussions and recurrence. Even those investigators who have found evidence of long-term fluctuations in economic trends have not agreed as to whether they should be identified with long waves of 50+ years duration, or shorter long swings of around 20 years. Thus, Rostow (1975) dismissed long swings as a limited historical phenomenon and concentrated on the long wave; conversely, Solomou (1988) found no evidence of long waves but did identify sequences of long swings in several industrialized economies. A third position was adopted by Berry (1991), who claimed that there is empirical evidence for the existence of both types of trend fluctuation; he argued that long swings drive the accumulation of technological infrastructure having a lifespan long enough for two successive long swings in real output to be combined within one long wave of price acceleration and deceleration.

Despite a lack of consensus about the existence of long waves, there is a school of analysts that continues to investigate the phenomenon, employing more sophisticated statistical techniques in an attempt to identify and describe the historical occurrence of the wave in a manner which meets the objections of the sceptics (see, for example, Kleinknecht, 1987; Kleinknecht et al., 1992). A parallel stream of simulation modelling of the long wave is based on the concept of 'self-ordering' by capital goods industries: their own outputs provide the additional means of production they require to sustain their expansion, creating a positive feedback loop which can generate alternating periods of over- and under-investment as a result of inventory adjustment and production lags (Sterman, 1985). Finally, some economic historians continue to employ a long-wave framework for analyzing the dynamic rhythm of capitalist development (Tylecote, 1991; Lloyd-Jones and Lewis, 1998; Freeman and Louca, 2001). They have extended the Kondratieff–Schumpeter chronology by terminating the Third Wave during the Second World War, identifying the upswing of the Fourth Wave with the mass production of a broad range of consumer goods, bringing this post-war wave to a close in the 1980s, and pointing to the upswing of a Fifth Wave, based on information technology and the internet, as we move into the twenty-first century.

Business cycle theory

Impulse and propagation: Multiplier–accelerator models

Theoretical modelling of the business cycle started in the 1930s, with key contributions being made by economists from several European countries. In various ways, these early models combine an investment equation with a consumption equation and incorporate two lagged responses, one of which is typically a gestation lag in the construction of capital goods. The models reduce to a second-order linear difference or differential equation with complex roots which can propagate endogenous oscillations under certain parameter conditions, though typically they depend upon occasional exogenous impulse shocks to maintain their endogenous momentum (Gabisch and Lorenz, 1989). The importance of investment gestation lags as a generator of cyclical behaviour had already been recognized by writers such as Robertson (1915) in the United Kingdom and Aftalion (1927) in France. They attributed alternating investment booms and slumps to expectations that are too optimistic and then too pessimistic because they are formed on the basis of current rather than future prices: '...the actual state of demand and prices is a bad index of future demand and prices, because of the long interval which separates the moment when new constructions are undertaken from that when they satisfy the demand' (Aftalion, 1927: 166).

An important early contribution was made by the Norwegian economist Ragnar Frisch (1933), who highlighted the crucial distinction between the exogenous impulses that can trigger cyclical fluctuations and the endogenous propagation mechanisms which determine subsequent cyclical behaviour. He modelled the propagation process by combining a consumption equation, in which limits on the money supply act to dampen the growth in demand, with an accelerator form of investment demand equation and an investment output equation that integrates the construction starts from several previous time periods. With these relationships expressed in differential form, characteristic equations with multiple complex roots are derived, yielding cycles of different periodicity in the levels of both consumer and capital goods output. Sensitivity testing shows the average length of the capital goods gestation period to be the key parameter determining cycle behaviour. The propagation equations yield damped cycles that die out unless external impulse shocks, such as technical innovations, renew the cyclical momentum; however, these do not need to be regular – erratic impulses can stimulate the propagation of regular cycles. Frisch (1933: 198) quotes an analogy drawn by the Swedish economist Wicksell: 'If you hit a wooden rocking horse with a club, the movement of the horse will be very different to that of the club.'

The Polish economist Michal Kalecki (1935, 1937) also developed a business cycle model in which the long gestation period required to construct fixed capital goods plays a crucial role. He distinguished three stages to investment activity: investment orders for the replacement and expansion of capital stock, production of the capital goods and delivery of the completed goods. The production of capital goods each year is a function of the sum of uncompleted orders issued in previous years divided by the average length of the gestation period. The investment function has a strongly Keynesian flavour, with the volume of investment orders relative to existing capital stock expressed as an increasing function of the prospective rate of profit earned on the investment and a decreasing function of the rate of interest. Crucially, investor 'myopia' is assumed – the prospective rate of profit is equated with the current return on capital. The model incorporates the dual nature of investment, as orders for future capital goods increase with the current level of capital goods production, acting as a component of aggregate demand, but decrease with the capacity of the capital stock already available for use. The investment equation with gestation lag produces cyclical fluctuations in new orders, whereby investment orders exceed production which exceeds deliveries during the upswing of the cycle, while in the downswing the reverse is true.

The Anglo-Saxon contribution to the first generation of business cycle models derived explicitly from Keynesian theory. Harrod (1936) was the first to propose the combination of Clark's accelerator and Keynes's multiplier as the cause of business cycles, and he built these mechanisms into his famous growth model (Harrod, 1939). Almost simultaneously, Samuelson (1939) published a paper setting out a full 'multiplier–accelerator model' of the business cycle; it is one of the most important economic papers published in the twentieth century, and the fact that he could compress his ideas into just four pages is a lesson to us all. Samuelson introduced two lags into his model, with a consumption equation that sets private consumption to be a proportion of the previous period's total income, fixed by the marginal propensity to consume, and an investment equation based on the accelerator response of induced investment to the increase in consumption spending between the previous and current periods. The model reduces to a second-order linear difference equation in total expenditure, and in response to an initial disturbance such as a surge in investment, its behaviour varies according to the values of its two key parameters – the marginal propensity to consume and the accelerator coefficient. As the values of the parameters vary, the system moves through four behavioural regimes: monotonic damping (after the initial disturbance, the economy moves smoothly back towards its equilibrium position), damped oscillation (the initial disturbance induces cyclical oscillations which progressively die away), explosive oscillation (the induced oscillations progressively increase in magnitude) and monotonic explosion (the initial disturbance causes the economy to move further and further away from its equilibrium position). For only one combination of parameter values, when the accelerator coefficient is equal to the inverse of the marginal propensity to consume, are stable and persistent harmonic cycles generated; otherwise the cycles either explode or are damped.

Several versions of the multiplier–accelerator model were developed. The variant put forward by Hicks (1950) relates investment to the lagged increase in total demand, rather than to the increase in consumption; it also incorporates a component of autonomous investment, in addition to induced investment, which introduces an equilibrium growth path around which induced investment fluctuates. Hicks elaborated his model to constrain its potentially explosive cyclical fluctuations within a full-capacity ceiling and an autonomous investment floor. Metzler (1941) used an alternative model structure to generate cycles in inventory investment; rather than current consumption being determined by income in the previous period, output is determined by sales in the previous period, with differences between current output and consumer demand being absorbed through changes in inventories. Output is produced not only for sale to consumers but also for investment in inventories, in order to maintain stocks at a 'normal' level that is directly proportional to expected sales in the current period. There is thus an accelerator relationship between changes in sales and inventory investment, with the level of investment varying according to the difference between actual and anticipated sales in the previous period.

The basic accelerator relationship incorporated into these cycle models was also the subject of modification. In the 'naïve' version first proposed by Clark (1917), the planned construction of new capital stock automatically meets the perceived gap between desired and actual stock, acting through the marginal capital–output ratio. This assumption has been much criticized, both theoretically for being unrealistically mechanistic in its assumptions about investment behaviour and empirically for not yielding plausible or significant results when tested statistically (Knox, 1952). These criticisms led to a more realistic refinement of the concept, the 'flexible accelerator', which assumes that each year's planned investment meets only some fraction of the gap between desired and actual capital stock, scaling down the naïve accelerator by a reaction coefficient that changes it from a purely technical ratio into a decision variable (Chenery, 1952). In another version of the multiplier–accelerator model, Goodwin (1948) spread the accelerator response over several time periods, introducing an investment lag structure which can again generate cyclical behaviour. There are two reasons for moderating the investment response to an increase in demand for fixed capital: the uncertainty of investor expectations about future demand conditions and the existence of surplus capacity, acting as a buffer stock for capital goods with a long gestation period: '…an industry with good reason for maintaining excess capacity also has a good reason to react slowly to changes in demand' (Chenery, 1952: 15).

Non-linear models

The models described so far are linear in structure, which facilitates the decomposition of an economic growth trajectory into its trend and cycle components. However, from the outset there has been a strand of non-linear business cycle modelling, in which trend and cycle are more closely integrated. In these models, cycles are propagated endogenously, in the absence of any exogenous shocks, because of the inherent instability of the economic system. Dynamic, non-linear models are much more difficult to solve analytically than linear models, and so their behaviour is usually explored by simulation (see Chapter 7). However, some well-known non-linear business cycle models can be re-framed using a special type of second-order differential equation called a Liénard equation, which yields an explicit solution defining the oscillatory behaviour of the system in terms of a unique 'limit cycle' (Gabisch and Lorenz, 1989: 156–61).

Non-linear business cycle modelling started with Kaldor (1940), who investigated how the interaction between savings and investment could generate self-sustaining cycles. He employed a Keynesian savings function, in which savings is a function of total income, and also defined investment to be a function of the level of income, not the change in income as in accelerator models. Both functions are defined to have non-linear, S-shaped forms, one the inverse of the other, which intersect to give three points of short-period equilibrium at any given level of capital stock: stable upper and lower bounds and an intermediate unstable position. As investment proceeds, the investment and savings functions move up and down according to the changing level of capital stock, which causes the economy to oscillate between the shifting upper and lower bound equilibrium points. Kaldor's solution of this simple but elegant model was essentially graphical, but Chang and Smyth (1971) subsequently reformulated the model in a mathematical form which can be solved analytically.

Non-linear versions of multiplier–accelerator models have also been developed, the most important being the growth and cycle model presented by Goodwin (1951). Like Hicks (1950), he introduced the idea of a full-capacity ceiling and an autonomous investment floor constraining the oscillations of the cycle, and like Kalecki (1935) he employed a gestation lag in investment. Gross investment is split into two components: autonomous investment, which is driven by technical progress, and induced investment, which is proportionate to the rate of change of total output. The accelerator relationship between induced investment and output change is quasi-non-linear in shape – it is zero at the upper and lower bounds, and has a constant slope in between – so that as output growth speeds up or slows down, induced investment will increase or decrease steadily within the thresholds. The relative lengths of the downswing and upswing phases of the cycle depend on the rate of technological progress: the faster it is the relatively shorter the downswing and the longer the upswing needed to accumulate sufficient capital to meet the requirements of economic growth. Goodwin showed that, for each combination of parameter values, the model tends towards a unique limit cycle that generates '...a stable, cyclical motion which is self-generating and self-perpetuating' (Goodwin, 1951: 14). This is because the explosive tendency generated by the lag mechanism is offset by the damping effect of the ceiling and floor thresholds. The crucial determinant of the period of the cycle is again found to be the length of the construction lag in the production of capital goods.

As the first generation of business cycle models became more sophisticated, attempts were made to reverse the de-coupling of growth and cycles that had been a feature of both neoclassical and Keynesian theory. The non-linear models proposed by Goodwin and Hicks build in a simple exogenous growth trend through the assumption of an autonomous rate of investment driven by technical progress.

An alternative model that combines growth and cycles within a non-linear structure was formulated by Smithies (1957). He introduced 'ratchet effects', such that consumption and investment not only depend on current income but also on the maximum level of income achieved in the past, so that a reduction in income leads to a less severe fall in demand. During the upswing of the cycle, these ratchet effects boost the growth in demand past the previous peak, at which point they become inoperable; during the downswing, they retard the fall in demand, creating a higher trough than in the previous cycle. Successively higher turning points thus introduce a growth trend into the cycle through the impetus provided by the ratchets, as past history influences the present in a hysteresis effect of the type discussed earlier in this chapter.

The idea that cyclical fluctuations give impetus to economic growth through repeated surges in investment was developed by Kaldor (1954), who suggested a more fundamental sort of ratchet effect based on a Schumpeterian model of endogenous technical progress in which bursts of innovation-led investment are followed by phases of accelerated obsolescence. He provided the most persuasive argument for the integration of growth and cycles by considering the operation of an innovative economy in which entrepreneurs indulge their animal spirits:

'The conclusion which emerges from this is that so far from the trend rate of growth determining the strength or duration of booms, it is the strength and duration of booms which shapes the trend rate of growth. It is the economy in which business-men are reckless and speculative, where expectations are highly volatile, but with an underlying bias towards optimism...which is likely to show the higher rate of progress over longer periods...It is when expectations are highly volatile that the expansionary phase of the cycle is likely to be vigorous and sustained; that it will inevitably lead to a strong boom which will burst through the pre-existing "external frame" of the economy and carry it to a new and higher plateau. Once such a higher plateau is reached, the subsequent slump, though severe, will not mean a return to the previous depression-level; it will in time produce a new expansionary process from a higher "floor", leading to a new "ceiling"' (Kaldor, 1954: 68–70).

During the later 1950s and 1960s, Richard Goodwin was almost alone in continuing to work on non-linear models of growth cycles. He developed his 1951 model to operate rather in the fashion described by Kaldor: bursts of investment combining induced demand with Schumpeterian innovation operate through a lagged multiplier–accelerator to carry the upswing past its previous peak, until it catches up with the rising full employment ceiling, while rising fixed outlays create a higher floor to constrain the subsequent downswing (see, for example, Goodwin, 1955). This work culminated in a seminal paper (Goodwin, 1967) which combined brevity and impact in the same measures as Samuelson's multiplier–accelerator paper almost 30 years earlier. In this model, the focus of attention shifts from the dynamics of investment to the dynamics of the labour market, with the business cycle driven by an almost Marxian process of competition for income shares between capital and labour. During the expansion phase, increasing real wages and employment lead to a rising wage share and falling profit share; the falling profit share leads to a cutback in investment and a slow down in employment growth; during the resultant contraction, downward pressure on wages and a falling employment share cause the profit share to rise; the rising profit share then spurs a recovery in investment and employment, initiating a new upswing. Goodwin's non-linear modelling approach continues to be developed (Goodwin et al., 1984; Velupillai, 1990), and its enduring appeal provides a strong link between the first generation of business cycle models and the second generation which was born in the mid-1970s.

Rational expectations

As indicated at the start of this chapter, there was a lull in the development of business cycle theory from the mid-1950s to the mid-1970s. Strong and sustained growth after the Second World War, allied with the apparent success of Keynesian demand management policies, created a consensus among economists that severe cyclical disturbances to growth were a thing of the past. The worldwide OPEC recessions of 1973–5 and 1979–82 destroyed that consensus and created the conditions for the emergence of several new strands of business cycle theory, each grounded in a particular school of contemporary economic thought (Phelps, 1990).

Modern business cycle theory has developed as part of a broader movement over the past 30 years to articulate the microeconomic foundations of macroeconomics (Weintraub, 1979). These neoclassical micro-foundations are expressed in terms of 'representative agents', such as profit maximizing firms and utility maximizing households, which operate rationally under conditions of flexible prices and market-clearing equilibria. The micro-foundations movement developed as a reaction to the perceived rigidities of Keynesian macroeconomics models such as the multiplier–accelerator, which were derived under the simplifying assumption of fixed prices. It is through a common micro-foundations approach that the search is being conducted to find a 'new consensus in macroeconomics' which can unite the competing schools (Arestis, 2007). However, though it is now widely accepted that the structure of macroeconomic models should rest on the micro-foundations of individual agent behaviour, the approach is open to the charge that it depends upon a 'fallacy of composition'. By arguing that what is true for each individual agent is also true for the economy as a whole introduces a confusion between regarding the totality of agents as a distribution of individuals and regarding it as a collective whole (Dore, 1993: 126).

Rational expectations provide the underpinning for the micro-foundations of modern cycle theories (see, for example, Barro, 1989). Representative agents make intertemporal decisions based on their expectations about the outcomes of future events and it is the way in which these expectations are formed that determines their optimizing behaviour. At their simplest, expectations may be 'naïve' or 'myopic', assuming that the future will be the same as the present; a more sophisticated approach is to assume 'adaptive' expectations which adjust in response to discrepancies between previous expectations and actual outcomes (Nerlove, 1958). The rational expectations hypothesis takes the further step of assuming that economic agents are able to make informed predictions of future events using a plausible model of the workings of the economy, subject only to the impact of stochastic shocks which they cannot anticipate (Muth, 1961). It is also assumed that agents are aware of the existence of such shocks and know their probability distribution, so that their expectations are not biased by systematic errors. Two crucial conditions are required for the rational expectations hypothesis to be valid. The first is that the economic system is continuously equilibrating: agents can predict equilibrium values, but if there is disequilibrium in the system, then uncertainty is attached to actual outcomes and their expected values cannot rationally be forecast. The second is that all economic agents operate according to a coherent economic model and, furthermore, they all operate according to the same model.

The rational expectations hypothesis remains controversial and continues to be attacked from a Keynesian standpoint (see, for example, Blinder, 1987). There is an alternative approach to the formation of expectations, termed 'bounded rationality', which requires less demanding assumptions about human capabilities when making decisions under conditions of uncertainty (Simon, 1992). The combination of bounded computational abilities and imperfect information means that economic agents must adopt straightforward decision rules within a more realistic 'satisficing' framework: '…either by finding optimum solutions for a simplified world, or by finding satisfactory solutions for a more realistic world' (Simon, 1979: 498). The formation of expectations under conditions of uncertainty is particularly relevant to investment in capital goods such as buildings which have a long gestation period, so that '…decisions have to be made by reference to unknown conditions considerably in the future, when there is little rational basis for knowing how these future conditions are correlated with present ones' (Driver and Moreton, 1992: 2). In such circumstances, one way in which bounded rationality might operate has been proposed by Shackle (1970), who suggested that investors evaluate opportunities within ranges defined by the best-case and worst-case outcomes that they find believable – each being a limit beyond which any further increase in the desirability/undesirability of the outcome is more than offset by the increase in 'surprise', or disbelief, at its occurrence.

In parallel to the adoption of rational expectations, a stochastic approach both to measuring and modelling the business cycle has gained favour since the mid-1970s (the separation and measurement of stochastic trends and cycles is covered in Appendix A). Stochastic business cycle models do not seek to reproduce the cycle as a deterministic oscillatory process, as was the objective of first generation models, but rather the cycle is conceptualized as a variable but persistent series of serially correlated deviations from trend that result from exogenous stochastic shocks (Blinder and Fischer, 1981: 277). As a result, the focus of attention has shifted from the endogenous processes of cycle propagation to the exogenous sources of cycle-inducing impulses. The origins attributed to these shocks distinguish the main schools of modern business cycle theory – unanticipated money supply changes (New Classical), technology-induced productivity shocks (Real Business Cycles) and nominal demand shocks (New Keynesian). For comparative surveys of the different schools see, for example, Dore (1993) and Arnold (2002).

New Classical theory

The foundations of modern business cycle theory were laid by the Monetarist challenge to the post-war Keynesian consensus. Milton Friedman's aim was to replace Keynesian income–expenditure theory with a new macroeconomics, based on the classical quantity theory of money. This approach reasserted the primacy of the supply side of the economy as the determinant of the equilibrium rates of growth in output and real wages and the 'natural' rates of interest and unemployment that maintain the equilibrium growth path. In Friedman (1968), he set out the ideas which formed the basis of the New Classical approach to business cycles. Friedman contended that the business cycle is essentially a monetary phenomenon: the necessary and sufficient condition for the generation of cycles is unanticipated changes in the rate of growth of the money stock, rather than the autonomous changes in investment highlighted in the Keynesian model. An increase in the rate of growth of the nominal money supply initially lowers the market rate of interest below its natural rate, thereby stimulating investment and consumption demand; this causes output and employment to expand, so that unemployment falls below its natural rate and upward pressure is exerted on real wages. However, the expansion in demand also exerts inflationary pressure on prices, which works through to reduce the real money supply, push the market interest rate back up and lower the real wage. The result is that workers demand a compensating increase in nominal wages, causing unemployment to rise, output growth to slow and the rate of inflation to fall. Furthermore, given the tendency for the economy to overreact, the correction in interest rates is likely to overshoot, setting in motion a cyclical adjustment process.

The New Classical school set Monetarist ideas within a rational expectations framework in order to develop an 'equilibrium' theory of the business cycle (see Lucas, 1981, and Barro, 1981 for discussions). This theoretical approach promoted the 'policy ineffectiveness' argument that only unanticipated policy shifts can affect aggregate demand, and even then their effect is only temporary, while Keynesian counter-cyclical policies are ineffectual because economic agents adapt their expectations to accommodate known policy rules (Sargent and Wallace, 1976). The 'misperceptions' model developed by Lucas (1975) and Barro (1976) incorporates the Monetarist argument that business cycles result from imperfect price information: economic agents are assumed to have current information about the prices of goods they trade directly, but only lagged information about prices in other markets and therefore about the general price level. Under these conditions, an unanticipated increase in the money supply produces an inflationary rise in the general price level that is misinterpreted by agents as an increase in the relative price of the goods they trade. Their rational response is to expand investment and output to meet the perceived excess demand, but as they subsequently realize their error they cut back on production, creating excess capacity that dampens down further investment.

In the Lucas model, the fluctuation of real output around its equilibrium path is translated into a persistent cycle through two mechanisms: a distributed lag structure created by the information lags, and an accelerator relationship between the size of the perceived demand shock and the investment demand for additional capital. Lucas stressed the importance of the accelerator in his model with an observation that has a stronger flavour of Keynes's animal spirits than might appeal to the tastes of many proponents of rational expectations:

'How can moderate cyclical movements in prices lead to the high-amplitude movements in durable goods purchases which are observed?...For individual investment projects, rates of return are highly variable, often negative, and often measured in hundreds of percent. A quick, current response to what seems to others a weak "signal" is often the key to a successful investment. The agent who waits until the situation is clear to everyone is too late; someone else has already added the capacity to meet the high demand' (Lucas, 1981: 232).

A key problem with the New Classical theory is that misperceptions and rational expectations are essentially incompatible, as was pointed out by Tobin (1980) and Okun (1980), and subsequently recognized by Lucas (1981: 15). 'Continual equilibrium with rational expectations and fully informed agents makes the model economy too good to be true' (Tobin, 1980: 789), so that the assumption of price information lags across markets is really no more than a device to introduce the imperfect information necessary to generate cyclical behaviour within the model. Recognition of this inconsistency led to the emergence of Real Business Cycle (RBC) theory, which aimed to overcome the defects of the misperceptions approach while remaining within the New Classical tradition of equilibrium cycle models. The RBC theorists, led by Kydland and Prescott (1982), sought the origins of their shocks and response lags not in the money economy but in the real economy – and found them in technology-induced productivity shocks to provide the impulse mechanism (echoes of Schumpeter) and transmission lags such as the investment gestation period to provide the propagation mechanism (echoes of Kalecki).

The main thesis of the 'time-to-build' model of Kydland and Prescott is that '...the assumption of multi-period construction is crucial for explaining aggregate fluctuations' (Kydland and Prescott, 1982: 1345). The model combines growth and cycles, employing a constant-returns production function with a technology parameter which is assumed to be subject to both permanent and temporary shocks that make total factor productivity a stochastic variable. New fixed capital goods are built over multiple periods and only add to productive capital stock at the end of their construction; investment in each period consists of the sum of the outlays on current fixed capital projects, plus an addition to inventories. In response to exogenous shocks, economic agents adjust their levels of consumption and labour supply, with inventory investment acting as a substitute for consumption while an intertemporal utility function allows leisure to be substituted for employment. Capital investment and labour supply decisions in each period are made contingent upon the past history of productivity shocks and a current productivity indicator, but not the current unanticipated productivity shock. A steady-state growth path is derived by allowing the technology parameter to increase smoothly over time without any shocks; cyclical fluctuations around this path are then generated by introducing the shocks, rendering the decision framework stochastic through the formation of conditional expectations. The persistence of the cycle stems from the multi-period construction technology and the serial correlation of the technology shocks, as they are transmitted from one period to the next via their permanent component.

Views differ about the significance of time-to-build lags as a cycle propagation mechanism. Kydland and Prescott calibrated their RBC model to obtain a good fit to quarterly US data on cyclical fluctuations between 1950 and 1979, finding the cyclical behaviour of the model very sensitive to the time-to-build parameter. King et al. (1988a) developed a similar RBC model with stochastic technology shocks, but in addition they introduced a deterministic exogenous rate of labour-augmenting technical progress into their production technology, in order to make capital accumulation the explicit driver of steady-state growth. They achieved a similarly close fit with quarterly US cycle data for the 1948–86 period, but again only under the assumption of persistent technology shocks. In King et al. (1988b), the model was adapted so that the growth trend itself is stochastic, following a random walk with drift that produces permanent shifts in the trajectory of capital accumulation, while as a further extension, technical progress was endogenously generated through the accumulation of human as well as physical capital. In contrast, Rouwenhorst (1991) introduced time-to-build lags into a neoclassical capital accumulation model and found that the multi-period construction technology was not a strong propagation mechanism, while Burnside and Eichenbaum (1996) introduced variable capacity utilization to strengthen the propagation mechanism by magnifying the cyclical volatility of aggregate output in response to exogenous shocks.

The dependency of RBC models on serially correlated technology shocks to generate persistent cyclical behaviour has prompted the observation that 'Many RBC models have weak endogenous propagation mechanisms...output dynamics are essentially the same as impulse dynamics' (Cogley and Nason, 1995a: 493). For discussions of how RBC theory has developed since its inception in the early 1980s, see Barro, (1989), Stadler (1994), Cogley and Nason (1995a) and Arnold (2002: 86–90).

New Keynesian theory

The New Keynesian critique of the RBC school started by questioning its underlying neoclassical premise '...that fluctuations in consumption and employment are the consequence of dynamic optimizing behaviour by economic agents who face no quantity constraints' (Mankiw et al., 1985: 225). The authors of this paper could find no empirical evidence for continuous optimizing behaviour when using postwar US data to estimate an RBC form of intertemporal utility function in which economic agents are allowed to trade-off consumption against leisure when making consumption and labour supply decisions. The shortcomings of RBC theory were seen to stem from its assumption of completely flexible wages and prices, and its belief that only shocks in real variables such as productivity are important, ignoring the impact of nominal shocks such as a sudden change in the interest rate or oil price (McCallum, 1986; Mankiw, 1989). Perhaps most fundamental of all, the equilibrium assumptions of RBC theory seem to offend common sense: 'Of all the implications of RBC theory, the optimality of economic fluctuations is perhaps the most shocking. It seems undeniable that the level of welfare is lower in a recession than in the boom that preceded it' (Mankiw, 1989: 83).

The New Keynesian alternative has, for the most part, incorporated the rational expectations of representative agents into its micro-foundations, but rejected the notion of continuous market-clearing equilibrium in a perfectly competitive economy. There is widespread evidence of departures from the New Classical ideal: for example, 'sticky' prices and excess capacity in imperfectly competitive product markets, profit maximizing or 'efficiency' wages that remain above the market-clearing rate, and oligopolistic financial markets with credit rationing (Dore, 1993: 101–16). In the search for greater economic realism, New Keynesian theory emphasizes the role of imperfect competition and price rigidities as cycle propagation mechanisms, and nominal demand shocks as the predominant impulse mechanism (see Mankiw and Romer, 1991 for a review). Some recent variants of the

New Keynesian model draw upon RBC theory by allowing technology shocks as well as monetary shocks to act as the impulse mechanism (Ireland, 2004).

An early example of New Keynesian business cycle theory is the 'menu cost' model presented by Mankiw (1985). This derives price rigidities as a consequence of the optimizing behaviour of monopoly firms operating with a constant cost function and facing an inverse demand function, both of which shift in proportion to changes in the level of aggregate demand. The firm chooses the price and output combination which maximizes its profits, on the basis of its expectation of the level of aggregate demand, and sets its price accordingly. If actual and expected demand do not coincide, for example because of an unexpected contraction in demand, the price can only be adjusted downwards by incurring a small menu cost, and the firm will not make the adjustment unless the gain in profits outweighs the menu cost. The result is downward price rigidity that restricts output to a socially suboptimal level by creating excess capacity and underemployment. Even if there are no explicit menu costs, 'near-rational' wage and price inertia can occur under conditions of monopolistic competition, if there are only small losses to the firm by not fully adjusting to a demand shock (Akerlof and Yellen, 1985).

Another source of market imperfection explored by the New Keynesians is 'coordination failure' among a multiplicity of economic agents whose collective actions would lead to higher levels of output through positive externality effects if they were coordinated. As an example, the 'implementation cycles' model presented by Shleifer (1986) explores the cyclical behaviour of a multi-sector economy in which long-term expectations determine the timing of innovations, creating innovation clusters that echo Schumpeter and Mensch. There is a constant stream of exogenous inventions produced within each sector which can cheapen its production technology; the choice for firms within a sector is when to adopt these inventions as innovations so as to maximize the temporary profits they generate before imitators follow suit and eliminate the additional profits. Firms will choose to innovate when demand and therefore temporary profits are highest – which is during a boom. They hold commonly shared expectations about the timing of the boom, and so they tend to innovate simultaneously, which boosts output and ensures that their expectations are realized; conversely, if a boom is not expected, the firms will all tend to delay innovation, prolonging a slump. The result is that the economy pursues an expectations-driven cyclical growth path.

Imperfections in the credit market have featured strongly in recent business cycle theory. This strand was initiated by Bernanke et al. (1996), who proposed a cycle model in which firms' balance sheets act as a 'financial accelerator' to amplify the impact of shocks. Higher net worth reduces the costs of financing investment, and because cycle upswings improve net worth they increase investment, which amplifies the upturn. Kiyotaki and Moore (1997) developed this idea into a cycle propagation mechanism in which capital goods act as collateral for loans as well as means of production, so that their value is an endogenous determinant of credit limits. A positive shock raises investment, which increases the value of collateral, thereby relaxing borrowing constraints and generating a further lagged increase in investment that amplifies the effect of the initial shock. Aghion and Banerjee (2005) have added credit rationing to a Schumpeterian growth model which is driven by R&D and subject to productivity shocks. The exercise of credit rationing by lenders means that firms cannot be certain of raising loans for profitable investment, and in an environment in which productivity shocks create uncertainty for firms about their future liquidity, their willingness to undertake long-term investments in new technology is reduced. Shock-induced fluctuations are thus combined with a sub-optimal credit-constrained growth path. Even in the absence of exogenous shocks, credit rationing can generate endogenous cyclical fluctuations around the growth path: a period of accelerated growth increases interest rates, which squeezes profits and reduces borrowing capacity in a constrained credit market, causing a reduction in investment and a slow down in the growth rate.

The convergence of modern business cycle theory with endogenous growth theory returns us to the concept of growth cycles which so engaged the classical economists. Evans et al. (1998) have presented a rational expectations model of growth cycles in which the economy switches stochastically between periods of low and high growth according to self-fulfilling shifts in investor sentiment. When economic agents expect growth to be slow, investment is depressed, returns are low and growth is sluggish; when the expectation is for rapid growth, enhanced investment stimulates high returns and a strong rate of growth. Indeterminacy of expectations and multiple equilibria are induced by a combination of monopolistic competition and complementarity between different types of capital goods. A self-reinforcing process is created such that an increase in the demand for one capital good boosts the demand for others, encouraging firms to incur the R&D costs necessary to launch new goods on to the market. Firms and consumers endeavour to forecast the behaviour of the economy under conditions of uncertainty, anticipating whether high or low growth will continue or whether there may be a switch to the alternative state. There are echoes here of the role that Keynes attributed to animal spirits in the fluctuation of investment (Howitt and McAfee, 1992).

Both the current schools of modern business cycle theory – the New Classical (RBC) and the New Keynesian – base their theories on micro-foundations defined by the rational expectations behaviour of representative agents. Where they differ is in whether business cycles are the equilibrium response of a perfectly competitive economy to unanticipated exogenous shocks (New Classical), or whether the impacts of shocks or uncertainty trigger cyclical behaviour that is propagated endogenously through market imperfections (New Keynesian). Because of their equilibrium assumptions, some lagged response mechanism, such as price information lags or multi-period investment lags, has to be introduced into New Classical models in order to propagate cyclical behaviour. Despite such lags, the endogenous propagation mechanisms of these models tend to be weak and their cyclical behaviour may depend upon an exogenous impulse mechanism of serially correlated shocks. In essence, their cyclical behaviour may be little more than a reflection of their impulse dynamics. The market imperfections assumed in New Keynesian models, such as monopolistic competition, price rigidities, credit rationing or coordination failures, strengthen their endogenous propagation mechanisms, and though exogenous shocks may still be required to trigger cyclical behaviour, they do not need to be serially correlated. In this sense they are closer to the first generation of business cycle models launched by Frisch, with his evocative distinction between the motion of the club and the motion of the rocking horse.

Summary: Theories of growth and cycles

Before moving on to review the specific body of research on building cycles, it is useful to summarize the key themes that have emerged from this survey of theories about economic growth and business cycles:

Investment as the driver of growth
Capital investment is the key driver of the growth process, expanding productive capacity, increasing the capital intensity of production, raising labour productivity through endogenously generated technical progress, generating increasing returns to scale and establishing new industries to produce new products.

Path dependence
As an economy develops, there is a tendency for increasing returns to lock it on to a particular growth path, and the extent of its path dependence increases with the sunk costs of its expanding stock of fixed capital and the interrelatedness of the different technological components embodied in its physical and human capital.

Growth cycles
The secular trend in economic growth is dependent on the growth rate of the labour force combined with the rate of labour-augmenting technical progress; in the shorter term, the growth process involves the interplay of equilibrating and disequilibrating forces, creating a historically dependent cyclical dynamic which propels the economy forwards in a wave-like motion in which past cycles influence the current direction of growth.

The dual function of investment
The dual function of investment as income generator and capacity augmenter creates a tension between the competitive pressure on producers to increase productive capacity and maintain profitability through labour-saving investment and their need for a level of effective demand sufficient to consume total output; when these conflicting demands move out of balance, an over-investment crisis results.

The dual function of capital goods
A similar tension is created between the dual function of capital goods as physical means of production and as financial assets: the producer interest is to invest in new technologies which reduce the income earning capacity of existing assets, causing their value to depreciate, while the investor interest is to maintain the monetary value of those existing assets.

The investment accelerator
The accelerator relationship between changes in output and the level of induced demand for capital goods is one of the key factors generating cyclical instability; the longer the life of the capital goods, the smaller the stabilizing component of replacement investment and the more volatile the investment cycle.

Cycle-inducing characteristics of capital goods
The long gestation lags and lumpiness of capital goods contribute to the volatility of investment cycles: there is a tendency for investors to make inadequate allowance for the competing supply of goods coming on stream during the gestation period of their investment, causing an overshoot, followed by a cutback in investment activity.

A profitability cycle
During the recovery stage of the business cycle, profitability increases as demand expands and the investment upswing boosts productivity; during the prosperity stage, profitability is eroded by rising costs, initiating a cutback in investment; during the subsequent recession, profitability continues to fall as demand shrinks and spare capacity grows; in the depression, obsolete capital stock is liquidated and the inducement to invest begins to increase again.

Speculative boom–bust cycles
During a prolonged phase of prosperity, a sequence of mild business cycles creates the conditions for a more severe boom–bust cycle, as inflating asset prices provide the security for progressively higher levels of debt until a liquidity crisis bursts the speculative bubble, setting off a deflationary spiral that plunges the economy into a severe depression.

A family of cycles
There is evidence for the existence of up to four economic cycles of different periodicity (minor cycles, major cycles, long swings and long waves); they have been identified as investment cycles involving capital goods with different gestation lags and durability, or alternatively as technology cycles reflecting waves of innovation operating over different timescales.

Long waves
The existence of long waves is disputed, but their proponents explain them in terms of periodic technological revolutions: a surge of investment in a cluster of major innovations generates a phase of economic prosperity marked by accelerated growth in labour productivity and output; as the new technologies mature and markets saturate, productivity and output growth slacken, leading the economy into a phase of depression out of which the next technological revolution emerges.

Impulse and propagation
Theories of the business cycle make a fundamental distinction between the exogenous impulse shocks which set the cycle in motion and the endogenous propagation mechanisms which maintain the subsequent fluctuations of the cycle around the growth trajectory; alternative theories assign different weight to the importance of impulse and propagation in cycle generation.

Exogenous impulses
Monetarist, New Classical and New Keynesian theories identify nominal demand shocks, such as unanticipated changes in the money supply or interest rates, as the

main source of exogenous impulses to trigger cyclical fluctuations, whereas RBC theory highlights supply shocks such as technology-induced shifts in productivity.

Endogenous propagation
Different theoretical schools assume different endogenous cycle propagation mechanisms: for New Classical theory, it is misperceptions stemming from price information lags; for RBC theory, it is time-to-build lags; for New Keynesian theory, it is price rigidities, coordination failures and imperfect competition.

Linear models of investment cycles
Linear models of the multiplier–accelerator type generate endogenous cyclical behaviour by combining investment and consumption equations that incorporate a minimum of two reaction lags; one of these typically involves the gestation lag in capital goods construction, which proves to be the key determinant of the length of the cycle.

Non-linear models
Non-linearities can be introduced into cycle models to improve their realism: the fluctuations of the cycle can be constrained within an autonomous investment floor and a full-capacity ceiling, while ratchet effects can couple together the motion of trend and cycle by propelling the economy through progressively higher peaks and troughs, along a trajectory which reflects previous cycle history.

Investor expectations and sentiment
The instability of economic cycles is reinforced by the difficulties of forming expectations under conditions of great uncertainty, which creates a tendency for investor sentiment to alternate between optimism and pessimism, particularly during speculative boom–bust cycles.

The formation of expectations
The extreme assumptions of the rational expectations hypothesis are difficult to justify in the case of investment decisions made in markets characterized by long gestation lags and an uncertain future; myopic or adaptive expectations, or some form of bounded rationality, are more realistic assumptions.

Market imperfections
Even under assumptions of rational expectations, market imperfections such as monopolistic competition, price rigidities or credit rationing can induce fluctuations along an endogenously generated growth path, creating a modern version of the growth cycle that signifies a reintegration of growth and cycle theory.

3

The Nature of Building Cycles

A long and violent cycle

Specific studies of the building cycle first started to appear in the 1930s. Until then, '...building has been neglected by economists, its statistics unassembled, its history unwritten, its organisation practically unknown' (Cairncross, 1934: 1). The Great Depression of the early 1930s changed all that. In an attempt to ensure that nothing as traumatic happened again, the search was on to find ways in which economic growth could be better managed and stabilized. Attention focused on investment as the most volatile component of aggregate output, and building construction as the most volatile component of aggregate investment. The pioneers who launched the study of building investment were hampered by a lack of consistent data, and so data assembly and interpretation formed a major part of their research agenda. It is also noticeable that leading figures in the vanguard, such as Homer Hoyt and Clarence Long in the United States, derived their insights about the unique nature of building cycles from their professional involvement in the real estate industry, as much as from their academic associations. A strong connection between academic study and professional practice continues to be a feature of research on real estate cycles.

Early studies identified both long and short building cycles in most sectors of construction activity, and also noted that these cycles were manifested in other aspects of the real estate market, such as vacancy rates, land values and building rents. From the outset, short building cycles were seen as a manifestation of the general business cycle, while long building cycles were associated with the long swings in economic growth that had been identified by Kuznets and Burns as discussed in Chapter 2. A causal explanation for these long swings in building was initially identified in the relationship between economic development, population growth and building investment. A surge in economic growth was believed to induce an increase in population growth through in-migration, in turn inducing a boom in 'population-sensitive investment', particularly the construction of dwellings and infrastructure. It was also recognized that the length and severity of the cycle could be attributed to the durability of building capital: 'Buildings, railroads and other types of construction generally have such a long life that a period of over-construction is usually followed by an extended period of severe liquidation, so that the cycles are long and violent' (Warren and Pearson, 1937: 97).

During the 1960s, it became accepted that a migration-based model could no longer be used to explain the long building cycle, and attention turned to the endogenous capital stock adjustment processes underlying building investment, with its cycle-inducing characteristics of prolonged construction lags and durable stock. Another avenue of theoretical investigation focused on the sticky rent adjustment processes which link changes in occupancy to the changes in rents and prices that provide market signals to developers. Given that lagged adjustment processes are a characteristic feature of real estate markets, modern building cycle theory accords an important role to the way in which developers form expectations in the face of an uncertain future. The volatile market cycles which have been experienced in the last 30 years have maintained the research impetus, with the growing integration of real estate and capital markets directing particular attention to the impacts of property cycles on the wider economy. Building cycles have also come to be seen as an international phenomenon, as globalization has linked local and national property markets through the cross-border movement of occupiers and investment capital.

The chapter starts by charting the historical evolution of building cycle research, distinguishing between those studies which concentrated primarily on empirical investigation and those which attempted causal explanations of the phenomenon. There follows a review of modern property cycle research, concentrating on the new perspectives which have been adopted for investigating issues such as the formation of expectations, the convergence of property and financial markets and the globalization of building supply and demand. This survey of historical and recent research provides the foundations for constructing a conceptual model of the building cycle, taking account of the particular characteristics of building investment while drawing upon the broader corpus of theory on economic growth and cycles, surveyed in the previous chapter.

Historical building cycle research

The first wave of empirical studies

The pioneers of building cycle research were German scholars, writing in the late nineteenth and early twentieth centuries (for a brief review of this literature, see Gottlieb, 1976: 1–2). They investigated the wavelike trajectory of urban development in a range of German cities, from the middle of the eighteenth century up to the First World War, as manifested through a repeating pattern of booms followed by slumps in construction activity which was reflected in the movement of land and property prices. Among the most notable of these studies were those by Reich (1912), who examined the development of Berlin between 1840 and 1910, and Mangoldt (1907) who synthesized a general description of the cycle-driven process of urban development.

The first case study of the building cycle in Britain was the paper by Spensley (1918), who plotted two house-building cycles in London between 1871 and 1916 and noted an inverse relationship between the levels of building and vacant dwellings. Following on from this, Cairncross (1934: 1) was struck by the 'extraordinary violence' of the house-building cycle in Glasgow over the same period, again identifying two long cycles, with a short cycle being superimposed upon it. He also noted the inverse relationship between building and vacancy, acting with a one-year lag, which he observed to be mediated through movements in rents. During an economic boom, both population growth and rising household incomes boost the demand for houses, reducing vacancy and increasing rents, so prompting an upsurge in building which may be reinforced by an expanded supply of cheap credit. However, because of the stickiness of rents, it can take several years before the effect of a change in vacancy fully works through to rents. He further suggested that the link between the business cycle and levels of house-building operated through migration: when the city's heavy industries were flourishing, in-migration increased, boosting the demand for dwellings.

At a more aggregate level, Shannon (1934) produced an early indicator of the building cycle in England between 1785 and 1849 by constructing an index of national brick production. This revealed four long cycles over the period, yielding an average period of some 16 years. The secular trend in building activity broadly tracked the growth in population, acting as the long-term driver of housing demand, while the cycle in building closely followed the inverse movement of interest rates, acting as the key determinant of the supply of construction finance. Bowley (1937) considered that there was not a simple monocausal transmission link between the general business cycle and the house-building cycle, since the positive influence of low interest rates on construction costs during a depression tended to offset the negative effect on housing demand of reduced household incomes.

American research on building cycles was launched by the ground-breaking case study of *One Hundred Years of Land Values in Chicago* by Hoyt (1933). He assembled sales data for land transactions in Chicago between 1830 and 1933 in order to create a land value index which could plot both the rise and fluctuation in values, as the city developed 'from a hamlet of a dozen log huts' in 1830 into an urban agglomeration with a population of 3.4 million in 1930 (Hoyt, 1933: 3). He used the index to relate the development of the city to the growth in its population and the construction of its building stock, demonstrating that its development trajectory had been punctuated by a sequence of vigorous booms and slumps in the land market and in building activity. The building cycle was used to divide the development history of the city into a sequence of eras, each boom being associated either with the impact of a new form of transport infrastructure or building technology, or else with exogenous events such as war. Thus, there was a canal boom (1830–42), a railroad boom (1843–62), a post–Civil War and Great Fire boom (1863–77), a first skyscraper and World Fair boom (1878–98), an unusual period of relatively steady growth (1899–1918) and a post–First World War boom (1919–33). Excluding the period of steady growth between 1899 and 1918 as atypical, the five identified building cycles had an average duration of 17 years. Three characteristics of these cycles were noted: the magnitude of their oscillations was far greater than that of other cycles in business activity, troughs in building and in other economic indicators tended to coincide whereas their peaks did not and the slumps in building typically lasted longer than the short lived but more extreme booms.

Following his historical analysis, Hoyt offered some concluding thoughts as to how the real estate cycle operates. While sustained population growth and industrialization are the fundamental drivers of the long-term rise in building activity, the trigger for each building boom is typically an upswing in business conditions which both accelerates population growth in response to new opportunities and creates a mood of optimism that reinforces future growth expectations. Such periods of optimism arose during the speculative fevers induced by canal and railroad construction and during the economic aftermath of the Civil War and the First World War. Each surge in population boosts the demand for housing and infrastructure, generating a rapid increase in rents and prices for existing buildings which creates a boom in the land market and in construction activity. The combination of excessive growth expectations and a plentiful supply of credit in periods of prosperity then leads to over-building; this is followed by a downturn in construction activity which may be reinforced by weaker economic and population growth, causing land and property values to slump, credit supply to tighten, mortgage foreclosures to increase and building to slow down to a virtual standstill.

A second US case study was provided by Long (1936), who examined the historical development of Manhattan between 1868 and 1934, using the values of planned buildings in five separate uses (residential, office, retail, industrial and hotel). He identified two types of cycles in building activity. Long cycles were obtained by a two-stage smoothing process using variable length moving averages, while short cycles were isolated as fluctuations around the smoothed long cycles. Although long cycles with a period in the range 15–20 years were identified, similar to those found in other empirical studies of the time, they seemed to combine into more pronounced long waves of 30–40 years duration. There was a high degree of synchronization of the long cycles across the different sectors, with the exception of industrial building, and in general they moved independently of the business cycle, except in severe recessions. The short cycles tended to be of similar length (6–7 years), but much greater amplitude (5–6 times larger), than the standard NBER reference cycle of industrial activity. Unlike the long cycle, the short cycle showed definite conformity with the cycle in industrial activity and even stronger conformity with the cycle in industrial stock prices. Combining the two types of building cycle, a general relationship emerged whereby the sectors with the highest secular growth rate in building activity (hotel, office and industrial) exhibited both long and short cycles with the greatest volatility.

US studies of building cycles at the national level started with Riggleman (1933). He created an index of building starts (excluding infrastructure construction) for the United States between 1875 and 1932, using the value of building permits issued in an increasing number of cities up to 1900, and a constant total of 52 cities thereafter. The index was derived in per capita constant price values and expressed as percentage deviations around a linear trend. Three long building cycles were identified, with shorter cyclical movements of business cycle length superimposed on each long cycle; the long cycles had an average period of 18 years and an amplitude 2–3 times that of the short cycles. Riggleman subsequently extended his index to cover the period 1830–1933 and include up to 65 cities; six long cycles were then identified, while their average period remained 18 years. Newman (1935) conducted a similar exercise, using building permit data for 17 cities, and produced much the same results. Other early US studies quoted by Warren and Pearson (1937) yielded long building cycles of similar length, amplitude and timing.

After his Manhattan case study, Long (1939) also became involved in the construction of national indices of US building activity. He assembled annual data on the number and value of residential and non-residential buildings that were included in plans filed, or in permits issued, between 1856 and 1935 for an increasing number of the main cities across the country, reaching a total of 29 for the number index and 27 for the value index. Consistent with his earlier case study, he identified a long cycle in building activity at national level, with an average period of 18–19 years for both types of construction, but with the severity of the residential fluctuations being twice as strong as those in non-residential building. Where there was a correspondence between the cycles in building and general business activity, building led in the downturn, due to the accelerator effect, and lagged in the upturn, because of the overhang of vacant buildings and the gestation lags for new buildings.

A year later, Long published *Building Cycles and the Theory of Investment* (1940), the second major contribution to the building cycle canon after Hoyt's Chicago case study. The empirical analysis expanded the approach developed in previous papers (Long, 1936, 1939). Focusing first on the short building cycle, he assembled an aggregate monthly building index for American cities between 1868 and 1940, rising from just one city (Manhattan) at the outset to 37 by the end of the period, and smoothed this index by a multi-stage moving average technique in order to eliminate random and seasonal fluctuations. This exercise revealed a short cycle with an average duration of just 4 years which was coincident with movements in the general US business cycle, but exhibited more severe fluctuations. He found no association between fluctuations in the short building cycle and movements in construction costs or interest rates; however, there was a strong association with movements in stock prices which could indicate the effect of fluctuating business confidence on building activity.

Switching attention to long building cycles, Long returned to the annual quantity and value indices for residential and non-residential building which he had previously presented (Long, 1939), and added a more disaggregated value index that distinguished five building types (detached dwellings, multi-family dwellings, public, private non-residential, alterations). His broad findings remained the same: a long building cycle with a period of just under 20 years appeared in all sectors of building across all cities, exhibiting much more severe fluctuations that those of the short cycle superimposed upon it. Alterations tended to lead new building, because of shorter delays, while public building tended to lag private building, probably because of a lack of speculative activity; however, there was a surprising degree of synchrony between the long cycles in new building across the individual cities. He found evidence of the cycle becoming more severe over time, which he attributed to heightened speculative development as a result of increased debt financing within the industry.

Stepping back, Long related the building cycle to the broader sweep of American history: 'Four great waves in the construction of new buildings have occurred since the Civil War and it is not too much to say that their turning points mark the most exciting and memorable episodes in the nation's history' (Long, 1940: 150). He linked successive building booms to recovery after the Civil War (late1860s/early 1870s), the railway boom (late 1880s/early 1890s), the economic boom preceding the First World War (late1900s/early 1910s) and the post-war recovery (mid/late 1920s), while building slumps were closely associated with economic depressions (late 1870s, late 1890s, late 1910s and early 1930s). This chronology provided evidence of how the long building cycle is tied to the more fundamental rhythm of economic prosperity and depression, rather than to the shorter term and milder fluctuations of the business cycle.

Theoretical perspectives

Several of the early empirical studies had identified two building cycles: a pronounced long cycle with an average length of between 15 and 20 years on which is superimposed a short cycle, with an average length varying between 4 and 7 years. The short building cycle seemed to be closely synchronized with the general business cycle, reflecting the impact of broader fluctuations in economic activity upon the demand for buildings, acting through increases in incomes, and upon their supply, acting through the availability of credit. However, the long building cycle appeared to be more autonomous, and commentators differed as to whether it should be seen as an independent phenomenon or a manifestation of more general economic fluctuations of longer duration than the business cycle.

As noted at the start of this chapter, an early association was made between the long building cycle and the 20-year long swing in economic growth that had been identified by Kuznets (1930) and Burns (1934). Whilst this association was first made during the 1930s, it was most clearly articulated in a later paper by Abramovitz (1961). He argued that the long building cycle was just one manifestation, if the most prominent, of a long swing in economic growth which affected all components of output, operating both through the expansion of productive capacity and the fluctuation of resource utilization. He further suggested that it was over the timescale of the long swing, rather than the shorter business cycle, that fluctuations in building investment could be attributed to the processes of capital stock adjustment via the accelerator.

It was one of the long swing pioneers who first put forward a conceptual framework to explain the propagation of long cycles in residential construction (Burns, 1935). He identified the particular aspects of housing market behaviour that make long swings in building activity particularly volatile:

- The demand for new housing derives from increases in population and the replacement of obsolescent stock, and it is the changes in the rate of population growth during an economic long swing which provide the main exogenous impulse, inducing fluctuations in residential construction.
- The construction lag between changes in demand and the completion of new dwellings creates a tendency for building to overshoot or undershoot, in response to changes in demand, while the durability of the housing stock reinforces the accelerator effect to produce fluctuations of especially large amplitude.

- Uncertainty about the magnitude of likely changes in demand and competing supply, compounded by imperfect market information about rents and prices, leads to the formation of volatile expectations among developers which can further amplify the fluctuations in building.
- The lower bound threshold of zero construction constrains the downswing of the cycle, by inhibiting any reduction in the buffer stock of vacant space when demand diminishes, and this prolongs the cycle by delaying the supply response when demand increases on the upswing.
- Liberal supplies of cheap credit tend to reinforce the volume of speculative building during boom periods, while tightening loan conditions exacerbate the subsequent slump.

During the 1950s, several writers worked on a long swing theory of the development of the 'Atlantic economy' in which the reciprocal movements of building cycles in Britain and the United States were linked through the flows of migrants and investment capital between the two countries. Kuznets himself set the process by which long swings are transmitted from economic growth to building activity within a wider historical context, defined by the forces of industrialization and urban development (Kuznets, 1958, 1961). He described four long swings in US population change between 1869 and 1955, which resulted primarily from long swings in immigration, providing a link between long swings in economic growth and population change on either side of the Atlantic. Inverse fluctuations in economic activity in Britain and America created the push–pull mechanism that led to increasing or decreasing flows of migrants and investment capital from the Old World to the New, with the pull factor of favourable economic conditions in America appearing to be the stronger influence. This two-country theory of inverse long swings was subsequently formalized in a mathematical model by Parry Lewis (1964).

Kuznets proposed that the particular genesis of the long building cycle lay in a direct lagged relationship between population swings and 'population-sensitive investment', comprising the construction of housing and infrastructure. Up until the First World War, fluctuations in other investment sectors within the US economy appeared to move inversely with the population-sensitive sectors, indicating that limits on total capital formation were acting either through the supply of savings or else construction capacity. Long swings in aggregate output also tended to move inversely with population and population-sensitive investment. This suggested a self-perpetuating long swing process, whereby the surge in productivity and output growth induced by non-residential investment acted to improve living standards, thereby attracting a new wave of immigration. The resultant upswing in population growth, in turn, generated a wave of population-sensitive investment that led to cutbacks in more productive non-residential investment, and therefore in aggregate output growth. However, from the 1920s onwards, immigration was a less powerful driving force in US development while the capacity constraints on aggregate investment seem to have weakened, with the result that the swings in all sectors of investment became more synchronized.

An alternative theoretical tradition identified the long building cycle as an autonomous economic cycle in its own right, rather than a manifestation of the long swing.

As a pioneer of this approach, Long (1940) set his empirical investigation of building cycles within a conceptual framework determined by three aspects of the theory of investment:

- The formation of aggregate demand for all buildings is determined by their price or occupancy cost, the income of their prospective occupiers and the relative price and income elasticities of their demand. At the margin, the accelerator relationship between changes in the level of economic activity and the volume of new building means that new building demand tends to be highly income elastic in the short-term, at least within the limits set by zero construction and full capacity utilization.
- On the supply side, the inducement to invest in the construction of new buildings is determined by the trade-off between construction costs and the discounted value of expected future rents allowing for depreciation. The uncertainties facing investors, when making this trade-off for any type of durable good, are compounded in the case of buildings by their lumpiness and heterogeneity, including their spatial fixity, their prolonged gestation period and the subsequent long lifespan over which expectations must be formed about their future income stream.
- While changes in income influence the level of new building through an accelerator relationship, so the feedback from changes in new building investment to changes in aggregate income occurs via a multiplier relationship. It is through this multiplier–accelerator interaction that the interplay between the business cycle and the building cycle is maintained.

Following the autonomous tradition, Hansen (1941) attributed the length of the long building cycle to the exceptional lags in building construction that delay the adjustment of supply to changes in demand. He inserted the building cycle as a fourth member of the multi-cycle schema as developed by Schumpeter (see Chapter 2), arguing that with an average length of 17–18 years, one building cycle was approximately twice as long as the major business cycle first identified by Juglar. According to Hansen, '...American experience indicates that with a high degree of regularity every other major business boom coincides roughly with a boom in building construction, while the succeeding major cycle recovery is forced to buck up against a building slump' (Hansen, 1941: 23). Put another way, every other economic recession tends to be reinforced by a building slump which turns it into a prolonged and deep depression, whereas intermediate recessions tend to be shorter and milder, because they are moderated by a building upswing (see also Hansen, 1951: 39–52).

Isard (1942) also viewed the long building cycle as a distinct and separate phenomenon. He named it a 'transport-building cycle' because its underlying causal force is '...the irregular emergence of transport innovation and the jerky development of the transport network...(so that) building represents more or less the culmination of the process of industrial, commercial and population adaptation to the changing character of transport' (Isard, 1942: 149). By making an explicit link between investment in transport infrastructure and built structures, he was stressing the crucial role of the building cycle in both economic growth and urban development. His empirical justification was based upon an examination of the Riggleman index of US building activity between 1830 and 1933, which exhibited six clear cycles, having an average duration of 18 years (see above). These long building cycles were explained in terms of successive Schumpeterian waves of transport innovation. The first cycle (1830–43) was associated with the canal-building boom that reached a peak in the early 1830s; the next three cycles (1844–64, 1865–78, 1879–1900) were attributed to three waves of investment in the railway network that peaked in 1856, 1871 and 1887; the fifth cycle (1901–18) was driven by the development of electric trams and railways, peaking in 1906; the sixth cycle (1919–33) tracked the growth of automobile use, with car registrations peaking in 1923. Isard traced the links between the transport-building cycle and the broader trajectory of US economic development: long cycles in immigration and urban population growth were identified as synchronous with the long building cycle, while related cycles were also apparent in selected indicators of industrial production.

A reconciliation of the 'dependent' and 'autonomous' perspectives on the origins of the long building cycle was proposed by Matthews (1959). He pointed to the common cycle-inducing characteristics of building construction and other forms of investment: they are subject to an accelerator form of capital stock adjustment in response to increases in demand, they generate multiplier effects that feed back to aggregate income and output and they must respond to erratic shocks. On the other hand, building has special characteristics that explain why its cycles are longer and more pronounced than those in other sectors of investment. In addition to those characteristics highlighted by previous writers – long gestation lags, the durability of the stock, its lumpiness and heterogeneity, the buffer stock provided by vacant space, the uncertainty of expectations – he identified three others:

- The typically fragmented and under-capitalized structure of the building industry creates supply inertia. Thus, many firms are liquidated during a slump, so that there is a considerable delay before the capacity of the industry can be rebuilt to meet a recovery in demand; conversely, as the number of firms increases during a boom, so competitive pressures will tend to prolong construction after demand has started to weaken.
- The stickiness of rents and prices in the occupier market, due to factors such as long fixed-term leases and tenant inertia, create a significant reaction lag between a change in market conditions and the perception of that change by the development industry, which is another reason why the supply response is both delayed and prolonged.
- Successive construction booms incorporate building innovations that accelerate the obsolescence of previous vintages of stock; this tends to create a replacement cycle as an 'echo-effect' of previous booms, reinforcing and prolonging the cyclical tendencies triggered by induced demand.

The post-war empirical tradition

After the pioneering work in Germany prior to the First World War, research on building cycles during the 1930s had been confined, almost entirely, to the American and British real estate markets. One of the few exceptions was the review of available international data by Warren and Pearson (1937), which revealed long building cycles in several European cities (London, Glasgow, Hamburg, Berlin, Stockholm and Amsterdam). Following the Second World War, the strong Anglo–Saxon bias to empirical studies continued, though research on markets in other parts of Europe started to appear again. One example was the investigation by Flaus (1949) of house-building activity in Paris during the century between 1830 and 1938. He identified 12 short building cycles ('oscillations de courte dureé') with troughs that were coincident with major business cycle depressions, but could find no clear long cycle in building. Rather, he distinguished three phase of movement in the secular trend ('fluctuations de longue dureé'), which rose, stabilized and fell over the study period. Flaus conceptualized the building cycle in terms of a four-phase schema which incorporated the economic factors that affect the profitability of development (interest rates, building costs), the demographic factors that affect the demand for dwellings and therefore vacancy and rents (especially in-migration to the city from rural areas) and the psychological factors that affect developer sentiment.

In Britain, work continued on the analysis of historical data series to describe the trend and cycle in building activity, especially the long cycle in house-building. Weber (1955) compiled a national index of residential construction between 1856 and 1950 using partial data series collected by local authorities. He used the index to describe the house-building cycle in Britain, charting four long cycles with an average length of 21 years between the middle of the nineteenth century and the start of the Second World War. Though there were inevitable local variations, '...the most striking fact to emerge is the general participation of all towns in the rhythm of the long cycles...' (Weber, 1955: 115). Cairncross and Weber (1956) examined the long cycle during the earlier period 1785–1849, returning to the index of brick production that had been assembled by Shannon (1934), extending its geographical coverage and checking its fluctuations against those recorded in the consumption of other building materials. They reaffirmed the close relationship between movements in population and house-building, observing that the supply of housing fluctuated much more strongly than its demand.

As already noted, several early post-war studies were undertaken to explore the Atlantic economy model of inverse building cycles in Britain and North America. Thus, Buckley (1952) identified a 17–18 year long building cycle in Canada between 1866 and 1946 that tracked the US cycle plotted by the Riggleman index and closely followed successive waves of immigration into Canada; furthermore, since most of this immigration came from Britain, the Canadian cycle in its earlier decades showed a clear inverse relation to the London building cycle as reported by Spensley (1918). By examining trends in Britain and North America between 1870 and 1913, Cairncross (1953) highlighted how capital outflows from Britain had complemented the emigration of labour, funding successive building booms in North America to house its immigrants, while reducing the available supply of building capital in Britain when housing demand was, in any case, depressed by emigration. Studying the same 1870–1913 period, O'Leary and Lewis (1955) generalized the investigation beyond Britain and North America to identify long swings in a range of economic variables, including building, in several other economies including Germany and France; however, they concluded that the long swing fluctuations in each major economy tended to move in an independent, rather than interrelated fashion.

The study by Brinley Thomas of *Migration and Economic Growth* (1954, revised edition 1973) offered the most comprehensive empirical treatment of the Atlantic economy model. Like Kuznets, Thomas viewed the phenomenon as largely a function of the development of the US economy from the middle of the nineteenth century up until the First World War, after which the United States had less need for immigrants or foreign capital to maintain its growth. Central to his analysis were the determinants of the international migration of population and capital between trading nations at different stages of economic and social development. Again, in a similar vein to Kuznets and Cairncross, he linked fluctuations in migration and investment to inverse long swings in urbanization in both Britain and America. In order to verify the model, Thomas drew together a large number of data sources to describe the secular trends and long swing fluctuations in Atlantic migration, capital flows, economic development, investment and building activity over the period 1830–1913, though data limitations confined much of his analysis to the 1870–1913 period. He found that 'There is a remarkable inverse relation between the course of building in the two countries...It is also clear that the long cycles in emigration from the British Isles are in harmony with those of building in the United States and run in the opposite direction to the course of domestic building' (Thomas, 1973: 103).

During the 1960s, some writers began to question the migration-based explanation for inverse long cycles in the Atlantic economy, at least as a recurrent phenomenon. It was noticeable that several long swing studies had focused much of their empirical analysis on the relatively short period between 1870 and 1913, though they discerned a reciprocal cycle relationship stretching back earlier in the nineteenth century. Cooney (1960) conceded that there had been a clear inverse relationship between long building cycles in Britain and the United States over the core period 1870–1913, but suggested that this was the outcome of a unique combination of circumstances in the two countries during the 1860s – the end of the British railway boom coinciding with the end of the American Civil War – which triggered considerable capital outflows from Britain to fund the post-war American boom. Habakkuk (1962b) went further by arguing that even during the core period of apparently clear inverse cycles, domestic rather than international factors played the more important role in generating the long cycle in Britain. In particular, he pointed to the growing importance of suburban development as the main form of urban expansion and the crucial role of credit supply as a regulator of domestic building activity. Saul (1962) made a similar point by examining the local evidence for house-building fluctuations in a range of English towns in the period between 1890 and 1914. He concluded that external considerations such as emigration and the growth of the American economy were much less important determinants of housing investment than domestic factors, again highlighting the role that ready supplies of cheap credit played in fuelling speculative building booms.

Several post-war studies focused on the short cycle, rather than the long cycle, in house-building. The key transmission mechanisms linking the short building cycle to the business cycle were generally accepted to be variations in household incomes and the supply of credit, though there were differing views as to whether their net effect was to make the building cycle pro-cyclical or counter-cyclical. Thus, Guttentag (1961) observed a pronounced counter-cyclical relationship between the short building cycle and the business cycle in the United States over the period 1946–59, and identified the impact of the supply of mortgage credit on housing demand as the main transmission mechanism, rather than the population or income changes which tend to affect demand more strongly over the longer term. During a phase of economic expansion, the supply of credit tightens because of competing demands for capital, and the negative effect of reduced credit supply upon housing demand outweighs the positive effect of rising incomes, with the result that house-building turns down while the rest of the economy is still expanding. Paradoxically, Vipond (1969) used the impact of credit availability on building supply, rather than housing demand, to explain why the post-war short cycle in British house-building followed a markedly pro-cyclical course relative to the general business cycle during the years 1950–66. On his argument, house-builders can draw upon a plentiful supply of credit during an economic upswing, only cutting back on starts when credit conditions tighten; however, because of construction lags, there is a delay before building completions also turn down, which tends to coincide with a general downturn in the business cycle.

Three key studies

Three major empirical studies marked the culmination of the first post-war wave of building cycle research in Britain and the United States. In the United Kingdom, Parry Lewis (1965) published *Building Cycles and Britain's Growth*, a work which combined economic history with some simulation modelling in order to investigate the genesis and role of the long building cycle as a driver of British economic growth from 1700 to 1950. His historical review started by highlighting how the strong upward trend in building during the eighteenth and early nineteenth centuries followed the growth in urban population, while the volatile fluctuations in building activity around this trend showed a clear inverse relationship with movements in the yield on Government Consols. Builders relied heavily on short-term credit and their sensitivity to its cost meant that building supply had a high interest elasticity; cheap credit tended to fuel speculative building booms, while shocks such as wars, bad harvests or bank failures led to the sharp increases in interest rates that were the cause of building slumps. From around 1830, the gathering pace of industrialization in Britain became the dominant influence on building activity and while national influences remained important, there emerged important local and regional differences in the building cycle. These reflected differences in the local trajectories of industrial development, infrastructure investment (especially railway construction) and institutional change (e.g. the growth of building societies as a source of housing finance). For the period 1870–1913, Parry Lewis focused attention on the manner in which the national long cycle in house-building was mirrored in equivalent fluctuations in its profitability, drawing upon separately constructed indices of rents (Weber, 1960) and building costs (Maiwald, 1954). The historical analysis concluded with a fairly brief survey of the inter-war and early post-war periods; for a similar, but more detailed treatment of building in Britain during the inter-war period, see Richardson and Aldcroft (1968).

  In the United States, two important building cycle studies were produced as part of the on-going programme of research into economic cycles sponsored by the NBER. In his *Evidences of Long Swings in Aggregate Construction since the Civil War*,

Abramovitz (1964) was following in the tradition established by Kuznets (1930) and Burns (1934). He used 38 previously published data series to construct a definitive chronology of the long cycle in aggregate building activity in the United States, over the century from 1858 to 1959. The separate data series were smoothed, using moving averages computed over successive business cycle periods, in order to remove the short building cycle and isolate the alternating phases of rising and falling building activity that were then aggregated into a long cycle reference chronology. This typical NBER methodology produced evidence of between five and six broadly coincident long cycles, affecting all the main branches of construction to varying degrees; they had a duration varying between 14 and 20 years, with the downswing shorter than the upswing, and such pronounced amplitude that the level of construction, typically, more than doubled from trough to peak. The long cycles were between four and five times as prolonged as the short cycles in the same series, and had an amplitude at least twice as large. Abramovitz concluded that the persistence and conformity of the long building cycle across different branches of construction pointed to the influence of external demographic and economic factors acting on the demand for buildings, helping to generate fluctuations in building investment which fed back to reinforce the long swing in the wider economy. Given the estimates by Kuznets (1961) that construction accounted for 50% or more of total US investment and 10% or more of its GNP, then these feedback effects were likely to be substantial.

The most comprehensive of the empirical NBER studies of the building cycle was *Long Swings in Urban Development*, published by Gottlieb (1976), who investigated long cycle fluctuations in over 200 historical data series on building, real estate activity and population change at urban and national level in North America, Europe and Australia. Though more recent data were available, he only analysed the European series up to 1914 and the American series up to 1939. The rationale for these limits was that the European real estate markets in the inter-war period were severely distorted by the consequences of the First World War, while all markets in the post-war period were functioning within a radically different macroeconomic environment in which the causal factors that had previously generated long swings no longer seemed to be operating. For the purposes of cycle identification, he combined the standard NBER reference cycle methodology, as discussed in the previous chapter, with autocorrelation analysis (see Appendix A) – in order to establish the duration and amplitude of local cycles and identify their specific turning points relative to reference chronologies derived from fluctuations in residential building. As Abramovitz had done, the expansion and contraction phases of each long cycle were smoothed in order to remove short cycle fluctuations, but the secular trend was not eliminated, since Gottlieb adhered to the Schumpeterian argument that cyclical motion was an intrinsic driver of long-run growth. Successive long cycles in each local series were then removed from their historical context by averaging then into a 'representative long swing' in a standardized form designed to capture the distinctive cycle profile generated by each market.

Gottlieb's main findings can be summarized as follows:

- National building cycles appeared to be a coalescence of urban cycles which tended to move in a coincident fashion because they were bound together by common economic inter-linkages and subject to common external shocks such as wars; there was also a broad conformity between cycles in residential and non-residential building.

- For 81 local long cycles identified across 30 cities in 8 countries, the average duration was 19.7 years, subject to a mean deviation of 5.0 years, while the 30 national long cycles identified across 7 countries had an almost identical average duration of 19.0 years, with a mean deviation of 4.4 years.
- Using a special measure of cycle amplitude, based on the sum of trough–peak–trough ranges, the local cycles had 'enormous' amplitudes that were on average three times the average level of building activity over the entire cycle period; because of the smoothing introduced through aggregation, the national cycles typically had average amplitudes around two-thirds those of their local cycles.
- Long cycles in migration and population growth with similar duration and amplitude to the cycles in urban building highlighted how demographic factors drove the demand for new building; as already discussed, the migration-based, inverse relationship between building cycles in Europe and North America was most obvious during the 1870–1913 period.
- A strong and lagged inverse relationship was apparent between fluctuations in building and vacancy in the existing building stock, mediated through equivalent fluctuations in real estate prices and rents; this confirmed the transmission mechanism whereby an increase in occupier demand reduces vacancy and increases rents, making development more profitable and triggering a cyclical upswing in new building that eventually feeds through to increase vacancy and reduce building.
- The building cycle was reflected in fluctuations in several other aspects of property market behaviour, in particular, the transactions volume and price for development land, and the transactions volume and yield differential relative to bonds for mortgages on both new and existing properties; long cycle fluctuations in building costs were more muted.

In conducting this exhaustive analysis, Gottlieb was clear that his aim was '…to bring out the general and essential characteristics of, and the interplay between, the different elements and processes at work in [long] swings…' (Gottlieb, 1976: xxii). He was neither attempting to develop a historical narrative of the influence of the building cycle on urbanization, nor constructing a theoretical model of its formation which could be tested by econometric methods.

Modern property cycle research

By the early 1960s, the apparently greater stability of developed economies in the post-war period was prompting some commentators to assert that the forces which had generated long swings and long building cycles before the Second World War were now much weaker (Hickman, 1963). The clearest statement of this view was advanced by one of the former champions of the long swing, when Abramovitz (1968) announced 'The passing of the Kuznets cycle' just one year before Bronfenbrenner (1969) asked, 'Is the business cycle obsolete?' Abramovitz was clear that the Kuznets cycle had existed, but contended that '…it is a form of growth which belonged to a particular period in history and that the economic structure and institutions which imposed that form on the growth process have evolved, or been changed, into something different' (Abramovitz, 1968: 349). By this, he meant that the migration link between economic expansion and population growth no longer operated, while the combination of much higher levels of government expenditure together with active fiscal and monetary policy had stabilized economic growth.

However, just as the global recession of the mid-1970s shattered complacency about post-war economic stability and led to a revival in business cycle studies, so the 1970s and 1980s boom–bust cycles in real estate markets were the genesis of a new wave of research on property cycles. If migration-based theories were no longer valid as explanations of the long building cycle, then alternative theoretical traditions had to be explored. The approach first developed by Long, Hansen and Isard offered a different avenue for analysis, concentrating on the endogenous capital stock adjustment processes underlying building investment, with its cycle-inducing characteristics of long construction lags and durable stock. A second and related avenue of investigation has focused on the sticky rent adjustment processes which link changes in occupancy to changes in rents and prices; it is these price changes that provide the market signals to which developers respond, thereby transmitting the rhythm of the building cycle to all aspects of market behaviour. Another strand of investigation has drawn upon the burgeoning interest in rational expectations theory to explore how the expectations of developers and other agents are formed in a market subject to the uncertainties and adjustment delays that are such a feature of property development.

The body of modern property cycle research differs from previous traditions in four ways:

1 The building cycle is viewed as just one aspect of a cyclical tendency apparent in all aspects of real estate market behaviour – in vacancy, rents and capital values as well as in construction starts and completions.
2 Greater attention is being paid to cycles in non-residential building, particularly in sectors such as office building, whereas previous research had tended to concentrate primarily on residential building.
3 The growing integration of real estate and capital markets means that the financial impacts of property cycles on investment performance are accorded as much importance as their real effects on the supply and occupancy of buildings.
4 It is recognized that property cycles have become an increasingly international phenomenon, as globalization has linked local and national real estate markets through the cross-border movement of occupiers and investment capital.

It is notable that part of the new wave of property research is being conducted in private sector consultancies rather than in academic institutions. As a consequence, there is a strong interest in models of property market behaviour, which can be used for the purposes of commercial forecasting; the development of such real estate models is reviewed separately in Chapter 7. The past 30 years has also seen the establishment of several specialist real estate journals in which the majority of property research is now published, rather than in the general economic journals that had previously been favoured. For general summaries of recent research on the real estate market, including its cyclical behaviour, see DiPasquale and Wheaton (1996) and Ball et al. (1998). For discussions of the unique nature of property development as a prolonged multi-stage process involving different economic agents, see Cadman and Topping (1995) and Guy and Henneberry (2002).

Long cycles: Fact or artifact?

This was the question raised by Adelman (1965), expressing a sceptical view about the reality of long cycles that was voiced by several post-war observers. In particular, she queried whether long cycles were a genuine economic phenomenon, or rather were a statistical artifact created by the smoothing procedures such as moving averages, which had been applied to remove the short cycles from data series (see also Bird et al., 1965). To test the question, she applied the recently developed technique of spectral analysis to a variety of economic series in which previous writers such as Kuznets and Abramovitz had claimed to observe long cycles. The advantage of the technique is that it simultaneously isolates the cyclical components of all frequencies that are contained within a series, once it has been detrended, so that short cycles do not have to be eliminated in order to isolate any long cycles (see Appendix A.4). For none of the series that Adelman tested did long cycles appear as significant components in the estimated frequency spectra, whereas there was evidence of short cycles with a period of 3–4 years. Her conclusion was that the long cycles which others had observed were more artifact than fact – though her results were subsequently criticized for procedural inadequacies (see for example, Soper, 1975).

   Subsequent investigations of the long cycle using spectral analysis have produced more positive results. However, even when long cycles are shown to exist, Howrey (1968) demonstrated theoretically that smoothing techniques applied to eliminate short cycles from a data series will tend to introduce a bias, by increasing the estimated period of the cycle that remains. Thus, a major cycle with a duration of between 7 and 11 years in the original series can display an apparent long swing period of between 15 and 25 years after smoothing. This cast doubt on the duration of the Kuznets cycles reported in previous studies – they may well have been facts, not artifacts, but their lengths were probably exaggerated. Howrey tested a range of US macroeconomic variables, detrended by using growth rates; while most exhibited a short cycle of 3–4 years, equivalent to the minor business cycle, residential construction stood out in revealing a prominent major cycle with a duration of up to 12 years, while other forms of investment and durable goods production also showed evidence of a longer cycle of 6–7 years duration in addition to the minor cycle.

   Studies which used spectral analysis to identify long cycles had to confront two technical questions. The first was the adequacy of the sample size. According to one of the early standard texts on the application of the technique (Granger and Hatanaka, 1964: 17), a data series needs to be at least seven times as long as the lowest frequency cycle being investigated – which, in the case of the 20-year long swing, would require a series spanning 140 years or more. The second question was the efficiency and bias of the detrending technique used to meet the stationarity requirements of spectral analysis, since these will influence the form of the cycles that are identified. Two main approaches were typically applied: using the deviations around an appropriately fitted trend, or deriving first differences or growth rates. The issues surrounding trend elimination and long cycle identification are explored in detail in Appendix A.

Harkness (1968) investigated the issue of detrending by applying spectral analysis to 48 series on the Canadian economy, extending up to 100 years in length. For the majority of series, including residential construction, he found clear evidence for long cycles that in most cases were more pronounced that the short business cycle. However, the duration of the identified long cycles varied markedly depending upon the method used to eliminate the trend. Applying a growth rate transformation, the long cycle in residential construction showed a duration of 12 years, but when expressed as deviations around a harmonic trend this increased to 16 years. Soper (1975) was particularly concerned with the question of sample size, testing the growth rates of 30 British data series, with lengths varying between 100 and 238 years. He found evidence of weak long swings in most series, but only in the two building construction series did the long cycle dominate cycles of higher frequency. This provided some confirmation of the often stated belief that building cycles are the most prominent form of long cycle to be found in economic data.

Specific applications of spectral analysis focused on the identification of building cycles started with Cargill (1971), who tested 43 American construction series, detrended using growth rates. The majority of series showed prominent long cycle components, though their duration varied from 12 to 20 years, averaging around 14–15 years. As part of a wider study of building cycles in Britain, the author undertook spectral analyses of annual data on investment in dwellings and other buildings between 1856 and 1983, and quarterly data on building starts in five sectors of development between 1958 and 1983 (Barras and Ferguson, 1985). Given the brevity of the post-war building starts series, only short cycles could be identified, whereas the long-run investment data provided the opportunity to isolate longer cycles. The quarterly data were transformed into deviations around a non-linear trend fitted by polynomial regression, and for all five building sectors (private commercial, private industrial, private housing, public housing and other public building) clear short cycles were identified. For three sectors (private housing, public housing and commercial), the dominant cycle was a major cycle of 7–9 years duration, while for the other two sectors, there was a dominant minor cycle of around 4 years duration. The annual building investment series were converted into growth rates, and spectral analysis identified prominent long cycles of average 19 years duration for non-residential building and 28 years for house-building. The fluctuations in each sector moved broadly in phase through five cycles of building; the difference between their estimated cycle periods arose because the first wave only showed up clearly in the non-residential series.

New perspectives and established traditions

The study of building cycles undertaken by the author during the 1980s had three aims: to apply techniques such as spectral analysis and error-correction models to analyse both national and urban data; to employ a theoretical framework which drew upon the approach adopted by the first generation of business cycle modellers; and to frame the discussion within a historical narrative of the type employed by the first generation of building cycle researchers. The results of the spectral analysis are summarized above; the theoretical modelling is described in Chapter 7. Here, the general approach can be outlined with reference to three papers that reported the main findings at different spatial levels and over different time frames (Barras, 1984, 1987, 1994); updated versions of these analyses are presented in subsequent chapters.

In Barras (1987), the results of the long-run spectral analysis reported above were used to develop a chronology of the five waves of building investment which have occurred in the British economy since the mid-nineteenth century (allowing for the interruptions caused by two World Wars). It was argued that the broadly coincident long cycles in residential and non-residential building can be treated as manifestations of the same urban development cycle, triggered by exogenous impulses deriving from successive Schumpeterian technological revolutions in the wider economy. Each wave of industrialization creates new demands for the development of the urban fabric and, following Isard (1942), it is the introduction of new forms of transport and communications infrastructure that provides the crucial impetus for successive waves of urbanization. As already noted, more detailed spectral analysis revealed shorter building cycles superimposed upon the post-war long cycle in UK urban development, with a major cycle of up to 9 years duration identified in all sectors of private building, while a minor cycle with a period of around 4 years was also apparent in private industrial and residential development. In Barras (1994), four major cycles between the early 1960s and early 1990s were described in terms of fluctuations in building starts, rents and capital values, and related to exogenous influences such as fluctuations in GDP growth and movements in interest rates. In Barras (1984), the operation of the first three of these cycles was illustrated by a case study of office development in London, paying particular attention to the manner in which levels of building responded to cyclical fluctuations in development profitability.

The analysis of these post-war cycles in the United Kingdom was based on the premise that the major cycle is the product of endogenous supply-side adjustment processes, whereas the minor cycle is largely a demand-side phenomenon which reflects the impact of the business cycle on all aspects of economic activity. The multi-stage nature of the development process, proceeding through site acquisition, planning permission, construction and letting, was identified as the key source of the adjustment delays which propagate major cycles. Special attention was paid to financial factors influencing the building cycle. The combination of low interest rates and plentiful credit supply from banks fuelled two speculative building booms, in the early 1970s and late 1980s, each of which was abruptly terminated when rising inflation necessitated sharp increases in interest rates that plunged the economy into recession. As a result, much more volatile market conditions obtained in these two cycles than in the intermediate cycles of the early 1960s and early 1980s; a long cycle rhythm was thereby generated through speculative over-building in alternate major cycles. Long-term investment in property by financial institutions, such as insurance companies and pension funds, was also identified as a powerful influence on the building cycle. Institutional investors create an investment demand that is distinct from occupier demand, acting principally through the yield, or capitalization rate, that determines the price of property in combination with its rent. Yields respond not only to the expected investment returns from property, but also to the expected returns from competing assets, such as equities and bonds.

The tradition of cycle analysis developed at the NBER continued to influence building cycle research in the United States. Thus, Grebler and Burns (1982) studied post-war short cycles in different sectors of US construction, in relation to reference cycles in GNP and business fixed investment. Their particular aim was to answer policy-related questions concerning the potential for counter-cyclical public building programmes to stabilize construction in particular and the economy in general. Using detrended quarterly data between 1950 and 1978, they identified six short cycles in the residential sector (average duration 4.5 years), four in private non-residential development (7 years) and four in state and local building (7 years), compared to four business cycles in their reference series. They considered that the differences between the timing of the construction cycles and the business cycle were sufficient to suggest that even the short building cycle is, in part, an autonomous phenomenon. In general, while congruence between the cycles in different sectors of construction was quite weak, there was little sign of that systematic counter-cyclical movement between public and private building that would reduce the volatility of total construction. Furthermore, rather than running counter-cyclically, state and local government construction tended to move pro-cyclically with GNP, reflecting the influence of general economic conditions upon the tax revenues which fund public building.

During the 1980s, American real estate research paid increasing attention to the office sector, in part because it was the market attracting the greatest investment interest, and in part because it was the market exhibiting the most volatile building cycle. Wheaton (1987) traced three office market cycles in the United States between 1960 and 1986, with an average period of around 10 years, illustrating how the dynamics of the cycle were manifested through fluctuations in office employment, net absorption of space, the vacancy rate, building starts and completions. He considered that the observed 18–24 month lag between building starts and completions was insufficient to explain the endogenous propagation of a 10-year building cycle, and put greater emphasis on the exogenous impulses generated by the business cycle in the wider economy. Estimation of a structural time series model suggested that the duration of the office cycle could be attributed to the slow adjustment of rents to a changed supply-demand balance, while the volatility of the cycle could be explained by the greater elasticity of supply compared to demand with respect to changed market conditions.

A substantial body of US research has focused on the slow adjustment of rents, rather than on construction lags, as the most important factor propagating cyclical instability in property markets. It is because of factors such as long leases and high search and transaction costs that rents adjust only slowly to a change in the supply-demand balance, as manifested in the vacancy rate. This stickiness of rents provides misleading signals to developers, creating a tendency for building to over- and then under-shoot in response to changes in demand. An increasingly sophisticated series of rent adjustment models were formulated in the 1980s and

1990s in order to capture this core dynamic of property market behaviour (these models are reviewed in Chapter 7). Their specification is based on the idea of an equilibrium vacancy rate and an equilibrium level of rent, at which supply and demand are balanced with just enough surplus space to allow for efficient occupier search and movement within the market. Clapp (1993) illustrated the operation of this rent adjustment process by adapting an equilibrium model of rent and capital value determination presented by DiPasquale and Wheaton (1992).

In contrast to the neoclassical framework used in most modern property cycle research, there has also been a strand of Marxist theory, initiated by Harvey (1978). He characterized the urban process under capitalism in terms of two interrelated 'circuits of capital'. The primary circuit involves the production of consumption goods through the employment of labour and fixed capital; the secondary circuit is devoted to investment in two types of fixed capital – means of production (plant and equipment) and the built environment for consumption and production (buildings and infrastructure). Harvey's hypothesis was that periodic over-accumulation in the primary circuit releases surplus investment capital and labour which can be switched into the secondary circuit in the search for higher profits. Capital switching thus creates the resources for those periodic phases of intensified urban building which characterize long cycles of the Kuznets type, fuelling speculative booms which turn into crises of over-building, in turn leading to devalued property assets and distressed financial markets. Because successive vintages of capital embody a fixed level of technology that is rendered obsolete by the next wave of investment, there is a contradiction in the urban process between the investor interest to preserve the value of existing buildings and the producer interest to replace them with new and more productive buildings (an argument previously developed by Veblen, as discussed in Chapter 2). Attempts to verify the capital switching hypothesis have proved inconclusive. A US study by Beauregard (1994) of trends in industrial production and building investment during the 1980s boom could find no empirical support for the idea, whereas a study by Lizieri and Satchell (1997) of the relative movement of investment returns in the United Kingdom property and equity markets appeared to offer some weak confirmative evidence.

The formation of market expectations

Property cycle theory has not remained immune from the 'rational expectations revolution' that has swept through economics during the past 30 years (see Chapter 2). Questions concerning the formation of expectations seem particularly relevant in a market subject to great uncertainty as a result of sticky adjustment processes, extended transmission mechanisms and prolonged gestation lags. To what extent are tenants able to anticipate changed market conditions when negotiating new leases? To what extent are developers able to predict the future market conditions into which they will be delivering their new buildings? To what extent are investors able to compare the future returns from property as against those from alternative asset classes? Is the assumption of rational expectations in property markets reasonable, or is a more restricted assumption such as bounded rationality more tenable? Answers to these questions have become an important goal of real estate research.

In this vein, Kling and McCue (1987) identified two characteristics of office development as reasons for the persistent over-building of offices in the United States during the first half of the 1980s. First, office development involves investment in real assets with high transaction costs, making projects irreversible once started; second, extensive construction lags mean that developers must start projects on the basis of expectations of future demand, rather than current observed demand. They explored the 'time to build' problem by modelling office construction against lagged output, nominal interest rates, money supply and aggregate prices, in an attempt to isolate the factors influencing developer expectations. Using monthly national data for the 1972–85 period, they identified the nominal interest rate, operating as a predictor of future output, to be the main explanation for the fluctuation in office construction: falling interest rates boost the output expectations of developers, and therefore their expectations of the future demand for space. Persistent over-building occurs because an increase in anticipated demand prompts developers to maintain high levels of office building, even when rising vacancy signals that supply is already adequate.

The informational efficiency of real estate markets has received considerable attention, particularly with regard to the housing market. The consensus view is that real estate markets do not in general satisfy the efficient capital markets hypothesis, which asserts that asset prices fully reflect all relevant available information (Fama, 1970). However, empirical studies suggest that there are differing degrees of inefficiency according to the type of real estate: the least efficient appears to be owner-occupied housing, while rental markets such as apartments and offices may be rather more efficient, although less so than corporate security markets (see the reviews in Cho, 1996, on housing markets and Gatzlaff and Tirtiroglu, 1995, on real estate markets in general). Several empirical studies of the housing market have found evidence that price changes exhibit positive autocorrelation in the short run, indicating informational inefficiency, whereas in the long run they do tend to show negative autocorrelation, indicating trend-reversion back to fundamental values. In other words, prices do correct after a disturbance, but only slowly. A study of the US housing market by Case and Shiller (1989) identified one source of inefficiency to be the failure of the market to price in 'predictable' movements in real interest rates. More generally, the informational inefficiency of real estate markets is often attributed to high transaction and information costs arising from factors such as the heterogeneity of buildings, the infrequency of transactions, the paucity of buyers and sellers and the common reliance on valuation rather than transaction data. As eloquently summarized by Evans (1995: 28): 'It is no accident that so many millionaires made their money in the property market – it is a result of its inefficiency'.

Informational inefficiency implies that real estate price expectations are not rational, in the sense that not all available information relevant to predicting future prices is incorporated into the current price. In other words, real estate markets tend to suffer from 'capital market myopia' (Sahlman and Stevenson, 1985). This was illustrated by Mankiw and Weil (1989), who investigated whether changes in residential demand due to predictable demographic shifts were being factored into US house prices, and found that a myopic or naïve expectations model reproduced observed price movements better than a rational expectations model with perfect foresight. Similarly, Clayton (1996) investigated whether short-run fluctuations in real house prices could be explained by a rational expectations model that is based on imputed rents. Using Canadian data between 1979 and 1991, he rejected the rational expectations hypothesis, since the model failed to capture fully observed price movements during two real estate booms, although it tracked movements well in less volatile periods. These results suggest that it is during unstable boom and bust cycles that prices deviate most markedly from their underlying equilibrium values.

Similar evidence of irrational investor behaviour has been found in commercial property markets. The yield applied to a property to calculate its capital value should reflect its expected real income growth, and since real commercial property rents are repeatedly shown to be trend-reverting, above average incomes at the top of the rent cycle signal below average future growth. This means that capitalization rates should be set at above average levels when real rents are above trend, in expectation of declining income growth, and at below average levels when real rents are below trend, in anticipation of a rebound. Recent empirical analysis suggests that UK investors have rationally built trend-reversion into their property pricing, but US investors have not. In other words, US investors have paid too much for property at the peak of the rent cycle, and too little at the trough (Hendershott and MacGregor, 2005).

Commentators who support the view that real estate markets are not efficient point to the importance of investor sentiment in the pricing of assets and suggest that alternative, more realistic, behavioural models are to be preferred to the rational expectations hypothesis. One alternative was proposed by Gardiner and Henneberry (1991), who introduced the concept of 'habit persistence' or adaptive expectations into a rent adjustment model for the office sector, such that changes in expected occupier demand are expressed as a function of the gap between the previous period's expectations and the actual outcome. This approach was developed further by Antwi and Henneberry (1995), who highlighted how developer behaviour in response to exogenous shocks can introduce asymmetries and non-linearities into the adjustment processes and transmission mechanisms at different stages in the development cycle. They used behavioural modelling of UK data to test alternative developer strategies for formulating profit expectations, and identified habit persistence as a common strategy. When developers' expectations are conditioned by past experience, their response to price signals is both delayed and exaggerated: in a cyclical upturn, the expectation that an established rental growth trend will continue creates inflated profit expectations, which lead to oversupply, followed by an asymmetrical cutback in development that is abrupt and violent – all of which amplifies the volatility of the development cycle.

Option pricing is another approach that has been suggested to explain the apparent irrationalities in behaviour that accompany persistent real estate cycles. Grenadier (1995) developed a model of leasing and construction in order to capture two aspects of the cycle: the stickiness of occupancy adjustment and the recurrence of over-building. The leasing stage uses the analogy of a financial option to explain the stickiness of vacancy in the face of changing occupier demand. For owners of a vacant unit in a rising market, there is the option to wait for a future letting at a higher rent, rather than make the letting now; by making the letting, the owner not only incurs the costs of leasing, he also loses the option to wait. The converse argument applies in a falling market: the costs of losing a tenant in a falling market may hold back the rise in vacancy as the owner offers concessions to hold on to tenants. The option concept is also applied to over-building under conditions of long construction lags and the virtual irreversibility of a development project once started. The uncertainty about future demand conditions means there is an option value on completing a development: if demand is strong, the owner will exercise the option to let; if demand is weak, the space can be held until the market turns. This option value encourages developers to take the decision to build rather than delay, and creates a tendency to over-building which increases with the length of the construction period and the volatility of demand.

The rational expectations orthodoxy that endogenous building cycles should not occur, if there is perfect foresight about the market outcomes of unanticipated shocks, was examined by Wheaton (1999). Using a multi-equation stock adjustment model of the type which is reviewed in Chapter 7, he tested the implications of two alternative assumptions about developer expectations of the price for a new development to be completed at a future date. There is either irrational or myopic pricing, when the expected price is based on the capitalization of current rents, or rational pricing with perfect foresight, when the expected price is the discounted present value of correctly predicted future rents. The assumption of rational expectations means that '...agents perfectly understand the equations that govern market behaviour and thus can make correct forecasts of rents...' once an unexpected shock has occurred (Wheaton, 1999: 215). With perfect foresight, no cyclical behaviour is generated by an initial shock, since estimates of future prices are by definition self-fulfilling, with the one qualifying condition that another unanticipated shock does not occur during the course of development (which may be quite likely). With this strict version of rational expectations, the only way that the market can exhibit the symptoms of a persistent cycle is for it to be subjected to a repeating pattern of exogenous shocks. Under conditions of myopic pricing, on the other hand, cyclical fluctuations in market behaviour are generated, as long as the price elasticity of supply is greater than the rent elasticity of demand. As the long-term rate of growth in demand increases, the cycle period shortens, but its amplitude increases; as the construction lag lengthens, both the period and amplitude of the cycle increase. A subsequent paper by McDonald (2002) reviewed empirical studies of the office market in the light of the Wheaton model, concluding that the available evidence supported the view that observed market cycles could be attributed to a combination of myopic pricing and relatively rent inelastic demand compared to price elastic supply.

The integration of real estate and capital markets

The wave of property research undertaken in the United Kingdom and United States during the 1980s was prompted in large part by the office-building booms that these countries had experienced during the early 1970s and early 1980s respectively. The next major building cycle that occurred in the late 1980s/early 1990s was the first truly global real estate cycle; so violent were the upheavals it caused that its impact was felt not only on the world's property markets, but also on the wider international economy (see Chapter 8). The inevitable result was the launch of a new and more extensive phase of research on real estate cycles during the 1990s. A particular focus of this research has been the growing integration of real estate and capital markets. This integration played a crucial role in shaping the late 1980s property boom, causing cycle volatility to increase (Coakley, 1994) and cycle timing in different cities and regions to converge (Leitner, 1994; Henneberry, 1999). Furthermore, as investors have adopted an ever more dominant role in real estate development and ownership, potential conflicts have arisen between user and investor demands for property which have had an impact upon development supply (Keogh, 1994).

The particular nature and causes of the late 1980s property boom attracted the attention of several writers, who sought explanations for the exceptional magnitude and duration of the cycle. In the United States, Hendershott and Kane (1992) pointed out that, by the end of the decade, vacancy rates in most markets had risen to twice their normal level, causing a rapid fall in rents and capital values which had resulted in a surge in non-performing loans and foreclosures that weakened financial institutions and threatened to depress economic growth for several years. They identified two aspects of government policy which they considered to be responsible for the persistence and extent of the over-building: the deregulation of banks and savings institutions, which encouraged them to finance the boom on highly favourable loan terms, and over-generous tax allowances for depreciation, which encouraged excessive levels of construction.

The 1980s boom–bust cycle hit the US office market particularly hard, so that by the beginning of the 1990s, it appeared to be in its most severe recession since the 1930s. Mills (1995) considered tax policy to have been a factor contributing to market instability, but he identified a Schumpeterian factor, that is the impact of the information technology revolution on service industries, as the prime cause of the over-building. The trigger for the boom had been the rapid growth in office demand during the first half of the decade, which created excessively optimistic expectations about the future rate of growth. However, the increase in office productivity due to the widespread introduction of information technology slowed the growth in office employment during the second half of the decade, so that the demand for additional space grew more slowly than the continued expansion of office activity would have suggested.

The housing sector was affected as much as the commercial markets by the late 1980s boom. In Britain, the recovery from the recession at the start of the 1980s saw strong income growth at a time when both real house prices and household debt levels were low; as a result, prices started to rise strongly from the middle of the decade. Demand was outstripping the growth in supply, and was further boosted by financial deregulation which increased permitted gearing levels and made equity withdrawal easier; when interest rates were cut in 1987–8, the price spiral was given a final twist. The subsequent bust resulted from a reversal of most of these factors. The economy moved into recession, interest rates rose sharply and mortgage lenders tightened their conditions, all of which caused demand and prices to collapse, leaving large numbers of households with negative equity and mortgage arrears, thereby leading to widespread repossessions (Muellbauer and Murphy, 1997).

The widespread repercussions of the late 1980s/early 1990s cycle prompted a major investment-led study by Key et al. (1994) of the post-war relationship between economic and property cycles in Britain. Using a unique data set on the returns from commercial property as compiled by the Investment Property Databank (IPD), the researchers defined a reference cycle of fluctuations in the United Kingdom all-property total return over the 30-year period 1962–92, tracked the movement of the all-property cycle relative to the economic cycle and decomposed the property cycle by sector and region, according to different aspects of market behaviour, such as building, rents and yields. Spectral analysis identified short cycles of 4–5 years duration in all aspects of market behaviour, while causality testing (see Appendix A) explored the associations between the component property cycles and those between the property and the economic cycles. Key findings suggested that the total returns cycle may lead the economic cycle, that the cycle in building starts tends to lag the total returns cycle, that investors behave with a modest degree of foresight, in that yield movements typically anticipate rental movements by a year or so and that inflows of institutional investment tend not to reinforce the volatility of the cycle, because they are constrained by target portfolio weightings.

A second phase of this study (Key et al., 1999) took a longer historical perspective, making use of an extended data series on UK all-property total returns, back to 1921, which had been compiled by Scott (1996). Spectral analysis now showed some evidence of a major cycle of 9 years duration, in addition to the minor cycle of 5 years duration that had previously been identified using the shorter data series; this combination of cyclical components is broadly in line with the findings in Barras and Ferguson (1985) outlined above. The analysis of the links between the property and the economic cycles was repeated using the extended data series, finding distinct differences between the linkages in the pre-war period, when the property cycle seemed to be more highly correlated with fluctuations in bond yields and inflation, and the post-1970 period, when the main relationships were with movements in GDP and inflation. A new strand of the analysis compared the investment returns from property with those from other assets over the period 1921–97. It was found that property had on average out-performed government bonds, but under-performed equities, and that the associations between the returns cycles in property and the other two asset classes had weakened considerably over time, boosting the diversification advantages of property within investment portfolios.

In the United States, the severity of the late 1980s/early 1990s boom and bust prompted Kaiser (1997) to examine the historical record for comparable events, and determine whether it was indicative of a much longer cycle in real estate behaviour than the typical major cycle of up to 10 years duration that had characterized the post-war period. Like the UK study by Key et al., he used total investment returns as a long-run indicator of the US real estate cycle, assembling data series stretching back to 1919. Only one other period, between 1929 and 1934, appeared to have suffered the negative total returns that had been experienced between 1990 and 1993, and he attributed both periods of market distress to the same combination of factors – an inflation spike in the general level of prices feeding through to a rapid increase in rents which triggered an excessive building boom. On the basis of historical records going back to the eighteenth century, Kaiser argued that there is evidence of a continuing long cycle in building of up to 20 years duration, and that every third occurrence of these cycles tends to culminate in a particularly spectacular boom and bust, as happened in the 1920s/30s and 1980s/90s, and is also likely to have occurred in the 1860s/70s. This rhythm creates a potential

50–60 year cycle, with echoes of the Kondratieff long wave that was discussed in Chapter 2.

The transmission of cyclical instability between the real estate and financial markets via the process of debt financing has come under increasing scrutiny since the early 1990s property crash. As described in Chapter 2, a recent strand of business cycle theory has been built around the concept of the 'financial accelerator', which implies that credit cycles and property cycles can interact through endogenously generated changes in credit market conditions over the course of the cycle (Bernanke et al., 1996; Kiyotaki and Moore, 1997). Borrowing conditions are determined by the net value of real estate and other assets acting as collateral, such that an increase in land and property prices during a cycle upswing tends to lower the costs of borrowing and increase credit supply, thereby boosting the investment demand for real estate. This amplifies the upswing by driving property prices even higher, while funding a surge in new construction, which leads eventually to over-supply as boom turns to bust. The transmission process operates in reverse on the cycle downswing, as falling asset prices intensify credit rationing to such a degree that a 'credit crunch' can severely restrict lending for further development, as happened between 1989 and 1992 (Fergus and Goodman, 1994).

Recent evidence for the interlocking of housing booms and consumer booms via the financial accelerator is of particular concern to policy-makers. During a housing boom, the wealth effect created by rising house prices encourages owners to take on increased levels of debt, which is used to invest in more property but also spills over into additional consumption. When house prices subsequently slump, collateral shrinks, borrowing is cut back and both investment and consumption are correspondingly depressed (Aoki et al., 2002; Iacoviello, 2005). A different type of transmission process amplifies cyclical fluctuations in closely integrated office markets, such as the City of London, where financial institutions are the main occupiers of the office space, the main owners of standing investments and the main sources of development finance. Such a highly concentrated structure creates the systemic risk that a failure in one part of the market can spill over into other parts through feedback and contagion effects. Thus, a shock to the financial system, such as the stock market crash of 2000/1, reduces the occupier demand for space, causing rents and capital values to fall; this depresses the asset base of the financial sector, curtailing both the investment demand for property and the supply of development finance (Lizieri et al., 2000).

Globalization and speculative bubbles

We have seen that the global impacts of financial deregulation and the integration of capital and real estate markets first became apparent during the late 1980s/early 1990s cycle. As barriers to cross-border investment have been lifted, there has been an acceleration of international investment flows into property and other assets, and these have stimulated an enhanced appetite for speculative risk. The proliferation of new financial instruments, such as mortgage-backed securities, and the central role of property assets as loan collateral, has tended to magnify the cross-border transmission of shocks between financial and real estate markets. The result has been that building cycles seem to have become more convergent, widespread and volatile, while the increasingly speculative nature of building investment appears to be generating more frequent real estate price bubbles of the type which affects other markets, such as equities (Björklund and Söderberg, 1999; Allen and Gale, 2000; Hunter et al., 2003). While there are conflicting views as to whether bubbles reflect investor behaviour that can be described as rational (Hendershott et al., 2003) or irrational (Shiller, 2005), they are unquestionably a phenomenon with extreme consequences – as vividly described by Charles Kindleberger in his classic study of *Manias, Panics and Crashes* (Kindleberger and Aliber, 2005).

Nowhere was the speculative nature of the 1980s property boom more apparent than in Japan, where spiralling investment in land and property by financial institutions was the key driver of the 'bubble economy' that collapsed in 1990 (Oizumi, 1994; Mera and Renaud, 2000). The boom was the result of three factors: first, economic restructuring was shifting the economy away from manufacturing towards services, creating a massive demand for office building; second, vast flows of savings into financial institutions were encouraging them to seek new investment outlets; third, the Government had introduced a series of policy measures designed to deregulate planning and to open up the development process to private capital. The redevelopment boom was turned into a classic asset price bubble by the deregulation of financial markets and relaxation of monetary policy between 1985 and 1987, which ratcheted up investment through the operation of the financial accelerator. The expansion of credit multiplied the flow of money into land and property speculation, creating an upward spiral in land prices which was reinforced by the restricted domestic supply of land and property. Speculative pressures caused large capital flows to be directed into overseas property markets with more abundant investment opportunities, particularly in the United States – which did not, however, turn out to be the real estate 'paradise' that Japanese investors had anticipated because of the inflated prices they paid for low yielding properties (Edgington, 1995). It was when the Government tightened monetary policy in 1990 and started to regulate lending to property companies, that the Japanese bubble burst. Land prices plunged and non-performing loans multiplied, there was a severe contraction in new lending and widespread 'bubble bankruptcies' among property companies and financial institutions, while multiplier effects transmitted the collapse to the wider economy, which moved into a prolonged depression.

The role of global financial markets in coordinating the real estate cycles that occurred in most developed and many developing countries, during the late 1980s/ early 1990s, was examined by Renaud (1997). The typical cycle consisted of an exceptionally strong boom which reached a peak in 1989, followed by a crash at the beginning of the 1990s; in his view, the resultant asset price deflation was both severe and widespread enough to cause a contraction in aggregate economic output that lasted until 1994. Thus in Europe as a whole, while property values virtually doubled between 1986 and 1990, most of this gain was lost in the subsequent four years. Renaud pinpointed the massive investment outflows from Japan during the late 1980s as the key international factor which led to the synchronization of different national cycles, while their volatility was dependent on the extent to which domestic policy-makers were embracing the current enthusiasm for capital market liberalization and the deregulation of financial and real estate markets. Goetzmann and Wachter (2001) suggested a reverse causality to explain the crash: rather than causing the global recession, it was the weakening of demand due to an exogenous economic slowdown that triggered the market collapse. Whatever the causality, the result was an 'asset market hangover' which depressed investment throughout the developed world during the early 1990s (Higgins and Osler, 1997).

An alternative, demand-side explanation for the global reach of the 1980s boom was proposed by Ball (1994). Drawing a parallel with the role of technology shocks in Real Business Cycle Theory (see Chapter 2), he identified the revolutionary impact of information technology on service industries as the fundamental driver of a world-wide upsurge in building demand that started in the mid-1970s. Growth in financial and business services employment not only provided a direct boost to the demand for new office space, but also fed through to higher household incomes, which increased the demand for population-sensitive investment in retail and residential property. Technology did not just increase the level of demand for new buildings, but innovation also changed their desired form and location, rendering existing stock obsolete. The conditions were thus created for a classic long cycle building boom, reinforced and coordinated globally by factors such as the loosening of credit supply and the deregulation of finance services and land use planning. However, the building boom reached its peak just as the global economy moved into recession, and the subsequent slump in demand was exacerbated by firms rationalizing their use of the new space which they had acquired during the expansion phase of the cycle.

The experience of the 1990s has reinforced the need for a global perspective on real estate cycles, and in particular, on the ever closer integration of financial and real estate markets – which means that instability in one local or national market can spread rapidly to many others (Brown and Liu, 2001). This contagion effect was all too apparent during the Asian crisis of 1997/8, when the heavy real estate exposure of major Asian banks transmitted the effects of falling property values to the rest of the region's financial sector (Mera and Renaud, 2000). In the view of Renaud et al. (2001), the immaturity and inadequate regulation of property markets in rapidly growing economies, such as Thailand, contributed to the severity of the Asian real estate bubble of the mid-1990s. By 1996 signs of distress were evident, as excessive lending and over-building were causing a sharp increase in vacancy and in the number of non-performing loans; when the currency crisis of 1997 pricked the real estate bubble, the outcome was a far more widespread financial and economic crisis. Collyns and Senhadji (2003) considered that a wave of optimism, deriving from a serious under-estimation of risk, was the crucial factor driving the lending boom which fuelled the Asian bubble. Investors were operating under conditions of considerable uncertainty, relying on imperfect information and prone to 'disaster myopia', a tendency to underestimate the probability of a low frequency economic shock occurring (Herring and Wachter, 2003). As ever, it was investor sentiment which created this asset price bubble – just as it did, during the Tulipmania in seventeenth century Holland and during the South Sea Bubble in eighteenth century England (Kindleberger and Aliber, 2005).

Towards a satisfactory theory of the building cycle

What we know about building cycles

The theories that were surveyed in Chapter 2 have been formulated to explain the motion of the business cycle as it affects the growth trajectory of the whole economy. The research reviewed in this chapter has been undertaken to describe and explain the motion of the building cycle as it affects the development of one particular sector of the economy. A satisfactory theory of the building cycle needs to draw upon both traditions. Because the subject is a single capital goods sector, the theory should focus on explaining the motion of the building cycle itself; however, the theory should also cover the way in which building influences, and is influenced by, aggregate investment and therefore economic growth as a whole. Furthermore, a perspective is needed as to the manner in which growth and cycles in building activity interact with the broader processes of urban development, since buildings and infrastructure constitute the physical fabric of our towns and cities.

The following are the main propositions which past research suggests should be integrated within a satisfactory theory of the building cycle.

Building investment as a driver of long-run growth

Building investment is a component of fixed capital formation, and capital accumulation is a key driver of overall economic growth. At the same time, building stock constitutes the principal fixed capital of cities, and so building investment is also a key driver of urban accumulation and innovation. Consequently, the secular trend in building activity tracks those long-run trends in economic and population growth that define the trajectories of industrialization and urbanization in a growing economy.

Technical progress and building activity

There is a dual relationship between technical progress and building activity. New buildings embody improvements in design and facilities which enable their occupying activities to function more productively, while the construction process is itself subject to technical progress which encourages the intensification of urban development through the provision of larger and taller buildings. New types of buildings can be likened to discontinuous major innovations which spread through the stock, replacing older, less effective types through a process of creative destruction. Each new vintage of buildings causes previous vintages to move closer to economic obsolescence, so that, the higher the rate of building investment, the shorter is the economic life of existing buildings.

Cycles as the impetus to growth

Building cycles are characterized by a burst of investment in new stock, induced by an increase in occupier demand, followed by a phase of accelerated obsolescence in the existing stock. Each cycle thus creates a distinctive vintage of buildings and urban forms which reflects its particular historical context in terms of prevailing technologies and occupier requirements. As each vintage reaches the end of its economic life, a replacement cycle is generated to reinforce the cycle that is induced by the growth in demand. It is by this process that the building cycle helps to ratchet both economic growth and urban development to successively higher levels of activity.

A family of building cycles

Three cycles in building activity of increasing duration and volatility have been identified, each associated with a member of the wider family of business cycles. These comprise relatively mild minor cycles of 3–5 years duration (equivalent to the Kitchen cycle), more pronounced major cycles with a period of 7–11 years (equivalent to the Juglar cycle) and especially violent long cycles lasting 15–25 years (equivalent to Kuznets long swings). Multiplier-accelerator effects link these building cycles to the business cycle: the accelerator translates changes in occupier demand into more pronounced fluctuations in building investment, while the multiplier feeds these fluctuations in building investment back into aggregate investment and output.

The propagation of building cycles

Minor building cycles are primarily a demand-side phenomenon, reflecting the influence of the business cycle operating through changing levels of occupier activity and credit supply. Major cycles are more of a supply-side phenomenon, generated by endogenous propagation mechanisms, such as long construction periods and sticky market adjustment processes. Long cycles appear as particularly pronounced major cycles, usually associated with speculative booms. The different cycles seem to be linked through a cumulative tendency for every other demand-led minor cycle to be intensified into a major cycle by supply-side forces, and for every other major cycle to be intensified into a long cycle by speculative pressures.

The importance of long cycles

Long cycles have historically been identified as the most prominent form of building cycle, and characterized as one manifestation of a long swing affecting all aspects of industrial and urban development. As part of a general technology-driven upswing in economic growth, each long building cycle is typically associated with a wave of innovation in construction methods and infrastructure provision. The upswing generates increased demand for population-sensitive investment in dwellings and social infrastructure, together with accelerated investment in industrial and commercial buildings to expand the means of production. The resultant building boom is reinforced by speculative pressures, which lead to substantial levels of over-building, followed by an inevitable deflationary slump and the liquidation of surplus stock.

The transport-building cycle

A particular characteristic of the long building cycle is the close link between infrastructure investment to implement new transport technologies and building investment to support the urban growth, stimulated by the new transport systems. Each revolution in transport technology generates a surge in suburban expansion, embodied in a new vintage of residential and commercial buildings which creates a distinctive component of the urban fabric. Successive transport revolutions can therefore be identified with both a long swing in economic growth and a long cycle in urban development.

The transmission of market cycles

The movement of the building cycle is transmitted through all aspects of property market behaviour. An exogenously generated increase in demand leads to an increase in take-up and a reduction in the stock of vacant space; this is translated into an increase in rents and prices, which boosts the profitability of development;

the result is an upswing in building starts which eventually feeds through to increased levels of completions and vacancy. Conversely, when supply overshoots, vacancy increases and rents and prices fall, causing a drop in development profitability which leads to a cutback in further building starts. The cycle operates within a lower bound constraint of zero construction, and an upper bound set by the capacity of the development industry.

The unique characteristics of building investment

Building cycles tend to be more prolonged and volatile than any other type of economic cycle because of the unique characteristics of building investment. These include the length of the construction lags and the lumpiness of the investments (which create a tendency to over-building), the stickiness of rent adjustment due to demand-side rigidities (which delays the transmission of market signals), the durability of building stock (which reduces the stabilizing effect of replacement investment on unstable induced demand), the existence of a buffer stock of vacant space (which slows the supply response on the upswing and prolongs over-building on the downswing) and the traditionally fragmented nature of the development industry (which means that many firms are liquidated in a slump, creating a delay while capacity is restored during an upswing).

Relative demand and supply elasticities

Except where strict planning or land supply constraints are operating, the development supply of new buildings tends to be quite price elastic, responding more to changes in expected rents and capital values than to construction costs. Conversely, the occupier demand for new and second-hand buildings tends to be less price elastic because of the rigidities caused by factors such as long fixed-term leases and high transactions and moving costs. The greater the difference between the price elasticity of supply compared to demand, the greater the propensity for supply to overshoot and consequently the more volatile the building cycle.

The formation of market expectations

The formation of expectations in real estate markets is uniquely difficult because of the uncertainties deriving from long lead times in construction, market rigidities, infrequent transactions, heterogeneous stock, imperfect information and the long asset life over which future investment returns must be projected. The informational inefficiencies created by these features of the property market make the formation of rational expectations all but impossible. Furthermore, the speculative nature of much development creates a tendency for confidence itself to be cyclical, reinforcing the cycle as sentiment switches between optimism on the upswing and pessimism on the downswing.

Speculative bubbles

Real estate markets are particularly prone to speculative bubbles because of two interrelated factors: the development industry is heavily dependent on loan capital to finance its activities, while buildings act not only as productive capital, but also as financial assets and loan collateral. Financial accelerator effects thus reinforce building cycles through parallel cycles in credit supply. During an economic upswing, credit tends to be cheap and plentiful, thereby funding a building boom which creates new assets to act as collateral for raising further loans; conversely, on a downswing, higher interest rates lead to falling asset values and shrinking collateral, giving rise to a credit crunch which causes building to slump. Inadequate regulation of lending institutions increases the risk of such bubbles occurring.

Conflicting occupier and investor demand

The dual function of buildings as productive capital and financial assets creates a potential conflict between occupier demands for investment in improved buildings and investor demands for the preservation of existing asset values. When there is a shortage of supply, the asset values of buildings may be inflated above their income-earning capacity. Conversely, as occupiers move into a new vintage of buildings after a development boom, previous vintages suffer a phase of accelerated obsolescence, during which their book values may be deflated below earning capacity. This tendency towards excessive inflation and then deflation of asset values reinforces the impact of the building cycle upon the investment market.

The integration of real estate and capital markets

The growing integration of real estate and capital markets is creating spillover and contagion effects which are increasing the volatility of the building cycle and translating its instability into more widespread economic and financial crises. Cycles in the housing market reinforce fluctuations in consumer expenditure through the financial accelerator link between housing equity and debt-financed spending. Similarly, there is a risk of systemic failure in closely integrated markets, such as big city offices, in which financial institutions are the major occupiers of space, owners of assets and providers of development finance.

The international convergence of cycles

Building cycles in different sectors and cities within a national economy have historically tended to move in a broadly coincident manner because they are subject to common propagation mechanisms and the same macroeconomic environment. But locational differences arising from variations in economic structure, and sectoral differences due to variations in secular growth rates, have meant that the duration, frequency and volatility of cycles have varied considerably between different countries. However, as the integration of financial and real estate markets increases, as new financial instruments proliferate and as investment flows are globalized, it seems that building cycles internationally are becoming not only more volatile and more frequent, but also more convergent.

A conceptual model of the building cycle

Drawing together some of the themes outlined above, the operation of the classic speculative building cycle is illustrated in Figure 3.1. The conceptual model encompasses the links between the real economy, the property market and the money economy, and moves through the four phases of the business cycle, first outlined by Schumpeter (see Chapter 2).

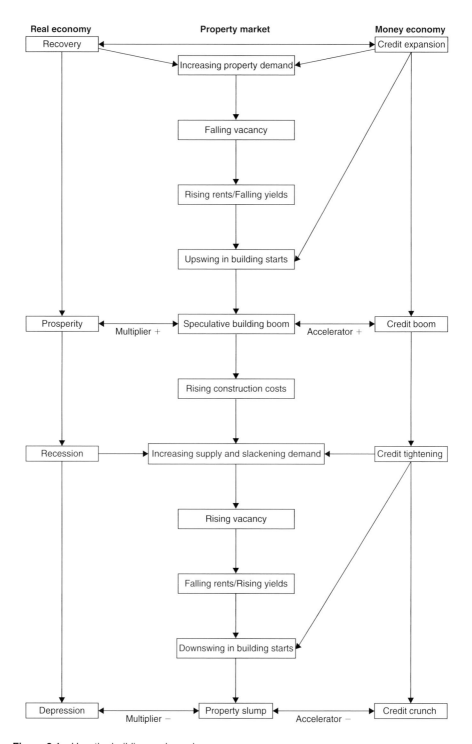

Figure 3.1   How the building cycle works.

Recovery

The process starts with an upturn in economic growth triggered by an exogenous shock, such as the adoption of a new technology or a fiscal stimulus to demand. The expansion in output and incomes induces increased demand for residential and commercial property, which is initially met from the stock of available space, so that vacancy falls below its equilibrium level. Rents overcome their initial stickiness and start to rise, while yields fall in expectation of increasing rental growth and reduced investor risk. Development profitability increases, prompting a first wave of building starts which is funded by the expansion in credit supply accompanying the economic upturn. The surge in building investment further boosts aggregate demand through multiplier effects, but because of construction lags, there is no short-term increase in building supply, so the growth in rents and prices accelerates.

Prosperity

During the prosperity phase, the economic boom continues to generate strong growth in demand for property, maintaining the growth in rents and prices and intensifying investor euphoria. The building boom is now in full swing, with financial accelerator effects sustaining the expansion of credit to fund a second wave of more speculative development starts through the rapid growth in collateral values. However, the first wave of development starts is now reaching completion, at last increasing the supply of available space, easing the upward pressure on rents and prices and boosting the productive capacity of the economy. As completed schemes continue to reach the market, rents and prices reach their peak and start to turn down. Development profitability is now falling, because of declining expectations of future returns, and because construction costs are rising as the development industry approaches its operating capacity. Consequently, the rate of new building starts turns down.

Recession

Overheating consumer demand is causing general inflationary pressures, so that interest rates are rising and the supply of credit tightening, which reinforces the cutback in building starts. An economic slowdown is now underway, reinforced by the multiplier effect on aggregate demand of cutbacks in investment, including building activity. However, because of the lags in development, high levels of building completions continue for some time, leading to a rapid rise in vacancy which is exacerbated by the slackening of demand due to the economic slowdown. The decline in rents accelerates, while yields rise in response to higher interest rates and deteriorating rental growth prospects. The shrinking value of existing assets sends the financial accelerator into reverse, further restricting the supply of building loans. Eventually, the supply of newly completed buildings tails off and vacancy stabilizes, though it remains well above its equilibrium level. As a result, the rate of rental decline starts to slow down.

Depression

With the economy now in depression, reduced occupier demand for buildings forces the liquidation of swathes of secondary stock. Demand for new building is mostly confined to the replacement of obsolete stock. Low construction activity feeds back to reinforce the depression, while property values have fallen so far that further development is no longer viable. Combined with the credit crunch, this means that building starts are close to zero. Vacancy begins to fall from its peak, but only slowly, given the depressed level of occupier demand, while rents and prices stabilize at levels far below earlier expectations. Many developers are left with unlet buildings or insufficient rental income to cover their increased interest charges, while many occupiers can no longer cover their loan or rent payments. The result is widespread loan defaults, bankruptcies and repossessions. However, as the property slump proceeds, the conditions for development begin to improve, as construction costs fall and expectations of future rental growth emerge once more. The stage is set for the start of the next building cycle.

Typically, the overhang of vacant space from such a property slump can last through much of the following business cycle, so that only a minor building cycle is generated in response to the next upswing in demand. When the next major building cycle gets underway, following the minor cycle, it may primarily be funded by owner occupiers and long-term institutional investors, rather than the banks and other credit institutions, which are still grappling with the bad debts left over from the last speculative boom. This major cycle may therefore be more demand-driven, with a smaller speculative component restricting the extent of the over-supply, so that rents and prices do not surge and collapse to the same extent as in a speculative boom. The repeat of the long cycle awaits one more major cycle upturn, by which time all the necessary conditions are in place for the onset of another speculative boom.

Herein lies the tendency for every second major cycle, and every fourth minor cycle, to turn into a speculative long cycle. It must be stressed that this is no more than a tendency; specific historical events or shifts in market conditions can substantially alter the phasing, duration and volatility of successive building cycles with respect to this idealized model. Nevertheless, while there is always a danger of too literal and mechanistic an explanation of observed cycles within their historical context, it is important to remember that these phenomena are not merely random events, but rather, they have explicable causes deriving from particular combinations of circumstances which tend to be self-replicating over varying timescales. Furthermore, the operation of the building cycle can only properly be understood within the broader dynamic of the growth process, as each cycle ratchets the productive capacity of the economy up through progressively higher levels, adding both to the quantity and quality of its fixed capital.

4

Building Investment and Economic Growth

Buildings as means of production

Investment and technical progress

In Chapters 2 and 3, we discussed how building capital forms part of the economic means of production, how building investment provides a component of fixed capital formation and how capital accumulation acts as a driver of economic growth. We also noted the dual relationship between technical progress and building investment: new buildings embody technical improvements which enable their occupying activities to function more productively, while the activity of building is itself subject to productivity improvements through technical progress in construction methods. Building investment helps to expand productive capacity, increase the capital intensity of production and raise labour productivity. As existing buildings age, their economic value depreciates relative to that of newer vintages, constructed with more productive techniques and embodying more advanced technologies. The depreciation of buildings can either be offset by investment in their renovation, or else allowed to run its course until the obsolete buildings are demolished and replaced.

A useful starting point for formalizing the role of building investment in economic growth is provided by the famous set of 'stylized facts' first proposed by Kaldor (1961: 178–9) to describe the long-term equilibrium growth path of an industrialized economy. These are as follows:

- Output and capital stock tend to grow in tandem, with their growth rate exceeding that of the labour force by a margin equal to the rate of growth of labour productivity, or output per worker, resulting from technical progress.
- The capital intensity of production, measured by capital per worker, thus tends to grow in line with labour productivity, as do real wages.
- The productivity of capital, the inverse of the capital–output ratio, remains broadly constant, as does the rate of profit on capital and thereby the shares of capital and labour in total income.

Clearly this is a highly idealized set of assumptions which presume that economies tend to follow balanced, steady-state growth paths that are unaffected in the long term by specific historical events. We have already seen that this is not the case, but rather the trajectories of real economies are marked by disequilibrium, cyclical instability and structural change. Nevertheless, empirical studies of the secular development of capitalist economies do reveal some approximations to Kaldor's stylized facts when conducted over a timescale long enough to minimize the influence of cyclical fluctuations and structural discontinuities (Maddison, 1991).

Technical progress is the key to understanding how investment drives the growth process through its dual impact on labour productivity. Productivity is not only boosted by the accumulation of an expanding volume of capital at a given state of technology, but it is also augmented by the technological improvements embodied in successive vintages of capital stock. Put another way, investment in new capital goods introduces improved techniques into production, enhancing the marginal productivity of the labour working with the new techniques; at the same time, technical progress in the construction of investment goods reduces their price relative to that of labour, encouraging the substitution of capital for labour which boosts capital per worker and thus average labour productivity. Technical improvements thus increase both the quality and quantity of capital employed in production, generating a twofold boost to labour productivity (Salter, 1966: 36). However, while the increase in capital per worker through substitution (termed capital deepening) reinforces the impact of technical improvements on labour productivity, it offsets their impact on the productivity of capital because of diminishing returns to additional increments of capital of constant quality. If the countervailing influences of substitution and technical progress balance out, then the productivity of capital will remain broadly constant, as suggested by Kaldor's stylized facts.

Technical progress can be both capital- and labour-saving, but while its labour-saving effects are obvious in rising labour productivity, its capital-saving impact is masked by the substitution of capital for labour as ever more capital-intensive methods of production are employed. Depending on the balance of these effects, technical progress can be identified as 'neutral', if the shares of capital and labour in total income stay constant through time, or as having a 'labour-saving' or 'capital-saving' bias if the income share of the respective factor is falling through time (Stoneman, 1983: 4–6). Different versions of neutrality have been defined, and that first proposed by Harrod (1948: 81–4) is the version which is consistent with Kaldor's stylized facts, since it is defined along an equilibrium growth trajectory with a constant capital–output ratio. Some writers have argued that the main thrust of technical progress is likely to be labour-saving, particularly in times of relative labour scarcity (Habakkuk, 1962a). A rationale for this can be proposed if it is assumed that firms are able to achieve a range of possible productivity improvements through their investment in new technology, and that they seek to implement those innovations which maximize their resultant cost savings or output gains. Since labour typically accounts for the dominant share of total production costs, there will be an 'induced bias' towards innovations which produce gains through augmenting labour, rather than capital, productivity (Kennedy, 1964).

In order to identify the potential capital-saving propensities of a new technology, it is necessary to separate out the impacts of technical progress and factor price change upon the productivity of capital. Thus, for example, technical progress in the construction of capital equipment or buildings may involve a strong labour-saving bias in their producer industries, through the introduction of more mechanization, but the resultant cheapening of these capital goods will have a capital-saving impact on the consumer goods industries which use them, because they need to invest less capital in the means of production needed to undertake a specific task. Furthermore, technical improvements in the specification of particular types of capital goods will also tend to improve their performance, reinforcing the capital-saving effect. In other words, capital can be saved in user industries because a particular task can be undertaken using capital goods which are both cheaper and of higher specification as a result of technical progress. However, because of these reductions in price and improvements in performance, a broader spread of firms in a broader spread of industries will tend to invest in more of such goods in order to save labour across a wider range of tasks. The likely net result is that aggregate capital per worker rises, even though strong capital-saving effects are in operation within individual firms and industries.

Building versus equipment capital

When aggregate capital stock is broken down into its main constituents, equipment and buildings, we need to recognize that different types of capital goods can make differential contributions to the growth process. Again, a dual effect is at work. First, the various types of capital goods enjoy differential rates of cheapening relative to labour, stemming from variations in the rate of technical progress achieved in their construction. At one extreme, equipment such as computers, produced in industries subject to continuous and rapid innovation, shows astonishing rates of cheapening for machines of equivalent performance; in the case of computers, the quality-adjusted rate of cheapening has been estimated to lie in the range 15%–20% per annum (Jorgenson, 2001). On the other hand, innovation and technical progress have been notoriously difficult to achieve in the traditionally fragmented, undercapitalized and craft-based construction industry, with the result that the rate of cheapening of buildings has been much more modest (Powell, 1980; Groak and Ive, 1986). With wide differentials in their rates of cheapening, equipment and building capital will tend to be substituted for labour at different rates. The result is a high rate of capital deepening with equipment such as computers (Jorgenson et al., 2008), together with pressures to substitute rapidly cheapening equipment for slowly cheapening buildings. These capital-saving pressures are manifest, for example, in attempts by office firms to save on space costs by employing information technology to allow their staff to work from home and to share desks in the office.

The second and related aspect of the differential impact of technical progress on the various constituents of capital is that those goods which enjoy the most rapid cheapening in their own manufacture also tend to embody the most dynamic technological improvements when employed in the production of other goods and services. As the shares of the different constituents of capital have shifted over time, so has the extent to which they have directly or indirectly contributed to productivity growth in the economy as a whole. Thus, the great wave of factory and railway building associated with the Industrial Revolution established the basic infrastructure for an industrializing economy, providing expensive buildings to house simple, relatively cheap steam-powered machines (Crouzet, 1972: 37–8). Buildings provided the dominant constituent of the stock of fixed capital and acted as the main embodiment of the new steam-powered technologies, whereas the stock of machinery played a more secondary role (Field, 1985).

In contrast, the modern economy is devoting an apparently ever-growing share of investment to electronic equipment, which is consequently acting as the principal carrier of the new information and communication technologies (ICTs) in all types of industrial and commercial buildings. In general, a new computer network is likely to increase output per worker more than a new office building, which is not to deny that the way in which office space is organized can have an important effect upon the well-being and effectiveness of the workforce. Hence, the anecdotal but widespread evidence that many firms now invest more in their computer systems than in their accommodation. This not only reflects the remarkable cost reductions which encourage companies to expand their computer systems to embrace an ever-wider range of tasks, but also the huge performance gains to be derived from applying the latest system enhancements to already computerized tasks.

In summary, this argument suggests another stylized fact of long-run economic growth to add to Kaldor's list: that because of higher rates of technical progress in its manufacture and use, the share of the equipment component of total capital stock tends to increase over time at the expense of the building component, and at the same time the locus of technical progress also switches progressively from building to equipment capital. The result is that building investment has a diminishing role as an engine of productivity growth in a maturing economy, even though it remains an essential and complementary factor of production. This proposition is examined further in the next section, using long-run growth data for the United Kingdom and United States and employing a simple growth model incorporating building and equipment capital.

Several empirical studies have explored the manner in which equipment capital has attracted a growing share of total investment and has functioned increasingly as the engine of productivity growth in the modern economy. De Long and Summers (1991) undertook a cross-sectional study of 61 countries between 1960 and 1985 which demonstrated that the share of equipment investment in GDP was a key driver of national productivity growth, whereas the influence of building investment was much weaker. This result was confirmed by a subsequent panel model of productivity growth in six industrialized economies using eight consecutive periods of growth between 1870 and 1980 (De Long, 1992). A strong negative relationship was also discovered between productivity growth and the real price of equipment in different industrialized economies. The lower the relative price of equipment because of technical progress in its manufacture, the higher the level of equipment investment via the substitution effect, and therefore the higher the rate of labour productivity growth as a result of increasing capital intensity and embodied technical change.

These findings suggest that 'If machinery and structures contribute differently to growth, then analyses of the relationship between total capital accumulation and growth are likely to be very misleading' (De Long and Summers, 1991: 452). However, in apportioning the major share of embodied technical progress to equipment rather than buildings, we must beware of making too artificial a distinction between what are essentially complementary forms of capital. A Victorian cotton mill was an imposing symbol of the Industrial Revolution, but it could make no contribution to the growth of national output without the installation of its mechanical looms; conversely, today's robotic car plant, however complex, must still be housed in a factory building designed to accommodate the latest technologies and work practices. In a similar vein, it should be recognized that built structures and infrastructure networks also act as complementary factors of production. Aschauer (1989) highlighted the importance of public investment in the core infrastructures of transport and utilities as a key driver of productivity growth, on the basis of a time series study of the US economy in the post-war period.

The shift in the locus of embodied technical progress from buildings to equipment appears to be accompanied by a growing fusion of the different constituents of capital in terms of their productive capacity. Thus, it is estimated that over 20% of total construction costs are now accounted for by the mechanical, electrical and information technology systems installed in buildings (Gann, 2000: 110). The process has gone furthest in manufacturing industry, where the modern 'design and build' plant integrates equipment and structure very closely. While traditionally lagging behind manufacturing, service industries are now following the same trend, as computer networks are integrated into the fabric of offices and other commercial buildings.

The integration of building and equipment capital has important implications for the obsolescence of commercial property. As discussed in Chapter 2, the vintage model of embodied technical change implies a direct relationship between the age of a capital good and its technological potential, with each new vintage of investment embodying an improved technique of production. This relationship may be clear for equipment capital such as computers, but it is less so for buildings – many service businesses are operating just as effectively in a 100-year-old office as they would be in a new building, but few would be satisfied with a computer system that is even 5 years old. Paradoxically, rapid innovation in information technology, moving in the direction of greater flexibility and portability, offers the opportunity to extend the economic life of buildings by reducing the technological demands on their fabric. A good example is the emphasis in the late 1980s building boom on providing new offices with large floor-to-ceiling heights and raised floors to accommodate cabling for computer networks; by the mid-1990s, many of the more extreme design solutions to this perceived need were rendered obsolete by the miniaturization of the technology, while older and apparently less suitable buildings were given a new lease of life (Barras and Clark, 1996). However, as building and equipment capital become more integrated, there is a risk that the rate of obsolescence of the building component could become more closely tied to that of the equipment component, shortening the life of the building and depressing its investment value.

Cyclical growth

The long-run trajectory of economic growth is propelled by the interplay of several dynamic forces: demographic growth and change, the exploitation of natural resources, the accumulation of human capital, investment in physical capital, the expansion of trade and the evolution of legal, financial and governmental institutions (Maddison, 1991). It can be said that technical progress in its generic sense helps to tie these forces of propulsion together, both influencing and responding to their development. If we adopt this long-run perspective, technical progress can be viewed as an evolutionary process in which new products and processes emerge to meet the changing needs of society (Basalla, 1988). It is important to recognize that the processes of invention, innovation and adoption which constitute techni- cal progress are not deterministic; rather they are subject to historical influences which are social and cultural as well as scientific and economic, and they involve human inspiration and creativity as well as physical investment and workforce training (Mokyr, 1990). In particular, we must avoid the pitfalls of a crude tech- nological determinism which in essence assumes that 'technology drives history'; instead it is more fruitful to characterize technology as a mediating factor within a historical process which links the economic, social, political and cultural spheres of human activity (Smith and Marx, 1994).

As discussed in Chapter 2, the forces which propel economic development do not operate smoothly and steadily through time, as is assumed in the idealized world of equilibrium growth. In reality, the growth process is punctuated by disequilibrat- ing shocks and discontinuities which can both shift the economy away from its secular trajectory and alter the direction of the trajectory itself, until compensating adjustment processes move the economy back towards its new trajectory. It is this historical interplay of equilibrating and disequilibrating forces which creates the conditions for the propagation of economic cycles in general and building cycles in particular. Furthermore, the motion of these cycles provides a crucial dynamic which propels economic development – not as a smooth and continuous process, but rather as a sequence of investment-led surges of growth interspersed with peri- ods of slowdown and retrenchment. Each expansion phase drives the economy to a new and higher peak, so that the next contraction is limited to a higher trough than was reached in the previous cycle.

According to Schumpeterian theory, technical progress itself is not achieved through a process of continuous evolution, but rather through a sequence of tech- nological revolutions. Each is initiated by the emergence of a new general purpose technology, consisting of a cluster of interrelated innovations with their associ- ated infrastructure, which diffuses throughout the economy, driving an investment boom which expands productive capacity until market saturation sets in. The sub- sequent slump is marked by a phase of creative destruction which accelerates the obsolescence of established techniques and products, thereby generating the con- ditions for the start of the next boom. Such technological revolutions are identi- fied as the source of the Kondratieff long wave in economic growth which was discussed previously in Chapter 2. Though far from generally accepted as a periodic phenomenon, the long wave does provide a helpful framework for analyzing the rhythm of capitalist development since the late eighteenth century. An illustrative long wave schema is presented in Table 4.1, drawn from Freeman and Louca (2001); similar chronologies are employed in Tylecote (1991) and Lloyd-Jones and Lewis (1998). The schema describes each long wave in terms of the suggested dates of its upswing and downswing, its cluster of dominant technologies, the sectors that led economic development and the associated infrastructure networks that carried the technology.

Some empirical evidence for the existence of long waves is provided by Hartman and Wheeler (1979) in their study of the evolution of the British and American economies since the late eighteenth century. They identified Schumpeterian waves

Table 4.1 A long wave schema.

Kondratieff	1	2	3	4	5
Upswing	1780–1815	1848–1873	1895–1918	1940–1973	??
Downswing	1815–1848	1873–1895	1918–1940	1973–	??
Technologies	Water power	Steam power	Electrification	Motorization	Computerization
Leading sectors	Textiles	Railways	Steel	Automobiles	Computers
	Iron	Machine tools	Engineering	Aircraft	Telecommunications
		Coal	Chemicals	Oil	Biotechnology
Infrastructure	Canals	Railways	Arterial roads	Motorways	Internet
	Turnpikes	Telegraph	Telephone	Airports	

Source: Freeman and Louca (2001: 141).

of innovation, as measured by the issue of patents, and associated waves of infrastructure investment, as measured by the installation of canal, railway and highway networks. These waves of innovation fitted within the Kondratieff long wave chronology, as revealed by movements in a range of economic indicators including aggregate output, consumption, investment, unemployment and prices.

As has already been discussed in Chapter 2, the long wave has been identified as the most extended of a whole family of investment cycles which also includes minor cycles, major cycles and long swings. It is argued that the generation of each type of cycle depends upon endogenous propagation mechanisms that derive from the durability, lumpiness and gestation periods of different types of capital goods. The extent to which such a family of cycles can be identified in the historical record remains a matter of some debate, with the long wave being the most controversial family member. In the final section of this chapter, we go on to investigate the existence of cycles of different duration in long-run investment data for the United Kingdom and the United States, making use of the recently developed technique of unobserved components modelling which can simultaneously decompose a data series into a stochastic trend and up to three stochastic cycles. Having isolated the significant cyclical components in both building and equipment investment, the interrelationships between the different cycles provide an indication of the manner in which successive waves of investment have propelled the growth of the two economies.

Building investment as driver of growth

Building investment and UK growth (1855–2005)

The way that capital investment in general, and building investment in particular, drive the growth process can be illustrated empirically using data for the United Kingdom between the mid-nineteenth century and the present, covering the whole period since Britain became a mature industrial economy. A unique dataset describing the long-run growth of the UK economy has been assembled by Feinstein (1976) for the years 1855–1965, and subsequently revised with improved capital stock estimates for the years up to 1920 (Feinstein and Pollard, 1988). The original version of this dataset underpins a detailed empirical study of UK growth up to 1973 produced by Matthews et al. (1982), and was used by Ball and Wood (1996a) in their study of building investment as a driver of economic growth in the UK economy between 1856 and 1992. For the purposes of our study, the revised Feinstein data have been extended forwards to 2005 using Office for National Statistics (ONS) National Accounts data; for some series, the ONS data stretch back to 1948, for others, it goes back to 1965. The analysis of the data presented here updates and modifies an earlier and more detailed version published in Barras (2001).

Annual indices have been extracted from the dataset to illustrate the trajectories of UK output, employment and capital stock growth between 1855 and 2005 (Figure 4.1). The indices used are the volume measure of GDP at constant factor cost (to 1948) or market prices (from 1948), the total number of people in employment, and volume measures of total gross capital stock and its main constituents – housing, other buildings (including infrastructure), machinery and vehicles (excluding those owned by households). The capital stock indices require interpolation to cover missing values in the years 1939–46. For much of the analysis, machinery and commercial vehicles are combined into a composite measure of equipment capital.

The use of the total number in employment as the labour input measure is inevitably crude, since no consistent time series measures of hours worked or labour force qualifications are available to make adjustments for the quantity and quality of labour inputs over the full time period (though Matthews et al., 1982 do attempt such adjustments). The gross capital stock measures are derived by the 'perpetual inventory method', whereby each year's new investments valued at their replacement cost are added to the stock total, while past investments are only deducted

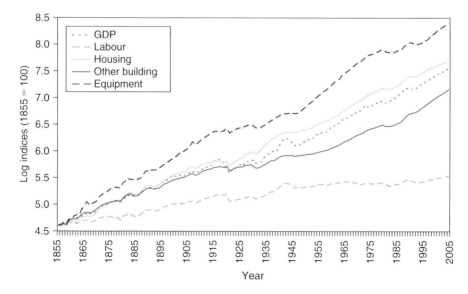

Figure 4.1   Growth in UK output, labour and capital stock 1855–2005.
Source: Feinstein (1976), Feinstein and Pollard (1988) and ONS.

when the assets are assumed to have completed their economic lives. In contrast to the net stock measure, the gross measure makes no allowance for the progressive depreciation of assets over their service lives (OECD, 2001). A comparison of the two measures shows similar long-run growth profiles. Griffin (1976) argues that the gross measure is the more appropriate indicator of the output potential of capital stock, as the constant depreciation assumption undoubtedly overstates the loss of productive capacity of capital assets as they age, whereas the net measure is the more appropriate for calculating the rate of return on capital. To be more consistent with the labour measure of total numbers in employment (rather than the total size of the labour force), the capital stock indices have been adjusted to provide a measure of 'utilized capital' by applying the labour force unemployment rate as a proxy for the capital utilization rate. Even so, the approximate nature of the capital stock series must be acknowledged, being dependent upon inevitably crude assumptions about the economic lives of different types of assets.

The UK data provide some confirmation that Kaldor's stylized facts of economic growth do hold approximately true over long periods of time (Figure 4.2). During the past century and a half, both output and total capital stock have grown at an average rate of around 2.0% per annum, while the employed labour force has expanded at only 0.6% per annum – and if allowance could be made for the progressive decline in working hours since the mid-nineteenth century, the growth of labour inputs would have been even smaller. These relative trends imply that labour productivity and capital intensity, or capital per worker, have been increasing on average by at least 1.4% per annum, while capital productivity as measured by the inverse capital–output ratio has remained broadly constant. Although such averages do capture the long-run characteristics of the growth process, they should not be taken to imply that it has proceeded along a smooth equilibrium path.

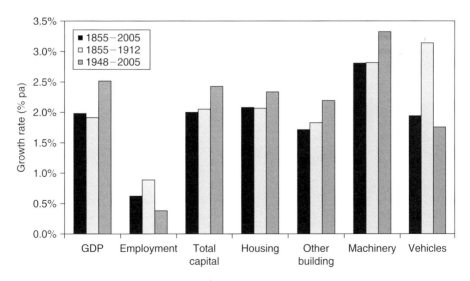

Figure 4.2 Growth rates for the UK economy 1855–2005.
Source: Feinstein (1976), Feinstein and Pollard (1988) and ONS.

An examination of Figure 4.1 shows that the trajectory of each macroeconomic indicator exhibits an oscillatory motion which will be examined more closely in the final section of this chapter when we come to explore the cyclical characteristics of UK growth.

While the long-run trends are broadly consistent with Kaldor's stylized facts, average growth rates and factor ratios have varied significantly as the United Kingdom has passed through different phases of growth. These differences can be illustrated most clearly by setting aside the turbulent period spanning the two World Wars and the inter-war years, and comparing the trends in two equal periods that define the phase of Victorian and Edwardian industrialization (1855–1912) and the phase of post-war development (1948–2005). During both phases, the trajectory of growth conformed reasonably well to the Kaldor facts. In the period leading up to the First World War, output (1.9%) and capital stock (2.1%) were growing at rates close to the long-run average, but the labour force (0.9%) was growing more rapidly. In contrast, the post-war period has been marked by higher rates of growth in output (2.5%) and capital stock (2.4%), but a lower rate of labour force expansion (0.4%). Consequently, when the two periods are compared, there has been a marked increase in the rates of growth of labour productivity, doubling from around 1.0% to 2.1% per annum, and the capital intensity of production, jumping from around 1.2% to 2.0% per annum. These increases reflect the changing nature of the growth process in the United Kingdom over the past 150 years. In particular, historically high rates of investment in the post-war period have generated above average rates of productivity and output growth by boosting both productive capacity and aggregate demand (Matthews et al., 1982: 515–22).

Let us now focus on the contribution to the growth process made by different constituents of the UK capital stock. As we have seen, aggregate capital stock has grown at a long-run average rate of 2.0% per annum over the whole 1855–2005 period, matching the growth of national output and income. The capital stock data show that this aggregate growth rate has been closely matched by both dwellings (2.1%) and vehicles (1.9%), indicating that the demands for housing and transport have grown broadly in line with national income over the past century and a half. Furthermore, the growth rate of housing capital has followed the rising trajectory of national income growth, increasing from 2.1% during the 1855–1912 period to 2.3% over the 1948–2005 period.

However, the two principal constituents of productive capital – machinery and non-residential buildings (comprising industrial and commercial buildings and infrastructure) – have exhibited more divergent trends relative to total capital. Over the whole period, machinery capital has grown at an above average rate of 2.8% per annum, while non-residential building capital has increased at the below average rate of 1.7% per annum. Similar differentials between the constituent growth rates can be observed over the shorter periods: 2.8% compared to 1.8% between 1855 and 1912, and 3.3% compared to 2.2% between 1948 and 2005. The result of these divergent trends is that the share of machinery in total capital stock has progressively increased, whereas the share of non-residential buildings has shrunk. Thus, in 1855, the share of non-residential buildings in total stock was 57% (at 1900 prices), whereas machinery accounted for only 12%; however, by 2005, the building share had dropped to 33% and had been overtaken by the machinery share which had risen to 37%.

As discussed in the previous section, the relative substitution of machinery for buildings within the productive capital of the United Kingdom can in part be attributed to divergent trends in their relative prices. To test this, the relative prices of the different capital components have been derived as 'implied deflators' from the long-run current and constant price gross capital stock data. The price indices which underlie these deflators are constructed as far as possible to measure changes in the price of a fixed quantity of capital goods of constant specification, thereby allowing for that technical progress in their manufacture which feeds through to reduce their costs of production. However, the indices do not allow for those improvements to the quality of capital goods which enhance their productive potential but are not reflected in changes to their costs of manufacture. It is these quality improvements, resulting for example from design enhancements or better operating procedures, which are embodied in capital goods as technical progress and translate into increases in output per unit of capital when the goods are employed as means of production (Feinstein and Pollard, 1988: 262–4).

The derived price indices for UK capital goods have been expressed relative to the price of labour, as represented by an index of average weekly earnings. The indices show that over the whole period 1855–2005, aggregate capital has cheapened relative to labour at an average rate of 1.0% per annum; furthermore, there has been a substantial increase in the rate of cheapening from 0.8% during the 1855–1912 period to 1.9% during the 1948–2005 period (Figure 4.3). This increase signifies a strengthening of the rate of technical progress enjoyed in the construction of capital goods which helps to explain the observed acceleration in capital investment during the post-war period. The averages for aggregate capital conceal a wide variation in the relative rates of cheapening of its different constituents, with housing showing the slowest rate (0.7%) over the whole period, followed by other buildings (1.0%) and vehicles (1.3%), while machinery exhibits the fastest rate (1.7%). It should be noted

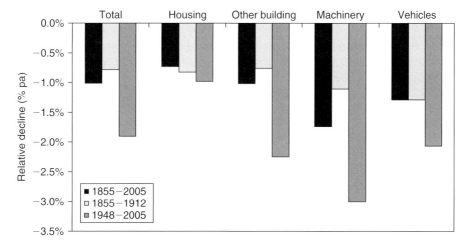

Figure 4.3 Rates of decline of UK capital goods prices relative to labour.
Source: Feinstein (1976), Feinstein and Pollard (1988) and ONS.

that the estimated differences between the rates of cheapening of machinery and building capital are understated, since no allowance is made for the costs of building land, which by its very nature, does not enjoy technical progress in production. Comparing trends over the two shorter periods 1855–1912 and 1948–2005, it can be seen that the rate of cheapening has barely increased for dwellings, whereas there has been a marked acceleration for the other constituents, with non-residential buildings registering an increase from 0.8% to 2.2% and machinery an increase from 1.1% to 3.0%.

Thus the construction of both the buildings and machinery used in production has benefitted from a comparable increase in technical progress during the post-war period, which explains why both types of capital have been substituted for labour at an accelerated rate since the Second World War. However, throughout the whole period since the mid-nineteenth century, the rate of cheapening of machinery has exceeded that of buildings, which explains why the growth of machinery capital has consistently outstripped that of building capital – because of a greater propensity to substitute machinery rather than buildings for labour. A comparison of the trends for residential and non-residential buildings reveals a different story. The construction of dwellings has not only witnessed a lower rate of technical progress than the construction of other types of buildings, but its productivity appears not to have improved significantly in the post-war period, unlike that of non-residential building (Needleman, 1965: 104–6). Yet the stock of residential capital has grown in line with the increasing rate of growth of national income, indicating that the demand for housing is determined not by its contribution to economic output, but rather by its status as an income-elastic consumer good (Meen, 1996).

In summary, housing is becoming relatively more expensive compared to commercial and industrial buildings, which in turn are increasing in price relative to equipment (vehicles and machinery). Qualitative observation confirms the differential rates of technical progress which underlie these relative price trends. The methods used to construct a house today do not differ fundamentally from those adopted in the Victorian era, since their choice is influenced at least as much by aesthetic and cultural concerns as by technological possibilities. More substantial have been the cost reductions achieved in the design and construction of contemporary industrial and commercial buildings; compare, for example, the rapid assembly of modern light industrial units with the painstaking construction of the brick-built mills of the mid-nineteenth century. But far more revolutionary is the contrast between the automated assembly techniques applied in the latest generation of computer factories and the primitive fabrication methods used to produce the steam plant of the early Industrial Revolution.

A growth model with building capital

As discussed in the previous section, the shift in the composition of productive capital stock from buildings to equipment reflects the quality effect of technical progress as well as its price effect. Not only has equipment become cheaper relative to industrial and commercial buildings, it tends to have embodied within it higher rates of technical progress to be exploited in the production of final output. In order to investigate the impact of the shifting composition of investment upon long-run economic development, a simple growth model incorporating building and equipment capital has been formulated (Barras, 2001). The model is based upon an aggregate production function in which the quantity of national output is expressed as a function of the factor inputs used in production, and it is formulated so as to allow for both embodied and disembodied technical progress. Such models are rightly criticized for being a crude simplification of real-world production relationships, but their simplicity does make them amenable to the type of long-run analysis presented here. (For an alternative approach, identifying the long-run sources of UK growth using a growth accounting methodology, see Matthews et al., 1982.)

The growth model is set out in the appendix at the end of this chapter. It has been estimated using the long-run data series on output, employed labour and utilized gross capital stock for the United Kingdom that are described above. Four versions of the model have been estimated according to equations (4.4)–(4.7); they comprise both the extensive and intensive production equations (with the variables expressed either as levels or ratios), each incorporating either aggregate capital or its two main components (non-residential buildings and equipment). While the full UK series cover the years 1855–2005, stable cointegrating models could not be derived over the full sample period because of a structural break in the model relationships at the end of the First World War, marking the transition from one growth regime to another (see Barras, 2001, for a formal methodology to identify such structural breaks). Consequently, separate models have been fitted for the sub-periods 1855–1912 and 1920–2005 and, for consistency with the earlier analysis, also for the shorter 1948–2005 sub-period. Each of the series used in the models tests as integrated of order one, and the models in all cases yield cointegrating relationships. The derived model coefficients are listed in Table 4.2.

The estimated rates of embodied and disembodied technical progress derived from the intensive models are summarized in Table 4.3. The disembodied rates are

Table 4.2 Coefficients of the estimated UK growth models[a].

	Aggregate capital[b]				Components of capital[b]				
Extensive models[c,d]	$\log A_0$	t	$\log K_t$	$\log L_t$	$\log A_0$	t	$\log B_t$	$\log E_t$	$\log L_t$
1855–1912	0.946*	0.006	0.561	0.238	0.886*	0.007	0.520	–	0.288
1920–2005	−1.232	0.004	0.813	0.381	−0.490*	0.009	0.386	0.194	0.416
1948–2005	−0.120*	0.008	0.623	0.307	0.934*	0.014	0.146	0.231	0.271
Intensive models[c,d]	$\log a_0$	t	$\log k_t$		$\log a_0$	t	$\log b_t$	$\log e_t$	
1855–1912	1.495	0.002	0.680		1.761	0.005	0.618	–	
1920–2005	0.988	0.006	0.711		1.415	0.009	0.387	0.195	
1948–2005	1.152	0.008	0.653		1.805	0.012	0.177	0.255	

Source: Feinstein (1976), Feinstein and Pollard (1988) and ONS.
[a]The coefficients refer to the model equations (4.4)–(4.7) set out in the appendix to this chapter; all model variables are expressed in logarithmic form.
[b]All the model variables test as I(1) at the 1% significance level using the augmented Dickey–Fuller (ADF) test.
[c]All model coefficients, except those marked *, are significant at the 1% level.
[d]All models produce a cointegrating regression, yielding residuals that are stationary according to the unit root test at the 1% level of significance using critical values from MacKinnon (1996).

Table 4.3   Estimated rates of technical progress in the UK economy.

Period	Aggregate capital (%)		Capital components (%)		
	Disembodied	Embodied	Disembodied	Embodied	
				Buildings	Equipment
1855–1912	0.2	0.9	0.5	0.8	–
1920–2005	0.6	1.6	0.9	0.6	0.8
1948–2005	0.8	1.6	1.2	–	1.5

Source: Feinstein (1976), Feinstein and Pollard (1988) and ONS.

Note: The estimates are derived from the intensive models listed in Table 4.1.

derived directly from the time trends in each model, following equations (4.5) and (4.7). The embodied rates are derived from the difference between each estimated capital coefficient and the estimated share of that capital component in national income: according to equation (4.3), this difference is the product of the average age of the capital stock and its rate of embodied technical progress. Data from Feinstein (1976) and the ONS show that the share of capital in UK national income averaged 0.4 in the 1855–1912 period and 0.3 in the 1920–2005 and 1948–2005 periods. These shares have in turn been allocated between building and equipment capital according to the average current price share of each constituent in the value of aggregate capital – yielding shares of 0.28 for buildings and 0.12 for equipment in the first period, and 0.18 and 0.12 in the two later periods.

As far as the average age of each component of stock is concerned, the gross capital stock series in the UK National Accounts have traditionally been constructed using assumed asset lives of around 80 years for commercial buildings and 25 years for plant and machinery (CSO, 1985: 200–1). Applied to the 1855–1912 period, these lives translate into approximate average ages of 40 years and 12.5 years for commercial buildings and equipment, and a weighted average of 31 years for aggregate capital using the average current price share of each component during the period. There is some evidence that the average age of capital assets has been decreasing, particularly after the Second World War, as the obsolescence of commercial buildings has speeded up and the introduction of computer technology has reduced the economic life of some constituents of equipment capital to as little as 5 years (ONS, 2007). For the purposes of this analysis, it has therefore been assumed that the average ages of building and equipment capital dropped to 35 and 10 years respectively during the 1920–2005 period, yielding a weighted average of 25 years for aggregate capital, and to 32.5 and 8.5 years respectively over the 1948–2005 period, yielding a weighted average of 22.5 years for aggregate capital.

The following are the main points to emerge about the drivers of growth in the UK economy since the mid-nineteenth century.

Embodied technical progress

The sum of the estimated output elasticities of labour and capital in the extensive models is typically quite close to unity, which would be consistent with the assumption of constant returns to scale in aggregate production over the long term. However, the estimated elasticities for each factor do not correspond closely with their historic shares of national income. Comparison of the model coefficients with the estimated income shares (0.6:0.4 for labour:capital in the 1855–1912 period, and 0.7:0.3 in the 1920–2005 and 1948–2005 periods) shows in all cases that the estimated output elasticities of labour are lower than their income shares, but the output elasticities of capital are higher – which is consistent with the findings of other empirical studies of long-run growth (Crafts, 1992: 392). These estimates suggest that a degree of technical progress has been embodied in the capital stock, but within the model this scale effect is offset by an apparent reduction in the output elasticity of labour. The output elasticities derived from the intensive model yield estimated rates of embodied technical progress in the aggregate capital stock that rise from an average of 0.9% per annum in the 1855–1912 period to 1.6% per annum during the 1920–2005 period, the latter rate also being maintained during the shorter 1948–2005 period.

Building versus equipment capital

The breakdown of the estimated rates of embodied technical progress between buildings and equipment confirms the argument developed in the previous section that it is equipment capital which has attracted the growing share of total investment and has functioned increasingly as the engine of productivity growth as the UK economy has matured. Thus, during the 1855–1912 period, building capital was so much the dominant component that its embodied rate of 0.8% contributes nearly all of the technical progress assigned to aggregate capital, with no significant contribution estimated to come from equipment capital. Moving on to the period from 1920 to 2005, the two components contribute broadly equally to the aggregate rate of embodied technical progress: 0.6% from buildings and 0.8% from equipment. However, when the analysis focuses on the post-war period 1948–2005, equipment capital has become established as the key driver of growth, with the model estimates suggesting that it is now the sole contributor to the technical progress assigned to aggregate capital, with its own embodied rate of 1.5%.

Disembodied technical progress

As well as the technical progress embodied in the capital stock, all the models yield significant estimates of disembodied technical progress as captured by their time trends. For the intensive models using aggregate capital, the estimates reveal an increase in the rate of disembodied progress from 0.2% per annum over the 1855–1912 period to 0.8% per annum during the 1948–2005 period. The equivalent models with capital disaggregated into its two constituents yield correspondingly higher rates of 0.5% per annum between 1855 and 1912, rising to 1.2% per annum between 1948 and 2005. The reason for the increase in the rate of disembodied progress when capital is split into its constituent parts is that the embodied progress assigned to the constituents does not fully account for that assigned to the aggregate stock.

These estimates must be treated with caution, given the limitations of the data (particularly the historic capital stock series) and the restrictions involved in using models based on an aggregate production function. Nevertheless, the broad implications of the analysis seem plausible and consistent. These are that the United Kingdom's capital stock has embodied technical progress at a slowly increasing rate since the mid-nineteenth century, but that a fundamental shift in the nature of that embodied technical progress occurred progressively during the first half of the twentieth century. Through the era of nineteenth century industrialization, commercial buildings and infrastructure were the dominant components of capital investment, both quantitatively and as carriers of the new technologies, while plant and machinery played a secondary role in the growth process. However, during the twentieth century, faster rates of technical progress in the manufacture of equipment compared to buildings ensured that the equipment share of capital investment increased, while its growing dominance as the engine of growth was reinforced by taking over as the main carrier of new technology. Nevertheless, whilst this has relegated commercial buildings to a secondary role as driver of productivity growth, the complementarity between structures and equipment investment means that the function of buildings as a constituent of business capital remains vital to the growth process.

The trajectory of US growth (1929–2005)

A comparison between the growth trajectories of the US and UK economies between 1929 and 2005 can be made using a set of macroeconomic data compiled by the US Bureau of Economic Analysis (BEA) which is broadly consistent with the data which have been used to analyze UK growth (Figure 4.4). The main difference between the two datasets is that the BEA presents only net capital stock estimates and so, for the sake of consistency, net stock is used to estimate capital growth rates in both countries, again adjusted to provide a measure of utilized capital by applying the respective national unemployment rates to scale down the totals. For the historical background to this brief analysis of US growth, Kuznets (1961) provides a detailed investigation of all sectors of capital formation going back to 1869, while Grebler et al. (1956) focus on residential capital formation between 1889 and 1953. Further light is shed by the growth accounting study presented by Abramovitz and David (2000), which covers both the nineteenth and twentieth centuries and highlights the impact of successive technological revolutions on US productivity growth.

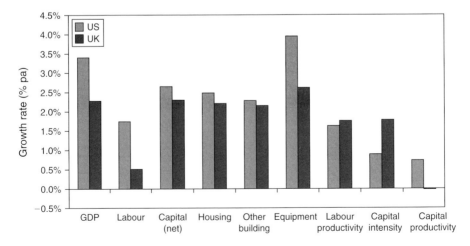

Figure 4.4   Comparison of US and UK growth rates 1929–2005.
Source: BEA, BLS, Feinstein (1976), Feinstein and Pollard (1988) and ONS.

Since 1929, the output of the US economy has grown at an average rate of 3.4% per annum, compared to a growth rate of 2.3% per annum in the United Kingdom. In terms of factor inputs, the difference in output growth rates can largely be ascribed to a much stronger rate of growth in the employed labour force in the United States (1.7% compared to 0.5% in the United Kingdom), which has been sustained by continuing high rates of in-migration that have persisted through the post-war period. Consequently, the average rates of labour productivity growth in the two economies appear to have been broadly similar (1.6% compared to 1.8%). Perhaps surprisingly, the rate of growth in the total volume of capital stock in the United States has not been much higher than that in the United Kingdom (2.7% compared to 2.3%), which means that US capital per worker has only grown at half the UK rate (0.9% versus 1.8%), whilst its capital productivity has been growing at 0.7% per annum compared to a zero rate of growth in the United Kingdom. The source of US capital productivity growth stands out in Figure 4.4: while the rates of growth of building capital in the two economies have been similar, equipment capital (combining machinery and vehicles) has grown by as much as 4.0% per annum, compared to only 2.6% per annum in the United Kingdom. The exceptional growth of economic output in the United States compared to the United Kingdom during the twentieth century can thus be attributed to two principal factors – a stronger and more sustained increase in the labour force and an exceptional rate of investment in equipment as compared to building capital (this latter point forms one of the key themes in Abramovitz and David, 2000).

A more disaggregated US dataset of private sector capital stock allows the contribution to the growth process of different components of building capital to be examined in more detail than the UK data allow (Figure 4.5). Of the four types of building capital that are distinguished, the slowest growing over the 1929–2005 period has

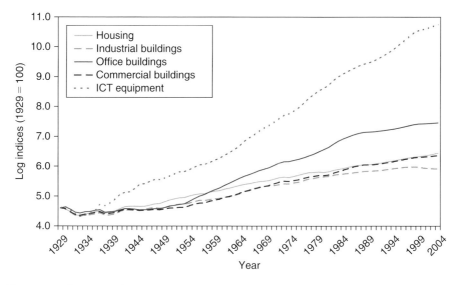

Figure 4.5 Growth in US private net capital stock 1929–2005.
Source: BEA and BLS.

been industrial buildings (1.7% per annum), reflecting the relative decline of manufacturing industry as the economy has become more service dominated. Next are
commercial buildings (2.3%), which include shops and warehouses, and dwellings
(2.4%), neither of which have kept up with the rate of GDP growth. This suggests
that housing demand may be less income-elastic in the United States than in the
United Kingdom, where the rate of growth of the dwellings stock has matched that
of national income. The fastest growing constituent of the US building stock has
been offices, with a 3.8% rate of growth since 1929, rising to 5.4% over the period
since 1955. Here is a clear illustration of how office-based services, and particularly
financial and business services, have provided a key dynamic of post-war economic
development, as manifested through high rates of office building (see Chapter 6).

Despite the relatively high rate of post-war investment in office buildings in the
United States, there has been a much higher rate of growth in the ICT component
of equipment capital which acts as the main form of productive capital for office-
based service industries. Over the whole period 1929–2005, the stock of ICT equipment has grown at an average rate of 8.4% per annum, and since 1955 this has risen
to 10.2% per annum. In other words, over the past 50 years, equipment capital in
the US office economy has been growing twice as fast as its building capital. In
turn, over the past 20 years, the computer hardware component has been growing
at more than twice the rate of ICT equipment as a whole – recording an extraordinary 22.2% per annum average growth rate between 1985 and 2005, compared to
9.2% for all ICT equipment and a mere 3.1% per annum for office buildings.

Once again, very different rates of cheapening of the various constituents of US
capital stock help to explain these differential growth rates. Over the past 50 years,
the price of office buildings relative to labour appears to have reduced at a very
modest average rate of 0.3% per annum, whereas ICT equipment has enjoyed relative cheapening at a rate of 5.0% per annum. An even starker differential is apparent over the last 20 years, which have seen the relative price of office buildings
remain virtually static, whilst ICT equipment as a whole has cheapened at 6.0%
per annum and computer hardware at an apparent rate of 17.2% per annum. It is
little wonder, therefore, that investment in information technology has become
the dominant driver of growth in the modern service economy, leaving the rate of
investment in increasingly expensive office buildings to trail way behind.

The extent to which investment in information technology has driven US productivity growth in recent years is highlighted in the growth accounting study
undertaken by Jorgenson et al. (2005, 2008). Their estimates show that over the
whole period 1959–2006, US private sector output grew on average by 3.6% per
annum, of which labour productivity growth accounted for 2.1%. The combination
of capital deepening through ICT equipment investment, together with increased
total factor productivity through technical progress in ICT production, contributed
0.7% to the overall rate of productivity growth; of the remainder, non-ICT investment and technical progress contributed 1.2% and improved labour quality 0.2%.
Having languished at around 1.5% between 1973 and 1995, there was a surge in
labour productivity growth up to a rate of 2.7% between 1995 and 2000, and nearly
80% of this increase can be attributed to the boom in ICT investment during the
late 1990s, as unprecedented rates of technical progress in the producer sectors
fuelled rapid capital deepening in the user sectors. After the internet investment

bubble burst in 2000, the resurgence in productivity growth was sustained at a rate of 2.5% by more broadly based capital deepening together with enhanced technical progress in the user sectors, particularly those employing ICT most intensively.

Amongst the user sectors enjoying substantial productivity gains in the US economy during the last decade are private sector services such as financial and business services and distribution services, including retailing. The ICT-driven productivity gains now being achieved in these industries match those obtained in the manufacturing sector (van Ark et al., 2008), countering the long-held concern that the growing share of services in national output inevitably means slower growth because of lower capital intensity, fewer scale economies and more restricted technical progress (Baumol, 1967). Recent research helps to answer the question as to why it took until the mid-1990s for the productivity benefits of installing ICT equipment to become apparent, despite accelerating rates of investment since the start of the 1980s. It seems that full realization of the benefits of ICT investment requires firms to undertake complementary investments and innovations in their working practices, business organization and human capital, and these take longer to reach fruition (Brynjolfsson and Hitt, 2000).

Building investment as generator of cycles

The identification of economic cycles

The development of techniques for identifying cyclical fluctuations around secular economic trends has a long history that stretches back to the work of Mitchell (1927). He explored the use of simple curve fitting or moving average methods to identify the variable trend in an economic time series, in order to isolate the cyclical fluctuations and measure their amplitude, based on standard deviations around the fitted trend, and their duration, based on the identification of peak and trough turning points (see the discussion in Chapter 2). Mitchell's first exercises in cycle measurement were subsequently developed at the NBER into the 'reference cycle' methodology that synthesizes a standardized representation of the general business cycle, against which the motion of specific cycles in individual economic variables can be compared (Burns and Mitchell, 1946). This relatively informal method of defining cycle chronologies remains a valuable complement to the more formal methods of trend and cycle identification which have come into favour more recently.

The use of sophisticated statistical methods in cycle studies started in the 1960s with the application of spectral analysis, a technique that can simultaneously decompose a detrended economic series into cyclical components of different frequency (the use of this technique was explored in Chapter 3). Such a technique is particularly valuable for identifying the long cycles which may coexist with short cycles in a building investment series. Since the 1980s, attention has focused on techniques that represent both the variable trend and the cycles around it as stochastic processes. One of the most recent and powerful of these techniques is structural modelling with unobserved components, which simultaneously fits a stochastic trend and stochastic cycles to a series, apportioning the variance of the series among the components by means of maximum likelihood estimation involving a procedure known as the Kalman filter (Harvey and Proietti, 2005).

Unobserved components modelling is the technique which has been adopted for trend and cycle identification in this and subsequent chapters, employing a customized software package named STAMP (Structural Time Analyser Modeller and Predictor) that fits structural time series models incorporating up to three separate stochastic cycles of differing frequency (Koopman et al., 2006). A detailed illustration of the use of unobserved components modelling and other cycle identification techniques is presented in Appendix A, along with discussions of how a detrended series can be tested for stationarity, decomposed into its cyclical components using spectral analysis and translated into a cycle chronology through the identification of peak and trough turning points.

The procedure that has been adopted for our analysis of investment cycles is as follows:

- An unobserved components model is fitted to the data series, with the modelling process interpolating for any missing observations. The fitted trend is defined to have a fixed level but variable slope, in order to ensure that it is smoothly varying. Starting from a model with no cycle, the number of possible cycles is progressively increased up to the permitted maximum of three. The significance of each identified cycle is evaluated by a likelihood ratio test that compares the maximum values of the likelihood functions of the models with and without the cycle. The model residuals are tested for heteroscedasticity, normality and serial correlation using the statistics described in Section A.2.7.
- The modelled trend is extracted to leave a stationary residual which is subjected to spectral analysis according to the procedure set out in Section A.4. The purpose of this exercise is to check whether the periods of the cyclical components identified by spectral analysis match those derived by structural modelling, and to ascertain which of the cyclical components dominate the decomposition of the detrended series in the frequency domain.
- A turning point chronology of successive peaks and troughs is constructed for each identified cycle. The average length of time between the turning points and their average deviations from the fitted trend provide informal measures of the cycle period and amplitude to compare with the equivalent parameters derived from the unobserved components model.
- When cycles of similar frequency are isolated in two or more related series, one is identified as the reference cycle and the phasing of each of the other cycles is measured in terms of the average leads or lags between its turning points and those of the reference cycle.
- The cross-correlations between corresponding cyclical components in the different series are derived in order to measure the strength of the relationships between the cycles at different lags. The existence of causal relationships between the different cycles is explored using the Granger causality test outlined in Section A.6.2.
- Where the data allow, the structural model fitted to each original series is extended by introducing one or more explanatory variables, in addition to the unobserved components, in order to establish the extent to which the fit of the model is improved and the specification of the cyclical components is altered.

UK investment cycles (1855–2005)

In the previous section, we observed an oscillatory motion propelling the secular trajectories of each macroeconomic indicator used to describe the long-run growth of the UK economy. The most pronounced cyclical fluctuations appear in the investment series used to construct the capital stock estimates. To explore the motion of these investment cycles, long-run data on gross domestic fixed capital formation at constant prices have been assembled from the same sources as those used to derive the capital stock series. Again, the analysis is conducted using total investment and its main constituents – housing, other (non-residential) building and equipment (combining plant and machinery with commercial vehicles) – together with GDP for comparison purposes. The investment trends are illustrated in Figure 4.6, showing fluctuations that are dominated by the severe impact of the two World Wars, particularly upon building investment.

Unobserved components models have been fitted to each series to separate out the investment and GDP cycles from their variable trends over the period 1855–2005. (For a similar analysis of UK industrial production between 1700 and 1913, see Crafts et al., 1989 and Mills and Crafts, 1996). The results of the modeling exercise are presented in Tables 4.3 and 4.4 and illustrated in Figures 4.7–4.9. The main findings can be summarized as follows.

Major cycles
One-cycle models of all the investment sectors, as well as GDP, yield highly significant major cycles with estimated periods varying between 9.5 and 12.5 years. Very similar major cycle components are retained in the two-cycle models, with

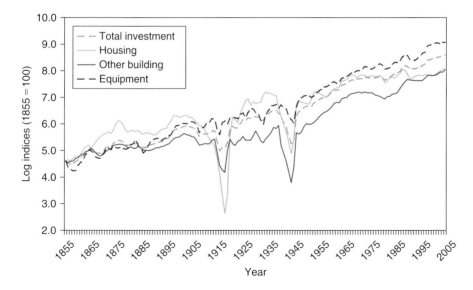

Figure 4.6 Growth of UK investment 1855–2005.
Source: Feinstein (1976), Feinstein and Pollard (1988) and ONS.

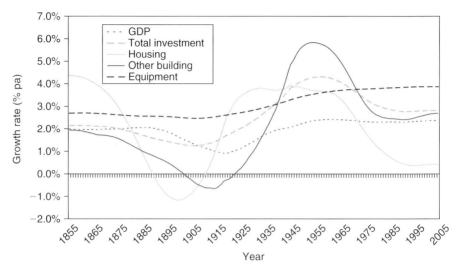

Figure 4.7   Trend rates of growth in UK investment 1855–2005.
Source: Feinstein (1976), Feinstein and Pollard (1988) and ONS.

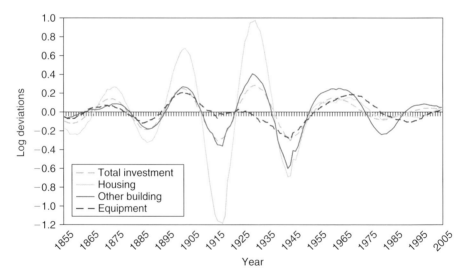

Figure 4.8   Long waves in UK investment 1855–2005.
Source: Feinstein (1976), Feinstein and Pollard (1988) and ONS.

the exception of the total investment cycle, the period of which increases from 11.3 to 15.3 years (Table 4.4 and Figure 4.9). The major cycle is most regularly defined in the 10-year equipment investment cycle, which has therefore been adopted as the reference cycle for this cyclical component. An examination of the turning point chronology for total investment shows that the reason why the period of its major cycle is longer than that of its constituents is that their combination smoothes out

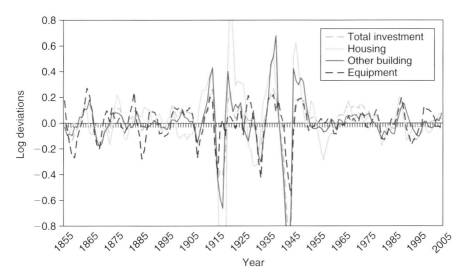

Figure 4.9 Major cycles in UK investment 1855–2005.
Source: Feinstein (1976), Feinstein and Pollard (1988) and ONS.

two of the nineteenth century cycles which are apparent in the constituents. As measured by their amplitudes, the least volatile major cycle is that in GDP, followed by total investment and then equipment investment, with non-residential and residential building being the most volatile – due in part to the extreme shocks delivered to building investment by the two World Wars (For a detailed investigation of the stylized facts of UK business cycles in the post-war period, see Blackburn and Ravn, 1992).

Long waves
For all the models, the addition of a second cycle separates out from the trend what can best be described as a long wave; it is of shorter duration than the much debated Kondratieff cycle, but more prolonged than the Kuznets long swing (Table 4.4 and Figure 4.8). All the two-cycle models are significant at the 5% level, and all but the equipment investment model are significant at 1%, as measured by the likelihood ratio test. The estimated period of this second cycle is around 30 years in all cases except equipment investment, for which two of the cycles affecting the other sectors merge into one, extending its period into the 50–60 year span typically assigned to the Kondratieff wave. The long wave in total investment is the most regular and so has been chosen as the reference cycle. The long wave in residential building is more volatile than those in the other sectors, especially during the turbulent years between the start of the First World War and the end of the Second World War.

Minor cycles
When the number of cycles in the models is increased to three, a minor cycle with a period of between 4 and 6 years is identified in GDP and in all investment sectors except equipment (Table 4.4). However, with the exception of non-residential

Table 4.4   Parameters of UK investment cycles 1855–2005.

	Period (years)[a]	Order[a]	Damping factor[a]	Amplitude[a]	Variance[a]	Likelihood ratio[b]	Spectrum[c]
Major cycles[d]							
GDP	12.8	2	0.679	0.0103	0.0003	38.40**	(Y)
Total investment	15.3	2	0.592	0.0338	0.0106	37.23**	
Equipment	10.1	1	0.830	0.0651	0.0223	66.11**	Y
Housing	9.8	2	0.655	0.0797	0.0297	51.16**	
Other building	11.1	1	0.855	0.0769	0.0531	46.46**	(Y)
Long waves[d]							
GDP	31.1	1	0.979	0.0172	0.0009	13.09**	Y
Total investment	30.3	1	0.983	0.0397	0.0234	23.86**	Y
Equipment	55.1	1	0.960	0.0491	0.0194	8.03*	Y
Housing	29.4	1	0.982	0.0682	0.1614	15.16**	Y
Other building	31.5	1	0.968	0.0725	0.0504	12.21**	Y
Minor cycles[d]							
GDP	6.0	1	0.945	0.0016	0.0001	5.52	(Y)
Total investment	3.6	1	0.979	0.0053	0.0004	7.00	
Equipment	–	–	–	–	–	–	
Housing	4.3	1	0.951	0.0085	0.0037	4.25	
Other building	4.6	1	0.726	0.0138	0.0081	8.69*	

Source: Feinstein (1976), Feinstein and Pollard (1988) and ONS.

Notes: For all models except GDP, the irregular disturbance is absorbed into the variance of the cyclical components.

Diagnostic statistics for the model residuals show that at the 5% level none of the models satisfy the normality test, due to the extreme irregularity of their cyclical components; the heteroscedasticity test is satisfied by the GDP, total investment and housing models; the serial correlation test is satisfied by the total investment and other building models (for a description of the test statistics, see Table A.1 in Appendix A).

[a]For definitions of cycle period, order, damping factor, amplitude and variance, see Appendix A (Section A.2.7 and Table A.2).

[b]The likelihood ratio compares the values of the likelihood functions for models with and without the specified cycle; ** denotes that the restriction of there being no cycle can be rejected at the 1% level, * denotes rejection at the 5% level. For major cycles, the comparison is between models with and without a single cycle component; for long waves, the comparison is between models with one and two cycle components; for minor cycles, the comparison is between models with three and two cycles.

[c]The spectrum is estimated using the residuals derived from the detrended series. Y indicates that the spectrum provides strong confirmation of the presence of a cyclical component with the same period as that obtained from the structural model; (Y) indicates weak confirmation.

[d]For all sectors, the parameters are derived from two-cycle models that isolate the major cycle and long wave components; where a three-cycle model for these sectors identifies a minor cycle, its parameters are separately listed.

building, the likelihood ratio test indicates that none of these minor cycles are significant at the 5% level.

Dominant cycles

Spectral analysis of the detrended series confirms the existence of cyclical components of similar frequency to those generated by the structural models (Table 4.4).

For all series, the estimated spectrum reveals a dominant cycle peak at the long wave frequency. For equipment investment, this is accompanied by an equally prominent peak at the major cycle frequency, while for GDP and non-residential building, there is also weak evidence of the major cycle. The spectra for total and residential investment show no clear evidence of the major cycle. Only the GDP spectrum shows any trace of the minor cycle.

Growth trends
GDP and equipment investment manifest the most stable growth trends, following parallel trajectories but with equipment investment enjoying consistently higher growth rates (Figure 4.7). Thus the estimated GDP growth rate is level at around 2.0% per annum during the second half of the nineteenth century, falls to only 1.0% during the First World War, then over the next 40 years rises slowly but steadily to a post-war plateau of around 2.3%. (This trajectory is consistent with the findings of the growth accounting study by Matthews et al., 1982: 497–507, which points to a similar U-shaped growth profile.) The equivalent growth trend for equipment investment runs at around 2.5% per annum up to the First World War and then rises steadily to a new plateau of around 3.8% which is maintained from the 1970s onwards. Non-residential building exhibits a markedly more volatile trend than equipment investment; its growth rate falls from 2.0% in the 1850s to below zero during the First World War, then embarks on a steep rise to a peak of nearly 6.0% in the 1950s, after which it settles back down to a level of around 2.5% from the 1980s onwards. Apart from the period between 1940 and 1970, the trend rate of growth of non-residential building investment consistently lags behind that of equipment investment. The trend in residential investment follows a rather different trajectory compared to the two constituents of productive capital: it falls from over 4.0% in the mid-nineteenth century to below zero in the run-up to the First World War, rises back close to 4.0% between the 1930s and early 1960s before collapsing back close to zero again during the last 15 years.

Cycle phasing
For both the major cycles and long waves, cross-correlation analysis reveals a set of pro-cyclical relationships between the constituents of investment but, more surprisingly, a set of counter-cyclical relationships between investment and GDP (Table 4.5). These counter-cyclical relationships between GDP and investment are captured by positive correlations lagged by 4–5 years for the major cycles and 9–10 years for the long waves. The explanation for their divergent phasing seems to lie principally with the two wartime periods, when national output surged but non-military investment was heavily curtailed. The strong pro-cyclical relationships between the cycles in non-residential building and equipment investment reflect the complementarity of these two constituents of productive capital, whilst those between the residential and non-residential cycles indicate that the endogenous and exogenous forces which generate building cycles tend to act simultaneously on both sectors.

Relationships between cycles
Causal analysis suggests that the especially pronounced major cycles and long waves in residential and non-residential building have a strong influence on the cyclical

Table 4.5   Interrelationships between UK investment cycles 1855–2005.

	GDP	Total investment	Equipment	Housing	Other building
Major cycle cross-correlations					
GDP	1.000	−0.444 (1)**	−0.275 (3)	−0.673 (1)**	−0.461 (1)*
Total investment	0.444 (4)	1.000	0.755 (0)*	0.734 (0)	0.894 (0)
Equipment	0.212 (5)	0.755 (0)*	1.000	0.325 (0)	0.609 (0)
Housing	0.546 (4)*	0.734 (0)	0.353 (1)	1.000	0.722 (0)
Other building	0.554 (4)**	0.894 (0)**	0.609 (0)**	0.722 (0)**	1.000
Long wave cross-correlations					
GDP	1.000	−0.747 (6)	−0.216 (6)	−0.688 (5)**	−0.770 (5)
Total investment	0.870 (10)*	1.000	0.588 (0)	0.932 (0)*	0.929 (0)**
Equipment	0.374 (9)	0.588 (0)	1.000	0.443 (1)**	0.633 (0)
Housing	0.854 (10)**	0.932 (0)**	0.435 (0)**	1.000	0.844 (0)**
Other building	0.850 (10)*	0.929 (0)**	0.633 (0)**	0.844 (0)**	1.000

Source: Feinstein (1976), Feinstein and Pollard (1988) and ONS.

Notes: The listed correlations are the closest peak positive or negative values reached in the cross-correlograms between each pair of cyclical components, measured at the lag shown in brackets. The rows represent the leading cycle, the columns the lagging cycle.
Significant causal relationships between pairs of cycles according to the Granger causality test are denoted by ** (1% level) or * (5% level), with two lags employed for the major cycles and four lags for the long waves. The rows represent the causal cycles, the columns the dependent cycles.

behaviour of equipment investment, and therefore total investment. The building cycles also seem to influence the cycles in GDP, despite their lagged phasing. Among the major cycles, it is non-residential building that appears to act as the key driver, strongly influencing all the other cycles, with some additional feedback from GDP to building investment. As far as the long waves are concerned, both residential and non-residential building are identified as causal influences on the other cycles, as well as interacting strongly with each other. These results must, however, be treated with caution, since the close interrelationships between the cycles mean that in several cases causal links are identified as operating in both directions.

The use of structural modelling to decompose UK investment into its variable trends and component cycles has confirmed several of the findings of previous research, as discussed in Chapters 2 and 3, as well as those of the growth analysis reported in the previous section:

- The variable trends reveal that there has been a secular increase in the overall rate of investment in the British economy since the 1920s, that there has been a shift in the composition of investment from building to equipment capital and that residential building has followed a different trajectory from non-residential building.
- These secular trends have been propelled by the combined motion of interacting long waves and major cycles, together with weaker minor cycles. A key driver of this cyclical motion appears to have been the particularly volatile and coincident fluctuations in residential and non-residential building investment. The building

cycle has fed through to equipment investment, aggregate investment and output and has been reinforced by feedback from output to building investment.

We have thus uncovered evidence of a family of investment cycles compatible with the Schumpeterian schema discussed in Chapter 2, with building cycles playing a dominant role in the motion of the whole system. While the identified components fit well within the general family of investment cycles recognized in the business cycle literature, can they also be reconciled with the more specific two-cycle dynamic suggested by building cycle research?

As was discussed in the historical review in Chapter 3, several studies have distinguished a pronounced long building cycle, with an average length of between 15 and 20 years, on which is superimposed a milder short cycle with an average length of around 5 years. The short building cycle can be identified with the minor business cycle, which shows up in the unobserved components models as a weak residual cycle after the other two components have been isolated. The long building cycle has often been identified with the Kuznets long swing, but as was pointed out in Chapter 3, some observers have noted that the smoothing techniques traditionally applied to eliminate short cycles from building data will tend to introduce a bias by increasing the estimated period of the long cycle. What is actually a major cycle with a duration of around 10 years can display an apparent long swing period of closer to 20 years after the data are smoothed. With structural modelling, the simultaneous identification of all the significant cyclical components in the building data overcomes the problem of smoothing bias. The result is the clear identification of a 10–11 year major cycle in both sectors of building.

What is perhaps more unexpected is the emergence of a strong long wave in building – and furthermore a long wave with a duration of around 30 years which is significantly shorter than the 45–60 year period traditionally ascribed to this cycle. A comparison between the long waves in building and equipment investment provides an explanation. As already noted, the equipment long wave is more extended than the building long waves, with an estimated duration lying within the typically quoted Kondratieff range. This is because the second and third building long waves are combined in a single equipment long wave, largely uninterrupted by the First World War. The result is an equipment long wave chronology broadly compatible with that suggested by Kondratieff historians (see Table 4.1). It would seem that the two World Wars interrupted the rhythm of the long wave in building much more severely than that in equipment investment, creating an extra trough during the First World War and an extra peak during the 1930s. This compression of the building long wave can create a tendency for the major cycle and long wave to amalgamate into an intermediate cycle which dominates the series spectrum in the frequency range typically associated with the Kuznets long swing (Barras and Ferguson, 1985; Ball et al. 1996).

US investment cycles (1901–2005)

A similar cycle analysis of US private sector investment over the shorter 1901–2005 period has been conducted using the BEA dataset which was employed for the growth analysis presented in the previous section. As was discovered in the growth analysis, the US data on private non-residential building provide a further

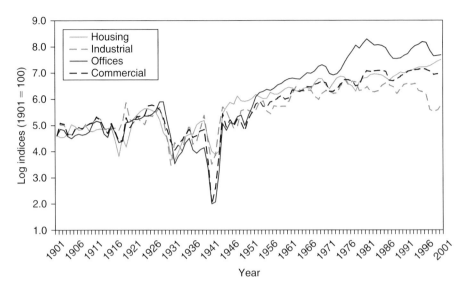

Figure 4.10 Growth of US private building investment 1901–2005.
Source: BEA.

breakdown into office, commercial (including shops and warehouses) and industrial building. The trends in the four sectors of building investment are illustrated in Figure 4.10. As with the UK data, the trends in US investment show the severe impact of the Second World War, particularly upon building investment. However, with the exception of residential building, the effect of the First World War is less marked than in the United Kingdom, whereas the shock of the Great Depression is much more pronounced in the United States (Galbraith, 1975).

The results of fitting unobserved components models to these US investment series are presented in Table 4.6 and illustrated in Figures 4.11–4.13. The main findings can be summarized as follows, making comparisons with the UK cycle analysis for the longer 1855–2005 period.

Major cycles
One-cycle models of all the US investment sectors plus GDP again yield highly significant major cycles with estimated periods varying between 7.3 and 14.9 years, a range wider than that produced by the UK one-cycle models. Similar major cycle components are retained in the two-cycle models, with the exception of non-residential building, with a cycle period that decreases from 14.9 to 10.4 years, and industrial building, which shows an increase from 7.3 to 10.2 years (Table 4.6 and Figure 4.13). Apart from residential building, all the major US cycles are slightly shorter in length than their UK equivalents. The relative volatility of these US cycles, as measured by their amplitudes, exhibits a similar ranking to that obtained from the UK cycles: the least volatile is GDP, followed by total investment, equipment investment, non-residential building and then residential building. The shocks delivered to building investment by the Great Depression and Second World War are especially apparent in the high volatility of the office and industrial building cycles.

Table 4.6   Parameters of US investment cycles 1901–2005.

	Period (years)[a]	Order[a]	Damping factor[a]	Amplitude[a]	Variance[a]	Likelihood ratio[b]	Spectrum[c]
Major cycles[d]							
GDP	7.6	1	0.904	0.0066	0.0011	18.78**	(Y)
Total investment	10.8	1	0.867	0.0540	0.0263	29.43**	(Y)
Equipment	8.0	1	0.727	0.0613	0.0222	40.65**	(Y)
Housing[e]	13.2	1	0.851	0.0914	0.1265	34.69**	Y
Other building	10.4	1	0.819	0.0627	0.0259	33.40**	(Y)
Offices	8.8	1	0.837	0.2329	0.1439	38.53**	Y
Industrial	10.2	1	0.869	0.2073	0.0533	51.27**	Y
Commercial	10.3	1	0.847	0.1072	0.1343	49.03**	Y
Long waves[d]							
GDP	21.6	1	0.925	0.0098	0.0064	8.17*	Y
Total investment	34.4	1	0.950	0.0517	0.0350	6.28	Y
Equipment	30.1	1	0.960	0.0805	0.0272	11.59**	Y
Housing[e]	41.6	1	0.947	0.0622	0.0495	2.50	
Other building	24.9	1	0.925	0.0165	0.0272	2.90	Y
Offices	31.0	1	0.973	0.0553	0.1304	3.94	Y
Industrial	–	–	–	–	–	–	
Commercial	–	–	–	–	–	–	
Minor cycles[d]							
GDP	–	–	–	–	–	–	
Total investment	5.6	1	0.933	0.0205	0.0043	11.27*	(Y)
Equipment	5.7	1	0.964	0.0310	0.0058	6.50	Y
Housing[e]	–	–	–	–	–	–	
Other building	5.3	1	0.927	0.0136	0.0032	6.57	Y
Offices	5.0	1	0.915	0.0390	0.0311	15.35**	Y
Industrial	5.1	1	0.801	0.0995	0.0524	7.41	Y
Commercial	4.9	1	0.913	0.0136	0.0261	8.92*	(Y)

Source: BEA.

Notes: For all models except GDP and housing investment, the irregular disturbance is absorbed into the variance of the cyclical components.

Diagnostic statistics for the model residuals show that at the 5% level none of the investment models satisfy the heteroscedasticity or normality tests, due to the extreme irregularity of their cyclical components, and only the industrial and commercial models satisfy the serial correlation test; the GDP model satisfies the normality and serial correlation tests (for a description of the test statistics, see Table A.1 in Appendix A).

[a]For definitions of cycle period, order, damping factor, amplitude and variance, see Appendix A (Section A.2.7 and Table A.2)

[b]The likelihood ratio compares the values of the likelihood functions for models with and without the specified cycle; ** denotes that the restriction of there being no cycle can be rejected at the 1% level, * denotes rejection at the 5% level. For major cycles, the comparison is between models with and without a single cycle component; for long waves, the comparison is between models with one and two cycle components; for minor cycles, the comparison is between models with three and two cycles, except with the industrial and commercial sectors for which the comparison is between one and two cycle models.

[c]The spectrum is estimated using the residuals derived from the detrended series. Y indicates that the spectrum provides strong confirmation of the presence of a cyclical component with the same period as that obtained from the structural model; (Y) indicates weak confirmation.

[d]For all sectors except industrial and commercial, the parameters are derived from two-cycle models that isolate the major cycle and long wave components; where a three-cycle model for these sectors identifies a minor cycle, its parameters are separately listed. For the industrial and commercial sectors, the parameters are derived from two-cycle models that isolate the major and minor cycle components.

[e]For the housing model, the slope is constrained to be variable, because otherwise a constant slope is fitted.

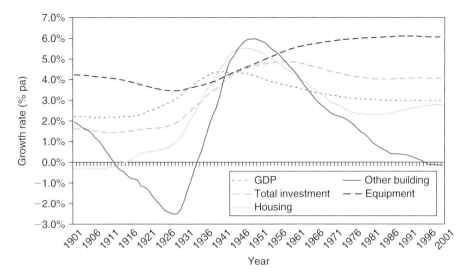

Figure 4.11   Trend rates of growth in US private investment 1901–2005.
Source: BEA.

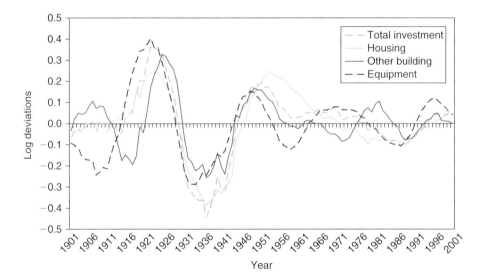

Figure 4.12   Long waves in US private investment 1901–2005.
Source: BEA.

Long waves

For all but industrial and commercial building, the introduction of a second cycle into the models also isolates a US long wave (Table 4.6 and Figure 4.12). However, because the series are too short for cycles of such duration to be identified properly, they are weaker than their corresponding UK components: only that for equipment

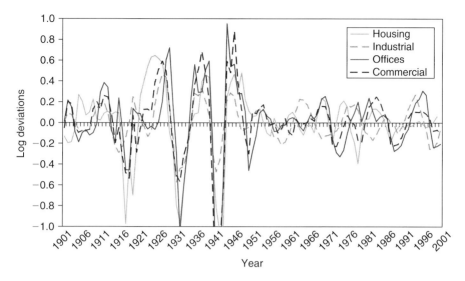

Figure 4.13   Major cycles in US private building investment 1901–2005.
Source: BEA.

investment is significant at 1%, and that for GDP at 5%. In all cases, these US long waves are dominated by a severe slump that merges the Great Depression with the Second World War. As with the UK series, the result is that the measured periods of these cycles fall short of the normally recognized Kondratieff span, ranging from a Kuznets swing of 22 years for GDP to a 42-year wave in residential building.

Minor cycles
While the relative lengths of the national series dictate that the US long waves are weaker than their UK equivalents, a correspondingly stronger set of 5–6 year minor cycles is identified in all the US series but GDP and residential building (Table 4.6). They are the second cycles to be identified in the industrial and commercial building models, in the absence of long wave components, while for the other sectors they emerge when the number of cyclical components is increased to three. For all sectors, these minor cycles are significant at least at the 10% level, while for total investment and commercial building, they can be accepted at the 5% level, and for office building even at the 1% level.

Dominant cycles
As with the UK data, spectral analysis of the detrended series confirms the existence of cyclical components of similar frequency to those generated by the structural models (Table 4.6). Despite their mostly insignificant likelihood ratios, if a long wave is identified in a series, then its estimated spectrum is dominated by a peak at that frequency in all cases but residential building. The residential, office, industrial and commercial building spectra reveal prominent peaks at their major cycle frequencies, while for GDP, total investment, equipment investment and non-residential building, there is weak evidence of the major cycle. The minor

cycle frequencies also show up in the estimated spectra, again with the exception of residential building. The spectrum for office building is unique in exhibiting peaks at all three cycle frequencies, whilst that for residential building is unique in only showing clear evidence of one component, the major cycle.

Growth trends

There are some marked similarities between the long-run trajectories of US and UK investment growth. Again, GDP and equipment investment manifest the most stable trends, following broadly parallel trajectories with equipment investment enjoying considerably higher average rates of growth (Figure 4.11). The trend rate of GDP growth is around 2.2% per annum during the early part of the twentieth century, rising to a peak of 4.4% during the Second World War, then gently subsiding to a new plateau of around 3.0% over the last 25 years. The equivalent growth trajectory for equipment investment fluctuates around 4.0% up to the Second World War, then rises steadily to a level of 6.0% which has been sustained since the mid-1970s. As in the United Kingdom, the trend in non-residential building is more volatile than the equipment investment trend, while generating a considerably lower rate of growth. This falls from 2.0% at the start of the twentieth century to a phase of absolute decline between the First World War and the mid-1930s, before rising steeply to a peak of 6.0% in the early 1950s and then plunging back down to around zero by the start of the new century. Only the trend in US residential building follows a trajectory substantially different from its UK equivalent, more closely tracking the other components of investment. From a level of around zero during the first years of the twentieth century, its growth rate rises to an early 1950s peak of 5.5%, coinciding with the peak in non-residential building, but then levels out at around 2.5% from the end of the 1970s, in contrast to the non-residential trend which continues falling towards zero.

Cycle phasing

The US investment cycles demonstrate the same pattern of phasing as the UK cycles. Thus the motion of both major cycles and long waves is in general governed by a set of strong pro-cyclical relationships between the constituents of investment and weaker counter-cyclical relationships between investment and GDP (Table 4.7). For both components, the counter-cyclical relationships between GDP and investment are captured by positive correlations lagged by between 3 and 5 years; the only exceptions are the relatively weak coincident relationships between the major cycles and long waves in GDP and equipment investment. Again, the explanation for the divergent phasing of the GDP and investment cycles lies principally with the high output/low civilian investment conditions which prevailed during the Second World War. The tendency for there to be strong pro-cyclical relationships between the investment cycles is maintained when non-residential building is broken down into its office, industrial and commercial constituents. The one exception to the general pro-cyclicality rule is that while the complementarity of US equipment investment and non-residential building is evident in their major cycles, their long waves tend to run out of phase during peace time periods (Figure 4.12). This perhaps suggests some switching of investment between the two main components of productive capital which is not apparent in the United Kingdom.

Table 4.7 Interrelationships between US investment cycles 1901–2005.

Major cycle cross-correlations (all investment)

	GDP	Total investment	Equipment	Housing	Other building
GDP	1.000	0.159 (4)	0.249 (0)	−0.216 (1)	0.219 (3)
Total investment	−0.158 (2)*	1.000	0.806 (0)**	0.831 (0)	0.892 (0)**
Equipment	−0.304 (3)**	0.806 (0)**	1.000	0.440 (0)	0.730 (0)
Housing	0.132 (4)	0.831 (0)*	0.440 (0)**	1.000	0.623 (0)**
Other building	−0.309 (2)*	0.892 (0)**	0.730 (0)	0.623 (0)	1.000

Major cycle cross-correlations (building investment)

	Housing	Other building	Offices	Industrial	Commercial
Housing	1.000	0.623 (0)**	0.598 (0)*	0.478 (0)	0.751 (0)**
Other building	0.623 (0)	1.000	0.881 (0)**	0.802 (0)**	0.845 (0)
Offices	0.598 (0)	0.881 (0)	1.000	0.611 (0)*	0.837 (0)*
Industrial	0.478 (0)*	0.802 (0)**	0.654 (1)**	1.000	0.692 (0)**
Commercial	0.751 (0)**	0.845 (0)*	0.837 (0)**	0.692 (0)	1.000

Long wave cross-correlations (all investment)

	GDP	Total investment	Equipment	Housing	Other building
GDP	1.000	0.564 (3)	0.491 (0)	0.477 (5)	0.587 (4)
Total investment	−0.679 (10)*	1.000	0.802 (0)**	0.927 (0)	0.800 (1)**
Equipment	−0.692 (12)**	0.837 (1)**	1.000	0.675 (2)*	0.714 (4)**
Housing	−0.489 (9)**	0.927 (0)	0.623 (0)**	1.000	0.665 (1)*
Other building	−0.825 (8)**	0.766 (0)**	−0.540 (8)**	0.663 (0)	1.000

Cross-correlations with UK cycles[a]

	GDP	Total investment	Equipment	Housing	Other building
UK major cycles	0.441 (−1)	0.585 (0)	0.536 (0)	0.650 (−1)	0.580 (0)
UK long waves	0.529 (−7)	0.698 (+7)	0.258 (+6)	0.526 (+7)	0.659 (+5)

Source: Feinstein (1976), Feinstein and Pollard (1988), ONS and BEA.

Notes: The listed correlations are the closest peak positive or negative values reached in the cross-correlograms between each pair of cyclical components, measured at the lag shown in brackets. The rows represent the leading cycle, the columns the lagging cycle.
Significant causal relationships between pairs of cycles according to the Granger causality test are denoted by ** (1% level) or * (5% level), with two lags employed for the major cycles and four lags for the long waves. The rows represent the causal cycles, the columns the dependent cycles.
[a]These correlations are the closest peak positive values reached in the cross-correlograms between corresponding cycles in the United States and the United Kingdom over the 1901–2005 period, measured at the lag shown in brackets (where '−' denotes the UK cycle leading; '+' denotes the US cycle leading). No causality tests are quoted for these cross-national comparisons.

Relationships between cycles

The pattern of linkages revealed by the causal analysis of the US cycles is less clear-cut than that obtained from the UK exercise, because it is conducted on shorter series which are all shaped by the major shocks of the Great Depression and Second World War. What does emerge is the dependency of the GDP major cycles and long waves on the various investment cycles, the autonomous nature of the residential building cycles and, rather surprisingly, an apparently strong influence exercised by the residential cycles on the cycles in productive investment. Amongst the constituents of building investment, there are significant interrelationships between the major cycles in residential and commercial building, and between those in office, industrial and commercial building.

Relative phasing of US and UK cycles

Cross-correlations between US and UK cycles over the period 1901–2005 indicate strong pro-cyclical relationships between their major cycles but equally strong counter-cyclical relationships between their respective long waves (Table 4.7). These perhaps unexpected results can be explained by the contrasting impact on the rhythm of the cycles resulting from the three most severe economic shocks of the twentieth century – the First World War, the Great Depression and the Second World War. To varying degrees, all three shocks generated investment slumps in both national sets of major cycles, so that the spacing of the shocks is a crucial factor determining both the duration of the major cycles within each national economy and their coordination across the international economy. The explanation for the inverse phasing of the long waves again seems to lie with the exogenous shocks. Because the First World War had a more severe impact on the UK economy than the US economy, whilst the reverse is true for the Great Depression, a counter-cyclical rhythm was established for the two national long waves which persisted through the rest of the century. (For a broader international comparison of the historical properties of business cycles over the last century in 10 countries, including the United States and the United Kingdom, see Backus and Kehoe, 1992.)

When we review the main findings of our analyses of UK and US investment cycles, the similarities are more striking than the differences:

- Secular trends in investment confirm the crucial role of equipment investment as the key driver of the long-run growth process, as explored in the previous section.
- Superimposed on the secular trends is a three-cycle schema of long waves, major cycles and minor cycles.
- Building cycles are the most volatile of the investment cycles, and they provide a crucial impetus to the cyclical propulsion of aggregate investment and output.
- Significant variations in cycle periodicity usually reflect the smoothing out of one or more peaks or troughs, due to particular circumstances in individual sectors of investment.
- The pro-cyclical motion of non-residential building and equipment investment reflects their complementarity as constituents of productive capital.
- The pro-cyclical motion of residential and non-residential construction indicates the broadly coincident operation of the forces of cycle generation in the different sectors of building.
- Residential building appears subject to the most autonomous cycles, by inference responding to demographic and social influences which lie outside the economic and technological spheres.
- The regularity and persistence of the cyclical components reveal the dynamic generated by strong endogenous cycle propagation mechanisms.
- However, cycle timing, duration and amplitude are also critically influenced by the incidence and severity of major historical events such as wars or financial crises.

This comparative historical analysis has concentrated on the role that building investment has played as driver of growth and generator of cycles in the industrial development of the UK and US economies. We now move on to the parallel role that building investment has played in their urban development.

Appendix: The growth model

The model is based upon an aggregate production function in which the quantity of national output is expressed as a function of the factor inputs used in production. The production function can be stated in a general factor-augmenting form, whereby technical progress increases the productivity of both labour and capital at differential rates (Stoneman, 1983: 4). Factor-augmentation is the inverse of factor-saving: because of technical progress, either the same quantities of inputs produce an increasing quantity of output, or the same quantity of output is produced by a decreasing quantity of inputs. With such a formulation, the quantity of national output Y_t at point in time t can be expressed as a function of the input quantities of labour L_t and capital K_t, augmented by technical progress multipliers a(t) and b(t) which increase the productivity of each factor through time, i.e.:

$$Y_t = F\left[a(t)L_t, b(t)K_t\right] \qquad (4.1)$$

The simplest interpretation of this form of production function is that technical progress is disembodied, accruing to the economy through improvements in technical knowledge. However, as discussed in Chapter 2, it can also be interpreted as expressing the factor inputs in a quality-adjusted form which implies that technical progress is embodied in each factor. On this basis, the term $a(t)L_t$ represents a quality-adjusted measure of labour inputs, equivalent to the concept of human capital, whereby the productivity of the labour force is augmented by investment in education and training. Similarly, $b(t)K_t$ represents a quality-adjusted measure of physical capital, as in the vintage version of the Solow growth model, whereby investment in improved production techniques augments the average productivity of capital. With differential factor augmentation, an equilibrium growth path with neutral technical progress can still be specified. Output and the physical measure of capital grow in tandem, while the rates of growth of quality-adjusted labour and capital exceed those of their physical measures by the rates of technical progress embodied in labour force training and new capital equipment. Allowance can also be made for disembodied as well as embodied technical progress to boost total factor productivity.

The interaction of embodied and disembodied technical progress in the growth process can be clarified if the production function defined in equation (4.1) is restated in the more restrictive but commonly used Cobb–Douglas form (Sorensen and Whitta-Jacobsen, 2005). The chosen specification for the growth model in this form is:

$$Y_t = A_0 e^{\delta t} L_t^{\lambda} K_t^{\kappa} \qquad (4.2)$$

Here, the term $A_0 e^{\delta t}$ is designed to capture the effect of disembodied technical progress on output growth at a rate δ, while the effect of technical progress embodied in the factor inputs is captured in their output elasticities λ and κ. If $\lambda + \kappa > 1$, then embodied technical progress is generating increasing returns to scale with respect to the physical

quantities of factor inputs. The extent of the technical progress embodied in each factor input can be isolated by comparison with the standard version of the growth model
which assumes profit maximization in competitive markets and constant returns
to scale in an economy in which all technical change is disembodied. Under these
restrictive assumptions, it can be shown that the elasticities of output with respect
to each factor are equivalent to the respective shares of capital ω and labour $1 - \omega$ in
national income. Thus, if $\lambda > (1 - \omega)$, labour productivity is boosted by the improving
skills and knowledge of the workforce; if $\kappa > \omega$, capital productivity benefits from the
improving specification of new investment goods. It can be shown (Barras, 1986: 945)
that the enhanced elasticity of output with respect to capital stock is a function of the
rate of technical progress embodied in successive vintages of the stock τ and the average age of the stock α, according to the approximation:

$$\kappa \cong \omega + \tau\alpha \tag{4.3}$$

This function breaks the overall output elasticity of the capital stock down into two
components, with ω representing the contribution to output growth of a growing
quantity of capital K_t acting as a factor input, and $\tau\alpha$ representing the contribution
which can be attributed to the increasing quality of the capital resulting from
embodied technical progress.

For estimation purposes, equation (4.2) can conveniently be restated in the logarithmic form:

$$\log Y_t = \log A_0 + \delta t + \lambda(\log L_t) + \kappa(\log K_t) \tag{4.4}$$

This represents an extensive form of the growth model, relating the level of output
Y_t to the levels of factor inputs L_t and K_t, the point in time t reached in the development of the economy, the rate of disembodied technical change δ and the elasticities of output with respect to labour λ and capital κ. If the production function is
restricted to the standard form, by assuming constant returns to scale $(\lambda + \kappa = 1)$,
then an equivalent intensive version of the model can be derived. This is expressed
in terms of ratios rather than level variables, relating output per worker, or labour
productivity, $y_t (=Y_t/L_t)$ to capital per worker $k_t (=K_t/L_t)$, i.e.

$$\log y_t = \log a_0 + \delta t + \kappa(\log k_t) \tag{4.5}$$

Finally, in order to investigate the relative contributions of building capital B_t and
equipment capital E_t to output growth, equation (4.4) can be expanded to replace
aggregate capital K_t with its components, i.e.

$$\log Y_t = \log A_0 + \delta t + \lambda(\log L_t) + \beta(\log B_t) + \varepsilon(\log E_t) \tag{4.6}$$

where β and ε are the output elasticities of building and equipment capital, respectively. Similarly, the intensive form of equation (4.5) can be expanded as:

$$\log y_t = \log a_0 + \delta t + \beta(\log b_t) + \varepsilon(\log e_t) \tag{4.7}$$

expressed in terms of building capital per worker $b_t (=B_t/L_t)$ and equipment capital
per worker $e_t (=E_t/L_t)$.

Long-run trended economic variables of the type incorporated into this model are typically non-stationary; in other words, their means and variances change over time as their magnitude increases. Rather, it is their first differences which tend to be stationary. In the parlance of time series analysis, variables which are stationary in their first differences are termed integrated of order one, and denoted I(1), in contrast to stationary variables which are integrated of order zero and denoted I(0). Non-stationarity can create problems when using classical least squares regression techniques to estimate long-run models, because of a tendency to identify spurious regressions between the trended level variables. However, the theory of cointegration which has been developed over the past 25 years provides a formal technique for modelling the relationships between I(1) variables. If the residuals derived from fitting the regression model to the trended level variables are stationary, then the variables are said to be cointegrated – which means that they are linked by a linear equilibrium relationship which is stable through time. The simplest way of estimating such models is first to use a unit root test to check that the original variables are I(1), and having fitted the regression model, then use the same test to check that the residuals are I(0), signifying that a cointegrating relationship has been derived (see Appendix A for a discussion of cointegration and stationarity testing).

5

Building Investment and Urban Development

Urban innovation and accumulation

The city in history

There is a distinguished tradition in urban studies, best exemplified by Lewis Mumford's *The City in History* (1961) and Peter Hall's *Cities in Civilization* (1998), of viewing cities as the product of their age, as manifestations of the technological, institutional, social and cultural conditions prevailing in each historical epoch. In this spirit, commercial cities such as eighteenth century Paris can be compared and contrasted with nineteenth century industrial cities like Glasgow and twentieth century suburban cities such as Los Angeles, while looking-forward attempts have already been made to delineate the 'informational cities' of the twenty-first century (Castells, 1989). Such typologies are not meant to imply a static classification; rather, they aim to capture the essence of cities during particular phases of their dynamic development. So it is that a city like London has evolved from being a classical city, through successive medieval, commercial and industrial phases to its latest materialization as a global financial centre. The aim of this chapter is to explore how the historical development of a city can be understood in terms of the twin processes of urban innovation and accumulation, and to highlight the crucial role that building cycles play in driving these processes.

In developing the argument, we need to distinguish between urban functions, the activities which are undertaken in cities, and urban forms, the physical fabric of cities within which urban activities are conducted. The processes of urban innovation operate on the activities of the city, altering and improving the way in which urban functions are performed. The processes of urban accumulation operate on the fabric of the city, modifying and developing urban forms in response to the changing needs of their occupying activities. To employ an example used later in this section, the mass ownership and use of motor vehicles has generated widespread innovation in the manner in which urban functions such as commuting and retailing are conducted. These innovations have created demands for investment in new urban forms such as business parks and out-of-town shopping centres. Through this interplay of urban innovation and accumulation, the form and function of cities as a whole have been irreversibly transformed.

From a morphological perspective, the buildings and infrastructure which make up the built environment can be seen as the physical expression of urban forms that have accumulated over a long period of time. Their design expresses the changing cultural and aesthetic norms of an urban society; their materials and construction indicate the different stages of its technological development; their disposition reflects the historical pattern of its spatial growth. At the same time, the built environment can be understood as an economic manifestation of urban function. Because investment in buildings and infrastructure is undertaken to accommodate the economic and social activities being pursued in the city, it represents a physical record of both the past history and present activity of city life. Indeed, urban form and function are both subject to the interlocking processes of innovation and accumulation. Urban innovation encompasses improvements to the technologies and institutions which regulate the activities of the city; urban accumulation involves investment in the building capital that supports these activities, in part embodying urban innovation and in part responding to it.

Urban innovation operates at several levels, through a process of 'interactive innovation' (Barras, 1990). New technologies can change urban forms and functions quite directly, as through investment in new modes of transport or the introduction of new building materials and construction methods (Powell, 1980). Examples include the impact of reinforced concrete and multi-lane highways on the appearance and organization of twentieth century cities. Slower acting, but more fundamental, are the indirect effects which technical change works upon the economy and society as a whole, which in turn feed through to steer the course of urban development. The Industrial Revolution did not just create new types of buildings and infrastructure, or new methods of manufacturing production; it was also instrumental in the mass migration of population from countryside to city, and in political reforms such as the Public Health Acts which were introduced as a response to the squalor and disease rife in Britain's industrial cities (Briggs, 1968). The impetus for urban innovation can equally originate in spheres other than the technological- as through new flows of investment channelled into private property ownership, through changes in the land-use planning system or even through shifts in cultural values, such as the defeat of the modernist experiment and the rise of post-modernism (Ellin, 1996).

Disequilibrium is inherent in urban development, arising from the tension between the rapid processes of innovation which transform the functions undertaken in cities, and the much slower processes of accumulation which expand their built form. Despite the powerful combination of forces promoting urban innovation, the physical permanence and rigidity of buildings acts as a constraint on the rate at which the physical structure of cities can change. Just as technical progress in the construction industry lags behind that in other capital goods industries, so does the rate of innovation in the urban built form lag behind that in its occupying activities. The problem is reinforced by the tendency for the life of buildings to be extended by repeated renovation, which acts as a brake on the rate at which the fabric of cities can be transformed. In contrast, changes in urban functions, or the emergence of completely new functions, may happen quite quickly as a new technological regime becomes established. In these circumstances, the changing life of the city must be accommodated within a physical fabric which can adapt only slowly and sometimes painfully to its altered demands.

Given the pronounced cyclical nature of the investment process which was revealed in the previous chapter, it is apparent that urban accumulation does not follow a steady-state growth trajectory. Rather, it proceeds through successive waves of development, each generating a unique vintage of building stock that is distinguished by the technologies and occupier demands which shaped it (Whitehand, 1987:11–29). The long cycles which have marked residential and non-residential building since the nineteenth century can be seen as manifestations of a single urban development cycle, in which successive technological revolutions have played a vital role. Each wave of industrialization has powered the accumulation of a new generation of building capital, while investment in new forms of transport and communications infrastructure has expanded the reach of urban activities. The result is that a distinctive pattern of urban development has evolved in association with each new technological regime and its associated institutional structures. Within each wave of urbanization, sequences of building cycles of shorter duration have been identified; these major cycles are propagated endogenously, but respond to irregular shocks emanating from a variety of sources such as wars and financial crises, or institutional reforms such as financial deregulation.

The manner in which urban innovation and accumulation interact with population growth, technological progress, industrialization and the expansion of trade is a thread that runs through several recent histories of urban development. *Cities and Economic Development* by Paul Bairoch (1988) is perhaps the most ambitious and wide-ranging of these studies, and one of its arguments concerns the crucial role that cities have played in generating and diffusing the technological innovations which have driven economic growth. In *The Making of Urban Europe*, Hohenberg and Lees (1995) discussed the Industrial Revolution in terms of a self-reinforcing process, in which industrialization both generated and was sustained by an accelerated rate of urbanization, accompanied by the accumulation of building capital in the form of railways and factories. A major theme in *The Cambridge Urban History of Britain* (Clark, 2000; Daunton, 2000; Palliser, 2000) is the manner in which the built form of today's towns and cities, as reflected in their topography and physical structure, is the product of a process of cumulative causation that stretches back through centuries of urban development, a process in which technological and institutional innovation has interacted continuously with the changing demands of society.

Urbanization as a whole can be characterized in terms of an innovation process, as population and economic activity have clustered together to benefit from the economies of agglomeration. In support of this view, the historical trajectories of urbanization in England and the United States are illustrated in Figure 5.1, showing the proportion of national population living in settlements of over a threshold size (10,000 in England and Wales; 2,500 in the United States). These trajectories exhibit the classic S-shaped logistic growth curve typical of a diffusion process. England experienced a long and slow initial phase of urbanization in pre-industrial era, with the proportion of the population living in towns of 10,000 or more rising from 6% in 1600 to 17.5% in 1750 and 24% in 1800 (Wrigley, 1987: 177). Under the impact

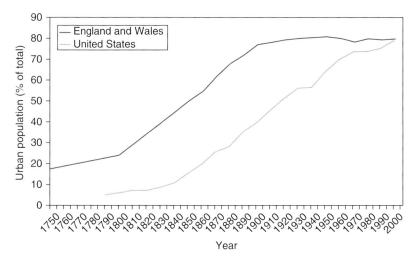

Figure 5.1   The urbanization of Britain and America.
Source: Hall et al. (1973), Wrigley (1987), ONS, USCB.

of industrialization, there was then a rapid take-off at the start of the nineteenth century, with the 50% point reached by 1850 and a near saturation level of 77% by 1900. Britain was then a mature urbanized economy, and its urban population share remained stable throughout the twentieth century at close to 80% for towns of 10,000 or more, rising close to 90%, when the threshold size is dropped to 2,500. The US trajectory closely tracks that for England and Wales, with a lag of around 70 years, which reflects its later history of urbanization and industrialization. The proportion of the American population living in towns of 2,500 or more was just 5% in 1790, rising slowly to 11% by 1840. It was around the time of the Civil War that the growth in the urban share took off at a similar gradient to that of England and Wales; it reached 25% by 1870, 50% by 1920 and a near saturation level of 74% as recently as 1970, with the impact of the Great Depression apparent in the flattening of the gradient during the 1930s (Heim, 2000: 139).

Urban agglomeration

Cities exist as economic entities because of agglomeration economies, the economies of scale which result from activities clustering in proximity to each other. A crucial dynamic of urban development is the tension between the centripetal forces of agglomeration and the centrifugal forces of dispersion. One of the first to recognize this tension was the German urban economist August Lösch: 'We shall consider market areas that…arise through the interplay of purely economic forces, some working towards concentration and others towards dispersion. In the first group are the advantages of specialization and of large-scale production; in the second, those of shipping costs and of diversified production' (Lösch, 1954: 105).

To understand the interplay of these opposing forces, space must be introduced into economic theory. However, this requires new types of models to deal with increasing returns and the indivisibilities created by the fixed supply of land and the costliness of transport. 'Because standard general equilibrium analysis abstains from the consideration of indivisibilities or increasing returns to scale, it will fail to capture the essential impact of transport and land use when one comes to study the spatial distribution of economic activities' (Fujita and Thisse, 2002: 13). Theories of the spatial economy must therefore be founded on imperfectly competitive markets: '...because of the monopoly elements which are almost invariably present in spatial relations, a broadly defined general theory of monopolistic competition can be conceived as identical with the general theory of location and space-economy' (Isard, 1949: 505–6). The thrust of the 'new economic geography' is to derive general equilibrium models of the space-economy within a framework of monopolistic competition that takes account of the uniqueness of location (Krugman, 1991a; Fujita et al., 1999).

As noted in Chapter 2, Alfred Marshall was one of the first economists to discuss increasing returns to scale in production, emphasizing how large industrial enterprises can achieve scale returns by investing in new technologies and improved organization. In addition to these internal scale economies, which benefit the growth of individual enterprises, he also pointed to the external scale economies that are generated when separate firms cluster together (Marshall, 1920: 267–77). Marshall identified three types of agglomeration benefits: knowledge spillovers among neighbouring firms who can exchange knowledge and experience, joint markets for intermediate inputs such as specialist services and the sharing of skilled labour pools (for recent discussions of these externalities, see Duranton and Puga, 2004; Rosenthal and Strange, 2004). An alternative way of explaining agglomeration economies is to express them in terms of linkages: as firms cluster together, they benefit from backward linkages to shared suppliers and from forward linkages to expanded product markets (Fujita et al., 1999: 5). There is an important distinction, first made by Hoover (1948), between 'economies of localization', the agglomeration economies which accrue to firms within the same sector, and the 'economies of urbanization' which accrue to firms across different sectors. Cities vary considerably according to their degree of specialization or diversity, as measured by the extent to which their economies are concentrated in a few or many sectors. In a specialized city, the economies of localization are uppermost; in a diverse city, it is the economies of urbanization that are dominant (Duranton and Puga, 2000).

The stronger the economies of agglomeration, the greater are the productivity gains made by firms operating in close proximity to one another (Lucas, 2001). This is a key factor in the trade-off between land rent and transport costs which is central to economic theories of location. The famous model of von Thünen, published in 1826, formulated this trade-off in terms of farmers spread over a uniform agricultural plain, selling their produce at a central market; the further the location of the farmer from the market, the higher his transport costs and therefore the lower the rent he is able to pay for his land. Alonso (1964) and Muth (1969) generalized this monocentric model to accommodate the location decisions of firms and households, allowing them to substitute between their use of land and other, non-spatial, goods. The city centre, or central business district (CBD), is assumed to be the location in which all goods are traded and all employment is concentrated; consequently firms incur distribution costs and households commuting costs which increase with distance from the centre. Under this simplifying assumption, the model generates convex bid rent curves such that rents and occupation densities decline at a decreasing rate away from the city centre, because firms and households choose to occupy more land the cheaper it becomes with increasing distance. As population rises, the urban fringe moves outwards and rents and densities rise; as incomes rise, the urban fringe again moves outwards and rents again tend to rise but densities fall; as transport costs fall, the urban fringe once more moves outwards, the rent gradient flattens and densities fall close to the CBD (Fujita, 1989: 75–83).

To make the monocentric model more realistic, we can treat the CBD as the source of endogenously generated agglomeration economies rather than the predetermined location of employment and market exchange. Mills (1967, 1972) emphasized the tension between the economies of agglomeration and the diseconomies of transport costs within the urban economy. Increasing distance from the city centre not only imposes transport costs on firms and households, but also reduces the impact of scale economies. Henderson (1974) incorporated this trade-off into a model of the urban economy based on the relationship between city size and the utility of its residents. Utility increases up to an optimal city size as the economies of agglomeration predominate and then declines as the diseconomies of scale take over, due to factors such as transport costs, congestion and pollution. Cities vary in size because the economies of localization mean that different cities tend to specialize in particular industries with different agglomeration economies, whereas the diseconomies of scale tend to be common to all cities, irrespective of their industrial structure.

The next step is to admit a multiplicity of production sectors, enjoying differing scale economies and supported by differently sized market areas, in order to conceptualize the polycentric structure which characterizes modern cities (Anas et al., 1998). Polycentric cities will tend to emerge when the opposing forces of agglomeration and dispersion are relatively balanced, but the range of the centripetal forces is shorter than that of the centrifugal forces, encouraging the emergence of sub-centres (Krugman, 1996: 24–5). The result is an urban structure with a CBD containing production activities with strong scale economies, serving the whole population of the surrounding city, while activities with lesser agglomeration economies locate in suburban sub-centres, supported by more local catchment populations.

The location of urban activities finds its echo in the spatial structure of building capital. Developers respond to agglomeration economies by substituting between land and structures in the overall cost of building investment, with the result that building heights typically decrease away from the city centre in parallel with the decline in land values (Grimaud, 1989). Towards the urban periphery, developers will tend to build on large sites at low densities, constructing relatively cheap, low-rise structures such as detached houses, office parks and retail warehouses. Conversely, in or near the city centre, they shift the composition of their investment towards more expensive, high-rise, high density structures such as apartment blocks, office towers and shopping centres. Through its influence on plot densities, construction technology therefore plays a crucial role in mediating between land rents and property rents, but both manifest the distance decay trend that reflects the influence of agglomeration economies.

The manner in which building rents decline away from the city centre can most clearly be illustrated by the office market, the spatially most concentrated sector of the urban economy. Office-based financial and business services tend to enjoy the strongest benefits from knowledge spillovers, serve the widest market area, draw on the largest skilled labour pool and are the most intensive users of land. Figure 5.2 illustrates the rent gradient of the London office market, stretching from the tower blocks of Central London to the business parks on the urban periphery delineated by the M25 orbital motorway. In 2007, the prime office rent at the peak of the market in the West End was £100 per square foot; this decayed rapidly to £65 in Midtown and £67.50 in the City, just 3 miles away, then fell more slowly to £20.50 in the suburban centre of Croydon, some 10 miles from the West End. However, beyond the 10-mile limit, office rents stopped falling, remaining within a band of between £20 and £30 up to 35 miles from the centre. Such rent gradients are typically modelled using a negative exponential function: the fitted rent curve out to the edge of Greater London has a coefficient of −0.140; beyond that, the relationship between rents and distance from the centre is much weaker, with a slope of only −0.0074. The implication of this flattening of the rent gradient is that beyond 10 miles the decline in agglomeration economies is no longer a significant influence on rents, while other more local factors such as quality of space and local amenities have come into play.

The growth of cities

A powerful stimulus to urban growth is provided by the interaction between innovation and agglomeration. Several observers have argued that cities act as engines of economic growth because they are the places in which new ideas are formed, knowledge is exchanged and learning is promoted (Jacobs, 1969; Bairoch, 1988;

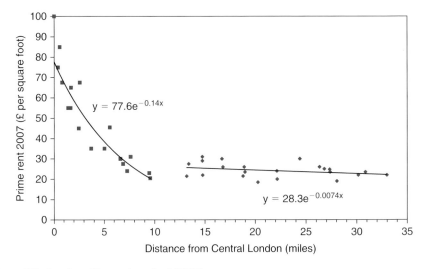

Figure 5.2 London office rent gradient (2007).
Source: Cushman and Wakefield, PMA.

Glaeser, 1999). The cross-fertilization of ideas within a concentrated mass of people creates knowledge spillovers which reinforce the accumulation of human capital, thereby providing a crucial link between theories of endogenous economic growth and urban agglomeration (Lucas, 2001). Models of endogenous urban growth which combine agglomeration and human capital formation are now being developed to formalize the idea that '...agglomeration can be considered the territorial counterpart of economic growth' (Fujita and Thisse, 2002: 389). In these models, agglomeration, innovation and growth are mutually self-reinforcing processes: agglomeration spurs growth because it reduces the costs of innovation, while growth fosters agglomeration by spawning new firms that cluster together. As human capital accumulates, the optimal size of cities increases, so that population growth is absorbed partly by increasing city size and partly by an expansion in the number of cities. In general, the more spatially agglomerated an economy, the faster will be its aggregate growth rate (Eaton and Eckstein, 1997; Black and Henderson, 1999; Martin and Ottaviano, 2001; Fujita and Thisse, 2002).

The dynamic behaviour of these models is broadly consistent with the stylized facts of urban growth which have been revealed by empirical studies. Cities of all types have been growing in size and increasing in number, yet a broadly stable relative distribution of city sizes has been maintained across the urban hierarchy (Black and Henderson, 2003). The larger a city, the more diversified it is, and diversity tends to stimulate urban growth while specialization hinders it (Glaeser et al., 1992). A city will tend to grow faster when its workforce contains a high proportion of the business professionals in whom is embodied much of its human capital (Simon and Nardinelli, 1996). Knowledge exchange, innovation and new business formation are fostered by diversified cities, which are able to supply most of their own needs, whereas specialized cities tend to be over-dependent on the export of a few staple industries (Jacobs, 1969). The invention and diffusion of technological innovations are most active in large cities, where learning is concentrated and knowledge spillovers are strongest (Pred, 1966; Robson, 1973). The knowledge base of a city is one of the key determinants of its competitiveness (Lever, 2002), and its creative industries such as design and the media have become important drivers of overall economic growth (Hall, 2000).

The correlation between diversity and growth is captured in models of the space-economy operating under conditions of monopolistic competition. In a multi-city version of the model, different industries are assigned different scale economies and transport costs, defining a ranking of industries which allows a hierarchical urban system to evolve, with higher order cities containing a more diversified economic structure than lower order cities (Fujita et al., 1999: 203–4). Urban growth is propelled by the twin forces of industrialization and transport innovation, with mass production increasing scale economies, while improvements in transport technology reduce distribution costs (Krugman, 1991a: 22–3). As cities grow in size, they produce a wider range of goods to satisfy consumer demand, and can produce these goods at lower cost which means that they capture larger market areas. This generates a process of positive feedback or 'circular causation' analogous to the principle of cumulative causation promoted by Kaldor (1972): '...manufactures production will tend to concentrate where there is a large market, but the market will be large where manufactures production is concentrated' (Krugman, 1991b: 486).

An important characteristic of monopolistic competition models of urban agglomeration is that they tend to generate multiple equilibria, so that outcomes are indeterminate and the trajectory of urban growth is historically dependent (see Chapter 2). 'Which equilibrium you get to depends on where you start: history matters' (Krugman, 1991a: 20). For example, a transport hub such as a port or railway interchange can provide the catalyst for the emergence of a new city which is then locked in to that location as it continues to grow through agglomeration economies, long after its transport function has lost its primary importance (Fujita et al., 1999: 227–36). A classic example of this phenomenon is the massive impetus given to the growth of Chicago by its role as the main rail hub in the heartland of America (Krugman, 1993). That urban development is particularly prone to historical path dependence is an argument advanced by Arthur (1994). His emphasis was on the factors determining the emergence of industrial clusters, which then act as nuclei around which cities evolve under the influence of agglomeration economies. In part at least, the initial location of such clusters may be determined by historical accident; multiple spatial orderings are possible and specific historical events determine which eventually emerges.

As urban activities cluster together, sharing knowledge, intermediate inputs and labour, they become increasingly interdependent. 'As an industry (or industrial economy) grows and adapts to changing and increasingly complex production methods, interconnections, more or less rigid, develop among its technological components – among machines, plant, transport network and raw material supplies...' (Frankel, 1955: 297). This phenomenon of interrelatedness reinforces the tendency for cities to lock on to historically determined trajectories of development, and makes it difficult for established cities, particularly those with specialized economies, to switch from an old to a new technological regime. As a consequence, periods of revolutionary technological change tend to cause 'an upheaval in the urban hierarchy' (Bairoch, 1988: 292).

New technologies can lead to the rise of new cities, in which start-up firms are able to take advantage of lower land and labour costs in order to exploit the new technological opportunities. The new industries may form a distinct growth pole, as in the case of the much-quoted microelectronics cluster in Silicon Valley, creating a wellspring of innovation which boosts the growth of the whole national economy (Scott, 1988; Castells and Hall, 1994). Conversely, existing cities can suffer relative decline if their established firms continue to rely on the experience they have accumulated in using more traditional technologies. As a consequence, specialized cities locked into a narrow range of industries and technologies may pass through a life cycle in which cumulative causation at first generates a virtuous circle of growth, but eventually switches to a vicious circle of decline (Brezis and Krugman, 1997). Such are the economic forces that drive the rise and fall of cities (Lawton, 1989).

There is an especially strong tendency for building investment to lock cities on to historically determined trajectories of urban accumulation. Because of the durability of building capital, we can depict '...urban growth as a layering process and urban spatial structure at any point of time as the result of a cumulative process spanning decades' (Harrison and Kain, 1974: 62). This cumulative development process produces a fixed, long-lived and highly interrelated urban fabric, embodying sunk costs that constrain the ways in which urban activities can develop in the future. Large-scale development may be required to counter the inefficiencies created by these sunk costs. Rauch (1993) explores the role of developers in overcoming the inertia of established industrial clusters through the phased construction of new industrial parks on the urban periphery. Several recent models of urban growth afford a prominent role to developers as 'large' agents who can facilitate expansion by operating on a scale sufficient to internalize some of the agglomeration benefits of creating a new business or residential neighbourhood (see, for example, Henderson and Mitra, 1996). This is one example of the more general role that land and property markets play as active mediators in the processes of urban change (D'Arcy and Keogh, 1997).

The indeterminacy of urban development is conducive to the propagation of cyclical fluctuations in building investment. The urban economy can switch between periods of low and high growth according to self-fulfilling shifts in investor expectations; in particular, when developers anticipate slow growth, building investment slumps, whereas when the expectation is for rapid growth, building investment will boom (Evans et al., 1998). Successive building booms act as endogenously generated shocks to the trajectory of urbanization. Each produces a new vintage of capital stock which adds another layer to the urban fabric, while past vintages are demolished when the expected returns from their continued operation are matched by the expected returns from their redevelopment (Brueckner, 1980). The discontinuous impact of development cycles on the built form of cities is an example of the process of 'urban morphogenesis' through which '...self-organizing systems tend naturally to be dominated by the most unstable fluctuations' Krugman (1996: 49).

The urban development cycle combines innovation and accumulation in two ways:

1 Innovations in *construction technology*, such as the use of steel-framing and reinforced concrete, reduce the costs of larger and taller structures, which steepens the bid rent curve because building can profitably be undertaken at higher densities, thereby providing an impetus to intensification through redevelopment. The result is successive vintages of buildings with improved technical specification and higher plot ratios in the city centre.
2 Innovations in *transport technology*, such as the construction of railway and highway networks, reduce the costs of moving goods and people, which flattens the bid rent curve and pushes out the urban boundary, thereby encouraging the extension of urban development through decentralization. The result is successive rings of buildings of progressively newer specification and lower density on the urban periphery.

Acting through the development cycle, innovation and accumulation create a self-reinforcing process of metropolitan growth in which intensification and extension operate in tandem. As cities grow, the intensification of development in their central areas creates congestion externalities and rising land costs. These generate pressures for the decentralization of residential and business activities through improvements in transport provision, leading to a corresponding extension of urban development. This, in turn, creates opportunities for new functions to occupy the central area, triggering a new round of intensification.

The interplay between intensification and decentralization within the urban development cycle is illustrated in Figure 5.3, using as an example, the evolution of the out-of-town office market in six major British cities (Birmingham, Bristol, Edinburgh, Glasgow, Leeds and Manchester). By the mid-1980s, most of Britain's motorway network had been completed, providing the catalyst for a wave of out-of-town retail and office development. Following earlier innovations in the United States (Lang, 2003), a new form of office building was developed around UK cities, consisting of landscaped business parks containing a number of low density office pavilions of light construction, typically rising no more than two or three storeys in height. During the office-building boom of the late 1980s/early 1990s, twice as much space was built out-of-town as in the centres of the six cities; the result was that the out-of-town share of their stock of modern (post-1980) office space increased from 38% in 1987 to 55% by 1992. Despite the greater supply, prime out-of-town rents converged on those in the city centre, the ratio between the two rising from 75% in 1991 to 85% in 1997. This flattening of the rent profile signified a weakening of agglomeration economies, as the new generation of business parks offered the benefits of convenient car access and an attractive working environment. However, during the next building cycle, in the late 1990s/early 2000s, levels of town centre office building matched those out-of-town, stabilizing their respective shares. Furthermore, the rent ratio dropped back sharply, from 85% to 70% by 2007. This suggests that the economies of agglomeration had strengthened again, as the combination of growing motorway congestion and a lack of services on isolated business parks shifted occupier preferences back towards a new generation of town centre offices.

Transport and suburbanization

The nature of technological change in transport systems and its impact on the evolution of cities are the subject of a valuable study by Grübler (1990).

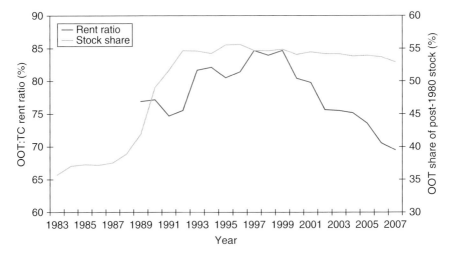

Figure 5.3 Evolution of the UK out-of-town office market (six provincial cities).
Source: PMA.

He visualizes each transport revolution as producing a radical reduction in the cost and increase in the speed of transport, which impart a 'growth pulse' to urban development. New modes of transport undergo a diffusion process such that initial introduction is followed by growing adoption until a saturation point is reached at which the network has achieved its full extension. This diffusion process stretches over space as well as time, as the new transport mode spreads out to compete with established forms of provision (Hägerstrand, 1967). Once the new mode achieves market dominance, the sunk costs of the infrastructure investment are an important factor locking the urban economy on to a particular development path, until disrupted by the next transport revolution. Krugman (1991a: 24–5) makes the point that '…there are economies of scale in transportation itself. A railway or a highway represents indivisible investments…It is possible in principle to imagine this transportation network effect as an independent source of geographical concentration of industry…' Because of the indivisibilities of transport investment, once an infrastructure network is installed, linking together existing urban centres, it will reinforce the agglomeration economies already in operation.

Grübler demonstrated how transport systems have evolved in a range of countries by plotting logistic diffusion curves to represent the spread of canals, railways, modern highways and automobiles. He observed a catch-up effect as the 'diffusion bandwagon' gathers pace, whereby the later adopters of a transport technology attain saturation network coverage more quickly than the pioneers. Following his example, Figure 5.4 illustrates the diffusion curves of three types of interurban transport networks for which comparable data are available for the UK and

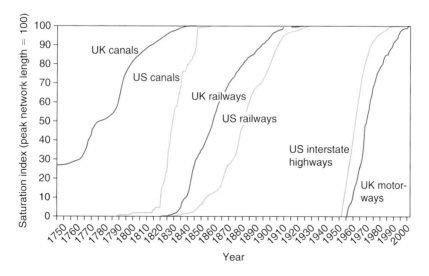

Figure 5.4   Growth of UK and US transport networks.
The labels read (left to right): UK canals; US canals; UK railways; US railways; US interstate highways; UK motorways
Source: Isard (1942), Chandler (1965), Feinstein and Pollard (1988), Mitchell (1988), Grübler (1990), DfT, FHWA, NBER.

US – canals, railways and modern highways. These diffusion curves are expressed in terms of the proportion of the peak network length reached in each year of installation. The relatively abrupt nature of each major wave of infrastructure investment is apparent. So is the catch-up effect, particularly for canals and, to a lesser extent, railways. With these networks, investment take-off occurred later in the United States, but was followed by a steeper rate of adoption, culminating in a completion date close to that reached in the United Kingdom.

Over the long term, the evolution of the whole urban transport system is characterized by successive waves of investment that mark the rise and fall of particular infrastructure networks. New transport modes of superior performance are substituted for existing modes that decline in competitiveness, face shrinking demand and pass into a final life cycle stage of network closures. These waves of infrastructure investment stimulate other forms of building investment, generating what Isard (1942) termed the 'transport-building cycle' as a key driver of urban accumulation (see Chapter 3). Figure 5.5 illustrates how the transport-building cycle can be represented as a process of interactive innovation: a new transport technology acts as a catalyst for both the extension and intensification of urban development, while the resultant development boom feeds back to underwrite the investment in the

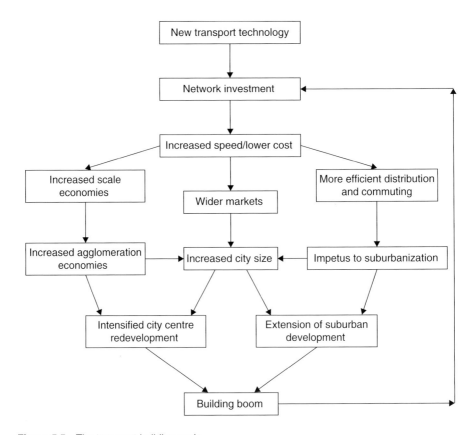

Figure 5.5   The transport-building cycle.

new transport infrastructure. An empirical link between transport investment and long waves in economic growth was suggested by Grübler (1990: 187), who showed that the three major waves of canal, railway and highway investment in the United States were separated by gaps of around 55 years, and that, in each case, the onset of network saturation coincided with periods of economic depression (in the 1870s, 1930s and 1980s).

The extent of the contribution that new modes of transport make to economic growth and urban development has been a hotly contested issue. Those who ascribe a leading role to infrastructure investment as an engine of growth point to its extensive backward and forward linkages, which place transport improvements at the centre of a self-reinforcing process of industrialization and urban agglomeration. Transport innovation contributes to growth by widening and integrating product markets, increasing the reliability and speed of distribution, facilitating the emergence of new industries and reinforcing economies of scale (Szostak, 1991). The most frequently discussed example is the extent to which the railways were the leading sector in the Industrial Revolution. Supporters of this view argue that the railways not only created massive demands on the coal, iron and steel and engineering industries, but also generated positive feedback links between falling transport costs and the emergence of the factory system (Rostow, 1971). The opposing view (Fogel, 1964; Hawke, 1970) is that the railways should be viewed as just one component of nineteenth century industrialization, since counterfactual analysis suggests that the 'social savings' they generated for the economy were relatively modest (measured as the difference between the actual cost of the services provided by the railways and their hypothetical cost, if the railways had not been built). That established modes of transport such as canals and roads could have delivered services of equivalent scope at a comparable cost to those provided by the railways is doubted by several critics of the counterfactual approach (see, for example, David, 1975).

Transport innovations affect urban growth in two interrelated ways: lower transport costs increase the aggregate size at which cities can function effectively, and they facilitate suburbanization by flattening the rent and density gradients. In other words, improvements in transport technology weaken the 'tyranny of distance' (Bairoch, 1988: 11). To demonstrate the effect, Henderson (1988: 54–9) outlined a model of urban development in which improvements in transport technology reduce commuting times and increase optimal city size, concentrating a growing population into cities of expanding size. He argued that the history of urbanization in the United States illustrates this process at work. The long-run tendency for the urban population to concentrate in large cities accelerated in the period 1890–1930, which can be related to the development of rapid transit systems at the turn of the century and the widespread adoption of automobiles after the First World War; a similar period of accelerated concentration occurred in the period 1950–70, coinciding with the construction of the interstate highway network.

In addition to lower transport costs, the suburbanization of residential population is driven by rising household incomes (Margo, 1992), together with the growing externality costs of living in inner areas, due to congestion, pollution and urban blight. Rising household incomes increase the demand for housing, which can be satisfied more easily and cheaply in suburban locations, while reductions in transport costs and travel times make longer-distance commuting and shopping trips more acceptable. The suburbanization of households and firms has tended to be mutually reinforcing. People move to the suburbs, to be followed by jobs and services, and because households and firms leave the inner city, urban decay sets in, which further reinforces decentralization.

As successive waves of suburban building extend the limits of a city, so the densities prevailing at the time of construction are embodied in concentric rings of durable housing stock: '...current spatial structure can be explained more adequately as the aggregation of historical patterns of development rather than as an equilibrium adjustment to current conditions' (Harrison and Kain, 1974: 63). The physical structure of a city reflects both the secular trend and the cyclical fluctuations in its building history, as it has been influenced by the technological possibilities, income levels and consumer tastes prevailing during each development cycle. The extent and orientation of each new residential ring are shaped by the reach of the commuter transport network and the duration of the construction boom, while its built forms reflect both the economic and social demands of its occupiers and the architectural fashions of the time (Adams, 1970). More intensive, higher value uses tend to predominate in a boom, while lower value uses are favoured by a slump (Whitehand, 1987: 39–59).

Suburbanization is a long established historical process. Estimated density gradients for London and Paris show consistent declines since the beginning of the nineteenth century (Clark, 1967: 349). A similar tendency has been observed in the United States since the late nineteenth century; it was particularly strong in the prosperous 1920s, when car ownership expanded rapidly, it slowed in the 1930s after the Great Depression, and it accelerated again during the post-war boom (Mills, 1972: 46). The flattening of density gradients has been paralleled by a flattening of land and property value gradients, as observed by Atack and Margo (1998) in nineteenth century New York, Edel and Sclar (1975) in Boston between 1870 and 1970 and Yeates (1965) in twentieth century Chicago. Anas et al. (1998) suggest that suburbanization has proceeded through three distinct stages. The first was the outward spread of the urban boundary as cities grew in size, which has occurred ever since urbanization began. Second was the emergence of polycentric rather than monocentric cities, as expanding cities absorbed free-standing towns and converted them into metropolitan sub-centres. Most recently, in the post-war era of mass car ownership, 'urban sprawl' has accelerated, particularly in the United States (Bruegmann, 2005), while suburbanization has taken on a new form – the 'edge city' (Garreau, 1991). These consist of large-scale, developer-led settlements on the periphery of established metropolitan areas, with residential neighbourhoods centred on low-rise office parks and shopping malls, linked to interchanges on the highway network.

The protracted and often painful adaptation of the built form of cities to the demands of the motor car was one of the dominant themes of twentieth century urbanization. It illustrates how the necessity of accommodating new urban functions to old urban forms can initiate a process of interactive innovation in urban development. The turn of the century saw the start of the mass production of motor vehicles, but for their pioneering users, the benefits were limited not only by the technical limitations of the early models, but also by the physical constraints of densely built-up industrial cities, which had not been designed for such a transport technology. As a result, the initial adoption of motor vehicles produced only modest, incremental innovations in urban activity. However, their performance improved as rapidly as their ownership expanded, creating congestion and strain on the existing urban fabric. In combination with continued population growth and the emergence of new consumer goods industries, the demands of the car created a growing pressure for the outward spread of lower density suburban development. By this means, automobile technology was instrumental in generating more radical urban innovations, as epitomized by the garden suburbs, arterial roads and trading estates of the interwar years. In the post-war period, rising real incomes and increasing leisure time fuelled the demand for private cars to such an extent that, through advertising and the entertainment media, their status was elevated from essential household commodity to potent cultural symbol (Flink, 1988). By achieving such a status, the car created an irresistible demand for those physical changes in urban structure which could best meet its needs – in turn generating political institutions such as the road lobby to ensure that these urban innovations were implemented. The response was a whole series of new urban forms, such as motorways, new towns, business parks and out-of-town shopping centres, which were designed explicitly, and almost exclusively, to accommodate a car-borne lifestyle. As we proceed into the twenty-first century, the environmental costs of such a lifestyle are becoming ever more apparent, and the pressures to invest in more sustainable transport technologies are intensifying.

A comparison of UK and US urban development cycles

The analysis of UK and US investment cycles in Chapter 4 identified both major cycles and long waves in all capital goods sectors including building investment. When these two cyclical components in building investment coalesce, the result is an intermediate cycle in the 15–25 year frequency range typically associated with the Kuznets long swing. This corresponds to the dominant long cycle widely identified in the building cycle literature reviewed in Chapter 3. It is this long building cycle that we shall examine in the remainder of this chapter, identifying it with the urban development cycle discussed in the previous section. The approach adopted is to construct composite indices of aggregate building activity for the United Kingdom and United States, apply structural modelling to the series to isolate their long building cycles, establish a chronology for the urban development cycle in each country and investigate the key historical influences which have shaped the trajectories of the two cycles.

The data

For each country, a composite long-run index of the total volume of building investment has been constructed by combining the residential and non-residential investment series used for the cycle analysis that was presented in Chapter 4, and extending the aggregate series, as far back in time as possible, using other available historical indices of building activity (Figure 5.6). Each series has been derived as follows:

- For the United Kingdom, the constant price residential and non-residential building series have been combined into an aggregate index that covers the years

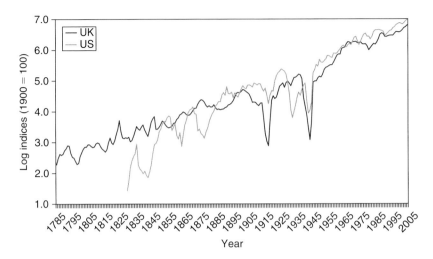

Figure 5.6 Total building investment in the United Kingdom and United States (1785–2005). *Source*: Riggleman (1933), Colean and Newcomb (1952), Cairncross and Weber (1956), Kuznets (1961), Feinstein (1976), Feinstein and Pollard (1988), BEA, NBER, ONS.

1851–2005. This has been extended back to 1785 by chaining it to the index of brick production in Great Britain between 1785 and 1849 published by Cairncross and Weber (1956), based on the earlier work of Shannon (1934), who considered it '…a direct measure of building in general' (Cairncross and Weber, 1956: 300). From 1855, the cyclical behaviour of total UK building can be compared directly with that of its housing and other building components that has already been reported in Chapter 4.

• For the United States, the constant price private sector residential and non-residential investment series have been combined into an aggregate index covering the years 1901–2005. This has been chained back to 1889 using comparable constant price data estimated by Kuznets (1961), and then to 1830 using the Riggleman index of the annual real value of new building permits (which excludes infrastructure). A current price version of this index was first assembled by Riggleman (1933) on a per capita basis; it was subsequently adjusted by Isard to produce an aggregate index and deflated by a building cost index also assembled by Riggleman (these data are published in Colean and Newcomb, 1952: Appendix N). The separate indices of US residential and non-residential building have also been extended: back to 1889 using constant price data from Kuznets (1961) and back to 1850 using current price data from Gottlieb (1965) to apportion the aggregate volume of constant price building between the two sectors. Several of these series are available from the US National Bureau of Economic Research Macrohistory database.

Structural models

Unobserved components models have been fitted to the building series in order to identify their variable trend and long building cycle. Two different modelling strategies have been adopted. First, a one-cycle model was used to decompose each

Table 5.1   Parameters of UK and US building investment cycles.

	Start year[b]	Period (years)[c]	Order[d]	Damping factor[d]	Amplitude[d]	Variance[d]	Likelihood ratio[e]
US long cycles (one-cycle models)[a]							
Total (1)[f]	1830	18.7**	1	0.898	0.0594	0.1130	44.82**
Total (2)[f]	1830	36.9**	2	0.700	0.0643	0.0298	46.33**
Housing	1850	21.6**	1	0.857	0.0898	0.1813	51.16**
Other building	1850	17.3**	1	0.842	0.0552	0.0743	46.79**
UK long cycles (one-cycle models)[a]							
Total	1785	25.1	2	0.647	0.0694	0.0306	91.78**
Housing	1855	23.2	2	0.686	0.0498	0.0799	57.82**
Other building[g]	1855	–	–	–	–	–	–
UK major cycles (two-cycle models)[a]							
Total	1785	12.3*	2	0.611	0.0699	0.0166	48.21**
Housing[h]	1855	9.8	2	0.655	0.0797	0.0297	51.16**
Other building[h]	1855	11.1*	1	0.855	0.0769	0.0531	46.46**
UK long waves (two-cycle models)[a]							
Total	1785	30.0**	1	0.979	0.0216	0.0426	49.49**
Housing[h]	1855	29.4**	1	0.982	0.0682	0.1614	15.16**
Other building[h]	1855	31.5**	1	0.968	0.0725	0.0504	12.21**

Source: Riggleman (1933), Colean and Newcomb (1952), Cairncross and Weber (1956), Kuznets (1961), Gottlieb (1965), Feinstein (1976), Feinstein and Pollard (1988), ONS: NBER, BEA.

Note:
Diagnostic statistics for the model residuals show that at the 5% level, none of the models satisfy the normality test, due to the extreme irregularity of their cyclical components; the heteroscedasticity test is satisfied by the UK housing and other building models; the serial correlation test is satisfied by all models but US other building and UK housing (for a description of the test statistics, see Table A.1.)
[a] The long cycle parameters are derived from one-cycle models; the major cycle and long wave parameters are derived from two-cycle models.
[b] All series end in 2005.
[c] The estimated period of each cycle component is checked by spectral analysis of the residuals derived from the detrended series; ** indicates that the spectrum provides strong confirmation about the presence of a cyclical component with the same period as that obtained from the structural model, * indicates weak confirmation.
[d] For definitions of cycle order, damping factor, amplitude and variance, see Section A.7 and Table A.2.
[e] The likelihood ratio compares the values of the likelihood functions for models, with and without the specified cycle; ** denotes that the restriction of there being no cycle can be rejected at the 1% level, * denotes rejection at the 5% level. For the long cycles and major cycles, the comparison is between models with and without a single cycle component; for long waves, the comparison is between models with one- and two-cycle components.
[f] For US total building investment, two separate long cycle models of order 1 and 2 have been derived.
[g] No one-cycle model of the long cycle in UK other building investment could be derived.
[h] These results for the two-cycle UK housing and other building investment models are as listed in Table 4.4.

series into a single building cycle accompanied by a smoothly varying growth trend. Second, a two-cycle model was employed to identify a separate major cycle and long wave which could then be aggregated into a composite building cycle (adopting the approach that was applied in Chapter 4). The results of this exercise, summarized in Table 5.1, are as follows:

- For the UK series, one-cycle models generate significant long cycles in total and residential building but not in non-residential building. However, the trends obtained from these models are unsatisfactory, tending to become linear and lose the variations in secular growth rates that were previously revealed by the analysis presented in Chapter 4. The two-cycle models yield better results for all three series, identifying a smoothly varying trend accompanied by a significant major cycle and long wave that combine well to create a composite long building cycle. (The two-cycle model results quoted for residential and non-residential building are taken from Table 4.4)

• All the US one-cycle models yield significant long cycles and variable trends that are broadly consistent with those derived from the shorter period analysis already reported in Chapter 4. Two versions of the one-cycle total investment model are reported, with the cycle component defined to be of either order 1 or order 2 (see Section A.2.7). The order 2 model is generally preferred as it generates a smoother trend and a more pronounced long cycle in the post-war period, although the smoothing extends its estimated period beyond the normal long cycle range. The results obtained from fitting two-cycle models to the US series are less satisfactory: it is difficult to extract a significant long wave, and, as with the UK one-cycle models, the trends tend towards the linear.

The following discussion is based upon the results derived from the UK two-cycle models and the US one-cycle models (referring to the total investment model of order 2 unless otherwise stated).

Growth trajectories

The growth trajectories for total UK and US building investment are illustrated in Figure 5.7 in terms of their trend rates of growth. The UK trend runs at around

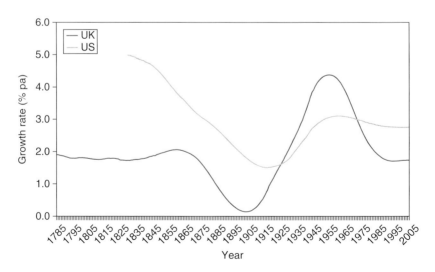

Figure 5.7   Trend rates of growth in UK and US total building investment (1785–2005).
Source: Riggleman (1933), Colean and Newcomb (1952), Cairncross and Weber (1956), Kuznets (1961), Feinstein (1976), Feinstein and Pollard (1988), BEA, NBER, ONS.

1.8% per annum during the late eighteenth and early nineteenth centuries, rises to a 2% peak in late 1850s/early 1860s and then subsides to a trough close to zero by the start of the twentieth century. This trough is followed by a compensating upswing during the first half of the century, to an early post-war peak of over 4%. During the three decades following the early 1960s, there is a sharp downward adjustment before the growth rate levels out again at around 1.7% in the early 1990s. This growth profile for total building investment is consistent with the shorter investment trajectories presented Chapter 4 (Figure 4.7): it is more volatile than investment as a whole, but less volatile than the separate building components. The recent return to the same average growth rate as prevailed two centuries earlier might suggest that, over the very long term, the equilibrium rate of growth in UK building investment is around 1.7%–1.8%; however, the displacement away from this level between the 1850s and 1990s was so protracted as to be considered a 'permanent' rather than 'temporary' effect.

The trend in total US building investment begins at a much higher growth rate of around 5% per annum in the 1830s, when the urbanization of the new country had barely begun (Figure 5.1). The investment growth rate declines during the remainder of the nineteenth century until a trough of 1.5% is reached around the onset of the First World War, a little later than the more severe UK trough. This is followed by a similar but less steep upswing, which reaches an early post-war peak of just over 3% compared to the UK peak of over 4%. However, the subsequent correction is far less marked, with the growth rate being maintained at close to 2.8% since the 1980s. Over the twentieth century, the growth profile of US building investment is not dissimilar to the shorter trajectories of GDP and total investment growth derived in the previous chapter (Figure 4.11).

Long cycles

The long cycles in UK total building investment since 1785 and US building since 1830 are illustrated in Figure 5.8, and their corresponding turning point chronologies are set out in Tables 5.2 and 5.3. As shown in Table 5.1, the average periods of the two cycles as estimated by the unobserved components models are 25.1 years for the United Kingdom and 18.7 years for the United States (from the order 1 model). These estimates are confirmed by the turning point chronologies. The more extended duration of the UK cycle, since 1830, is reflected in there being only six identified cycles in the United Kingdom compared to nine in the United States, with the difference deriving from one and a half extra US cycles in the nineteenth century, one more in the inter-war period and an additional half cycle in the post-war period. Including the war years, the average deviations of the turning points in the UK and US cycles since 1830 are similar; excluding the war years, the average deviations of the US cycle are greater. This is because US building investment was more volatile during the nineteenth century, when the economy was in its rapid initial growth phase, and also during the Great Depression; in contrast, more extreme shocks were delivered to UK building in the twentieth century by the two World Wars.

It should be stressed that the quoted averages conceal considerable variation in the duration and amplitude of successive building cycles in the two countries. These variations support the argument that the motion of any one cycle can be properly

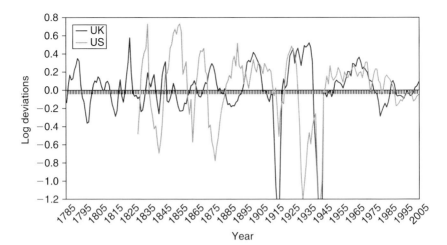

Figure 5.8 Cycles in UK and US total building investment (1785–2005).
Source: Riggleman (1933), Colean and Newcomb (1952), Cairncross and Weber (1956), Kuznets (1961), Feinstein (1976), Feinstein and Pollard (1988), BEA, NBER, ONS.

Table 5.2 Long cycle turning points for UK building investment 1785–2005.

Total investment Cycle number		Date[a]			Duration (years)		Housing timing[c]		Other building timing[c]	
T–T	P–P	T	P	Amplitude[b]	T–T	P–P	T	P	T	P
	1		1792	0.349						
1		1798		0.361		13				
	2		1805	0.148	18					
2		1816		0.287		20				
	3		1825	0.577	16					
3		1832		0.235		22				
	4		1847	0.313	24					
4		1856		0.228		29	−1		0	
	5		1876	0.293	32			0		0
5		1888		0.181		26	−2		0	
	6		1902	0.417	30			−1		0
6		1918		1.467		35	0		0	
	7		1937	0.521	26			3		−2
7		1944		1.828		31	0		0	
	8		1968	0.362	37			0		0
8		1981		0.285		21	0		0	
	9		1989	0.105				1		−1
Averages				**0.310[d]**	**26.1**	**24.6**	**−0.6**	**0.6**	**0.0**	**−0.6**

Source: Cairncross and Weber (1956), Feinstein (1976), Feinstein and Pollard (1988), ONS.
[a] T = trough, P = peak.
[b] The amplitude is measured as the proportionate deviation of each turning point from the fitted trend, excluding the war years. This is typically a more extreme measure than the stochastic estimate derived with the structural model (see Table A.2).
[c] The cycle leads (+) or lags (−) compare the timing of each component turning point with the equivalent turning points in the reference long cycle of total building investment.
[d] The average deviation of total building investment over the shorter 1855–2005 period is 0.299, compared to 0.417 for housing and 0.281 for other building.

Table 5.3 Long cycle turning points for US building investment 1830–2005.

Total investment Cycle number		Date[a]		Amplitude[b]	Duration (years)		Housing timing[c]		Other building timing[c]	
T–T	P–P	T	P		T–T	P–P	T	P	T	P
	1		1836	0.728						
1		1843		0.693		20				
	2		1856	0.729	21			0		+3
2		1864		0.573		15	0		0	
	3		1871	0.462	14			2		0
3		1878		0.776		21	−1		+1	
	4		1892	0.518	21			3		0
4		1899		0.021		10	−1		0	
	5		1902	0.336	19			−3		0
5		1918		0.509		24	0		0	
	6		1926	0.486	15			1		−3
6		1933		1.205		15	0		0	
	7		1941	0.258	10			0		0
7		1943		1.286		31	−1		0	
	8		1972	0.309	32			0		+6
8		1975		0.019		13	−7		−1	
	9		1985	0.166	16			−1		0
9		1991		0.172			0		−1	
Averages				0.466[d]	18.5	18.6	−1.3	0.3	−0.1	+0.8

Source: Riggleman (1933), Colean and Newcomb (1952), Kuznets (1961), Gottlieb (1965), NBER, BEA.
[a]T = trough, P = peak.
[b]The amplitude is measured as the proportionate deviation of each turning point from the fitted trend, excluding the war years. This is typically a more extreme measure than the stochastic estimate derived with the structural model (see Table A.2).
[c]The cycle leads (+) or lags (−) compare the timing of each component turning point with the equivalent turning points in the reference long cycle of total building investment.
[d]The average deviation of total building investment over the shorter 1850–2005 period is 0.437, compared to 0.537 for housing and 0.363 for other building.

understood only in relation to its specific historical context. For example, Figure 5.7 confirms that during the second half of the nineteenth century, the UK and US building cycles tended to move counter-cyclically. It was this counter-cyclical relationship that prompted the development of the 'Atlantic economy' model of inverse long swings in the two economies, driven by reciprocal flows of labour and capital. However, as noted in Chapter 3, a growing body of opinion has concluded that it is the combination of particular domestic events, such as the end of the second British railway boom in the 1860s coinciding with the end of the American Civil War, which better explains the origins of this apparent inverse relationship between the national building cycles.

During the twentieth century, the two national cycles became more convergent, partly through the common impact of the two World Wars, and partly through the influence of the more open global economy that evolved in the post-war period. Nevertheless, important differences in cycle duration and timing have remained. It has already been observed in the previous chapter that, while building in both

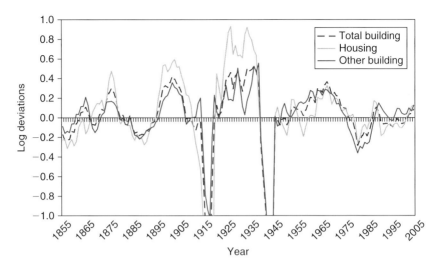

Figure 5.9   UK building investment cycles (1855–2005).
Source: Cairncross and Weber (1956), Feinstein (1976), Feinstein and Pollard (1988), ONS.

countries was severely depressed during the Second World War, the impact of the First World War was much greater in Britain, whereas the Great Depression had a much more severe effect in America – interrupting building investment to such an extent that the whole trajectory of urbanization stalled (see Figure 5.1). The cycle in both countries became less volatile after the Second World War, particularly during the long period of stable post-war growth between the 1950s and the mid-1970s, when cycle peaks and troughs are quite difficult to distinguish. However, national differences are still apparent: the post-war building boom was sustained for longer in the United States than in the United Kingdom, peaking in 1972 compared to 1968, while the subsequent slump in the late 1970s/early 1980s was more severe in the United Kingdom.

Cycle phasing

Let us now examine the behaviour of the residential and non-residential components of total building investment, using the series commencing in 1855 in the United Kingdom and in 1850 in the United States. Table 5.1 summarizes their structural modelling results; Figures 5.9 and 5.10 compare the component long cycles with the total building cycle in each country; Tables 5.2 and 5.3 relate the chronologies of the component cycles to the reference cycle of total building; Table 5.4 presents the cross-correlations between the three cycles within each country, and between corresponding cycles in the two countries.

As measured by the average deviations of their turning points, the residential cycle in both countries is more volatile than the non-residential cycle, and in general, the fluctuations in total building more closely track those in non-residential building. The component cycles are broadly coincident with the aggregate cycle in each country, more strongly so in the United Kingdom than in the United

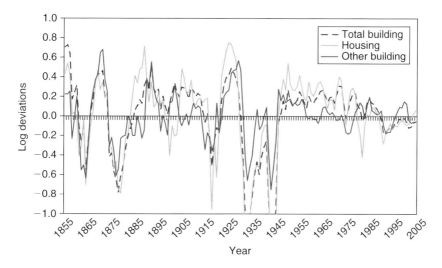

Figure 5.10   US building investment cycles (1855–2005).
Source: Riggleman (1933), Colean and Newcomb (1952), Kuznets (1961), Gottlieb (1965), BEA, NBEA.

Table 5.4   Interrelationships between UK and US building investment cycles.

UK long cycles[a] (1855–2005)

	Total	Housing	Other building
Total	1.000	0.910 (0)	0.949 (0)
Housing	0.910 (0)	1.000	0.767 (0)
Other building	0.949 (0)	0.767 (0)	1.000

US long cycles[a] (1850–2005)

	Total	Housing	Other building
Total	1.000	0.882 (0)	0.753 (0)
Housing	0.882 (0)	1.000	0.625 (0)
Other building	0.753 (0)	0.625 (0)	1.000

Cross-correlations between UK and US long cycles[b] (1855–2005)

	Total	Housing	Other building
	0.354 (+9)	0.223 (0)	0.389 (+9)

Source: Riggleman (1933), Colean and Newcomb (1952), Cairncross and Weber (1956), Kuznets (1961), Gottlieb (1965), Feinstein (1976), Feinstein and Pollard (1988), ONS: NBER, BEA.
[a]The listed correlations are the peak positive values reached in the cross-correlograms between each pair of long cycles, measured at the lag shown in brackets. The rows represent the leading cycle, and the columns the lagging cycle.
[b]These correlations are the peak positive values reached in the cross-correlograms between corresponding long cycles in the United Kingdom and United States, measured at the lag shown in brackets (where + denotes the US cycle leading).

States. This is because there is a more coincident relationship between housing and other building in the United Kingdom, as measured by their higher cross-correlation coefficient, and the closer correspondence of their turning points to the reference cycle chronology. The main divergences between the component cycles in the United Kingdom took place in the 1860s, when there was a strong boom in non-residential building that was not matched in the housing sector, and in the 1950s, when a more volatile major cycle interrupted the upswing of the housing long cycle. In the United States, the main divergences took place in the periods 1885–1905 and 1960–90, when the component cycles tended to move out of phase. The counter-cyclical movement of the UK and US building cycles, particularly in the nineteenth century, is confirmed by the cross-correlations between corresponding cycles in the two countries. For total and non-residential building, the peak positive values occur with a 9-year lead, which is approximately half the period of the US long cycle; for residential building, the peak value occurs when the cycles are coincident, but it is very weak.

Explanatory variables

The structural models fitted to UK and US total building investment have been extended to incorporate explanatory variables as well as the unobserved components (see Section A.6 for the detailed methodology). The results of this modelling exercise are summarized in Table 5.5. For both countries, three explanatory variables have been assembled: indices of GDP and industrial production provide alternative measures of macroeconomic growth to act as positive drivers of building investment, while the government bond yield is used to represent the negative effect of interest rates upon building activity. The sources used to construct the explanatory data series are as follows:

• The index of UK industrial production from 1785 is based on the 'revised best guess' series published in Crafts and Harley (1992) for the years up to 1913, extended forward to 1948 using Feinstein (1976) and the ONS database from then on. The GDP index from 1855 is that used in Chapter 4, drawn from Feinstein (1976) up to 1948 and the ONS thereafter. The UK bond yield series from 1785 is drawn from Homer and Sylla (2005), updated from the ONS, based on the 3% Consols yield until 1888, an estimated 2.75% Consol until 1903, and the 2.5% Consols yield after that (see Section A.6 for more detailed analysis of the industrial production and bond yield series).
• The US index of industrial production uses the series constructed by Davis (2004) for the years from 1830 to 1915, and the series available on the Federal Reserve Board (FRB) database from 1919 to the present, with the two series chained together using the Miron–Romer index taken from the Historical Statistics of the United States (HSUS) database (Carter et al., 2006). The HSUS database is the source of the GDP index from 1830 to 1928; after that, it is the BEA index used in Chapter 4. The HSUS database is also the source of the US long-term government bond yield for the years 1842–99 and 1919 onwards, with the years 1900–18 interpolated using a corporate bond series from Homer and Sylla (2005).

Structural models fitted to the three UK explanatory variables indicate the presence of a major cycle in each series, with a period of 13.1 years for industrial production, 12.5 years for GDP and 11.7 years for the bond yield. Industrial production and total building investment both test as stationary in their first differences, their trends are cointegrated, and causal analysis indicates that production causes building

Table 5.5   Cycles in total building investment with explanatory variables.

	Coefficients[a]	Period (years)[b]	Order[b]	Damping factor[b]	Amplitude[b]	Variance[b]	Likelihood ratio[c]
UK 1785–2005							
Industrial production[d]							
Major cycle[e]		13.1	1	0.646	0.0484	0.0025	72.06**
GDP[f]							
Major cycle[e]		12.5	1	0.870	0.0078	0.0016	38.40**
Bond yield							
Major cycle[e]		11.7	1	0.639	0.2640	0.4511	48.43**
Total building investment							
Major cycle[g]		12.6	2	0.606	0.1137	0.0159	7.00*
Long wave[g]		30.3	1	0.976	0.0503	0.0403	8.94*
Industrial production (0)[h]	0.704 (3.86)						
Industrial production (−1)[h]	0.616 (3.38)						
US 1830–2005[i]							
Industrial production							
Long wave[e]		39.2	1	0.838	0.0493	0.0202	58.28**
GDP							
Long cycle[e]		25.6	1	0.853	0.0115	0.0075	55.33**
Bond yield[j]							
Long cycle[e]		22.0	1	0.809	0.3475	0.5992	38.73**
Total building investment							
Long cycle[g]		18.2	1	0.891	0.0750	0.1006	11.33**
Industrial production (0)[h]	0.656 (4.29)						

Source: Riggleman (1933), Colean and Newcomb (1952), Cairncross and Weber (1956), Kuznets (1961), Gottlieb (1965), Feinstein (1976), Feinstein and Pollard (1988), Crafts and Harley (1992), Davis (2004), Homer and Sylla (2005), ONS: NBER, BEA, HSUS: FRB.
[a] These are the estimated coefficients of the explanatory variables (with t-statistics in brackets).
[b] For definitions of cycle period, order, damping factor, amplitude and variance, see Section A.7 and Table A.2.
[c] For the explanatory variables, the likelihood ratio compares the models with and without the specified cycle; for building investment, the ratio compares equivalent models with and without the explanatory variables; ** denotes that the restriction of there being no significant explanatory can be rejected at the 1% level, * denotes rejection at the 5% level.
[d] The UK industrial production series has seven missing values (1939–45), which are estimated from its one-cycle model.
[e] These parameters relate to separate one-cycle models fitted to the explanatory variable.
[f] The UK GDP series starts in 1855.
[g] These parameters relate to a two-cycle model (UK) or a one-cycle model (US) fitted to the building investment series with the explanatory variables included.
[h] These are the explanatory variables used in the building model (with lags shown in brackets).
[i] The US bond yield series starts in 1842.

investment, but not vice versa. There are significant cross-correlations between the major cycle in production and both the long and major cycles in building investment. The introduction of unlagged and lagged industrial production into the two-cycle building model improves model performance, with a significant of 5% as measured by the likelihood ratio test, while the coefficients on the explanatory variables are significant at 1%. The effect of the explanatory variables is marginally

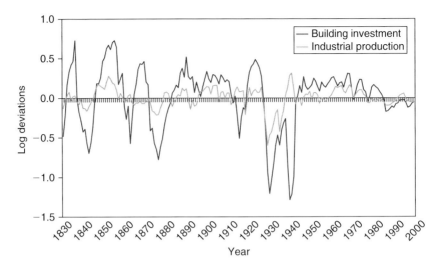

Figure 5.11 Long cycles in US building investment and industrial production (1830–2005). *Source*: Riggleman (1933), Colean and Newcomb (1952), Kuznets (1961), Gottlieb (1965), Davis (2004), BEA, FRB, HSUS, NBER.

to increase the period of the major building cycle from 12.3 years to 12.6 years, and the period of the long wave from 30.0 years to 30.3 years. In contrast, neither GDP nor the bond yield has a significant effect when tested as an explanatory variable.

The performance of the three US explanatory variables is similar to that of their UK counterparts. Structural modelling yields a significant long wave in industrial production, with period of 39.2 years, and significant long cycles in GDP and the bond yield, with periods of 25.6 years and 22.0 years respectively. Industrial production and total building investment are both stationary in their first differences; their trends are cointegrated, and causal analysis indicates that while production causes building investment, there is also a weaker feedback effect. There is a strong coincident relationship between the production and building cycles, particularly when allowance is made for the divergence between production boom and building slump during the Second World War (Figure 5.11). The introduction of unlagged industrial production into the one-cycle building model of order 1 produces an improvement in model performance that is significant at the 1% level, slightly reducing the estimated period of the long building cycle from 18.7 to 18.2 years. Neither GDP nor the bond yield work as well as an explanatory variable. When introduced into the building model, their coefficients are significant at 5%, but the likelihood ratio test shows that neither variable produces a significant improvement in overall model performance.

In summary, the trend and cycle in industrial production have been found to be the strongest explanatory influences on the trend and cycle in building investment, both in the United Kingdom and the United States. Industrial production is a better measure than GDP for capturing the growth in manufacturing activity which was integral to the inter-linked processes of industrialization and urbanization. The bond yield has not been found to be a consistent long-term influence on building investment, largely because there were sustained periods when its cyclical fluctuations were weak – between the 1830s and the First World War in the United Kingdom, and between the 1890s and the 1950s in the United States. However, when exploring the UK building cycle in detail below, we shall highlight the crucial influence that cheap credit exerted on the building cycle during the eighteenth and early nineteenth centuries.

Cycle histories

Variations in growth

Our analysis of the urban development cycles in Britain and America has, in each case, started around the times associated with their industrial 'take-off' – the 1780s/1790s in the United Kingdom and the 1840s/1850s in the United States (Rostow, 1971: 38). We can now consider the historical forces which have helped to shape the trajectories of building investment in the two economies since the start of industrialization. Rich sources of background material on their economic development are provided by *The Cambridge Economic History of Modern Britain* (Floud and Johnson, 2004) and *The Cambridge Economic History of the United States* (Engerman and Gallman, 2000). Focussing on the urban development of Britain, *The Cambridge Urban History of Britain* (Clark, 2000; Daunton, 2000; Palliser, 2000) includes the whole of our study period, while Briggs (1968) and Dennis (1984) concentrate on the nineteenth century. Turning to the urbanization of America, Monkkonen (1988) reviews the two centuries 1780–1980 with a special emphasis on public policy; Glaab and Brown (1967) pay particular attention to the interplay between technical change and urbanization, while Duncan and Lieberson (1970) stress the interrelationship between industrialization and urban development. The most comprehensive, yet vivid historical narrative of urbanization within the context of successive building cycles remains the case study of Chicago by Hoyt (1933).

The derived growth trend for building investment in the United Kingdom shows no clear evidence of a take-off associated with industrialization, with a stable growth rate of just under 2% per annum being maintained between 1785 and the start of the 1840s (Figure 5.7). The absence of any rapid upward shift in the building growth rate during the late eighteenth or early nineteenth centuries is broadly consistent with the current view of most economic historians that the United Kingdom enjoyed a gradual acceleration in industrialization, rather than a sudden 'take-off'. Most recent estimates suggest that the annual rate of growth of UK industrial production slowly increased from under 1% per annum between 1700 and 1770, through an intermediate range of 1.5%–2% between 1770 and 1815, up to a peak of 3%–3.5% between 1815 and 1841 (Crafts and Harley, 1992; Jackson, 1992). Take-off is more apparent in the growth trend of US building investment, starting at a rate of around 5% per annum in the 1830s. Davis (2004: 1196) identifies two phases to the US take-off: the increasing adoption of the factory system in the 1830s, when he estimates that industrial productivity growth peaked around 6% per annum, and the first wave of railway investment in the 1850s, when productivity growth reached a second and even higher peak of nearly 8%.

The rising rate of growth of UK building investment from the 1840s through to the early 1860s can be explained by the two railway construction booms which occurred during those decades. This expansionary phase peaked during the late 1850s/early 1860s, coinciding with the height of what has traditionally been termed the 'Great Victorian Boom' (Church, 1975). The subsequent slowdown in building growth from the 1870s to the 1890s similarly corresponds to the downswing of what has been identified as the 'Great (Victorian) Depression', a deflationary period that culminated in the severe recession of 1891–3 (Mathias, 1983: 361–9). The recent consensus is that a climacteric, a slowdown from sustained boom to long depression, did not occur in Britain during the second half of the nineteenth century (Saul, 1985; Crafts et al., 1989); however, our derived trend in building investment growth does appear to lend some credence to the idea. The progressive reduction in the rate of growth of American building investment during the second half of the nineteenth century can be attributed to two factors: first, as industrialization and urbanization gathered pace, the stock of built capital accumulated so rapidly that the rate of investment inevitably declined; second, episodes such as the Civil War during the 1860s and the depressions of the 1870s and 1890s further moderated the secular growth rate (Gallman, 2000: 9).

The zero growth trough in UK building investment at the start of the twentieth century reflects the weakest phase of British economic performance during the past century and half (see the previous discussion in Chapter 4). The economy had become locked in to technological and institutional regimes established during the Industrial Revolution (Setterfield, 1997), with the result that the pace of industrial innovation and productivity growth began to slacken and the economy became increasingly reliant on its mature staple industries and ageing stock of Victorian buildings and infrastructure (Mathias, 1983: 369–93; Pollard, 1989: 49–57). No such problems affected the US economy, which helps to explain why the slowdown in building investment growth reaches a later and much milder trough around the start of the First World War.

During the inter-war period, the upswing in UK building investment growth tracked the improving growth rate of the economy as a whole, as the structural decline of the old staple goods industries was at least partly offset by the emergence of a new generation of lighter consumer goods industries and the expansion of the service sector (Crafts, 2004: 19–21). The 1950s/early 1960s peak in building investment growth is a manifestation of the 'Golden Age' of post-war economic performance in which historically high levels of investment in new consumer goods industries were combined with the adoption of Keynesian demand management policies that maintained stable full employment levels of aggregate demand (Crafts and Wooward, 1991). As the post-war boom ended in the OPEC recessions of 1974/5 and 1980/1 (Dow, 1998), so the rate of UK building investment growth slumped back below 2% by the late 1980s. The much less severe trough in US building investment at the start of the century required a correspondingly milder inter-war upswing to reach its early post-war peak. While this is lower than the equivalent UK peak, the subsequent correction is far less marked because the US economy has maintained a rate of building investment sufficient to support an economy with a trend rate of aggregate growth close to 3.5% per annum, compared to 2.5% in the United Kingdom.

The transport-building cycle

Because of the scale of the continent and the speed of its industrialization, there is a long tradition of describing the history of American urbanization in relation to successive revolutions in transport technology. Among the first was Isard (1942), who illustrated his theory of the transport-building cycle by associating six long cycles in US urban development between 1830 and 1933 with successive waves of investment in the canal, railway, tram and highway networks. Similar perspectives were adopted by Borchert (1967), who presented a chronology of American metropolitan evolution based on four epochs defined by their dominant transport and power generation technologies; Warner (1972), who discussed the urbanization of the United States in terms of the constraints and opportunities presented by its evolving transport systems and Jackson (1985), who examined the close historical relationships between suburban development and transport innovation. Fishlow (2000) provides a recent example of the approach, with a narrative of nineteenth century urbanization that proceeds through four overlapping phases of the Turnpike Era (1800–20), the Age of Canal Expansion (1815–43), the Ascendancy of the Railroad (1830–60) and the Reign of the Railroad (1860–1910). To illustrate the progress of successive waves of US infrastructure investment, Figure 5.12 shows the growth of three transport networks – canals, railways and electric trains/trams – measured in terms of annual network additions.

Three cycles of US canal investment have been distinguished by Goodrich (1961), covering the periods 1815–34, 1834–44 and 1844–60. The origins of these long cycles in canal building were attributed to their long construction periods, the clustering of project starts which arose from the rivalry between cities wishing to capture canal-borne trade, and the fluctuating supply of loan finance. The second cycle, in particular, was an integral part of a wider speculative investment boom, in which the opening of new canals accelerated land speculation, while the demand for

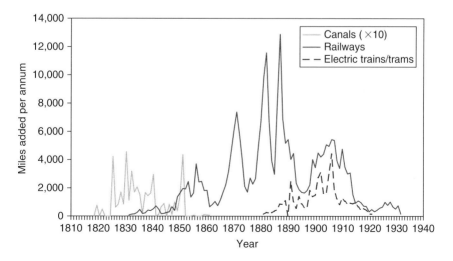

Figure 5.12   Additions to US transport networks (1810–940).
Source: Isard (1942), Chandler (1965), NBER, USCB.

construction loans strained the resources of the money markets. A financial panic in 1839 precipitated the collapse of this canal boom, contributing to a general economic depression at the beginning of the 1840s. There is evidence that the spread of the US canal network accelerated economic growth in the ante-bellum economy by facilitating the movement of goods between the industrializing eastern seaboard and the agricultural interior, integrating their markets and expanding inter-regional trade, promoting the settlement of the interior and even boosting the rate of technical invention and innovation (Goodrich, 1961: 221–46; Sokoloff, 1988).

Construction of the US railway network proceeded through five distinct cycles. The first major boom lasted through the 1850s, quadrupling the length of the network. The subsequent three waves of investment reached progressively stronger peaks in 1868–73, 1879–83 and 1886–92. These three cycles, plus a final cycle at the start of the twentieth century, propelled the expansion of the network from 30,000 miles in 1860 to nearly 170,000 miles in 1890 and over 250,000 miles by 1916. At the end of the First World War, the length of the US railway network accounted for over one-third of world mileage and exceeded the whole European total (Youngson Brown, 1951: 59).

The construction of the railways had a profound influence on the development of North America. They further accelerated the settlement of the central and western parts of the continent that had been given initial impetus by the canals. Agricultural products and industrial goods could now be traded from coast to coast. Radical reductions in freight charges enlarged the market areas of manufacturing firms, enabling them to realize previously untapped scale economies through the expansion of the factory system. The increased benefits of agglomeration and large-scale production reinforced the expansion of established metropolitan centres such as New York, and created an unrivalled growth dynamic for rail hubs such as Chicago (Cronon, 1991). Railroads were 'the nation's first big business', generating far-reaching institutional innovations in the organization of its capital markets and the management of its business corporations (Chandler, 1965). The fortunes made by the railway builders became the stuff of legend; when the Union Pacific and Central Pacific railways were joined in Utah in 1869 to create a continuous transcontinental line 'The greatest railroad in the world was completed, and a crowd of millionaires emerged from the adventure, idolised by a grateful population' (Youngson Brown, 1951: 63–4).

While the construction of the canal, railway and highway networks were vital to the development of the whole American economy, innovations in intra-urban transport were equally essential to the growth of its individual cities (Glaab and Brown, 1967: 147–57). The horse-drawn omnibus was introduced into cities in the late 1820s; from the 1840s, steam railways provided commuter services on the eastern seaboard; in the 1850s, horse-drawn streetcars appeared; steam-powered elevated railways and cable cars were installed in large cities from the 1870s; electric streetcars became operational from the late 1880s and the electric-powered subway from the 1890s. Between 1880 and the First World War, the suburban expansion of America's large cities was closely interwoven with the spread of their rapid transit networks (Cheape, 1980). The intensification and extension of urban development proceeded apace, as inner city housing was redeveloped to provide higher density tenement blocks, while extensive residential suburbs developed around the urban core. Moving through the horse-car, electric streetcar and automobile eras, each vintage of suburban building in American cities bears the imprint of the intra-urban transport system prevailing at the time (Adams, 1970).

Rapid improvements in transport systems were matched by the pace of innovation in construction technology, which acted as an equally important catalyst for American urbanization (Glaab and Brown, 1967: 142–6). In the 1830s, house construction was made more efficient by the adoption of the standardized balloon-frame; during the 1840s, large factories and warehouses of up to eight stories were supported using cast-iron columns rather than load-bearing walls; from the 1850s, entire commercial buildings were prefabricated in cast-iron; the adoption of steel frames combined with the installation of elevators made it possible to build the first generation of skyscrapers in the 1880s (the development of skyscrapers is considered further in Chapter 8). 'The steel frame greatly simplified difficult construction problems and proved an enormously efficient form for taking advantage of valuable urban land sites...But the skyscraper from the beginning contributed to greatly intensified land speculation and increasing traffic congestion...' (Glaab and Brown, 1967: 146).

The combination of cheap electric power, the telephone, mass car ownership and a major highway construction programme accelerated the suburbanization of American cities in the twentieth century (Jackson, 1985). Between 1920 and 1980, the suburban population grew from 9% to 45% of the national total (Abbott, 1987:7). The automobile began to change the morphology of cities such as Los Angeles, which were shaped by their expanding highway networks (Banham, 1971). Mass ownership of private passenger and commercial vehicles took off in the 1920s, with the number of registered vehicles nearly tripling over the decade. This encouraged a major wave of decentralization in which commerce and industry, in the form of multiple stores and factory estates, followed the movement of population to new residential suburbs (Abbott, 1987: 36–45). Suburbanization accelerated after the Second World War, as urban sprawl gathered pace and edge cities proliferated. Major scale economies were achieved through the integrated development of office parks, shopping malls and residential neighbourhoods, enabling large developers to play a leading role in shaping urban growth (Checkoway, 1980; Weiss, 1987). 'Development gain was reaped on the spatial frontier by acquiring cheap land and making large, one-time, not-easily-reversible investments in infrastructure and buildings' (Heim, 2000: 150).

The influence that transport improvements have exerted on the development of British cities is also apparent, if less dramatic than in the United States. This can be attributed to two factors: as a much smaller country, there were far smaller distances to conquer; and in any case, urbanization was already much further advanced when the major nineteenth century innovations in transport technology were introduced. Investment in a new transport system such as electric streetcars was much more rapid and extensive in an American city such as Boston than it was in a British city such as Leeds, so that it inevitably had a stronger influence on suburban development (Ward, 1964). Nevertheless, several authors have examined the links between transport innovation, industrialization and urbanization in Britain, as manifested through the development of canals (Turnbull, 1987), railways (Kellett, 1969; Simmons, 1986), trams and underground trains (Jackson, 1973; Thompson, 1982).

British urban historians tend to take the view that while new transport networks have stimulated suburban development, it is too simplistic to propose a direct causal link from one to the other (Kellett, 1969: 354–82). The classic US study of transport-led suburban growth by Warner (1962) argued that the development of Boston's electric streetcar network was a crucial catalyst for the accelerating suburban expansion of the city between 1880 and 1900. Railway building similarly preceded the development of several outer London suburbs, with new lines being promoted ahead of suburban house-building by speculative landowners as well as by railway companies (Thompson, 1982). However, UK counter-examples are offered by Simpson (1972), who demonstrated that the western suburbs of Glasgow were already half built when the tramway and railway networks arrived after 1870, and Dyos (1961: 39), who made a similar point about the development of the London suburb of Camberwell during the Victorian era.

The conceptual model of the transport-building cycle presented in Figure 5.5 suggests that the links between transport and building investment can best be viewed as mutually reinforcing – transport improvements facilitate suburban expansion, while the development of new suburbs underwrites the profitability of the network investment. By adopting this perspective, we can endeavour to avoid the charge of technological determinism which Monkkonen (1988: 162) levels at American urban geographers who '...have claimed that the history of transportation has been the backbone of the American city's history'.

Turning points

Moving from the longer to the shorter term, the impact of specific historical events on the urban development cycle comes into sharper focus. To illustrate these impacts, Table 5.6 indicates the historical events which can be associated with particular troughs in the long building cycles of each country, together with the leading property and transport sectors which powered each building boom.

The building cycle troughs tend to be associated either with severe and general economic depressions, often following a financial panic, or with external events, such as wars or the recent oil price shocks, which have induced or exacerbated a building slump. Several depressions of the nineteenth century have been labelled 'Great Depressions', but here that title is reserved for the depression of the early 1930s. The cycle peaks appear to occur towards the end of economic booms, because as noted by Rostow (1948: 53), there is a tendency for 'long-term investment decisions to concentrate in the latter stages of the upswing of the major cycles', when business confidence is well established. Furthermore, once the investment decisions have been made, the long gestation period of development projects means that the peak in building output may be reached after other economic indicators have started to turn down. Such building booms have normally been reinforced by plentiful supplies of cheap credit, often fuelling speculative manias that in some cases have been specifically related to transport investments such as the construction of the canals and railways (Matthews, 1972: 106). A financial crisis has usually followed speculative booms of this type, as happened in 1792/3, 1825, 1847 and 1974/5 in England, and 1836/7, 1856/7, 1892/3, 1926 and 1974/5 in the United States (Kindleberger and Aliber, 2005: 256–65).

Table 5.6   UK and US long building cycle events and leading sectors.

Trough		Event	Peak		Leading sectors
UK	**US**		**UK**	**US**	
			1792		Canals; turnpikes
1798		Revolutionary Wars			
			1805		Industrial
1816		Napoleonic Wars			
			1825		Housing, industrial
1832		Depression			
				1836	Land, canals
	1843	Depression			
			1847		Railways
1856		Crimean War		1856	Railways, housing
	1864	Civil War			
				1871	Railways, industrial
			1876		Housing, industrial
	1878	Depression			
1888		Depression			
				1892	Railways, housing
	1899	Depression			
			1902	1902	Trams, housing
1918	1918	First World War			
				1926	Housing, offices
	1933	Great Depression			
			1937		Housing
				1941	–
1944	1943	Second World War			
			1968		Housing, commercial
				1972	Highways, housing, commercial
	1975	First oil shock			
1981		Second oil shock			
				1985	Offices
			1989		Offices
	1991	Global recession			

Source: Riggleman (1933), Isard (1942), Colean and Newcomb (1952), Gayer et al. (1953), Cairncross and Weber (1956), Kuznets (1961), Gottlieb (1965), Parry Lewis (1965), Aldcroft and Fearon (1972), Feinstein (1976), Feinstein and Pollard (1988), Dow (1998), Gallman (2000), Davis (2004), Kindleberger and Aliber (2005). ONS: NBER, BEA.

A historical example from each country can serve to illustrate how speculative building booms have typically unfolded. Following the end of the Napoleonic Wars, there was a strong upswing in all sectors of the British economy which reached a cycle peak in 1825. 'The prosperity that reached its climax in 1825 has often been referred to as the first truly modern cyclical boom in British economic history' (Gayer et al., 1953: 171). The post-war recovery was founded on expanding exports of manufactured goods from the world's leading industrial economy to markets across the globe. The export-led upswing in national output generated abundant domestic savings which, combined with lower peacetime interest rates, funded a surge in capital market issues which included large volumes of infrastructure stocks for docks, railways and utilities development. The parallel upswing in investment that took off in 1819/20 led to an enormous but short-lived boom in the construction of housing, factories and infrastructure. Buoyant investor optimism fuelled feverish stock market speculation until the bubble burst in the crash and panic of December 1825, when there was such a severe run on the banks that the Bank of England almost ran out of notes. Building investment took a decade to recover (Gayer et al., 1953: 185–92; Parry Lewis, 1965: 33–9; Kindleberger and Aliber, 2005: 95).

As Aaron Sakolski remarks in his preface to *The Great American Land Bubble* (1932) 'Land speculation in the United States has been a national business'. The 1920s boom and bust provides a spectacular example (Heim, 2000: 169–71). Total new construction nearly doubled in the first half of the 1920s, sustained by a combination of the backlog of demand from the First World War, the suburban expansion stimulated by rising automobile ownership and the migration of population to new cities and regions. The growth of specialist financial institutions, such as savings and loan associations, provided a ready supply of mortgage finance. The result was a speculative fever of residential, hotel and office development which reached its height in the famous Florida land boom, marked by the usual mixture of fantasy and fraud (Sakolski, 1932: 331–52). The speculative housing bubble burst in 1926, although non-residential building did not peak until 1929. Vast numbers of building lots were left undeveloped and houses unsold, unleashing negative multiplier effects throughout the economy. Mortgage debt had more than tripled, but most loans were short term and could not be re-financed in the credit crunch that followed the stock market crash of 1929. By 1933, nearly half the nation's home mortgages were in default and new housing starts had dropped by 90% from their 1925/6 peak. The property market collapse played a major role in the Great Depression: its severity intensified the initial downturn, while its persistence helped to prolong the slump. Unlike the United Kingdom, the United States did not enjoy a resurgence in house-building during the 1930s to help to lift the economy out of depression, in part because of the sheer magnitude of the economic shock, and in part because of the uncontrolled nature of the previous building boom. 'By encumbering locationally choice areas with poorly planned neighborhoods, partially completed developments, and diffuse and uncertain ownership, the uncoordinated boom laid the groundwork for a collapse in construction spending, disrupted intermediation and a prolonged depression' (Field, 1992: 803).

A UK building cycle chronology (1785–2005)

Long cycles and major cycles

In this section, we shall examine in more detail the chronology of the urban development cycle in Britain since the late eighteenth century, as it has interacted with the trajectories of population growth, technological change and industrialization. Emphasis is placed on the way in which each technological revolution has been translated into a fresh wave of investment in new infrastructure networks and new types of built structures. The fabric of today's towns and cities reflects this history of urban development, as manifested in the distinctive vintages of buildings which can be observed moving from the Georgian inner city through the Victorian, Edwardian and inter-war suburbs to the post-war satellite towns beyond the urban periphery.

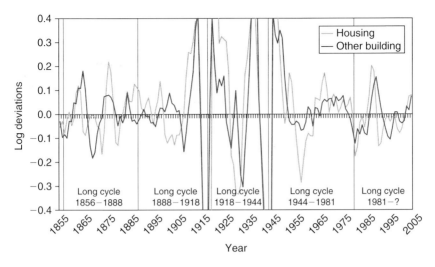

Figure 5.13   Major cycle chronology for UK building (1855–2005).
Source: Cairncross and Weber (1956), Feinstein (1976), Feinstein and Pollard (1988), ONS.

As summarized in Table 5.1, unobserved components modelling has demonstrated that the long cycle in UK building investment, with an average duration of 25 years, can be decomposed into a 30-year long wave and a 12-year major cycle. It is clear both from the spectral analysis and from a comparison of turning points that it is the long wave which dominates the motion of the composite long building cycle. However, the major cycle also imparts a distinctive shorter period rhythm to the fluctuation of building investment. Consequently, while the framework for our historical narrative is provided by the long cycle chronology set out in Table 5.2 and illustrated in Figure 5.9, it is also instructive to introduce the chronologies of the residential and non-residential major cycles which were previously discussed in Chapter 4. These major cycles are displayed in Figure 5.13 and their chronologies set out in Tables 5.7 and 5.8. A reference chronology of 16 major cycles has been identified since 1855, the date from which the component building cycles start. The chronology for total building is missing four of these cycles, through aggregation of divergent component cycles; the residential chronology is missing two cycles and the non-residential chronology three cycles. This explains the variation in the duration of the different major cycles, as estimated by the structural models and confirmed by the turning point chronologies – a total building cycle of 12 years, a residential cycle of 10 years and a non-residential cycle of 11 years.

The first industrial revolution (1785–1856)

By the mid-nineteenth century, Britain had already enjoyed the first phase of an Industrial Revolution which had transformed a predominantly agricultural economy into the world's 'first industrial nation' (Mathias, 1983). Industrialization

Table 5.7   Major cycle turning points for UK housing investment 1855–2005.

Cycle number		Date[a]			Duration (years)		Timing[c]	
T–T	P–P	T	P	Amplitude[b]	T–T	P–P	T	P
1		1857		0.079			−1	
	1		1863	0.119	9			2
2		1866		0.088		6		
	2		1869	0.003	7			
3		1873		0.166		7	−4	
	3		1876	0.219	7			0
4		1880		0.129		11	0	
	4		1887	0.126	15			−3
5								
	5							
6		1895		0.045		11	0	
	6		1898	0.137	9			0
7		1904		0.129		16	+4	
	7		1914	0.395	14			0
8		1918		1.932		7	0	
	8		1921	1.032	13			0
9								
	9							
10		1931		0.335		17	+1	
	10		1938	0.531	13			0
11		1944		1.085		9	0	
	11		1947	0.623	7			0
12		1951		0.039		6		
	12		1953	0.171	7			
13		1958		0.285		15	0	
	13		1968	0.171	12			0
14		1970		0.008		11		
	14		1979	0.070	11			
15		1981		0.176		9	0	
	15		1988	0.202	10			+1
16		1991		0.133		9	+5	
	16		1997	0.011	9			+1
17		2000		0.079		0		
Averages				**0.204**	**10.2**	**10.3**	**+0.4**	**+0.1**

Source: Cairncross and Weber (1956), Feinstein (1976), Feinstein and Pollard (1988), ONS.
[a]T = trough, P = peak; where no dates are shown, that cycle does not appear in the series.
[b]The amplitude is measured as the proportionate deviation of each turning point from the fitted trend, excluding the war years. This is typically a more extreme measure than the stochastic estimate derived with the structural model (see Table A.2).
[c]The cycle leads (+) or lags (−) compare the timing of each turning point with the equivalent turning points in the reference major cycle of total building investment; if no comparison is shown, that turning point does not appear in the reference series.

was achieved through the diffusion of a cluster of fundamental technological innovations, starting in the cotton, coal and iron industries, which generated scale economies that were realized through the progressive mechanization of production and the development of the factory system. Further impetus to growth was

Table 5.8 Major cycle turning points for UK other building investment 1855–2005.

Cycle number		Date[a]		Amplitude[b]	Duration (years)		Timing[c]	
T–T	P–P	T	P		T–T	P–P	T	P
1		1858		0.099			−2	
	1		1865	0.181	11			0
2								
	2							
3		1869		0.183		11	0	
	3		1876	0.081	11			0
4		1880		0.048		8	0	
	4		1884	0.090	8			0
5		1888		0.040		7		
	5		1891	0.021	8			
6		1896		0.052		11	−1	
	6		1902	0.088	12			−4
7		1908		0.156		12	0	
	7		1914	0.429	10			0
8		1918		0.663		6	0	
	8		1920	0.402	10			+1
9		1928		0.142		10	0	
	9		1930	0.098	5			0
10		1933		0.303		9	−1	
	10		1939	0.679	11			−1
11		1944		1.163		7	0	
	11		1946	0.423	14			+1
12								
	12							
13		1958		0.068		30	0	
	13		1976	0.077	23			−8
14								
	14							
15		1981		0.123		14	0	
	15		1990	0.155	15			−1
16		1996		0.106		9	0	
	16		1999	0.008	5			−1
17		2001		0.038			−1	
Averages				**0.164**	**11.0**	**11.2**	**−0.4**	**−1.1**

Source: Cairncross and Weber (1956), Feinstein (1976), Feinstein and Pollard (1988), ONS.
[a]T = trough, P = peak; where no dates are shown, that cycle does not appear in the series.
[b]The amplitude is measured as the proportionate deviation of each turning point from the fitted trend, excluding the war years. This is typically a more extreme measure than the stochastic estimate derived with the structural model (see Table A.2).
[c]The cycle leads (+) or lags (−) compare the timing of each turning point with the equivalent turning points in the reference major cycle of total building investment; if no comparison is shown, that turning point does not appear in the reference series.

provided by investment in the turnpike roads and canals which provided the enabling infrastructure for the first phase of industrialization (Szostak, 1991).

Since only approximate estimates of output and investment growth are available for this period, the manner in which the Industrial Revolution unfolded in Britain remains a matter of vigorous debate among economic historians (Hudson, 1992; Mokyr, 1999). It is clear, however, that there was a fundamental shift in the structure of the British economy between the late eighteenth and mid-nineteenth centuries. The share of agriculture in the national product shrank from 33% in 1801 to 20% by 1851, while the share of the production industries (manufacturing, mining and construction) grew from 23% to 34%. More spectacularly, between 1770 and 1831, the share of industrial output accounted for by the cotton industry is estimated to have multiplied from 3% to 22% (Crafts, 1985: 22), while the first half of the nineteenth century saw a more than fourfold increase in coal output and a more than eightfold increase in the production of iron and steel (Deane and Cole, 1962: 216–25). These leaps in production support the view that Britain truly underwent a technological revolution which transformed every aspect of its economy and society (Landes, 1969).

The Industrial Revolution was accompanied by rapid population growth, providing the supply of labour and the market for consumption goods which industrialization demanded. Wrigley and Schofield (1989: 208–9) estimate that the population of England more than doubled between 1781 and 1851, from 7.0 million to 16.7 million. Urbanization started to gather pace towards the end of the eighteenth century, prompting investment in the buildings and infrastructure which formed the fabric of a whole new generation of industrial towns and cities in the Midlands and North (Langton, 2000). By the middle of the nineteenth century, around 50% of the population was living in towns and cities, and England was experiencing the highest level of urbanization in Europe (Wrigley, 2004: 88–9). One graphic example of the pace and increasing intensity of urbanization is provided by Manchester, the locational and operational heart of the cotton industry: between 1774 and 1831 its population increased nearly eightfold, from 29,000 to 228,000, while its housing stock grew by a factor of six (Vigier, 1970: 139).

Between 1785 and 1856, four clear urban development cycles have been identified, peaking in 1792, 1805, 1825 and 1847, with an intermediate major cycle peak in 1836 (see Figure 5.8 and Table 5.2). Parry Lewis (1965: 12–39) observes that a common feature of these building cycles was a clear inverse relationship with movements in interest rates: cheap credit triggered speculative building booms, while sharp increases in the cost of money precipitated building slumps. There were, however, marked regional differences in the building cycle, according to structural variations in the pattern of industrial growth. The volatility of the house-building cycle was exacerbated by the organizational structure of the building industry. Large numbers of small local firms undertook precariously financed speculative developments to supply rapidly growing urban markets that swung between shortage and glut (Rodger, 1989: 20–2).

A building cycle chronology for the period can be constructed as follows. The first great wave of canal construction occurred during the late 1760s and 1770s, and was followed by the 'canal mania' of the 1790s (Hadfield, 1974: 107–31). Investment in the buildings and machinery used in cotton and iron manufacture took off at the start of the nineteenth century, but was checked by outbreak of the Napoleonic Wars. Because the war effort was in part funded by the sale of government securities, rising interest rates tended to 'crowd out' domestic investment, particularly building investment (Williamson, 1984). Though the extent of the crowding out is disputed (Hudson, 1992: 58–61), it is clear that investment resumed at an intensified rate after the wars were over. As we saw in the previous section, the mid-1820s building boom included both housing and industrial infrastructure (Gayer et al., 1953: 186), and was followed by investment booms in the cotton, coal, iron and railway industries during the 1830s. The 'railway mania' of 1845–7 created a massive construction boom which at its peak accounted for as much as half of all UK domestic capital formation, and employed a quarter of a million men in laying nearly 6,500 miles of track (Deane and Cole, 1962: 231; Gourvish, 1988: 58–67).

The second industrial revolution (1856–88)

The second phase of the Industrial Revolution was the age of steam power. This general purpose technology was associated with the rapid spread of the railway network, the expansion of coal mining and metal manufacture and the establishment of heavy engineering industries such as machine tools and shipbuilding. The interlinkages between these growth industries provided a further powerful impetus to technological innovation, creating significant scale economies within the leading sectors and agglomeration economies in the emerging industrial regions. By stimulating export demand, the expansion of world trade acted as an engine of growth for Britain's manufacturing industry and for its capital markets based in London. However, other nations were beginning to catch up with Britain as they, in turn, embarked on industrialization (Bairoch, 1982).

During the second half of the nineteenth century, population in Britain continued to increase rapidly, from 20.9 million to 37.1 million, at an average rate of 1.2% per annum compared with 1.4% in the first half of the century (Mitchell, 1988: 12–13). The long-run rate of growth of the national product continued at around 2.0% per annum, similar to the estimated rate for the first half of the century (Crafts, 1985: 45). The share of agriculture contracted further, from 20% in 1851 to just 7% in 1901, while the share of the production industries as a whole increased from 34% to 40% and the output of the metal and engineering industries more than quadrupled (Feinstein, 1976: 114). In 1851, there were some 6,270 miles of railway track in use, and by 1901 this had tripled to 18,870 miles (Mitchell, 1988: 541). Though not approaching the peak of activity reached in the mid-1840s, there was a further railway building boom between 1862 and 1866 which accounted for one-third of all UK domestic investment (Gourvish, 1988: 58–67).

The pace of urbanization accelerated. By 1891, the urban share of population in England and Wales reached 72%, some 40% lived in the six largest conurbations (Hall et al., 1973, vol. 1: 61–4) and there were 23 towns outside London with a population of 100,000 or more, whereas at the beginning of the century there had been none (Briggs, 1968: 59). The production requirements of manufacturing industry were a key influence on the form and location of the new industrial towns and cities (Reeder and Rodger, 2000). The scale economies achieved through factory production led to the establishment of major industrial centres like Glasgow, Sheffield and Birmingham in key locations such as estuaries, coalfields and railway interchanges which offered the lowest costs of raw material assembly and the easiest access to domestic and overseas markets. These manufacturing centres attracted a rapidly growing industrial workforce, which migrated in from the countryside to be accommodated in densely packed developments of working-class housing

(Daunton, 1983). The railway network provided a crucial catalyst for urban development in the second half of the nineteenth century, helping to determine the compact form of the new industrial cities and the directions for suburban expansion around established cities such as London (Kellett, 1969; Simmons, 1986).

This long cycle in total building investment starts from a trough in 1856, reaches a peak in 1876 and terminates in an 1888 trough. Four residential and three non-residential major cycles are contained within the long cycle, with the 1858–69 non-residential cycle and the 1873–80 residential cycle being particularly pronounced. The strong peak in non-residential building investment in 1865 reflects the impact of the 1860s railway boom, while the subsequent 1876 major cycle peaks in both sectors of building reinforce the crest of the long cycle and mark the climax of the mid-Victorian building boom (Weber, 1955: 112; Parry Lewis, 1965: 106–39). The supply of credit continued to influence the movement of the building cycle in the later nineteenth century, but it was a less dominant factor than in the first half of the century (Habakkuk, 1962b). The downswing of the long building cycle during the 1880s was a manifestation of the wider depression that gripped the British economy, and was marked by widespread bankruptcies and low levels of output in the building industry (Rodger, 1989: 52).

The age of electricity (1888–1918)

This era was dominated by the emergence of electric power as the new general purpose technology. The spread of the electricity transmission network encouraged a new phase of industrial development based on steel, chemicals, electrical engineering and automobiles. However, the pace of industrial growth in Britain was slowing, as leadership in the new technologies passed to the United States and Germany. Over the whole period, the rate of UK population growth dropped from 1.2% to 0.9% per annum, while output growth dipped from around 2.0% to 1.5%; the share of production industries in the national product peaked at around 46%, and was now matched by the share of services which had moved up to 47% by 1920 (Feinstein, 1976).

The Late Victorian and Edwardian age saw a decisive shift from urbanization towards suburbanization across Britain's towns and cities. The steam railway network had already facilitated residential decentralization with the construction of the first generation of 'railway suburbs'. The installation of telegraph networks alongside railway lines had similarly encouraged the establishment of geographically more dispersed business enterprises, and this impetus was intensified by the subsequent spread of the telephone network (Hall and Preston, 1988: 37–54). The technological key to a more universal wave of suburbanization at the start of the twentieth century was another infrastructure revolution, as mass transit systems based on electric trains and trams were installed across the country (Barker, 1988: 155–60). These networks were instrumental in reducing the density and improving the quality of urban development, compared to the crowded conditions prevailing in most industrial inner cities. New and more spacious suburbs were constructed, centred on public transport nodes that allowed workers to commute directly to their city centre jobs (Jackson, 1973: 35–51).

Starting from the 1888 long cycle trough, there was a strong upswing in building investment during the 1890s, encouraged by a combination of cheap money and rising rents which boosted development profitability (Parry Lewis, 1965: 160). Favourable market conditions were reinforced by the expansion of the transport network, which created large-scale development opportunities on land previously in rural use. This phase of suburban development culminated in the Edwardian building boom which is marked by the long cycle peak of 1902 (Saul, 1962). This building boom was supported by strong growth in the effective demand for housing resulting from a sustained period of rising real wages (Ashworth, 1960: 200). The subsequent house-building slump in the decade leading up to the First World War was more severe than the downswing in non-residential building, creating a long cycle trough of unparalleled severity. Two residential and three non-residential major cycles are contained within this long cycle, mostly running out of phase. However, the run-up to the First World War coordinated the two major building cycles, so that they both exhibit strong 1914 peaks, followed by exceptionally severe 1918 troughs. The long cycle trough in 1918 combines both major cycle and long wave troughs, because the structural model apportions the wartime collapse in building activity between the two cyclical components.

During these decades, there was growing specialization in the form and provision of industrial and commercial buildings, in response to changing economic conditions and new technological opportunities (Scott, 2000). The structure of the built environment became more differentiated, as custom-built offices and shops clustered in city centres, while factories migrated to the urban periphery. An increasingly sophisticated property development industry evolved, as financial institutions extended development loans, specialist property companies were established and the building sector became more concentrated. Developers began to employ technologies imported from the United States and France to construct a more advanced generation of buildings to satisfy the demands of manufacturing, retailing and office-based service companies that were growing in size and becoming more complex and diversified in their operations. In particular, the introduction of steel-framed and reinforced concrete structures incorporating electric lifts and telephone networks made it possible to build office towers, department stores and multi-storey factories on a scale never previously realized in Britain (Bowley, 1966: 3–35). The scale as well as the extent of the urban fabric was being transformed.

Inter-war turbulence (1918–44)

The inter-war period laid the foundations of the automobile age, based on the mass production of motor vehicles in large assembly-line plants using techniques and forms of industrial organization pioneered in the United States. Britain suffered two severe recessions, in 1920/21 and 1930/31 (Dow, 1998: 133–233), which depressed the average rate of output growth to only 1.4%. During the 1920/21 recession, caused principally by the run-down of the war economy, industrial output fell by nearly 20%. The Great Depression, triggered by the stock market crash and subsequent banking failures in the United States, caused another fall in industrial output of over 10% between 1929 and 1932 (Feinstein, 1976: 112). During the 1930s, the establishment of a new generation of lighter consumer goods industries produced a decisive shift in the regional location of manufacturing, from the traditional heavy industrial areas in the North to new concentrations of light industry in the Midlands and South (Pollard, 1983: 76–82).

It was during the inter-war period that the transition from an industrial to a service-based economy became apparent in the United Kingdom: the share of production industries in the national product fell from 46% to 41% by 1938, while the services share further increased from 47% to 55%. This was the era when market services began to be industrialized through the introduction of early forms of information technology, such as data processing machinery, and the reorganization of service delivery away from low volume, high margin customization towards high volume, low margin standardization. However, as was the case in the new consumer goods industries, Britain lagged behind the United States in introducing such innovations, with the result that it lost the productivity advantage in service industries it had enjoyed over its international competitors since the mid-nineteenth century (Broadberry, 2006).

The long cycle in building investment which spans this turbulent inter-war period is defined by the two wartime troughs, separated by an intervening aggregate peak in 1937. Within this long cycle, there are two extremely volatile major cycles in residential and non-residential building, running in phase with peaks in 1920/1 and 1938/9, together with a weak intermediate cycle in non-residential building that peaks in 1930. Both sectors exhibit a severe major cycle trough in 1931–3, caused by the shock of the Great Depression. The slump caused by the Second World War has a similar impact to that generated by the First World War. Simultaneous troughs appear in both the major cycles and long waves in 1944, comparable to those produced in 1918, though this time the downturn in non-residential building is as severe as that in residential building.

Population growth continued to slow in the inter-war period, down to a rate of only 0.5% per annum, while the urban share of total population stabilized at around 80% and the proportion living in the six largest English conurbations levelled out at around 41%. Infrastructure investment in the road and telephone networks, together with the electrification of suburban railway lines, encouraged both a fresh wave of suburban housing-building and the decentralization of new light industries based on electric power, which had less need for the mass transport of bulky raw materials and finished products. The inter-war building boom benefited particularly from the growth of motor transport for both goods and passengers (Barker and Savage, 1974: 160–81), encouraging the spread of lower density housing estates, shopping parades, factories and industrial estates along the new arterial roads radiating out from the major cities, particularly London (Scott, 2001).

Strong levels of house-building were maintained through much of the 1930s by the favourable combination of a high rate of net household formation, rising real incomes for those in work, falling costs of building materials and, most importantly, low interest rates (Richardson and Aldcroft, 1968; Broadberry, 1987). This expansion in housing output was achieved principally by a new generation of building firms, established in response to the advantageous market conditions. The outcome was that house-building accounted for the largest share (36%) of total domestic investment between 1932 and 1937 (Feinstein, 1976: 86). There is, therefore, some justification for the argument that the inter-war housing boom helped to lead the British economy out of the Great Depression (Richardson and Aldcroft, 1968: 269).

The post-war consumer boom (1944–81)

The upswing of the post-war boom generated a sustained rise in household incomes, creating a widespread demand for mass-produced consumer goods, based on durables such as motor vehicles and new technologies such as electronics, synthetic materials and pharmaceuticals. After the turbulence of the inter-war years, average output growth over the whole 1944–81 period returned to the same 2.0% per annum rate which had prevailed up until the First World War. However, this average is depressed by the adjustment to a peacetime economy in the immediate post-war years, and by the impact of the two oil price shocks which triggered the recessions of 1974/5 and 1980/1 (Dow, 1998: 273–320). Over the 25 years starting in 1948 and ending with the 1973 boom, the UK economy achieved average growth rates of 3.0% in GDP and 2.6% in output per worker, higher than in any equivalent period since the mid-nineteenth century (Kitson, 2004).

Despite the expansion of the new consumer goods industries, British firms in these sectors were still less successful at innovation and mass production than their overseas competitors (Broadberry, 1997), while the old heavy industries which had been in the vanguard of the Industrial Revolution were in terminal decline. The result was the accelerating de-industrialization of the British economy (Blackaby, 1978), such that the share of manufacturing in UK output shrank from around 34% in the early post-war years to 26% by 1981, while the output share of services rose to 58%. The growth of the new service economy (Gershuny and Miles, 1983) was led by major investments in public services, such as health and education, as part of the establishment of the post-war Welfare State, and by the burgeoning of private sector financial and business services in response to the diversification and specialization occurring within all sectors of the economy. Financial, professional and business services were internationally the most competitive of Britain's service industries (Broadberry, 2006: 29–30), which helps to explain why, having accounted for an unchanging 6% of the national product up until the mid-1960s, they then began a phase of rapid expansion that doubled their share to 12% by 1981.

The explosion of car ownership during the post-war boom led to a major programme of motorway construction, starting at the end of the 1950s (Bagwell, 1988: 353–67). This new transport revolution facilitated another vigorous wave of urban decentralization (Hall et al., 1973). In the search for better housing and social facilities, more mobile households deserted the major cities for the smaller satellite towns surrounding them, leaving behind a decaying infrastructure and obsolete housing stock that required wholesale regeneration. The out-migration from the cities was reinforced by planning policies such as the development of new towns and the imposition of green belts around the major metropolitan areas. The result was that the proportion of the population living in the six largest English conurbations fell from 39% in 1951 to 32% by 1981. The new consumer goods and service industries were equally footloose, with many seeking development sites on the motorway network which located them close to growing centres of population that provided them with both their workforce and their customer base.

The post-war long cycle in building investment begins at the end of the Second World War, peaks in 1968 and terminates in the 1981 recession. Due to the relative stability of economic growth during this period, both the long cycles and the major cycles in building are considerably more subdued than they are in the inter-war years, reverting to fluctuations of comparable volatility to those exhibited by the cycles prior to the First World War. Whilst four major cycles in house-building can be identified within the long cycle, only two major cycles in non-residential building are apparent. Vipond (1969) demonstrated that these post-war fluctuations in house-building moved pro-cyclically with the business cycle in national output, and were again closely related to the availability of credit. After more than two decades of demand-led building investment, the post-war long cycle culminated in a speculative development boom in 1972/3 which was ended suddenly and dramatically by the first OPEC recession of 1974/5. There was then a sharp decline in development activity down into the trough of the second OPEC recession of 1980/1 that marks the end of this long cycle.

The surge in housing development after the Second World War was initiated by a massive public sector building programme that encompassed the redevelopment of inner city slums, the provision of overspill estates on the urban periphery and the establishment of new towns outside the major conurbations. From the 1960s onwards, the level of house-building was sustained by a growing demand for owner–occupier dwellings as household incomes steadily rose (Short, 1982). The upswing in non-residential building began with the abolition of post-war building controls in the early 1950s, and gathered pace in the 1960s and 1970s with the construction of light industrial and warehousing estates along trunk roads and the commercial redevelopment of city and suburban centres with new office buildings and shopping centres.

The computer age (1981–2008?)

With this long cycle, we enter the era of the computer, the internet and the 'knowledge economy'. What is unique about the new information technologies is that they constitute a general purpose technology which is changing the mode of production of all sectors of the economy, not just the manufacturing sectors which were the principal beneficiaries of previous technological revolutions. In particular, computer technology is generating a fundamental transformation of the service industries that now dominate advanced economies, not only by boosting the productivity of existing service delivery, but also by introducing innovation through the provision of wholly new types of services (Barras, 1990).

In general, the ICT-led productivity resurgence which has been enjoyed in the United States since the mid-1990s (see Chapter 4) has not occurred to the same extent in Europe, where the emergence of the knowledge economy has been markedly slower. However, the United Kingdom has been an exception, exhibiting recent rates of output and productivity growth much closer to American than average EU rates – particularly, in distribution, finance and business services (van Ark et al., 2008). The result has been an accelerating expansion of the UK service sector at the expense of the production industries. Between 1981 and 2004, the share of output contributed by service industries rose from 58% to 70%, while the manufacturing share shrunk further from 26% down to 19%. Led by the City of London, financial and business services were in the vanguard of this service revolution, their share of the national product doubling again between 1981 and 2004, from

12% to 25%. The dynamic provided by these service industries maintained a 2.7% rate of growth in national output, despite the intervention of the early 1990s recession.

Since 1981, there has been another powerful wave of urban decentralization, driven first by the completion of the motorway network and more recently by the universal reach of the internet. British versions of the 'edge city' have been developed around the major conurbations, particularly the area known as M25West on the western periphery of London. There has been a parallel wave of redevelopment designed to regenerate decayed inner areas and attract households and businesses back into the cities (Healey et al., 1992). This investment in urban regeneration seems finally to have halted the flight from the cities: the proportion of the population living in the six largest conurbations levelled out at around 32% between 1981 and 2001.

The latest long cycle in building investment starts in the 1981 recession, and appears to have reached a spectacular finale in the crash of 2008, which is considered further in Chapter 8. Each sector of building exhibits three major cycles within this long cycle, occurring during the 1980s, 1990s and 2000s. The late 1980s cycle generated the second speculative building boom of the post-war period, following that of the early 1970s, with residential building peaking in 1988 and non-residential building in 1990. In both markets, strong economic recovery during the mid-1980s was accompanied by unchecked credit expansion; this generated a growing demand for property which translated into a rapid increase in rents and prices that fed the building upswing. However, by the time the new space was reaching completion towards the end of the decade, rising inflation and interest rates were choking off demand, leading to falling prices, a surge in vacancies, developer bankruptcies and widespread housing repossessions (Muellbauer and Murphy, 1997). As already discussed in Chapter 3, the late 1980s building boom was a global phenomenon, driven by speculative flows of investment from the capital markets, and the subsequent crash was a major contributor to the worldwide recession of the early 1990s (Dow, 1998: 321–63). Following the crash, both sectors of UK building experienced a weaker major cycle during the remainder of the 1990s, followed by a new upswing through to 2005 that marks the onset of the third speculative boom of the post-war period – which came to such an abrupt end in the 2008 crash.

The London building cycle (1714–2005)

At the start of the eighteenth century London was the largest city in Europe; by the mid-nineteenth century it had grown to become the largest city in the world. Central to the urban history of Britain over the past three centuries is London's transformation from mercantile metropolis through industrial and imperial capital to global financial centre.

We are able to trace the development of London over these three centuries by means of two overlapping building series. The first comprises the annual totals of registered deeds of land and building transactions in the County of Middlesex between 1714 and 1900, compiled by Sheppard et al. (1979). This is the building series that was introduced for illustrative purposes in Chapter 1 and used as a case study example in Appendix A to illustrate the application of alternative techniques for trend and cycle analysis. The second series consists of the estimated volume of annual house-building completions in Greater London between 1856 and 2005, which can be compared with an equivalent national series for Great Britain. Though the two datasets are not directly compatible, the earlier transactions series does relate predominantly to house-building, and so broadly complements the later housing completions series. In this section, we start by identifying the long cycles in each building series, examine possible causal influences on construction activity, develop a combined turning point chronology that spans the whole period 1714–2005 and use this chronology as the framework for presenting a short narrative of London's building history since the beginning of the eighteenth century.

Middlesex deeds (1714–1900)

The trajectory of building in London over the two centuries covered by the Middlesex deeds series is illustrated in logarithmic form in Figure 1.1. Structural modelling of this series, as described in detail in Section A.7, identified the following trend and cycles in building activity:

- A one-cycle model of order 1 yields a strong long cycle with a period of 15.9 years, together with a smoothly varying trend that shows clear evidence of a residual long wave (see Table 5.9 and Figure A.5).

Table 5.9   Parameters of London building cycles.[a]

	Dates	Period (years)[c]	Order[d]	Damping factor[d]	Amplitude[d]	Variance[d]	Likelihood ratio[e]
London							
Deeds (1)[b]	1714–1900	15.9**	1	0.904	0.2803	0.0321	43.62**
Deeds (2)[b]	1730–1900	15.2**	1	0.900	0.2416	0.0216	31.45**
House-building	1856–2005	22.8**	2	0.720	0.0869	0.2486	50.74**
Great Britain							
House-building	1856–2005	20.3**	2	0.755	0.3962	0.0799	53.04**

Source: Spensley (1918), Weber (1955), Sheppard et al. (1979), DCLG, GLA.

Note:
Diagnostic statistics for the model residuals show that at the 5% level, the Deeds model satisfies the normality test; the heteroscedasticity test is satisfied by the GB house-building model and the serial correlation test is satisfied by the Deeds model (for a description of the test statistics, see Table A.1).
[a] The parameters relate to long cycles derived from one-cycle models in all cases.
[b] Version 1 of the London Deeds model is without an explanatory variable; the second version includes the Consols yield as the explanatory variable (see Section A.6.4).
[c] The estimated period of each cycle component is checked by spectral analysis of the residuals derived from the detrended series; ** indicates that the spectrum provides strong confirmation about the presence of a cyclical component with the same period as that obtained from the structural model, * indicates weak confirmation.
[d] For definitions of cycle order, damping factor, amplitude and variance, see Section A.7 and Table A.2.
[e] For all but the Deeds (2) model, the likelihood ratio compares the values of the likelihood functions for models, with and without the long cycle; for the Deeds (2) model, the comparison is between one-cycle models, with and without the explanatory variable; ** denotes that the restriction of there being no cycle can be rejected at the 1% level, whereas, * denotes rejection at the 5% level.

- A one-cycle model of order 2 isolates the long wave with a period of 45.1 years, subsuming the long cycle within the upswings and downswings of the long wave.
- With the long wave removed, the growth trend in London building activity shows a slow secular rise from around 1.2% per annum in the first half of the eighteenth century to 2.4% in the second half of the nineteenth century.
- A two-cycle model identifies a separate major cycle of 8.0 years duration within the building long wave, but it is a relatively weak component that does not improve model performance significantly.

The long cycle turning points in the Middlesex deeds series between 1714 and 1900 are illustrated in Figure 5.14 and listed in Table 5.10, together with the duration and proportionate deviation of each cycle, and its timing relative to equivalent turning points in the bond yield cycle. Twelve complete cycles are identified with an average trough-to-trough duration of 14.3 years and an average deviation at the turning points of 0.246. These turning point statistics compare with the fitted cycle period of 15.9 years and amplitude of 0.280 derived from the structural model (see Table 5.9). Nine out of the twelve individual cycles have trough-to-trough periods in the range 15–17 years; the exceptions result from two shorter period cycles, Cycle 5 and Cycle 9, superimposed respectively on the downswing and upswing of longer cycles. If they are removed, the average cycle duration increases to 17.2 years and the average deviation to 0.262 – closer to the values obtained from the structural model.

Exogenous influences on the London building cycle have also been investigated (see Section A.6). Of the two explanatory variables introduced in the previous comparison of UK and US urban development cycles, UK industrial production can be extended back to 1714 and the Consols yield to 1729. There is a cointegrating relationship between the levels of industrial production and London building, and the direction of causality runs from production to building. Both explanatory variables

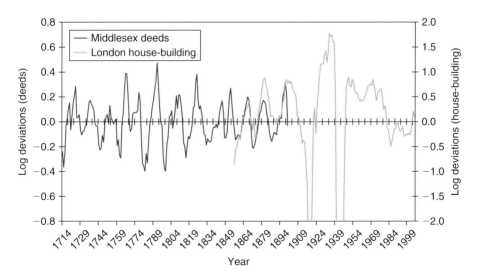

Figure 5.14 London building cycle chronologies (1714–2005).
Source: Spensley (1918), Weber (1955), Sheppard et al. (1979), GLA.

Table 5.10 Long cycle turning points for London building 1714–1900.

Cycle number		Date[a]		Amplitude[b]	Duration (years)		Timing versus Consols[c]	
T–T	P–P	T	P		T–T	P–P	T	P
1		1715		0.365				
	1		1725	0.284	15			
2		1730		0.106		12	0	
	2		1737	0.171	15			0
3		1745		0.227		16	+2	
	3		1753	0.131	17			0
4		1762		0.292		13	0	
	4		1766	0.389	8			+2
5		*1770*		*0.078*		*11*	*0*	
	5		1777	0.235	12			−2
6		1782		0.398		15	−1	
	6		1792	0.472	17			0
7		1799		0.397		18	−1	
	7		1810	0.218	17			−1
8		1816		0.291		15	0	
	8		1825	0.383	17			−1
9		1833		0.186		21	−2	
	9		*1846*	*0.168*	16			−2
10		*1849*		*0.130*		7	−1	
	10		1853	0.268	*8*			−1
11		1857		0.145		14	+9	
	11		1867	0.197	15			+1
12		1872		0.212		13	+2	
	12		1880	0.171	15			+1
13		1887		0.158		18	+1	
	13		1898	0.313				−1
Averages								
All cycles				0.246	14.3	14.4	0.8	−0.3
Excl. cycles 5 T–T and 9 P–P				0.262	17.2	17.3	1.0	0.0

Source: Sheppard et al. (1979), Homer and Sylla (2005).

Note:

Shorter cycles are shown in italics (Cycle 5 T–T and Cycle 9 P–P).

[a]T = trough, P = peak.

[b]The amplitude is measured as the proportionate deviation of each turning point from the fitted trend, excluding the war years. This is typically a more extreme measure than the stochastic estimate derived with the structural model (see Table A.2).

[c]The cycle leads (+) or lags (−) compare the timing of each building cycle turning point with the equivalent inverse turning points in the Consols yield cycle (i.e. building peaks coinciding with yield troughs).

contain strong cyclical components, but only the yield cycle has a significant causal relationship with the building cycle (see Figure A.13). When added as an explanatory variable to the one-cycle building model, industrial production has a significant positive coefficient, but its inclusion does not improve model performance overall. However, inclusion of the bond yield, with a strong negative coefficient, does produce a significant improvement in the performance of the model (the parameters of the long cycle model with and without the bond yield are

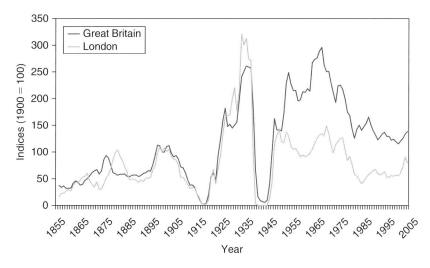

Figure 5.15   House-building in London and Great Britain (1856–2005).
Source: Spensley (1918), Weber (1955), DCLG, GLA.

compared in Table 5.9). With one exception (the 1857 building trough), there is a close correspondence between the turning points in the building and yield cycles (Table 5.10).

   In summary, the level of building in London during the eighteenth and nineteenth centuries exhibits strong long wave and long cycle fluctuations, as well as a weaker major cycle. The secular trend in building activity rose in response to the growing industrialization of the British economy. However, the major cycle in industrial production only became established in the early part of the nineteenth century (Crafts et al., 1989), which helps to explain why it did not act as a consistent influence on the London building cycle over the period as a whole. In contrast, cyclical fluctuations in the government bond yield do seem to have had a strong impact on the building cycle, particularly during the eighteenth and early nineteenth centuries. The inverse relationship between the building and yield cycles supports the argument put forward by Ashton (1959) and Williamson (1984) that during war periods high levels of Government borrowing crowded out the private investor, particularly the private builder. As the price of Consols fell and their yield rose, the rate of interest on commercial loans and mortgages also tended to rise, increasing the cost of borrowing and choking off the level of building activity until interest rates declined to affordable levels once more.

London house-building (1856–2005)

Indices of the annual volumes of house-building completions in Greater London and Great Britain between 1856 and 2005 are illustrated in Figure 5.15. The Great Britain index has been created from the series published by Weber (1955) covering the years up to 1945, and extended forward to 2005 using government statistical sources (DCLG). For the years up to 1937, the London index is similarly derived from Weber (1955), who in turn draws on Spensley (1918) for the years 1871–1916. From 1945 to 2005, the data are from Central Government (DCLG) and Greater London Authority (GLA) sources, with annual values for the years 1945–55 scaled up from data for the smaller London County Council (LCC) area. Missing London values for the war years (1917–19 and 1938–44) have been interpolated by scaling down from the national series.

Structural modelling of the log-transformed indices has identified the following trends and cycles in national and metropolitan house-building since the mid-nineteenth century:

- One-cycle models identify strong long cycles with a period of 22.8 years in London and 20.3 years in Great Britain (Table 5.9).
- The London and national cycles are strongly correlated, with a peak unlagged cross-correlation coefficient of 0.888.
- Almost constant trend rates of house-building growth are derived in both models, with the Greater London growth rate of 0.4% per annum, averaging under half the national rate of 1.0%, as new development has decentralized beyond the metropolitan boundary.
- Two-cycle models offer weak evidence that the long house-building cycle can be split into a major cycle and long wave, but at neither national nor city level is the decomposition significant.
- Neither UK industrial production nor the Consols yield improve the performance of either model over the estimation period 1856–2005.

The turning points of the London house-building cycle between 1856 and 2005 are illustrated in Figure 5.14 and listed in Table 5.11, together with its timing relative to the national cycle. Six complete long cycles are identified with an average trough-to-trough duration of 22.4 years, close to the period estimated by the structural model. The relative phasing of individual turning points shows that the high cross-correlation between the metropolitan and national cycles conceals some important divergences. During most of the second half of the nineteenth century, the two cycles moved out of phase, only converging in the building trough of 1890. The two World Wars imposed greater convergence on their phasing during the first half of the twentieth century, though the inter-war housing boom was even stronger in London than in the country as a whole. In the post-war period, the two cycles have drifted apart again, with the London cycle tending to lag the national cycle since the late 1950s.

Available data on the operation of the London housing market in the late nineteenth century throws some light on the formation of the house-building cycle. For the period 1871–1915, covering the late Victorian and Edwardian cycles, Spensley (1918) documented the lagged inverse relationship between the proportion of the London dwelling stock that was vacant and subsequent levels of house-building. Falling levels of vacancy caused rents to rise, making new building more profitable, thereby triggering a building upswing (Figure 5.16). The first recorded vacancy trough in 1876 led to a peak in building completions 4–5 years later in 1880/1; in

Table 5.11   Long cycle turning points for London house-building 1856–2005.

Cycle number		Date[a]			Duration (years)		Timing[c]	
T–T	P–P	T	P	Amplitude[b]	T–T	P–P	T	P
	1		1868	0.399				
1		1873		0.304		13	−12	
	2		1881	0.886	17			−5
2		1890		0.026		18	0	
	3		1899	0.852	28			−1
3		1918		3.371		35	0	
	4		1934	1.778	26			+2
4		1944		5.863		16	0	
	5		1950	0.898	17			+4
5		1961		0.407		20	−3	
	6		1970	0.853	24			−2
6		1985		0.498			−3	
Averages				**0.690**	**22.4**	**20.4**	**−3.0**	**−0.4**

Source: Spensley (1918), Weber (1955), Sheppard et al. (1979), DCLG, GLA.
[a] T = trough, P = peak.
[b] The amplitude is measured as the proportionate deviation of each turning point from the fitted trend, excluding the war years. This is typically a more extreme measure than the stochastic estimate derived with the structural model (see Table A.2).
[c] The cycle leads (+) or lags (−) compare the timing of each component turning point with the equivalent turning points in the reference long cycle of GB house-building.

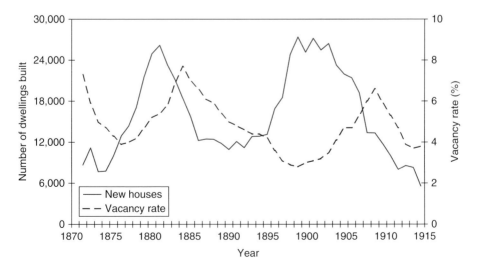

Figure 5.16   London house-building and vacancy cycles (1871–1915).
Source: Spensley (1918).

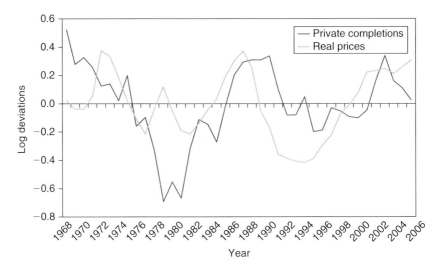

Figure 5.17   London house-building and price cycles (1968–2007).
Source: Nationwide, GLA, ONS.

contrast, the second vacancy trough in 1898/9 created a more contemporaneous building peak that lasted from 1899 to 1903.

Since the late 1960s, a similar lagged relationship can be observed between fluctuations in London house prices and private building completions, measured as deviations around their logarithmic trends (Figure 5.17). Real house prices grew at an average rate of 3% per annum over the period, in excess of the 1.9% trend rate of growth in the private sector completions, which is consistent with the long-term tendency for the price of dwellings to rise relative to the prices of other investment goods and to the general price level (see Chapter 4). When real prices peaked in 1972, the volume of private completions was already falling, but the subsequent drop in prices over the five years to 1977 triggered a much more severe building slump that terminated in a deep trough between 1979 and 1981. The short-lived rise in prices from 1977 to 1979 initiated the first stage of a building recovery at the start of the 1980s, while the strong upswing in prices between 1982 and 1988 precipitated the surge in building that culminated in the extended 1988–91 boom. The subsequent collapse in prices from 1988 to 1992 was more severe than the 1972–7 fall, but nevertheless it induced a milder building slump during the first half of the 1990s than that of the late 1970s. Similarly, the sustained recovery in prices from 1996 generated a quite feeble and short-lived building response that reached a peak in 2004 when prices were considerably above trend and still rising. Clearly, the response of private sector house-building in London to changes in the price level has not been consistent over the past 40 years. The price elasticity of supply appears to have weakened markedly since the start of the 1990s, reflecting the increasing difficulty faced by house-builders when trying to obtain planning permission and community support for new developments within the already densely developed metropolitan area (Meen, 1996).

A London building cycle chronology

The overlap between the Middlesex deeds cycle and the London house-building cycle is reasonably consistent, as illustrated in Figure 5.14 and Tables 5.10 and 5.11. A composite chronology can therefore be constructed using the troughs in the deeds cycle up to 1857 and the house-building troughs thereafter. The chronology provides a narrative framework for summarizing London's building history since the beginning of the eighteenth century, following the thread laid down by Sheppard et al. (1979). Two recent histories of London by Porter (1994) and Inwood (1998) offer a helpful background to this story; Ball and Sunderland (2001) analyse the economic development of the metropolis in the nineteenth century; Summerson (1978), Olsen (1976) and Jackson (1973) describe the building of the city during the eighteenth, nineteenth and twentieth centuries respectively; Barker and Robbins (1963, 1974) provide an exhaustive history of London Transport since the early nineteenth century.

1715–30

The feverish pace of development in both the City and West End during the 1660s to 1680s (see Chapter 1) led to over-supply and a building lull in the 1690s and 1700s. The ending of the Wars of Spanish Succession in 1713 and the founding of the Hanoverian dynasty a year later were catalysts for a phase of intensive building in the 1720s, as population increased and the city pushed westwards. At its peak in 1725, this building boom caused Daniel Defoe to comment on 'an amazing Scene of new Foundations, not of Houses only, but as I might say of new Cities, New Towns, new Squares, and fine Buildings, the like of which no City, no Town, nay, no Place in the World can shew' (Defoe, 1929: 97).

1730–45

High levels of building continued into the 1730s, with another peak in 1737. However, modest economic and population growth in Britain during the first quarter of the eighteenth century had given way to stagnation in the second quarter (Deane and Cole, 1962: 61). This created a housing over-supply in London, with high levels of vacancy bringing building to a halt. It was reported in 1739 that 'at least fifteen hundred houses now uninhabited in St Martin's and other adjacent Parishes will be rebuilt' (Summerson, 1978: 111).

1745–62

Building levels remained relatively low throughout the later 1740s and the 1750s. The cycle began with a severe trough in the period 1745–8, when the Government was engaged in war with France while at the same time putting down the Jacobite Rebellion in Scotland, precipitating a financial crisis which placed tight restrictions on the supply of credit. A second slump occurred in 1759–62, when another period of war with France (the Seven Years War) combined with bad domestic harvests to cause a new financial crisis, with the yield on Consols reaching a peak of 4.3%.

1762–82

The Peace of Paris in 1763 precipitated a strong 20-year building boom in London, fed by revived population and economic growth in second half of the century.

This launched the 'golden age' of Georgian building, when elegant districts were developed on the great aristocratic estates in the West End of the capital, encouraged by government planning and investment in public buildings, road improvements and bridge construction (Summerson, 1978). The boom peaked quickly in 1766–7, as interest rates fell to 3.3%, and the exceptional pace of construction activity is attested by several contemporaries: the Morning Chronicle in 1764 referred to 'the many piles of new buildings that are daily arising in the metropolis' (Ashton, 1959: 98). Continuing low interest rates sustained building at a high level for another decade, until the American War of Independence forced a prolonged downturn, starting in 1778, as Government demand for war finance forced interest rates up to over 5%, once more severely restricting the supply of private loan capital.

1782–99

The building recession between 1780 and 1784 was especially severe because it coincided with a sustained period of exceptionally high interest rates. Following the end of the American War in 1783, the Consols yield fell sharply from a peak of 5.4%, leading the building cycle into an upswing which culminated in a feverish peak in 1792, when interest rates bottomed out at 3.3% (Ashton, 1959: 101–2). This new phase in the development of London was relatively short lived, however, as Britain's entry into the Revolutionary Wars with France in the following year led to renewed credit tightening. The yield on Consols climbed to an all-time high of 5.9% in 1797/8, plunging the building cycle into a second deep recession in 1798–9.

1799–1816

By the start of the nineteenth century, the population of London had grown to 1.1 million, amounting to 12% of the England and Wales total. In partial contradiction to Summerson (1978: 154), building in London does not appear to have remained depressed throughout the long period of war with France. The lull between the Revolutionary and Napoleonic Wars at the start of the century helped to stimulate a new building upswing, fed by a combination of accelerating population growth, the onset of industrialization, rising real wages and some easing of the credit supply (Parry Lewis, 1965: 25–6). From the boom years of 1808–11, the cycle downswing led to another trough in 1816, as credit supply again grew tighter because high deficit spending by the Government towards the end of the war pushed interest rates back up to 5% (Matthews, 1972: 111).

1816–33

After the war, the pent-up demand created by continued strong population growth fuelled the Regency building boom that peaked in 1824/5. As previously noted, this building boom formed part of a wider speculative boom that gripped the whole economy. London enjoyed a new wave of development centred on the redesign of the West End by John Nash, the most comprehensive exercise in planned urban redevelopment ever attempted in London. Speculative developers such as Thomas Cubitt built new residential estates to the north and west in areas such as Bloomsbury, St John's Wood, Belgravia and Pimlico (Summerson, 1978: 177–97), and began the development of suburbs south of the Thames (Dyos, 1961). Following the Regency boom, building in London fell once more into a severe slump, with population growth slowing and the economy depressed, so that the new supply created in the 1820s outstripped subsequent demand. 'Many builders who started in the boom years of 1817–25 went under in the severe slump of 1826–32, when... London brick production fell to a sixth of its 1825 peak' (Inwood, 1998: 574).

1833–57

The recession in London's building activity lasted from 1833 to 1837. Building recovery during the 1840s was assisted by a strong upswing in the UK industrial cycle powered by the railway boom. The building cycle upswing was interrupted by the financial crisis of 1847, which led to widespread bankruptcies and loss of business confidence (Gayer et al., 1953: 333). However, plentiful supplies of credit fuelled a rapid recovery after 1849, sustaining the upswing through to the next peak in 1853. The subsequent slowdown to 1857 reflects the effect of the Crimean War in tightening credit supply again. There was a strong wave of speculative house-building in London during the late 1840s and 1850s which drove a new phase of metropolitan expansion (Parry Lewis, 1965: 85–7). This expansion was linked to two transport innovations in the 1830s and 1840s: the introduction of the horse omnibus (Barker, 1980: 81), and the first wave of railway construction (Kellett, 1969: 244–83). By 1851, London had grown to be the world's largest city, with a population of 2.7 million, some 15% of the national total.

1857–73

A second wave of railway building took place in London during the 1860s, as the mainline network expanded and the first underground lines in the world were built, creating the infrastructure for the next stage in the intensification and extension of London's development (Kellett, 1969: 365–82). This involved both suburban expansion, as house-building followed the new rail routes out of the city, and redevelopment of the central area, replacing overcrowded housing with new commercial buildings to accommodate its burgeoning commuter workforce (Waller, 1983: 28). The progressive extension of the railway network acted as a transmission mechanism by which this and the two subsequent building booms were communicated to the outer suburbs of London (Jahn, 1982). During the 1860s '...London was more excavated, more cut about, more rebuilt and more extended than at any time in its previous history' (Summerson, 1973: 7). Building activity peaked in 1867/8, then turned down ahead of the rest of the country, as the financial crisis caused by the collapse of bankers Overend, Gurney & Co. in 1866 brought London's railway boom to an abrupt halt. The expansion of the railways stalled, fares rose, housing vacancy increased and rents fell, causing a new slump in building (Parry Lewis, 1965: 136).

1873–90

The London house-building recession at the start of the 1870s was short lived, and the remainder of the 1870s saw another cyclical recovery, stronger than that of the 1860s, which peaked in 1880/1 when the rest of the country had already entered a long building trough (Spensley, 1918). This metropolitan cycle was fuelled by further rapid growth in commuting from suburban homes to city centre workplaces as a result of two transport innovations: more frequent and cheaper services on the established rail network (Kellett, 1969: 178–97) and a new network of horse-drawn trams introduced in the 1870s (Barker and Robbins, 1963: 98–104). During this boom, speculative builders played a crucial role, operating on a larger scale than hitherto in London (Dyos, 1961: 125). The result was widespread over-supply of housing by the early 1880s, leading to a repeat of the market conditions which had prevailed a decade or more earlier. Vacancy rose to a new peak in 1884, rents fell and many development schemes were abandoned (Parry Lewis, 1965: 137). In the words of a contemporary observer in 1885 'An array of unoccupied houses meets the eye in all directions…and even, where some few of the newest buildings have recently succeeded in finding tenants, at greatly reduced rentals' (Dyos, 1961: 82).

1890–1918

Accelerating growth drove the population of the metropolis to 6.6 million by the turn of the century, raising its share of the national total to a peak of 20% which was maintained up until the Second World War. The final building recession of the Victorian era lasted from 1886 to 1895, during which period the London cycle converged with the national cycle. A rapid upswing then led into the Edwardian building boom which lasted from 1898 to 1903, to be followed by a long downswing which terminated in the collapse of house-building at the onset of the First World War. The cause of the downswing has been attributed to weaker demand, resulting from rising prices, falling incomes, a slowdown in household formation and increased emigration (Parry Lewis, 1965: 207). During this cycle, a new outward wave of suburban expansion in London was unleashed by another transport revolution, involving the electrification of existing underground lines and tramways, the construction of new tube lines and the introduction of the first motor buses (Barker and Robbins, 1974). The new suburbs were developed at lower densities than their Victorian predecessors, through the construction of that archetypal dwelling – the Edwardian villa (Jackson, 1973: 44).

1918–44

The inter-war housing boom reached dramatic heights in London. Over the decade 1928–37, nearly 600,000 dwellings were completed in the metropolis, amounting to 22% of the national total, compared to a long-run average of 12% since the mid-nineteenth century. This unprecedented level of building was caused by two factors: the favourable market conditions for private developers mentioned in the previous section, and the obligation placed on local authorities by Act of Parliament in 1919 to provide low-rent housing in their areas. The resultant housing boom, combined with the outward extension of the underground electric train, tram and bus networks, fuelled an accelerated rate of suburban expansion. The inter-war housing estates of 'metro-land' dominate the landscape of Outer London to this day (Jackson, 1973). Accompanying this wave of suburban house-building was the construction of large numbers of factories and industrial estates on the urban periphery, particularly along the arterial roads leading out to the west. Over 80% of the large factories built in Britain between 1932 and 1937 were located in the Greater London area, as the focus of industrial activity in the national economy shifted from north to south (Richardson and Aldcroft, 1968: 308).

1944–61

Second World War bombing destroyed over 100,000 dwellings in London, and rendered another 1.3 million in need of repair (Inwood, 1998: 823). Private building was at a virtual standstill in the aftermath of the war, due to shortages of labour and materials and tight government controls. The massive demand for repair and rebuilding could only be met by the public sector. Between 1945 and 1960, nearly 400,000 dwellings were constructed in Greater London, over 70% by local authorities. Many of these schemes involved the comprehensive redevelopment of run-down inner city areas, replacing terraced housing with tower blocks clustered in high density estates. Within 20 years, many of these estates had degenerated into a new generation of slums. Despite the rebuilding, the population of London began to decline, both in absolute terms and as a proportion of the national total. It fell from a peak of 8.3 million in 1951 to 7.5 million by 1971, causing its national share to drop from 19.1% to 15.2%. The shrinkage in population was associated with a parallel decline in manufacturing industry, attributable to a weakening of the agglomeration economies which had previously driven metropolitan growth (Crampton and Evans, 1992). Both households and firms were moving out of Greater London to locate in dormitory settlements and new towns beyond the green belt (Coppock and Prince, 1964).

1961–85

During the two decades from 1961 to 1980, local authorities continued to be the main developers of new housing in London, completing on average nearly 20,000 dwellings a year and maintaining their share of total completions at close to 70%. However, the final stage of this cycle witnessed a collapse in total house-building because of the decision by the Conservative government elected in 1979 to cease further funding of local authority housing development (Inwood, 1998: 888). By 1985, the annual public sector contribution had dropped to under 3,000, creating a trough in total completions which marked the lowest point in the London house-building cycle since the late 1880s/early1890s, leaving aside the exceptional years around the two World Wars. The collapse of house-building highlighted the rapid growth of private sector investment in the redevelopment of Central London and suburban centres with new office blocks and shopping centres. The renewal and expansion of the commercial building stock provided the infrastructure to support the service industries which now dominate the metropolitan economy, as London has evolved into a global financial centre (Frost and Spence, 1993). Between 1972 and 2006, a loss of 777,000 manufacturing jobs in Greater London was offset by an increase of 824,000 in service employment, over 80% of which was concentrated in the financial and business services sectors.

1985–2008?

The population of Greater London stabilized at close to 7.7 million between 1981 and 1991, around 15% of the national total, then climbed again to 8.3 million by 2001, as higher density redevelopment by private sector builders and housing associations expanded the metropolitan housing stock once more. The commercial redevelopment of Central London has increased in both intensity and volatility, as typified by the spectacular office-building boom of the late 1980s. Meanwhile, the terminal decline of the city's traditional manufacturing industries has been offset by the development of a large growth pole of high-tech industries located on business parks in the M25West region – outside the Greater London boundary, but very much part of the metropolitan economy.

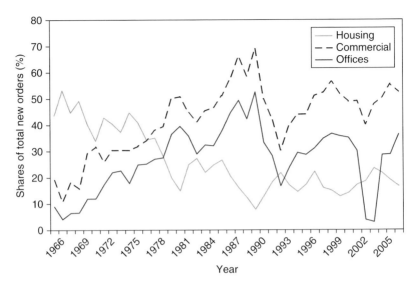

Figure 5.18   Sector shares of London building (1966–2007).
Source: ONS

Looking back over the past 50 years, the focus of building activity in Greater London has moved progressively away from housing towards commercial development, as the shares of the two sectors in the total value of building new orders have been reversed (Figure 5.18). In the mid-1960s, housing accounted for as much as 50% of building starts by value, while the share of commercial building was less than 20%. By 1980, the housing share had dropped to 20%, where on average it has stayed ever since due to the weakening of private sector supply, the cessation of local authority building and the expansion of the suburbs beyond the metropolitan boundary. Over the same period, there was a compensating rise in the commercial building share to 50%, an average which has again been maintained subsequently, allowing for cyclical variation. The largest and most volatile component of this commercial share has been contributed by office building, with an average of over 30% of the total since 1980 and a peak which reached 50% in the late 1980s boom. It is to the office development cycle in the Central London that we now turn.

6

Case Study: The City of London Office Market

The development of the City economy

City of capital

A visitor to the City of London at the start of the twenty-first century is confronted by a dense mass of office blocks that blanket and overflow the famous 'Square Mile'. They stand at the commercial heart of the largest city in Europe, and they house one of the three great nodes in the global network of international finance, together with New York and Tokyo. The City is not only the largest office market in Europe, it is also the most liquid, the best documented and the most intensively measured. It therefore provides an ideal case study for testing out the theoretical ideas about the building cycle which are being developed through this book.

In Chapter 1 we observed that although the modern City appears to be the quintessential central business district of a modern metropolis, contained within its boundaries are a scattering of survivors from a two thousand year building history. While the Great Fire of 1666 and the wartime bombing raids of 1940/1 destroyed much of the historic fabric of the City, these disasters were the catalysts, not the root causes of change. The real driving force behind the physical transformation of the City has been its changing economic and social base, reflecting the growth of London as the hub of a global empire and trading network. The metropolis has overflowed the old City boundaries, in concentric rings of urban development which now stretch up to twenty miles from the centre. One by one the traditional functions of the medieval City have decentralized – residential, manufacturing, commercial – to leave its economic structure now dominated by a closely interlocking set of financial and business service industries: a 'City of capital' rather than a 'capital city' (Coakley and Harris, 1983).

It is necessary to summarize briefly the economic history of the City before focusing in more detail upon the development of its office stock. This is because external economic conditions have provided a crucial influence on the office-building cycle which has operated in the City for the last 150 years. Two recent surveys of the

City economy, by Michie (1992) and Roberts (2004), provide a useful background; far more depth is provided in the monumental study produced by Kynaston (1994, 1995, 1999 and 2001) which follows the fortunes of the City between 1815 and 2000; Cassis (2006) sets the development of the City within a broader historical analysis of the world's main financial centres over the past three centuries. The more general recent histories of London by Porter (1994), Inwood (1998) and Ball and Sunderland (2001) are also useful sources of information about the development of the City.

The City in the sixteenth to eighteenth centuries

As noted in Chapter 1, the city and City of London were still synonymous in the sixteenth century. Every urban land use was to be found within the medieval walls of London – dwellings, shops, taverns, markets, warehouses, workshops, hospitals, churches and even market gardens. All that was missing was the seat of national government, moved outside the city to Westminster in the eleventh century, leaving the City of London to develop its own autonomous government, a Corporation based on local wards represented by aldermen who each year elected a Mayor. The City had been granted the privileges of raising its own taxes and administering the law to its citizens, which gave it considerable autonomy in its dealings with national government (Barron, 2000).

As the suburban expansion of London accelerated during the seventeenth century, the resident population of the City went into decline and its economy became increasingly dominated by commercial activities. This was the first of several waves of decentralization which have taken place in the City over the past four centuries, offering a textbook illustration of the economics of location discussed in Chapter 5. Progressively, more profitable and intensive land uses have derived agglomeration benefits from a City location, enabling them to outbid lower value, more extensive uses that could no longer afford the rising central area rents, forcing them to decentralize to lower cost locations outside the City.

By the end of the seventeenth century, the City was established as the commercial heart of the British economy. The establishment of the Bank of England, the Stock Exchange, Lloyd's underwriters and several insurance companies during the last two decades of the century then provided the springboard for the take-off of the City as an international financial centre. During the eighteenth century, the financial revolution in Britain was driven by two forces: the requirement of successive governments to finance their overseas wars, and the spectacular growth of overseas trade, which stimulated the growth of the commodity markets, insurance and banking. London's banking system grew first through the use of bills of exchange to finance international trade and then through the issue of loans to overseas governments (Cassis, 2006: 16–20). Between 1760 and 1800, the number of commercial banks in the City nearly doubled from 40 to close to 80 (Porter, 1994: 146), and London was overtaking Amsterdam as the world's leading financial centre.

The Victorian and Edwardian City

Just as Victorian London had become the world's largest city by the middle of the nineteenth century, so the Victorian City had become the global hub of world trade and finance. At the end of the Napoleonic Wars in 1815, the main elements of the City's core financial activities were already in place – a government bond market, a money market trading domestic bills, a central bank, a rudimentary national banking system, a few joint-stock insurance companies, Lloyd's underwriters, ship-broking and marine insurance and several commodity markets (Roberts, 2004: 27). The railway investment boom in Britain during the 1840s boosted the growth of the capital markets, enabling the Stock Exchange to broaden its capital-raising across a much wider range of infrastructure, utilities and transport sectors in the second half of the century.

The technological revolution in communications wrought by the introduction of the international telegraph in the 1860s and the telephone in the 1880s transformed the speed and cost of exchanging financial information and executing transactions. Previously, decentralized markets became more integrated, providing an agglomeration boost to the concentration of financial services within the Square Mile (Garbade and Silber, 1978; Ball and Sunderland, 2001: 347). The City economy became ever more international and diversified, as its banks funded overseas governments, foreign investment, international trade and imperial expansion; in 1873, total deposits in London banks were three times as great as those in New York and nearly ten times higher than those in Paris (Inwood, 1998: 483). During the second half of the nineteenth century, there was a parallel expansion in insurance and professional services, while the global demand for investment capital, particularly to fund railway construction, transformed the scale and scope of the London Stock Exchange; by 1913, it accounted for half the world's overseas investment and handled a third of all the world's quoted securities (Inwood, 1998: 480–1). These were truly the City's 'golden years' (Kynaston, 1995).

Despite the rapid growth of London as a whole, the resident population of the City shrank dramatically during the second half of the nineteenth century, from 128,000 in 1851 to 75,000 in 1871, 38,000 in 1891 and only 20,000 in 1911. In contrast, its working population continued to rise, from 200,000 in 1871 to 301,000 in 1891 and 364,000 in 1911 (Dunning and Morgan, 1971: 34). The railway boom of the 1860s helped boost this growth in the City's workforce, as swelling flows of commuters passed through its five newly built termini. While a substantial proportion of businesses in the Victorian City were still involved in manufacture and trade, they were giving way to the rapidly expanding financial and professional services sector, which accounted for nearly 30% of the workforce by 1911 (Michie, 1992: 16–7). Office-based services became the most dynamic component of the City economy, deriving exceptional externality benefits from their central location which enabled them to displace older-established manufacturing and commercial activities (Cowan et al., 1969; Goddard, 1975). This economic transformation spawned a corresponding transformation of the City's building stock, as custom-built offices were developed to accommodate its growing population of clerical workers and its increasingly complex business operations.

The inter-war City

As the British economy was overtaken by that of the United States and then Germany during the decades leading up to the First World War, so London's pre-eminent position as the world's largest city was eroded during the early years of the twentieth century. By 1925, New York had caught up, and Tokyo, Paris and Berlin were closing the gap (Chandler and Fox, 1974: 335). During the inter-war period, Britain's relative economic decline also undermined the supremacy of the City, with New York challenging its position as the world's leading financial centre and the dollar taking over from the pound as the main international trading and reserve currency. Nevertheless, the City retained its unrivalled expertise in the provision of international financial services and established a new predominance in rapidly developing markets such as foreign exchange (Cassis, 2006: 162–4).

However, the Wall Street crash of 1929 and subsequent Great Depression affected the City severely. The slump in world trade, plus widespread loan defaults by overseas governments, hit the markets for international finance, shipping, marine insurance and commodities (Roberts, 2004: 33). These setbacks to its international activities forced the City to become more inward-looking during the 1930s, so that its continued expansion became more dependent upon domestic savings and investment. The growth of new light manufacturing industries was in part funded by City banks, while domestic banks and insurance companies underwent a process of concentration which saw the larger conglomerates centralize their operations within the City (Michie, 1992: 162).

The City's working population reached a recorded peak of around 500,000 in 1935, nearly 40% higher than in 1911. By then, some 60% of the workforce was in office occupations, as financial and business services supplanted all other activities to become the dominant force in the City economy (Inwood, 1998: 736), while some 45% of its floorspace was in office use (Dunning and Morgan, 1971: 32). It was during the inter-war period that new technologies previously pioneered in the United States began to revolutionize the financial and business services industries, transforming the counting house into the modern office (Broadberry and Ghosal, 2002). The introduction of various types of office machinery facilitated the automation of data processing and other routine tasks, generating productivity gains which heralded the eventual demise of the clerical workers who had formed the backbone of the City's workforce. A case study of office automation in the Prudential Assurance Company, one of the largest employers in the City, offers a good illustration of how this transformation was achieved, and the resulting competitive advantage it brought to the company (Campbell-Kelly, 1992).

The post-war City

Though Britain's relative economic decline continued and even accelerated after the Second World War, the City of London took on a new lease of life as the premier financial centre in Europe, operating in an increasingly detached fashion from the rest of the economy – still very much 'a world of its own' (Kynaston, 1994). The nexus of complementary banking, fund management, insurance, commodities and currency markets, which developed in the City over the previous two centuries, together with their supporting professional services such as law, accountancy and management consultancy, have created a strongly interlinked and functionally specialized economy. To add to its unique pools of capital, skilled labour, financial expertise, business relationships and support services, the City has enjoyed the further benefits of long-established reputation, a shared language with the world's most powerful economy and a strategic location midway between the North American and Asian time zones. These advantages have placed London in a uniquely favourable position to exploit the growing globalization and centralization of financial markets, enabling it to take its place alongside New York and Tokyo as one of the world's three leading 'global cities' (Sassen, 2001).

The clustering of financial firms and their associated services within a flexible institutional framework has generated a strong dynamic in the City economy, in which agglomeration, innovation and growth operate in the mutually self-reinforcing manner described in Chapter 5. The rapid creation and diffusion of knowledge within a highly competitive business environment has encouraged service innovation, productivity growth, new firm formation and the creation of new markets. Integral to the success of the City has been the universal adoption of ICT , ushering in the era of electronic financial trading (Siegel, 1990). This technological revolution has created a new wave of innovation and agglomeration economies to benefit the City economy, comparable to those generated by the introduction of the telegraph and telephone a century earlier. Though the electronic trading of financial services is now a ubiquitous 'virtual' activity, the advantages deriving from the concentration of these activities in one physical location remain as strong as ever (Clark, 2002). The continuing success of the City economy indicates that the centripetal forces which encourage the clustering of financial firms remain stronger than the centrifugal forces which might encourage their dispersion (Cook et al., 2007).

The strongest impetus for the post-war growth of the City economy has been provided by the expansion of international trade, investment and finance (King, 1990). The output of international financial services in the City has grown at an estimated 7% per annum (Lombard Street Research, 2003), while the number of foreign banks represented in London rose from 73 to 383 between 1960 and 1980, and to 567 by 1997, more than in any other international financial centre (London Chamber of Commerce and Industry, 1998). During the 1960s and 1970s, London became the main location for the fast-growing Euromarkets, while the abolition of exchange controls in 1979 opened the floodgates to international securities investment (Roberts, 2004: 37–42). Deregulation of the Stock Exchange in the 'Big Bang' of 1983–6 led to the creation of integrated investment banks through merger and acquisition, and further opened up the City to international capital (Michie, 1992: 142–3). The result has been the creation of an oligopolistic structure of international financial conglomerates, operating through global networks centred on a highly concentrated nodal location (Amin and Thrift, 1992).

Though its domestic markets are much smaller than those in the United States and Japan, the extent of the City's dominance of international financial markets can be seen from 2004 data for the United Kingdom (which overwhelmingly means the City) collated by the Corporation of London (2005). On this evidence, the United Kingdom accounted for over 40% of the total value of wholesale financial services produced within the European Union, more than twice the output of Germany (mostly Frankfurt) and three times that of France (mostly Paris). On a global scale, the City accounted for 20% of cross-border bank lending and 31% of foreign exchange dealing (in both cases more than the United States and Japan combined), 43% of foreign equities turnover (compared to a 31% share in the United States) and a massive 60%–70% of the market in international bonds. Furthermore, with the exception of foreign equities turnover, these global shares had been stable or rising over the previous decade. The City has also captured a commanding market share of the latest generation of financial industries such as derivatives, hedge funds and private equity (Gieve, 2007).

The post-war dominance of the financial sector in the City means that office activities of all types now account for over 90% of its employment and floorspace. Though overall City employment was only around 320,000 in 2005, much lower than its pre-war peak of 500,000, employment in the core office sectors of financial and business services had risen from around 185,000 in 1970 to 268,000 in 2005. Furthermore, an additional 64,000 financial and business services jobs were located in the satellite office centre of London Docklands, centred on Canary Wharf, developed during the 1980s and 1990s to accommodate overspill activity from the City (Daniels and Bobe, 1993). As the most profitable front-office activities of international firms have concentrated within the City, so less profitable domestic services and more routine back-office functions have followed manufacturing and commercial activities in decentralizing to lower cost locations outside the City, while universal computerization has replaced most clerical tasks altogether.

The growth trajectory of the City economy (1970–2005)

We can now examine the extent to which the post-war trajectory of the City office economy corresponds to the 'stylized facts' of steady-state growth introduced in Chapter 4, drawing upon trends in City output, employment and floorspace which have been constructed for the years between 1970 and 2005 (Figure 6.1). For the purposes of this trend analysis, the 'City' economy is assumed to include the office activities in Docklands, since these function very much as an extension of the core

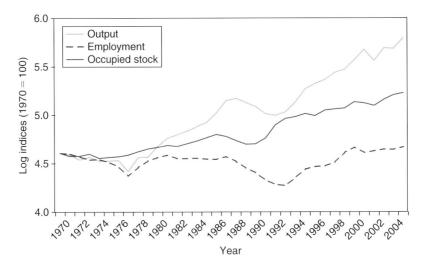

Figure 6.1   Growth trajectory of the City office economy 1970–2005.
Source: ONS, City Corporation and PMA.

activities located within the Corporation boundary. Though the illustrative data are particular to the City of London, the broad trends they reveal are common to modern office economies as a whole.

The chosen measure of City office employment is all workers less those employed in retailing; this has shown a broadly flat trend since 1970, though its composition has changed markedly in terms of business sectors and occupations. The share of financial and business services within total office employment increased from 55% to 89% between 1970 and 2005, as this sector has come to dominate the City economy, while there has been a corresponding increase in the share of higher order managerial and administrative occupations, as the majority of clerical jobs have been lost to computer technology. Owing to this occupational shift, the value of the labour inputs to the City economy has been growing much faster than their volume.

A crude income-based measure of City output (excluding profits and rents) has been derived by multiplying office employment by the average real wages of a full-time, male, non-manual worker in the City. The derived output trend does not follow a steady trajectory, but rather exhibits two phases of accelerated growth. The first occurred in the early to mid 1980s, as the City economy responded to the institutional and technological boost provided by deregulation and computerization in the run-up to 'Big Bang'. There was then a setback to growth following the stock market crash of 1987 and the subsequent recession of 1990–2. Output growth accelerated for the second time through the remainder of the 1990s and first half of the 2000s, as the City established its dominant position as the world's leading centre for international finance, checking only briefly after the stock market crash of 2001/2. Over the whole period 1970–2005, this constructed measure of City output yields an average growth rate of 3.5% per annum; however, the accelerated growth phases saw rates of 7.5% between 1979 and 1987, and 6.8% between 1993 and 2005.

Occupied office floorspace in the City (including Docklands) nearly doubled between 1970 and 2005, growing on average by 1.8% per annum. With virtually no growth in office employment, the increase in occupied space is almost entirely attributable to growth in floorspace per worker at an average rate of 1.5% per annum, from 114 square feet per worker in 1970 to 194 square feet in 2005 (Figure 6.2). This rise in space standards is consistent with the expectation of increasing building capital per worker along a steady-state growth trajectory. It is worth noting that the rise has not primarily been generated by increases in space standards for individual office workers, but rather by the additional floorspace allocated to ancillary uses such as conference and meeting rooms, corporate catering, plant and machinery and information technology. In other words, the increase in the capital intensity of office activities reflects the growing complexity of the working practices undertaken within an office building, the more sophisticated floorspace layouts required to accommodate these functions and the technological support they must receive from the building's mechanical and electrical systems (Duffy, 1997).

The rate of growth of occupied floorspace has been only half that of output over the whole period since 1970, while the gap has been far greater since 1993 – 2.2% for floorspace compared to 6.8% for output. Their growth rates first diverged in the early to mid 1980s; they converged in the early 1990s, as output slumped while over-supply made space cheap to occupy, but they have diverged strongly again since. The result is that not only has building floorspace per worker been growing,

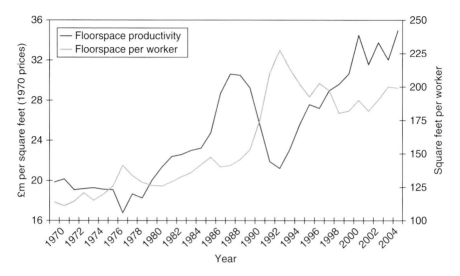

Figure 6.2   City office floorspace productivity and floorspace per worker 1970–2005.
Source: ONS, City Corporation and PMA.

but so has the productivity of building capital (the inverse of the capital–output ratio), with a growth rate averaging 1.7% since 1970 and as much as 4.4% since 1993 (Figure 6.2).

The reason for the growing productivity of building capital lies in the massive investment that City businesses have been making in information technology since the 1980s, which is boosting the productivity not only of office workers but also of office buildings. As has already been discussed in Chapter 4, the relative switch of office investment from buildings to computer equipment partly reflects the extraordinary rates of cheapening being achieved in the manufacture of ICT systems, and partly the greater productivity gains to be enjoyed from investing in a new or upgraded computer system rather than a new or refurbished office building. Consequently, as in all office economies, it is ICT investment which is now the driver of growth in the City economy and the dominant component of new office investment, relegating investment in office buildings to a secondary role (see Chapter 4 for an analysis of similar trends in the US economy over the past twenty years).

Nevertheless, there remain strong pressures to expand and upgrade the City's office stock – particularly as ICT systems become more integrated into the fabric of buildings. The leading financial firms are engaged in a competitive process of merger and restructuring, which involves enhancing their labour force and upgrading their technology, thereby creating a continuous occupier demand for new buildings of higher quality, larger size and improved technical specification. Since financial institutions are the main source of development finance and the main owners of City office property, as well as the main occupiers of the buildings, they generate a dual investment and occupational demand for prime offices which has encouraged developers to expand the total office stock in the City at a rate slightly ahead of the growth of the occupied stock. Since 1970, total stock has grown at an

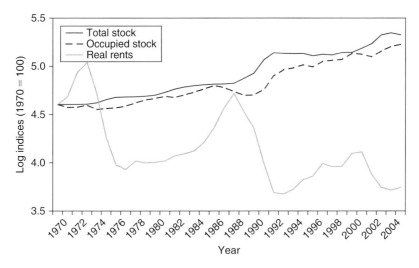

Figure 6.3 City office stock and rents 1970–2005.
Source: City Corporation, Ingleby Trice, Hillier Parker, Richard Ellis and PMA.

average rate of 2.1% per annum compared to 1.8% for occupied stock – with total stock moving ahead particularly strongly following the development booms of the late 1980s and late 1990s (see Figure 6.3). This tendency towards over-building in the City has been abetted by a loosening of planning controls during the 1980s; in contrast, in the neighbouring West End office market, restrictive planning and conservation policies have produced the opposite effect – a constrained development market in which there has been a persistent tendency towards under-supply.

The interlocking of investment and occupational demand in the City has not only produced a tendency towards over-supply but has also contributed to a particularly volatile market cycle (see the discussion of the cycle chronology below). The result has been an unfavourable combination of below average returns and above average risk for the investor (Lizieri et al., 2000: 1110). The propensity to over-development has resulted in two interrelated structural trends, which will be explored further in Chapter 7 using the simulation model:

- The first is for average levels of City vacancy to rise, causing real rents to suffer a secular decline. It can be seen in Figure 6.3 that each successive rental peak and trough has tended to hit a lower level, as the building cycle has ratcheted up the vacancy rate and depressed the real rent level. This provides a good illustration of historical dependency in the cyclical growth process, as discussed in Chapters 2 and 5. (In the supply-constrained West End market, there has been the opposite trend – a secular rise in real rents).
- The second is for declining real rents in the City to accelerate the rate of obsolescence, as occupiers can afford to upgrade their space more frequently, so that progressively younger office buildings are demolished and replaced by new vintages of larger buildings of the latest specification (Barras and Clark, 1996: 76–7).

Though these are secular trends, they are the cumulative result of the cyclical forces at work in the City office market, and it is to these that we should now turn.

The City office-building cycle

Modelling the cycle

Until the middle of the nineteenth century it was normal for office activities in the City of London to be accommodated in dwellings, counting houses and coffee houses (Baum and Lizieri, 1999: 88). It was during the 1840s that customized offices started to appear, and thereafter these became the dominant building form to be constructed in the City (Olsen, 1976: 118–22). While there exists no consistent historical record of the development of the City's office stock since the mid-nineteenth century, it has been possible to trace that historical record through the vintages of buildings which have survived until the present day.

A database has been constructed to provide information on the almost 1,000 office buildings of over 5,000 square feet (465 square metres) standing or under construction within the City Corporation boundary at the end of 2005. The basic schedule of information on each building comes from the Estates Gazette (EGi) London Office Database, amended and supplemented using additional information collected by Property Market Analysis (PMA) and obtained from Bradley and Pevsner (1997), who provide a comprehensive gazetteer of City buildings which contains valuable information about the dates at which buildings were constructed and refurbished. For each building (where known), the resulting database lists its location, size, construction start and completion dates, refurbishment dates and construction dates for previous buildings on the site.

Many, if not most, of the City office buildings which were constructed during the nineteenth and early twentieth centuries have been demolished and replaced by more modern buildings. Nevertheless, the survivors do preserve an 'echo' of the early building cycles which drove the development of the City's office stock. Figure 6.4 plots in logarithmic form the quantities of office floorspace standing or under construction in the City at the end of 2005 by their original year of completion (rather than the year of any subsequent refurbishment) or their planned year of completion (for the years 2006–7). Inevitably, these annual totals exhibit considerable irregular fluctuation during the early decades of the series, with several years of 'missing values' for which no surviving buildings have been identified. Furthermore, the series is interrupted by the two World Wars, with the impact of the Second World War being prolonged into the middle of the 1950s by the strict controls which were imposed on commercial building during the years of post-war austerity in Britain. In order to smooth out the extreme fluctuations in the building series and interpolate individual missing values, a simple symmetric 3-year moving average has been constructed from the annual data. As discussed in Section A.2.6, any such smoothing process risks introducing 'spurious cyclicality' into the data; however, the subsequent analysis shows that the chosen filter is short enough to preserve and enhance the cyclicality inherent in the original data. This smoothed series is also plotted in Figure 6.4.

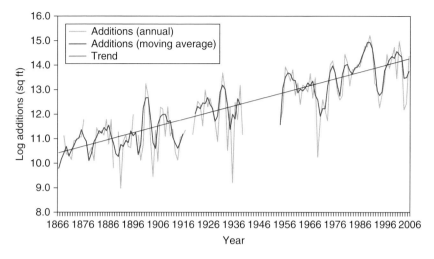

Figure 6.4   City office building 1866–2007.
Source: EGi London Office Database, PMA and Bradley and Pevsner (1997).

Table 6.1   Stochastic parameters for the City of London office-building cycle.

Interval	Period (years)	Damping factor[a]	Amplitude[a]	Variance[a]	Likelihood ratio[b]
(i) Annual values					
1866–2007	9.4	0.656	0.465	0.357	7.01
1866–1916	7.4	0.835	0.226	0.144	1.53
1955–2007	14.3	0.512	0.566	0.871	10.72*
(ii) Three-year moving averages					
1866–2007	10.6	0.827	0.600	0.335	76.16**
1866–1916	7.8	0.841	0.435	0.216	37.43**
1955–2007	11.8	0.891	0.726	0.468	14.28**
(iii) Three-year moving averages with ODP restrictions					
1866–2007	10.0	0.825	0.711	0.306	4.74*
1955–2007	10.5	0.887	0.527	0.373	3.84*

Source: EGi London Office Database, PMA and Bradley and Pevsner (1997).

Notes:

1. The residuals from the full period annual model satisfy the heteroscedasticity and serial correlation tests, but just fail the normality test at the 5% level; the full period moving average model residuals satisfy the normality and heteroscedasticity tests but fail the serial correlation test because of the smoothing process.

[a] For definitions of cycle damping factor, amplitude and variance, see Appendix A (Section A.2.7 and Table A.2); all cycles are of order 1.

[b] For models in groups (i) and (ii), the likelihood ratio statistics compare models with and without the specified cycle, for models in group (iii) the comparison is between cycle models with and without the ODP dummy variable; ** denotes that the restriction can be rejected at the 1% level, ˙ denotes rejection at the 5% level.

The process of structural time series modelling with unobserved components which is described in Appendix A and used in Chapters 4 and 5 has been applied to the derived City office-building series in both its annual and moving average forms (Table 6.1). The models are fitted from 1866, the point at which there is sufficient data for cyclical fluctuation first to become apparent, and estimation is continuous through to 2007, with the modelling process interpolating for missing values including the war periods. With both the annual and smoothed series, the model fits a deterministic linear trend (see Figure 6.4) on which is superimposed a stochastic cycle. The likelihood ratio test for the moving average model shows that the restriction of there being no cycle component can be rejected at the 1% level; however, with the more irregular annual model, the ratio test just fails at the 5% level. For the annual series the majority of the stochastic disturbance is assigned to the irregular component, whereas for the smoothed series it is all assigned to the stochastic cycle, which explains why the cycle is more strongly identified in the moving average model.

The slope of the linear trend fitted to both log series yields a 2.7% per annum long-term average rate of growth of office building in the City between 1866 and 2007. As will be elaborated in Chapter 7, this growth rate comprises the sum of the expansion rate of the office stock and its replacement rate. It was noted in the earlier section on the development of the City economy that the occupied stock of office space in the City grew on average by 1.8% per annum between 1970 and 2005; if this were the average over the full estimation period, it implies an average replacement rate of just under 1% per annum to make up the average building rate of 2.7%. This in turn implies that since the mid-nineteenth century the average life of a City office building may have been around 100 years, although the evidence suggests that this has not been constant but rather has been shortening progressively during the post-war period (see below).

Around the constant growth trend, the annual model fits a building cycle with an average period of 9.4 years, while the moving average model produces a cycle with a slightly longer average period of 10.6 years. The damping factor for the moving average cycle is 0.826, compared to 0.656 for the annual cycle, indicating a greater degree of regularity in the smoothed cycle; similarly, the proportionate amplitude of the moving average cycle is 0.600 compared to 0.465 for the annual cycle, confirming that a more pronounced cycle has been fitted to the smoothed series. These model results are confirmed by autocorrelation and spectral analysis applied to the detrended moving average series with missing values omitted; both exercises indicate the presence of a cycle component having a period of around 9 years. This average periodicity identifies the fundamental City office-building cycle with the major cycle within of the family of cycles discussed in previous chapters.

In addition to the commercial building controls exercised in the immediate post-war decade, there was a period between 1965 and 1970 when office building in the City was restricted by the imposition of Office Development Permits (ODPs), a policy that will be discussed below. This policy depressed City office completions most markedly between 1969 and 1973, and so the moving average model has also been fitted with a dummy variable for that period to capture the impact of these restrictions on development. A likelihood ratio test shows their inclusion to be significant at the 5% level (Table 6.1). The effect of their inclusion is slightly to reduce the period of the fitted cycle from 10.6 to 10.0 years and further boost its amplitude from 0.600 to 0.711; however, the damping factor remains virtually unchanged. The coefficient fitted to the dummy variable suggests that ODP restrictions may have depressed office-building levels during the period on average by around 40%.

Shorter term models have also been fitted to both the annual and smoothed series over the periods 1866–1916 and 1955–2007, to exclude the missing war years from the analysis and to test the stability of the full period models:

- For the early years 1866–1916, the periods of the fitted cycles shorten significantly to 7.4 years with the annual model and 7.8 years with the moving average model, while their amplitudes also reduce proportionately to 0.226 and 0.435 respectively. The moving average cycle remains significant at the 1% level, though now with a smoothly varying stochastic trend, but the annual cycle becomes weaker than that fitted over the full period, because of the preponderance of missing values during the opening decades.
- For the more recent years 1955–2007, the periods of the fitted cycles lengthen substantially to 14.3 years with the annual model and 11.8 years with the more stable moving average model, while their amplitudes increase proportionately to 0.566 and 0.726 respectively. Again, the moving average cycle remains significant at the 1% level, while the annual cycle is now significant at the 5% level. Both cycles are once more fitted to a deterministic linear trend, with average growth rates which increase slightly from 2.7% in the full period models to 2.8% in the annual model and 3.2% in the moving average model, which is consistent with an increase in the replacement rate during the post-war period (see below).
- The 1955–2007 moving average model has also been fitted with the ODP restrictions that were applied to the full period model. The inclusion of the restrictions over the shorter period is just significant at the 5% level. Compared to the equivalent model without the ODP dummy, the cycle period reduces from 11.8 to 10.5 years, which is closer to the estimates derived from the moving average models fitted over the full period 1866–2007. The growth trend is no longer linear, but rather reduces from a rate of 3.5%–4% per annum in the 1960s down to 1%–1.5% per annum in the late 1990s/early 2000s, reflecting the exceptional conditions which prevailed in the early post-war period when above average rates of office building were required to replace the stock lost to war damage (see below).

Cycle turning points

The parameters of the City office-building cycle derived by unobserved components modelling have been compared with those obtained by detrending the building series and locating the peak and trough turning points that delineate successive cycles. The deterministic linear trend shown in Figure 6.4 has been removed from both the annual and moving average series, as has the irregular component in the case of the annual series, to produce the stochastic cycles plotted in Figure 6.5. Cycle peaks and troughs have been located on the moving average cycle, and successive trough-to-trough cycles are marked in Figure 6.5. The turning point chronology identified from the moving average cycle is listed in Table 6.2, together with the duration and extreme amplitude of each cycle, the amplitudes being measured as the proportionate deviation of each turning point from the fitted trend.

The period between 1866 and 2007 has been divided into 12 major office-building cycles, allowing for the interruptions of the war years. In addition, two minor cycles have been identified within Cycles 1 and 11, the latter reflecting the impact of the economic

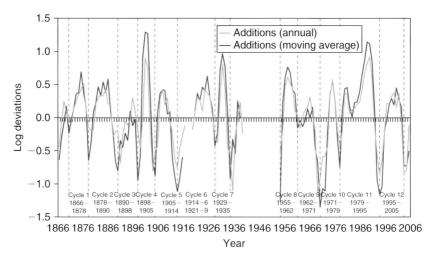

Figure 6.5   City office-building cycle 1860–2007.
Source: EGi London Office Database, PMA and Bradley and Pevsner (1997).

recession of 1980/1 as it interrupted the upswing of the major cycle. Over the full period, the major cycles yield an average trough-to-trough period of 9.5 years and an average turning point amplitude of 0.750. These estimates compare reasonably closely with the parameters derived from the unobserved components models (see Table 6.1): an annual cycle with period 9.4 years and amplitude 0.465, and a moving average cycle with period 10.6 years and amplitude 0.600. The closest correspondence to the turning point chronology comes from the moving average model with ODP restrictions imposed, which produces an average cycle period of 10.0 years, compared to 9.5 years, and a cycle amplitude of 0.711, compared to 0.750 from the turning points.

For the early years 1866–1916, there is a close correspondence between the modelled moving average cycle, with period 7.8 years, and the turning point chronology including the minor cycle within Cycle 1, which yields an average trough-to-trough cycle period of 8.0 years. This correspondence indicates that when the structural model is confined to the early period, it picks up shorter term fluctuations in the cyclical component. If the minor cycle is excluded, the turning point chronology produces an average trough-to-trough period of 9.6 years, which is very close to the average of 9.5 years estimated for the whole period 1866–2007.

Over the recent years 1955–2007, the closest correspondence is between the major cycle chronology, with an average trough-to-trough period of 10.0 years, and the moving average model with ODP restrictions imposed, which yields a cycle period of 10.5 years. Without the imposition of the ODP restrictions, the period of the moving average cycle increases to 11.8 years, which can best be matched by combining Cycles 8 and 9 in the turning point chronology to yield an average trough-to-trough period of 12.5 years. This reflects the effect of the ODP restrictions in the late 1960s, which suppressed the upswing of Cycle 9 and reduced it almost to the status of a minor cycle; by accentuating this cycle, the inclusion of the ODP restrictions in the moving average model is better able to distinguish Cycle 9 from Cycle 8.

Table 6.2 City of London office-building cycle turning points.

Cycle number T–T	P–P	Date T	P	Amplitude[b]	Duration (years) T–T	P–P
1a		1866		0.635		
	1a		1869	0.174	4	
1b		1870		0.238		6
	1b		1875	0.690	8	
2		1878		0.645		11
	2		1886	0.581	12	
3		1890		0.804		9
	3		1895	0.099	8	
4		1898		0.948		6
	4		1901	1.290	7	
5		1905		0.882		7
	5		1908	0.426	9	
6		1914		1.116		
	6		1926	0.626		
7		1929		0.425		6
	7		1932	0.966	6	
8a		1935		0.919		
8b		1955		1.269		
	8		1958	0.764	7	
9		1962		0.157		10
	9		1968	0.156	9	
10		1971		1.348		8
	10		1976	0.559	8	
11a		1979		0.749		6
	11a		1982	0.456	5	
11b		1984		0.011		9
	11b		1991	1.116	11	
12		1995		1.154		11
	12		2002	0.450	10	
13		2005		0.727		
Averages						
1866–2007						
All cycles				0.679	8.0	8.1
Major cycles				0.750	9.5	9.2
Major cycles (8/9 combined)				0.800	10.4	10.4
1866–1916						
All cycles				0.656	8.0	7.8
Major cycles				0.738	9.6	8.3
1955–2007						
All cycles				0.686	8.3	8.8
Major cycles				0.769	10.0	11.0
Major cycles (8/9 combined)				0.904	12.5	14.7

Source: EGi London Office Database, PMA and Bradley and Pevsner (1997).

Notes:

1. Where minor cycles are identified, the major cycle is split into phases a and b.
2. The chronology is interrupted by the impacts of the First World War (1917–20) and Second World War plus post-war building restrictions (1940–54).

[a] T = trough; P = peak.

[b] The amplitude is measured as the proportionate deviation of each turning point from the fitted trend, excluding the war years. This is typically a more extreme measure than the stochastic estimate derived with the structural model (see Table A.2).

In summary, formal structural modelling and informal turning point analysis have identified a major office-building cycle in the City of London since the middle of the nineteenth century, superimposed upon a steady growth trend that combines the expansion of the building stock with its replacement rate. The City building cycle has a long-term average period of between 9 and 10 years, its duration having tended to increase from around 8 years during the second half of the nineteenth century to over 10 years during the second half of the twentieth century. The individual cycles exhibit marked differences in behaviour in terms of their duration and volatility, reflecting the operation of variable market conditions and the impact of specific historical events. In particular, policy interventions such as the imposition of ODP restrictions on City development during the late 1960s/early 1970s can mask the rhythm of the cycle, while the impact of economic shocks such as the UK recession of 1980/1 can choke off an upswing and prolong the cycle, as happened during Cycle 11.

The cycle chronology

We can now consider the trajectory of the City office market since the 1860s, as it has moved through the sequence of 12 building cycles identified in the previous section. At each stage, the interaction of office technology, occupier demand, development supply, market conditions and planning policy will be examined.

Victorian and Edwardian cycles (1866–1914)

Customized office buildings became the dominant City building form in the first major phase of Victorian office development which spanned Cycles 1 and 2, stretching from the 1860s to the end of the 1880s (Summerson, 1977). These imposing new buildings met the demands of financial institutions '...both to house their various operations and to serve as architectural expression of their wealth, respectability and reliability...The office building as a specific type was a nineteenth-century invention and its proliferation a Victorian phenomenon' (Olsen, 1976: 120). At first, these offices were primarily purpose-built for the occupier, but by the later 1860s large speculative offices housing several tenants had begun to appear. Banks and insurance companies both occupied and financed much of this office-building boom in the City. The first specialist property companies were formed, gearing up with fixed-interest loans to purchase land or acquire ground leases, develop office buildings and lease them to tenants; among the pioneers were the City of London Real Property Company and the City Offices Company, both founded in 1864 (Scott, 1996: 22–6).

After a muted Cycle 3 during the 1890s, there was a second major phase of City office development in the Edwardian era, manifested as Cycles 4 and 5 and covering the period from 1898 to 1914. This wave of building not only received the technological boost of another transport revolution, with electrification of the underground railway and tram networks, but also benefitted from the introduction of lifts into office buildings, which became widespread from the 1880s. This 'vertical transport revolution' facilitated the construction of taller buildings, thereby intensifying the use of valuable City sites and enhancing their value because higher rents could be charged for upper floors in buildings with lifts (Turvey, 1998: 62–5). As building intensified within the area of the City Corporation, so office development also began to spread beyond its boundaries (Inwood, 2005: 214–6). By the end of the Edwardian building boom, office development dominated the City property market: between 1907 and 1912, some 60% of new buildings were for office or part-office use, and by 1911, office uses accounted for perhaps 30% of all buildings in the City (Turvey, 1998: 57).

Overall, it has been estimated that the cumulative impact of successive waves of Victorian and Edwardian building between 1855 and 1905 was the demolition and reconstruction of as much as 80% of the building stock in the City, increasing its floorspace area by at least 50% (Holden and Holford, 1951: 173). The cyclical behaviour of the City office market during this period can be illustrated by means of an analysis undertaken by Turvey (1998: 57–61), using original records from the City Offices Company of over 900 lettings and year-end vacancies in the period between 1869 and 1910. From this company data, Turvey constructed an annual office vacancy rate and index of achieved rents, observing that 'The considerable fluctuations in the rent index display a degree of inverse movement with the vacancy index…' These data provide a valuable historical example of the inverse rent adjustment process that is incorporated into the simulation model presented in the next chapter (an estimated rent equation based on the Turvey data is presented in Chapter 7).

Figure 6.6 illustrates the relationship between Turvey's estimated annual vacancy rate and a rental growth rate based upon a 3-year moving average of his rent index, to smooth out short-term fluctuations. The key phases of the inverse relationship can be summarized as follows:

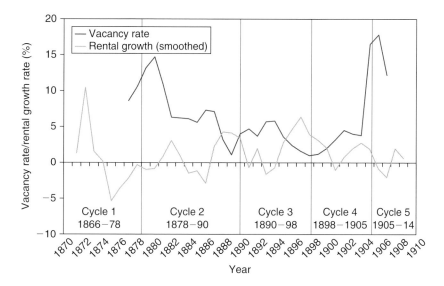

Figure 6.6 City of London office market cycle 1871–1909.
Source: Turvey (1998).

- There was a strong surge in rental growth during the early 1870s which triggered the wave of building that peaked towards the end of Cycle 1. The result was a rapid rise in vacancy and a switch to rental decline during the later 1870s. Between 1873 and 1880, the annual rent index records a cumulative fall of 19%, as vacancy rose to a recorded peak of 15%, though in real terms, the decline in rents was only 6% because of price deflation during the period.

- Having peaked soon after the start of Cycle 2, vacancy declined during most of the remainder of the 1880s, probably due to a combination of lower building completions and stronger demand. As vacancy fell below 5%, rental growth resumed strongly between 1888 and 1890. This rental increase appears to have stimulated development towards the end of the cycle, with the result that vacancy rose again in the early stages of the next cycle, to a modest peak of nearly 6% in 1893/4.

- It would seem that strong demand stayed ahead of increasing supply during much of the 1890s, causing vacancy to fall again during the second half of Cycle 3, to reach a low of just 1% in 1898–9. This prompted another surge in rental growth between 1895 and 1900, with the annual index recording a cumulative increase of 26% in nominal terms and 22% real. Once again, it can be assumed that rental growth led to increased levels of office development in the later stages of the cycle, setting vacancy on a rising trend at the start of the following cycle.

- During Cycle 4, there appears to have been an exceptional surge in office building in the City (see Figure 6.5). Consequently, vacancy continued to rise, and then leapt to a peak of around 17% in 1905/6 (although this peak is exaggerated by the completion of one very large building by the City Offices Company). Nevertheless, demand must have remained strong, because it was not until the start of Cycle 5, with vacancy at apparently record levels, that the rent index again registers a significant fall.

Inter-war cycles (1921–35)

The two inter-war office development cycles in the City took place against a background of exceptional turbulence in the national and international economy (see Chapter 5). The upswing of Cycle 6 was interrupted by the First World War and the subsequent savage recession of 1919–21. Once development resumed, there was a strong phase of office building up until 1927, after which the cycle was terminated by the onset of the Great Depression, starting in 1929. Despite this global depression continuing well into the 1930s, office building in the City appears to have recovered quickly during Cycle 7, reaching a strong peak as early as 1932. Building then declined equally swiftly to a trough in 1935/6, after which a new cycle upswing was interrupted by the onset of the Second World War (see Figure 6.5). Office rents in the City are reported to have been fairly stable during the 1920s, then to have fallen during the deflationary period 1929–33, before partially recovering during the later 1930s (Dunning and Morgan, 1971: 186).

A new generation of office buildings was constructed in the City during the inter-war period, involving 'the erection of several hundred large steel-framed buildings' (Holden and Holford, 1951: 181). This construction technology had been pioneered some 30–40 years earlier in the first generation of skyscrapers built in Chicago and New York (see the skyscraper analysis presented in Chapter 8); its belated introduction in Central London boosted the intensification of development through taller buildings which had been started by the introduction of lifts in the 1880s. Banks, insurers and commercial companies built themselves new City headquarters, and bespoke office building moved westwards into Midtown and the West End (Inwood, 1998: 738–9). By 1939, it is estimated that offices accounted for around 45% of floorspace in the City (Dunning and Morgan, 1971: 32) and that some 20% of the buildings which had existed in 1905 had been rebuilt (Holden and Holford, 1951: 178).

Early post-war cycles (1955–79)

As we move into the post-war period, the available sources of information about office development in the City of London increase considerably, both in quantity and quality. These data will be employed in Chapter 7 to test the operation of the building cycle simulation model. As an illustration, Figure 6.7 compares annual volumes of completed space, taken from development pipeline statistics for the post-war period, with the annual additions recorded from the completion dates of standing buildings, as used to develop our long-run cycle chronology. Both annual series are expressed as proportions of the total office stock at the end of the previous year; for the completions series, the data up to 1960 refer to the whole of Central London, from 1961 onwards, they refer to the City only. Allowing for discrepancies in the dating of individual buildings, there is a close correspondence between the two series, the main difference being that up to around 1970 the completions totals are significantly in excess of the standing additions, because some of the buildings completed in the early post-war period have since been demolished (see below).

Some six million square feet of office space in the City of London was destroyed or damaged by bombing during the Second World War, amounting to around 16%

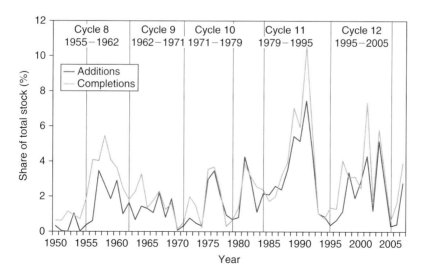

Figure 6.7 City office additions and completions 1950–2007.
Source: EGi London Office Database, PMA, City Corporation, Cowan et al. (1969), Bradley and Pevsner (1997).

of the total stock (Dunning and Morgan, 1971: 32). Nevertheless, the 1947 Town and Country Planning Act imposed strict controls on office development in the immediate post-war period through a highly regulated system of building licences (Cowan et al., 1969: 162–5). The City Development Plan adopted in 1951 set the stage for post-war rebuilding, imposing restrictions on building heights combined with maximum plot ratios of 5:1 across most of the City and 5.5:1 in the vicinity of the Bank of England. The progressive loosening of building controls during the 1950s, combined with the pent-up demand created by a rapidly growing office economy, triggered the start of the first post-war development cycle in the City, denoted as Cycle 8 in our chronology. In response to sustained demand growth, top City rents grew from around £1.25 per square foot in 1950 to £2 in 1960 and £3 in 1965 (Dunning and Morgan, 1971: 186–7). Strongly rising rents triggered such a wave of development that by 1964 the stock of office space in the City had been increased by nearly 50% compared to its immediate post-war level, and office uses accounted for 62% of all City floorspace (Dunning and Morgan, 1971: 32).

The abundance of cleared bomb-sites speeded up this first post-war cycle. Much of the redevelopment occurred on land taken over by the City Corporation and let out to developers on long building leases at low ground rents, echoing the approach pioneered by the Earl of Southampton three centuries earlier (see Chapter 1). Boom conditions in the property market encouraged a major institutional shift in the structure and dynamic of the development industry. Property companies replaced the old landed estates as the main Central London developers, funding their schemes principally through short-term bank loans which were subsequently refinanced through long-term mortgages issued by pension funds and insurance companies. This was a 'golden age' for the new breed of entrepreneurial developers, as vividly described in Marriott (1967); one illustration of the explosion in market activity is that between 1958 and 1962 the share value of listed property companies rose nearly eightfold (Marriott, 1967: 313).

At the peak of Cycle 8 in 1958, the volume of new office space completed in Central London reached 5.5% of total stock – a proportion not attained again for another 30 years. By the early 1960s, the development boom was cooling, as the market moved towards over-supply, so that completions dropped to a trough of just under 2% of stock in 1962. The second post-war wave of development in Cycle 9 had barely got underway when in 1965 the incoming Labour Government introduced ODPs, in an attempt to curb further development in Central London and encourage office activities to relocate outside the capital (Scott, 1996: 175–6). As a result of these restrictions, completions progressively declined from the modest level they had reached in 1964, just prior to the introduction of ODPs, shrinking virtually to zero by the time the cycle ended in 1970/1. The structural modelling exercise reported above suggests that building levels towards the end of this cycle might have been some 40% higher had ODP restrictions not been imposed.

By artificially restricting supply, ODPs contributed to the especially turbulent market conditions which accompanied the next wave of City office development in the 1970s, during Cycle 10. Unsustainable economic growth generated in the 'Barber boom' of the early 1970s intensified demand pressures in an already under-supplied office market. The result was that prime rents exploded from £5 per square foot in 1968 to £12 in 1970 and £22 by 1973 – more than twice as high as rents in

Paris, the next most expensive office location in Europe (Committee on Invisible Exports, 1974). The inevitable outcome was a speculative boom in office development, assisted by the progressive relaxation of ODP restrictions implemented by the returning Conservative government.

The economy and the property market crashed simultaneously in 1973/4, as boom turned to slump in a matter of months in the face of a quadrupling of oil prices, a rise in short-term interest rates from 5% to 13% and a government imposed freeze on commercial rents (Harris, 2005: 73–9). Economic recession meant that demand for City office space fell by one-third just as the majority of projects started in the building boom reached completion, so that vacancy soared from 2.6% in 1973 to 11.5% in 1976. During the same period, prime rents fell from £22 per square foot to £13, prime yields doubled from 3.9% to 7.7% and the capital value of prime City offices fell by as much as 60%. By 1975, office building starts had dropped back to only a quarter of their peak level at the start of the building boom in 1971. Many over-borrowed property companies with unlet space were unable to cover their escalating interest charges and were forced into receivership, while the Bank of England was forced to bail out the secondary banking sector which had grown up specially to service the property industry with cheap loan finance (Reid, 1982).

The last two cycles (1979–2005)

By the end of the 1970s, the economy and the City office market had recovered sufficiently for take-up to have reached record levels, vacancy to have dropped below 5% and nominal (but not real) rents to have risen back to their previous peak level. These improved market conditions were the trigger for a new development upswing to launch Cycle 11. This upswing was interrupted, however, by the onset of a second post-war recession in the United Kingdom during 1980/1, more severe than that of 1974/5, and again induced by an oil price shock (see the discussion of the national building cycle chronology in Chapter 5). This interruption prolonged the duration of Cycle 11, splitting it into two sub-cycles 11a and 11b and making it the longest cycle of the post-war era (see Table 6.2).

The upswing of Cycle 11b resumed in the mid-1980s with increased vigour, due to a combination of financial deregulation, new technological demands on office buildings and a relaxation of development controls (Diamond, 1991). Big Bang plus computerization unleashed a surge in demand from the emerging financial conglomerates for a new generation of much larger, air-conditioned office buildings, incorporating open-plan dealing rooms and raised floors to accommodate computer cabling. Take-up peaked at over 4 million square feet in 1987, while prime City rents soared to £70 per square foot by 1988 – some 50% higher than peak rents in Paris in this cycle and over twice the peak level reached in New York and Frankfurt; only in Tokyo was office space more expensive.

To meet this explosion in demand, the City Corporation relaxed its planning guidelines in 1986, removing conservation controls from some areas and increasing the permitted density of development through higher plot ratios. The result was another speculative boom in office development which because of construction delays did not reach a peak until 1991, when 5.2 million square feet of newly completed space came on stream in the City, amounting to an unprecedented

10.5% of total stock. Part of the reason for the relaxation of development controls by the Corporation in the mid-1980s was a fear that financial firms would otherwise relocate en masse to modern, lower cost accommodation in Docklands (Harris, 2005: 150–4). The establishment of the London Docklands Development Corporation (LDDC) in 1981, offering generous tax incentives and a favourable planning regime to encourage development, caused the emergence of a new growth pole to the east of the City, centred on Canary Wharf (Fainstein, 2001, chapter 9). This major office complex was started in 1985, and by 1992 some 3.2 million square feet had been completed, offering prime institutional-quality space at only 60% of the top rents prevailing in the City.

As had happened in the previous cycle, boom once more turned to bust in Cycle 11b under the impact of the 1991/2 recession, the third of the post-war era (for an entertaining chronicle of this most volatile property cycle, see Goobey, 1992). The onset of recession coincided almost exactly with the completion of the main wave of development schemes in the City; again take-up fell by more than one-third when compared to its late 1980s' peak, while vacancy soared to a post-war high of 20%. As a consequence, prime rents more than halved, from £70 per square foot in 1988 to £32.50 in 1992/3, while prime yields rose from 4.2% to 6.4%. The turnaround in market fortunes was even more damaging in Docklands, where the developers of Canary Wharf, Olympia and York, were declared bankrupt in 1992, with as much as 80% of their office space still not let (Ghosh et al., 1994).

The extreme volatility of the late 1980s/early 1990s cycle can be attributed to a unique combination of three factors: the surge in demand generated by Big Bang, the loosening of development controls by the City Corporation and the subsequent impact of the global economic recession. As has already been noted in Chapter 3, market instability also seems to have been increased by feedback and contagion effects arising from the triple role of financial institutions as occupiers, funders and owners of City office property (Lizieri et al., 2000). The dual nature of investor and occupier demand was reinforced by the increasing involvement of overseas financial institutions in City office development, reflecting the accelerating globalization of the financial markets (Pryke, 1994; Baum and Lizieri, 1999).

With vacancy at record levels, office building in the City virtually ceased between 1993 and 1995. This development trough heralded the beginning of Cycle 12, which took off as demand strengthened and market conditions steadily improved during the second half of the 1990s. By 1997/8, take-up had increased to well over 5 million square feet per annum, and this record level of demand combined with low levels of building meant that vacancy fell rapidly – from 20% in 1991 to under 3% by the end of the decade. Nevertheless, when prime rents peaked at £62 in 2001 they were still 11% below the previous cycle peak of £70 in nominal terms, and as much as 45% lower in real terms. The development response to improved market conditions was more orderly and better phased than in the previous cycle, with three successive waves of building completing in 1997/8, 2001 and 2003. The strongest of these three Cycle 12 peaks reached 7.3% of total existing stock, compared with the more concentrated 10.5% peak in Cycle 11b.

There was a parallel recovery in development activity in Docklands during Cycle 12, following the re-floatation of the Canary Wharf Group by an international financial consortium in 1995. A second phase of building yielded a further

9.5 million square feet of new offices between 1999 and 2004, space that now commanded rents as high as 80% of top City rents. The success of the venture was assured by the completion of the Jubilee Line extension of the underground network in 1999 to serve this new office location – a recent example of the symbiotic relationship between infrastructure investment and urban development which has been so important to the growth of London and other major cities (see Chapter 5).

Just as the development response during Cycle 12 was more orderly than that during Cycle 11b, so was the manner in which the cycle ended. This time there was no national recession to choke off demand as the new supply was coming on-stream. However, the stock market crash of 2001/2 did administer a short, but very nasty, shock to the City market, causing take-up in 2002 to drop to under 2 million square feet – its lowest level in absolute terms since 1975 and the lowest since 1970 when expressed as a proportion of total office stock. Though demand recovered strongly in 2003/4, the combination of lower take-up and a new wave of over-supply had already driven vacancy back up to nearly 18% and prime rents down by 27% to £45 per square foot. Building starts again dropped virtually to zero, and the stage was set for the start of Cycle 13.

Looking back through the post-war sequence of five major office-building cycles in the City of London, the outlines of a longer cycle rhythm can be observed. Three of the major cycles – those denoted 8, 9 and 12 – proceeded in a fairly orderly fashion, driven by sustained growth in occupier demand during periods of relatively stable economic growth. By contrast, Cycles 10 and 11b were more volatile, each exhibiting the classic characteristics of a speculative boom–bust cycle. These cycles shared three exceptional features: supply was boosted by a relaxation in planning constraints, demand was boosted by an inflationary economic boom and the main wave of building reached completion just as the economy moved into a recession in which the property crash played a significant role. The contrast between these two unstable cycles and the three more orderly demand-led cycles of the post-war period provides some empirical confirmation of the idea that was advanced at the end of Chapter 3 – that there is a tendency for every second major cycle to turn into a speculative long cycle. As boom once more turned to bust in 2007/8, the unfolding Cycle 13 was emerging as the third such speculative cycle of the post-war period (see Chapter 8).

Vintages of City office stock

Each development cycle in the City of London since the mid-nineteenth century has produced a distinct vintage of office buildings with a unique bundle of characteristics comprising location, size, specification and design. For an illustration of the succession of building styles in the City since the 1830s, see the Corporation of London (1984); for a more general architectural history of London, including the City, see Sutcliffe (2006). The manner in which the building stock has changed through the vintages offers a valuable illustration of the dynamic behaviour of the City office market over the past 140 years, as it has moved through successive growth cycles.

The profile of each vintage of building stock has been derived from our City database, covering 984 office buildings of over 5,000 square feet providing a total of

Table 6.3   Characteristics of City office vintages.

Vintage (cycles)	Years	Concentration in Core (%)	Average size (sq ft)	Average redevelopment age (years)	Average rent ratio
1–3	1867–1898	46.5	18,128		48.9
4–5	1899–1914	29.4	30,459		54.8
6–7	1921–1935	62.5	44,134		56.3
8–9	1956–1971	44.5	66,238	110.9	57.1
10–11a	1972–1984	32.4	58,123	93.9	60.7
11b	1985–1995	25.5	83,538	79.4	65.6
12	1996–2005	46.7	131,130	60.3	90.1
Total	1867–2005	38.8	66,071	75.3	64.4

Source: EGi London Office Database, PMA and Bradley and Pevsner (1997).

60.9 million square feet of space. For the robustness of the analysis, the individual cycle periods have been aggregated into the following broader vintages:

- Nineteenth century: Cycles 1–3 (1866–98)
- Early twentieth century: Cycles 4–5 (1898–1914)
- Inter-war period: Cycles 6–7 (1921–35)
- The 1950s and 1960s: Cycles 8–9 (1955–71)
- The 1970s and early 1980s: Cycles 10–11a (1971–84)
- Late 1980s and early 1990s: Cycle 11b (1984–95)
- Late 1990s and early 2000s: Cycle 12 (1995–2005).

The summary characteristics of each vintage are presented in Table 6.3, designating the trough years as the final year of each cycle.

Locational clusters

The location of City office buildings by cycle vintage shows a clear clustering pattern, with concentrations of buildings of similar vintage found in different localities (Figure 6.8). The distribution of these clusters reflects the interaction between historical patterns of urban development and the recent planning policies of the City Corporation.

As has previously been discussed in Chapter 5, agglomeration economies of localization are particularly strong in a specialized economy such as the City of London, where concentrated clusters of firms in related industries derive considerable benefits from knowledge spillovers and easy access to specialist services, skilled labour and well-funded capital markets. These clusters of business activities have also helped to create distinctive clusters within the office stock, by generating demands for particular types of buildings in their chosen locations. A pioneering study by Goddard (1968) about the linkages between different sectors in the City showed that historical clusters of interrelated activities could clearly be identified, each with a unique location pattern, while a more recent research study by the RICS (2000) showed that clustering still persists as a distinctive feature of the City economy.

Figure 6.8 City office buildings by cycle vintage.
Source: PMA.

There is a concentration of traditional banking and insurance buildings in the core of the City, close to the Bank of England – the location which was the earliest to be developed, contains the most valuable sites and is now the most strongly protected from redevelopment by listed building policy. A second major concentration of period buildings is to be found in the south-west corner of the City, in the area of the Temple, where the legal profession has located in the Inns of Court since medieval times. A few other pockets of early vintage buildings survive in scattered locations around the edge of the Corporation boundary; these have typically been occupied by less profitable commercial uses now displaced from the City, and they await redevelopment in the next building cycle. At the other end of the age spectrum, strong concentrations of recent buildings mark where redevelopment was most active in Cycles 11 and 12. These clusters include Broadgate, a major new office area developed in the north-east of the City, and the London Wall/Gresham Street, Paternoster Square and Queen Victoria Street localities to the north and south of St Paul's Cathedral, where widespread redevelopment of early post-war buildings has recently taken place to provide new, top quality space for financial and professional services firms.

One aggregate indicator of the shifting location of office development in successive cycles is the proportion of schemes of each vintage to be found within the central City Core, as defined by the Corporation Planning Department, compared to the proportion in the surrounding Rest of City zone (Table 6.3). There would appear to have been significant shifts in the Core–Rest balance of development activity in different cycles; however, the relatively small sample sizes of buildings in the early vintages means that their estimated proportions cannot be given too much weight. Concentrating on the post-war period, some 44% of all schemes that were built in Cycles 8 and 9, spanning the 1950s and 1960s, are located within the Core. The location of these early post-war developments was largely determined by where the bomb-sites were situated, and their distribution made no concessions to planning policy. During the 1970s and early 1980s, as the supply of bomb-sites ran out and planning constraints were tightened, so a higher proportion of development schemes were forced out of the protected Core into the Rest of City. The result was that the proportion of Core schemes dropped to 32% in Cycles 10 and 11a, and to only 25% in Cycle 11b.

The relaxation of planning constraints in 1986 (see above) was too late to shift the balance of development back to the Core in Cycle 11b, but it certainly had an impact in Cycle 12, when the share captured by the Core nearly doubled to 47%. This increased level of building in the historic central area during the late 1990s and early 2000s was not a function of planning policy alone. As will be seen below, much of the construction activity in Cycle 12 comprised the redevelopment of the first generation of post-war office buildings, so that the Core concentration in Cycle 12 in part echoes that created in Cycles 8 and 9. The indications are that these factors will lead to at least as high a proportion of development activity being located in the Core during Cycle 13.

Building size

The average size of City office buildings has increased vintage by vintage, from a little under 20,000 square feet in the late nineteenth century to just over 130,000 square feet in Cycle 12 (Table 6.3). The nearly 60% increase in average size between

Cycle 11b and Cycle 12 is particularly marked, and an examination of the size dis-tribution of buildings completed in each post-war vintage shows that this increase reflects a qualitative as well as quantitative shift in the scale of building during the 1990s (Figure 6.9). Prior to the last cycle, the distributions for each vintage show a similar and expected profile, with the number of buildings decreasing as the size band increases. However, in Cycle 12, the distribution is dominated by large build-ings in the 100,000–250,000 square feet band, with a much smaller proportion of buildings of under 50,000 square feet. Three reasons can be identified to explain the tendency for City office buildings to have increased in size and for that tendency to have intensified during the 1990s.

Construction technology

Improvements in construction technology have progressively increased the poten-tial height and size of office buildings in the City since the late nineteenth century (see Bowley, 1966 and Powell, 1980 for histories of technical progress in the British building industry). Following the discussion in Chapter 5, these improvements have created a trajectory of urban innovation which can be described in terms of a sequence of discrete stages:

- As described above, the first improvement was the introduction of lift technology towards the end of the nineteenth century, facilitating the construction of taller buildings and helping to explain the increase in average size between the vintages of the late nineteenth century (Cycles 1–3) and the early twentieth century (Cycles 4–5).
- Following the First World War, the second major improvement was the belated introduction to the City of the steel-framed construction methods pioneered in the United States. These allowed for more flexible internal layouts and a further increase in building heights, leading to another increase in average size between the vintages of the early twentieth century and the inter-war period (Cycles 6 and 7).

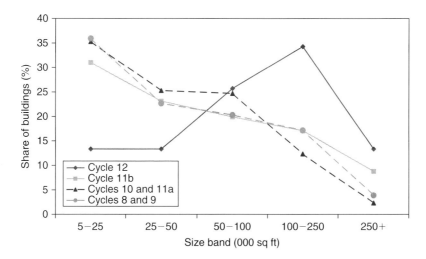

Figure 6.9   City office size distributions by post-war cycles.
Source: EGi London Office Database, PMA and Bradley and Pevsner (1997).

- The substantial increase in average building size in the early post-war period (Cycles 8 and 9) in part reflects the availability of large cleared bomb-sites, but can also be attributed to the widespread adoption of curtain-wall techniques to construct office tower blocks in which lightweight glazed external walls were hung from a reinforced concrete frame (Goobey, 1992: 24).
- The introduction of 'fast-track' construction methods, again originating in the United States, is the most recent enhancement of construction technology to have benefitted the City, increasing both the scale and productivity of office building since the mid-1980s (Cycles 11b and 12). These methods rely upon sophisticated project planning to run the design and construction processes in parallel, organizing the delivery and assembly of prefabricated modular components for a 'shell and core' structure. This consists of a central services core, a steel framework, metal-deck floors and light external cladding, with the internal finishes left to the occupier (Gann, 2000: 169–71). Not only do these methods improve construction productivity, they are also ideally suited to the integration of increasingly complex mechanical and electronic services into the fabric of a building, while allowing for the flexible reconfiguration of the space as demands change.

Economies of scale

Increasing returns to scale, closely related to technical progress in construction, is a second factor which has driven the increase in the size of City office buildings. Scale returns are to be expected in the construction of large and complex buildings such as office blocks, because parts of the operation such as the clearance of the site and the laying of foundations involve a relatively fixed resource cost, however many storeys are constructed. Building productivity is difficult to measure directly, but the data used for the vintage analysis allow a crude proxy measure to be derived as 'floorspace per construction year', dividing the size of the building by the length of its construction period. This measure has been plotted for different size bands of buildings in each post-war vintage, and the results show clear scale economies operating within each vintage (Figure 6.10). Indeed, not only does this measure of productivity increase with building size, but it does so with an upward-sloping curve, indicating that the scale benefits in office building tend to increase with size. Furthermore, there is a tendency for the curve to shift upwards with each successive vintage, reflecting the extent to which technical progress through time has improved building productivity in each size band. The one apparent exception to this rule is that the curve for Cycles 8 and 9 is higher than that for Cycles 10 and 11a; however, this can be explained by the fact that the first post-war vintage was largely built on bomb-sites for which site clearance was a 'gift of war', not the necessary first phase of the construction process.

Planning policy

The third and final factor which has encouraged the development of larger buildings in the last 15–20 years is the relaxation of planning policy by the City Corporation. The acceptance of higher plot ratios, together with a growing predisposition in favour of tall towers, helped to boost average building size in Cycle 11b, and more obviously in Cycle 12 (Corporation of London, 2006: 14). The rash of applications

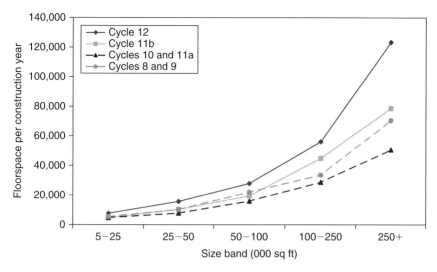

Figure 6.10 City office-building productivity by size and cycle.
Source: EGi London Office Database, PMA and Bradley and Pevsner (1997).

which have been made by developers to build 'landmark' towers in the next few years suggests that Cycle 13 will witness a further substantial increase in average building size in the City.

Redevelopment and obsolescence

For nearly 200 of the buildings in the database, the construction date of the previous building on the site is known, providing some indication of the changing rate of economic obsolescence in the City office stock as manifested through the age of redeveloped buildings. The data show that the average age of the buildings demolished for redevelopment has steadily reduced through each post-war cycle (Table 6.3), which is another way of saying that obsolescence has been accelerating and the replacement rate has been increasing.

During the 1950s and 1960s, the average age of buildings demolished in Cycles 8 and 9 was 111 years; this meant that typically it was the first generation of mid-nineteenth century office buildings which was being replaced. By the time we reach the late 1990s and early 2000s, the average age of buildings demolished in Cycle 12 had nearly halved, to 60 years. Furthermore, the distribution of demolished buildings by vintage shows a marked and qualitative shift when Cycle 12 is compared with the previous Cycle 11b, covering the late 1980s and early 1990s (Figure 6.11). The profile of demolished buildings in Cycle 11b is still dominated by the pre-war vintages, contributing some 86% of the known total, with only a handful of early post-war buildings also being redeveloped. However, in Cycle 12, the focus of replacement moves decisively to the first post-war vintage, with almost 60% of the known total of demolished buildings having been constructed in Cycles 8 and 9. Available evidence on the schemes planned or under construction at the start of Cycle 13 suggests that the redevelopment focus on the earlier post-war vintages is set to continue: a high proportion of Cycle 8 and 9 buildings is again being targeted,

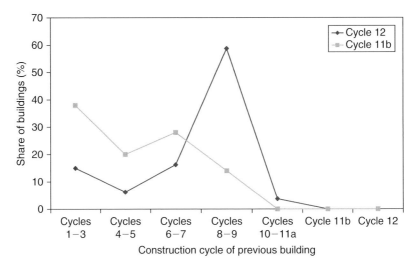

Figure 6.11   Vintages of City office buildings redeveloped in last two cycles.
Source: EGi London Office Database, PMA and Bradley and Pevsner (1997).

together with a significant number of 1970s' buildings constructed in Cycle 10 and even one or two 1980s' buildings from Cycle 11.

What has emerged in Cycle 12, and is set to be repeated in Cycle 13, is a replacement cycle, whereby a new building cycle tends to replace stock of a particular previous vintage, thus creating a tendency for the cycle to reproduce itself (see Knox, 1952). While Ball (2003) could not find evidence for a replacement cycle when testing aggregate data on UK office stock, this City of London case study shows that the phenomenon is more apparent when examining a single urban market using disaggregated building-level data. The experience in the City has been that the replacement cycle also tends to be an intensification cycle: in other words, an increased area of lettable floorspace is achieved following redevelopment. The increase in plot ratios permitted by the City Corporation from the mid-1980s onwards created conditions which encouraged intensification through redevelopment, and developers have taken full advantage of the opportunity by employing the latest construction techniques to achieve more efficient site cover and increased building heights. The result has been that for the 100 or so redevelopment schemes completed in Cycle 12, the average intensification ratio was 1.63, measured as the ratio of the new to old floorspace area.

Given that particular building vintages tend to cluster spatially, the effect of the replacement cycle can be traced across different localities in the City. This is particularly apparent in those locations around St Paul's which saw a concentrated phase of redevelopment in Cycle 12. There were seven redevelopment schemes in Gresham Street in Cycle 12, all but one of which replaced a building constructed in Cycle 8, with an average intensification ratio of 1.50. In Queen Victoria Street, five early post-war buildings from Cycles 8 and 9 were similarly replaced in Cycle 12 at an intensification ratio of 1.78. London Wall and Paternoster Square were two of the iconic early post-war developments on prominent City bomb-sites (Marriott,

1967: 85–91; Goobey, 1992: 25), and these are being redeveloped in a similar intensi-fied fashion. Paternoster Square, built between 1962 and 1967, was totally replaced by a new office complex in 1999–2003, with an intensification ratio of 1.80; London Wall, flanked by eight large office slabs erected between 1957 and 1965, saw two replaced in Cycle 11b, one in Cycle 12 and two in the early phases of Cycle 13.

The predominant dynamic behind the accelerating redevelopment of the City's office stock has undoubtedly been the economic incentive for landlords to increase rental income by upgrading the quality of the floorspace and expanding its letta-ble area. However, cultural and aesthetic factors have also played their part in the last twenty years. The early post-war vintage of office buildings was unashamedly Modernist in style, and highly regarded at the time. In 1973, Britain's most eminent architectural historian, Nikolaus Pevsner, described the Paternoster Square devel-opment to the immediate north of St. Paul's as 'outstandingly well conceived'. By 1997, the view was very different – the precinct was now considered 'draughty and harsh' (Bradley and Pevsner, 1997: 595–6). Between these two dates, tastes and fash-ions had changed, Post-Modernism was in the ascendant (Ellin, 1996) and a profes-sional and popular reaction had turned the demolition of Modernist buildings into a crusade. Nowhere was this reaction better encapsulated than in the campaign orchestrated by the Prince of Wales to ensure that the replacement of Paternoster Square was 'traditional' in style – favouring designs that mixed Neoclassical, Neo-Georgian and Neo-Gothic elements. The scheme that was finally built was an attempt 'to reconcile tastes and values' producing an outcome which is 'an art-ful framing of views of the cathedral that has been criticized as "stage scenery"' (Allinson, 2003: 50). One suspects that within another twenty years, fashion may have turned as savagely against the replacement as it did against the original.

Rent formation

For 519 of the office buildings in the database, amounting to a little over half the total, PMA has compiled records of the rents achieved on lettings of space in part or all of the buildings for one or more years in the period 1995–2005. For each of the nearly 1,200 recorded lettings, the achieved rent has been expressed as a per-centage of the prime City rent fixed in that year (typically an average of the top 5% of deals), with the intention of deriving rent relativities across the market which are independent of the timing of transactions in relation to the rent cycle. For each building, the relative rents derived from its individual lettings have been averaged over the years 1995–2005 in order to produce a rent ratio that expresses the market rating of the building during the period covered by Cycle 12.

When the rent ratios are averaged across the buildings within each vintage, the rent profile exhibits the expected upward slope, with higher relative rents achieved on more recent buildings (Table 6.3). However, the slope is not linear, but rather shows only a gradual increase from Cycles 1–3, with an average ratio of 49% of prime rents, to Cycles 10–11a, averaging 61%, before there is a slightly steeper rise to 66% for Cycle 11b buildings and then a far more pronounced jump to 90% for the Cycle 12 vintage. The distribution of relative rents by rent band for each post-war vintage illustrates why the latest vintage stands out from the others (Figure 6.12). The modal peak for buildings in Cycles 8 and 9 is in the 50%–60% band,

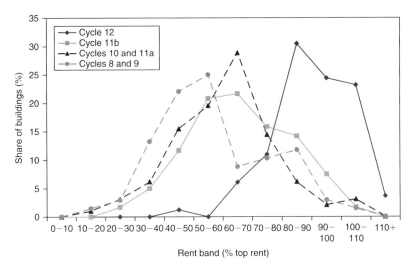

Figure 6.12   City office rent distributions by post-war cycle.
Source: EGi London Office Database, PMA and Bradley and Pevsner (1997).

for Cycles 10 and 11a it is in the 60%–70% band, and for Cycle 11b it is also in the 60%–70% band but with more of a skew towards the higher bands. However, for Cycle 12, the mode shifts up to the 80%–90% band, and furthermore there are substantial proportions of buildings in the 90%–100% band and even in the 100%–110% band.

What these rent distributions imply is that the latest vintage of space, built to the highest specification, dominates the prime market, meeting the current requirements of those occupiers who are prepared to pay the top rents. As soon as a new cycle is underway, delivering a new generation of buildings, the previous vintage suffers substantial depreciation, such that the relative rent it can achieve drops sharply. Comparing the average relativities in Cycle 12 and Cycle 11b, this depreciation effect has been reinforced by the higher proportion of Cycle 12 buildings which are situated in the City Core and can therefore command higher rents by virtue of their location as well as their age. The tendency for rental depreciation to be non-linear with respect to age has been noted in previous studies of the City office market, though because of differing methodologies and property samples these studies do not agree as to the timing of the most severe phase of depreciation (Salway, 1986; Baum, 1991; Barras and Clark, 1996; Dixon et al. 1999).

The spatial distribution of relative office rents across the City is shown in Figure 6.13. This shows clusters of buildings in the same rent band concentrated in different localities, reflecting in part the distribution of buildings by cycle vintage shown in Figure 6.8. However, although the age of a building is an important determinant of the relative rent it can achieve, other factors also have an influence. The most important is location within the City; rents tend to be highest close to the historic centre (the Bank of England) and decrease with increasing distance from the centre, following a bid-rent curve of the type that was described in Chapter 5. Other factors which have an influence on relative rents include the size of the building (also correlated with vintage) and the date of any refurbishment it has enjoyed. To explore the influence of these

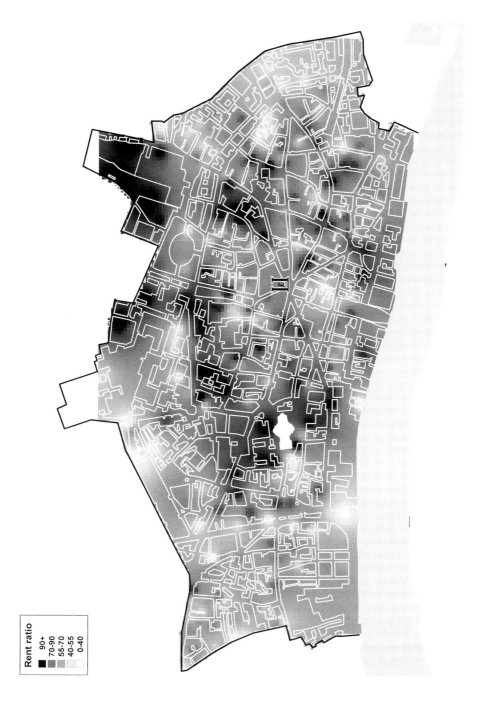

Figure 6.13 City office buildings by rent band.
Source: PMA.

different factors, a hedonic regression model has been estimated to explain the distribution of relative rents by building characteristics (t-statistics of the coefficients are in brackets):

$$r = -182.4 + 0.14c + 14.3v_0 + 6.0v_{11} + 26.9v_{12} + 0.007f + 0.057s - 5.9d + 23.8b$$

$$(-4.13) \quad (6.06) \quad (0.03) \quad (3.17) \quad (11.84) \quad (8.62) \quad (7.10) \quad (-5.89) \quad (3.96)$$

$$n = 519; \ R^2 = 0.538; \ adjR^2 = 0.531; \ SER = 14.11. \tag{6.1}$$

Here r is the relative rent ratio; c is the completion date; v_0, v_{11} and v_{12} are dummies for vintages 0 (pre-1867), 11b and 12 respectively; f is the refurbishment date (if any); s is building size ('000 square feet); b is a dummy for buildings in the Broadgate complex; d is the (log) distance from the Bank of England. What this model says about the determinants of City rent relativities is as follows:

• There is an underlying linear relationship between rent ratio and building age, but it has a very shallow gradient, with each 10 years of age reducing the ratio by just 1.4%.
• The nonlinearities in the age–rent relationship are introduced through the vintage dummies. Buildings surviving from before the start of Cycle 1 enjoy a 14% rent premium, as a result of their historic 'trophy' status. Consistent with the profile shown in Table 6.3, the rents of Cycle 11b buildings are boosted by a modest 6% above the linear trend, while the rental premium for Cycle 12 buildings is a far greater 27%.
• Recent refurbishment of older vintage buildings boosts their rent ratio by around 14%.
• Each additional 100,000 square feet in the size of the building adds 5.7% to the rent ratio. This size effect is independent of age, and an inference may be drawn that bigger buildings can attract higher rents because of the scale benefits which large occupiers are able to derive from being located within a single building, whatever its age.
• There is an exponential decay function linking the rent ratio to the distance of the building from the Bank of England: as the distance from the centre of the City increases, the rent ratio falls, but at a decelerating rate.
• For buildings located within the massive Broadgate complex, under development on the edge of the City since the mid-1980s, there is a substantial rent premium of 24%, reflecting the extent to which the high quality and specification of these buildings compensate for their fringe location.

Despite the range of significant variables incorporated into the model, it accounts for only 54% of the estimated variance in rent ratios across the building sample. What this means is that nearly half the variance is attributable to building-specific and lease-specific factors, confirming the importance which investors assign to individual stock selection when constructing their portfolios. In a broadly similar cross-sectional analysis of office rents in Chicago in 1990, location and building size were found to be strong determinants of rent levels, but the influence of age was less clear-cut because most of the buildings in the sample were constructed after 1945 (Mills, 1992).

Occupier profiles

The London Office Database provides information about the occupiers of around three quarters of the existing City office buildings at the end of 2005, spread among 1,234 units of occupation. Of the identified total of 41.3 million square feet of occupied space, 89% is assigned to the key sectors of financial, professional and business services, with the main occupiers consisting of foreign banks (17%), insurance (12%), other finance (18%) and legal firms (19%).

The relationship between clusters of activities and clusters of buildings of the same vintage within the City has already been noted. In aggregate terms, this relationship is manifested through differences in the average age of buildings occupied by each sector; more specifically, the separate sector distributions of occupied units by vintage show distinct peaks where strong clustering occurs (Table 6.4). Three financial sectors – foreign banks, other banks and other finance – dominate occupation of the latest vintages of office space built in the last 20 years. The average age of units they occupy is around 38 years, compared to an overall average of 49 years, with other banks (principally investment banks) and other finance particularly concentrated in Cycle 12 buildings, and foreign banks concentrated in Cycle 11b space. In contrast, other professional and other activities are concentrated in the early, pre-1914 vintages of Cycles 1–5, pushing up the average age of buildings they occupy to over 50 years. The insurance and accountancy sectors favour the intermediate vintages, with insurance concentrated in the inter-war buildings of Cycles 6–7, and accountancy choosing the early post-war buildings of Cycles 8–9. The legal sector is the only one to be spread fairly evenly across the vintages;

Table 6.4   Occupation profiles for City office buildings.

Sector	Share of space (%)	Average unit size (sq ft)	Average unit age (years)	Main vintage[a]	Average rent ratio	High rent share[b] (%)
Foreign banks	17.1	49,542	38.9	11b	74.0	40.9
Other banks[c]	8.6	61,063	38.5	12	75.2	51.6
Insurance	11.9	32,943	44.9	6–7	65.0	28.2
Other finance[d]	18.2	39,074	37.9	12	70.9	36.2
Accountancy[e]	4.3	25,781	45.3	8–9	66.0	22.6
Legal	18.8	36,075	68.1	–	66.8	27.7
Other professional[f]	9.9	19,259	52.8	1–5	61.3	16.1
Other	11.2	23,807	51.2	4–5	64.6	24.5
Total	100.0	33,482	49.2	–	66.9	28.5

Source: EGi London Office Database, PMA and Bradley and Pevsner (1997).

Notes:
[a] Main vintage is that in which there is an exceptionally high relative concentration of the sector.
[b] High rent share denotes the proportion of units occupied by the sector which have a rent ratio of 80%+.
[c] Other banks includes merchant banks, investment banks and UK clearing banks.
[d] Other finance includes pension funds, investment managers, investment trusts, stockbrokers and securities houses.
[e] Accountancy includes management consultants.
[f] Other professional includes a wide range of professional and business services covering media, property and construction.

the high average age of the buildings occupied by this profession stems from its unique mixture of a large number of small barristers' chambers in period buildings in the Temple and a smaller number of large firms of solicitors in modern office blocks.

As has already been seen, newer buildings tend to be larger and more highly rented; consequently, sector differences in average unit size and average rent ratio follow the distributions to be expected from the relative concentrations of the sectors across the vintages. Foreign banks, other banks and other finance occupy units of above average size in newer buildings with an above average rent ratio, while other professional and other activities are concentrated in units of below average size in older buildings with a below average rent ratio. Differences in rent-paying propensity among the sectors are highlighted more starkly by examining the proportion of units occupied by each sector which have a rent ratio of 80% or more. Out of all the occupied units in buildings with a known rent ratio, 29% have a ratio of 80% or more; however, this proportion rises to 36% for other finance, 41% for foreign banks and 52% for other banks.

It is the leading firms in the banking and investment industries which are currently driving the City office market. They occupy the latest buildings commanding the highest rents, out-bidding other occupiers and forcing them into the older, lower rented space. Through the competitive processes of merger and restructuring, they are creating a continuous demand for larger units with enhanced technical specification. The result is a three-tier market. The leading financial firms move into the new prime buildings, paying top rents; vacancy migrates into the secondary stock to be occupied by less profitable firms in other sectors paying lower rents; meanwhile, the poorest quality, lowest rented tertiary buildings drop into the pool of vacant schemes awaiting redevelopment. In the next chapter we turn to the supply-side processes which generate a cyclical development response to this demand-side dynamic.

7

A Simulation Model
of the Building Cycle

Real estate models

We are now in a position to draw upon the theories of cycle formation which were
explored in Chapters 2 and 3 in order to construct a simulation model which can
reproduce the observed real world behaviour of the building cycle as described in
Chapters 4, 5 and 6. To provide a context for the specification of the model, it is
necessary first to review the operational models of the real estate market which
have been published to date.

Modern property cycle research relies upon mathematical modelling to articulate
its theoretical underpinnings. In part, the models draw upon exemplars developed in
the wider field of business cycle research, and in part, they have grown out of ideas
formulated through the specific study of real estate markets. These strands are represented by two convergent modelling traditions, each of which is concerned to
represent property market behaviour in terms of lagged adjustment processes. One
is the stock adjustment process, common to all sectors of capital investment, by
which building responds to changes in occupier demand; the other is the rent adjustment process specific to real estate markets, through which the stock adjustment
process is mediated. A third tradition, of multi-equation modelling, has evolved
to combine these adjustment processes into a circular transmission process which
propagates cyclical fluctuations across all aspects of property market behaviour.
For general reviews of the different strands of real estate modelling, see Ball et al.
(1998) and McDonald (2002).

Stock adjustment models

In Chapter 3, we saw that a persistent theme in discussions about the propagation
of real estate cycles is the capital stock adjustment process which drives building
investment, and in particular, the accelerator relationship which translates changes
in occupier demand into levels of investment. Two aspects of this process have
been identified as responsible for the especially volatile and prolonged nature of the

building cycle. The first is the long gestation lag involved in construction, which creates a tendency for building to alternate between over-shooting and under-shooting in response to increases in investment demand. The second is the durability of built structures, which means that the more stable replacement component of investment demand is insufficiently large to offset the volatile component of induced demand driven by fluctuating increases in occupier activity. One strand of real estate modelling captures these aspects of building investment through the specification of lagged accelerator models, drawing upon the multiplier–accelerator tradition which dominated the first generation of business cycle models (see Chapter 2).

Derksen (1940) published an early lagged accelerator model of the long cycle in residential construction. His building equation relates rates of construction to the levels of existing and required housing stock, introducing a delay between changes in requirements and additions to stock which combines a reaction lag between changes in rents and the start of construction with a construction lag between building starts and completions. A separate rent equation expresses rents in terms of the supply–demand balance as represented by the housing occupancy rate, determined by the number of households plus a 'normal' vacancy rate. Rents rise if supply falls short of the normal level of demand, which leads to an increase in the level of new building. Exogenous factors include the influence of household incomes on rents and of construction costs on the level of building. By holding the exogenous variables constant, Derksen showed how the building and rent equations could be combined into a single second order equation in building starts which generates damped oscillations with a period of around 12 years under the conditions determined by his estimated model parameters.

The first generation of real estate models was mainly designed for the house-building sector. A lagged stock adjustment model was adopted by Maisel (1963) for simulating the fluctuation in US residential construction as an inventory process. He defined housing inventories to be the sum of units vacant and under construction, made building starts a function of net household formation and removals (induced plus replacement demand), allowed the equilibrium level of vacancy to vary according to market circumstances and inserted a lag between starts and completions which propagated an inventory cycle. Smith (1969) developed a stock-flow model in which house prices and vacancy are determined by the interaction of the available stock of housing and the level of household demand, which in turn depends on demographic factors, incomes, house prices and the cost of mortgage finance. Housing starts are a function of prices, vacancy, development costs and the availability of mortgage finance. Bischoff (1970) provided an early application of the lagged accelerator to model fluctuations in non-residential building. He defined desired building stock to be a function of past levels of industrial output, building starts to be a function of the gap between desired and available stock moderated by a flexible accelerator and building output to be a function of past levels of starts. To improve the performance of the model, he extended his distributed lag equation for desired building stock to include the relative price of industrial output as well as its quantity, drawing upon the neoclassical model of investment first proposed by Jorgenson (1963).

The author developed a lagged accelerator model of the UK office development cycle, concentrating on a sector in which the construction lags are particularly prolonged, and the building cycles especially volatile (Barras, 1983). In a similar vein to Bischoff, desired building stock is defined to be a simple function of the current level of user output, development starts are a flexible accelerator function of the gap between desired and available stock, allowing for replacement of obsolete stock at a constant rate of depreciation, while building starts and completions are separated by a construction lag. As with multiplier–accelerator models of the business cycle, the model reduces to a second order difference equation which generates alternative behavioural regimes around a steady-state growth path, depending upon the parameter values. The crucial model parameters are the flexible accelerator coefficient, the rate of depreciation and the length of the construction lag. Under plausible assumptions about the values of these parameters, the model can generate cyclical fluctuations with a period in the range 8–10 years, consistent with the duration of major office cycles observed in the post-war period. An expanded version of this lagged accelerator model, incorporating a rent adjustment process, is presented below and in Appendix B.

Wheaton and Torto (1990) presented a flexible accelerator model of the US industrial market–a market they considered suitable for this type of approach because it is largely owner occupied, so that the development of new industrial plants can be assumed to be the outcome of investment decisions by occupying firms. The basic demand variable is the change in industrial employment, while the negative influence of the cost of capital is also included. The model allows for depreciation of the existing stock and a construction lag between an increase in demand and delivery of the new buildings. The estimated adjustment rates suggest that whilst investment in new industrial plants tends to be phased over several years, the construction period for each phase is relatively short. For this reason, industrial development is less prone to long building cycles than sectors such as offices for which construction periods are substantially longer; instead, the industrial market can exhibit more pronounced short cycles reflecting business cycle fluctuations in occupier activity and therefore property demand.

A similar flexible accelerator model of industrial development in the United Kingdom was constructed by Giussani and Tsolacos (1994). They employed an adaptive expectations framework (see Chapter 2) and chose manufacturing output rather than industrial employment as their demand variable. Building starts are expressed as a function of lagged changes in output and vacancy, to capture owner occupier expectations of investment requirements, lagged levels of rents, to capture the speculative component of industrial building, and a constant fraction of existing stock, to capture replacement investment. In Tsolacos (1995), the model was used to analyse industrial building at the regional rather than national level, expanding the set of explanatory variables to include more general proxies of regional economic conditions such as GDP and unemployment. In Tsolacos (1998), the model was adapted to analyse building in the retail rather than the industrial sector, using consumer spending as the demand variable and again including rents as an indicator of expected development profitability.

Rent adjustment models

A particular aspect of the real estate market which contributes to cycle propagation is the indirect relationship between the construction and use of new buildings, which means that the adjustment of capital stock to changes in occupier demand is mediated through the adjustment of vacancy and rents. An increase in occupier demand for space is met in the short run from the inventory of vacant space within the existing stock; a reduction in the level of vacancy leads to an increase in rents and prices, providing the market signal to which developers respond by constructing new stock in excess of replacement demand. This rent adjustment process tends to be sticky because of factors such as long leases and high search and transaction costs. Models of rent adjustment incorporate an equilibrium or natural vacancy rate which balances supply and demand, and helps rents and prices to revert to their equilibrium levels by maintaining just sufficient surplus space to ensure efficient turnover within the market. As a general rule, the higher the elasticity of occupier demand for space, the higher the equilibrium vacancy rate needs to be, because economic shocks will generate a greater change in turnover. Conversely, the higher the elasticity of developer supply of new space, the lower the equilibrium vacancy rate because supply can respond more rapidly to changes in demand (Sanderson et al., 2006).

The first rent adjustment models were developed for the housing market. Blank and Winnick (1953) formulated an equilibrium model in which housing rents and occupancy are determined by the interaction of two adjustment relationships: that between the level of rents and the rate of utilization of the standing stock, under short-run conditions of fixed supply and sticky rents, and that between construction levels and rents, as supply shifts in response to exogenous changes in demand. Smith (1974) developed the Blank and Winnick rent–occupancy relationship into a partial rent adjustment equation. In this formulation, the change in rents, rather than their level, is an inverse function of the vacancy rate, in recognition of the market friction which means that rents and vacancy can deviate from their equilibrium values for considerable periods of time. The natural vacancy rate is defined to be the rate at which rental growth is zero under conditions of fixed supply, while demand is made partly endogenous by allowing it to vary inversely with rents as well as directly with household incomes.

Various refinements have been made to the partial rent adjustment model. Rosen and Smith (1983) expressed rental change as an inverse function of the gap between the current and natural vacancy rates, moderated by an adjustment parameter which is equivalent to the reaction rate in a flexible accelerator model. They estimated the model for rental housing in 17 US cities over the period 1969–80, finding wide variation in the derived values of the natural vacancy rate, ranging from 5.5% to 16.7%; cross-sectional modelling suggested that this variation was a function of the turnover rate, the level and dispersion of rents and the rate of house-building in each city. Shilling et al. (1987) used the same vacancy gap model to estimate the natural vacancy rate for offices in a different set of 17 US cities between 1960 and 1975, again deriving a wide range of estimates across the cities. They tested the assumption that the natural vacancy rate increases directly with the expected growth in demand for office space, and inversely with the marginal cost of holding vacant space, but obtained inconclusive results. Wheaton and Torto (1988) fitted the model to the national office market in the United States between 1968 and 1986, allowing the natural vacancy rate to vary through time in order to capture a structural increase due to higher occupier turnover and shorter leases. Sivitanides (1997) generalized the approach to express the natural vacancy rate as a time-dependent function of lagged variables such as net absorption and the rate of building; when the model was tested for 24 US office markets, the addition of one or other of the possible explanatory variables was found to improve model fit in nearly all cases.

Some analysts have pointed to the incomplete nature of the partial rent adjustment model, due to the omission of an explicit equilibrium or natural rent level to complement the natural vacancy rate. As a result, rents do not necessarily revert to their equilibrium level when vacancy returns to its natural rate, forcing the market to overshoot in response to supply or demand shocks. To counter this problem, Wheaton and Torto (1994) suggested an improved model based on the tenant search process. Rental change is expressed as a function of the gap between the equilibrium rent and the lagged level of actual rent, so that rents are trend reverting, while the equilibrium rent is determined by the lagged rate of net absorption as well as market vacancy. The inclusion of net absorption captures the effect that the faster the turnover rate, the lower the search cost and, therefore, the higher the equilibrium rent that both tenants and landlords will accept. In a similar vein, Hendershott (1995) proposed a generalized rent adjustment equation in which rental growth is a function of both the vacancy gap and the rent gap, with the rent gap acting as a stabilizing feedback mechanism. He fitted this generalized equation to data on real effective rent movements in the Sydney office market between 1970 and 1992, and found that it gave a considerably better fit than the partial model based on the vacancy gap alone, with addition of the rent gap doubling the explanatory power of the model.

More recently, Hendershott et al. (2002a) have embedded the rent adjustment model within a more general theoretical framework which captures the supply and demand determinants of the equilibrium rent level. They specified a long-run reduced form equation to determine the equilibrium level of rent in terms of output or employment on the demand side and the vacancy rate and building stock on the supply side. To complement the equilibrium equation, they derived a short-run error correction form of adjustment equation for rental change expressed in terms of changes in the explanatory variables plus the lagged residuals from the long-run equation (see, for example, Engle and Granger, 1991 on error correction models). By this means, the rent adjustment relationship captures not only the feedback effects of the deviation in rents and vacancy around their equilibrium levels, but also the impact of the exogenous supply or demand shocks which triggered the departure from equilibrium. In Hendershott et al. (2002b), this model was applied using panel data to explain the movement of real office and retail rents in 11 UK regions over the period 1971–99; in Mouzakis and Richards (2007), it was applied to the panel data modelling of office rents in 12 European markets between 1980 and 2001.

The linear structure of rent adjustment models has also come into question. Farrelly and Sanderson (2005) argue that the behaviour of real estate actors can alter during different phases of the property cycle, particularly near unstable peaks and troughs, and that this should be captured by introducing non-linearities into the model specification through the use of a 'regime switching' approach. They tested a non-linear rent adjustment model for the City of London office market and found that it reproduced market behaviour better than the equivalent linear model, particularly during the turbulent late 1980s/early 1990s cycle.

Multi-equation models

The endogenous propagation of building cycles involves a combination of rent adjustment and capital stock adjustment processes, creating a circular transmission process which links vacancy to rents, rents to building starts, starts to completions and completions to vacancy. The lags which contribute to cycle generation can occur at each stage in this transmission process, either due to technical factors such as construction periods, which delay capital stock adjustment, or institutional factors such as fixed leases, which slow the rent adjustment process. It is to represent this transmission process that the third real estate modelling tradition has emerged – the formulation of multi-equation models to produce forecasts which can help developers and investors to anticipate the future course of the property cycle.

Although the various multi-equation models which have been developed show individual differences, there is a common structure to which most adhere in whole or in part (Ball et al., 1998: 223–8). The following are the three core behavioural equations which most models incorporate in one form or another:

- *Occupier demand* for building space is typically expressed as the direct function of an appropriate measure of occupier activity, such as household income or economic output, and an inverse function of the real rent level, representing the user cost of capital.
- *Rental change* is normally represented by some form of rent adjustment equation, which in its most extended form is defined in terms of the gaps between the actual and equilibrium vacancy rates and the actual and equilibrium levels of rents.
- *Development supply* can be expressed either as a stock adjustment model of the gap between desired and actual space, allowing for depreciation, or as a profitability model based on expected rents or capital values, construction costs and the cost of capital.

Two accounting relationships complete the basic model circuit:

- *Development starts and completions* may be separately specified, so that the development supply equation defines starts, and completions are expressed as a distributed lag function of starts.
- *Vacancy change* captures the opposing impacts of net absorption (increases in occupier demand) and net additions (development completions less demolitions) upon the buffer stock of vacant space.

In addition, some models also allow for the determination of capital values by incorporating property within a multi-asset framework:

- *Yields* are usually expressed as a function of expected rental growth and the yields on alternative investment assets, in particular bonds and equities.

The main exogenous inputs to the model are income or output, construction costs, the cost of capital and investment yields on other assets; the main endogenous variables are vacancy, rents, yields and the level of building. Lags can be introduced at each stage of the model, producing a dynamic structure which is able to capture the disequilibrium behaviour of property markets.

The office market focus of US real estate research in the 1980s is reflected in the early multi-equation models. Rosen (1984) was the first in the field with a model of office building at city level which employs the three core behavioural equations outlined above. The desired level of office stock takes the standard form, using office employment as the measure of occupier activity, while the rent adjustment equation takes the form proposed in Rosen and Smith (1983), with real rental change determined by the vacancy gap between the current and natural rates. The development supply equation is of the standard profitability type, except that it includes lagged vacancy rates as well as expected future rents, construction costs and interest rates; however, when the model was estimated using data for San Francisco between 1961 and 1983, only vacancy appeared to be a significant influence on new construction.

A different approach to modelling office building was adopted by Hekman (1985), who employed cross-sectional estimation of a two-equation panel model across 14 US cities, in order to capture both local and national influences on the market. As well as rents, construction costs and the interest rate, his development supply equation also includes the expected growth of the local market, to capture the delay between the decision to develop and the completion of construction. The rent equation is expressed in terms of the level of rent, rather than the rate of rental change, expressed as a function of the local vacancy rate, the local unemployment rate (a local demand measure), national GNP (a national demand variable) and total city employment (to account for city size). For estimation purposes, the local growth expectations variable was represented by the historic 10-year growth of office employment in each city, and this was found to be a highly significant influence on development supply, as was the rent level; however, construction costs and the interest rate were not significant.

The model used by Wheaton (1987) to replicate the national office market cycle in the United States employs the core supply and demand equations, plus a separate net absorption equation and an explicit distinction between building starts and completions separated by a construction lag. The demand equation includes an expectations variable about future space needs that is represented by the current rate of employment growth. Net absorption is specified as an adjustment equation in which only a portion of the increase in demand is realized each year, reflecting the inertia introduced into the market by long leases and high moving costs. As well as the standard variables, the development supply equation includes a growth expectations variable (as in the Hekman model) and vacancy (as in the Rosen model). Estimation of the model for the United States over the period 1967–86 was hampered by a lack of rent data, and so lagged vacancy was used as a proxy in the demand and supply equations. The slowness of the reaction lags in the office market was highlighted by an estimated 3-year delay between vacancy change and its impact on demand, and a 2½-year delay in its impact on supply. The growth expectations variable had a strong influence on both demand and supply but, as found in many other modelling exercises, neither construction costs nor the interest rate was a significant influence on supply. Pollakowski et al. (1992) used a cross-sectional model with the Wheaton structure to test for structural differences in the behaviour of 21 city office markets in the United States over the period 1981–90, finding significant differences which tended to support the hypothesis that larger, and therefore more competitive, markets exhibit more responsive adjustment processes.

Multi-equation models of the housing market have also been constructed by US researchers. A paper by Poterba (1984) presented a two equation asset-market model, defined in terms of real price changes and net investment in new housing stock. The price equation equates the marginal rental value of the housing services generated by a fixed supply of dwellings with the marginal cost of those services expressed in terms of the real house price and the user cost of housing. The user cost of housing is defined in terms of the sum of depreciation, repair costs, property taxes, mortgage interest payments and the opportunity cost of housing equity, less the capital gain from home ownership. The net investment in new housing is defined by the level of new construction, defined as a function of real prices, less the depreciation of the existing stock. The model was used to simulate the effects of changes in the expected inflation rate on real house prices and the equilibrium size of the housing stock.

DiPasquale and Wheaton (1994) modified and extended the traditional housing stock adjustment model developed by Maisel (1963) and Smith (1969) among others. Owner-occupier demand is expressed as an increasing function of household income and the expected home-ownership rate, and a decreasing function of the real price of housing and the user cost of home ownership. The development supply equation combines stock adjustment with profitability: supply adjusts to the gap between the actual and equilibrium levels of stock, and the equilibrium level is determined by house prices and building costs. Again the problem of insignificant construction and land costs was encountered when fitting the model to national data between 1963 and 1990. A three equation model of the rental housing market was developed by Chinloy (1996), incorporating the concept of a 'construction trigger vacancy rate' – the vacancy rate at which new construction is initiated. The level of construction is expressed as a direct function of the gap between the actual vacancy rate and the construction trigger, and an inverse function of construction costs. Rents adjust to the gap between the actual and equilibrium vacancy rates, while the vacancy gap that triggers construction in turn adjusts to the difference between the current rental growth rate and the equilibrating growth rate.

Turning to research in the United Kingdom, the lagged accelerator model developed by the author (Barras, 1983) was inserted into a model framework encompassing interrelated occupier and investment submarkets (Barras and Ferguson, 1987a, b). The model comprises three equations – for occupier demand, developer supply and investment demand – which are combined into a reduced equation in building activity expressed in error correction form so as to reproduce both the short-run dynamics of the adjustment process and the long-run equilibrium relationships between the market variables. The model was calibrated using quarterly UK data between 1958 and 1984 for three sectors of private construction: commercial, industrial and residential. The main drivers of occupier demand were found to be manufacturing output for industrial building, GDP for commercial development and both consumer spending and mortgage advances for house-building. Business cycle fluctuations in manufacturing output and consumer spending explained the minor cycles in industrial and residential building, while the model generated endogenous major cycles in all sectors. In the industrial and commercial sectors, there was evidence that the competing returns from investment in equities had an impact on the investment demand for property; in contrast, the influences of construction costs and interest rates on levels of building were again found to be weak, except in the case of house-building.

In their study of the post-war property cycle in the United Kingdom, Key et al. (1994) combined occupier demand and rent adjustment equations into a reduced form equation for the rent level; this incorporated occupier activity, total stock and lagged development starts as well as lagged rents. The rent model achieved good fits for all three sectors of commercial property (office, industrial and retail) when fitted to national data from the mid-1960s to 1992. The profitability form of the development supply equation was estimated for each sector using capital values rather than rents as the main driver. Unusually, construction costs, interest rates and lagged capital values acting as a proxy for land costs all turned out to be significant negative influences on building activity. An all-property yield equation was also specified in which the main factors reducing yields were found to be expected future returns, the inflow of investment funds and the inflation rate; the main factors increasing yields were short and long-term interest rates together with lagged building starts, which act to dampen investor expectations about future rental growth.

A rather different approach to modelling commercial real estate markets was presented by Tsolacos et al. (1998). They sought to capture the cyclical dynamics of the UK office market within an adaptive expectations framework in which the model equations are specified in terms of a lag structure of first differences in the explanatory variables. One equation is defined for each of the occupation, investment and development markets. Rental change is expressed as a function of changes in output, employment and new building; capital value change is a function of changes in rents, other asset prices (equities) and new building; new building change is determined by changes in rents, capital values and development costs (interest rates). A similarly defined rent equation was also tested for the UK industrial market by Thompson and Tsolacos (1999), using vacancy rather than new building as the supply variable. In a refinement of their approach, Tsolacos and McGough (1999) defined a rational expectations form of new building equation for the office market which incorporates the dampening effect of uncertainty upon future levels of development. Changes in the level of new building are expressed as a direct function of lagged changes in output and rents, and an inverse function of the uncertainty surrounding future output and rental changes, using measures of their historic volatility as proxies. When the model was fitted to quarterly data between 1979 and 1996, rental uncertainty was found to have exerted a significant negative influence on the rate of UK office development during the 1990s.

Two case study exercises to model the cyclical behaviour of the London office market were published in the late 1990s. Wheaton et al. (1997) applied a modified version of the Wheaton (1987) model to the Greater London office market. Compared to the original model, their demand equation omits the growth expectations term, but does include the product of employment and real rent levels to capture the impact of rents on the occupancy rate. The supply equation also omits the growth expectations term and there is no construction lag between starts and completions; when fitted to the London data between 1970 and 1995, the interest rate was as usual not significant, but construction costs were. An explicit rent adjustment process is included, with rental change expressed as a function of the gap between the equilibrium rent and the actual last period rent, while the equilibrium rent is determined by the interaction of the net absorption and vacancy rates. A similarly structured model was applied to the City of London office market by Hendershott et al. (1999). This model equates the equilibrium rent level to the user cost of capital, expressed as the product of the replacement cost with the sum of the real interest rate (based on the bond yield), the depreciation rate and the operating cost ratio. Rental adjustment is determined by both the vacancy gap and the real rent gap (as in Hendershott, 1995), development supply reduces to an equation in the lagged rent gap, while net absorption is defined as a stock adjustment process which includes lagged rental growth as well as the gap between the desired and available stock.

Finally, Meen (2000) developed a model of the UK housing market based upon the asset-market approach pioneered by Poterba (1984). House prices are derived by capitalizing the imputed rental price of housing services, allowing for the capital gain obtained from home ownership, while the rental price is in turn derived from the marginal rate of substitution between housing and a composite consumption good. Demand is driven by the excess return to housing, expressed as the difference between the total gains from investing in housing (capital gain plus imputed rent) less the costs (mortgage costs plus depreciation) relative to the return on an alternative risk-free asset. On the supply side, a standard profitability equation expresses housing starts as a function of new house prices, construction costs and interest rates, allowing for adjustment costs and construction lags. The dynamic interaction between demand and supply generates a strong market cycle, with development profits varying over the cycle.

Specification of the model

Underlying assumptions

Drawing upon the cycle literature reviewed in Chapters 2 and 3, and the modelling literature surveyed above, the following assumptions have been made as the starting point for specifying our simulation model.

A growth cycle
The aim of the model is to describe how building cycles are generated and sustained around the equilibrium growth path of an economy. For this purpose, it is helpful to convert extensive market variables such as the level of building starts into ratios with respect to one growth variable, chosen here to be occupied stock, so that the magnitudes of the cyclical fluctuations are not growth dependent. With this approach, market quantities fluctuate relative to their 'natural values' defined by the equilibrium growth path.

Interlocking submarkets
The model is formalized in terms of three interlocking submarkets, in which the occupier demand for property is met by a development sector undertaking building

construction and an investment sector engaged in building finance and ownership. Occupier demand, investment demand and development supply determine the main structural equations of the model, linked together through a circular transmission process which determines market rents and prices.

Impulse and propagation
Impulse and propagation are combined within the model. Once an initial shock has displaced the property market away from its equilibrium growth trajectory, a self-sustaining cycle is endogenously propagated in building and related market variables. Occasional random impulse shocks are necessary to maintain the momentum of the cycle, but these need not be regular in occurrence.

Adjustment lags
The dynamic behaviour of a property market is critically dependent upon the speed and strength of its adjustment response to a shock: the slower the speed of adjustment, the more likely it is that persistent cyclical fluctuations will be generated. The model incorporates adjustment lags at different stages in the transmission process linking an initial demand shock to the subsequent building response, as mediated through changes in vacancy and rents.

Myopic expectations and inelastic demand
Two conditions necessary for cycle propagation are assumed in the model. The first is that market agents form myopic expectations about future prices, since the requirements for expectations to be rational are too severe to be realistic in markets characterized by long construction periods, sticky adjustment processes and products that are durable, lumpy and heterogeneous. The second condition is that demand is relatively price inelastic compared to supply because of rigidities such as long fixed leases and high transaction and moving costs.

Model structure

Based on these underlying assumptions, the structure of the model that has been developed to reproduce the behaviour of the building cycle can be summarized as follows. The full equation system is set out in Appendix B.

Occupier demand
- Economic output grows at a constant secular rate, given by the sum of the labour force growth rate and the rate of labour-saving technical progress; this determines a steady-state growth trajectory on to which exogenous business cycle fluctuations can be superimposed.
- The occupied building stock in each time period is a product of the current level of economic activity and the occupancy rate; this occupancy relationship can either be defined in terms of the aggregate stock of buildings in all uses or the separate stocks occupied by different sectors of the economy.
- In the basic model, the occupancy rate is treated as a rent inelastic fixed parameter set at its natural rate; in more complex versions, it is time dependent and rent elastic – the higher the level of rents, the more intensively do occupiers utilize their building space.

- The desired level of total building stock consists of the occupied stock supplemented by an increment of available space sufficient to accommodate the natural vacancy rate which maintains the efficient turnover of the occupier market.
- During each time period, the take-up of building space by occupiers consists of two components – the net absorption of stock resulting from the additional demand created by economic growth, and the turnover generated by existing occupiers moving between buildings to satisfy their changing requirements.

Investment demand
- The level of building investment required to maintain total stock at its desired level consists of the sum of two components: induced investment and replacement investment.
- Induced investment is a function of the difference between the level of occupier demand for building stock in the current period and the actual stock available from the previous period.
- Replacement investment is a response to the loss of stock retired or demolished by building owners at the end of each period, and is expressed as the product of a depreciation rate applied to the total building stock available in that period.
- Like the occupancy rate, the depreciation rate can be made to vary around its natural rate according to whether rents are rising or falling – the higher rents rise, the more slowly do building owners retire their least profitable space.
- The planned level of building starts during each period consists of the required level of investment adjusted down by a reaction coefficient, acting as a flexible accelerator to allow for uncertain expectations about the future demand for space.
- Expressed relative to occupied stock, there is a unique natural rate of building starts which maintains the equilibrium growth trajectory; it is a function of the economic growth rate, the depreciation rate, the natural vacancy rate and the length of the development lag.

Rent adjustment
- Since most building investment is not undertaken directly by occupiers, but indirectly by a separate development sector, investment demand signals must be transmitted to developers through movements in the vacancy rate and levels of rents and prices.
- Investment demand for new building is translated into a relationship between the actual level of vacant space at the start of a period and the level required to maintain vacancy at its natural rate.
- When the market moves away from its equilibrium path, the actual vacancy rate deviates from the natural rate and this imbalance is reflected in an inverse adjustment to real rents and prices which takes them away from their equilibrium level.
- Along the equilibrium growth trajectory, there is a unique natural rent and price level which makes it just profitable enough for developers to supply the natural level of building starts and just affordable enough for occupiers to utilize the total stock of space up to its natural vacancy rate.

- The market clearing equilibrium, which defines the unique natural rate of building starts and the natural levels of rents and prices, can shift according to influences exogenous to the property market, such as other input costs, construction costs and investment returns in other asset markets.

Development supply
- Building supply by the development sector is driven directly by rent or price signals: if rents are above their natural level, or if they are growing, then the rate of starts exceeds the natural rate in order to boost total stock back towards its desired level, and vice versa.
- The combined transmission coefficient, which translates vacancy into building starts, is the product of a rent adjustment coefficient, determining the extent of the rental response to a given vacancy rate, and a development reaction coefficient, acting as a form of supply elasticity to determine the extent of the development response to a given rent signal.
- The level of building completions is equated to the level of starts lagged by the average construction period.
- The quantity of building stock available in each time period is equal to the previous period's stock less retirements, augmented by current period completions.
- An absolute floor on development is determined by the constraint that the level of starts in any period cannot be less than zero; more realistically, the development floor can be set to a minimum level of starts corresponding to some volume of 'autonomous development' that tends to be undertaken irrespective of current market conditions.
- There is a ceiling on development activity determined by the constraint that the level of development underway at any time, equal to the sum of the uncompleted starts from the current and previous periods, does not exceed the capacity of the development industry, which is assumed to grow in line with the economy as a whole.

Determinants of model behaviour

The model relationships presented in Appendix B have been formulated as a system of difference equations, an approach that is currently much in vogue for reproducing the dynamic behaviour of a wide variety of oscillatory systems in both the natural and social sciences (see, for example, Strogatz, 1994; Pikovsky et al., 2001). Appendix B presents analytic solutions for a simplified, second order, linear version of the model, with inelastic demand and a single period construction lag. These solutions indicate the conditions under which cycles will be generated and the factors which determine the subsequent behaviour of the cycle. More complex, non-linear forms of the model are much more difficult to solve analytically. Instead, this chapter reports the results of applying a numerical simulation approach, implementing the equations as a spreadsheet model and demonstrating how this behaves under a variety of more realistic conditions which allow for elastic demand, multi-period construction lags, composite rent adjustment processes and development floor and ceiling constraints. There are similarities to the simulation approaches adopted in Wheaton (1999) and Kummerow (1999) and, though the model structure is rather different, the results achieved are broadly consistent with those derived in these earlier studies.

The mathematical solution of the basic model set out in Appendix B shows that the equilibrium growth trajectory determines the natural rate of building starts as the product of three factors:

1 The sum of the output growth rate and depreciation rate, representing the induced and replacement components of investment demand for new space.
2 A scaling factor which boosts total development supply to meet the demand for an additional increment of spare capacity, on top of the occupied stock, at the natural vacancy rate.
3 A scaling factor which anticipates the growth in demand over the construction lag separating starts from completions, providing an additional increment of supply at the growth rate of the economy for each year of the lag.

When the model is initialized so that the actual rate of building starts equals the natural rate, then the model follows the equilibrium path without cyclical disturbance. However, any deviation away from the natural rate has the potential to generate cyclical fluctuations in building activity. The subsequent behaviour of the model, after an initial displacement, is shown to depend upon six parameters:

1 The size of the initial displacement;
2 The length of the construction lag;
3 The rate of output growth;
4 The rate of depreciation;
5 The value of the transmission coefficient which translates deviations in vacancy into compensating deviations in starts, via movements in real rents;
6 The elasticity of occupier demand with respect to movements in real rents.

It is the combination of these parameters which determines the conditions under which cycles will be generated, whether they will be damped or explosive, and the magnitude of the period and amplitude of the cycle.

As the transmission coefficient increases, so the behaviour of the model passes through a sequence of behavioural regimes that is well documented in the literature on business cycle models (see, for example, Gabisch and Lorenz, 1989: 48):

• For low values of the transmission coefficient, below its critical value, an initial displacement is followed by monotonic damping, as the rate of building starts moves smoothly back to its natural equilibrium rate.
• For intermediate values of the transmission coefficient, lying between its critical value and the crossover point, an initial disturbance produces damped oscillations in starts that die away progressively.
• When the transmission coefficient is equal to its crossover value, a stable harmonic cycle of building starts is generated.
• For high values of the transmission coefficient, above the crossover point, an initial disturbance generates explosive oscillations in starts which progressively increase in magnitude.

We have seen that it is the movement of real rents which plays the crucial intermediate role in the transmission process from vacancy to building starts. Appendix B sets out three alternative adjustment processes by which rents can respond to vacancy and building starts to rents – full adjustment, when real rents move to a new level above or below the natural rent, partial adjustment, when they undergo growth or decline away from their equilibrium level, and composite adjustment, which combines the two. The inverse relationship between vacancy and the rate of starts, as captured by the combined transmission coefficient, is unaffected by the choice of adjustment process; what do change are the separate relationships between vacancy and rent movements (acting through the rent adjustment coefficient), and rent and starts movements (acting through the development reaction coefficient). As indicated in the previous section, early rent models typically employed a partial adjustment mechanism, though more recently a composite formulation has been favoured. Partial adjustment has been chosen as the basic adjustment mechanism in the following simulations, although the effects of the three alternatives are separately assessed.

Model simulations

Equilibrium and displacement

Let us start with the model in its most basic, unconstrained form. For illustrative purposes, it is assumed that economic output is growing at a steady 2% per annum, building stock is depreciating at 1.5% per annum, the natural vacancy rate is 10%, real rents are indexed to a natural level of 100 and the average construction lag is 2 years. Building starts and completions during each time period are expressed as rates of building relative to the quantity of occupied stock at the beginning of the period. Occupier demand is assumed to be rent inelastic, so that the occupancy rate is a fixed coefficient; building activity is not constrained by a floor or ceiling, except for the absolute condition that starts cannot be negative; partial rent adjustment is assumed to be operating. The simulation is run over a period of 50 years.

The combination of the chosen output growth rate, depreciation rate, natural vacancy rate and construction lag produces a natural rate of building starts of 4.0%, according to equation (B.58). When the initial rate of starts is set to this value, the model stays on its equilibrium path, with the starts and vacancy rates staying constant at their natural rates, and the real rent remaining constant at its natural level. Furthermore, this equilibrium path is maintained irrespective of the size of the combined transmission coefficient relating starts to vacancy.

However, even a slight displacement of the initial rate of starts away from its natural rate is sufficient for the model to generate cyclical fluctuations in building activity, vacancy and rents, as long as the transmission coefficient is above its critical value. For relatively low values of the transmission coefficient, the fluctuations die away; however for values at or above the crossover point, they persist and magnify. The behaviour of the building cycle thus depends crucially upon the value of the transmission coefficient: for values below the crossover point, the cycle is stable, whereas for values above that point, it is unstable. This result holds true irrespective of the size of the initial displacement to the rate of building starts.

The larger the displacement, the larger the initial cycle amplitude, but whether or not subsequent cycles die away or explode still depends upon the value of the transmission coefficient.

Cycle transmission

With the construction lag set to 2 years, the crossover value of the transmission coefficient at which stable cycles are generated is found to be 0.66. With the transmission coefficient set to this value, the initial rate of building starts displaced from its natural rate by −2% and the other model parameters fixed at the values listed above. Figure 7.1 illustrates the timing and amplitude of the resultant harmonic cycles in building starts, vacancy and rental growth, each oscillating around its natural rate. The chosen parameter settings produce a starts cycle with an amplitude of 2.5% around the natural rate of 4%, a vacancy cycle with an amplitude of 3.7% around the natural rate of 10% and a rental growth cycle with an amplitude of 7.5% around the natural rate of zero.

The transmission process begins with the initial downward displacement of starts applied in years −1 and 0, reducing completions below their natural rate in years 1 and 2 because of the 2-year construction lag. Depressed completions reduce the vacancy rate below its natural rate at the end of years 1 and 2, because insufficient new space is added to total stock to meet the growth in occupier demand. Allowing for the lag in the transmission process, reduced vacancy at the end of years 1 and 2 generates rental growth in years 2 and 3, which boosts starts above their natural rate to compensate for their initial shortfall. This above average level of building in turn increases vacancy and reduces rents, moving the cycle into reverse.

The relative timing of these cycles follows from the transmission process just described, whilst their period is principally a function of the length of the development lag (see below). The amplitude of all three cycles varies with the magnitude of

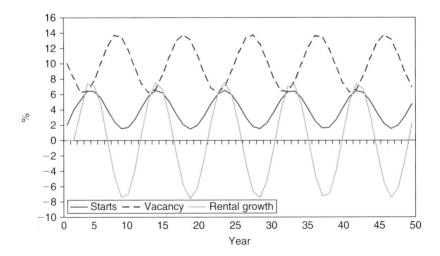

Figure 7.1   Market cycle transmission (development lag = 2).

the initial displacement to building starts. In addition, the amplitude of the rental growth cycle is dependent upon the size of the rent adjustment coefficient that is one of the two components of the combined transmission coefficient. As the rent adjustment coefficient is increased, so the amplitude of the rent cycle increases; however, this implies a compensating reduction in the development reaction coefficient if the transmission coefficient is to be maintained at its fixed crossover value. Consequently, the amplitudes of the vacancy and starts cycles are unchanged, as long as the value of the combined transmission coefficient which links the two remains unaltered.

Damped and explosive cycles

By steadily increasing the value of the transmission coefficient, each market cycle progresses through the sequence of behavioural regimes that was outlined in the previous section. For this exercise, the model parameters and initial displacement are set to the same values as in the previous simulation, and the value of the transmission coefficient is increased from 0.2 to 1.0 in steps of 0.2. The resultant impacts on building starts, vacancy rate, real rental growth and the real rent level are illustrated in Figures 7.2–7.5.

Monotonic damping

For low values of the transmission coefficient (i.e. 0.2), building starts, vacancy and real rental growth follow trajectories characterized by monotonic damping. The initial downward displacement of starts depresses vacancy below its natural rate (down to 6.3%) and causes a surge in real rental growth (peaking at 7.4%). There is then a compensating shift in starts to a rate above their natural rate (4.7%), after which they

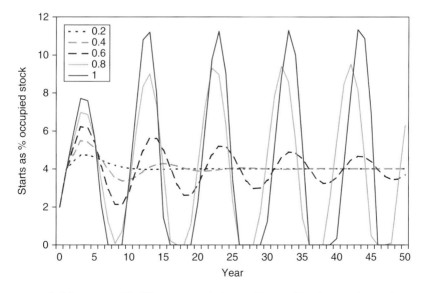

Figure 7.2   Building starts with different transmission coefficients (development lag = 2).

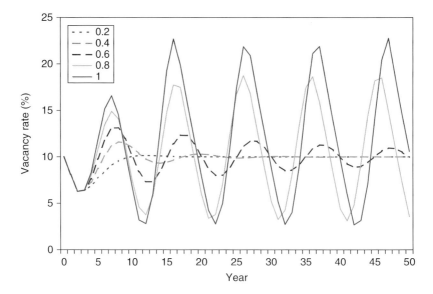

Figure 7.3 Vacancy rate with different transmission coefficients (development lag = 2).

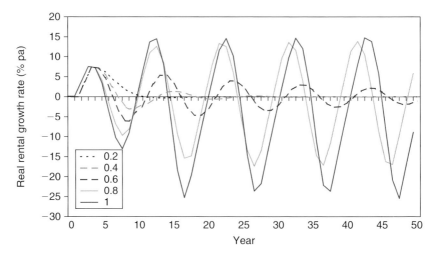

Figure 7.4 Real rental growth rate with different transmission coefficients (development lag = 2).

revert to their natural rate of 4%, vacancy reverts to its natural rate of 10% and the rental growth rate reverts to zero. Because of the initial surge of rental growth, real rents are displaced from their natural level of 100 to stabilize at a new higher level (settling at 139); they are then maintained at a level above their natural rate because the rent adjustment process used in this simulation is only partial (see below).

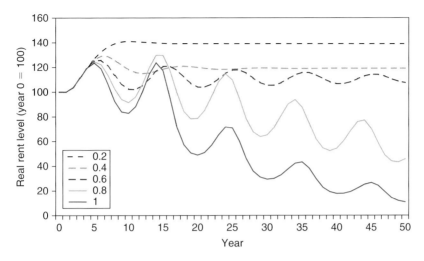

Figure 7.5   Real rent level with different transmission coefficients (development lag = 2).

Damped oscillations

As the transmission coefficient increases above 0.2, it passes through the critical value at which cyclical fluctuations begin to appear. If the model is specified with the chosen parameter settings but a development lag of only 1 year, the analytical solution set out in Appendix B predicts a critical value of 0.24 for the transmission coefficient, and simulation shows that the critical value with a development lag of 2 years is close to this.

With intermediate values of the transmission coefficient (0.4 and 0.6) starts, vacancy and real rental growth exhibit damped oscillations in response to the initial displacement. Unless reinforced by subsequent disturbances, these oscillations die away through successive cycles, the rate of dampening decreasing as the transmission coefficient increases. For building starts, the compensating adjustment after the initial displacement determines the first cycle peak, with an amplitude which is dependent upon the size of the transmission coefficient: the larger the coefficient, the greater the amplitude. This first cycle is followed by a damped oscillation around the natural rate that dies away within two cycles when the transmission coefficient is set at 0.4, but persists throughout the simulation period when the coefficient is set at 0.6. As the transmission coefficient increases, so the cycle frequency also increases, as predicted by the analytical solution to the model presented in Appendix B.

After the initial displacement, the vacancy rate and real rental growth rate experience damped oscillations around their natural rates similar to those exhibited by building starts, with the same pattern of increasing cycle persistence and amplitude as the transmission coefficient is increased. Real rents continue to show a shift above their natural level, resulting from the initial downward displacement of building supply; however, as the transmission coefficient is increased, so it generates a stronger building response to the initial shortfall which reduces the upward displacement. Once a new average level is established, the rent level exhibits the damped oscillations which are transmitted from vacancy to rental growth.

Explosive oscillations

For high values of the transmission coefficient (0.8 and 1.0), lying above the cross-over point (0.66), the initial displacement generates explosive oscillations in building starts which progressively increase in magnitude. However, at some point, these explosive oscillations hit the absolute floor that starts cannot be less than zero. Importantly, this is a sufficient constraint to transform an explosive cycle into one which is stable and persistent with constant frequency, as shown by Hicks (1950) and Goodwin (1951) when they introduced such constraints into their multiplier–accelerator models of the business cycle (see Chapter 2). The larger the transmission coefficient, the more quickly does the cycle hit the absolute floor, and the greater the range of the constrained oscillations which result. With the coefficient set to 0.8, the range of the starts cycle is around 9.5%, whilst with a coefficient of 1.0, it reaches 11.3%. Furthermore, because of the zero floor, the constrained building cycle is no longer symmetrical around the natural starts rate, but rather its unconstrained upswing is greater in magnitude than its constrained downswing.

The corresponding cycles in vacancy and rental growth exhibit a similar pattern of initially explosive and then asymmetrically constrained oscillation once the starts cycle stabilizes. The asymmetry of the starts cycle is transmitted directly to the constrained vacancy cycle: for example, with a transmission coefficient of 0.8, the vacancy rate oscillates between approximately 3% and 18.5%, producing an average a little higher than the natural equilibrium rate of 10%. Because of the inverse relationship between vacancy and rental growth, the asymmetry of the constrained rental growth cycle works in the opposite direction. With a transmission coefficient of 0.8, the rental growth rate oscillates between approximately −17.5% and +13.5%, averaging below the natural equilibrium rate of zero. As a result, there is a secular downward trend to the level of real rents through successive cycles.

Different construction lags

With the model parameters set as before, the average construction lag is varied through 1, 2, 3 and 4 years. For each construction period, the transmission coefficient is adjusted until the crossover point from damped to explosive oscillations is reached, generating a stable and persistent building cycle without the intervention of the absolute floor of zero starts. The results of these simulations are summarized in Table 7.1.

As the construction period increases, the crossover transmission coefficient that generates a stable harmonic cycle decreases in value: from 1.04 with a lag of

Table 7.1   Stable building cycles with different construction lags.

Lag (years)	Transmission coefficient	Cycle period (years)	Cycle amplitude (starts as % stock)
1	1.04	5.9	2.2
2	0.66	9.7	2.5
3	0.50	13.3	2.7
4	0.40	17.0	2.7

1 year, through 0.66 for the 2-year lag and 0.50 for the 3-year lag, to 0.40 with the 4-year lag. This implies that the shorter the construction lag, the stronger can be the development response to a given demand signal without an explosive cycle being generated, because there is a shorter backlog of uncompleted building schemes to disturb the supply–demand balance. The finding that the derived crossover coefficient is 1.04 with a 1-year lag is consistent with the analytic prediction presented in Appendix B.

In line with expectations, the longer the average construction lag, the longer the cycle period. It increases from 5.9 years with a 1-year lag, to 9.7 years with a 2-year lag, 13.3 years for a 3-year lag and 17.0 years with a 4-year lag. The close to 6-year cycle generated by a 1-year lag also confirms the estimates derived in Appendix B. This relationship between the period of the cycle and the length of the construction lag can be advanced as an explanation of the existence of a family of cycles of different duration: the rhythm of each cycle is a manifestation of the delays involved in different types of investment processes. As discussed in Chapters 2–5, there is empirical evidence for the existence of a 4–5 year minor cycle, an 8–11 year major cycle and a composite long cycle of 15–25 years in building activity. The simulation model suggests that the major building cycle is consistent with a construction process which on average lasts for around 2 years.

As the construction lag increases from 1 to 3 years, there is a slight increase in the amplitude of the harmonic building cycle, but between 3 and 4 years there is no further increase. This means that the reduction in the transmission coefficient necessary to achieve a stable cycle broadly offsets the tendency to more explosive cycles of increased amplitude as the construction lag increases. Another way of looking at this is to increase the construction lag while holding the transmission coefficient constant, and observe how cycle behaviour changes. Figure 7.6 illustrates the shift in cycle behaviour when the transmission coefficient is held constant at 0.5:

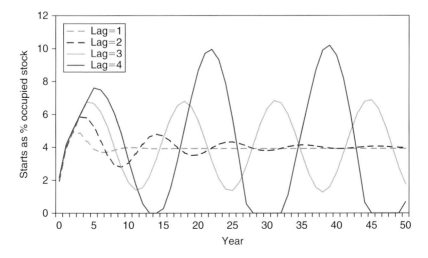

Figure 7.6 Building cycle with fixed transmission coefficient and different lags.

- With a 1-year construction lag, there is only a small damped oscillation which dies away after one cycle.
- For a 2-year lag, the cycle is still damped, but it has greater amplitude and persists through several cycles.
- With a 3-year lag, the transmission coefficient of 0.5 is at its crossover value, thus generating a stable cycle.
- When the construction lag reaches 4 years, the transmission coefficient is large enough to generate an explosive cycle until stabilized by the zero floor.
- The period of the cycle progressively increases with the length of the lag, even though the transmission coefficient is held constant.

Floor and ceiling constraints

It has already been shown that the introduction of an absolute floor such that development starts cannot be less than zero is sufficient to constrain a potentially explosive building cycle to become stable and persistent, albeit with a large amplitude. Cycle volatility can further be reduced if additional constraints are introduced for greater realism, whereby the floor is set not at zero but at some minimum rate of autonomous development, and a ceiling derived from the capacity of the development industry is also imposed.

These effects can be illustrated using the same fixed parameter settings as before, with a 2-year construction lag and the transmission coefficient set at 0.8, which has already been demonstrated to generate an explosive cycle (Figure 7.7):

- When the absolute zero floor is the only constraint, the starts rate oscillates asymmetrically between 0% and 9.5%, around its natural rate of 4%.
- If the floor is lifted to accommodate a minimum rate of autonomous starts equivalent to 1.5% of occupied stock, then the cycle oscillates between 1.5% and 7.4%, reducing its range from 9.5% to 5.9%.

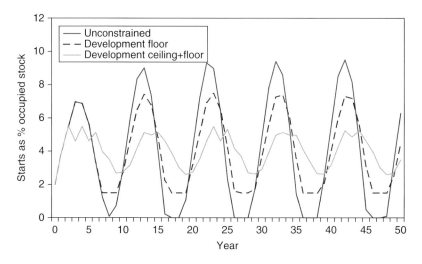

Figure 7.7   Building cycle with floor and ceiling constraints.

• The introduction of a capacity ceiling, such that the volume of building under construction in any period cannot exceed 10% of occupied stock, further reduces the range of the cycle down to around 2.6%. Because the ceiling operates on the sum of two years of starts, due to the development lag, the building peak is considerably reduced, it takes on an erratic profile and the cycle now spends longer at its peak than in its trough.

Persistent under- or over-supply

So far it has been assumed that after an initial disturbance, the development industry adjusts its rate of building above or below the true natural rate of starts when compensating for fluctuations in market conditions. However, as was discussed previously in Chapter 6 with respect to the Central London office markets, there are some property markets in which there is a tendency towards persistent over-supply, due to the pressure of investor demand (e.g. the City of London), and some with a tendency to persistent under-supply, for example due to restrictive planning policies (e.g. the West End of London). To simulate such historically dependent effects, we can introduce a continuous upward or downward displacement of building starts away from their natural rate, once the initial displacement has set the building cycle in motion.

Using the model with a 2-year construction lag, the transmission coefficient set to its crossover value of 0.66, and an initial starts displacement of 2%, further continuous displacements of 0.5% above and below the natural starts rate are introduced. The effect of this sequence of shocks is that the building cycle still oscillates around the natural rate of starts, but for this positioning to be maintained, there is a compensating upward displacement of the vacancy cycle and downward displacement of the rental growth cycle relative to their natural rates, when an over-supply bias is introduced, and vice versa with an under-supply bias. The effect of these displacements on the level of real rents is illustrated in Figure 7.8. With no continuous displacement,

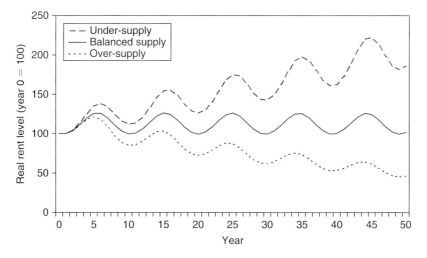

Figure 7.8 Effect of persistent over- or under-supply on real rents.

balanced building supply can be maintained without the secular trend in real rents deviating from its natural level; the rent cycle thus oscillates around a zero growth trend. With over-supply, the downward displacement of the rental growth cycle relative to its zero natural rate means that the cycle in real rents is superimposed upon a downward sloping secular trend (compare with Figure 6.3 in the previous chapter, showing the real rent trend in the City of London between 1970 and 2005). With under-supply, there is a converse upward secular trend to the real rent cycle.

Alternative rent adjustment processes

As already noted in the previous section, the nature of the rent adjustment process does not affect either the timing or amplitude of the building and vacancy cycles; however, it does affect the rental growth cycle and the relationship between rent levels and vacancy rates at different points in the cycle. This can be illustrated using the simulation model set to produce stable cycles with a 2-year construction lag, and incorporating a composite rent adjustment process as specified by equation (B.28c). At one extreme, this composite equation yields a pure partial adjustment process, when there is a zero feedback coefficient on the gap between actual and natural rent levels acting as a stabilizing influence on rental growth. At the other extreme, with a feedback coefficient of unity, the composite equation equates to an instantaneous full adjustment process, with the rent gap rather than rental growth reacting to the gap between the actual and natural vacancy rates. With intermediate values of the feedback coefficient, the composite adjustment process expresses rental growth as a function of both the rent gap and the vacancy gap, as first proposed by Hendershott (1995).

The impact of choosing alternative rent adjustment processes can best be illustrated by examining the non-linear relationships they generate between the vacancy rate and the real rent level, plotted on a phase diagram of model behaviour. With the simple partial adjustment process, used in all the previous simulations, the relationship between vacancy rate and rent level circles around the equilibrium point defined by their natural values (vacancy rate = 10%; rent level = 100 with the chosen model settings). With instantaneous full adjustment, the vacancy–rent relationship is a backward sloping straight line through the equilibrium point with a gradient determined by the rent adjustment coefficient. Figure 7.9 illustrates how a composite adjustment process, with rental growth responding to both the vacancy and rent gaps, produces intermediate vacancy–rent trajectories, with the circular path of simple partial adjustment attenuating to a narrower oval around the full adjustment line as the feedback coefficient on the rent gap increases. By following a closed loop rather than an open line, this composite adjustment process manifests a classic hysteresis effect of the type described in Chapter 2. With full adjustment, the current rent level is uniquely determined by the vacancy rate; with composite adjustment, the current rent can be at one of two levels in relation to the vacancy rate, and is indeterminate without knowing the previous level of rent.

Rent elastic occupier demand

The simulations presented so far all assume that the occupier demand for building space is inelastic with respect to rent. This restriction can be relaxed by allowing

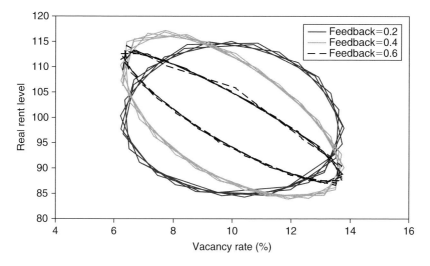

Figure 7.9 Real rent levels and vacancy rates with composite adjustment.

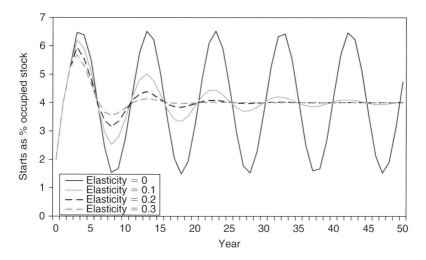

Figure 7.10 Building cycle with variable demand elasticity.

the occupancy rate to vary inversely with rental growth (partial adjustment) or the rent level (full adjustment). If occupiers vary their use of space as rents vary, this absorbs some of the fluctuation in vacancy, in turn reducing the volatility of the induced demand for new building. In other words, occupiers are absorbing some of the inherent cyclical tendency in the market which would otherwise be borne by developers. The strength of this dampening effect is illustrated in Figure 7.10, with the transmission coefficient set to its crossover value for a 2-year construction lag, and different elasticities applied to the inverse relationship between the occupancy rate and rental growth, assuming a partial adjustment process.

With the occupancy elasticity set to zero, the familiar harmonic building cycle is generated. As the elasticity is increased above zero, the volatility of the cycle progressively decreases such that an elasticity of 0.3 is sufficient to eliminate the oscillations after two cycles. This is achieved by only a 1.5% initial corrective reduction in the occupancy rate – which, because it applies to all occupied stock and not just new stock at the margin, is sufficient to offset the vacancy fluctuation and eliminate the cycle. Further increases in the occupancy elasticity above a value of around 0.32 produce a sudden phase change in model behaviour, with over-compensation in the occupancy rate creating a positive rather than negative feedback effect which generates unstable seesaw fluctuations in starts. Such sudden phase transitions from stable to unstable behaviour are typical of non-linear dynamic systems (Elaydi, 1996).

What these results demonstrate is that for a persistent building cycle to be generated through the medium of development lags, there must be some stickiness in the building occupancy rate as a result of long leases and high transaction and moving costs. This is why the elasticity of occupier demand with respect to rents is one of the parameters which determine model behaviour, as noted in the previous section. These results are consistent with the finding by Wheaton (1999: 221) that for cyclical behaviour to be generated in his model, the elasticity of demand for space with respect to rents must be less than the price elasticity of its supply.

Elastic depreciation

It is also possible to allow the depreciation rate to vary with market conditions. The argument is that as vacancy increases and rents fall during a market depression, a greater amount of poor quality space becomes unprofitable in use, which encourages owners to speed up the rate of depreciation and increase the level of replacement demand (see the discussion of the behaviour of the City office market in Chapter 6). By this means, building owners rather than developers absorb some of the volatility of the cycle.

This is tested as in the previous example, by holding the other model parameters constant and varying the depreciation rate around its natural value in inverse proportion to the rate of rental growth, with different elasticities applied to the relationship (Figure 7.11). As with the rent elastic occupancy rate, cycle volatility decreases as the depreciation elasticity increases away from the zero value which maintains a stable building cycle. However, unlike the occupancy rate which affects the aggregate demand for building stock, the depreciation rate only determines the replacement component of demand, and so has to vary proportionately much more to damp down the cycle. In this example, even an elasticity as high as 15 does not entirely eliminate the cycle within the 50-year simulation period, although its amplitude is much reduced. With the elasticity set this high, the depreciation rate has initially to oscillate between a trough of 0.2% and a peak of 2.4%, before progressively converging to the chosen natural rate of 1.5% through successive cycles.

Business cycle in demand

As a final illustrative simulation, the assumption that the demand for property is expanding at a steady rate of economic growth can be elaborated to superimpose an exogenous business cycle on to the constant output growth trajectory. A 5-year

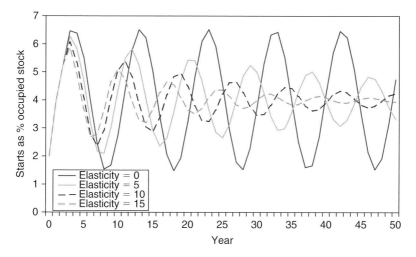

Figure 7.11 Building cycle with elastic depreciation rate.

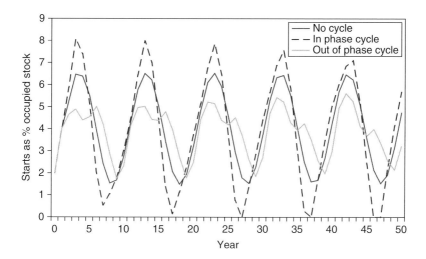

Figure 7.12 Building cycle with business cycle in demand.

business cycle has been chosen, varying economic growth between a trough of 0.5% and a peak of 3.5% around the average long-term growth rate of 2% per annum. With the construction lag set at 2 years, this means that a 5-year demand cycle interacts with an approximately 10-year supply cycle.

If the business cycle is running in-phase with the vacancy cycle (here meaning that every other business cycle peak coincides with a vacancy trough), then this reinforces the amplitude of the building cycle, since alternate points of maximum demand for space are coinciding with a point of minimum supply. With this simulation example, the amplitude of the building starts cycle is boosted from 2.5% of occupied stock with steady-state output growth, to nearly 4% under the influence of the in-phase business cycle (Figure 7.12). When the business and vacancy cycles are running out-of-phase, then the amplitude of the main building cycle is reduced and an additional intermediate building cycle, of lesser amplitude, is also created by the intermediate business cycle. We then have the situation in which a minor demand-driven cycle is superimposed on to a major supply-driven cycle. The empirical evidence for such a phenomenon was discussed in Chapter 3; for a more general simulation model of the interaction of economic cycles of different periodicity, see Mosekilde et al. (1992).

Modelling the City of London office market

In Chapter 6 we examined the historical course of the building cycle in the City of London office market since the mid-nineteenth century. Since the City is such a well documented and intensively measured market, it provides an ideal case study for testing the applicability of the building cycle model presented in this chapter and Appendix B.

Consistent data series measuring the key indicators of City office market behaviour are available back to 1970 in all cases, while some series stretch back well into the 1960s. These data allow estimation of the model equations for occupier demand, vacancy change, rental adjustment, development supply and building completions (see the study published by RICS, 2000, for a multi-equation model of the City market with a broadly similar structure). It should be stressed that the aim of the analysis presented here is to estimate the basic a priori relationships incorporated into our theoretical model of the building cycle; an error correction model that is better able to capture short-run market dynamics is presented in the next chapter.

For consistency with the model equations set out in Appendix B, the variables in the estimated equations are expressed either as ratios with respect to the level of occupied stock in the City (take-up, vacancy, vacancy change, starts and completions) or as rates of change (output and rents). Consequently, normal rather than logged variables have been used as there are no appreciable heteroscedasticity effects. Estimation is by ordinary least squares; the estimation period has an end date of 2007 and is varied to capture the most stable model relationships (with the particularly volatile 1970s period being omitted from some equations); the t-statistics for each coefficient are quoted in brackets; the adjusted R-squared and Durbin–Watson statistics for each model are also quoted. Earlier versions of the equations were presented in Barras (2005); they differ slightly from those presented here because they were estimated to 2004 rather than 2007, using data which have subsequently been revised in some cases.

Take-up and occupier demand

The rate of take-up of office space in the City, comprising net absorption plus the turnover of occupiers within the existing stock, shows the impact of the business cycle as it has affected the London economy, as well as special demand shocks such as the stock market crash of 2001/2 (Figure 7.13). Unlike take-up, the rate of net absorption is not a directly measured statistic, but can only be derived from estimated changes in occupied stock. The derived net absorption series for the

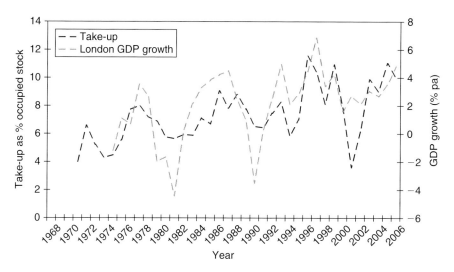

Figure 7.13 City office take-up and London output growth.
Source: Ingleby Trice, ONS, PMA.

City is highly volatile and shows little or no relationship with either London GDP growth or the rate of take-up, particularly during the late 1980s/early 1990s. This highlights the difficulty of using derived net absorption as a demand indicator.

Following equation (B.11), the rate of take-up u_t can be expressed as a function of the output growth rate $\Delta Y_t/Y_{t-1}$, the occupancy rate α_t and the turnover rate τ. Furthermore, if it is assumed that the occupancy rate varies with market conditions, as stated in equations (B.41a and b), then rental change can be introduced into the take-up equation to act as an influence on the occupancy rate. On this basis, the rate of take-up in the City has been estimated over the period 1975–2007, with London GDP growth found to be the best available indicator of demand growth:

$$u_t = 5.815 + 0.077t + 0.339\Delta Y_t/Y_{t-1} - 5.202\text{dum}02$$
$$\quad\ (14.15)\quad(3.02)\quad\ \ (3.49)\qquad\qquad(-4.16)\qquad\qquad\qquad(7.1)$$

$$\text{adjR}^2 = 0.602; \ n = 33; \ DW = 1.986$$

To achieve this level of fit, it was necessary to introduce a time trend and a dummy for the year 2002, when City take-up collapsed in response to the shock of the stock market crash of 2001/2. No rent variable, whether level, first difference or growth rate, was found to be significant. Estimation of the equivalent equation using net absorption rather than take-up produced no significant coefficients.

The equation offers a plausible explanation for the drivers of the take-up rate. The combination of the constant and the time trend suggests a rising turnover rate, while net absorption responds to variations in the London GDP growth rate. The estimated turnover rate τ rises from 5.8% in 1975 to 8.3% in 2007, indicating an increasingly active occupier market consistent with the fact that typical lease lengths for City offices shortened from 25 years down to 15 or even 10 years during the period. The lack of any significant negative rent effect in the demand equation confirms that there is considerable rent inelasticity in the occupier market, because of long leases and high moving costs, which hampers its potential to dampen down the building cycle through variations in the occupancy rate (as demonstrated by the simulation in the previous section).

The extent of the inelasticity of demand with respect to rents can be illustrated by separately estimating the occupancy rate α_t over the period 1971–2007 as an inverse function of real rental growth $\Delta r_t/r_{t-1}$, according to equation (B.41b), using floorspace per office employee as the measure of occupancy rate:

$$\alpha_t = 117.2 + 2.248t - 0.603(\Delta r_t/r_{t-1})_{-2}$$
$$(22.71) \quad (9.10) \quad (-3.56)$$

$$\text{adjR}^2 = 0.741; \, n = 37; \, DW = 0.326$$

(7.2)

As the chosen occupancy rate is measured against office employment rather than output, there is a positive time trend reflecting rising building capital per worker. As a result, the natural occupancy rate α^* rises from 117 square feet per employee in 1971 to 198 square feet in 2007, at an average growth rate of 1.5% per annum. Around this rising natural occupancy rate, there is an inverse relationship between the actual occupancy rate and real rental change, but lagged by 2 years as an indicator of the stickiness of the demand response.

Vacancy change

Vacancy change Δv_t is negatively related to the rate of take-up u_t, and positively related to the rate of completions c_t. When rates of take-up have been high and/or completion rates low, then vacancy in the City has fallen; conversely, low take-up and/or high completions have typically meant rising vacancy. In particular, there is quite a close relationship between the cycles in completions and vacancy, as newly completed space feeds back to boost vacancy (Figure 7.14). The vacancy change relationship has been estimated from equation (B.35) over the full period 1971–2007 as:

$$\Delta v_t = 5.446 + 0.962c_t - 0.679u_t - 0.312v_{t-1}$$
$$(3.31) \quad (5.64) \quad (-3.17) \quad (-4.05)$$

$$\text{adjR}^2 = 0.564; \, n = 37; \, DW = 1.665$$

(7.3)

This long-run accounting relationship captures the determinants of vacancy change reasonably well, although there is inevitably a considerable amount of unexplained short-term variation due to the erratic nature of the dependent variable. The equation shows vacancy to be boosted by the rate of completions, with a coefficient very close to the expected value of unity, and reduced by the rate of take-up, with a coefficient less than unity because only a part of take-up consists of net absorption as distinct from turnover. There is also a self-correcting negative feedback from the

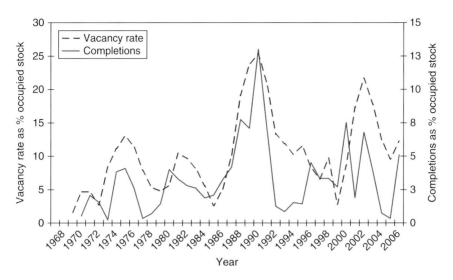

Figure 7.14 City office vacancy and completions.
Source: ICHP, CBRE, Ingleby Trice, City Corporation, PMA.

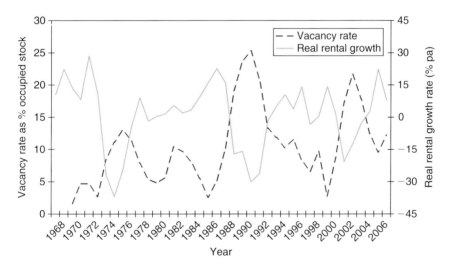

Figure 7.15 City office rent adjustment.
Source: ICHP, CBRE, Ingleby Trice, City Corporation, PMA.

lagged vacancy level v_{t-1} to vacancy change: the higher the existing level, the more likely it is to fall.

Rent adjustment

A clear inverse rent adjustment relationship linking real rental growth to vacancy levels can be observed in the City office market (Figure 7.15). When vacancy has

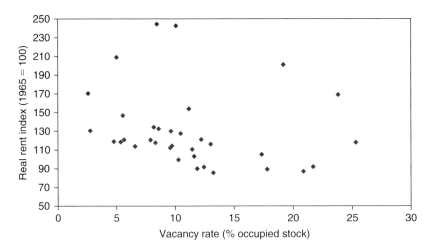

Figure 7.16   City rent–vacancy relationship 1974–2007.
Source: ICHP, CBRE, Ingleby Trice, City Corporation, PMA.

been at a trough, rental growth has been at a peak (1972/3, 1986/7, 2000 and 2006); conversely vacancy peaks have coincided with rental decline troughs (1975/6, 1991 and 2002/3). In contrast, the relationship between real rent levels and vacancy (Figure 7.16) follows a broad oval orbit around the equilibrium point, tracing out a hysteresis loop of the type illustrated in the Figure 7.9 phase diagram derived from the simulation model. As discussed in the previous section, this is characteristic of a predominantly partial rent adjustment process with weak feedback from rent levels to rental growth. The weakness of the relationship between vacancy and rent levels reflects the historic tendency for each supply cycle in the City to ratchet average real rents to successively lower levels (see Figure 6.3 and the discussion in the previous Chapter).

   Alternative rent adjustment equations have been estimated for the City, according to the full, partial and composite formulations set out in equations (B.28a)–(B.28c). The regression estimates confirm the observations made above: the partial adjustment equation is much stronger than the full adjustment equation, and the rent gap term is insignificant in the composite adjustment equation (though as discussed in Chapter 8, estimates for several other global office markets, particularly in Europe, do reveal a significant negative feedback from rent levels to rental growth). The partial rent adjustment equation for the City has been estimated over the period 1982–2007 as:

$$\Delta r_t/r_{t-1} = 24.56 - 1.942 v_t$$
$$\qquad\quad (7.40) \quad (-7.94) \tag{7.4}$$

$$\text{adjR}^2 = 0.713; \text{ n} = 26; \text{ DW} = 1.417$$

This version relates proportionate real rental change $\Delta r_t/r_{t-1}$ to the vacancy rate v_t at the end of the period; it gives a considerably stronger model than that fitted to the vacancy rate at the beginning of the period, which is the typical form of the rent adjustment relationship incorporated in equation (B.28b). Because of the lag structure of the model, the estimated form of the rent adjustment equation does not create a problem of co-determination between rents and vacancy. It yields estimates of 1.94 for the rent adjustment coefficient ρ, and 12.6% for the natural vacancy rate v^* at which rental growth is zero in the City. This natural vacancy rate is calculated with respect to occupied space; the equivalent rate measured against total stock is 11.2%. Estimates of the natural vacancy rate in other European office markets are typically lower, while those for most US and Asian markets are higher (see Table 8.3).

Comparison with the late Victorian period

In the previous chapter, we introduced the historic rent and vacancy series constructed by Turvey (1998) for the City of London office market between 1869 and 1910. These data provide a unique historical illustration of the rent adjustment relationship in the late Victorian period to compare with that observed over the past quarter century.

The best relationship for the Victorian period was found to be between unlagged vacancy and smoothed rental growth, derived from a 3-year moving average of the rent index. The equation has been estimated over the shortened period 1884–1904 to exclude the extreme vacancy spikes at the beginning and end of the period, which are seemingly distorted by one or two buildings (see Figure 6.6). The estimated equation is:

$$\Delta r_t / r_{t-1} = 5.530 - 1.020 v_t$$
$$\qquad\qquad (6.84) \quad (-5.44)$$

$$\text{(7.5)}$$

$$\text{adjR}^2 = 0.588; \, n = 21; \, DW = 2.181$$

The equation yields estimates of 1.02 for the rent adjustment coefficient and 5.4% for the natural vacancy rate (measured against total stock). Extension of the estimation period back to 1877, to include the first vacancy spike, lowers the estimated rent adjustment coefficient to 0.48 but increases the natural vacancy rate to 7.6%. These estimates for the late Victorian period are considerably lower than those obtained for the post-war period 1982–2007 as derived from equation (7.4); the rent adjustment coefficient is reduced because of the smoothing applied to the Turvey rent index, and the natural vacancy rate is depressed by the removal of the vacancy spikes. Nevertheless, given the partial nature of the data and the heroic assumptions required to derive the indices, it is encouraging that a plausible rent adjustment relationship can be derived for this historical period at the very start of the modern office era.

Development supply

The development supply relationship links real rental change to the rate of building starts: the higher the rate of rental growth, the more the profitability of development is increasing and therefore the higher the rate of starts initiated by

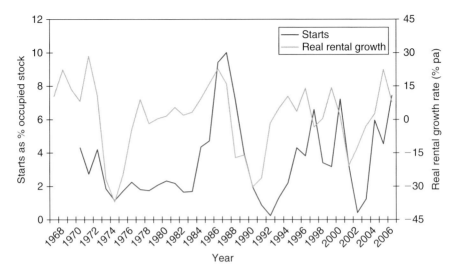

Figure 7.17   City office development reaction.
Source: ICHP, CBRE, EGi LOD, City Corporation, PMA.

developers. Figure 7.17 shows that peak periods of real rental growth in the City (1972, 1987, 1997/2000 and 2006) have generated a subsequent peak in development starts, typically with a 1-year lag (1973, 1988 and 1998/2001 and 2007). There is some evidence here of developer expectations anticipating future rent levels, insofar as current rental growth is an indicator of higher future rent levels.

Like rental growth, the development supply relationship has been formulated using alternative adjustment processes, as set out in equations (B.29a)–(B.29c). Unlike the rent adjustment equation, all three versions of the development supply equation produce significant relationships when estimated for the City. Corresponding to rental growth equation (7.4), the partial adjustment development supply equation has been estimated over the shortened period 1985–2007 as:

$$s_t = 4.168 + 0.155(\Delta r_t/r_{t-1})_{-1}$$
$$(13.05) \quad (7.14)$$

$$(7.6)$$

$$\text{adjR}^2 = 0.694; \; n = 23; \; DW = 1.297$$

This version of the partial adjustment equation expresses the rate of development starts s_t as a function of lagged real rental growth $\Delta r_t/r_{t-1}$; again this gives a considerably stronger model than the unlagged relationship assumed in equation (B.29b). The constant in the equation corresponds to a fixed natural rate of starts; the equation was also expanded to include the interest rate and an index of construction costs, to allow the natural rate of starts to vary with development costs, but as is usually found when estimating such development equations, neither variable was found to be significant.

Equation (7.6) yields estimates of 4.2% for the constant natural rate of starts s*
around which the building cycle oscillates, and 0.16 for the development reaction
coefficient μ. These regression estimates can be compared with the results derived
by inserting appropriate parameter values into the simulation model equations:

- The estimated natural rate of starts of 4.2% in the City is remarkably close to
  the equilibrium value of 4.3% which can be obtained from model equation (B.58).
  This equilibrium value is derived by using estimated parameter values of 12.6%
  for the natural vacancy rate v*, 2.5 years for the average construction lag q as
  estimated below, an average output growth rate ε of 2.1% per annum for London
  GDP over the period, and an average City office depreciation rate δ which has
  been estimated to be around 1.5% per annum (Barras and Clark, 1996: 75).
- The product of the estimated rent adjustment and development reaction coefficients
  yields a combined transmission coefficient $\mu\rho$ with a value of 0.30. Though the lag
  structure of the individual equations differs from that adopted in model equations
  (B.28b) and (B.29b), their combined effect is to produce the same 1-year lag between
  the vacancy signal and development starts as that derived in equation (B.30). The
  estimated value of the transmission coefficient is above the critical value of 0.24
  derived from equation (B.62) but below the crossover point with a construction lag
  of 2–3 years (see Table 7.1). It therefore lies in the range in which damped cycles
  are generated. This suggests that the persistent severity of the building cycle in the
  City is the result of occasional irregular shocks which destabilize the tendency for
  the market to return towards equilibrium through a sequence of damped cycles.

An improved development supply equation, with better adjusted R^2 and less autocorrelation, was obtained using a composite adjustment equation, similar in form
to equation (B.29c) but with a different lag structure combining the unlagged real
rent level r_t with lagged real rental growth:

$$s_t = 0.776 + 0.112(\Delta r_t/r_{t-1})_{-1} + 0.027 r_t$$
$$\quad (0.81) \quad (5.40) \qquad\qquad (3.69) \qquad\qquad\qquad (7.7)$$

$$\text{adjR}^2 = 0.809; \, n = 23; \, \text{DW} = 1.931$$

Based upon the value of the natural rate of starts derived from equation (7.6), this
equation yields an estimate of 0.19 for the feedback coefficient β^s in the composite
adjustment process, and an index value of 126 for the constant level of the natural
rent r* over the estimation period (with real City rents indexed to a value of 100 in
1965). The derived relationship suggests that developers in the City respond both to
rental change, feeding expectations of improving or worsening market conditions,
and the prevailing rent level, indicating current levels of development profitability.

Again, the addition of the construction cost variable produced no significant
improvement to equation (7.7), and neither did the addition of the real interest
rate, a potential influence on the natural rent level acting as a user cost of capital
(Hendershott et al., 1999). Equivalent versions of equations (7.6) and (7.7) were also

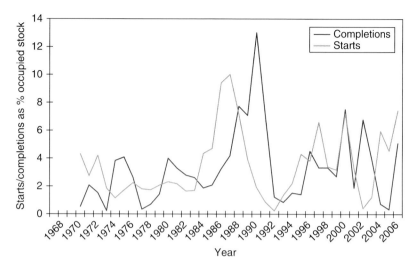

Figure 7.18   City office construction delays.
Source: EGi LOD, City Corporation, PMA.

estimated using real capital values rather than real rents; with both formulations, rents appeared to be the stronger trigger for development activity. Current output growth was also tried in each equation as a proxy for developer expectations about future demand growth, but in neither case was found to be significant, which tends to confirm the assumption of myopic pricing adopted for the model.

Building completions

Because of the scale of the building projects being undertaken in the City, there is a substantial construction delay between starts and completions (Figure 7.18). Thus, peaks in starts (1973, 1988 and 1998/2001) have been followed by peaks in completions 2–3 years later (1975/6, 1991 and 2001/2003). In passing, it is worth noting again the contrast between the profile of development activity in the most recent Cycle 12 compared to Cycle 11b in the late 1980s (see Chapter 6). While Cycle 11b produced a single massive surge in development, Cycle 12 was more orderly and better phased, with three successive waves of building completing in 1997–8, 2001 and 2003. This 'saw-tooth' profile of building activity in the latest cycle bears some similarity to the results of the model simulation with a capacity ceiling imposed (see Figure 7.7). It is as if the development industry in the City was operating within a self-imposed ceiling during Cycle 12, in an attempt to avoid the extremes of over-supply and market turbulence associated with Cycle 11b.

The construction lag relationship has been estimated from equation (B.32) over the period 1975–2007 as:

$$c_t = 0.495s_{t-2} + 0.567s_{t-3}$$
$$(3.80) \qquad (4.25) \qquad\qquad (7.8)$$

$$adjR^2 = 0.669; \; n = 33; \; DW = 2.338$$

The coefficients on the lagged rate of starts terms add to 1.06, close to the expected long-run average of 1; a weighted average of the two coefficients suggests an average construction lag in the City of just over 2.5 years. This estimate of the construction lag derived from the aggregate starts and completions data is broadly confirmed by a building-level analysis of all office development schemes of over 5,000 square feet completed in the City within the last cycle, drawing on the database utilized in Chapter 6. Between 1996 and 2005, there were 103 development schemes with a known start and completion date, yielding an average construction delay across all schemes of 22 months, rising from 15 months for buildings of under 25,000 square feet to 28 months for buildings of over 250,000 square feet. When the average construction delay is weighted by floorspace area, it rises from 22 to 25 months.

By interpolation from Table 7.1, the simulation model generates a building cycle period of 10.0 years using the weighted scheme-by-scheme construction lag of 2.1 years, and a period of 11.6 years using the aggregate construction lag of 2.5 years derived from equation (7.8). These model estimates apply when the transmission coefficient is at its crossover point; when it is below that point, as indicated above, then the cycle period is a little longer (see Appendix B). These model estimates correspond well with the results of the building cycle analysis for the City office market presented in the previous chapter. The structural time series model produced an average post-war cycle period of 10.5 years with ODP restrictions imposed, and 11.8 years without; the turning point analysis produced a post-war trough-to-trough period of 10.0 years, increasing to 12.5 years when Cycles 8 and 9 are combined.

In conclusion, using data covering the period 1970–2007, it has been shown that plausible transmission equations can be estimated for the City of London office market which corroborate the assumptions underlying the simulation model presented in this chapter and in Appendix B. Furthermore, when substituted into the simulation model, the parameter values and lag structures derived from the estimated equations generate cyclical behaviour that is consistent with the historical analysis of the City office building cycle presented in Chapter 6. As indicated at the start of this section, these results have been obtained for the best documented commercial property market in Europe; in the next chapter, we shall explore the extent to which the model is able to capture the post-war behaviour of a variety of office markets in Europe, North America and Asia, as they have come under the increasing influence of global investor and occupier demand.

8

Property Cycles in Global Investment Markets

Instability and growth in real estate investment

The crash of 2008

> 'Nothing was wrong in the country, but the over-dominant spirit of speculative commerce...' (Anthony Trollope in *Phineas Finn*, 1972: 357)

Trollope wrote these words shortly after the London discounting house of Overend, Gurney & Co. crashed on 'Black Friday', 11 May 1866, setting off a chain of bankruptcies across the British economy, which included many speculative building firms. To come across these words in July 2008 was a salutary reminder that there is nothing new about the destabilizing effects of imprudent bank lending in general, and imprudent lending to the property sector in particular. The extraordinary global financial crisis, followed by deep worldwide recession, which was triggered by the collapse of overheated housing markets has ensured that 2008 will go down in history as another of those years when a reckoning must be made for the 'over-dominant spirit of speculative commerce'. Kindleberger and Aliber (2005: 35) quote Walter Bagehot's remark about the Overend and Gurney crash: 'These losses were made in a manner so reckless and so foolish that one would think a child who had lent money in the City of London would have lent it better'. Equally withering remarks were common currency during 2008, directed at the modern leviathans in the City and on Wall Street. This unfolding story suggests that history does tend to repeat itself, in the sense implied by Braudel: although specific events are unique in their surface phenomena, they share common features attributable to the intrinsic instability of cyclical growth.

The global financial crisis of 2008 is an event of comparable magnitude to the crash of 1929, and it may have long-term structural consequences as profound as those that unfolded in the 1930s. Drawing on the experience of what he termed the 'financial panic-deep depression combination' of 1929–33, Minsky (1964) identified a combination of three conditions likely to generate a financial crash: speculative asset price inflation, unsustainable debt–income ratios and a liquidity shortage. All three conditions lay at the heart of the 2008 crisis, a crisis that marked the culmination of nearly three decades of market deregulation. Furthermore, the crisis reaffirmed the enduring capacity of property cycles to generate much more widespread financial and economic instability.

The problem stemmed from the 'sub-prime mortgage' crisis in the US housing market: a classic case of excessive lending on inadequate collateral in an overheated property market. The precursor to the crisis was the long housing boom that had been enjoyed in the United States and many other advanced economies, including Britain. In the decade 1996–2006, nominal average house prices in the United States more than doubled; in the United Kingdom, they tripled. As prices soared, mortgage banks relaxed their credit limits and lending standards to such an extent that large numbers of households with insufficient income and poor credit histories were encouraged to borrow heavily at variable interest rates in order to buy into the rising market. The risk attached to these sub-prime mortgages was spread throughout global financial markets by means of complex securitized assets, such as mortgage-backed securities, underwritten by even more complex derivatives such as credit default swaps (Syz, 2008). The advocates of these innovative financial instruments argued that by packaging up debt in the form of tradeable securities, lending risk could be hedged, loans could be extended to borrowers with weaker collateral and market fluctuations could be smoothed (Dynan et al., 2006).

However, when the US housing market bubble burst in 2007, it became apparent that far from spreading risk these instruments had amplified it, because investment banks and hedge funds had leveraged the value of the securities many times over, while the very complexity of the credit derivatives had reduced market transparency to the point at which banks became uncertain as to the extent of their exposure to bad debt. Risk had not so much been hedged as obscured. Having previously stimulated economic growth, financial innovation was now propagating instability (Augar, 2009). Two years of rising interest rates, designed to combat an overheating economy, had been sufficient to trigger the first fall in US house prices since the early 1990s, causing home sales and construction starts to slump. In the face of rising borrowing costs and falling prices, millions of households sank into negative equity and defaulted on their loans, forcing their banks to repossess the properties and write off the debt. During 2008 these deteriorating market conditions crossed from the United States to Europe, as the new derivative instruments provided the perfect transmission mechanism for amplifying a national housing crisis into a global financial disaster. The contagion of toxic debt spread rapidly, as many previously top-rated mortgage-backed securities were downgraded to junk status by the rating agencies. The world economy was seized by a severe credit crunch, as inter-bank lending all but ceased in the face of universal uncertainty and fear about counter-party risk, and the financial system was only kept functioning by repeated injections of liquidity from central banks. As the extent of the bad debt became apparent, a growing number of banks were faced with insolvency. The casualties of the crisis were spectacular indeed.

Northern Rock, a UK mortgage bank relying more on short-term borrowing than on investor deposits to fund its operations, was the first large domino to fall.

Its collapse in September 2007 precipitated the first run on a British bank since the Overend and Gurney crash, and forced its belated nationalization five months later. Next was Bear Stearns, one of America's big five investment banks; its plunge towards insolvency was only halted when the Federal Reserve Bank underwrote its takeover by JP Morgan Chase in March 2008. There then followed a lull, with only two further mortgage bank failures during July, encouraging some commentators to suggest that the worst of the crisis had passed. However, what had gone before was a mere prologue to the astonishing events of September and October 2008.

During September, a second British bank HBOS, much larger than Northern Rock but saddled with a similarly flawed business model, was only saved by a government-engineered merger with the more solvent Lloyds TSB, in defiance of competition law. Across the Atlantic, the US government effectively nationalized half of the nation's mortgage industry, in the form of giant lending institutions Freddie Mac and Fannie Mae, together with the country's largest insurance company AIG, which had underwritten a large slice of the sub-prime mortgage risk. In the largest bank failure in America's financial history, its sixth largest bank Washington Mutual suffered a massive run, ended only by receivership and another fire sale to JP Morgan Chase. Meanwhile, a second of the giant investment banks, Merrill Lynch, was rescued through a takeover by Bank of America, while a third, Lehman Brothers, collapsed and was not saved. The fall of Lehman Brothers on 15 September proved to be the defining moment of the whole crisis. The remaining representatives of this once Olympian industry, Goldman Sachs and Morgan Stanley, struggled on, but were forced to convert themselves into conventional commercial banks in order to survive. The era of buccaneering Wall Street banking appeared to be over.

In the week beginning Monday, 29 September, the crisis passed from being a cyclical shock to a more fundamental structural upheaval. The long experiment in financial deregulation was ending in catastrophe, and governments around the globe were struggling to lay the foundations for a new financial world order. There was a growing awareness that lack of solvency as much as illiquidity was the root cause of the banking problem: banks were over-leveraged, under-capitalized and exposed to massive levels of bad debt. The American government proposed a rescue plan to purchase all of this bad debt, to a potential extent of $700 billion, but with an election imminent, Congress voted down the measure as a bailout of Wall Street not Main Street. Investors panicked, stock markets collapsed and the wounded banking system froze. The British government was forced to nationalize Bradford and Bingley, the last remaining demutualized building society; the Benelux governments bailed out the Fortis banking and insurance group; the German government extended a credit lifeline to the collapsing commercial real estate lender Hypo Real Estate; the struggling American bank Wachovia was taken over by Wells Fargo. So severe were these repercussions that the US Congress was forced to pass a modified version of the rescue plan by the end of the week.

The focus of the crisis shifted to Europe in the week starting Monday, 6 October. The German government offered unlimited guarantees to depositors in contravention of EU competition rules. The entire banking system of Iceland faced insolvency. As the value of banking stocks slumped, the British government launched an ambitious and far-reaching £500 billion restructuring plan, covering up to eight major banks and building societies. The scheme consisted of three main elements: a £50 billion equity stake to recapitalize the banks, a £200 billion injection of public loan capital into a special liquidity scheme and £250 billion of funding guarantees to underwrite inter-bank lending. This was followed by coordinated interest rate cuts across the world, led by the United States, United Kingdom and eurozone countries. However, the panic in stock markets was unabated; by the end of the week, there had been market falls of 18% in New York, 21% in London, 22% in Frankfurt and 24% in Tokyo. At the weekend, the G7 group of leading industrialized economies together with the 15 eurozone economies announced coordinated plans to underpin the global financial system. These plans followed the British example, involving recapitalization through part-nationalization, further liquidity injections, a strengthening of depositor protection schemes and the provision of guarantees to underwrite inter-bank lending. On Monday, 13 October, the British government took major equity stakes worth £37 billion in three of the country's largest banking institutions: Royal Bank of Scotland, Lloyds TSB and HBOS. This was followed a day later by the American government taking equity stakes totalling $250 billion in nine banks, including Bank of America, JP Morgan Chase, Citigroup, Goldman Sachs and Morgan Stanley. The first step towards stabilizing the global banking system had been taken, just as the scale of the damage to the real economy began to emerge.

The property cycle and the business cycle

As the cataclysmic events of 2008 pass into history, they will spawn an enormous literature in the years and decades to come, just as did the Wall Street Crash of 1929 and the Great Depression of the 1930s. Attention will focus on the systemic failure of global capital markets and the need for improved regulation 'to ensure that this never happens again'. However, we should not lose sight of the crucial role that the property cycle played in the drama, just as it has in many past financial crises. To emphasize the point, Kindleberger and Aliber (2005: 26) observe that 'In the twentieth century most of the manias and bubbles have centered on real estate and stocks'. In Chapter 3 we discussed how the growing integration of deregulated real estate and capital markets has increased the risks of 'bubble contagion' transmitting instability across global investment markets – as was dramatically highlighted during the global real estate cycle of the late 1980s/early 1990s and the Asian cycle of the late 1990s (Kindleberger and Aliber, 2005: 123–42). The recurrence of these risks had been widely recognized in recent years – particularly the inevitability, if not the precise timing, of the bursting of the housing market bubble and the financial crisis that would result (Harrison, 2005; Shiller, 2005).

Each crisis of the past 30 years had offered a painful lesson about the dangers inherent in the free-market philosophy of deregulation, a philosophy which had been the dominant orthodoxy of Western capitalism since the early 1980s. It was a lesson which had to be learned again in 2008: that when credit bubbles burst, only prompt action by governments and central banks can save the global banking system from the disaster that followed the Wall Street crash of 1929. The experiences of Japan and Sweden in the early 1990s provided contrasting illustrations of the costs of inactivity and the benefits of direct intervention.

Following the collapse of Japan's property-based bubble economy in 1990, the hangover of non-performing loans in the banking system lingered through the 'lost decade' of the 1990s because regulators and the Bank of Japan failed to take strong and immediate countermeasures in the wake of the crisis. As a result, the whole economy became locked into a deflationary spiral which lasted until 1998, when a new government finally took decisive action to guarantee the deposits of failed banks, nationalize and liquidate the insolvent banks and recapitalize the weak but solvent banks using public funds (Kanaya and Woo, 2000). In contrast, there was swift action when Sweden's deregulation-induced credit and property bubble burst in 1990, and five of the country's six largest banks required support (Englund, 1999). The government provided a blanket guarantee to all creditors, but not equity-holders, set up a publicly owned 'bad bank' to take over all the non-performing loans and established a national agency to acquire equity stakes in the struggling banks in exchange for injections of fresh capital. The government followed the principle of '...saving the banks but not the owners of the banks' (Englund, 1999: 92), and by 1994 performance indicators for the Swedish banking system were back at pre-crisis levels. As governments grappled with the 2008 crisis, they drew upon the experience of these 1990s crises, as well as the 1980s collapse of the inadequately regulated and under-capitalized savings and loan industry in the United States (Eichler, 1989).

Of course, the crisis of 2008 was not confined to the money economy. Inevitably, the housing market collapse and the subsequent credit crunch fed through into the real economy. The slump in construction starts had a negative impact on investment and output; the combination of shattered confidence and the spiralling cost of debt severely depressed both household consumption and business investment; the lack of liquidity precipitated business failures across the economy. Despite deep and unprecedented cuts in interest rates, the advanced economies led by the United States, United Kingdom and Japan slid into recession for the first time since 1991, the growth of the developing economies as a whole was severely checked and some smaller emerging economies had to be rescued from bankruptcy. Fears of a prolonged global slump grew, as eminent observers proclaimed 'the return of depression economics' (Krugman, 2009). The preceding period of uninterrupted growth had prompted the same question that had been raised in the 1920s and the 1960s: 'Has the business cycle been abolished?' (Zarnowitz, 1998). Again, the answer turned out to be no, and for much the same reasons as it did in the early 1930s and mid-1970s – a financial shock precipitating the collapse of a speculative boom at the culmination of a strong period of economic expansion.

The links between the property cycle and the business cycle were discussed in Chapter 3, and explored empirically in Chapter 4. These links operate in both directions: fluctuations in building investment help to propagate the business cycle in the wider economy, while instability in the wider economy generates shocks that destabilize building investment. Since it is the most volatile and unstable component of total investment, building investment has a strongly cyclical influence on aggregate demand, acting through the investment multiplier. Similarly, real estate cycles are transmitted to credit markets, and thereby to the real economy, through the medium of the financial accelerator. A good example of these transmission mechanisms was provided by Case (1992), who described how a dramatic cycle in the real estate market amplified the local business cycle in Massachusetts during the late 1980s, both on the way up and on the way down. A house price boom boosted consumer spending, leading to an expansion of the local service sector. This in turn triggered a building boom which generated a surge in demand for local labour and capital. Inflation in rents and wages, together with problems in the over-extended banking sector, combined to weaken the regional economy and intensify the economic downturn when the real estate boom turned to bust. The result was that the State went from having the lowest unemployment rate in the United States in 1987 to the second highest in 1991.

Several commentators have pointed to the role of speculative property investment as a source of macro-economic instability (Dow, 1998: 160–80; Heim, 2000: 162–76). In particular, bank failures triggered by over-exposure to non-performing property loans will transmit knock-on effects throughout an economy. In Chapter 5 we discussed how the 1920s development boom and bust in the United States created a legacy of widespread loan foreclosures, a huge over-supply of unsold property and severe cutbacks in construction activity – all reminiscent of the 2008 crisis. The bad debt generated in the property market was a major factor contributing to the bank failures that followed the Wall Street Crash of 1929, unleashing a credit crunch of unparalleled severity. This credit crunch induced deep cuts in private expenditure and corporate failures on a massive scale, leading Dow (1998: 178) to observe that 'Bank failures thus provide a mechanism that powerfully amplifies a recession, and by so doing generalizes it'. Similar links between speculative property bubbles and economic instability can be observed in the run-up to the global recessions of the mid-1970s and early 1990s (Dow, 1998: 296–7, 347–8).

One of the crucial transmission mechanisms between the property cycle and the business cycle operates through the role that property plays as an asset on corporate balance sheets (McWilliams, 1992). According to ONS national accounts data, buildings and infrastructure accounted for 57% of non-financial assets on the balance sheets of UK industrial and commercial companies (non-financial corporations) in 2007. These property assets constitute a major part of the collateral for corporate borrowing, so that changes in their values acting through the financial accelerator have a strong influence on activity in the wider economy. According to both Keynesian and Monetarist theory, there is both a direct and an indirect effect of changes in asset prices upon the level of economic activity. The direct effect is that changes in property values alter the level of borrowing by companies and therefore their investment expenditure; the indirect effect is that corporate borrowing itself influences the money supply, in turn affecting the level of economic activity. Consequently, by boosting asset prices, a property boom reinforces an economic upswing, while the subsequent crash reinforces the downswing.

As was noted in Chapter 3, the interlocking of housing booms and consumer booms has been a phenomenon attracting growing attention in the past 20 years. Several commentators have suggested that the wealth effect created by rising house prices during a boom encourages owners to take on increased levels of debt, which is used to invest in more property but also spills over into additional consumption. These linkages were extensively investigated following the 1980s economic boom, particularly in the United Kingdom and United States. It was observed that in economies undergoing credit liberalization and rapid house price inflation, the average household propensity to consume had increased markedly, while there was a corresponding drop in the personal savings rate.

In the United Kingdom, Muellbauer and Murphy (1990) demonstrated a close link between increases in the consumption–income and wealth–income ratios

during the 1980s, attributing the link to the manner in which financial liberalization had made it easier for households to access the wealth tied up in their houses.
They further argued that macroeconomic instability is intensified by a speculative
'frenzy effect', which reinforces the acceleration of house prices in a rising market,
and by house-building booms, which reinforce the collapse of prices after the bubble has burst. A US study by Skinner (1989) presented a model in which house price
increases cause a substantial short-term decline in the aggregate savings rate, as
homeowners spend their windfall gains, unless they are strongly motivated to pass
on the gains to the next generation. Miles (1992) pointed out that new mortgage
products introduced in the United Kingdom and United States during the 1980s
explicitly encouraged equity withdrawal, by allowing households to raise loans
backed by the collateral of their existing house which could be used for consumption rather than further property investment. Using UK data, Attanasio and Weber
(1994) found that for older cohorts of households, much of the 1980s consumption
boom could be explained by the wealth effect derived from surging house prices,
whereas for younger households it was increases in expected lifetime incomes
which appeared to be the more important factor.

Since the end of the 1980s housing boom, further innovations in housing finance
systems have linked the property cycle ever more closely to the business cycle. As
we have seen, these innovations have lowered the cost and widened the availability of mortgage loans, multiplying both the volume of housing debt and the risks
attached to that debt. This has served to reinforce the role of the housing market as
a source of instability and a channel through which shocks are transmitted to the
wider economy. Against the background of growing turbulence in world financial
markets, the International Monetary Fund (IMF) published a special study of 'The
changing housing cycle and the implications for monetary policy' in April 2008.
Drawing on previously published research covering a variety of advanced economies, they set out four key stylized facts about the links between the housing market and the broader economy. First, movements in real house prices are closely
correlated with the economic cycle. Second, there is a clear connection between
aggregate economic activity and residential investment. Third, the link between
consumption and housing wealth is stronger in economies with more developed
mortgage markets. Fourth, economies with more flexible systems of housing
finance tend to experience stronger spillovers from the housing market. In an admi-
rably restrained conclusion to the study, they stated that '...innovations in housing
finance systems in advanced economies over the past two decades have altered the
role of the housing sector in the business cycle...these changes have broadened the
spillovers from the housing sector to the rest of the economy and have amplified
their impact by strengthening the role of housing as collateral' (IMF, 2008: 103).
The full impact of these spillover effects became all too apparent in the months to
follow.

Property as an investment medium

Investment in land and buildings has a dual purpose. As we saw in Chapters 4 and
5, building investment is a process of capital accumulation which enhances the
productive capacity of economies and the physical fabric of cities. However, land
and buildings also act as a repository of wealth; they form the largest component

of the tangible assets which constitute the wealth of nations. This duality is the source of an inherent contradiction between the economic interests of the owners and occupiers of buildings – who may be one and the same entity. The owner interest is to maximize the value of a building as an investment asset, while the occupier interest is to maximize the accommodation services provided by a building at minimum cost. This contradiction is most apparent in the housing market, as rising house prices benefit existing owners in their capacity as investors, but penalize tenants and first-time buyers by reducing the quantity and quality of housing services which they can afford. The result is that owners and renters have conflicting economic and political interests (Saunders, 1978). In Chapter 2 it was noted that Veblen identified a similar contradiction in the industrial sector as one cause of the business cycle. The producer interest is to invest in new capital stock embodying the latest technologies, which tends to reduce the earning capacity of previous vintages through economic obsolescence, whereas the investor interest is to maintain or even enhance the monetary value of existing assets.

The interrelationships between the ownership of land and property, the formation of rents, the accumulation of capital and investment in the means of production are a recurrent theme in Marxist analyses of urban development (see, for example, Massey and Catalano, 1978; Harvey, 1985; Smyth, 1985). At each stage of economic development, the dominant mode of production is associated with a particular type of economic surplus and a particular structure of land ownership. It is through the urban accumulation process that the origins of the surplus and the pattern of land ownership influence the built environment. Thus, the combination of feudal land ownership and the agricultural and mercantile origins of the economic surplus was a crucial influence on the form of the medieval city, as created by the building programmes of the monarchy, aristocracy and church. In a similar fashion, the combination of a capitalist structure of land ownership and an economic surplus derived principally from manufacturing was a crucial determinant of the form of the industrial city, as built by the factory owners, railway magnates and speculative landlords of the nineteenth century. With the rise of capitalism, land and buildings became commodities to be owned and traded like any other, binding ever more closely together their dual functions as investment assets and means of production. These interrelationships have reached their most developed form in the post-industrial city, in which financial institutions dominate the ownership of commercial land and buildings, both as investors and occupiers, while also providing the capital to fund property development across all sectors of the economy.

The growth of real incomes in advanced economies during the post-war period has given rise to what may be termed the 'rentier economy'. As was noted in Chapter 2, Keynes feared that as societies became richer, their propensity to consume would tend to decline, so that savings could outstrip the investment opportunities available in the economy. Empirical studies have shown that these fears were seemingly unfounded: in the short run the average propensity to consume does decrease with increasing household income, but in the long run it remains broadly constant. These findings prompted economists to relate consumption and savings not simply to income but also to wealth, and not to current income but rather to lifetime income or 'permanent income' excluding transitory fluctuations (Friedman, 1957). Nevertheless, the combination of rising volumes of savings and inflating asset prices has meant that the volume of household wealth has been

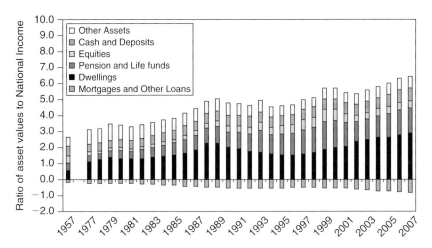

Figure 8.1   Growth and structure of assets held by UK households 1957–2007.
Source: Revell (1967) and ONS.

growing more rapidly than national income, while the ownership of that wealth has broadened, as an increasing proportion of households have invested in pension schemes and home ownership (Hamnett, 1999).

The growth and spread of household wealth in general, and housing wealth in particular, is illustrated in Figure 8.1, using UK balance sheet data from ONS for the years 1977–2007, and from an earlier pioneering study by Revell (1967) for the year 1957. The asset values are expressed as a ratio of national income in current prices; thus the net wealth of UK households in 2007 was valued at £7,523 billion, some 5.3 times the value of national income of £1,408 billion. As personal wealth has accumulated over the past 50 years, so the wealth to income ratio has more than doubled, from 2.3 in 1957 to 2.7 in 1977 and 5.3 in 2007. Superimposed on this secular trend are strong cyclical fluctuations, as the values of assets such as housing and equities have fluctuated with their market cycles. In 2007 the largest components of total assets were dwellings at 45% and pension and life funds at 24%; as a share of net wealth, the value of dwellings less mortgages was 39%. In contrast, in 1957 dwellings only accounted for 21% of total personal assets and pension and life funds 16%, while cash deposits, equities and other financial assets accounted for larger shares than they did in 2007. The growth of dwellings as the main component of household wealth mirrors the rise of owner-occupation in Britain, from 34% of the total housing stock in 1953 to 70% in 2001 (Holmans, 2005: 143). Not only does housing constitute the largest component of personal wealth, it also induces the most pronounced cyclical fluctuations in its value. Thus, at the height of the 1980s housing boom in 1988, the share of dwellings in total household assets peaked at 46%; seven years later, in the depths of the subsequent slump, this share had dropped to 32%.

As well as direct investment in dwellings, household savings are also directed into property through investments in pension and life funds, the second most

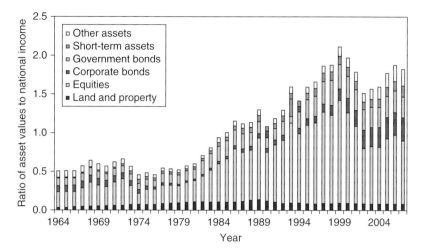

Figure 8.2   Growth and structure of assets held by UK financial institutions 1964–2007.
Source: ONS.

important component of personal wealth. These funds have been growing even more rapidly than household wealth as a whole: according to ONS data, the total assets of UK insurance companies, pension funds and trusts grew from a multiple of 0.5 times the national income in 1964 up to 1.8 times in 2007 (Figure 8.2). The portfolios of these financial institutions are dominated by investments in UK and overseas equities, acting both as the major component of their asset balances and the main source of volatility in their net worth. When a stock market boom turns into a crash, the share of equities in the total value of institutional funds can fall dramatically – as witnessed by the drop from 52% to 31% between 1972 and 1974, and from 63% to 47% between 1999 and 2002. Direct investment in land and property, mainly industrial and commercial buildings, forms a smaller proportion of institutional portfolios, but has proved equally volatile as the investment strategies of the funds have evolved (Scott, 1996). The property share rose from 6% in 1964 to a peak of 18% in 1981, as the institutions sought to diversify away from equities, particularly after the 1973/4 crash. However, as equity values surged again during the 1980s and 1990s, so direct property investment dropped back proportionately, until in the early 2000s it accounted for only 4%–5% of portfolio values.

These direct property holdings, now substantially under-estimate the overall property exposure of financial institutions, because of their recent shift towards indirect investment in a variety of property equity and debt vehicles. The attractions of holding property within a multi-asset investment portfolio are its unique risk-return characteristics, intermediate between bonds and equities, its relatively stable rental income stream and the diversification benefits derived from the low correlation of its returns with those on the other asset classes. The disadvantages are its lumpiness and heterogeneity, its high transaction costs, the illiquidity of the market and the lack of market transparency due to the shortage of direct transactions evidence. For these reasons, direct property investment has mainly been confined to large financial institutions investing principally in their domestic markets.

However, indirect investment vehicles overcome several of the problems of direct investment. In particular they enable investors to take an interest in pooled property portfolios which offer greater liquidity and risk diversification combined with reduced transaction costs. These vehicles include equity instruments such as Real Estate Investment Trusts (REITs) and Property Unit Trusts (PUTs), debt instruments such as Commercial Mortgage-Backed Securities (CMBSs) and derivative instruments in the form of futures, options and swaps (Hoesli and MacGregor, 2000). The recent proliferation of these indirect vehicles has opened up the market to a much broader range of investors and has stimulated an explosion of cross-border investment. Thus, estimates produced by data publishers Property Data show that out of the £58 billion of UK property traded during 2006, at the height of the recent investment boom, some 25% was purchased by UK financial institutions, 27% by property companies, 29% by overseas investors and 19% by other investors.

The unprecedented volumes of savings that have been flowing into property, both directly and indirectly, have greatly boosted the investor interest in its performance as a source of income and capital value growth. The investor interest in maximizing property returns is not only opposed to the tenant interest in minimizing them, but it can create investment demand pressures that are partly independent of movements in user demand (Keogh, 1994). For example, as we saw in Chapter 6, investment demand can run ahead of occupier demand in a prestige market such as City of London offices, creating a self-defeating tendency towards over-development and falling rents. Autonomous investment demand also adds another transmission mechanism to the links between the business cycle and the property cycle. Economic shocks can destabilize the investment demand for property, causing rapid adjustments to real estate yields and prices, which in turn affect development profitability and therefore the supply of new buildings.

As revealed by the City of London case study, an inevitable result of excess investment demand and over-building is the accelerated economic obsolescence of existing buildings. This process has been characterized as the devaluation of building capital due to over-accumulation (Harvey, 1978). In general terms, urban obsolescence is a necessary corollary of the dual processes of urban innovation and accumulation that have already been discussed in Chapter 5. New or improved urban functions require to be accommodated in new or improved built forms, thereby generating user demands for the renewal of the physical capital invested in cities. As new buildings are constructed, embodying the latest production technologies, the continued operation of the older vintages of buildings eventually becomes uneconomic – even though they may still be far from the end of their physical life. Furthermore, as the rate of investment in the building stock increases, so the economic life of each vintage shortens (Salter, 1966: 66). The economic obsolescence of buildings is tending to accelerate for two reasons: the first is the gathering pace of urban innovation; the second is the growing demand for property as an investment asset. Accelerated obsolescence in the urban fabric facilitates innovation by the activities occupying buildings, which in turn encourages the more rapid renewal or replacement of the building stock. Following the argument that was developed in Chapter 4, a higher rate of obsolescence is capital-saving for the users of buildings, since each new vintage is relatively cheaper to produce, as a result of improved construction techniques, and more productive to occupy, in terms of the technologies embodied within it. However, it is capital-using for the owners of buildings, since they must re-invest more in their assets to maintain their income stream.

Complex institutional structures have evolved to articulate the agency relationships that link investment demand, occupier demand and development supply in property markets (Healey, 1991). A variety of funding arrangements tie development supply to investment demand. For example, a property company will fund a development through some combination of its own capital resources, short-term loans from a bank and the mortgage or equity capital provided by a long-term investor. Development supply and occupier demand interact differently, according to whether a development is undertaken speculatively or to meet the requirements of specific occupiers. As was discussed in Chapter 3, the extent to which development projects are undertaken speculatively, rather than for pre-letting or owner-occupation, can affect the volatility of the building cycle itself. The classic long building cycle is typically driven by the pressures of speculative investment demand, which tend to create a price and construction boom followed by collapsing property values, loan defaults, bankruptcies and repossessions. In order to understand how occupier demand, investment demand and development supply interact within the property cycle, let us now examine the course of the post-war property cycles in the UK and US residential and non-residential markets.

The post-war property cycle in the United Kingdom and United States

A model of the national property cycle

A comparison of post-war property cycles in Britain and the United States can be developed directly out of our previous long-term analysis of growth and cycles in the two economies. That analysis demonstrated the dual role that building investment plays as driver of growth and generator of cycles in industrial and urban development. The growth model presented in Chapter 4 incorporated the concept of an equilibrium growth path along which output and capital stock grow in tandem, while real prices remain constant in aggregate, but diverge for individual goods according to relative shifts in consumer tastes and production technologies. This equilibrium growth model was incorporated into the building cycle model employed in Chapter 7, in which external shocks displace the economy away from its equilibrium path, and the lag structure of the model captures the adjustment processes that propagate cyclical fluctuations in building starts, vacancy, rents and prices.

The full building cycle model formulated in Appendix B is more suited to the analysis of an urban property market for which a complete set of data are available, as demonstrated in Chapter 7 by application to the City of London office market. A simplified version of the model, better suited to the analysis of national property markets with more limited data availability, is presented in the appendix at the end of this chapter. It takes the form of an error correction model in which a long-run equilibrium growth path is combined with the short-run adjustment processes that generate price and building cycles. The role of vacancy as a transmission mechanism between changes in the supply–demand balance and changes in prices is implicit in this version of the model, but vacancy is not included as a model variable because of a lack of suitable data for the national markets.

Two cointegrating relationships between trended variables define the equilibrium growth path of the property market. First, the real price or capital value of property is dependent upon the balance between occupier demand and building supply, represented by measures of economic output or income and building stock. Second, the level of construction activity is dependent upon the level of economic activity and the real price or capital value of property, which acts as a determinant of development profitability. The residuals derived from each cointegrating equation represent the deviations in actual price and construction levels around the fitted equilibrium trends.

The residuals derived from the equilibrium equations are incorporated as error correction terms in the adjustment equations, which determine incremental changes in market variables. The change in property prices is related to changes in output and building stock, together with the lagged price change and the error correction term, while the change in construction activity is related to changes in output and prices, together with the lagged construction change and the error correction term. To complete the transmission process, construction activity feeds additions to building stock, allowing for a development lag. The lagged dependent variables introduce serial correlation into the price and construction equations, which has the effect of positively reinforcing a cyclical shift away from market equilibrium. In contrast, the error correction terms introduce negative feedback, capturing the trend-reverting tendencies that dampen cyclical growth. Using a terminology adopted by Abraham and Hendershott (1996), the serial correlation terms act as 'bubble builders', whereas the error correction terms are 'bubble bursters'. In the theoretical model, the coefficients on the serial correlation and error correction terms are identical, so that the cyclical forces of reinforcement and damping are balanced, and the larger these coefficient values the stronger the cyclical fluctuations that are generated.

In order to implement the model, four data series have been assembled for the residential and non-residential markets in each country. Economic activity as a driver of user demand is represented by real disposable household income in the housing market and GDP in the combined industrial/commercial market. Building stock is represented by the fixed asset value of housing and other building capital in constant prices, as employed in the Chapter 4 growth analysis; for the United Kingdom the data cover gross total assets, for the United States they cover net private assets. Construction activity is represented by the annual volume of constant price private sector new orders in the United Kingdom, and by the annual volume of private sector building output in the United States. Regression modelling indicates that UK building new orders are translated into additions to building stock, with an average lag of 1 year in the residential market and 2 years in the non-residential market; in the United States, there is no measurable lag because the data refer to building output, not starts. House prices in each country are represented by transactions-based, quality-adjusted indices: for the United Kingdom, the series is based on a mix-adjusted index derived from mortgage lending survey data, as published in Holmans (2005: 279) and updated from government sources; for the United States, it is based on the S&P/Case-Shiller repeat sales index, extended prior to 1987 using a constant quality index from the Census Bureau. Non-residential capital values, combining industrial and commercial property, are represented by valuation-based indices derived from institutional investment portfolios; the UK series is constructed from IPD data, extended prior to 1971 using data published in Scott (1996: 278); the US series is constructed from National Council of Real Estate Investment Fiduciaries (NCREIF) data available from 1977.

Both residential and non-residential datasets for the United Kingdom cover the period 1957–2007; for the United States, the residential data cover the years 1963–2007, while the non-residential data cover the years 1977–2007. Each data series has been transformed into a logarithmic constant price index, so that growth rates are expressed as trend gradients and model coefficients as elasticities. The trends and cyclical fluctuations in each market are illustrated in Figures 8.3–8.6, the datasets being indexed to their start dates and updated to include the 2008 cycle downswing. The average growth rates derived by fitting linear trends to the logarithmic indices are presented in Table 8.1, together with the standard deviations of the price and building cycles around these linear trends. The results of estimating the property cycle model using each dataset are also summarized in Table 8.1 which lists the significant coefficients and overall performance measures for the separate equilibrium and error correction components of the model. Despite sometimes divergent trends in the different variables, all the equilibrium models produce a cointegrating regression, yielding residuals that are stationary according to the unit root test at the 1% significance level. The income/output and price elasticities of demand and supply have been estimated from the coefficients of the equilibrium models; these are also listed in Table 8.1, except in those cases where the relevant explanatory variable proved to be insignificant.

We can now compare the post-war behaviour of the UK and US property cycles using the illustrated trends and estimated models.

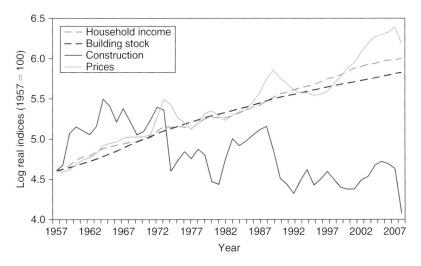

Figure 8.3   UK residential market cycles 1957–2008.
Source: Holmans (2005), Nationwide, DCLG and ONS.

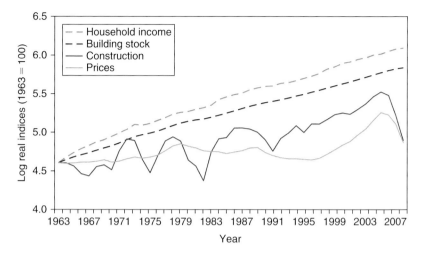

Figure 8.4   US residential market cycles 1963–2008.
Source: S&P/Case-Shiller, BEA and USCB.

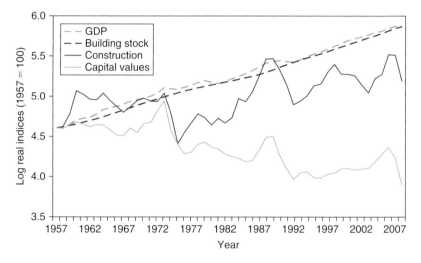

Figure 8.5   UK industrial/commercial market cycles 1957–2008.
Source: Scott (1996), IPD and ONS.

The housing market

Over the 50-year period 1957–2007, real household income in the United Kingdom grew on average by 2.7% per annum, compared to a 2.5% average rate of growth in the real asset value of the housing stock; the equivalent growth rates in the United States over the slightly shorter 1963–2007 period were 3.1% and 2.7% per annum, respectively (Figures 8.3 and 8.4; Table 8.1). Conditions in the two national housing markets diverge much more markedly, when we come to examine their relative trends in real prices and construction activity. In the UK real house prices have

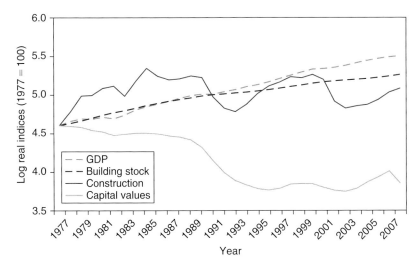

Figure 8.6   US industrial/commercial market cycles 1977–2008.
Source: NCREIF, BEA and USCB.

Table 8.1   Models of post-war UK and US property cycles[a].

	Variable	UK housing	UK Industrial/ Commercial	US Housing	US Industrial/ Commercial
Start date[b]		1957	1957	1963	1977
Trend growth rates[c]					
Income/Output[d]		2.7%	2.4%	3.1%	3.0%
Building stock[e]		2.5%	2.4%	2.7%	2.1%
Construction[f]		−1.5%	1.1%	2.0%	0.0%
Price/capital value[g]		3.0%	−1.3%	0.9%	−3.3%
Cycle standard deviations[c]					
Construction		0.249	0.205	0.146	0.182
Price/capital value		0.144	0.146	0.118	0.152
Price/Capital value models[h]					
Equilibrium model[i]	$\log p_t$				
Constant	ω_1		6.787**	3.249**	11.976**
Income/output	$\log Y_t$	1.548**	2.614**	0.280**	
Building stock	$\log K_t$	−0.539*	−3.105**		−1.572**
Adjusted R^2		0.922	0.713	0.482	0.778
Error correction model	$\Delta\log p_t$				
Constant	α_3			−0.015	
Lagged price/cap value	$\Delta\log p_{t-1}$	0.349**		0.742**	0.753**
Income/output	$\Delta\log Y_t$	1.585**	3.706**	0.453	0.814**
	$\Delta\log Y_{t-1}$		−1.307*		
Building stock	$\Delta\log K_t$		−2.968**		−1.310**
	$\Delta\log K_{t-1}$	−0.822			
Error correction term[j]	u_{t-1}				
	u_{t-2}	−0.154*		−0.160**	
	u_{t-3}		−0.351**		−0.098*
Adjusted R^2		0.530	0.537	0.566	0.788
Durbin–Watson statistic		1.608	1.640	1.728	1.273

Table 8.1   (*continued*)

	Variable	UK housing	UK Industrial/ Commercial	US Housing	US Industrial/ Commercial
Construction models[h]					
Equilibrium model[i]	$\log S_t$				
Constant	α_2				
Income/output	$\log Y_t$	0.456	0.648**	0.521**	0.527**
Price/capital value	$\log p_t$	0.662*	0.367**	0.438**	0.579**
Time trend[k]	t	−0.047**			
Adjusted R^2		0.500	0.507	0.785	0.066[l]
Error correction model	$\Delta\log S_t$				
Constant	α_4		−0.061*	−0.085*	−0.230**
Lagged construction	$\Delta\log S_{t-1}$			0.314*	
Income/output	$\Delta\log Y_t$		3.159**	2.311*	3.982**
	$\Delta\log Y_{t-1}$				3.600**
Price/capital value	$\Delta\log p_t$	1.872**	0.444*	1.473**	
	$\Delta\log p_{t-1}$	−1.710**			
Error correction term[j]	v_{t-1}	−0.340**		−0.669**	
	v_{t-2}		−0.229**		−0.339**
Adjusted R^2		0.603	0.532	0.586	0.756
Durbin–Watson statistic		1.549	2.344	2.025	1.597
Elasticities[m]					
Demand					
Income/output	β_1	2.87	0.84		
Price/capital value	γ_1	1.86	0.32		0.64
Supply					
Income/output	β_2	0.46	0.65	0.52	0.53
Price/capital value	γ_2	0.66[l]	0.37	0.44	0.58

Source: Scott (1996), Holmans (2005), S&P/Case-Shiller, BEA, DCLG, IPD, NCREIF, ONS and USCB.

[a] All series are modelled as real indices in logarithmic form.

[b] All series end in 2007.

[c] The growth rates are derived from linear trends fitted to each logarithmic series; the standard deviations are calculated on the residual fluctuations around the fitted linear trends.

[d] For the housing models, the economic growth variable is disposable household income; for the industrial/ commercial property models, it is GDP.

[e] Building stock is represented by the fixed asset value of building capital; for the United Kingdom, the indices cover gross total assets, for the United States, they cover net private assets.

[f] For the United Kingdom, the indices of construction activity represent the annual volume of private sector building starts; for the United States, they represent the annual volume of private sector building output.

[g] For housing, the indices refer to transactions-based, quality-adjusted house prices; for industrial/commercial property, the indices refer to valuation-based capital values for non-residential property in institutional investment portfolios.

[h] The coefficients refer to the model equations (8.1)–(8.4), set out in the appendix to this chapter; coefficients marked ** are significant at the 1% level, while those marked * are significant at the 5% level.

[i] All the equilibrium models produce a cointegrating regression, yielding residuals that are stationary according to the unit root test at the 1% significance level.

[j] The error correction terms are lagged by 1, 2 or 3 years.

[k] A negative time trend is included in the equilibrium model of UK housing construction to capture the effect of non-market constraints on house-building; this distorts the estimated price elasticity of supply.

[l] The equilibrium model for US industrial/commercial construction is fitted from 1979, but is very weak because of the zero growth trend; the error correction model is fitted from 1983.

[m] The demand and supply elasticities are estimated from equations (8.1) and (8.2) in the appendix, using the coefficients of the equilibrium models.

grown on average by 3.0% per annum over the past 50 years, whereas there has been an average 1.5% rate of decline in the real value of private construction starts. In contrast, since 1963, real house prices in the United States have only grown on average by 0.9%, with virtually all of that growth attributable to the housing boom of the last decade, whereas the real value of construction output has grown at a rate of 2.0% per annum. In other words, the UK housing market has been characterized by a declining supply of new dwellings and strong growth in real prices, whereas the US market has maintained a sufficient rate of growth in new supply to hold real prices close to a constant level, at least until the latest boom (Shiller, 2005: 12). As a result, the tendency has been for the house price/income ratio to exhibit a slowly rising trend in the United Kingdom and a falling trend in the United States, although in both countries the trend has been overlaid by strong cyclical fluctuations (Figure 8.7).

Two points about the real price of housing emerged from the growth analysis presented in Chapter 4. The first is that of all components of capital stock, housing has benefitted the least from technical progress in construction methods. The second is that housing, or at least owner-occupied housing, is primarily an income-elastic consumption good rather than an investment good. As demonstrated in the appendix, the relative trends in real house prices and household income depend upon the price and income elasticities of demand and the elasticity of supply, split between price and income components which in turn are determined by the elasticities of land supply and of substitution between land and other inputs to housing construction (Ermisch, 1990: 22–4; Meen, 1996: 437). A secular rise in the house price/income ratio is more likely the larger the income elasticity of demand compared to the price elasticity of demand and the elasticity of supply. The divergence between the trends in this ratio in the United Kingdom and United States suggests that the income elasticity of housing demand may be higher in the United Kingdom,

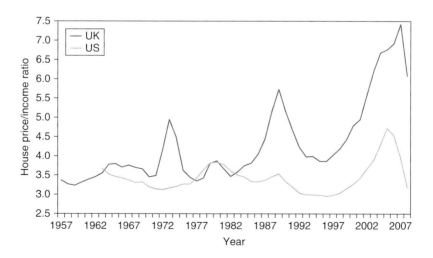

Figure 8.7 UK and US average house price/income ratios 1957–2008.
Source: Feinstein (1976), Holmans (2005), Nationwide, S&P/Case-Shiller, BEA, DCLG, ONS, and USCB.

while the elasticity of supply is lower (see also the growth analysis presented in Chapter 4).

The estimates presented in Table 8.1 broadly support the inference that it is the combination of highly income-elastic demand and relatively inelastic supply that has fuelled the stronger post-war rate of house price inflation in Britain than in America. Based upon the equilibrium price models, the estimated ratio of the income to price elasticity of demand is much higher in the United Kingdom when compared to the United States, although the US value is an under-estimate because it is derived from an incomplete price model lacking a significant stock variable. The equilibrium construction models appear to yield similar combined estimates of the price and income elasticity of supply in the United Kingdom and United States, but the UK estimates are artificially boosted by the inclusion of a negative time trend in the model to capture the non-market constraints which operate on the supply of housing land in Britain. These constraints stem from three interrelated causes: a small and crowded land mass, generally restrictive planning policies and community resistance to new development, all of which mean that British house-builders tend to construct 'rabbit hutches on postage stamps' (Evans, 1991). In contrast, the vastness of the continental land supply in North America has helped to hold down real land and property prices, as its expanding cities have sprawled ever outwards (Edel and Sclar, 1975; Atack and Margo, 1998). The restricted supply of development sites in the United Kingdom inevitably inflates land prices, which serves to explain why house prices in the United Kingdom are relatively more expensive than those in the United States, when compared to average levels of income (Figure 8.7).

The high income elasticity of demand that is apparent in the UK housing market can be attributed to the importance attached to home ownership as the principal source of household wealth accumulation in Britain. Moving through the life cycle, individual households seek to upgrade their accommodation as their incomes rise. However, because of relatively inelastic supply, the majority of the aggregate demand generated by rising incomes tends to feed asset price inflation rather than an expansion of the quantity or quality of available dwellings. Thus, while there was a 2.6% per annum rate of growth in the real asset value of the housing stock in Britain between 1961 and 2001, there was only a 1.1% rate of growth in the number of households and dwellings over the same period (Holmans, 2005: 43). Furthermore, on a size-adjusted basis, the physical increase in the UK housing stock will have been even more modest. The average floor area of all categories of dwellings has been decreasing in the more recent vintages of stock, reducing from an average of 90 square metres for pre-1900 dwellings, down to 78 square metres for those built between 1900 and 1980 and to just 73 square metres for those built after 1980 (Holmans, 2005: 56). In contrast, while the real value of the American housing stock grew at a similar 2.7% per annum between 1966 and 2000, there was a substantially higher 1.8% rate of growth in the number of households and dwellings (Simmons, 2001: 68). The extent to which real increases in household income are being translated into dwellings of improved size or specification in the United Kingdom is limited not only by the constraints on house-building but also by cultural preferences for period rather than modern homes. As a result, in Britain, to a greater extent than in America, we are living not in better or larger houses, but merely in more expensive houses.

So far we have concentrated upon the secular trends in the post-war growth of the UK and US housing markets. However, reverting to our main theme, the growth of each market has been far from smooth, but rather has been propelled by a sequence of strongly articulated boom–bust cycles (Hamnett, 1999; Bramley et al., 2004). In the United Kingdom, there have been three major house price bubbles in the post-war period, associated with the economic booms of the early 1970s, the late 1980s and the mid-2000s, together with a more subdued price cycle in the late 1970s (Figure 8.3). House-building booms have accompanied each of these price cycles, following an earlier building cycle in the mid-1960s. However, because successive building cycles have been superimposed on a declining secular trend, they have delivered a diminishing volume of new dwellings to the market (see Figure 5.15). Since the start of the 1970s, the same four cycles can be distinguished in the US housing market, although the intermediate cycle in the late 1970s is relatively stronger (Figure 8.4). The standard deviations of the US price and building cycles are smaller than those of their UK counterparts, partly because the constrained supply of new housing in Britain has tended to intensify market volatility. It also appears that a greater degree of smoothing has been introduced into the national data series for the United States: construction is represented by output, not starts, while the price index is aggregated across a far wider spread of metropolitan markets than the UK index.

The error correction models of price adjustment in the two national markets have a similar structure (Table 8.1). Both include a strong serial correlation effect, whereby the current year's proportionate change in real prices is influenced by the direction and size of the previous year's change, with the effect being twice as strong in the US model. Such serial correlation is a commonly observed feature of cyclical price behaviour across a wide range of housing markets in different countries (Case and Shiller, 1989; Abraham and Hendershott, 1996; Englund and Ioannides, 1997). To a considerable extent, the larger serial correlation term in the US model seems to reflect the degree of smoothing introduced into the national price index. Both national models incorporate the cycle generating shocks that result from shifts in household income, though the effect is more pronounced in the UK model, which also includes the impact of short-term changes to the housing stock. Finally, the error correction terms in both models have a similar but relatively low value, indicating that quite a slow trend reversion process corrects the price cycle in each market. With regard to the formation of house price cycles, these estimates suggest that the reinforcement processes embodied in the serial correlation term may be stronger than the damping processes which act through the error correction term.

There are more marked differences in the structure of the error correction models for the house-building cycle in each country. There is a serial correlation term in the US model, but none in the UK model. The US model incorporates shocks emanating from changes in both income and prices, whereas in the UK model shocks to building are generated solely through the accelerator effect of variations in the rate of change of prices. The error correction term in each building model is stronger than that in the equivalent price model; the coefficient on the feedback term is twice as large in the UK building model compared to the price model and four times as large in the US model. It seems that the forces of negative feedback are relatively stronger than the forces of positive reinforcement, when comparing the cyclical behaviour of house-building to that of house prices.

These error correction models embody the transmission processes that link together price and building cycles in the housing market. An increase in household income generates stronger demand and rising prices, particularly if exacerbated by a shortage of supply. Stronger demand and rising prices stimulate an upswing in building activity, which feeds through to boost supply at the same time as the house price/income ratio becomes unsustainable. The feedback from unaffordable prices and increased supply causes the rate of price growth to moderate and then to reverse, in turn choking off further new supply. This simple model structure by no means captures all the influences on the housing market cycle. The mortgage rate can be introduced as an influence on the user cost of housing: in the UK model it replaces the effect of stock changes; in the US model it has a less significant effect. Fiscal or institutional shocks such as tax changes or the liberalization of mortgage credit are more difficult to include formally within the model, but their role in triggering price bubbles can easily be observed.

Despite its simple structure, the exogenous demand shocks and endogenous adjustment processes embodied within the model are capable of replicating the essential dynamics of the housing market cycle as an economy moves along its secular growth path. These dynamics have been operating particularly forcefully during the latest boom–bust cycle. The scale of the price correction that is likely to follow the latest crash is all too apparent from Figure 8.7. The double digit falls in prices recorded during 2008 mark only the first stage in a prolonged and severe adjustment, an adjustment that may turn out to be structural as well as cyclical.

The industrial and commercial property market

The UK industrial and commercial market has exhibited a relatively stronger trend in construction activity and a weaker trend in capital value growth compared to the housing market. In contrast in the US market, both construction and real capital values have exhibited more negative trends than those in the housing market (Figures 8.5 and 8.6; Table 8.1). Thus, between 1957 and 2007, non-residential construction starts in the United Kingdom grew on average by 1.1% per annum, compared to the 1.5% rate of decline in housing starts, while the real capital values of industrial and commercial property declined on average by 1.3% per annum, compared to the 3.0% rate of growth in real house prices. In the United States, over the shorter 1977–2007 period, the real value of non-residential construction output showed a flat trend, compared to an average growth rate in housing construction of 2.4% over the equivalent period, while real industrial/commercial capital values declined on average by 3.3% per annum, compared to the 1.0% rate of growth in real house prices.

Three reasons can be suggested to explain the very different price and building trends in non-residential compared to residential markets. First, as demonstrated in Chapter 4, industrial and commercial building has enjoyed a higher rate of technical progress than house-building, thereby generating a stronger rate of cheapening relative to the labour used in construction. Second, non-residential buildings are investment not consumption goods, and occupiers have been substituting away from buildings towards equipment because of the more rapid cheapening and higher rates of embodied technical progress enjoyed by equipment capital. Third, industrial and commercial buildings are a more intensive land use than dwellings, with the result that land supply constraints have a less powerful effect upon the elasticity of non-residential compared to residential building supply. The differential operation of these supply and demand forces in the two markets is better illustrated by the UK elasticity estimates presented in Table 8.1, since these are clearer than the US results which have been derived from an incomplete price model lacking a significant output variable.

The contrast between rising construction levels and falling real prices in the non-residential market and the reverse combination in the residential market implies that there has tended to be too much industrial and commercial development and insufficient housing development in post-war Britain. Such a tendency towards over-supply and falling prices was previously noted in the City of London office case study presented in Chapter 6. The behaviour of the industrial/commercial market compared to the housing market can be explained by a combination of lower output and price elasticities of demand and higher output and price elasticities of supply. The estimated output elasticity of demand from industrial and commercial occupiers is considerably smaller than the income elasticity of demand from households, reflecting the capital-saving tendencies operating on non-residential building investment. Industrial/commercial demand also appears to be much less price elastic than housing demand, which means that increases in supply are translated into a much stronger downward pressure on prices. The combined output and price elasticities of supply appear to be similar in the two markets, but as indicated above, the elasticity of housing supply is artificially boosted by the inclusion of a negative time trend in the housing construction model to replicate non-market land supply constraints.

Though the US elasticity estimates are incomplete, a slightly different combination of forces seems to have been at work in the American markets. Unlike in the United Kingdom, the supply elasticities in the US residential and non-residential markets appear to be broadly similar, indicating that the reason for the flat trend in industrial/commercial construction is the exceptionally severe decline in real capital values that has occurred over the past 30 years. In order to explain this decline in prices, we must infer that in the US non-residential market the ratio of the output to price elasticity of demand is lower than that in the United Kingdom, as also appears to be the case when comparing the two national housing markets.

Over the past 50 years the UK non-residential market has experienced the same three boom–bust cycles that were apparent in the housing market. The three cycles are marked by peaks in real capital values and construction starts in 1973, 1988/9 and 2006 (Figure 8.5). Each was a classic speculative long cycle of the type conceptualized in the final section of Chapter 3, with an unstable price cycle closely tracked by an unstable construction cycle. The build-up of speculative demand is indicated by the strong increase in bank lending to the property industry which occurred in each of these cycles, typically rising from a floor of around 4% of total outstanding bank debt up to a peak of between 8% and 10% at the height of each boom (Figure 8.8). Interspersed with the dominant speculative cycles, there were less volatile intermediate cycles in the early 1960s, late 1970s and late 1990s. All six of the identified national cycles in building starts fed through to completions cycles that are apparent in the postwar cycle chronology established for the City of

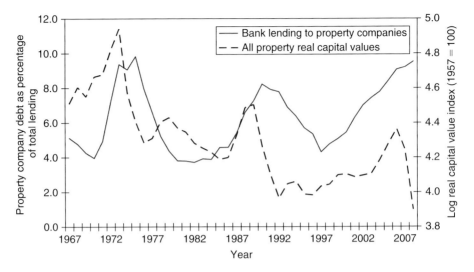

Figure 8.8   Bank lending and real capital values in the UK non-residential market 1967–2008. *Source*: Bank of England, ONS and IPD.

London office market in Chapter 6. This chronology is marked by the alternation between relatively orderly demand-led cycles and unstable speculative boom–bust cycles, such that a 15–20 year long cycle rhythm is superimposed on an 8–10 year sequence of major cycles.

The speculative cycles of the late 1980s and mid-2000s, together with the intermediate cycle of the late 1990s, are also apparent in the shorter capital value and construction series available for the US non-residential market (Figure 8.6). However, as in the housing market, the cycles are less clearly defined, again suggesting that the US series are more smoothed than their UK counterparts. In addition to the smoothing effects of greater aggregation, the US capital value index is based on compounded quarterly valuations, whereas the UK index is based on year end valuations. To some extent, the smoothed series conceal the severity of the boom–bust cycles which have affected the US non-residential market, and in particular the office market, during the past 30 years (Wheaton, 1987; Hendershott and Kane, 1992; Mills, 1995).

As measured by their standard deviations, the volatilities of the non-residential price and building cycles in the two countries are much closer in value than they are in the residential market. This is partly because neither national market is subject to the supply constraints which operate in the UK housing market. In both countries the non-residential capital value and construction series can be disaggregated into their component sectors. The standard deviations of the component series establish that the office sector exhibits the most volatile market cycles and the industrial sector the least volatile, with the retail sector typically occupying an intermediate position.

There are significant differences in the error correction models of non-residential cycle behaviour in the two national markets, although in part at least these reflect differences in the length and smoothing of the data series (Table 8.1). The US price

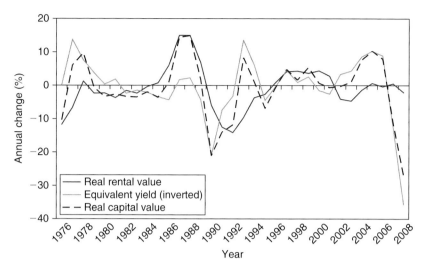

Figure 8.9   Cycles in UK non-residential capital value and its components 1976–2008.
Source: IPD.

adjustment model incorporates a strong serial correlation term, but a weak error correction term, whereas the UK model contains no significant serial correlation term, but a strong error correction term. Comparing the dynamics of non-residential price formation in the two countries, the estimates imply that the 'bubble building' reinforcement process may be stronger in the US market while the 'bubble bursting' damping process is weaker. However, this result may in part be a statistical artifact, arising from the smoothing applied to the US capital value series. Both national price adjustment models incorporate the cycle generating shocks that result from business cycle shifts in output, and both also include the impact of short-term changes to the building stock. Neither model of the industrial/commercial building cycle includes a serial correlation term, while the coefficients on the error correction terms in the two national models are closer in value than those in the corresponding price models. The UK building cycle model allows for shocks due to changes in both output and prices, whereas in the US model building responds only to exogenous changes in output.

The interaction of occupier and investment markets

The non-residential models discussed so far are all based on property capital values. However, the IPD series used in the UK model also allows for capital value changes to be broken down into their two components: changes in rental values and movements in the equivalent yield, calculated as the discount rate which equates future rental income to the current capital value. For total UK non-residential property, Figure 8.9 illustrates the annual changes in real capital values and real rental values, together with the inverted yield movements that have occurred since 1976, the date from which the rental value and yield data are available. The decomposition of the capital value cycle into its constituent rent and yield cycles is valuable, because it reveals the operation of user demand on the movement of rents and investor demand on the movement of yields – demand forces that operate at least partly autonomously because of the different factors which can influence the behaviour of the occupier and investment markets.

An alternative version of the national property cycle model is presented in the appendix, specified in terms of real rents and yields, rather than real capital values. The equilibrium and error correction equations for capital values and construction activity are formulated using rents rather than prices, and separate equilibrium and error correction equations are defined for the yield in relation to conditions in other investment markets. The property yield is assumed to be a negative function of the real rent level, since the higher the rent the stronger the investment demand, a negative function of the equity yield, since property and equities are investment substitutes, and a positive function of the bond yield, since this represents the expected risk-free rate of return. In the error correction equation, movements in yields respond to expected as well as current changes in the explanatory variables. The results derived by estimating this model for total UK non-residential property over the 1975–2007 period are displayed in Table 8.2.

The error correction model of the rent cycle has a better structure and higher explanatory power than the equivalent capital value model over this shorter period. Consistent with the theoretical model, it incorporates reinforcement and damping processes of comparable strength, as embodied in the serial correlation and error correction terms, respectively. Its overall performance confirms that movements in occupier demand operate more directly on rents than capital values, and that the occupier market contains pronounced cycle propagation properties. The building cycle model is slightly improved when estimated using rents rather than capital values, but it would seem that either rents or prices can provide developers with the necessary market signals concerning construction profitability. Like the rent model, the yield model incorporates reinforcement and damping processes of similar magnitude, indicating that there are strong cyclical tendencies in the investment as well as occupier market. Property yields respond to expectations of changes in rental values and the equity yield 1 year ahead, together with current changes in the bond yield. This confirms that the yield cycle, and therefore the capital value cycle, is partly driven by conditions in the occupier market and partly by conditions in the investment market.

It is apparent from Figure 8.9 that over the past 30 years rent and yield movements have made differential contributions to the dynamic of the capital value cycle in UK non-residential property. The chronology of market movements can be summarized as follows:

- Following the frenzied boom of the early 1970s, the consequent slump in capital values was driven principally by rental decline, reflecting the impact of the subsequent economic recession on occupier demand. The real level of industrial and commercial construction starts virtually halved between 1973 and 1975.
- As real rental values stabilized during the late 1970s, there was a period of strong investor demand for commercial property, which was seen to be out-performing equities as an investment asset. The result was a sustained fall in yields and an entirely investor-driven spike in real capital value growth during 1977/8.
- During the first half of the 1980s property yields began slowly to move out again, as the equity market embarked upon a decade-long boom. Real capital and rental

Table 8.2   Models of the UK industrial and commercial property cycle 1975–2007[a].

Equilibrium rent model[b]

$$\log r_t = 4.915 + 3.348 \log Y_t - 3.474 \log K_t$$
$$\quad\quad (15.07) \quad (6.28) \quad\quad (-6.66)$$

adjR^2 = 0.617; n = 33; DW = 0.493

(8.1)

Error correction rent model[c]

$$\Delta \log r_t = 0.508 \Delta \log r_{t-1} + 1.303 \Delta \log Y_t - 1.360 \Delta \log K_t - 0.308 u_{t-1}$$
$$\quad\quad\quad (7.80) \quad\quad\quad (4.65) \quad\quad\quad (-4.47) \quad\quad (-4.44)$$

adjR^2 = 0.880; n = 31; DW = 1.835

(8.3)

Equilibrium construction model[b]

$$\log S_t = -4.178 + 1.121 \log Y_t + 0.714 \log r_t$$
$$\quad\quad (-2.94) \quad\quad (8.87) \quad\quad (3.02)$$

adjR^2 = 0.705; n = 33; DW = 0.455

(8.2)

Error correction construction model[d]

$$\Delta \log S_t = 1.848 \Delta \log Y_t + 1.181 \Delta \log r_t - 0.445 v_{t-1}$$
$$\quad\quad\quad (3.33) \quad\quad\quad (4.12) \quad\quad (-3.78)$$

adjR^2 = 0.491; n = 32; DW = 1.574

(8.4)

Equilibrium yield model[b]

$$w_t = 7.344 - 0.367 e_t + 0.398 g_t$$
$$\quad (18.06) \quad (-4.26) \quad\quad (5.31)$$

adjR^2 = 0.459; n = 32; DW = 1.126

(8.5)

Error correction yield model[e]

$$\Delta w_t = 0.504 \Delta w_{t-1} - 2.938 \Delta \log r_{t+1} - 0.130 \Delta e_{t+1} + 0.209 \Delta g_t - 0.431 z_{t-1}$$
$$\quad\quad (4.13) \quad\quad\quad (-2.61) \quad\quad\quad (-2.57) \quad\quad (4.00) \quad\quad (-4.57)$$

adjR^2 = 0.635; n = 29; DW = 1.703

(8.6)

Net additions model

$$\Delta \log K_t = -0.056 + 0.016 \log S_{t-2}$$
$$\quad\quad (-6.91) \quad (10.01)$$

adjR^2 = 0.756; n = 33; DW = 1.038

(8.7)

Source: IPD and ONS.

[a] The models are based on equations (8.1)–(8.7), set out in the appendix to this chapter, fitted over the period 1975–2007; the t-statistics for each coefficient, the adjusted R-squared and the Durbin–Watson statistic for each equation are quoted.

[b] All the equilibrium models produce a cointegrating regression, yielding residuals that are stationary according to the unit root test at the 1% significance level.

[c] In the rent models, the rent variable is the IPD All Property real rental value, output is GDP and building stock is represented by the fixed asset value of non-residential building capital.

[d] In the building models, construction activity is represented by the annual volume of private sector industrial and commercial building starts.

[e] In the yield models, the yield variable is the IPD All Property equivalent yield, the equity variable is the earnings yield and the bond variable is the yield on 10-year gilts.

values experienced mild decline, but remained relatively unaffected by the early 1980s recession.

- As the speculative boom of the late 1980s got under way, real rents started to rise in 1985, while capital values took off a year later. This boom was almost entirely driven by the expansion of demand in the occupier market, with the rate of growth in both capital and rental values peaking in 1987/8 at around 15% per annum, while the upswing barely registered on the yield cycle. The building boom peaked a year later in 1988/9, at a real level of starts more than twice that at the beginning of the decade.
- The slump at the start of the 1990s was a dramatic event in both the occupier and investment markets. With the onset of recession, a sharp rise in yields to a 1992 peak of 10.6% combined with a sudden drop in rents to generate a cumulative fall of 40% in real capital values between 1989 and 1992.
- However, as had happened after the mid-1970s crash, yields moved in quickly again, as investors realized that the market had over-corrected and property had become under-valued. The result was another brief investor-driven spike in capital value growth during 1993/4.
- During the late 1990s, the occupier market took over again as the main driver of the capital value cycle. Steady real rental growth underpinned the growth of real capital values between 1997 and 2000, as the economy and property market moved into a sustained phase of prosperity. The accompanying boom in construction new orders peaked in 1998.
- Though rental growth faltered in the early 2000s, a new speculative boom was launched by an unprecedented surge in investor demand during a period when property was generally out-performing equities. The all-property equivalent yield fell from 7.8% in 2001 to 5.4% by 2006, some 2% lower than at any point in the past 30 years. The consequences of this overheated investment market were a cumulative 28% rise in real capital values between 2003 and 2006, and a new upswing in development starts that peaked in 2006/7.

During 2007/8 the inevitable reaction occurred, as yields switched rapidly back to more sustainable levels, causing a steep decline in real capital values. Paralleling the collapse of house prices, this equally abrupt reversal of conditions in the non-residential market illustrates once more how a speculative investment boom can turn into a spectacular bust.

The globalization of the property cycle

The growth of the transnational investment market

Three broad trends within the world economy are combining to spur the growth of the transnational property investment market:

Shifting economic power
The composition of global economic output is shifting steadily from the advanced economies towards the emerging and developing economies, due principally to the

rapid industrialization that is taking place in Asia. The IMF estimate that global GDP measured on a purchasing-power-parity basis was worth $65 trillion in 2007, having grown on average in real terms by 3.4% per annum since 1980 (IMF, 2008). The split in total world output between the advanced economies and the emerging and developing economies was 64% to 36% in 1980; by 2007 it had narrowed to 56% against 44%, and by 2013 the contribution of the emerging and developing economies is projected to reach parity with that of the advanced economies. Between 1980 and 2007, the United States maintained its leading share of global output at between 22% and 23%, whereas the relative contributions of the slower growing advanced economies shrank, with the EU share dropping from 29% to 23%, and that of Japan from 9% to 7%. It was of course China, with its astonishing rate of industrialization, which produced the most dramatic increase in economic output over the period, its share of global output jumping from just 2% in 1980 to 11% by 2007. The increase in India's share from 2% to 5% over the same period seems almost sedate in comparison. By 2013, the rise of China is projected to take its share of world output up to 15%, while the US and EU shares contract to 19% and 20% respectively. If current rates of convergence continue, China could even overtake the United States as the world's largest economy by 2020.

Accelerating urbanization

The world's population has been growing at an accelerating rate, and it has been urbanizing at an even faster rate. According to estimates by the United Nations (2007), global population increased from 2.5 billion in 1950 to 6.1 billion in 2000, and is projected to reach 8.0 billion by 2025 and 9.2 billion by 2050. Nearly 60% of this global total lives in Asia. In 1950, only 29% of the world's population lived in urban areas; by 2000 this share had risen to 47%, and the UN estimates that it will reach 57% by 2025 and as much as 70% by 2050. The extent of this urban explosion can be gauged by the fact that in 1950 there were only two cities in the world with a population of more than 10 million (New York and Tokyo, with London lying third at 8.4 million), and 78 cities with a population of 1 million or more. By 2000, the number of cities with 10 million or more inhabitants had risen to 16, half of them in Asia, while the number of cities with a population of 1 million or more had increased to 378, again half of them in Asia. By 2025, it is estimated that there will be 27 cities with a population of more than ten million, with 16 in Asia, and 599 cities of 1 million or more, with 332 in Asia. Of the ten largest cities in the world in 2000, five were in Asia (Tokyo, Mumbai, Shanghai, Kolkata and Delhi) three in Latin America (Mexico City, Sao Paulo and Buenos Aires) and two in the United States (New York and Los Angeles). By 2025, it is estimated that seven of the top ten will be in Asia (Tokyo, Mumbai, Delhi, Dhaka, Kolkata, Shanghai and Karachi), two in Latin America (Sao Paulo and Mexico City) and just one in the United States (New York). The balance of global economic power and human resources is tilting decisively towards Asia.

Proliferating investment

Investment in all types of assets has become an increasingly global activity in response to the growth of transnational corporations, the liberalization of capital flows and the integration of financial markets. Property investors have responded to the forces of globalization by developing international property portfolio strategies (Lizieri and Finlay, 1995), as a result of which there has been a rapid growth in global property investment in general, and cross-border investment in particular. According to real estate adviser DTZ (2008), the value of the global real estate capital market reached $11.7 trillion in 2007, an almost threefold increase over the decade since 1997, compared with a less than twofold increase in global output over the same period. In terms of international spread, the US market accounted for 35% of the total, the UK for 12%, the rest of Europe 29% and Asia-Pacific 24%. During 2007, around $720 billion of property investments were transacted worldwide, and around $100 billion of this total flowed between the three main continental markets of the United States, EU and Asia-Pacific. Although the transnational property investment market has been growing rapidly, it still represents only a small proportion of the total global value of real estate assets. According to Syz (2008: 149), the investible global property market in 2002 may have accounted for only around 10% of the total value of residential and non-residential real estate assets, the remainder being held in owner-occupation by households and firms. However, the example of the United Kingdom, one of the world's most developed property investment markets, indicates how high the investible share can rise. Estimates from the Investment Property Forum (IPF, 2005) suggest that, in 2003, the value of the commercial property investment market in the United Kingdom was as high as 43% of the total value of all non-residential property in the national economy, and that this proportion was over 60% in the case of retail and office property.

One of the most striking manifestations of globalization is the way in which the world economy can now be viewed as an interlocking network of cities, linked together by flows of goods and services, knowledge, labour and capital. The perception that the world economy consists of a hierarchical system of cities originated with writers such as Berry (1964), who developed a pioneering theoretical model to represent 'cities as systems within systems of cities'; Pred (1977), who explored the inter-urban linkages generated by multi-locational organizations and Friedmann (1986), who put forward a 'world city hypothesis' expressed as a set of theses linking urbanization to global economic development. More recently, Sassen (2001, 2006) has argued that information technology is facilitating a combination of geographic dispersal and economic integration which creates a new strategic role for global cities, while Castells (2000) has examined how the information age is transforming the global economy into a 'network society'.

To paraphrase the metaphysical poet John Donne, no city is an island, entire of itself; rather it is part of the wider whole. Innovations originating in one part of the global urban system are diffused through the remainder of the network by the outward flow and returning feedback of ideas and investment, in the manner of the transport improvements discussed in Chapter 5. Perhaps the clearest illustration of the phenomenon is provided by the 'world city network' which has been created by the operations of transnational financial and business services companies (Taylor, 2004b). The nodes of this system are the world's metropolitan office centres, interconnected by sophisticated ICT networks which intensify the agglomeration economies within each centre, while simultaneously facilitating 24 hour financial trading between separate centres in different time zones. Waves of real estate investment flow around this world city network, feeding economic growth and urban development but at the same time propagating market instability.

As the transnational investment market has evolved, so it has become apparent that the property cycle itself is becoming a global phenomenon. The behaviour of the cycle varies across national and urban economies according to differences in local market conditions and institutional structures. Nevertheless, the processes that propagate the property cycle, and link it to the wider business cycle, appear to be common to all economies irrespective of their location, market structure and stage of economic development. This argument can most clearly be demonstrated by examining the convergence of market cycles across a range of international office centres during the past 25 years.

Global cities, global cycle

The office market is the most globally integrated real estate market in terms of occupier demand, investment demand and development supply. Transnational corporations are generating relatively homogenous demands for office space in whichever city they locate. Office buildings constitute the largest component of global property investment in general and cross-border investment in particular. Architects and developers are producing office buildings of similar design and specification in every continent of the world. Consequently, the office market is at the forefront of the transformation of the world economy into an interlocking network of global cities. Furthermore, of all real estate sectors, it is the office market that exhibits the most volatile price and building cycles. As the office market becomes more integrated, so its volatile behaviour is more readily transmitted between the cities of the world.

We have previously identified three major cycles in the commercial property market over the past 25 years. These consist of the strong speculative cycles of the late 1980s and mid-2000s, together with the more stable intermediate cycle of the late 1990s. As discussed in Chapter 3, the boom–bust cycle of the 1980s was the office market cycle *par excellence*. The widespread diffusion of information technology throughout the financial and business service industries combined with a wave of financial deregulation and a weakening of land use planning controls to create a potent demand stimulus. As vacancy plunged and rents soared, the resulting building boom saw the construction of unprecedented volumes of new office space, which reached completion just as the onset of global recession severely weakened demand, causing vacancy to surge and rents to collapse. Cyclical instability was reinforced by feedback and contagion effects deriving from the close interlocking of the occupier and investment markets in the world's major office centres, with financial institutions acting as the main occupiers of the newly built office space, the main sources of long-term development funding and the main purchasers of the completed developments.

The manner in which these three cycles have manifested themselves in different global office markets can be illustrated using data series compiled by PMA from a variety of sources published by government agencies and real estate firms. The analysis covers the 25 office markets listed in Table 8.3; of these 9 are in Europe, 9 in the United States and 7 in the Asia-Pacific region. These cities include the main financial centres of the world, together with other major urban economies with a dominant office sector. Four data series have been used for the analysis of each market: office employment, total office floorspace, vacant space and real rent levels for prime city centre offices. No direct measures of building activity are available

Table 8.3   Cycle parameters for global office centres 1986–2007.

	Cycle volatility (%)[a]			Rent cycle correlation[b]		Rent transmission	
	Rents	Vacancy	Building	Coefficient	Lag (years)	Natural vacancy[c] (%)	Feedback coefficient[d]
Europe[e]	*13.18*	*2.86*	*1.60*	*0.796*		*7.52*	*0.205*
Amsterdam	6.30	4.04	2.06	0.641	0	10.56	0.120
Barcelona	19.84	3.37	1.97	0.793	0	6.65	0.227
Brussels	5.21	1.33	2.16	0.784	−1	7.63	0.124
Frankfurt	12.60	3.84	1.43	0.784	0	9.90	0.235
London	14.68	4.83	2.22	0.823	0	10.98	
Madrid	19.26	2.83	2.27	0.972	0	5.97	0.226
Munich	8.67	2.08	0.84	0.844	0	4.14	0.227
Paris	17.78	2.70	0.86	0.769	0	5.93	0.312
Rome	14.29	0.72	0.65	0.757	−1	5.88	0.168
United States[e]	*8.85*	*3.69*	*1.90*	*0.753*		*14.17*	*0.218*
Atlanta	3.47	4.67	3.04	0.630	−1	9.91	
Boston	14.14	5.10	2.32	0.922	0	14.52	0.182
Chicago	6.73	3.51	1.81	0.698	0	14.42	
Dallas	5.00	3.74	2.04	0.750	0	19.45	
Houston	12.42	3.15	0.74	0.591	0	19.33	
Los Angeles	5.20	2.22	1.85	0.696	0	14.45	
New York	8.49	2.53	0.85	0.884	0	11.40	0.274
San Francisco	18.45	5.68	1.69	0.884	0	12.79	0.197
Washington	5.74	2.65	2.77	0.726	0	11.28	
Asia-Pacific[e]	*22.94*	*6.85*	*2.29[f]*	*0.666[g]*		*12.35*	*0.352*
Beijing	22.68	11.36	22.18	0.386	−6	16.39	
Hong Kong	31.85	2.66	2.08	0.793	0	9.97	0.525
Melbourne	16.67	7.25	3.51	0.294	7	11.14	0.238
Shanghai	25.69	14.49	22.34	0.406	−5	20.13	
Singapore	34.28	4.20	2.37	0.659	0	14.90	0.604
Sydney	15.05	5.67	2.25	0.426	0	9.18	0.222
Tokyo	14.33	2.33	1.25	0.787	0	4.72	0.171

Source: PMA.

[a]Cycle volatility is measured as the standard deviation around a fitted linear trend of the real rate of rental change, the vacancy rate and the rate of net additions, the latter two being expressed as a proportion of total stock.

[b]Rent cycle correlation is measured as the coefficient and lag on the highest positive cross-correlation between the rental change cycle for the city and the aggregate cycle for its corresponding continental region; for Asia-Pacific, the regional aggregate excludes Beijing and Shanghai.

[c]The natural vacancy rate is estimated from the partial rent adjustment equation (B.28b) in Appendix B.

[d]The feedback coefficient is estimated from the composite rent adjustment equation (B.28c), using the results set out in Table 8.5.

[e]The continental parameters are simple arithmetic averages of the values for the individual cities in the region.

[f]The Asia-Pacific average for building cycle volatility excludes Beijing and Shanghai.

[g]The Asia-Pacific average for the rent cycle correlation coefficient excludes Beijing, Shanghai and Melbourne.

on a consistent basis across the centres, and so annual additions to stock are used as a proxy measure, which tends to reduce the volatility of the building cycle to some extent because of the delays and smoothing inherent in the stock data. All series cover the period 1985–2008, and some stretch back to the start of the 1980s. The building, vacancy and rent cycles obtained by combining the individual city trends into their three continental aggregates are illustrated in Figures 8.10–8.12.

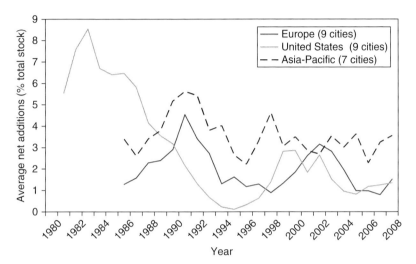

Figure 8.10   Building cycles in global office markets.
Source: PMA.

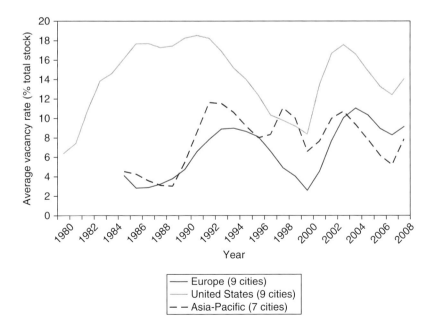

Figure 8.11   Vacancy cycles in global office markets.
Source: PMA.

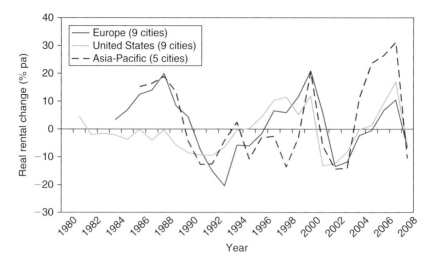

Figure 8.12   Rent cycles in global office markets.
Source: PMA.

The building cycle

Four building cycles are apparent from the trends in net additions, expressed as a proportion of total stock (Figure 8.10). As already noted, the most prominent of the office-building cycles of the past three decades occurred in the 1980s. However, it is clear that there were two separate phases to this building cycle: there was a huge building boom in the United States which peaked between 1983 and 1986, whereas in Europe and Asia-Pacific the cycle did not reach a completions peak until 1991. Several American cities featured prominently in this cycle, with newly emerging markets such as Dallas and Houston generating levels of building as high as those in established centres such as New York and Chicago. In contrast, in Europe and Asia-Pacific it was the established centres of London, Paris and Tokyo that tended to dominate. It would appear from the relative timing of the continental cycles that the demand stimulus created by information technology and financial deregulation originated in the United States in the first half of the 1980s, and spread to Europe and Asia in the second half of the decade (Mills, 1995).

Differences in timing are still apparent in the late 1990s office-building cycle, although the continental cycles were more convergent than they were in the 1980s. Net additions peaked first in Asia-Pacific in 1998, followed by the United States in 1999/2000 and Europe as late as 2002. In each continent, this was a less volatile cycle than its predecessor, generating substantially less construction activity in most cities. The main exceptions were the German cities of Frankfurt and Munich, where late 1980s building levels were exceeded, and Beijing and Shanghai, which experienced massive building booms in the second half of the 1990s, following the opening of the Chinese economy to overseas investors and occupiers in the earlier part of the decade. Because of construction lags, the building cycle which took off in the mid-2000s only began to have an impact on net additions in 2007/8. At the end of 2007, the top five global cities in terms of the quantity of total office floorspace under construction consisted of the three Asian cities of Beijing, Shanghai and Tokyo, plus London and Washington, these being closely followed by New York, Paris and Singapore.

The vacancy cycle
The impact of the building cycle on the vacancy cycle is clear across all the centres (Figure 8.11). The massive building boom of the early 1980s forced the average vacancy rate across the nine US cities to rise from just over 6% in 1980 to nearly 18% in 1986, while in Dallas and Houston vacancy reached as high as 30%. The late 1980s building boom produced rather more modest vacancy peaks of 9% in Europe and 11.5% in Asia-Pacific during the early 1990s, although again exceptional peaks of 20% or more were recorded in London, Sydney and Melbourne. In all three continents, vacancy reached a trough in 2000, although the downswing of the vacancy cycle in Asia was interrupted by a spike in 1998/9, as the spectacular Chinese building boom during the second half of the decade caused vacancy in Beijing and Shanghai to soar above 40%.

As the cycle of the late 1990s fed through to completions and then vacancy, so the vacancy rate rose once more in all continents, reaching a cycle peak in 2003/4 which was far more coordinated than that of the previous cycle. Despite generally more modest levels of building in this cycle, the US and Asia-Pacific vacancy peaks still matched the levels reached in the previous cycle, while the European peak in 2004 exceeded that recorded in 1993/4 with Frankfurt and Amsterdam experiencing unprecedented vacancy rates of 20%. As building slumped, vacancy dropped to a new 2007 trough in all three regions, although in Europe and America this trough was substantially higher than that reached seven years earlier. The global office cycle was so convergent by then that only 5 of the 25 cities did not register a vacancy trough in 2007.

The rent cycle
As previously noted, the transmission process within the property market means that the rent cycle and the vacancy cycle are inversely related (Figure 8.12). The demand stimulus that triggered the early 1980s office-building cycle in the United States had generated a phase of strong real rental growth during the late 1970s and the start of the 1980s (Clapp, 1993: 59). As US vacancy rose to record levels during the first half of the decade, real rents switched from growth to a prolonged period of decline which lasted from 1982 to 1995 (Wheaton, 1987). In the cities of Europe and Asia-Pacific, the later demand shock is reflected in the surge of real rental growth which peaked during 1988 at around 20% in both regions, when their markets were close to a vacancy trough. At their late 1980s peak, four of these cities achieved an annual real rental growth rate of 50% or more – Paris (56%), Barcelona (50%), Hong Kong (60%) and Singapore (54%). (The Asia-Pacific rental series excludes Beijing and Shanghai because their exceptional recent development history means that their rent cycles have followed a different chronology.)

As economic boom turned to recession at the start of the 1990s, real rents in the European and Asian office markets collapsed as rapidly as they had previously surged. With vacancy peaking in 1992/3, real rental decline reached a simultaneous trough in all three continents, averaging −10% in the United States, −12.5% in Asia-Pacific and −20% in Europe. Particularly severe rental troughs were recorded in Barcelona (−45%), Madrid (−38%), Melbourne (−47%) and Singapore (−39%). In total contrast, Beijing and Shanghai were manifesting extraordinary rates of real rental growth at this time, peaking at 65% and 52% respectively in 1994, as burgeoning international demand was confronted by an almost non-existent supply of modern office space. The inevitable result was the building boom that engulfed the Chinese markets during the remainder of the decade.

During the second half of the 1990s, strong economic growth combined with reduced levels of new building to produce a rapid improvement in office market conditions. Real rental growth resumed in the United States for the first time in 14 years, and all three continents enjoyed a rental cycle upswing that peaked in 2000 just as vacancy reached its trough. Remarkably, Europe and Asia-Pacific again achieved an average rate of real rental growth of 20%, identical to that reached 12 years earlier, while the US markets peaked at an average rate of 12%. In this cycle, growth rates of 40% or more were experienced in San Francisco (44%), Madrid (45%), Paris (40%) and Hong Kong (50%). The counter-cyclical movement of the two Chinese markets meant that while the rest of the world was enjoying rental growth in the late 1990s, Beijing and Shanghai were suffering several years of real decline in response to over-building and soaring vacancy rates.

The stock market crash of 2001/2, and the subsequent economic slowdown, administered a short but severe demand shock to the world's office markets. Within two years, the rent cycle had switched from peak to trough, with all three continental markets averaging around 13% real decline in 2002/3. There then followed a new upswing, as the global economy boomed and office vacancy fell. By 2007, average real rental growth peaked once more at 10% in Europe, 17% in the United States and 31% in Asia-Pacific. For most of the American cities, this was the strongest period of rental growth since the beginning of the 1980s, with recorded growth rates of 40% in Boston, 39% in Houston and 27% in New York. However, their exceptional performance was overshadowed by the extraordinary rental growth being achieved in some Asian cities. In particular, between 2003 and 2007 real rents in both Hong Kong and Singapore quadrupled in response to the classic combination of low vacancy and strong economic growth. Rarely have office markets exhibited such extreme rental bubbles.

The determinants of market behaviour

Despite the global convergence of market cycles over the past 25 years, there remain considerable differences in the behaviour of individual office markets. These differences can be attributed to a variety of local factors such as economic structure, land supply, planning policies and market maturity (Keogh and D'Arcy, 1994; Berry and McGreal, 1995). For the purposes of our analysis, we shall focus on the determinants of five aspects of market behaviour: cycle co-movement, cycle volatility, the rent adjustment process, cycle dynamics and the formation of prime rents. Under each heading, we shall endeavour to uncover the stylized facts which encapsulate common features of market behaviour across centres subject to very different local conditions (for some stylized facts concerning recent UK commercial building cycles, see McGough and Tsolacos, 1997; for investigations of the determinants of office rents in different European cities, see D'Arcy et al., 1997 and Mouzakis and Richards, 2007).

Cycle co-movement

The simplest method for examining the co-movement of cycles is cross-correlation analysis at different time lags (see Section A.6.3). Technically more sophisticated methods are provided by cross-spectral analysis in the frequency domain (Chatfield, 2004: 159–66), and the identification of common features and common cycles in the time domain (MacGregor and Schwann, 2003).

For the three regional rent cycles illustrated in Figure 8.12, the strongest cross-correlation measured over the 1986–2007 period is the coincident relationship between the European and Asia-Pacific cycles (coefficient 0.664). This is followed by an almost equally strong relationship between the American and European cycles (0.651), with the US leading by one year, and by a significantly weaker coincident relationship (0.500) between the United States and Asia-Pacific. The cross-correlations between the rental cycles in each city and the corresponding cycles in their continental regions are listed in Table 8.3. In general, there is quite strong and coincident co-movement between the individual city cycles within Europe and within the United States: the averages of their city/region cross-correlation coefficients are quite similar (0.796 and 0.753 respectively) and for most cities the strongest relationship with the regional average is unlagged. It is a different story in the Asia-Pacific region. Only three of the cities, Tokyo, Hong Kong and Singapore, show reasonably strong and coincident co-movement; Sydney exhibits a weaker coincident relationship, while Beijing, Shanghai and Melbourne have all been moving counter-cyclically to the other cities in the region. Clearly, the greater integration of the American and European economies, compared to the more heterogeneous economies of the Asia-Pacific region, is reflected in the movement of their office market cycles.

It has already been noted that the co-movement of cycles in the three regions has not remained constant over the past 25 years, but rather has been increasing. To illustrate the extent of cycle convergence, Figure 8.13 plots the distribution of peak and trough turning point dates for the rent cycles in 23 of our sample set of

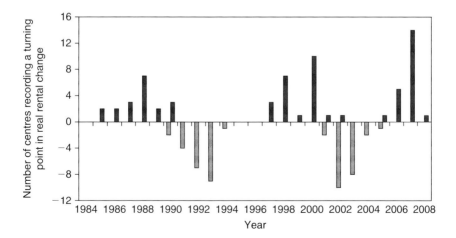

Figure 8.13   Rent cycle turning points in global office markets.
Source: PMA.

centres (excluding Beijing and Shanghai). The earlier incidence of the 1980s cycle in the United States means that the late 1980s peak in rental growth is not sharply defined, for although there is a concentration of turning points in 1988, the distribution is spread over the six years of 1985–90 and four of the US centres show no discernable peak at all. The early 1990s trough is more clearly defined; although the distribution is spread over the five years of 1990–4, 16 out of the 23 turning points occur in 1992/3. The late 1990s peak exhibits a bimodal distribution in which the main mode occurs in 2000, but there is an earlier secondary mode in 1998 concentrated among the American centres. Moving into the 2000s, the convergence of the cycles becomes more apparent. The trough at the start of the decade is more concentrated than that of the previous cycle, with 18 out of 23 centres recording a turning point in 2002/3, while 14 out of 21 centres register the subsequent peak in 2007 (two centres show no cycle peak in this period).

The feedback and contagion effects that reinforce volatility in the office market also appear to encourage cycle coordination. The integration of occupier and investor demand through the activities of financial institutions provides a transmission process whereby shocks emanating from the wider global economy, or from other asset markets, feed through to cause rapid adjustments to demand and supply conditions in office markets across the world. In this vein, Edgington (1995) and Renaud (1997) argue that massive investment outflows from Japan were a key factor in the synchronization of different national real estate cycles during the late 1980s, while Mera and Renaud (2000) and Brown and Liu (2001) discuss how the integration of financial and real estate markets was responsible for the contagion effects that spread so swiftly amongst Asian markets during the late 1990s cycle. More generally, Krugman (1996: 71–3) has used a physical sciences analogy with coupled oscillators to suggest how the linkages between interdependent economies can transmit shocks which synchronize the global business cycle through a process of 'phase locking' (see also Pikovsky et al., 2001 on the synchronization of oscillating systems).

Cycle volatility

The volatilities of the building, vacancy and rent cycles in each office market are displayed in Table 8.3. These volatilities are measured by the standard deviations of real rates of rental growth, vacancy rates and rates of net addition to stock, all estimated around linear trends fitted over the period 1986–2007. For most cities, the rent cycle is the most volatile, followed by the vacancy cycle, with the building cycle being the least volatile. This ranking is reproduced by the simulation model presented in Chapter 7; it is also consistent with the results of the City of London office market analysis presented in the same chapter, which compares the volatility of real rental change to that of vacancy and building starts over the longer period 1970–2007. Across our set of global cities, the main exceptions to the normal volatility ranking are provided by Beijing and Shanghai, which show very high building cycle volatilities because net additions are expressed as a proportion of their small but fast-growing stock of modern office space.

Comparing the continental averages, Asia-Pacific emerges as the most volatile regional market on all three cycle measures. Europe is more volatile than the United States, when measured in terms of rental volatility, whereas the US exhibits higher vacancy and building volatility. However, there are wide variations in volatility

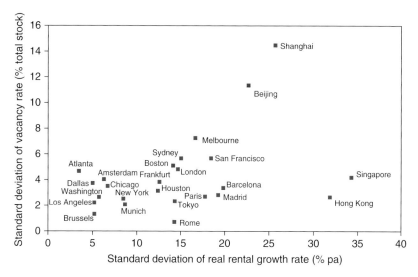

Figure 8.14 Volatility of rent and vacancy cycles in global office markets 1986–2007. *Source*: PMA.

within each continental grouping, as illustrated by the scatter plot of rent and vacancy volatilities shown in Figure 8.14. For example, within the Asian region, high rent volatility is associated with high vacancy volatility in the Beijing and Shanghai markets, but relatively low vacancy volatility in Hong Kong and Singapore.

Measured across the 25 global centres, there is a strong correlation (0.893) between the volatility of the building and vacancy cycles, although this is reduced (0.609) when the two Chinese cities are excluded. In contrast, there is weak correlation between the rent and vacancy cycle volatilities (0.394) and the rent and building cycle volatilities (0.361). These results suggest that there is a relatively straightforward linkage from building to vacancy, as net additions feed into the buffer stock of available space, but the transmission processes that flow from vacancy to rents and from rents to building are more complex.

Simple cross-sectional models have been estimated to explain the determinants of rent, building and vacancy cycle volatility across 23 of the global centres, again excluding Beijing and Shanghai because of their exceptional market conditions (see Table 8.4). Rent cycle volatility is weakly related to vacancy volatility but more strongly related positively to the average rate of net absorption of office space (expressed as a proportion of occupied stock) and negatively to the average rate of net additions (expressed as a proportion of total stock). In other words, the higher the level of demand, the more volatile the rent cycle, whereas the higher the level of supply, the less volatile the cycle. In addition, the average rent cycle volatility of all US centres is shifted downwards relative to the global average. Building cycle volatility is positively related to the average rate of growth of the total office stock and to the estimated natural vacancy rate (see below). This means that the faster the growth of the office centre and the higher the average rate of vacancy at which the market operates, the more volatile the building cycle. In this model, the average building cycle volatility of all Asia-Pacific centres is shifted upwards, relative to

Table 8.4   Models of global office market behaviour 1986–2007[a].

Rent cycle volatility[b]

$$\tilde{r}_c = 12.61 + 17.36n_c - 16.51d_c + 1.074\tilde{v}_c - 13.98\text{dumUS}$$
$$(3.37) \quad (4.27) \quad (-4.12) \quad (1.43) \quad (-5.19)$$

$R^2 = 0.638$; $\text{adjR}^2 = 0.557$; $n = 23$

where: $\tilde{r}_c$ is the volatility of the real rate of rental change in centre c.
   n_c is the average rate of net absorption of space in centre c (% occupied stock).
   d_c is the average rate of net additions of new space in centre c (% total stock).
   $\tilde{v}_c$ is the volatility of the vacancy rate in centre c.
   dumUS is a dummy for all US centres.

Building cycle volatility[b]

$$\tilde{d}_c = 0.129 + 0.451g_c + 0.053v_c^* + 0.468\text{dumAP}$$
$$(0.30) \quad (4.38) \quad (1.95) \quad (1.72)$$

$R^2 = 0.568$; $\text{adjR}^2 = 0.499$; $n = 23$

where: $\tilde{d}_c$ is the volatility of the net additions rate in centre c.
   g_c is the average rate of growth of the total office stock in centre c.
   v_c^* is the natural vacancy rate in centre c.
   dumAP is a dummy for all Asia-Pacific centres.

Vacancy cycle volatility[b]

$$\tilde{v}_c = 1.701 + 2.106\tilde{d}_c - 0.878d_c$$
$$(2.91) \quad (5.60) \quad (-3.51)$$

$R^2 = 0.611$; $\text{adjR}^2 = 0.572$; $n = 23$

Natural vacancy rate[b]

$$v_c^* = 10.56 + 7.582n_c - 7.977d_c + 0.748\tilde{v}_c - 0.031r_c$$
$$(4.23) \quad (3.97) \quad (-4.22) \quad (1.84) \quad (-1.72)$$

$R^2 = 0.624$; $\text{adjR}^2 = 0.541$; $n = 23$

where: r_c is the average level of real rents in centre c.

Rent level 2000[c]

$$r_{c0} = -39.74 + 20.72e_{c0} + 2.082w_{c0} + 0.579x_{c0} - 6.304\acute{v}_{c0} - 84.83\text{dumUS}$$
$$(-1.99) \quad (3.83) \quad (2.84) \quad (2.23) \quad (-3.31) \quad (-5.29)$$

$R^2 = 0.677$; $\text{adjR}^2 = 0.587$; $n = 24$

where: r_{c0} is the real $ rent level in centre c in year 2000.
   e_{c0} is the level of office employment in centre c in year 2000.
   w_{c0} is national GDP/capita in year 2000.
   x_{c0} is an index of airport connectivity in centre c in year 2000.
   $\acute{v}_{c0}$ is the vacancy gap in centre c in year 2000.

Source: Haver Analytics, IATA (2000) and PMA.

Notes:
[a]All models are fitted over the period 1986–2007; the t-statistics for each coefficient, the R-squared and adjusted R-squared statistics for each equation are quoted.
[b]The volatility and natural vacancy rate models are estimated for 23 centres excluding Beijing and Shanghai; the real rent, vacancy and net additions volatilities plus the natural vacancy rate for each city are listed in Table 8.3.
[c]The rent level model is estimated at the year 2000, the year for which the connectivity index in available; it is fitted over 24 centres, excluding Washington, because no connectivity index is available for that city.

the global average. Vacancy cycle volatility is positively related to building cycle volatility and negatively related to the average rate of net additions. This confirms that the volatility of building feeds directly through to vacancy, whilst the higher the level of supply the less volatile is the vacancy cycle as well as the rent cycle.

Rent adjustment
The low correlation between the volatility of the vacancy and rent cycles across our centres has indicated that the transmission process which links the vacancy rate to the real rate of rental change in the office market is not straightforward. As noted in Chapter 7, the simplest adjustment process assumes an inverse relationship between the real rate of rental change and the vacancy gap, as measured by the difference between the current vacancy rate and the natural rate. With this partial adjustment formulation, the level of rents does not necessarily revert to its natural or equilibrium level when vacancy returns to its natural rate, which creates a tendency for the market to overshoot in response to supply or demand shocks. As specified in equation (B.28b), the partial adjustment equation has been used to estimate the natural or equilibrium vacancy rate in each office centre over the 1986–2007 period, giving the values listed in Table 8.3.

The estimated natural vacancy rates show wide variation across the cities and continents. On average, the highest rates are found in the American cities and the lowest in the European cities; however, there is also considerable variation within each region. Estimated US rates vary from 9.9% in Atlanta to 19.4% in Dallas; in Asia-Pacific there is a more extreme range from 4.7% in Tokyo to 20.1% in Shanghai; in Europe rates vary from 4.1% in Munich to 11.0% in London. Clearly, specific local factors such as rates of building and take-up of space are influencing the equilibrium vacancy rate at which each market functions most effectively (see the discussion in Chapter 7 on the factors that influence the level of natural vacancy).

A simple model of the determinants of the natural vacancy rate in the 23 centres over the 1986–2007 period is presented in Table 8.4. It has a similar structure to the model of rent cycle volatility. The natural vacancy rate is again positively related to the volatility of the vacancy rate and the average rate of net absorption of office space, and negatively related to the average rate of net additions. It is also negatively related to the average level of real rents over the period (these rents being measured in 2007 prices and converted to US dollars using 2007 exchange rates throughout to exclude the effects of currency movements). The model indicates that the stronger the level of demand and the more volatile the market cycle, the higher the equilibrium vacancy rate at which the office market operates. Conversely, the stronger the level of supply of new space and the higher the cost of holding space empty, the lower the equilibrium vacancy rate. (For a comparable study of natural vacancy rates in 29 global office centres between 1990 and 2004, see Sanderson et al., 2006.)

For the majority of our sample set of centres, the relationship between rental change and vacancy is better captured by the composite adjustment process specified in equation (B.28c), rather than by the simple partial adjustment process that yields the estimates of natural vacancy rates. In the composite form of the adjustment relationship, the rate of rental change is expressed as an inverse function of both the vacancy gap and the rent gap (the difference between the current and equilibrium levels of rents). The inclusion of the rent gap introduces a stabilizing feedback mechanism: the higher the level of real rents relative to their equilibrium level, the stronger the tendency for rents to decline in the next period (see the simulation exercise in Chapter 7). The strength of this mechanism is expressed through a feedback coefficient, such that the higher the coefficient the closer the market is to operating with full rather than partial rent adjustment. The model coefficients derived by estimating the composite rent adjustment equation

Table 8.5 Rent cycle models for global office centres 1986–2007[a].

	Rent adjustment model[b]			Rental change model[c]		
	Constant	Vacancy rate[d]	Rent level (−1)	Serial correlation	Error correction	Average[e]
Europe[f]				*0.450*	*−0.401*	*0.425*
Amsterdam	24.52	−0.936	−0.136	0.582	−0.378	0.480
Barcelona	60.41	−4.613	−0.294	0.402	−0.473	0.438
Brussels	27.70	−1.614	−0.141	0.665	−0.213	0.439
Frankfurt	52.67	−1.651	−0.307	0.416	−0.397	0.407
London	29.60	−2.696		0.563	−0.301	0.432
Madrid	57.49	−5.212	−0.292	0.532	−0.458	0.495
Munich	41.64	−2.030	−0.294	0.333	−0.409	0.371
Paris	65.51	−4.141	−0.454	0.204[#]	−0.618	0.411
Rome	75.71	−9.204	−0.202[#]	0.350[#]	−0.359	0.355
United States[f]				*0.599*	*−0.308*	*0.454*
Atlanta	5.699	−0.575		0.803	−0.228	0.516
Boston	43.84	−1.804	−0.223[#]	0.651	−0.277	0.464
Chicago	18.59	−1.289		0.533	−0.401	0.467
Dallas	18.38	−0.945		0.672	−0.183	0.428
Houston	28.57	−1.478		0.381[#]	−0.299	0.340
Los Angeles	23.20	−1.605		0.750	−0.215	0.483
New York	58.90	−2.875	−0.378	0.595	−0.370	0.483
San Francisco	51.16	−2.323	−0.246	0.293[#]	−0.514	0.404
Washington	13.02	−1.154		0.714	−0.285	0.500
Asia-Pacific[f]				*0.426*	*−0.571*	*0.499*
Beijing	18.55	−1.132		0.415[#]	−0.235[#]	0.325
Hong Kong	141.17	−8.470	−1.107	0.201[#]	−0.791	0.496
Melbourne	57.35	−2.241	−0.312	0.166[#]	−0.888	0.527
Shanghai	19.69	−0.978		0.577	−0.367	0.472
Singapore	157.20	−6.588	−1.523	0.594	−0.849	0.722
Sydney	49.54	−2.370	−0.286	0.349	−0.573	0.461
Tokyo	36.75	−4.104	−0.206	0.683	−0.293	0.488

Source: PMA.

Note:
All coefficient estimates are significant at 5%, except where marked [#].
[a]The models use indices of prime city centre office rents adjusted for inflation.
[b]The rent adjustment models are based on the composite adjustment equation (B.28c) in Appendix B, expressing proportionate real rental change as a function of the current vacancy rate and the lagged real rent level; where the lagged rent level makes a negligible contribution, estimates based on the partial adjustment equation (B.28b) are quoted.
[c]The rental change models are based on the logarithmic error correction model set out in the appendix to this chapter; the equilibrium equation (8.1a) expresses the real price or rent level as a function of the levels of occupied and total office floorspace, while the restricted form of the error correction equation (8.3a) expresses the current period change in real prices or rents as a function of the change in the previous period (the serial correlation term) and the lagged residual from the equilibrium model (the error correction term), without the intervention of any explanatory variables.
[d]Vacancy rates are expressed as a proportion of total stock.
[e]The average coefficient is the average of the absolute values of the serial correlation and error correction coefficients.
[f]The continental coefficients are simple arithmetic averages of the values for the individual cities in the region.

for each centre are listed in Table 8.5; for those cities for which the inclusion of the rent level has a negligible effect, the results of estimating the partial adjustment equation are quoted. The feedback coefficients derived from the estimated composite adjustment equations are listed in Table 8.3.

Of the nine European office centres, only London does not yield a rent adjustment equation in which the lagged rent level makes a significant contribution to the stabilization of the rent cycle (as was already discovered in the City of London case study reported in Chapter 7). Similarly, with the exception of Beijing and Shanghai, the rent adjustment equations for the Asia-Pacific centres also include a feedback effect. In contrast, for only three of the American cities (Boston, New York and San Francisco) does the lagged rent level have a significant negative influence upon rental growth. In this respect, the Central London office market (particularly the City market) appears to behave more like an unconstrained American market than a constrained European market. Even for those markets in which the rent gap effect is significant, the feedback coefficients are in most cases quite small – typically averaging around 0.2. This suggests that partial adjustment is the dominant rent transmission process throughout our sample of office centres. The main exceptions are Hong Kong and Singapore, already identified as exhibiting exceptionally high rental volatility allied with relatively low vacancy volatility (see Figure 8.14). The high values of their feedback coefficients reveal the important role that the rent gap plays in correcting the large rental movements which occur in these markets in response to modest shifts in vacancy.

Cycle dynamics

The dynamics of rent cycle generation have been explored using the restricted error correction model set out in the appendix to this chapter. A cointegrating equilibrium relationship in logarithmic form has been estimated between the real rent level and the levels of total and occupied space in each centre between 1985 and 2007; the rent level is a positive function of occupied space, acting as the demand variable, and a negative function of total space, the supply variable. Real rental change in the current period is then expressed as a function of the change in the previous period (the serial correlation term) and the lagged residual from the equilibrium model (the error correction term), without the intervention of any first differenced explanatory variables. The values of the serial correlation and error correction coefficients estimated for each city, together with the absolute average of each pair of coefficients, are listed in Table 8.5.

As noted in the previous section, the serial correlation term positively reinforces a cyclical shift away from market equilibrium, while the error correction term introduces negative feedback, capturing the trend-reverting tendencies that dampen cyclical growth. In the idealized version of the restricted model, the coefficients on the two terms are identical, balancing the cyclical processes of reinforcement and feedback. This cycle generation coefficient is based upon the transmission coefficient which links vacancy to building starts via the rent adjustment process: the higher the value of the coefficient, the stronger the cycle, with a value of between 0.2 and 0.25 defining the critical threshold above which cyclical fluctuations first appear (see the simulation exercise presented in Chapter 7).

The values of the cycle generation coefficient derived by averaging the estimated serial correlation and error correction coefficients suggest some structural similarity in the cycle dynamics of office markets across the world. The average value of the coefficient across all 25 centres is 0.46, substantially above the critical threshold for cycle generation derived from the simulation model. Furthermore, the cycle coefficient lies within the 0.4–0.5 range for all three continental regions and for 18 out of 25 of the individual office centres. The one centre with a value lying well above this range is Singapore, the market exhibiting the highest rent cycle volatility among all our centres.

The separate values of the serial correlation and error correction coefficients appear reasonably well matched at the regional level. This indicates that the cyclical processes of reinforcement and feedback are in broad balance, as suggested by the theoretical model. However, moving down to the level of the individual cities, the disparities widen. As a general rule, the higher the serial correlation coefficient, the lower the (negative) error correction coefficient, which is why the average of the two tends to remain within a narrow range. In general, the American markets appear to embody stronger reinforcement and weaker feedback processes, whereas the reverse tends to be true for the Asia-Pacific markets. However, at the individual city level, too much should not be read into the separate coefficient estimates, as they will be influenced by local supply and demand factors that are unique to each market. In a further exercise, the error correction models for each city were expanded to include the influence of changes in the explanatory variables, as represented by net additions and net absorption of stock. In most cases, this produces some improvement in the performance of the model, with the values of the serial correlation and error correction terms tending to reduce, but their relativities remaining the same.

Prime rent formation

Moving through the office cycle of the past 25 years, the ranking of global cities in terms of their prime rent levels measured in US dollars has varied according to their economic status, the phasing of their local market cycle and the relative movements of exchange rates. Throughout the period 1986–2007, with only isolated exceptions (Paris in 1992/3 and San Francisco in 2000), the three leading financial centres of London, New York and Tokyo were pre-eminent in their respective regions. Of the three regional leaders, Tokyo exhibited the highest rents throughout the 1980s and 1990s, but has been overtaken by London during the 2000s (the London rents quoted here refer to the higher values achieved in the West End rather than the City market).

The distributions of prime office rents in the 25 global cities at the major cycle peaks of 1989 and 2007 are illustrated in Figure 8.15. The rent levels are again measured in 2007 prices and converted to US dollars using 2007 exchange rates at both points in time in order to exclude the effects of currency movements. Most of the markets exhibit somewhat lower rents in 2007 than in 1989 because there was a general tendency for real rents to experience a downward trend over the period; the main exceptions are New York and Singapore, both of which enjoyed an exceptional phase of rental growth in 2006–7. The secular decline of real office rents since the 1980s, indicative of a propensity towards over-building, has already been observed in the City of London case study in Chapter 6 and in the analysis of the UK and US commercial markets in the previous section. Since the US dollar was particularly weak in 2007, the rents in the American centres appear depressed relative to those in Europe and Asia-Pacific.

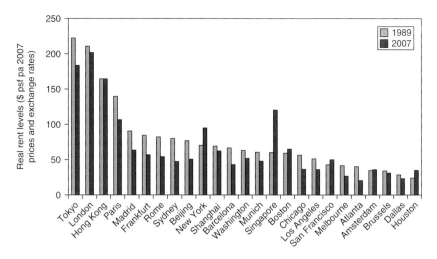

Figure 8.15   Peak real rent levels in global office markets.
Source: PMA.

As already indicated, the global rent hierarchy shown in Figure 8.15 is topped by Tokyo and London, which switched positions between 1989 and 2007. New York, the highest American centre, was back in tenth position in 1989, but by 2007, had climbed to sixth place behind Hong Kong, Singapore and Paris. At the bottom of the hierarchy are second tier centres such as Melbourne, Amsterdam, Brussels, Atlanta, Dallas and Houston. To identify some of the key factors that determine the position of a centre within the hierarchy, a cross-sectional model of the formation of global office rents has been estimated for the year 2000. The model contains four explanatory variables, as set out in Table 8.4:

- The *size* of the office economy in each city is represented by its total level of office employment.
- The *productivity* of the national economy in which each centre is located is represented by GDP per capita.
- The *connectivity* of each city within the world city network is represented by an indexed measure of the number of other cities to which it is linked by direct airline routes (taken from a study published by IATA, 2000).
- The influence of current *market conditions* is represented by the vacancy gap (the current vacancy rate less the natural rate).

With this model structure, the absolute level of prime office rents is positively related to the size and connectivity of a centre and the productivity of its national economy, and negatively related to the vacancy gap as a measure of excess supply in the market. A downward adjustment is made to the estimates for the US centres to account for exchange rate relativities. The 'structural rent' specified by the model explains two-thirds of the variation in the global office rent distribution as recorded in 2000. The main outliers are London and Hong Kong, both of which achieved actual rents substantially higher than their modelled values. In each case, their 'over-renting' can be attributed to special factors which depress the local supply elasticities for new office space: restrictive development control policies in the West End of London and restricted land supply in Hong Kong. If allowance is made for these two centres, the variation left unexplained by the model is halved.

Some stylized facts about the global office cycle

The stylized facts that have emerged from the preceding analysis can be summarized as follows:

- The greater integration of the United States and European economies, compared to the much more heterogeneous Asia-Pacific region, is reflected in the stronger and more coincident movement of their office market cycles.
- The phasing of the cycles in the three continental regions has converged over the past 25 years, as the growing integration of the world economy has been transmitted to its office markets.
- Of the three office market cycles, the rent cycle is typically the most volatile, followed by the vacancy cycle, with the building cycle being the least volatile.
- The higher the level of demand, as represented by the average rate of net absorption of office space, the more volatile the rent cycle; the higher the level of supply, as represented by the average rate of net additions, the less volatile the rent cycle.
- The faster the growth of the office centre, as represented by the average rate of growth of the total office stock, and the higher the average rate of vacancy at which the market operates, as represented by the natural vacancy rate, the more volatile the building cycle.
- The volatility of the building cycle feeds directly through to the vacancy cycle, whilst the higher the level of supply the less volatile is the vacancy cycle as well as the rent cycle.
- Partial rather than full adjustment of rents to the gap between the current and equilibrium vacancy rates is the main driver of the transmission process in office markets, and helps to explain their exceptional volatility.
- In the majority of office markets, particularly in Europe and Asia-Pacific, the level of rents relative to their equilibrium level acts to some degree as a stabilizing mechanism, such that the higher the current rent level the stronger the tendency for rents to decline in the next period.
- The higher the level of demand and the more volatile the market cycle, the higher the equilibrium or natural vacancy rate at which an office market operates; conversely, the higher the level of supply of new space and the higher the cost of holding space empty, the lower the natural vacancy rate.
- The dynamics of the rent cycle are embodied in the opposing forces of reinforcement and feedback: current period rental change responds positively to the previous period change, and negatively to the deviation of rents from their equilibrium level as defined by the long-run balance of supply and demand for space.
- The cyclical processes of reinforcement and feedback are broadly in balance across the regions, although there are disparities at the level of individual cities which reflect the influence of local supply and demand factors unique to each market.
- The structural level of office rents is positively related to the size of the urban economy, the productivity of the national economy and the connectivity of the

city within the world city network; it is negatively related to the vacancy gap as a measure of excess supply in the market.

- Markets in which the elasticity of new office supply is restricted by planning policy or land availability tend to achieve rents substantially above their structural rent.

The global diffusion of property innovation

In this chapter, the principal focus so far has been on the property cycle as a source of instability. However, we must not lose sight of its vital function as a driver of innovation and growth, a theme that has been repeated throughout this book. The motion of investment cycles in general, and building cycles in particular, provides the crucial dynamic which propels both economic growth and urban development. In this section, we examine the role of the building cycle in the diffusion of two major property innovations – high-rise offices and covered shopping centres – as they have spread out from their source in North America into Europe and on to Latin America, the Middle East and Asia. The rise of the skyscraper and the spread of the shopping centre provide noteworthy examples of the interaction between innovation and accumulation in the process of urban development that was explored in Chapter 5. As the service economy has evolved, so the occupier demands of financial institutions and retail chains have intersected with the investment demands of property funds to develop these two iconic building types in homogenous forms that present a remarkably similar appearance throughout the cities of the modern world.

The rise of the skyscraper

The skyscraper is the most dramatic physical manifestation of the impact of construction technology on urban agglomeration. As was previously discussed in Chapter 5, progressively more profitable and intensive land uses derive agglomeration benefits from a city centre location, enabling them to outbid lower value, more extensive uses which can no longer afford the rising central area rents. Developers respond to these agglomeration economies by substituting between land and structures in the overall cost of building investment, with the result that building heights and densities typically increase towards the city centre in parallel with the rise in land values. High land values encourage the development of high rise, high density and high cost structures. Each innovation in construction technology reduces the costs of larger and taller structures, which steepens the bid rent curve because building can profitably be undertaken at higher densities. Thus, technological innovation provides an impetus to urban intensification through redevelopment. As cities evolve, their centres are populated by successive vintages of buildings embodying improved specification and higher site density, occupied by the most profitable urban activities of the time. Today, the most profitable urban functions are financial and business service industries, occupying ever taller office buildings located on ever more valuable city centre sites.

Beyond an economically rational desire to maximize the lettable floorspace occupying valuable city centre sites, the construction of skyscrapers is motivated by a more basic human yearning – the desire to be the tallest. Throughout the history of skyscraper development, the race to erect the tallest building has been fierce.

A classic example, vividly chronicled in Bascomb (2003), is the epic 1920s race between the architects and developers of the Manhattan Company, Chrysler and Empire State Buildings to construct the tallest skyscraper in the New York, and therefore in the world. So powerful is the desire to be the tallest that Helsley and Strange (2008) include it as a separate factor in their theoretical model of sky-scraper development. They argue that the contest for the prize of being the tallest leads to 'dissipative competition', such that the value of the prize is lost in the poor economics of skyscrapers, with developers '...topping each other with structures of undeniable symbolic significance but doubtful economy' (Helsley and Strange, 2008: 52). Indeed, the authors suggest that the desire to be the tallest contributes to the seemingly endemic over-building that characterizes commercial property mar-kets in general, and office markets in particular – a tendency which contributes to the extreme volatility of the office market cycle.

The time and place of birth of the skyscraper remains the subject of a hotly con-tested debate between the champions of Chicago and New York. What is more generally agreed upon is that conception was achieved through the combination of two technologies: the steam-powered elevator and the steel-framed skeleton, the latter constituting '...the most radical transformation of the structural art since the development of the Gothic system of construction in the twelfth century' (Condit, 1964: 79). Prototype high-rise buildings were developed in New York during the 1870s, but it was the architects and engineers of the Chicago School who perfected the technology of skyscraper construction in a series of pioneering buildings con-structed during the 1880s and early 1890s (Randall, 1999). There were two crucial catalysts for the first Chicago skyscraper boom. One was the Great Fire of 1871, which by destroying much of the existing urban fabric presented a unique redevel-opment opportunity; the other was the outward spread of cable, elevated rail and electric tram networks, which radically improved access to the city centre from suburban labour markets (Hoyt, 1933: 128–95). When the new construction tech-nology was adopted wholesale in New York during the 1890s, the concentration of corporate headquarters in the city, together with the exceptionally high value of city centre land, propelled the skyscraper to new heights. In 1890, the New York World Building rose to a height of 18 storeys; by 1913, the Woolworth building had soared to 55 storeys (Landau and Condit, 1996).

'Form follows function', an idea first articulated by Plato in *The Republic*, was the dictum adopted by the Chicago School led by the architect Louis Sullivan (Condit, 1964: 36–7). These pioneers understood function in a much broader sense than the structural; it should embrace the social, cultural and even spiritual as well as the technical. New urban forms should be designed to accommodate their occupying activities as harmoniously as possible; in the case of the skyscraper, this means the wide variety of business functions undertaken by the modern corporation. However, as was noted in Chapter 5, urban functions can change quite rapidly in response to the processes of innovation, whereas urban built forms are subject to the much slower processes of accumulation, and once completed are relatively rigid in oper-ation. A subsequent architect, Mies van der Rohe, who also worked in Chicago, recognized this problem, and went so far as to suggest that Sullivan's dictum should be reversed. He believed that the solution lay in creating large, open, unencumbered spaces which can be used flexibly for a variety of functions (Cohen, 1996: 98–100). Just such an approach informs office design today.

During the first half of the twentieth century, Chicago and New York evolved into quintessential 'skyscraper cities', each locked on to a distinctive and different development trajectory determined by the interaction of local market conditions and zoning policies. Skyscraper development acted as a magnet for speculative investment, reinforcing the extreme volatility of the office-building cycle. Each building boom saw city centre sites redeveloped at progressively higher densities; redevelopment every 25–30 years was the norm in Chicago (Hoyt, 1933: 335). Each phase of over-supply tended to spur a political reaction. Thus, after the first Chicago skyscraper boom ended in a slump in 1893, the city council capped the height of future buildings, an ordinance that was not rescinded until 1923. In consequence, during the second boom of the early 1910s, the volume of office building in Chicago was controlled, whereas laissez-faire development continued unabated in New York. By 1920, New York had over ten times as many tall buildings as Chicago, despite an urban population that was only just over twice as large (Willis, 1995: 9).

There then followed the great skyscraper building boom of the 1920s, which formed part of the much more widespread wave of land and property speculation that gripped the United States during the decade (see Chapter 5). As the speculative boom intensified, the average height of New York's office towers rose in tandem with land prices: from 30–40 storeys in 1925 to 40–50 storeys by 1930, with a dozen or so buildings exceeding 50 storeys. The higher the site value, the taller had to be the tower to maximize developer returns. The climax of the 1920s building boom coincided with the onset of the Great Depression, with some 26 million square feet of space delivered to the Manhattan market between 1931 and 1934. As boom turned to bust, vacancy in New York's financial district shot up from just 1% in 1929 to 22% by 1933. The ensuing lack of demand condemned many of the newly completed trophy buildings to a prolonged period of high vacancy: following its opening in 1931, the Empire State Building remained three-quarters empty for a decade, and did not return a profit until 1950 (Willis, 1995: 85–90, 155–82).

Much more than just a new urban form, the skyscraper became a powerful cultural symbol for the optimism and energy of American capitalism (Domosh, 1988). As one of the Chicago pioneers observed 'The skyscraper is the most distinctively American thing in the world...so far surpassing anything ever before undertaken in its vastness, swiftness, utility, and economy that it epitomizes American life and American civilization...' (Starrett, 1928: 1–2). In particular, the vertical architecture of Manhattan's skyscrapers, its 'skyline perspective', became a cultural symbol not just in America, but throughout the world (Taylor, 1992: 23–33). Its aesthetic appeal has perhaps best been summarized by Starrett (1928: 3). 'Who can look on the majestic skyline of New York in sunshine or shadow and not be moved, both by the tremendous power of its mass and the beauty and richness of its detail?'

Between the 1890s and the 1990s, the United States remained the world leader in the development of skyscrapers. Helsley and Strange (2008: 52) list a succession of twelve American office buildings of increasing height that won the accolade of the world's tallest building, starting with the 1890 New York World Building, reaching a height of 309 ft, and finishing with the 1974 Chicago Sears Tower, built to a

Table 8.6 Global cities included in the high-rise office analysis.

North America	Europe	Asia-Pacific	Latin America	Middle East
Atlanta	Amsterdam	Bangkok	Bogota	Abu Dhabi
Boston	Barcelona	Beijing	Buenos Aires	Dubai
Chicago	Berlin	Guangzhou	Caracas	Qatar
Dallas	Brussels	Hong Kong	Mexico City	Tel Aviv
Houston	Frankfurt	Jakarta	Rio de Janeiro	
Los Angeles	Istanbul	Kuala Lumpur	Santiago	
Miami	London	Melbourne	Sao Paulo	
Montreal	Madrid	Osaka		
New York	Milan	Seoul		
San Francisco	Moscow	Shanghai		
Toronto	Munich	Singapore		
Vancouver	Paris	Sydney		
Washington	Stockholm	Tokyo		

height of 1,451 ft. However, the crown passed to Asia in 1998 with the completion of the Petronas Towers in Kuala Lumpur to a height of 1,483 ft, posting a decisive landmark in the shift of global economic power from west to east. The battle to be the tallest in the world is now being fought in Asia and the Middle East. In 2004, the Petronas Towers were supplanted by Taipei 101 (1,671 ft), which in turn is being far surpassed by the Burj Dubai (2,684 ft) still under construction at the start of 2009. Future buildings are planned to raise the world record to a height of over 1 km (3,281 ft).

In order to illustrate how the skyscraper evolved within the United States and then spread out to the rest of the world, use has been made of a unique global database of some 45,000 office buildings compiled by Emporis, which concentrates on high-rise offices of 12 or more storeys. From this database, a subset of information has been extracted for 50 leading office centres grouped into 5 global regions (see Table 8.6). The dataset identifies all the high-rise buildings in sole or predominant office use, which have been demolished, completed or are under construction, and for which the number of storeys and completion date are known. In order to create an index of skyscraper building activity for each city, an annual time series has been created by aggregating the total number of floors in buildings completed in each year. Estimated completion dates for schemes under construction carry the time series through to 2012, although the data for the final years are inevitably only an estimate. The coverage of buildings is partial, and the completeness of the information varies considerably by city. In particular, for some cities in Asia and Latin America, the completion date is known for only a minority of buildings, especially the older, smaller buildings. Comparisons between individual cities must therefore be treated with caution, but for broader aggregations of cities within global regions, the data provide a fascinating record of the diffusion of the skyscraper through time and space.

The history of high-rise office building in the pioneer cities of New York and Chicago since the start of the 1870s is illustrated in Figure 8.16. Identification of turning points reveals seven skyscraper cycles in New York and six in Chicago. These informal observations are partially confirmed by the results of a structural modelling exercise undertaken with the two time series; a significant long building cycle of 21

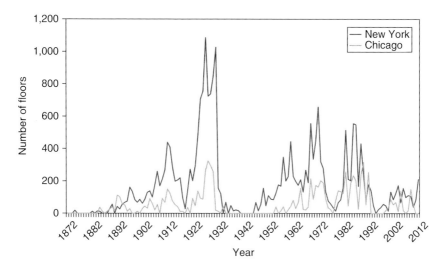

Figure 8.16 New York and Chicago high-rise office-building cycles 1872–2012.
Source: Emporis.

years duration is obtained for New York, but the results for Chicago are less clear. The progression of skyscraper development in the pioneer cities can be related to the multi-stage model of the diffusion of innovations which was described in Chapter 2. The first cycle shows up in the 1892/3 completions peak in Chicago, followed by the 1897 peak in New York. Though modest in scale, this constituted the introductory innovation phase that launched the whole process of high-rise office development. The second cycle, peaking in 1912, was of greater magnitude, particularly in New York. It was during the third cycle of the 1920s that skyscraper development reached the take-off phase. The Chicago building boom that peaked in 1928 was matched in subsequent post-war cycles, but the New York boom, with its twin peaks in 1927 and 1931, was of a scale that has never been approached since in the city.

During the post-war period, there have been four further cycles in New York and three in Chicago, representing the maturity phase of skyscraper development. During the introduction phase up to 1920, the number of floors in high-rise office buildings in the two cities averaged around 16; during the inter-war take-off phase, the average rose to around 22; during the post-war maturity phase, the average has settled down at between 32 and 34 floors per building. The first post-war cycle was confined to New York, peaking in 1961; the second peaked in Chicago in 1969, followed by New York in 1972. The 1980s cycle discussed in the previous section shows up clearly in both cities, with peaks in 1986/7 in New York and 1990 in Chicago which are later than those for office building as a whole, because larger buildings take longer to complete. The mid-2000s cycle is only partially captured, because it will not complete until the early part of the next decade.

At the end of the Second World War, New York and Chicago accounted for 75% of the cumulative total of all the floors in high-rise offices built up to that date throughout the world, as recorded in our 50 city database. Of the remainder, 17% was located in other North American cities such as Boston, Los Angeles,

San Francisco and Toronto, and just 8% was to be found in the rest of the world, in a few scattered cities such as London, Rio de Janeiro and Sydney. It was during the post-war period that the global diffusion of the skyscraper really took off. Just as the revolutionary structural design of Gothic cathedrals spread out from their birthplace in the Île de France to crown the skylines of medieval European cities during the twelfth and thirteenth centuries (Pevsner, 1970), so has the skyscraper spread out from New York and Chicago to dominate city skylines throughout the modern world during the second half of the twentieth century. The rate and reach of this global diffusion process has been boosted by further technological improvements, such as curtain-walling, shell and core and fast-track construction methods, which have considerably extended the scale economies in office building (see the City of London case study in Chapter 6).

The post-war skyscraper cycles in the five global regions – North America, Europe, Asia-Pacific, Middle East and Latin America – are illustrated in Figure 8.17. The aggregate North American trend shows three substantial building cycles: the first spans the 1960s and early 1970s (subsuming the early post-war cycle in New York), reaching a peak in 1972; the second is the more sharply defined 1980s cycle, with an early peak in 1983; the third is a fusion of the late 1990s cycle and the partially completed cycle of the mid-2000s, with a possible peak in 2009. It was during the 1980s cycle that other North American cities began to catch up with the two pioneers. Particularly prominent were Los Angeles, San Francisco, Dallas, Houston and Toronto, with the 1983 peak in Houston being the largest recorded for any individual US city in the post-war period.

To varying degrees, the same post-war skyscraper cycles can be distinguished in Europe and Latin America – though the late 1990s and mid-2000s cycles are more clearly differentiated, and in general the cycles are more muted than those in North America. Prominent among the European cities embracing high-rise office

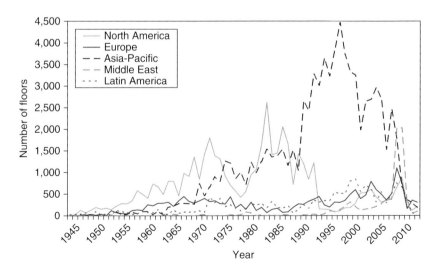

Figure 8.17   Global high-rise office-building cycles 1945–2012.
Source: Emporis.

development through the post-war period are London, Frankfurt and Madrid; in contrast, cities such as Paris and Rome have resisted the skyscraper in order to preserve their historic skylines. The recent building peaks achieved in Istanbul and Moscow, in 2000 and 2008 respectively, exceed any previously reached in the more established European office centres, highlighting the eastward shift in the centre of gravity of the European economy, and the intensification of the building cycle in response to the growing integration of the world economy. In Latin America, Sao Paulo stands out from the other cities in the region, recording exceptionally strong building peaks in both 2000 and 2008.

Asia-Pacific has exceeded all the other global regions in terms of both the scale and volatility of its skyscraper building cycles over the past 20–30 years. During the 1970s cycle, the more established office centres of Sydney, Singapore and Hong Kong were prominent. During the late 1980s cycle, Tokyo and Seoul, together with Hong Kong, were involved in unprecedented levels of development. During the late 1990s and mid-2000s cycles, enormous levels of building again occurred in Asian cities, with Shanghai and Beijing joining Tokyo, Seoul and Hong Kong in the leading group. The extent to which the focus of high-rise office development has shifted from North America to Asia can perhaps best be illustrated by the case of Hong Kong: during the decade of the 1990s, some 23% of all the recorded office floors completed in our 50 global cities were constructed in that one city. We have noted that the Middle East is now battling with Asia for the prize of being 'the highest', which serves to explain the extraordinary spike in completions in that region in 2008/9, due almost entirely to the skyscraper extravaganza that is being orchestrated in Dubai.

The skyscraper diffusion trajectories for each global region are plotted in Figure 8.18, aggregated from the cumulative annual floor totals for completed buildings in each city in the region. Thanks to its two pioneer cities, North America exhibits

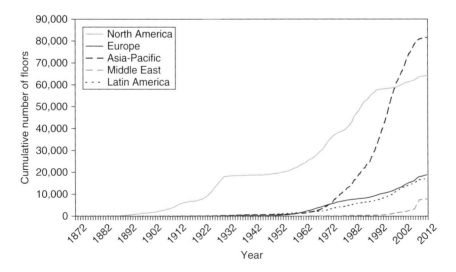

Figure 8.18 Global high-rise office stock 1872–2012.
Source: Emporis.

the most mature trajectory, clearly demonstrating an 'escalator effect' whereby successive building booms have ratcheted up the office stock to progressively higher levels. The Asia-Pacific trajectory has been far steeper; it overtook North America in terms of its cumulative total of high-rise office floors in the year 2000, and the crash of 2008 seems to mark the first time there has been a discernible slackening in its meteoric rise. Overall, it is Asia-Pacific that exhibits the clearest S-shaped logistic growth curve normally associated with diffusion trajectories (see Chapters 2 and 5). The European and Latin American trajectories speak of an altogether more sedate rate of skyscraper diffusion.

These diffusion trajectories determine the vintage composition of the high-rise office stock in each region, as measured by the proportion of floors constructed in different time periods. Four time periods have been distinguished: pre-1947, 1947–78, 1979–95 and 1996–2012. The most even distribution is the North American, with a spread of 29%, 31%, 30% and 10% between the vintages; because of the region's much earlier take-off, the most modern vintage accounts for a far smaller share than it does in the other regions. Next come Europe and Latin America; their smaller total stocks are weighted much more towards the three post-war vintages, with the most recent vintage accounting for the highest share in both regions. Owing to its steeply accelerating trajectory, Asia-Pacific exhibits a strongly increasing distribution, rising from only 1% in the pre-1947 vintage through 12% and 39% in the first two post-war vintages, up to 48% in the most recent vintage. These regional vintage distributions are reflected in the structure of the high-rise office stock in individual cities. Figure 8.19 depicts the ranking of the top 25 of our sample of 50 global cities, according to their cumulative totals of recorded office floors, broken down into the four vintage bands. New York remains at the top of the hierarchy, by virtue of its early start, but is rapidly being caught up by Hong Kong. Next come Tokyo and Seoul, followed by Sao Paulo and Chicago. Five of the top ten cities are in the Asia-Pacific

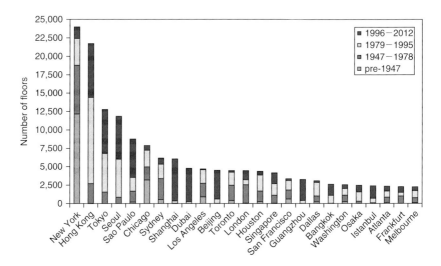

Figure 8.19   High-rise office vintages in global cities.
Source: Emporis.

region, once more confirming the shift in the balance of real estate investment towards the Asian economies that has occurred since the start of the 1990s.

The spread of the shopping centre

Shopping centres have spawned none of the eulogistic literature that has accompanied the rise of the skyscraper. Is it too fanciful to suggest that the contrast between the obvious phallic imagery of the skyscraper and the womb-like nature of the shopping centre offers a Freudian explanation for this disparity? The former overwhelms through external effect, the latter seduces through the offer within. The outside appearance of shopping centres is prosaic; it is the enticing atmosphere created by their interior layout, finishes and amenities that is their attraction. Shoppers are nourished by their food courts and soothed by their waterfalls. Size matters, not because of the egotistical drive to be the highest, but because of the desire to afford the most enticing experience.

Nevertheless, though the impact of shopping centres on urban form has been less spectacular than that of skyscrapers, their influence on urban function has been more profound. By transforming the scale and efficiency of retail distribution, shopping centres have revolutionized a crucial urban function as it is exercised throughout the city, in the central area, in the suburbs and on the urban periphery. Furthermore, the modern shopping centre aims at more than just scale and efficiency; it is designed and marketed to promote shopping as a pleasurable as well as a necessary function, so that the shopping trip becomes an end in itself, not just an opportunity to purchase. Hence the emphasis on shopping as an experience and shopping centres as 'retail destinations', as locations where the delights of 'festival shopping' can be sampled. The 'call of the mall' is heard beyond the consumer economy; it echoes around the social and cultural spheres of modern life (Underhill, 2004).

Retail development epitomizes the process of interactive innovation which was discussed in general terms in Chapter 5. Each improvement in the efficiency and organization of retail activity stimulates some innovation in the form of retail buildings, and each innovation in built forms feeds back to reinforce the improved operational efficiency of retailing. An evolutionary process is set in train as successive waves of retail investment promote new forms of provision which become established by out-competing existing forms, forcing them into decline. Each form of provision therefore tends to move through a life cycle of introduction, growth, maturity and decline (Gibbs, 1987). Thus, for example, a new shopping centre built in proximity to an old-established town centre will divert sales away from the traditional high street shop units, often to the point at which they can no longer trade profitably and the whole town centre is devastated. Such is the force of the Schumpeterian gale of creative destruction.

There is long history of interactive innovation in retailing. The nineteenth century shopping galleries still to be found in European cities such as Paris, London and Milan offer a good example. These structures were designed to provide elegant pedestrianized shopping streets which were covered but enjoyed natural lighting, and the glass and cast iron technology subsequently used to construct the great railway termini provided the ideal form of construction. During the late nineteenth and early twentieth centuries, the main innovation in retail activity was the growth of multiple trading, while the great innovation in shop building was the multi-storey department store, bringing together under one roof a far wider range of merchandise than ever before (Jefferys, 1954; Scott, 1994).

Scale economies in retailing have been taken to a new level by the post-war development of the enclosed shopping centre. Now large numbers of separate traders are brought together under one roof, occupying increasingly luxurious interior spaces which offer additional attractions such as cafés, restaurants, cinemas and health clubs. The town centre has become heated, air-conditioned and weather-proofed. It has also moved out of town. As car-based suburbanization has gathered pace, so covered shopping centres have been built in the suburbs and on the urban periphery, adding ease of access and parking to their other attractions. New types of functional, lower cost retail buildings have also appeared in suburban and peripheral locations, firstly in the form of stand-alone superstores and retail warehouses, selling food and non-food goods, respectively, and then as clusters of such units grouped together on retail parks (Guy, 1994). Meanwhile, the concentration of retail activity has intensified, as the dominant multiple traders have exploited their scale economies to increase market share (Basker, 2007), in particular, through massive investment in new 'lean retailing' technologies such as computerized inventory management (Abernathy et al., 1999). A crucial source of the productivity gains which have been made in the sector derives from the entry of new and more efficient traders, displacing established and less productive firms (Foster et al., 2006).

The enclosed shopping mall, like the skyscraper, was an American invention. It was born in the 1950s out of the opportunity created by suburban development, the expansion of the highway network, mass car ownership and cheap land (see Chapter 5). During the 1960s, it crossed the Atlantic, landing first in north-west Europe and then moving south and east in successive waves of development. Aggregate shopping centre building cycles in the United States and Europe since 1950 are illustrated in Figure 8.20, using annual totals of floorspace completed in each year.

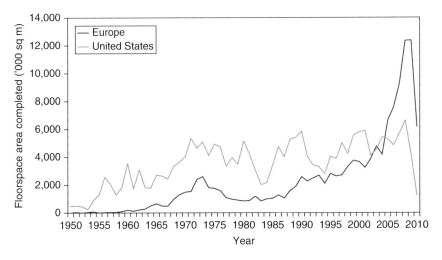

Figure 8.20   Shopping centre building cycles in Europe and the United States 1950–2010.
Source: Directory of Major Malls Inc. and PMA.

The US series is taken from a database of around 4,500 centres of over 10,000 square metres (100,000 square feet), compiled by Directory of Major Malls Inc.; the European data derive from a database of around 7,800 centres of over 5,000 square metres compiled by PMA. Estimated completion dates for schemes under construction carry the time series through to 2010, although as with the high-rise office series the data for the final years are inevitably only an estimate. The difference in average size of shopping centres in the two continents is striking – 48,000 square metres in America compared to only 17,200 square metres in Europe. The disparity in scale is highlighted by the fact that in the United States there are some 400 shopping malls of over 100,000 square metres in size, compared to only 40 in Europe.

The introductory phase of US shopping centre development during the 1950s culminated in a first cycle peak in 1960. Take-off was achieved during the 1960s, and four subsequent building cycles can be observed as the market matured – in the early 1970s (with a 1971 peak), the late 1980s (peaking in 1990), the late 1990s (peaking in 2001) and mid-2000s (with a probable peak in 2008). These US shopping centre cycles track fairly closely the cycles in high-rise office development that were discussed previously, indicating that the same general forces of cycle propagation have been operating in both commercial markets.

In Europe, the picture is less clear cut because the cyclical rhythm of development in each region is masked by the spread of shopping centres from the older established markets of the north and west to the more recently established markets in the south and east (see Skinner, 2007, on the growth of the European retail investment market). The 1970s cycle is apparent in the aggregate European series, peaking in 1973, but the three subsequent cycles are subsumed within a strongly rising trend that culminates in an extraordinary spike in completions in 2008/9. To uncover the interaction of cyclical movement and regional spread, the aggregate European series has been decomposed into the five regional cycles illustrated in Figure 8.21. The chosen

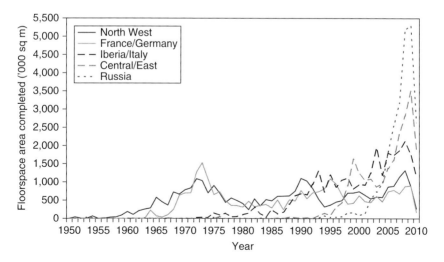

Figure 8.21 Shopping centre building cycles in European regions 1950–2010.
Source: PMA.

regions are North West (United Kingdom, Ireland, Benelux and Scandinavia), France/Germany (plus Austria and Switzerland), Iberia/Italy (including Spain and Portugal), Central and Eastern Europe (including Greece, Turkey and Ukraine) and Russia.

There is a sharp distinction between the development histories of the mature markets of the North West and France/Germany, and the still emerging markets of Iberia/Italy, Central/Eastern and Russia. The development of enclosed shopping centres began in the early 1960s in the North West region and in the late 1960s in France/Germany. In both regions, this initial phase of development culminated in the early 1970s boom, with a 1972 peak in the North West and a 1973 peak in France/Germany. Two more cycles are apparent in each region as their markets moved into the maturity phase. The North West shows the impact of the late 1980s boom, peaking in 1990, while France/Germany exhibits a later 1995 peak; both regions experienced the mid-2000s boom with peaks in completions in 2008/9.

Moving further south and east, we can observe increasingly rapid take-off trajectories, as shopping centres have become established in the last 20 years. The initial development phase in the Iberia/Italy region began in the 1980s, but take-off did not occur until the 1990s, leading to a sequence of progressively stronger cycle peaks in 1993, 2003 and 2008. In the Central/Eastern region, the initial phase of development did not start until the mid-1990s, but this immediately turned into a major building boom which peaked in 1999, to be followed by an even more spectacular mid-2000s boom. The rapidly modernizing Polish economy was the main driving force behind the late 1990s boom, while the transformation of the Turkish economy was the dominant contributor to the mid-2000s boom. Finally, there is Russia, in a league of its own. Here, shopping centre development did not start until the beginning of the 2000s, but immediately exploded in a building boom on a scale that is unprecedented in Europe and is comparable to the peak levels of building that have occurred in the United States. Between 2002 and 2010, the available information suggests that some 23 million square metres of new shopping centre space could be completed in Russia, including 14 out of the 40 individual centres of over 100,000 square metres built in Europe during the whole of the last 50 years.

Owing principally to the enormous building boom in Central and Eastern Europe, up to one half of all the shopping centre space built in Europe since 1950 will have been completed between 2002 and 2010. Furthermore, in much the same way as was observed in the global office market, the mid-2000s boom is the first to have been truly coincident across all the regional retail markets of Europe. The manner in which European shopping centre development has accelerated over the past 50 years is demonstrated by the cumulative regional floorspace profiles plotted in Figure 8.22. The accumulation of stock through successive building cycles in the different regions provides a classic example of the spatial diffusion process that was explored in Chapter 5. As the adoption of this innovative built form has spread south and east, so the slope of successive regional diffusion trajectories has steepened. The result is that the Iberia/Italy region has overtaken France/Germany, despite taking off nearly 20 years later, while Russia has already overtaken the rest of Central and Eastern Europe, despite taking off a cycle later.

So far we have examined the spread of one type of retail innovation, the covered shopping centre, as it has spread from the United States to Europe, and diffused south and east within Europe. An alternative perspective on innovation in

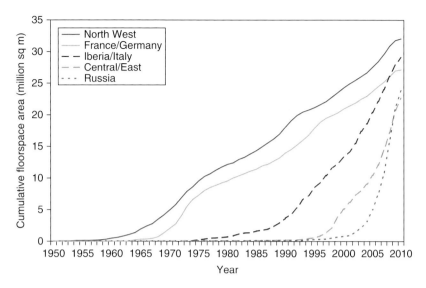

Figure 8.22 Cumulative shopping centre stock in European regions 1950–2010.
Source: PMA.

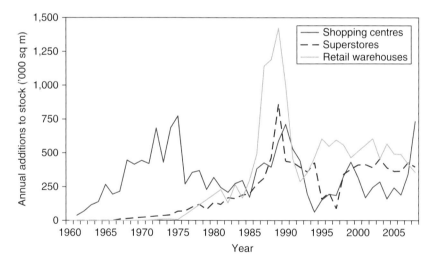

Figure 8.23 UK retail building cycles 1960–2008.
Source: PMA.

retailing is provided by the shifting market shares within one market, which result from successive waves of investment in different forms of retail provision. Analysis of the UK retail market by PMA demonstrates the extent to which investment in four types of provision – shopping centres, superstores, retail warehouses and the internet – has over the past 50 years progressively diverted sales away from the traditional form of provision in high street shop units. Figure 8.23 charts building investment in the three new types of physical provision since 1960, while

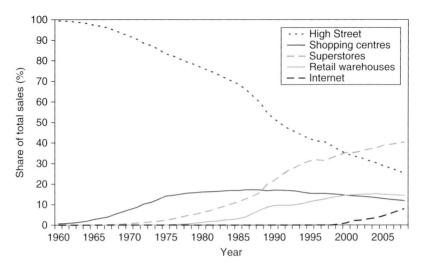

Figure 8.24   Shares of UK retail sales by type of provision 1960–2008.
Source: PMA and ONS.

Figure 8.24 reveals the shifting shares of total sales captured by the new forms of provision at the expense of the traditional high street (the analysis excludes neighbourhood shopping).

The late 1960s/early 1970s retail building boom in the United Kingdom was confined to the first wave of covered shopping centre development. By 1975 shopping centres had captured some 14% of total UK sales from the high street. The late 1980s building boom involved all three new types of physical provision, and in this cycle the volume of shopping centre development was matched by that of superstores and outstripped by the volume of new retail warehouse development. By 1990, the shopping centre share of total sales had reached a 17% plateau, while the shares of the two more recent formats were still on the upswing: the retail warehouse share had reached 10%, while superstores had already captured a 22% share. During the 1990s and first half of the 2000s, retail warehouse and superstore development outpaced the rate of building in the more established shopping centre market. The shopping centre share of total sales was now in decline, dropping to just 12% by 2008, retail warehouse sales had in turn reached a plateau of around 15%, while only the superstore share continued to increase, rising to 40% by 2008 under the impetus of continued innovation, as the superstore offer was broadened to include non-food goods. By now the traditional high street accounted for only a quarter of total sales, compared to its total dominance of the retail market half a century earlier.

With the modern physical forms of retail provision moving into their maturity phases, a new and fundamentally different competitor has entered the market. Though internet shopping in Britain only started at the end of the 1990s, online sales already accounted for nearly 8% of the total by 2008. This rate of growth in market share during the introductory decade of a retail innovation is unprecedented in Britain; previous innovations have typically captured no more than a 3% share after 10 years. The extent to which the internet may render the newer physical forms of shopping provision obsolete, just as they in their turn have out-competed the high street, raises fundamental questions about the possible path that building investment may follow in the twenty-first century.

Into the twenty-first century

As globalization gathers pace, two technologies will play a key role in shaping economic growth and urban development in the coming decades. It is already apparent that the universal applicability of information technology makes it unique as an instrument of change. Equally wide-ranging technological forces are being unleashed in response to the challenges posed by climate change and rising energy costs. The scope and impact of the general purpose technologies of information and sustainable energy will be reinforced because of the interactions between them: the knowledge economy has the potential to be a sustainable economy. As twin engines of growth and change, these technologies will generate complementary innovations in every aspect of economic and social life. Their impacts on urban development and building investment will be especially far-reaching. The perpetual tension between the rapid transformation of urban functions and the rigidities of urban forms may be heightened as never before, as the cities of the world, locked into their evolving global networks, endeavour to adapt to the demands of being both knowledge cities and sustainable cities.

The knowledge city

Information is the most valuable commodity traded within the knowledge economy (Foray, 2004), and the internet provides the infrastructure for its transmission within and between the cities of the world. With the explosive growth of the internet, the balance in the global economy is shifting from the material to the virtual realm. This shift has fundamental implications for the future pattern of economic growth and investment. In particular, an increasing share of fixed capital is being devoted to the electronic storage and transmission of information rather than the physical accommodation and transport of goods and people.

With regard to urban development, the knowledge economy is generating opposing forces that are simultaneously strengthening and weakening the economies of agglomeration. On the one hand, the role of cities as crucibles of new ideas has become more important than ever, reinforcing the interplay between urban agglomeration, innovation and growth that was discussed in Chapter 5. For example, the creative industries which are being formed to service the growth of the internet seem to be locating in highly concentrated clusters to obtain the agglomeration benefits of knowledge spillovers and convenient access to venture capital (Zook, 2005). Conversely, because ICT allows almost costless communication, irrespective of distance, many economic activities can be conducted efficiently without producers and consumers coming into any direct contact, as manifested by the growth of remote working, distance learning and internet shopping. These contradictory forces of concentration and dispersal underpin the argument advanced by Sassen (2006) that ICT is facilitating a combination of geographic dispersal and urban concentration within the global economy.

The rise of the knowledge economy is creating opportunities for economies to switch to a more capital-saving growth trajectory, along which an increasing share of investment is devoted to intangible, rather than tangible assets. In part, these opportunities are crystallizing into choices about the future form of buildings and the future organization of cities. We noted in Chapter 4 that the capital-saving effects of technical progress tend to be masked by the substitution of capital for labour, as ever more capital-intensive methods of production are employed across the economy. Substitution therefore conceals the strong capital-saving tendencies that are continuously at work, as economic activities are undertaken using capital goods which are both cheaper and of higher specification as a result of technical progress. The incentive to save capital is particularly strong with respect to building investment, favouring the substitution of rapidly cheapening equipment embodying the latest technologies for slowly cheapening buildings with less dynamic rates of embodied technical progress.

The most recent urban development cycle offers clear evidence as to how the adoption of ICT is altering the pattern of urban accumulation. This cycle has been marked by the construction of office parks, distribution centres, retail warehouses and leisure complexes on relatively cheap land in peripheral locations close to motorway junctions (see the UK building cycle chronology reported in Chapter 5). What these buildings have in common is a light, relatively inexpensive fabric, housing large investments in state-of-the-art information technology for tasks such as data processing, inventory control and multimedia entertainment. They provide a clear example of the capital-saving potential of ICT, offering low cost, functionally efficient buildings, in which the structure is subordinated to its services in such a way that the occupier can maximize their operational effectiveness while minimizing their accommodation costs. These new forms of commercial building are far cheaper to construct than their traditional city centre equivalents: the unit construction cost of a business park office may only be one-third that of a prestige city centre office block, even before allowance is made for the differential in land cost.

A reduction in the structural costs of modern commercial buildings is the least of the adjustments being made to the urban fabric in response to the demands and opportunities presented by ICT. Far more radical are the potential capital-saving effects of a reduction in the aggregate demand for such buildings. An already historical example is provided by the cutback in numbers of bank branches on the high street, partly owing to the switch of investment from branch buildings to automated teller machines; the second wave of cutbacks resulting from the spread of internet banking is proving to be much greater. Equivalent savings in retail outlets will occur as internet shopping gains in market share; the requirement for shop premises will reduce in favour of a greater demand for lower cost warehousing space to support home delivery services. A similar argument can be applied to the impacts of ICT on the workplace. Activities such as teleworking and teleconferencing are making work itself more mobile and flexible; again the net result will almost certainly be capital-saving in terms of the amount of floorspace required per worker, as more office activities are undertaken from home or in transit.

Undoubtedly, the most fundamental impact that ICT will have upon the form of cities is not on the specification or the number of their individual buildings, but rather on their overall spatial organization. As discussed in Chapter 5, automobile technology has transformed the trade-off between distance and location cost within cities, accelerating the processes of suburbanization. With the universal adoption of ICT, a more fundamental trade-off has been created between transportation and telecommunications. The debate about this trade-off has tended to polarize between two views of the urban future. Some commentators have highlighted the capital-saving substitution effect, whereby flows of information replace flows of goods and people as part of a wider process of 'dematerialization' which is weakening the agglomeration benefits of cities (Bernardini and Galli, 1993). Others stress the capital-using complementarity of ICT and transport technologies, such that telecommunications can induce more demand for transportation through increased interaction and efficiency gains within the wider economy (Mokhtarian, 1990). In reality, both substitution and complementarity effects are operating – the knowledge city encompasses a rising volume of both physical and electronic flows, but because of relative substitution a growing share of the flows is electronic rather than physical (Graham and Marvin, 1996). While improvements in transport technology have progressively weakened the 'tyranny of distance', progress in telecommunications technology does not yet appear to be challenging the 'tyranny of proximity' – the continuing demand for direct personal contact in so many aspects of urban life (Duranton, 1999). We can confidently assert that reports of the death of the city are greatly exaggerated (Gaspar and Glaeser, 1998; Glaeser, 1998).

The sustainable city
The threats posed by climate change and diminishing supplies of fossil fuels will require as far-reaching a shift in the future trajectory of economic growth as that already effected by the information revolution. The combination of global warming and higher energy prices is providing the catalyst for the development of new low-carbon technologies for transport, power generation and industrial production. Furthermore, the rising costs of producing and distributing material goods are boosting the growth of the virtual economy. In the same way that the information revolution is capital-saving, the sustainability revolution will be energy-saving. And, like the information revolution, the sustainability revolution will have a major impact upon both the future form of buildings and the future organization of cities. Improved energy efficiency in the construction and use of buildings is already a priority goal for developers, investors, occupiers and governments. It is likely that as the energy-saving performance of new buildings improves, so previous vintages of less energy efficient buildings will suffer accelerated obsolescence, stimulating the replacement building cycle.

Beyond the performance of individual buildings, the search for a more energy efficient trajectory of economic growth could fundamentally change the overall form and function of cities. For urban form, transportation systems and sustainability are inextricably linked (Breheny, 1992; Brotchie et al., 1995). Across the cities of the world, a strong inverse relationship exists between automobile dependence and metropolitan density, while there is a strong direct relationship between metropolitan density and energy efficiency. In other words, sprawling cities with high automobile dependence are relatively energy inefficient and emit above average levels of air pollution and greenhouse gases; conversely, more densely developed cities with high mass transit use are relatively energy efficient and environmentally friendly (Kenworthy and Laube, 1999). Reduced automobile dependence combined with greater investment in energy efficient mass transit systems is therefore seen as one key element in the development of more sustainable cities (Newman and Kenworthy, 1999). A wave of infrastructure investment in new mass transit systems could have a comparable impact to those produced by the development of the railways in the nineteenth century and highway networks in the twentieth century.

The corollary of a shift in the balance of urban transportation towards improved mass transit systems is a shift towards urban forms which are more compact, because transit systems cannot operate economically in sprawling, low density cities (Bertaud, 2003). The sustainable city is therefore likely to be a more compact city (Jenks et al., 1996; Williams et al., 2000). Such a shift would have profound implications for real estate investment. As we have already seen, much of the thrust of urban innovation over the past 30 years has been directed towards the development of new built forms inhabiting the urban periphery. Out-of-town office and retail parks have supplied the growing demands of a suburbanizing population: car-borne commuting trips have lengthened while the number of car-borne shopping trips has increased. Meeting these demands through the provision of low cost structures on cheap land has proved highly profitable for developers and investors. IPD data on average annual total returns in the UK investment market show that between 1980 and 2007, retail warehouses and retail parks were the best performing retail sector, while distribution warehouses and business parks were the second best performers in their respective industrial and office categories (behind the London industrial and West End office markets, in both of which returns were boosted by limited supply). If the future pattern of urban development tilts back towards in-town provision within more compact cities, the era of superior out-of-town investment performance may draw to a close.

Since the knowledge city is a capital-saving city, it also has the potential to be a more sustainable city. Perhaps the most important contribution that the knowledge economy can make to sustainability concerns the organization of business activity. The impact of ICT upon corporate organization is paradoxical. On the one hand, like telephone networks before them, computer networks render large organizations more efficient by reducing the costs of internal communication, thus expanding the effective span of ownership and control. To counter this, the technology is also a stimulus to more flexible and decentralized management structures, since it allows for more efficient communication between functionally and locationally separate units of business activity (Brynjolfsson and Hitt, 2000). Hence firms can adopt a structure of smaller and more dispersed operating units, creating a 'distributed workplace' which allows workers to live closer to their jobs and reduces the demands for capital-intensive transport infrastructure (Harrison et al., 2004). This suggests the possibility of a more sustainable pattern of future urban development in which smaller scale, more compact cities act as complementary nodes on regional and global information networks, enjoying agglomeration economies while avoiding the worst diseconomies of pollution and congestion that bedevil large metropolitan agglomerations (Batten, 1995). There would be more mixed-use development, combining homes, offices, shops and leisure facilities, assisting the return of residents to the inner city and opposing the migration of jobs to the urban periphery. Rather than a monocentric pyramid, the sustainable knowledge city of the future might more closely resemble a polycentric network (Castells, 2000).

The capital-saving potential of the knowledge economy, acting upon building investment and urban form, therefore complements the search for more energy efficient types of urban development. One likely outcome of these dual capital-saving and energy-saving trends is a shift in the balance of real estate investment from commercial to residential buildings, as more economic activities are conducted from home. Such a shift in the locus of economic activity towards the domestic sphere would reinforce two previously discussed trends in building investment. The first, explored in Chapter 4, is the tendency for commercial buildings to act as a diminishing source of economic growth, as equipment investment has taken over as the main engine of expansion in the business economy. The second, discussed in the first section of this chapter, is the growing importance of dwellings as the main repository of domestic wealth and the main asset underwriting the expansion of the household economy. If these trends continue, investment in residential buildings of improved specification and performance could constitute perhaps the most important driver of urban accumulation in the sustainable knowledge cities of the twenty-first century. What can confidently be asserted is that whatever the precise trajectory followed by building investment in the coming decades, it will be propelled by the same cyclical dynamic which has characterized economic growth and urban development in ages past.

Appendix: An error correction model of the property cycle

In Chapter 4, we explored the stylized facts of long-run economic growth in the UK and US economies using a growth model that expresses the trend in national output Y_t as a function of the labour L_t and capital K_t used as factor inputs to production. The stylized facts suggest that output and capital stock grow in tandem along the equilibrium growth path, with real prices remaining constant in aggregate but diverging for individual goods according to relative shifts in consumer tastes and production technologies. These elements of the equilibrium growth model were incorporated into the building cycle model set out in Appendix B and employed in Chapter 7. In this model, a steady-state growth path for total building stock K_t^*, occupied stock B_t and construction starts S_t^* is defined in terms of an exogenously determined rate of growth in output Y_t, so that with supply and demand in balance, the rate of construction s_t, vacancy rate v_t, real rent r_t and real price of property p_t remain constant at their natural levels s^*, v^*, r^* and p^*. External shocks displace the economy away from this equilibrium path, with the lag structure of the model capturing the adjustment processes which propagate cyclical fluctuations in the actual levels of building starts, vacancy, rents and prices.

A reduced form of the full building cycle model is presented in Section A.2.4. This allows the dynamic behaviour of the property market to be represented parsimoniously by an error correction model, in which a long-run equilibrium growth path is combined with the short-run adjustment processes that generate price and building cycles. In its simplest form, this type of model comprises two basic equations. The first is a cointegrating equilibrium relationship between non-stationary trends in the level variables, yielding a stationary residual which captures the deviations in actual levels around the fitted trend. The second equation incorporates this residual as a trend-reverting feedback mechanism in a first difference model of the short-run changes in market variables. For the theory and application of cointegrated error correction models in general, see Engle and Granger (1991) and Phillips and Loretan (1991); for applications of the approach to modelling real estate markets, see Abraham and Hendershott (1996), Munro and Tu (1996) and Hendershott et al. (2002a).

The proposed error correction model of the property cycle is based on long-run demand and supply relationships, each defined in logarithmic form in order to express growth rates as trend gradients and model coefficients as elasticities. Following the model structure set out in Appendix B, assume that at each point in time t along the steady-state growth path there is a fixed supply of total building stock K_t^*, with the occupancy of this stock determined by the natural vacancy rate v^*, so that the occupied stock at time t is defined by $B_t = K_t^*/(1 + v^*)$. The current real market price of this occupied stock p_t is determined by the demand conditions in the market, which are a function of the current level of economic output or income Y_t, the fixed building supply K_t^* and the natural vacancy rate v^*. A simple log form of the demand function can be expressed as:

$$\log B_t = \alpha_1 + \beta_1 \log Y_t - \gamma_1 \log p_t$$

where β_1 is the output or income elasticity of demand and γ_1 is the price elasticity of demand. This demand equation can be inverted to define a long-run price equation in terms of total stock K_t^*, i.e.

$$\log p_t = \varphi_1 + (\beta_1/\gamma_1)\log Y_t - (1/\gamma_1)\log K_t^* \tag{8.1}$$

where the constant $\varphi_1 = 1/\gamma_1[\alpha_1 + \log(1 + v^*)]$. When real prices remain constant at their natural level ($p_t = p^*$) and the output/income elasticity of demand is unity ($\beta_1 = 1$), this demand equation reduces to an equilibrium growth relationship between stock and output.

An alternative version of the equilibrium price equation can be derived in terms of the natural vacancy rate $v^* = (K_t^* - B_t)/B_t$. It is assumed that there is an inverse relationship between the actual rate of vacancy v_t at time t and the level of price p_t, such that the lower the vacancy rate, the higher the price level. This inverse relationship can be generalized to give a long-run price equation of logarithmic form:

$$\log p_t = \alpha_1' + \beta_1' \log B_t - \gamma_1' \log K_t^* \tag{8.1a}$$

The long-run supply equation defines the rate of building starts to be a direct function of the price level: the higher the price level, the higher the rate of starts. In the Appendix B model, the natural rate of starts $s^* = S_t^*/B_{t-1}$ is expressed as the ratio between the equilibrium level of starts and the level of occupied stock at the beginning of the period; for the purposes of the error correction model, the rate of starts can be defined relative to the level of output Y_t at the end of the period. The supply equation can therefore be expressed as:

$$\log S_t^* - \log Y_t = \alpha_2 + \gamma_2 \log p_t$$

where γ_2 is the price elasticity of supply. This supply equation can be generalized to define a long-run starts equation of the form:

$$\log S_t^* = \alpha_2 + \beta_2 \log Y_t + \gamma_2 \log p_t \qquad (8.2)$$

where β_2 is the output or income elasticity of supply. When real prices remain constant at their natural level and the output elasticity is unity, this supply equation reduces to an equilibrium growth relationship between starts and output. An alternative version of the supply equation can be defined using occupied stock B_t rather than output Y_t to provide a supply equation (8.2a) equivalent to price equation (8.1a).

The residuals u_t and v_t derived from estimating the long-run demand and supply relationships in terms of actual levels of stock K_t and starts S_t provide the error correction feedback terms for the short-term models, where

$$u_t = \log p_t - [\varphi_1 + (\beta_1/\gamma_1)\log Y_t - (1/\gamma_1)\log K_t]$$

and

$$v_t = \log S_t - (\alpha_2 + \beta_2 \log Y_t + \gamma_2 \log p_t)$$

A first difference model of changes in building prices $\Delta \log p_t$ can be expressed in terms of output changes $\Delta \log Y_t$ and stock changes $\Delta \log K_t$, together with a serial correlation term in the lagged dependent variable $\Delta \log p_{t-1}$ and the error correction term u_t:

$$\Delta \log p_t = \alpha_3 + \lambda_3 \Delta \log p_{t-1} + \sum_0^1 \beta_{3n} \Delta \log Y_{t-n} - \sum_0^1 \gamma_{3n} \Delta \log K_{t-n} - \sigma_3 u_{t-1} \quad (8.3)$$

The equivalent model for changes in building starts $\Delta \log S_t$ introduces price changes $\Delta \log p_t$ as explanatory variables:

$$\Delta \log S_t = \alpha_4 + \lambda_4 \Delta \log S_{t-1} + \sum_0^1 \beta_{4n} \Delta \log Y_{t-n} + \sum_0^1 \gamma_{4n} \Delta \log p_{t-n} - \sigma_4 v_{t-1} \quad (8.4)$$

The lagged dependent variables introduce serial correlation into the adjustment equations, which has the effect of positively reinforcing a cyclical shift away from market equilibrium. In contrast, the error correction terms introduce negative feedback, capturing the trend-reverting tendencies that dampen cyclical growth. The simplified version of the full building cycle model presented in Section B.2.4 is identical in form to equations (8.3) and (8.4), with the independent explanatory variables omitted. For example, the restricted form of price equation (8.3) is given by:

$$\Delta \log p_t = \alpha_3 + \lambda_3 \Delta \log p_{t-1} - \sigma_3 u_{t-1} \qquad (8.3a)$$

In the idealized version of the restricted model, the coefficients on the serial correlation term (λ_3) and the error correction term (σ_3) are identical, balancing the cyclical processes of reinforcement and feedback. The coefficient on each term is based on the transmission coefficient that links vacancy to building starts via the rent adjustment process. The higher the value of the coefficient, the stronger the cycle, with a value of between 0.20 and 0.25 defining the critical threshold above which cyclical fluctuations first appear (see Chapter 7).

Rather than formulating the model using real prices p_t, it can alternatively be specified in terms of real rents r_t and yield w_t, where $p_t = r_t/w_t$. With this approach, equations (8.1)–(8.4) are formulated using $\log r_t$ rather than $\log p_t$, and separate equilibrium and error correction equations defined for the yield. The equilibrium level of the property yield is expressed as a function of the real rent level and the yields on alternative investment assets. There is assumed to be a negative relationship with the real rent level, since the higher the rent the stronger the investment demand, a negative relationship with the equity yield e_t, since property and equities are investment substitutes, and a positive relationship with the bond yield g_t, since this represents the expected risk-free rate of return. These assumptions give a long-run yield equation:

$$w_t = \alpha_5 - \gamma_5 \log r_t - \chi_5 e_t + \psi_5 g_t \qquad (8.5)$$

and a corresponding error correction equation:

$$\Delta w_t = \alpha_6 + \lambda_6 \Delta w_{t-1} - \sum_0^1 \gamma_{6n} \Delta \log r_{t+n} - \sum_0^1 \chi_{6n} \Delta e_{t+n} + \sum_0^1 \psi_{6n} \Delta g_{t+n} - \sigma_6 z_{t-1} \qquad (8.6)$$

where z_t is the error correction term derived from equation (8.5) and yield movements respond to expected as well as current changes in the explanatory variables.

To complete the transmission process, building starts S_{t-q} feed the subsequent increase in stock ΔK_t, allowing for a construction lag q and a rate of depreciation δ applied to the existing stock. Expressed in logarithmic form, the increment of additional stock $\log \Delta K_t$ has an increasing trend, whereas the change in log transformed stock $\Delta \log K_t$ has a constant mean. To allow for these divergent trends, it is necessary to introduce a negative time trend into the logarithmic relationship between starts and additions to stock, i.e.

$$\Delta \log K_t = \alpha_7 + \lambda_7 \log S_{t-q} - \delta \log K_{t-1} - \kappa t \qquad (8.7)$$

In this formulation of the model, building stock, starts and prices are the endogenous market variables, subject to the exogenous influence of output/income growth and yields in other asset markets. The influence of interest rates on demand and that of construction costs on supply can be introduced into the error correction models as additional exogenous factors. Rather than using simple property prices, the models can be defined in terms of a measure of the real user cost of building capital, based upon factors such as price or rent, mortgage interest payments, depreciation and repair costs, property taxes and the expected rate of capital gain (see, for example, DiPasquale and Wheaton, 1994; Muellbauer and Murphy, 1997; Meen, 2000).

9

Understanding the
Building Cycle

'The essential point to grasp is that in dealing with capitalism we are dealing with an evolutionary process...Capitalism, then, is by nature a form or method of economic change and not only never is but never can be stationary...[a] process of industrial mutation...that incessantly revolutionizes the economic structure *from within*, incessantly destroying the old one, incessantly creating a new one. This process of Creative Destruction is the essential fact about capitalism'

(Schumpeter, 1943: 82–3).

Having opened this book with an early quotation from Joseph Schumpeter, it would seem appropriate to conclude it with a later quotation on the same theme, of capitalism as a process of creative destruction. Confronted with the economic crash of 2008, observers can be forgiven for concentrating on the destructive aspects of capitalist development, whereas in the preceding boom years, all the talk was of its creative potential. It is a vital lesson of history, however, that growth and instability, creativity and destruction, are two aspects of the same evolutionary process. That has been the central theme of this book, with a particular focus on the role that investment cycles in general, and building cycles in particular, play in the generation of growth and the propagation of instability.

Let us now synthesize the main themes from previous chapters into a theoretical framework which can guide our understanding of the building cycle.

Building cycles and economic growth

Cyclical growth

Capital investment is simultaneously the main motor of growth and the key source of instability within an economy. As a motor of growth, the effect of investment is to expand productive capacity, increase the capital intensity of production, raise labour productivity through endogenous technical progress, generate increasing returns to scale and establish new industries producing new or improved goods and services. However, the growth process is punctuated by disequilibrating shocks and discontinuities which shift the economy away from its equilibrium trajectory until compensating adjustment processes move it back towards equilibrium. It is the interplay of equilibrating and disequilibrating forces which generates investment cycles, and it is the motion of these cycles which propels economic growth – as a sequence of investment-led surges interspersed with periods of slowdown and retrenchment. The dynamic of cyclical growth is that each expansion phase drives the economy to a new and higher peak, so that the next contraction is constrained to a higher trough than was reached in the previous cycle.

Technological revolutions

The trajectory of economic growth is determined by the interplay of several dynamic forces: demographic growth and change, the exploitation of natural resources, the accumulation of human capital, investment in physical capital, the expansion of trade and the evolution of social and political institutions. Technical progress is a crucial common factor tying these forces together, operating as an evolutionary process in which new products and methods emerge to meet the changing needs of society. This evolutionary process is not continuous, but rather tends to progress through a sequence of technological revolutions. Each technological revolution is initiated by the emergence of a new general purpose technology, consisting of a cluster of interrelated innovations together with their associated infrastructure and institutions, which diffuses throughout the economy, triggering an investment boom that expands productive capacity until market saturation sets in. The subsequent slump is marked by a phase of creative destruction which accelerates the obsolescence of existing techniques and products, thereby establishing the conditions for the start of the next boom.

Historical dependence

Specific historical events determine how and when a particular general purpose technology is adopted and what institutions emerge to facilitate its adoption. Once a technological and institutional regime is established, there is a tendency for increasing returns from the continuing use of the technology to lock the economy on to a particular growth path. The extent of the path dependence of an economy increases with the interrelatedness of its technological and institutional structures, and the sunk costs of its growing stock of fixed capital. When a subsequent set of events creates the conditions for a new general purpose technology to emerge, and new institutional structures to arise, the economy may shift on to a different trajectory, but only at the cost of destroying parts of its obsolete productive capacity. The trajectory of cyclical growth is therefore historically dependent; its current and future direction is determined by the cumulative contribution of past growth cycles and past technological and institutional regimes.

Growth and technical progress

Technical progress has a dual impact on the productivity of an economy. Productivity is not only boosted by the accumulation of an expanding volume of capital at a given state of technology, but it is also augmented by the technological improvements embodied in successive vintages of capital stock. Investment in new capital goods introduces improved techniques into production, enhancing the marginal productivity of the labour working with the new techniques. At the same time, technical improvements in the construction of investment goods reduces their price relative to that of labour, encouraging the substitution of capital for labour, which boosts capital per worker and thus average labour productivity. As existing vintages of stock age, their economic value depreciates relative to that of newer vintages, constructed with more productive techniques and embodying more advanced technologies. Eventually, the older vintages depreciate to the point at which they are no longer profitable to operate, and become economically obsolete. The higher the rate of new investment, the shorter is the economic life of the existing capital stock. By this process, technical progress increases both the quality and quantity of capital employed in production.

Building investment and productivity growth

Building and equipment capital constitute complementary components of the means of production. However, the components of capital make differential contributions to productivity growth. First, they enjoy differential rates of cheapening relative to labour, stemming from variations in the rate of technical progress achieved in their construction. Technical progress in the construction of housing has been slower than that in the construction of commercial buildings, which in turn has been slower than that achieved in the manufacture of equipment, particularly ICT equipment. Consequently, rapidly cheapening equipment is being substituted for labour at a faster rate than slowly cheapening buildings. Second, those capital goods which enjoy the most rapid cheapening in their own construction also tend to embody the most dynamic technological improvements when employed in the production of other goods and services. For this reason, estimated rates of embodied technical change in equipment are higher than those for commercial buildings. The result is that the share of equipment in total capital stock tends to increase over time at the expense of buildings, while the locus of technical progress also switches from building to equipment capital. Building investment therefore tends to have a diminishing role as an engine of productivity growth in a maturing economy.

Technical progress in construction technology

Despite lower rates of technical progress than those achieved in equipment manufacture, significant advances have been made in construction technology, particularly for non-residential buildings. The introduction of new building techniques allows larger and taller structures to be erected, while the realization of scale economies increases construction productivity and speeds up the development process. The achievement of technical progress in construction is most apparent in the office sector. Since the late nineteenth century, successive vintages of office buildings of improved specification and increased size have been constructed at progressively faster rates of completion. Thus, the introduction of elevators, steel-framed then reinforced concrete skeletons and curtain walling have allowed for major increases in height and more flexible internal layouts of office buildings.

More recently, the introduction of fast-track construction methods has increased both the scale and productivity of office building, while ever more complex mechanical and electronic services have been integrated into the building fabric.

Building cycles as driver of growth

Of all the components of fixed capital formation, building investment exhibits the most prolonged and volatile cyclical fluctuations. Even though its role as an engine of productivity growth may be diminishing, building investment therefore makes a crucial contribution to cyclical growth. As the economy expands, building investment both augments an essential factor of production and is the source of the most acute instability in the growth process. Building cycles are characterized by a burst of investment in new stock, induced by increases in occupier demand, followed by a phase of accelerated obsolescence in the existing stock. Each cycle thus creates a distinctive vintage of buildings which reflects its particular historical context in terms of prevailing technologies and occupier requirements. The economic life of buildings is longer than that of other components of capital, because buildings can be adapted and reused productively in a way that equipment cannot. When each vintage does reach the end of its economic life, a replacement cycle reinforces the cycle induced by the growth in occupier demand. It is by this process that the building cycle helps to ratchet economic growth to successively higher levels of activity.

Propagation of the building cycle

The trajectory of building investment

The equilibrium growth trajectory of building investment is driven by the demand for additional stock combined with replacement demand. The increase in demand for residential and commercial buildings derives from the growth in incomes and output, moderated by the substitution between residential buildings and other consumer goods, and between commercial buildings and other capital goods. In general, the demand for housing is highly income elastic, because of its dual role as consumption good and store of wealth, while the demand for commercial buildings is less output elastic, because of the relative substitution of equipment for buildings which occurs during the growth process. The higher the income/output elasticity of demand, and the lower the price elasticities of demand and supply, the greater are the pressures for building rents and prices to rise, and vice versa. In income elastic housing markets where supply is relatively price inelastic due to limited land supply and restrictive planning policies, there is a tendency towards under-building and rising prices. Conversely, in commercial markets with a combination of more price elastic supply and less output elastic demand, the tendency is towards over-building and falling prices.

Impulse and propagation in cycle generation

Occasional exogenous shocks provide the impulses which divert building investment away from its equilibrium growth trajectory until compensating adjustment processes move it back towards equilibrium. These impulses can consist of a demand-side shock such as a shift in technology, or a supply-side shock such as a change in planning policy. However, it is the endogenous propagation mechanisms within the building process which translate these irregular impulses into the persistent fluctuations that characterize cyclical growth. There are several cycle-inducing features of building investment which explain its particular volatility:

- The long lead times in the development process together with the lumpiness and heterogeneity of buildings create a tendency for development to over-shoot and then under-shoot in response to increases in demand.
- The durability of building stock reduces the stabilizing effect of replacement demand on the unstable investment demand induced by the growth accelerator.
- The existence of a buffer stock of vacant space slows the supply response on the cycle upswing and prolongs over-building on the downswing.
- The stickiness of rent and price adjustment due to infrequent transactions and demand-side rigidities such as long leases and high moving costs delays the transmission of market signals.
- The difficulties of forming development decisions under conditions of future uncertainty mean that investor sentiment tends to oscillate between optimism and pessimism.

A circular transmission process

Property markets incorporate a circular transmission process in which the construction response to changes in occupier demand is mediated through the adjustment of vacancy and prices. There is an equilibrium vacancy rate which balances supply and demand and maintains real prices at their equilibrium level, by providing just sufficient surplus space to ensure efficient turnover within the market. However, delays in price adjustment and lags between the start and completion of construction create a strong endogenous cycle propagation mechanism in which the positive and negative feedback forces of cycle reinforcement and trend reversion are broadly in balance. An increase in occupier demand is met in the short run from the existing buffer stock of vacant space; a reduction in the level of vacancy leads to an increase in rents and prices; rising prices boost development profitability and therefore levels of construction starts; completion of the new buildings replenishes the vacant stock. Conversely, when supply overshoots, vacancy increases and rents and prices fall, causing a drop in development profitability which leads to a cut back in further building starts. The result of this cycle propagation process is that building investment fluctuates around its equilibrium growth trajectory, while vacancy, real rents and prices and development profitability fluctuate around their equilibrium levels.

Determinants of cyclical behaviour

The behaviour of the building cycle is dependent upon three sources of market imperfection. The first is the speed and strength of the market response to an exogenous shock: the slower the speed of adjustment, the more likely it is that persistent cyclical fluctuations will be generated. The second is the degree to which market agents form myopic expectations about future prices in an industry characterized by long construction periods and considerable future uncertainty. The third is the extent to which the demand for buildings is relatively price inelastic because of rigidities such as long fixed leases and high transaction and moving costs. The duration or period of the building cycle is dependent upon the construction delay between starts and completions; the volatility or amplitude of the cycle is dependent upon the strength of the transmission process which translates changes in vacancy into changes in building starts via movements in rents and prices. As the transmission process increases in strength, the building cycle moves from damped to explosive oscillations; however, even if explosive, the cycle is constrained within the absolute floor that starts cannot be less than zero and a ceiling set by the current capacity of the development industry.

A family of building cycles

There is evidence of up to four building cycles of different duration. The basic endogenously generated building cycle is a major cycle of 8–10 years, consistent with a construction process that on average lasts for around two years. Building investment also shows some evidence of a shorter 4–5 year minor cycle, reflecting the demand-side influence of the business cycle, and a 40–50 year long wave, revealing the impact of intermittent technological revolutions. The most prominent cycles in building activity are the long cycles which occur every 15–20 years. These are in part a result of the coalescence of the major cycle and the long wave, and in part a product of the tendency for every other major cycle to be subject to speculative investment pressures which create a particularly volatile boom–bust cycle.

The rhythm of post-war cycles

During the post-war period, a sequence of up to six major cycles in building activity can be identified, with alternate cycles manifesting the classic characteristics of speculative long cycles. The three long cycles – occurring in the early 1970s, the late 1980s and the mid-2000s – are apparent in different economies and all sectors of building. Each was triggered by strong growth in occupier and investment demand; each created a price bubble which fed a building boom; each ended with a recession-induced slump in demand accompanied by over-supply, leading to a collapse in prices and building activity. During these long cycles, the movements of residential and non-residential building have tended to coincide, indicating that similar forces of cycle generation have been at work, with the housing and office market cycles typically displaying the most extreme volatility. However, despite their generic similarities, each building cycle in each sector and locality has progressed in a unique fashion, due to the operation of particular market conditions and the intervention of specific historical events.

Building cycles and urban development

The urban development cycle

Building stock constitutes the principal fixed capital of cities, and so building investment is a key driver of urban development as well as of economic growth. The trajectory of urban development is shaped by the interlocking processes of innovation and accumulation which act upon urban forms and functions. Disequilibrium is inherent in urban development, arising from the tension between the rapid processes of innovation which transform the functions undertaken in cities, and the slower processes of accumulation which expand their built form. Urban accumulation does not follow a steady-state trajectory, but rather proceeds through successive long cycles of development, each of which is typically associated with a wave of innovation in construction methods and infrastructure provision. The urban development cycle is fuelled by investment demand from households for dwellings and social infrastructure, and from businesses for commercial buildings and other means of production. Each cycle produces a unique vintage of building stock which adds another layer to the fixed urban fabric within which urban activities must operate.

Urban growth and agglomeration

A crucial dynamic of urban development is the tension between the centripetal forces of agglomeration and the centrifugal forces of dispersion. It is the agglomeration economies generated when urban activities cluster together which underlie the trade-off between land rent and transport costs. The city centre offers the strongest agglomeration benefits and attracts the most profitable and intensive land uses, while lower value, more extensive uses decentralize away from the city centre. As distance from the centre increases, so land values, property rents and occupation densities fall while transport costs rise. A powerful stimulus to urban growth is provided by the interaction between innovation and agglomeration. Cities act as engines of economic growth in which new ideas are formed, knowledge is exchanged and learning is promoted, thereby creating knowledge spillovers which reinforce the accumulation of human capital. Agglomeration, innovation and growth are mutually reinforcing processes: agglomeration spurs growth because it reduces the costs of innovation, while growth fosters agglomeration by spawning new activities which cluster together.

Innovation and accumulation in urban development

The urban development cycle combines innovation and accumulation through successive improvements in construction and transport technologies. Developers respond to agglomeration economies by substituting between land and structures in the overall cost of building investment, with the result that building densities typically increase towards the city centre in parallel with the increase in land values. High land values support high-rise, high density and high cost structures. Each innovation in construction technology reduces the costs of larger and taller structures, steepening the bid rent curve and providing an impetus to intensification through redevelopment. The result is successive vintages of buildings with improved technical specification and higher plot ratios in the city centre. Each countervailing innovation in transportation technology reduces transport costs, flattening the bid rent curve and encouraging the extension of urban development through the decentralization of firms and households. The result is successive vintages of buildings of progressively newer specification and lower density on the urban periphery.

A self-reinforcing process of metropolitan growth

Innovation and accumulation create a self-reinforcing process of metropolitan growth in which intensification and extension operate in tandem. As cities grow, the intensification of development in their central areas creates congestion externalities and rising land costs. These generate pressures for the decentralization of residential and business activities through improvements in transport provision, leading to a corresponding extension of urban development. This in turn creates opportunities for new functions to occupy the central area, triggering a new round of intensification. Metropolitan growth is a historically dependent process. Each round of intensification and extension locks a city on to a unique trajectory of growth, as its fixed, long-lived and highly interrelated physical fabric accumulates through successive building cycles, embodying sunk costs which constrain the future direction of the city's development.

The transport-building cycle

Infrastructure investment acts as an engine of economic growth because of its extensive backward and forward linkages, which place transport improvements at the centre of an interactive process of industrialization and urbanization. Transport innovation contributes to growth by widening and integrating product markets, increasing the reliability and speed of distribution, facilitating the emergence of new industries and reinforcing economies of scale. Through successive waves of infrastructure investment, new transport modes of superior performance are substituted for existing modes that decline in competitiveness, face shrinking demand and pass into a final life cycle stage of network closures. These waves of infrastructure investment stimulate other forms of building investment, creating a transport-building cycle which acts as a key driver of urban accumulation. The transport-building cycle can be conceptualized as a process of interactive innovation: each new transport technology acts as a catalyst for both the extension and intensification of urban development, while the resultant development boom feeds back to underwrite the profitability of the infrastructure investment.

Transport investment and suburbanization

Transport innovations affect urban growth in two ways. Lower transport costs increase the aggregate size at which cities can function effectively, and they facilitate suburbanization by flattening urban rent and density gradients. The suburbanization of population is reinforced by rising household incomes, together with the growing externality costs of living in inner areas, due to congestion, pollution and urban blight. Rising household incomes increase the demand for housing, which can be satisfied more easily and cheaply in suburban locations, while reducing transport costs and travel times make longer distance commuting and shopping trips more acceptable. Successive waves of suburban development are embodied in concentric rings of durable housing stock. The extent and orientation of each residential ring are shaped by the reach of the commuter transport network and the duration of the construction boom, while its built forms reflect the technological possibilities, income levels, consumer tastes and architectural fashions of the time.

The urban office economy

The modern metropolitan economy is dominated by office-based financial and business service industries, and the office sector provides the clearest examples of the operation of the locational forces of both agglomeration and decentralization. Office-based services derive the strongest agglomeration economies from a city centre location, as clusters of firms in related industries benefit from knowledge spillovers and easy access to specialist services, skilled labour and deep capital markets. The most profitable office firms can therefore afford to occupy the latest city centre buildings commanding the highest rents, out-bidding other occupiers and forcing them into older, lower rented space. However, information technology also facilitates efficient communication between geographically dispersed but functionally integrated business units, encouraging large organizations to decentralize some of their activities away from the city centre. Combined with innovations in the technology of office construction, these opposing locational forces have generated a distinctive pattern of urban development. The command functions of the office economy occupy ever larger and taller skyscrapers in city centres, whilst back office functions have decentralized to business parks on the urban periphery, occupying inexpensive structures housing large investments in the latest ICT equipment.

Integration of real estate and capital markets

Property as an investment medium

Investment in land and buildings has a dual purpose. Building investment is a process of capital accumulation which enhances the productive capacity of economies and the physical fabric of cities. However, land and buildings also act as a repository of wealth; they form the largest component of the tangible assets which constitute the wealth of nations. In the corporate sector, real estate constitutes the main asset on the balance sheet, thereby providing the crucial collateral for loans to fund business expansion. In the household sector, dwellings make up the main component of personal wealth, which has been growing more rapidly than incomes due to the combination of rising savings volumes and inflating asset prices. Pension and life funds now comprise the second largest component of personal wealth, and the financial institutions managing these funds have built up substantial long-term property holdings, in the form of both direct investments and indirect vehicles, because of the diversification benefits and attractive risk-return characteristics of real estate. Whilst building capital may be making a diminishing contribution to productivity growth, it is making an increasing contribution to wealth accumulation.

The contradiction between investor and occupier demand

The dual function of building capital as financial asset and physical means of production is the source of an inherent contradiction between the economic interests of the owners and occupiers of buildings – who may be one and the same entity. The owner interest is to maximize the value of a building through the returns it generates as an investment asset; the occupier interest is to maximize the accommodation services provided by a building at minimum cost. This contradiction is most apparent in the housing market, as rising house prices benefit existing owners in their capacity as investors, but penalize tenants and first-time buyers by reducing the quantity and quality of housing services which they can afford. Similarly in the corporate sector, the producer interest is to invest in new capital stock embodying the latest technologies, which tends to reduce the earning capacity of previous vintages through economic obsolescence, whereas the investor interest is to maintain or even enhance the monetary value of existing assets. The investor interest in maximizing the returns from real estate assets can create investment demand pressures which are to some extent independent of movements in occupier demand. For example, in prestige markets such as city centre offices, investment demand can run ahead of occupier demand, creating a self-defeating tendency towards over-development and falling rents, manifested through the ratcheting down of successive peaks and troughs in the rent cycle.

The cyclical movement of real estate values

The capital value cycle in real estate markets is jointly influenced by the action of occupier demand on the movement of rents and investor demand on the movement of yields. These demand forces operate at least partly autonomously because of the different factors which influence the behaviour of the occupier and investment markets. The cyclical movement of rents is a manifestation of the cycle propagation mechanisms inherent in the occupier market, created through the circular transmission process linking vacancy to rents, rents to building starts, building starts to completions and completions to vacancy. The movement of yields is determined in part by investor expectations of future movements in rents, and in part by the movements of yields in other asset markets, subject to their own cyclical fluctuations. When a capital value cycle is decomposed into its component rent and yield cycles, its various phases typically exhibit differential contributions from rent and yield movements, reflecting the particular conditions and events which have separately affected the occupier and investment markets.

The intensification of the commercial building cycle

The growing integration of real estate and capital markets has tended to intensify the commercial building cycle. Two pressures are causing this intensification: accelerating innovation in occupier activity and growing investment demand for real estate assets. The result has been the creation of a three-tier market in which the average age of commercial buildings has been decreasing while their average size has been increasing, as rates of obsolescence and replacement have accelerated. Each building cycle delivers a new vintage of prime space, built to meet the latest technological and organizational requirements of those occupiers able to pay the top rents. The vintage which commanded the prime market in the previous cycle suffers rapid depreciation, while older secondary vintages also continue to depreciate, though at a slower rate. The profile of achieved rents drops progressively through the vintages. Occupiers in the older vintages can then afford to upgrade the quality of their space, moving from older to newer buildings and leaving vacant the poorest quality tertiary buildings to await the next upswing in market conditions that will make their redevelopment profitable. Redevelopment contributes to intensification because developers take advantage of improvements in construction technology to increase the lettable floorspace area on the site, when new buildings replace old.

The property cycle and the business cycle

The integration of real estate and capital markets is also strengthening the links between the property cycle and the business cycle, potentially increasing the volatility of both. Instability in the wider economy generates shocks which destabilize the property market; these shocks act principally through changes in occupier activity, transmitted to building investment via the growth accelerator, and changes in interest rates, which affect development profitability and investment returns. The cyclical behaviour of the property market acts on the business cycle through various channels. First, the volatility of building activity is transmitted directly to aggregate demand through the investment multiplier. Second, the housing market cycle influences consumer behaviour through the wealth effect and through equity withdrawal. Third, through the role of real estate as loan collateral, property cycles are transmitted to credit markets, and thereby to the real economy, through the medium of the financial accelerator. Property booms therefore reinforce economic booms by boosting investment, consumption and borrowing, while the reverse effects operate during a property slump.

Speculative boom–bust cycles

The conditions for a classic long building cycle are created when rising occupier demand combined with cheap credit triggers a surge in speculative investment demand. The result is a real estate price bubble and construction boom, to be followed by collapsing property values, a building slump, loan defaults, bankruptcies and repossessions as demand contracts and interest rates rise. Such speculative real estate cycles are typically associated with equally volatile economic cycles, as positive and then negative multiplier and accelerator effects transmit property market instability to the wider economy. During a prolonged phase of prosperity, a sequence of mild business cycles creates the conditions for a more severe boom–bust cycle, as inflating asset prices provide the security for progressively higher levels of debt until a liquidity crisis bursts the speculative bubble, setting off a deflationary spiral that plunges the property market and the economy into a severe depression. It was just such a sequence of events that defined the crash of 2008, confirming once again the capacity of property cycles to generate much more widespread financial and economic instability.

Globalization of the building cycle

The growth of the transnational investment market

The transnational property investment market is fast expanding in response to the global forces of industrialization and urbanization, particularly in Asia. Investment in all types of assets, including real estate, has become a global activity in response to the growth of transnational corporations, the liberalization of capital flows and the integration of financial markets. The recent proliferation of indirect property investment vehicles, offering greater liquidity and risk diversification combined with reduced transaction costs, has opened up the market to a much broader range of investors, stimulating an explosion of cross-border real estate investment. One of the most striking manifestations of globalization is the way in which the world economy now functions as an interlocking network of cities, linked together by flows of goods and services, knowledge, labour and capital. Waves of real estate investment are flowing around this world city network, feeding economic growth and urban development but at the same time propagating market instability.

The international convergence of cycles

As the transnational investment market has evolved, it has become apparent that the property cycle itself is becoming a global phenomenon. The behaviour of the cycle varies between national and urban economies according to differences in economic conditions, land supply, planning policies and market maturity. Nevertheless, the processes which propagate the property cycle, and link it to the wider business cycle, appear to be common to all economies irrespective of their market structure and stage of economic development. As the integration of real estate and capital markets increases, as new financial instruments proliferate and as investment flows are globalized, it seems that building cycles are becoming not only more volatile and more frequent, but also more convergent.

The global office market

The office market is the most globally integrated real estate market in terms of occupier demand, investment demand and development supply. Transnational corporations are generating relatively homogenous demands for office space in whichever city they locate. Office buildings constitute the largest component of global property investment in general and cross-border investment in particular. Architects and developers are producing office buildings of similar design and specification in every continent of the world. Furthermore, of all real estate sectors, it is the office market which exhibits the most volatile price and building cycles. The volatility of the office cycle is reinforced by feedback and contagion effects resulting from the close interlocking of occupier and investment demand in the office market. Financial institutions are the main occupiers of newly built office space, the main sources of long-term development funding and the main purchasers of completed developments. As the office market becomes more integrated, so its volatile behaviour is more readily transmitted between the cities of the world.

The global office cycle

There is clear evidence of the convergence of the global office cycle during the three major cycles which have occurred over the past 25 years. These consist of the volatile speculative cycles of the late 1980s and mid-2000s, together with the more stable intermediate cycle of the late 1990s. Convergence is apparent in the progressively stronger coincidence of peak and trough turning points in the building, vacancy and rental growth cycles in different global cities. The feedback and contagion effects which reinforce volatility in the office market also appear to encourage cycle coordination. The integration of occupier and investor demand through the activities of financial institutions provides a transmission process whereby shocks emanating from the wider global economy, or from other asset markets, feed through to cause rapid adjustments to demand and supply conditions in all office markets. Of course, there remain considerable variations in the behaviour of individual markets, as manifested in their different rates of building, rates of absorption, equilibrium vacancy rates, prime rent levels, rent adjustment processes and cycle volatilities. Nevertheless, the stylized facts of the global office cycle highlight common features of market behaviour across cities subject to very different local market conditions.

The global diffusion of property innovation

Property cycles are acting as a motor for the global diffusion of innovation through the technical progress embodied in successive vintages of building stock. The rise of the skyscraper and the spread of the covered shopping mall provide noteworthy examples of the role of the building cycle in the diffusion of major property innovations, propelling the spread of each building type from its source in North America into Europe and on to Latin America, the Middle East and Asia. With the growth of the service economy, the occupier demands of financial institutions and retail chains have intersected with the investment demands of property funds to develop these two iconic building types in homogenous forms that present a remarkably similar appearance throughout the cities of the modern world. As these property innovations have spread through time and space, their diffusion trajectories have steepened, illustrating how their development has accelerated and intensified under the coordinating impact of globalization.

Interactive innovation in retailing

Retail development epitomizes the process of interactive innovation in the property market. Each improvement in the efficiency and organization of retail activity stimulates some innovation in the form of retail buildings, and each innovation in built forms feeds back to reinforce the improved operational efficiency of retailing. An evolutionary process is set in train as successive waves of retail investment promote new forms of provision which become established by out-competing existing forms, forcing them into decline. Scale economies in retailing were taken to a new level by the post-war development of the covered shopping centre. At first, these were built in town centres, but as car-based suburbanization has gathered pace, so they have been constructed in the suburbs and on the urban periphery. New types of functional, lower cost retail buildings have also appeared in suburban and peripheral locations: firstly in the form of stand-alone superstores and retail warehouses, and then as clusters of such units grouped together on retail parks. One by one, the new forms of retail provision are passing through a life cycle of introduction, growth, maturity and decline, as reflected in their rising, stabilizing and then falling market shares.

Into the twenty-first century

As the modern physical forms of retail provision move into their maturity phases, a new and fundamentally different competitor has entered the market. During the past decade, internet shopping has taken off at a rate which has few if any precedents among previous retail innovations. The extent to which the internet may render the newer physical forms of shopping provision obsolete, just as they in their turn have out-competed the traditional high street, raises fundamental questions about the path that building investment may follow in the twenty-first century. With globalization gathering pace, two technologies will play a key role in shaping economic growth and urban development in the coming decades. It is already apparent that the universal applicability of information technology makes it unique as an instrument of change. Equally wide-ranging technological forces are being unleashed in response to the challenges posed by climate change and rising energy costs. The scope and impact of the general purpose technologies of information and sustainable energy will be reinforced because they are to some extent complementary technologies. Their impacts on urban development and building investment will be especially far reaching. The perpetual tension between the rapid transformation of urban functions and the rigidities of urban forms may be heightened as never before, as the cities of the world endeavour to adapt to the demands of being both knowledge cities and sustainable cities.

Our story concludes in 2008, during the most severe property crash of the post-war period and at the onset of possibly the most severe economic slump since the Great Depression. We have developed a historical narrative of the building cycle which started in eighteenth century Britain, spread to the rest of Europe and America during the nineteenth century, and became a truly global phenomenon during the second half of the twentieth century. The locus of the most rapid economic growth and urban development has shifted to Asia, and so inevitably this is where the most massive and volatile flows of building investment are now to be found. Just as the building booms of the nineteenth century helped to create the distinctive fabric of European cities, and the twentieth century building cycle shaped North American cities, so the iconic urban forms of the early twenty-first century are now under construction in Asia. However, while the location, scale and character of each wave of urban development have changed through time, the fundamental processes which propel the building cycle remain broadly the same. In consequence, the lessons we have learnt from the past three centuries should still be relevant to the authors of the next volume of the narrative.

The flows of information and capital which now bind the global economy together have greatly increased its capacity for amplifying and propagating the gales of creative destruction. Instability in a single sector of one national economy can reverberate across every sector of the world economy, ensuring that we can all participate in manias, panics and crashes, wherever they originate. Because of its inherent instability, and its multiplicity of interconnections with the wider economy, there is no more effective transmission mechanism for unleashing a perfect global storm than the property cycle. At the start of the twenty-first century, this explains why the consequence of a small proportion of American households defaulting on their mortgage payments was bankruptcy and recession on a global scale. But although the property cycle is a potent source of instability, we must never forget its vital function as a driver of innovation and growth. For growth and instability are two faces of the same dynamic process, and the one is not possible without the other. Just as each boom contains the seeds of its own destruction, so each slump creates the preconditions for the next boom. Within the crucible of the worst economic crisis since the Second World War, the instruments of the next recovery are already being forged. If the price of growth is instability, then out of instability there comes growth.

Appendix A

Building Trend and Cycle Analysis

A.1 Introduction

The formal analysis of long cycles within a time series of building data requires a similar general approach to that which has been developed for studying shorter business cycles. In order to establish the 'stylized facts' about the behaviour of the series, it is desirable to separate out the secular growth trend from the cyclical fluctuations around it, either through an economic approach, in which the trend and cycles are determined by an a priori theoretical model, or through a statistical approach, in which different stochastic assumptions are applied to the components. A crucial assumption of the decomposition is that the trend is non-stationary while the cycles are stationary (i.e. they have constant mean, variance and covariance at different lags). Once the trend has been removed, the cyclical characteristics of the series can then be explored informally, by identifying peak and trough turning points, and formally, by a technique such as spectral analysis which decomposes the series into cyclical components of different frequency. For a standard overview of the techniques used to analyse time series data, see Chatfield (2004); for an empirically based treatment of trend and cycle separation which follows a broadly similar approach to that presented here, see Mills (2003).

Care should be taken not to make too rigid a distinction between trend and cycle. The longer the time series, the more likely it is that the trend itself will be variable, as structural changes resulting from forces such as technical progress alter the dynamics of long-term growth. Once the possibility of a variable trend is recognized, it becomes more difficult to separate out cyclical fluctuations from changes in the trend: a phase of accelerating or decelerating growth may be attributed to a cyclical upswing or downswing, or alternatively to a secular shift in the trend. As Stock and Watson (1988: 150) put it: '…one economist's "trend" can be another's "cycle"…' Ideally, therefore, the approach adopted to building cycle analysis should aim to separate out variable trends from cyclical fluctuations simultaneously, in a manner that is consistent with economic theory, yet at the same time assigns stochastic variation to each component in recognition of the disturbances that accompany real-world economic processes.

Owing to these uncertainties, there is no consensus in the economic literature as to the 'correct' method for detrending a time series in order to isolate its cyclical components. Rather, the choice of method is to some extent a matter of judgement, depending upon the aims of the analysis. A heuristic approach is therefore required, recognizing that '...different detrending methods are alternative windows which look at series from different perspectives' (Canova, 1998: 477). This is to accept that alternative approaches to detrending can lead to the identification of very different cycles, as has been emphasized from the early years of business cycle research (see, for example, Frickey, 1934). For the purposes of building cycle analysis, it is vital that the chosen detrending method is capable of isolating long cycles, rather than subsuming them within the trend to leave shorter business cycle fluctuations as the residual component.

Traditionally, two approaches to economic cycle analysis have been adopted. The first has been to fit a deterministic trend, usually of a linear or log-linear form that conforms to a theoretical model of economic growth, and then derive the cyclical component as fluctuations around the secular trend. However, Nelson and Kang (1981) identified the risks of identifying spurious periodicity in a series if the chosen model applied to the data fails to capture variations in the trend. Because of such critiques, the fitting of a stochastic trend has become widely favoured in empirical cycle analysis. The second traditional approach, widely used to identify long building cycles, is to smooth the economic series by some procedure such as moving averages, so as to eliminate high frequency fluctuations and isolate lower frequency cycles. Again, as Adelman (1965: 447) pointed out '...these procedures are open to the charge that...they will tend to introduce spurious cyclical fluctuations into the basic series', while Harvey (1975: 13–4) demonstrated that the smoothing procedures used by Kuznets (1930) in his pioneering work on long swings would have tended to induce a 20-year long cycle as a statistical artifact. Therefore, as far as possible, the aim of modern cycle analysis is to identify stochastic cycles in a time series without making a priori assumptions about the frequencies at which those cycles might be located.

Since the early 1980s, much attention has been paid to exploring the stationarity of economic time series and its implications for economic growth theory. A seminal paper by Nelson and Plosser (1982) distinguishes between a series that is 'trend stationary' (i.e. it consists of a deterministic growth trend around which stationary cyclical residuals fluctuate) and one that is 'difference stationary' (i.e. it consists of a stochastic process with stationary first differences that is not trend-reverting). This distinction implies a fundamental difference in the operation of the growth process. Trend stationarity means that exogenous shocks can create cyclical disturbances around the growth trend but do not permanently alter its fixed trajectory; difference stationarity means that shocks can have a cumulative and permanent effect upon the growth trend, shifting it in a stochastic fashion so that it behaves like a random walk with drift. However, to some extent, the distinction depends upon how the trend is formulated (Perron, 1989). If it is assumed that occasional exogenous shocks can create permanent shifts in the level or slope of the growth trend, as well as transitory fluctuations around it, then the series may behave in a trend stationary manner as long as the trend is allowed to vary in order to capture these permanent shifts.

To illustrate the issues that arise when identifying and analysing building cycles, an example data series is used as a test case. The chosen series is that introduced in Chapter 1 and Figure 1.1, and discussed in detail in the final section of Chapter 5, describing the trend and cycle in building activity in London during the eighteenth and nineteenth centuries. As noted in Chapter 1, the series is based on a dataset of registered deeds, relating to land and building transactions, predominantly for house-building, in the County of Middlesex, covering virtually all of London north of the River Thames, excluding the City of London itself. The full series runs from 1709 to 1914, but the period of most consistent reporting falls in the range 1714 to 1900 (Sheppard et al., 1979).

A.2 Alternative detrending procedures

A growth cycle in economic activity can be characterized in general form as a variable growth path along which are superimposed regular cyclical fluctuations, possibly of several different frequencies, plus some white noise disturbance. On this basis, an observed building time series y_t with n observations can be decomposed into a stochastic process with two unobserved components, a non-stationary growth trend g_t and a stationary cyclical component c_t, plus an independent and normally distributed irregular disturbance term ε_t (with zero mean and constant variance σ_ε^2):

$$y_t = g_t + c_t + \varepsilon_t \qquad\qquad t = 1,...,T \qquad\qquad (A.1)$$

All the variables are expressed as natural logarithms, for the convenience of expressing the decomposition as an additive linear process. This is the basic model to be fitted to the data series, in order to separate out the trend and cycle components by the application of one of a number of alternative detrending procedures.

A.2.1 Linear growth trend

The simplest a priori economic procedure for specifying the model is to assume that building activity follows an equilibrium growth path along which capital stock, including building stock, increases at a constant rate of output growth determined by the sum of the labour force growth rate and the rate of labour augmenting technical progress (see, for example, King et al., 1988a, and the cycle model developed in Appendix B). This neoclassical growth model defines a deterministic log-linear trend in building activity, driven by a constant rate of exponential growth λ from an initial fixed value g_0, such that:

$$g_t = g_0 + \lambda t \qquad\qquad (A.2)$$

The deterministic growth trend assumes that the long-run evolution of the time series is perfectly predictable and unaffected by current or past events. Under this assumption, the cyclical component c_t can be defined as a transitory stochastic process that incorporates the irregular white noise term ε_t and satisfies the conditions for stationarity.

Equation (A.1) can now be re-expressed as:

$$y_t = g_0 + \lambda t + c_t \qquad (A.3)$$

and the cyclical component estimated from the residual deviations around the fitted trend as:

$$\tilde{c}_t = y_t - (\tilde{g}_0 + \tilde{\lambda}t) \qquad (A.4)$$

where $\tilde{g}_0$ and $\tilde{\lambda}$ are the parameter estimates derived from fitting trend equation (A.3) to the data.

The following log-linear time trend is obtained by fitting equation (A.3) to the full London building series, using ordinary least square (OLS) regression with the t-statistics of the coefficients given in brackets:

Period 1714–1900 (T_0 = 187)

$$\tilde{g}_t = 6.998 + 0.0182t$$
$$(146.4) \quad (42.9)$$
$$\qquad (A.5)$$

$$\text{adjR}^2 = 0.908; \ \text{RSS} = 18.11; \ \text{SER} = 0.3129$$

On the basis of this equation, the average rate of growth in London building activity fitted as a single linear trend between 1714 and 1900 is estimated to be 1.8% per annum.

A.2.2   Linear growth trend with structural breaks

Though the full period linear growth trend appears to fit the London building data relatively well, informal observation suggests that there may have been a structural break during the 1830s, with the average growth rate following the Industrial Revolution being substantially higher than that prevailing during the eighteenth and early nineteenth centuries. For illustrative purposes, the break point has been chosen to be between 1836 and 1837, with separate linear trends fitted to the two sub-periods as follows:

Period 1714–1836 (T_1 = 123)

$$\tilde{g}_t = 7.294 + 0.0131t$$
$$(147.5) \quad (20.0)$$
$$\qquad (A.6)$$

$$\text{adjR}^2 = 0.766; \ \text{RSS} = 7.98; \ \text{SER} = 0.2567$$

Period 1837–1900 (T_2 = 64)

$$\tilde{g}_t = 5.244 + 0.0297t$$
$$(24.6) \quad (22.5)$$

(A.7)

$$adjR^2 = 0.889; \; RSS = 2.36; \; SER = 0.1950$$

These separate sub-period estimates suggest that the growth rate in London building activity averaged only 1.3% per annum during the eighteenth and early nineteenth centuries, but accelerated strongly to 3.0% per annum during the subsequent Victorian period.

There is a simple statistical test of the significance of the structural break in a growth trend which uses an F-statistic to compare the unrestricted residual sum of squares of the separate trends fitted to the two sub-periods with the restricted residual sum of squares obtained from a single trend fitted to the whole period (Chow, 1960). In order to be valid, the test requires that the error variances of the two sub-period models are equal – the homoscedasticity assumption. Applying the Chow test to the linear trend models fitted to the London building series, the derived F-statistic has a value of 68.8, compared with a 1% significance value of around 4.75, indicating that the structural break is highly significant. However, the derived F-statistic for testing the equality of the sub-period error variances has a value of 1.73, which means that the equality condition can be rejected at the 5% significance level (F-value: 1.47). Nevertheless, the presence of some heteroscedasticity in the residuals does not undermine the basic finding that there is a significant structural break in the secular growth rate.

The residual cyclical deviations derived from the fitted linear trends in London building activity are illustrated in Figure A.1. For the full period 1714–1900, two log-linear residual cycles are shown – that derived from the full period equation (A.5) and a composite of those derived from the two sub-period equations (A.6) and (A.7). Both show strong cyclical fluctuations with coincident turning points; the main difference between them derives from differential positioning around their respective linear trends, which imparts greater volatility to the cycles derived from the full period trend.

A.2.3 Polynomial growth trend

With any long time series such as the London building series, there are likely to be variations in the trend growth rate. However, imposition of one or more structural breaks in the trend requires subjective judgement as to their position that can only be tested by trial and error; furthermore, the imposition of sudden breaks may be an artificial and misleading device to capture what in reality are more gradual changes in the slope of the trend (see Section A.2.7). An alternative approach is to fit a deterministic polynomial trend to the log transformed series, which allows for smooth variation in the trend growth rate. Such trends can also be segmented, by allowing for break points that can be determined by best fit estimation rather than a priori choice – see, for example, Mills and Crafts (1996), who fit a segmented quadratic trend with three break points to the growth in British industrial production between 1700 and 1913.

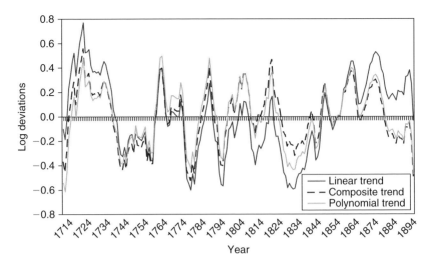

Figure A.1 Deviations in London building around deterministic trends.
Source: Sheppard et al. (1979).

The general formulation of a polynomial growth trend of order p is:

$$g_t = g_0 + \sum_1^p \lambda_j t^j \qquad j = 1,...p. \tag{A.8}$$

For the London building series, it was found that a second-order polynomial captures the increase in trend growth rate during the nineteenth century as well as any higher level polynomial. When fitted to the full period 1714–1900, the estimated quadratic trend equation is:

$$\tilde{g}_t = 7.527 + 0.00296t + 0.000077t^2$$
$$\quad (127.3) \quad (2.16) \qquad (11.4)$$

$$\tag{A.9}$$

$$T = 187; \text{ adjR}^2 = 0.946; \text{ RSS} = 10.61; \text{ SER} = 0.2401$$

The residual cycle derived from this polynomial trend is also shown in Figure A.1. It closely tracks the cycle derived from the composite linear trend, apart from the period during the 1830s and 1840s when the structural break occurs in the linear trend.

A.2.4 First-order differencing

So far, we have followed the traditional view that the secular component of the building time series can be described as a broadly stable deterministic trend, around which transitory and trend-reverting cyclical fluctuations oscillate. However, following the study by Nelson and Plosser (1982), it has become common practice to represent the non-stationary trend in an economic time series as a stochastic process, allowing the impact of random disturbances to have a cumulative and permanent effect on the system as the time horizon increases. For this assumption to hold, the first differences of the series must be stationary, so that it behaves as a random walk; such series are described as integrated of order one and denoted as I(1). Empirical support for this model of time series behaviour has come from a variety of studies which appear to suggest that many economic time series behave like random walks, or at least approximate to them.

A trended I(1) model can be defined by first differencing the log transformed series and introducing a drift term equivalent to the constant average rate of growth of building activity λ:

$$y_t = y_{t-1} + \lambda + c_t \tag{A.10}$$

with the cycle component c_t again defined as a stationary stochastic process incorporating the irregular white noise term ε_t. The stochastic trend can be isolated as:

$$g_t = y_{t-1} + \lambda \tag{A.11}$$

and an estimate of the cycle component obtained from:

$$\tilde{c}_t = (y_t - y_{t-1}) - \tilde{\lambda}, \tag{A.12}$$

where the first difference of the log transformed series is equivalent to the actual rate of growth in building activity over time period t, with an estimated trend value of $\tilde{\lambda}$.

When the cyclical component c_t reduces to the irregular white noise disturbance term ε_t, equation (A.10) reduces to a basic *random walk with drift*:

$$y_t = y_{t-1} + \lambda + \varepsilon_t \tag{A.13}$$

This stochastic first difference model can be compared with the deterministic trend model by accumulating the first differences over time from an initial value y_0 as:

$$y_t = y_0 + \lambda t + \sum_1^t c_k \tag{A.14}$$

A comparison with deterministic equation (A.3) shows that while both models are linear functions of time, there are two crucial differences between them (Nelson and Plosser, 1982: 142):

• The intercept g_0 in the deterministic model is a fixed parameter, whereas intercept y_0 in the stochastic model is a function of previous events.
• The deviations from trend in the deterministic model are by definition stationary, whereas in the stochastic model they are accumulations of stationary changes with a variance that increases as t increases.

The second of these points offers an empirical basis for testing which is the more appropriate detrending model to adopt. If the residuals derived from fitting a deterministic trend are shown to be stationary, then this can be accepted as the appropriate detrending procedure and the process is identified as *trend stationary*. If the trend residuals are not stationary, but the first differences of the original series are, then a stochastic trend is to be preferred and the process is identified as *difference stationary*.

By representing the stochastic trend in its simplest first difference form, much of the volatility of a time series may be captured by the trend. There are two problems with this outcome:

• It runs counter to the theoretical concept of a secular trend for it to exhibit rapid fluctuations; rather the trend may be expected to change slowly and relatively smoothly, as a result of changing economic fundamentals.
• Long cycles may be absorbed into the trend, leaving the detrended residual to capture only high frequency fluctuations.

The shortcomings of the difference stationary representation can be observed in Figure A.2, which plots the residual component derived by first differencing the London building series according to equation (A.12), adjusting the differences by an estimated drift term λ of 0.0184, equivalent to the average trend rate of growth in building activity of 1.8% per annum over the whole period. Compared to the cyclical residuals derived from the deterministic linear and polynomial trends, as illustrated in Figure A.1, the residual deviations from the stochastic first difference trend appear both smaller in magnitude and apparently dominated by higher frequencies, showing less evidence of the long building cycles that show up clearly in the residuals derived from the deterministic trends. The stationarity of these alternative sets of residuals, and therefore the applicability of the alternative models for detrending the building series, is examined in Section A.3.

A.2.5   ARIMA models

The first difference model defined by equations (A.10) and (A.13) is the most basic form of stochastic process which can be specified for detrending an economic series. More generally, the series can be defined as an autoregressive integrated moving average (ARIMA) process, in which a lagged polynomial function of the differenced series is expressed as lagged polynomial function of the white noise disturbance term (for a detailed treatment of such models see, for example, Chatfield, 2004, chapters 3 and 4).

Following Beveridge and Nelson (1981), a non-stationary time series y_t can be defined as an ARIMA process of order (p,d,q) in the form:

$$w_t = \lambda + \Psi(L)\varepsilon_t \qquad (A.15)$$

where

$$\Psi(L) = \Theta(L)/\Phi(L) \qquad (A.16)$$

Here $w_t = \Delta^d y_t$ is the dth order difference applied to render the original series stationary, λ is the expected value of w_t equivalent to its long-run mean, $\Phi(L) = (1 - \Sigma_1^p \varphi_m L^m)$ is a pth order polynomial in the lag operator L defining an autoregressive process on past values of the differenced variable, and $\Theta(L) = (1 + \Sigma_1^q \theta_n L^n)$ is a qth order polynomial defining a moving average process in the white noise disturbance term. It is usually assumed that the first differences of the series are stationary, i.e. the series is I(1); the basic random walk with drift model defined by equation (A.13) is thus equivalent to a reduced ARIMA(0,1,0) version of the general form.

Beveridge and Nelson (1981) show that the trend component in this ARIMA formulation reduces to:

$$g_t = g_{t-1} + \lambda + \left(\sum_0^\infty \psi_i\right)\varepsilon_t \qquad \psi_0 \equiv 1 \qquad (A.17)$$

where the parameters ψ_i are the coefficients of polynomial $\Psi(L)$. This trend is equivalent to a random walk with the same rate of drift λ as the observed series, but a noise term having a larger or smaller variance than the original series depending on the signs and values of the ψ_i parameters; typically, the variance of the trend noise term is larger. The stationary cyclical component can also be expressed as function of the disturbance term:

$$c_t = \Psi^\star(L)\varepsilon_t \qquad (A.18)$$

where the coefficients $\psi_i^\star$ of lag polynomial $\Psi^\star(L)$ are functions of the parameters ψ_i from the original difference equation polynomial. Estimates of the trend and cycle are derived by fitting equation (A.15) to the data to obtain estimates of the difference variable $\tilde{w}_t$, then creating one-step-ahead forecasts on y_{t-1} using $\tilde{w}_t$ to obtain estimated trend $\tilde{g}_t$, while deriving the estimated cyclical component $\tilde{c}_t$ from the gap between the observed and fitted differences w_t and $\tilde{w}_t$.

There are two often-voiced criticisms of ARIMA models (Canova, 1998: 481). The first is that they are better at capturing the short-run behaviour of a time series than its long-run properties; the second is that several alternative specifications may fit a data series reasonably well, yet produce significantly different decompositions into trend and cycle components. Harvey and Jaeger (1993: 242) go further, arguing that a parsimonious ARIMA model may be perfectly adequate for short-term forecasting, but 'as a descriptive device it may have little meaning and may even be misleading' when applied to series exhibiting slow long-term change. For an example exercise in which alternative ARIMA models are estimated to isolate the trend and cycle in long-run economic data, see Newbold and Agiakloglou (1991).

To explore the suitability of the technique for isolating building cycles, alternative ARIMA models have been tested on the logged London building series, under the assumption that its first differences $w_t = y_t - y_{t-1}$ are stationary (see Section A.3). These models thus incorporate alternative stochastic assumptions about the variability of the year-on-year growth rate in building activity.

OLS estimation shows there to be an autoregressive relationship in w_t which is significant in the first, but not in higher, orders:

$$\tilde{w}_t = 0.0118 + 0.338\, w_{t-1}$$
$$\quad\;\; (1.58) \qquad (4.75)$$

$$\text{(A.19)}$$

$$T = 186;\; \text{adjR}^2 = 0.104;\; \text{RSS} = 1.847;\; \text{SER} = 0.1002$$

In this ARIMA(1,1,0) model, the expected full period growth rate in building activity of 1.8% is split between the constant drift term of $\lambda = 0.0118$ and the coefficient of 0.338 on the lagged first difference term, whereas in the most basic first difference model examined in Section A.2.4, the whole of the expected growth rate is captured by the drift term.

An alternative moving average formulation of the example building series is significant up to order two, with maximum likelihood estimation producing the ARIMA(0,1,2) model:

$$\tilde{w}_t = 0.0175 + 0.321\varepsilon_{t-1} + 0.173\varepsilon_{t-2}$$
$$\quad\;\; (1.62) \qquad (4.46) \qquad (2.28)$$

$$\text{(A.20)}$$

$$T = 187;\; \text{adjR}^2 = 0.106;\; \text{RSS} = 1.836;\; \text{SER} = 0.0999$$

Estimation of a combined autoregressive moving average model in the building first differences does not produce a significant moving average error term when the first-order autoregressive term is present.

The trends and residual deviations produced by these alternative models differ little from each other, which is a reflection of the invertibility of autoregressive and moving average models, whereby one can be expressed as the inverse of the other under certain conditions (Chatfield, 2004: 39–40). Furthermore, their detrended residuals seem to differ relatively little from those derived from the simple first difference model explored in the previous section (see Figure A.2). As an approach to detrending, the same observations therefore apply to ARIMA modelling as to basic first differencing – it tends to absorb most of the building cycle fluctuation into the stochastic trend, leaving predominantly high frequency fluctuations to be captured by the residual.

A.2.6   *Moving average filters*

There is a long-established tradition of using moving averages as a linear filter for smoothing and detrending non-stationary economic time series (Osborn, 1995). Assume that the original series y_t is smoothed by a two-sided set of symmetric weights a_k such that $a_k = a_{-k}$, $k = 1,\ldots,K$. Then trend g_t can be defined as:

$$g_t = \sum_{-K}^{K} a_k y_{t-k} = a(L)y_t \tag{A.21}$$

where L is the lag operator. The residual cyclical component is then derived as:

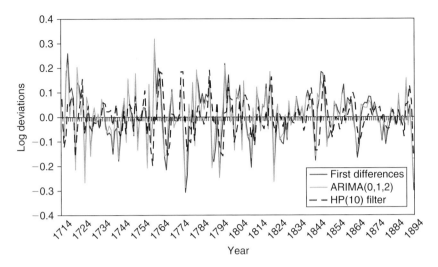

Figure A.2   Deviations in London building around stochastic trends.
Source: Sheppard et al. (1979).

$$c_t = y_t - g_t = d(L)y_t \qquad\qquad (A.22)$$

where $d(L) = [1 - a(L)]$ is the detrending filter.

The weights polynomial $a(L)$ can be defined in such a way that its coefficients sum to unity, i.e. $\Sigma_{-K}^{K}a_k = 1$, so that for a simple moving average filter with equal weights, $a_k = 1/(2K + 1)$, $k = 0, \pm 1, ..., \pm K$. Under these conditions, the coefficients of the detrending filter $d(L)$ sum to zero, in which case it can be shown that $d(L)$ can be factored into the expression $d(L) = (1 - L)(1 - L^{-1})d^*(L)$, where $d^*(L)$ is a symmetric moving average with $K - 1$ leads and lags (Baxter and King, 1999: 592). What this means is that a symmetric moving average detrending filter $d(L)$, with weights that sum to zero, contains both a backward and forward differencing term which can render stationary a series that is not only I(1) but also I(2), that is it is stationary in its second rather than first differences.

It has already been pointed out that moving average filters can create cycles as a statistical artifact (Harvey, 1975: 13–4). This is because they alter the relative importance of the periodic components in a series when it is analysed in the frequency rather than the time domain. The process by which a detrended series in the time domain can be transformed into cyclical components of different periodicity in the frequency domain will be discussed in Section A.4.1. Here it is sufficient to note that the use of moving average filters for trend and cycle estimation has been expanded to allow for the elimination of some frequency components and the enhancement of others (Baxter and King, 1999; Gomez, 2001; Christiano and Fitzgerald, 2003). Thus, *low-pass filters* eliminate components with frequencies above a certain threshold, typically retaining only the low frequency components that make up the variable trend in a series, while *high-pass filters* have the reverse effect, cutting out low frequency fluctuations. Combining the two, *band-pass filters* retain only those components with periodic frequencies lying within a preset range – for example those that encompass short business cycles or alternatively those that contain longer building cycles. The problem of a priori assumption remains, however, in that the choice of bandwidth for the filter will tend to determine the cycle frequencies which are identified.

One type of filter that has been widely used to separate out trend from cycle components in economic time series is the curve fitting procedure promoted by Hodrick and Prescott (1997). Drawing upon economic growth theory, the procedure is designed to identify a stochastic trend that varies 'smoothly' over time, in contrast to the ARIMA modelling approach that absorbs a considerable amount of fluctuation into the trend. The derivation of a smooth trend is achieved by minimizing the combined variability of both the trend g_t and cycle component c_t of equation (A.1) according to the expression:

$$\text{Min} \left\{ \sum_1^T c_t^2 + \kappa \sum_1^T [(g_{t+1} - g_t) - (g_t - g_{t-1})]^2 \right\} \tag{A.23}$$

where the first term captures the variability of the cyclical component and the second captures the smoothness of the growth trend as measured by its second differences. The smoothing parameter κ penalizes the variability of the growth trend: the larger the value of κ, the more the minimization is dominated by the trend component, and therefore the smoother the fitted trend. At the limit, as κ tends towards infinity, the fitted growth path tends towards a linear trend.

It can be shown (Harvey and Jaeger, 1993: 233) that the solution to this minimization problem is a linear filter which transforms the original series y_t into trend and cycle components g_t and c_t according to the expressions:

$$g_t = y_t/(1 + \Omega) \tag{A.24a}$$

$$c_t = \Omega y_t/(1 + \Omega) \tag{A.24b}$$

where $\Omega = \kappa(1 - L)^2(1 - L^{-1})^2$ is a function of the lag operator L. The minimization is performed using a smoothing algorithm known as the Kalman filter, a recursive procedure for computing the optimal estimator of a function at each point in time t, based on the observations up to and including y_t (Harvey, 1989). For an assessment of the properties of the Hodrick–Prescott (HP) filter, see King and Rebelo (1993) and Cogley and Nason (1995b), who demonstrate that the filter can act to amplify cyclical components at chosen frequencies while removing others outside the desired range. For applications of the HP filter to the analysis of business cycles, see Backus and Kehoe (1992) and Blackburn and Ravn (1992); for an application to the identification of real estate cycles, see Witkiewicz (2002).

With this method it is clear that the choice of value for the smoothing parameter will affect how much of the variability of a time series is captured by the trend and how much by the cyclical component. The lower the value of κ, the more volatile and less smooth the fitted trend, and the more it resembles the stochastic trend defined by a random walk with drift. Conversely, a high value of κ produces a smoother, less volatile trend that more closely resembles a deterministic polynomial function. Hodrick and Prescott (1997: 4) use a probability model to suggest that the appropriate value of κ should be determined by the variances of the cyclical component σ_c^2 and trend second differences σ_g^2, such that $\kappa = \sigma_c^2/\sigma_g^2$. On this basis, they estimate a representative value of $\kappa = 1{,}600$ for use with quarterly data, while a value of $\kappa = 100$ has been suggested for use with annual data (Backus and Kehoe, 1992: 886).

To demonstrate how the value of the smoothing parameter affects the shape of the fitted trend, the London building series has been run through the HP filter

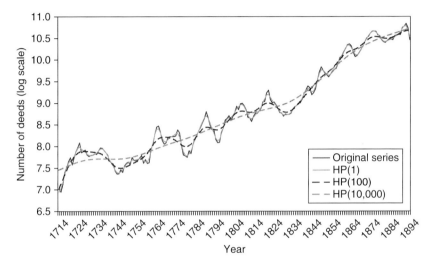

Figure A.3 Fitted trends in London building using HP filter.
Source: Sheppard et al. (1979).

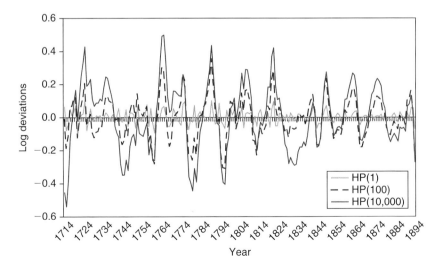

Figure A.4 Residual deviations in London building using HP filter.
Source: Sheppard et al. (1979).

with values of κ varying from extremes of 1 to 10,000 (Figures A.3 and A.4). At low values of the smoothing parameter, in the range 1–10, the fitted curve closely follows the original series, incorporating the long building cycle into the trend and leaving short frequency, low amplitude fluctuations to be captured by the residual deviations. For comparison, with the parameter set to 10, the HP residuals resemble the short cycle fluctuations produced by the first difference and ARIMA trends, as can be seen in Figure A.2. At the other extreme, high values of the smoothing parameter, in the range 1,000–10,000, produce a much slower changing trend and higher amplitude, longer frequency fluctuations in the residuals, more closely resembling the pronounced building cycles derived from the deterministic linear and polynomial trends illustrated in Figure A.1.

It is also worth noting that the trends and cycles in London building activity derived using the HP filter with different values of the smoothing parameter can be approximated reasonably closely by applying simple moving averages with different lag lengths, as defined in equations (A.21) and (A.22). Thus, for example, the HP(10) trend and cycle can be approximated by a 2 lag (5 period) moving average applied to the original series, while the HP(1,000) components can be approximated using a 7 lag (15 period) filter.

A.2.7 Structural time series models

On a recurrent theme, Harvey and Jaeger (1993: 231) argue that the use of 'mechanical' detrending procedures such as the HP filter to isolate the cyclical component '...can easily give a spurious impression of cyclical behaviour', depending on the choice of smoothing parameter. They suggest a more general approach, based on the specification of a structural time series model, which makes use of the stochastic properties of the data by fitting a separate trend and cycle simultaneously and apportioning series volatility between the two unobserved components. By defining an explicit stochastic cycle, as well as a stochastic trend, this approach introduces another layer into the analysis which is particularly useful for separating out long building cycles from shorter term disturbances around the fitted trend.

To the basic structural model for y_t given by equation (A.1) they add two equations defining a generalized linear trend as an ARIMA(0,2,1) process, with both *stochastic level and slope*:

$$g_t = g_{t-1} + \lambda_{t-1} + \eta_t \tag{A.25}$$

$$\lambda_t = \lambda_{t-1} + \xi_t \tag{A.26}$$

where λ_t is the variable slope of the trend and η_t and ξ_t are normally distributed white noise disturbances, with zero mean and variances σ_η^2 and σ_ξ^2, that are uncorrelated with each other and with the irregular component ε_t in equation (A.1). The effect of η_t is to allow the level of the trend to shift up and down, while ξ_t allows the slope to change; their combined effect is to define a process that is integrated of order two, that is, it is stationary in its second differences.

Alongside the stochastic trend, a *stochastic cycle* is generated recursively from wave equations that incorporate a damping factor and disturbances:

$$c_t = \mu \cos \omega \, c_{t-1} + \mu \sin \omega \, c_{t-1}^{\cdot} + \chi_t \qquad \text{(A.27a)}$$

$$c_t^{\cdot} = -\mu \sin \omega \, c_{t-1} + \mu \cos \omega \, c_{t-1}^{\cdot} + \chi_t^{\cdot} \qquad \text{(A.27b)}$$

where μ is the damping factor such that $0 \leqslant \mu \leqslant 1$; ω is the frequency of the cycle lying within the range $0 \leqslant \omega \leqslant \pi$, such that its period is $2\pi/\omega$; χ_t and $\chi_t^{\cdot}$ are normally distributed white noise disturbances with common variance σ_χ^2 that are uncorrelated with each other and with the other disturbances in the model. The variance of the stochastic cycle σ_c^2 is a measure of its regularity, and is related to the variance of the disturbance terms σ_χ^2 by the expression $\sigma_c^2 = \sigma_\chi^2/(1 - \mu^2)$. The cyclical component can be shown to be stationary if $\mu < 1$, and equivalent to an autoregressive moving average process of order ARMA (2,1), in which both the AR and MA parts are subject to restrictions – see Harvey (1985: 219).

Following Harvey and Trimbur (2003), the first-order cycle defined by equations (A.27) can be generalized to specify higher order, smoother cycles in the recursive form:

$$c_t^r = \mu \cos \omega \, c_{t-1}^r + \mu \sin \omega \, c_{t-1}^{r\cdot} + c_t^{r-1} \qquad \text{(A.28a)}$$

$$c_t^{r\cdot} = -\mu \sin \omega \, c_{t-1}^r + \mu \cos \omega \, c_{t-1}^{r\cdot} + c_t^{r-1\cdot} \qquad \text{(A.28b)}$$

where r is the order of the cycle, and $c_t^0 = \chi_t$ and $c_t^{0\star} = \chi_t^{\cdot}$ are the white noise disturbance terms defined in equations (A.27). With this formulation, the disturbances to second and higher order cycles are themselves cyclical; the higher the order r, the smoother the cycle. Typically, the smoothing of the cycle leads to an increase in the variance captured by the irregular component.

The model parameters to be estimated are the four disturbance variances (trend level, slope, cycle and irregular) plus the cycle frequency and damping factor. Parameter values are derived by maximum likelihood estimation and employed to derive optimal estimates of the trend, cycle and irregular components via the recursive Kalman filter smoothing process. At each point in time t, the smoothed component estimates are derived as weighted linear functions of the original observed series, with observations in the vicinity of t having more weight than those further away (see Harvey, 1989 and Durbin and Koopman, 2001 for detailed explanations of the methodology).

For recent reviews of the theory and practice of structural or unobserved components modelling, see Harvey et al. (2004) and Harvey and Proietti (2005). Instructive examples of the use of the methodology for economic analysis include Crafts et al. (1989), who investigate variations in the trend rate of industrial growth in Britain between 1700 and 1913; Ball et al. (1996), who isolate building cycles in eight OECD economies since the mid-nineteenth century; Solomou (1998), who searches for business cycles in four national GDP series between 1870 and 1913; and Scott and Judge (2000), who examine the cycle in British commercial property values between 1956 and 1996 under the assumption of a deterministic level trend subject to step changes and impulse shocks.

The generality of the structural modelling approach lays it open to the criticism of Newbold and Agiakloglou (1991: 342), who point out that 'an attempt is being made to disentangle *four* white noise series that jointly generate a *single* time series'. Furthermore, an empirical investigation of the use of structural modelling by Ball and Wood (1996b) highlights how different restrictions on the stochastic variability of the model can lead to the identification of very different trend and cycle components. In other words, the observer can still influence the results obtained. However, this can also be seen as a key attraction of the technique: it provides a general stochastic modelling framework for testing alternative assumptions about the unobserved components.

By imposing selected restrictions on the stochastic trend and cycle, the model reduces to one or other of the simpler specifications already considered in previous sections:

- If $\sigma_\eta^2 = \sigma_\xi^2 = 0$, but $\sigma_\varepsilon^2 > 0$, then the model is restricted to a *deterministic linear trend* with constant growth rate, as already introduced in equation (A.2), with all the white noise disturbance left to be captured by the irregular residual in the components equation.
- If $\sigma_\xi^2 = \sigma_\varepsilon^2 = 0$, but $\sigma_\eta^2 > 0$, the trend level varies stochastically but the growth rate λ becomes a constant, producing a trend model equivalent to the *random walk with drift* defined in equation (A.17). Following the ARIMA example, this suggests that the trend level may absorb much of the long cycle volatility of the time series, leaving the residual component to reflect shorter run disturbances around the trend. However, when this restricted form of the unobserved components model is compared with equivalent ARIMA models, its short-run behaviour is similar but its long-run properties may be quite different, producing very different estimates of the trend and cycle components (Watson, 1986).
- If $\sigma_\eta^2 = 0$ but $\sigma_\xi^2 > 0$ and $\sigma_\varepsilon^2 > 0$, the trend is constrained to have a constant level but stochastic slope. This produces a theoretically attractive *smooth trend* with variable growth rate, still integrated of order two, leaving most of the long cycle volatility of the time series to be picked up by the stochastic cyclical component. Harvey and Jaeger (1993: 233) demonstrate that this version of the model reduces to the *HP filter* defined by equations (A.24) under the further restrictions that the cyclical and irregular components are combined into a single residual around the trend, and that the ratio of the white noise variances $\sigma_\varepsilon^2/\sigma_\xi^2$ is fixed in the value of the smoothing parameter κ.
- If the damping factor $\mu = 1$, then cycle disturbance variance $\sigma_\chi^2 = 0$ and the stochastic cycle reduces to a *deterministic wave equation* of order AR(2) (see Harvey, 2004, who proposes tests to distinguish the presence of stochastic, as distinct from deterministic cycles in a data series). More generally, as $\mu \to 1$, then a stochastic cycle will approach a deterministic wave form, exhibiting an increasingly regular period and amplitude (see Appendix B for the solution of a model of the building cycle which generates a deterministic second-order autoregressive wave equation).

A customized software package named STAMP is available for fitting structural time series models of the type outlined above, incorporating up to three separate stochastic cycles of differing frequency (Koopman et al., 2006). Four alternative model specifications were tested using the example London building series over the full period 1714–1900, producing the estimation results shown in Tables A.1 and A.2. The significance of the identified cyclical components in the different models is examined using the likelihood ratio test (Maddala, 2001: 118).

Table A.1 Diagnostic results for alternative structural models of London building (1714–1900).

	Model 1	Model 2	Model 3	Model 4	5% value
Number of parameters	3	6	6	9	
Number of restrictions	1	1	1	1	
Disturbance variances ($\times 10^{-3}$)					
Level (σ_η^2)	0.000	0.000	0.000	0.000	
Slope (σ_ξ^2)	6.431	0.105	0.001	0.001	
Cycle 1 ($\sigma_{\chi_1}^2$)		5.876	6.044	4.318	
Cycle 2 ($\sigma_{\chi_2}^2$)				0.512	
Irregular (σ_ε^2)	1.454	0.000	0.874	0.982	
Log-likelihood	402.56	424.37	427.74	427.81	
Likelihood ratio[a]		43.62	50.36	6.88/0.14	7.81
Goodness of fit [b]	−0.1354	0.1143	0.1592	0.1599	
Standard error	0.1128	0.0997	0.0971	0.0970	
Normality[c]	3.97	5.23	5.13	5.35	5.99
Heteroscedasticity[d]	0.460	0.466	0.505	0.498	0.654
Durbin–Watson[e]	1.941	1.849	1.924	1.926	1.78
Box–Ljung statistic[e]	20.09	10.20	8.94	10.48	21.03

Notes:

See also Koopman et al. (2006).

[a] Likelihood ratio statistics compare Models 2 and 3 to Model 1 (restriction of having no cycle) and Model 4 to Models 2 and 3 (restriction of having one rather than two cycles) against the chi-square value with 3 degrees of freedom.

[b] Goodness of fit statistic R_d^2 with respect to first differences can be interpreted as the proportionate improvement in fit over a random walk with drift model.

[c] Normality test is the Bowman–Shenton statistic for the normality of model residuals based on their sample skewness and kurtosis, and has a chi-square distribution with 2 degrees of freedom.

[d] Heteroscedasticity test statistic compares the ratio of the squares of the last h residuals to the squares of the first h residuals, and has a (reciprocal) F distribution with (h, h) degrees of freedom (for this series h = 61).

[e] Serial correlation in the residuals is measured by the classical Durbin–Watson statistic, and also by the Box–Ljung portmanteau statistic Q(p,q), based on the first p autocorrelations and having a chi-square distribution with q degrees of freedom; for this series q = 12.

Table A.2 Parameters of stochastic cycles from alternative structural models of London building (1714–1900).

Cycle type	Period (years)[a]	Damping factor	Amplitude[b]	Variance[c]
Model 2				
Long cycle	15.9	0.904	0.280	0.0321
Model 3				
Long wave	45.1	0.705	0.306	0.0120
Model 4				
Long wave	40.6	0.735	0.299	0.0094
Major cycle	8.0	0.864	0.042	0.0020

Notes:

See also Koopman et al. (2006: 154–7).

[a] Cycle period $= 2\pi/\omega$.

[b] Cycle amplitude $= (c_T^2 + c_T^{*2})^{1/2}$ where c_T and c_T^* are the final state estimates of the cycle component derived by the Kalman filter with T observations.

[c] Cycle variance $\sigma_c^2 = \sigma_\chi^2/(1 - \mu^2)$.

Model 1: Fixed level, stochastic slope, no cycle
This model has just two estimated parameters – the variances of the slope and irregular disturbances – since the trend level is fixed. There being no explicit cycle component, the fitted trend closely follows the original series, with the stochastic slope subsuming most of the long cycle volatility, leaving only short-run noise to be picked up by the irregular component. With this specification, the structural model behaves rather like the HP filter when its smoothing parameter is set to low values (see Section A.2.6). A comparison of this model with Model 2, incorporating a cycle component, produces a likelihood ratio statistic of 43.6, which compares with a 5% critical value of 7.8 and a 1% value of 11.3. In other words, the restriction of there being no cycle component can be firmly rejected at the 1% level (Table A.1).

Model 2: Fixed level, stochastic slope, 1 stochastic cycle (order = 1)
This model has five estimated parameters, with three cycle parameters in addition to the two Model 1 parameters. Whatever the starting value for the first-order stochastic cycle period, the resultant iterations are very strongly convergent, generating a long building cycle of period 15.9 years around a smoothly varying trend, with the irregular disturbance absorbed into the cycle component (Figure A.5). The variance of the slope disturbance is much reduced compared to Model 1, being mostly captured by the cycle disturbance. The estimated cycle damping factor of 0.904 suggests that the cycle, while not deterministic, has considerable regularity.

The model residuals satisfy the normality and serial correlation tests at the 5% level of significance; however, they do exhibit significant heteroscedasticity, reflecting a decrease in their variance over time which suggests that the log transformation of the building series may be over-compensating for the increasing variance

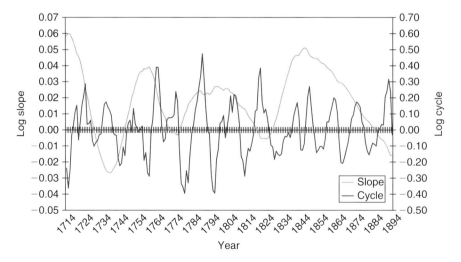

Figure A.5 Stochastic cycle and trend slope in London building from structural model.
Source: Sheppard et al. (1979).

of the original series (Table A.1). When the model is separately applied to the two sub-periods 1714–1800 and 1800–1900, the stochastic trend and cycle fitted to each sub-period closely match the corresponding portions of the full period components. The two sub-period models produce similar estimates for the duration of the long cycle, at 15.8 years and 15.4 years respectively, and the residual diagnostics are similar; the one difference between the sub-periods is that the heteroscedasticity problem is confined to the nineteenth century model.

As illustrated in Figure A.6, the stochastic building cycle derived from this one cycle structural model is comparable to the cyclical residuals produced by the deterministic polynomial trend (Section A.2.3) and the stochastic HP filter with high values of the smoothing parameter (Section A.2.6). In particular, the structural model cycle tracks very closely that produced by the HP(1000) filter, because the cyclical and irregular components in the structural model have been compressed into one, as is assumed a priori in the HP model. From observation, the cycles generated by all three detrending methods have very similar peak and trough turning points, as discussed below in Section A.5.

Model 3: Fixed level, stochastic slope, 1 stochastic cycle (order = 2)
The slope of the fitted trend in Model 2 itself shows clear cyclical variation (see Figure A.5). The trend rate of growth in building activity completes three and a half cycles, with an average period of close to 50 years during the 187 years of the series, passing through four peaks averaging +4.4% per annum, and four troughs averaging −1.3% per annum. An alternative one cycle model, of order 2 rather than 1, absorbs this cyclical variation in the trend into a long wave with an average period of 45.1 years, subsuming the long cycle within the upswings and downswings of the long wave. Owing to the smoothing of the cycle component,

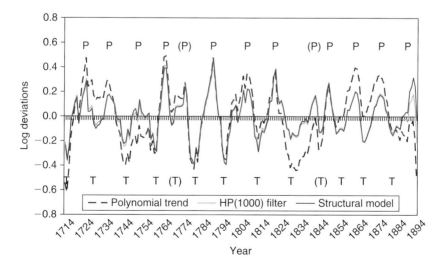

Figure A.6   Cycles in London building obtained by alternative detrending methods.
Source: Sheppard et al. (1979).

the irregular component reappears. The slope of the trend is no longer cyclical, but rather exhibits a slow secular rise from an average growth rate of around +1.2% per annum before 1750 up to around +2.4% per annum after 1850. Compared to Model 2, this model has a slightly improved goodness of fit, its residuals perform similarly and the log-likelihood test again confirms that the restriction of there being no cycle component can be rejected at the 1% level (Table A.1).

Model 4: Fixed level, stochastic slope, 2 stochastic cycles (orders = 1/2)
The introduction of second stochastic cycle into Model 3 generates a smaller amplitude major cycle, with a period of 8.0 years, in addition to the dominant long wave (Table A.2). The major cycle smoothes out some of the irregularities in the long wave – the value of its damping factor increases, its variance and amplitude decrease slightly and its period decreases to 40.6 years, while the slope of the trend remains unchanged. However, the major cycle is relatively weak; the likelihood ratio test between Models 2 and 4 shows that the restriction of there being no second cycle can only be rejected at the 10% level, while the same test between Models 3 and 4 indicates that the second cycle is not significant even at the 10% level (Table A.1).

A.3   Stationarity tests

The detrending procedures tested in the previous section can be divided into two groups:

- *Smooth trends* – linear growth trend; polynomial trend; HP filter with high values of the smoothing parameter; structural model trend with fixed level and variable slope.
- *Fluctuating trends* – first differencing; ARIMA models; HP filter with low values of the smoothing parameter.

What has been observed about these two types of detrending procedures is that the pronounced long cycle in the London building series is left to be captured as deviations around the smooth trends, but in contrast is largely absorbed into the fluctuating trends, leaving predominantly shorter run disturbances to be picked up by their residuals (Canova, 1998: 488–90, reports similar comparative results). In other words, different detrending methods isolate cycles of different frequency and amplitude, with the cycles derived from the smooth trends not only having longer periods but also larger amplitudes than those derived from the fluctuating trends, as measured by their standard deviations (Figure A.7).

For the purposes of building cycle identification, it is therefore clearly preferable to fit a smooth rather than fluctuating trend; the question is whether the cyclical fluctuations so identified satisfy the stationarity condition imposed upon the cyclical component of the model. Put another way: can the building series be classified as trend or difference stationary? To explore whether the stationarity condition is satisfied, two commonly used techniques have been applied: autocorrelation functions and unit root tests (see, for example, Pindyck and Rubinfeld, 1998, chapter 16).

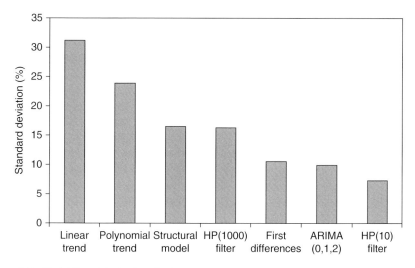

Figure A.7   Variability of derived cyclical residuals in London building activity.
Source: Sheppard et al. (1979).

A.3.1   Autocorrelation functions

The stationarity of a detrended series c_t can be assessed informally from its sample autocorrelation coefficients, expressing the degree of correlation between pairs of observations at different lags k. Stationary series tend to fluctuate frequently around their mean, whereas non-stationary series are relatively smooth and slow-changing. Consequently, series c_t is likely to be stationary if the *correlogram* plot of the estimated sample autocorrelation coefficients drops quickly from one towards zero as the length of the observation lag increases, whereas if it does not decline rapidly, the series is likely to be non-stationary. Furthermore, any regular and strong cyclical component in the detrended series should show up as a peak in the correlogram, the lag at which the peak occurs indicating the period of that cyclical component.

Figure A.8 plots the autocorrelation functions of the cyclical components derived from the four smooth trends that have been fitted to the log transformed London building series over the period 1714–1900, while Figure A.9 plots the correlograms of the residuals derived from the three fluctuating trends that have been fitted. The key points to note from these plots are as follows.

Cycles around smooth trends
- The autocorrelation function of the detrended cycle derived from the simple linear growth trend shown in Figure A.8 declines only slowly; it reaches zero for the first time at lag 22. This suggests that the residual series is not linear trend stationary, because of the structural breaks in the trend that were identified in Section A.2.2.
- The correlogram of the residuals derived from the polynomial trend reaches zero by lag 7, indicating that a deterministic trend with variable slope is an improvement on the linear trend, because it can capture structural changes in the trend rate of growth.

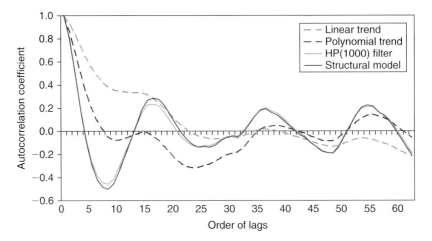

Figure A.8   Autocorrelation functions for cycles around smooth trends in London building.
Source: Sheppard et al. (1979).

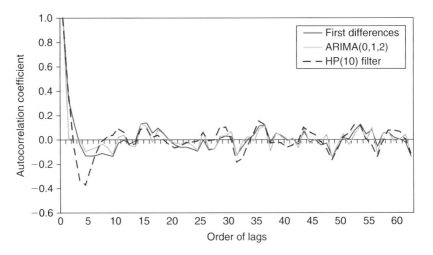

Figure A.9   Autocorrelation functions for residuals around fluctuating trends in London building.
Source: Sheppard et al. (1979).

- The correlograms of the stochastic cycles produced by the HP(1000) filter and the structural model (Model 2) track each other closely, and both decline faster than that of the polynomial function, reaching zero by lag 4. This suggests that these smooth stochastic trends are better able to produce stationary cyclical residuals than a deterministic polynomial trend.
- All the correlograms in Figure A.8, but particularly those derived from the smooth stochastic trends, show clear evidence of a regular cycle with a period in the range 15–17 years which reappears at harmonic multiples of that period (35–37 years and 53–55 years). This is consistent with the period of the stochastic long cycle estimated using the structural model (see Table A.2).

Deviations around fluctuating trends

- The autocorrelation functions of the residuals derived from all three fluctuating trends shown in Figure A.9 cut off very rapidly, within two to three lags. However, they show much less clear-cut evidence of cyclical components at any frequency compared to the correlograms derived from the smooth trends.
- The first difference correlogram reaches zero by lag 3, whereas the ARIMA(0,1,2) correlogram reaches zero by lag 1. This suggests that the original building series is not strictly difference stationary as defined by Nelson and Plosser (1982: 147) in terms of a model having a first differences correlogram that is close to zero after lag 1. The observed pattern of first difference autocorrelations in the building series tends therefore to support the validity of fitting a more general trend plus cycle model to the data (Harvey, 1985: 219).
- These correlograms have the general appearance of white noise residual processes, which tends to confirm that the long cycle in building activity has to a considerable extent been absorbed into the fluctuating trends.

A.3.2   Unit root tests

A more formal test for the stationarity of cyclical component c_t is to define it as the following first-order autoregressive process with intercept but no time trend (since the series is assumed to have been detrended):

$$c_t = \alpha(1 - \rho) + \rho c_{t-1} + \varepsilon_t \qquad (A.29)$$

The purpose of the test is to estimate by regression whether or not the value of parameter ρ is less than one. If the restriction $\rho = 1$ holds, the process is said to have a unit root and constitutes a non-stationary random walk with drift; this means that the effect of any shock to the process is permanent. With $\rho < 1$, the effect of a shock fades over time, so that the process is trend-reverting and satisfies the stationarity conditions.

For testing purposes, equation (A.29) can be re-expressed in terms of the first difference Δc_t:

$$\Delta c_t = \alpha(1 - \rho) - (1 - \rho)c_{t-1} + \varepsilon_t \qquad (A.30)$$

The classic unit root tests developed by Dickey and Fuller (1981) use either the t-statistic on the estimated coefficient of c_{t-1}, or an F-test on the restricted and unrestricted estimates of equation (A.30), to accept or reject the unit root as the null hypothesis (i.e. that the coefficient on c_{t-1} is zero), with both the t and F statistics having non-standard distributions.

With the DF test, the disturbance term ε_t is assumed to consist of a stationary sequence of independently and identically distributed random variables. The more general Augmented Dickey–Fuller (ADF) test relaxes this condition, assuming instead that the disturbance term includes a stationary autoregressive process of order p in the differenced cycle variable Δc_t. Under this assumption, equation (A.30) can be expanded into the generalized ADF regression equation:

$$\Delta c_t = \alpha(1 - \rho) - (1 - \rho)c_{t-1} + \sum_1^p \theta_i \, \Delta c_{t-i} + \varepsilon_t \tag{A.31}$$

Tests are normally conducted for increasing values of order p up to a level sufficient to generate white noise residuals. Model selection criteria such as the Akaike information criterion (AIC) or the Schwarz Bayesian criterion (SBC) can be used to identify the most appropriate order of augmentation, indicated by the regression model that minimizes information loss and thus maximizes the criterion score; this amounts to a more sophisticated version of minimizing the residual sum of squares and maximizing the adjusted R-squared (Chatfield, 2004: 256).

The results of the unit root tests conducted on the cyclical deviations derived from the detrended London building series over the period 1714–1900 are summarized in Table A.3. The t-statistics derived from the Dickey–Fuller regressions fitted to each series can be compared with the corresponding 95% critical values, with the most appropriate model being chosen by the AIC and SBC selection criteria. It should be noted that though the quoted results refer to unit root models fitted without time trend, for those series derived as residuals around a fitted trend, it is appropriate to use the critical value associated with models that include a time trend as a test of trend stationarity (Pesaran and Pesaran, 1997: 116).

The key findings confirm the observations made from the correlogram plots in the previous section:

Table A.3 Unit root tests for London building cycles.

(i) Smooth trends

	Linear trend	Polynomial trend	HP(1000) filter	Structural model
ADF(0)	−2.567	−2.748	−4.328	−4.354
ADF(1)	−3.455*	−4.078*	−6.227	−6.360
ADF(2)	−3.656	−4.446	−7.026*	−7.299*
ADF(3)	−3.338	−4.096	−6.776	−7.130
ADF(4)	−3.057	−3.797	−6.501	−6.925

(ii) Fluctuating trends

	First differences	ARIMA(0,1,2)	HP(10) filter
ADF(0)	−9.356*	−13.22*	−8.514
ADF(1)	−7.312	−9.194	−9.660
ADF(2)	−7.215	−7.544	−10.18
ADF(3)	−7.101	−7.267	−9.658*
ADF(4)	−6.691	−6.983	−8.848

95% critical values −3.436 (with time trend)
−2.878 (without time trend)

Notes:
Original series is log transformed, and the tests are conducted over the full period 1714–1900 (180 observations) for models with intercept but no time trend.
ADF(p) indicates the order of the autoregressive process in the augmented tests.
* denotes the most appropriate model as indicated by the AIC and SBC selection criteria.

- For the residuals derived from the single linear growth trend, the unit root hypothesis can only just be rejected at the 95% level for the chosen first-order ADF model when compared to the critical value for a model with time trend, which is the appropriate test in this case. This confirms that the stationarity of the cycle derived from the deterministic linear trend is uncertain; in comparison to the autocorrelation plot, it also suggests that the unit root is quite a weak test of stationarity.
- The stationarity of the cyclical residuals derived from the polynomial trend is more firmly established at the 95% level for the chosen model, confirming that a deterministic trend with variable slope may offer an acceptable procedure for isolating the cyclical component when there are variations in the secular growth rate.
- The stochastic cycles produced by the two smooth stochastic trends [the HP(1000) filter and the structural model] are more emphatically stationary, comparing their chosen ADF(2) statistics with the 95% critical values. This confirms what the correlograms indicate: that smooth stochastic trends are better able to produce stationary cyclical residuals than deterministic trends.
- The unit root hypothesis can clearly be rejected for the residuals derived from each of the fluctuating trends, confirming that these detrended series approximate to white noise residual processes left after their main cyclical component has been absorbed into the trend.

Though these unit root tests reinforce the previous informal observations on cycle identification and stationarity, it should be noted that they are considered to have relatively poor power, and may be misleading unless set within a broader framework for testing which detrending method is the most appropriate for a particular time series (Maddala, 2001: 550 and Chatfield, 2004: 263).

A.4   Spectral analysis

This technique is designed specifically to decompose a detrended time series into cyclical components of different frequency. It complements in a more formal manner those indications of cyclical components that can be derived by plotting the estimated autocorrelation function of the detrended series. For an introduction to spectral analysis, see Chatfield (2004, chapters 6 and 7), while for a more detailed and theoretical treatment of the subject, see Priestley (1981). As discussed in Chapter 3, applications of the technique to the identification of long cycles are to be found in Howrey (1968), Harkness (1968), Cargill (1971), Soper (1975) and Barras and Ferguson (1985).

A.4.1   Spectral density functions

The autocovariance function $\gamma(k)$ is a basic tool for describing the behaviour of a data series in the time domain, measuring the covariance of observations separated by different time lags k. Its complement in the frequency domain is the spectral density function $f(\omega)$, which measures the variability of the series across different frequencies ω when it is decomposed into a sequence of sinusoidal wave functions. Such wave functions have already been introduced in Section A.2.7 with the definition of the stochastic cycle component of the structural time series model.

Following Chatfield (2004: 107ff), assume that the detrended building time series c_t can be represented as a Fourier series consisting of $j = 0,...J$ cyclical components with angular frequency ω_j, such that:

$$c_t = \sum_0^J [\alpha_j \cos(\omega_j t) + \beta_j \sin(\omega_j t)] + \chi_t \qquad (A.32)$$

where $\alpha_j = R_j \cos \nu_j$ and $\beta_j = -R_j \sin \nu_j$; $R_j = (\alpha_j^2 + \beta_j^2)^{1/2}$ is the amplitude and ν_j is the phase of cyclical component j and χ_t is a white noise disturbance term. By letting the number of cyclical components $J \to \infty$, a continuous sequence of frequencies contributes to the variation in process c_t. Assuming that c_t is a discrete-time process measured in unit intervals of time, the frequency range can be confined between the limits $(0, \pi)$. This is because $\cos(\omega_j + n\pi)t = \cos(\omega_j t)$ for even values of n and $\cos(\pi - \omega_j)t$ for odd values of n, so that variation at frequencies higher than π cannot be distinguished from variation at a corresponding frequency within the range.

The variation of stationary stochastic process c_t within the frequency domain can be represented by a monotonically increasing *spectral distribution function* $F(\omega)$, which measures the cumulative contribution of frequencies in the range $(0, \omega)$ to the overall variance of the series. The spectral distribution function in the frequency domain is linked to the autocovariance function $\gamma(k)$ in the time domain by the relationship:

$$\gamma(k) = \int_0^\pi \cos(\omega k) dF(\omega) \qquad k = 0, 1...... \qquad (A.33)$$

which is termed the spectral representation of the autocovariance function. It can be seen that, by setting lag $k = 0$, the autocovariance function equates to the variance function and $\gamma(0) = \sigma_c^2 = F(\pi)$; in other words, the whole variance of the series σ_c^2 is captured by the spectral distribution function over the full range of frequencies $(0, \pi)$.

Since the spectral distribution is a continuous function over the range $(0, \omega)$, it can be differentiated with respect to frequency ω to define the *spectral density function* or *spectrum* as $f(\omega) = dF(\omega)/d\omega$. This allows equation (A.33) to be re-expressed as:

$$\gamma(k) = \int_0^\pi \cos(\omega k) \ f(\omega) d\omega. \qquad (A.34)$$

Again setting $k = 0$, the total area underneath a plot of spectrum $f(\omega)$ can be seen to be equal to the overall variance of the series, while that portion covered by increment $f(\omega)d\omega$ represents the contribution to the overall variance of components with frequencies in the range $(\omega, \omega + d\omega)$. A peak in the spectrum indicates an important contribution to variance at that frequency, identifying it as the frequency of a strong cyclical component within the series.

The inverse of equation (A.34) expresses the spectral density function in terms of the autocovariance function, and can be derived by means of a process known as the Fourier transform (Chatfield, 2004: 295–6):

$$f(\omega) = 1/\pi \sum_{-\infty}^{\infty} \gamma(k)e^{-i\omega k} \tag{A.35}$$

Since $\gamma(k)$ is an even function of k (i.e. it is symmetrical around k = 0), this equation can be re-expressed in the equivalent form:

$$f(\omega) = 1/\pi[\gamma(0) + 2\sum_{1}^{\infty} \gamma(k)\cos(\omega k)] \tag{A.36}$$

A normalized form of the spectral density function is often defined as $f^*(\omega) = f(\omega)/\sigma_c^2$, such that $f^*(\omega)d\omega$ represents the proportion of the overall variance captured within the interval $(\omega, \omega + d\omega)$. This normalized form of the spectrum is defined as in equation (A.36), substituting the autocorrelation function $\gamma^*(k)$ for the autocovariance function $\gamma(k)$ and setting $\gamma^*(0) = 1$.

The theoretical spectrum of the detrended series defined by equation (A.36) is a continuous function of frequency ω. For estimation purposes, it is assumed that the total variance of the series is partitioned across a discrete set of cyclical components with *harmonic frequencies* ω_j chosen for ease of estimation. It has already been observed that if the series is a discrete-time process measured in unit intervals of time, then the highest frequency at which the spectrum can be defined is $\omega_j = \pi$. At the other extreme, the lowest frequency at which it can be defined, termed the *fundamental frequency*, is determined by the cycle which has a period matching the length of the observed series (since there are insufficient observations to capture fully any lower frequency component). With a sample of t = 1,...,T observations, the fundamental frequency thus has period T and angular frequency $2\pi/T$. Between these upper and lower bounds, the harmonic frequencies are defined as a sequence of integer multiples of the fundamental frequency $\omega_j = 2\pi j/T$, j = 1,...,T/2.

The contribution of each harmonic cyclical component to total series variance is measured by a *periodogram* $\tilde{f}(\omega_j)$, which is the least squares estimator of the spectral density function $f(\omega)$. Following Chatfield (2004: 126–9), the periodogram $\tilde{f}(\omega_j)$ can be derived from equation (A.36) as a function of the estimated sample autocovariance coefficients $\tilde{\gamma}_k$ for values of lag k up to maximum value T−1, setting $\tilde{\gamma}_k = 0$ for k ⩾ T, that is:

$$\tilde{f}(\omega_j) = 1/\pi[\tilde{\gamma}_0 + 2\sum_{1}^{T-1} \tilde{\gamma}_k \cos(\omega_j k)] \tag{A.37}$$

The normalized form of the periodogram $\tilde{f}^*(\omega_j)$ is derived by substituting sample autocorrelation coefficients $\tilde{\gamma}_k^* (\tilde{\gamma}_0^* = 1)$ for the autocovariance coefficients in equation (A.37).

As defined by equation (A.37), periodogram $\tilde{f}(\omega_j)$ is not a consistent estimator of spectrum $f(\omega)$, since its variance does not decrease as the length of the time series increases. The raw periodogram tends to fluctuate wildly and requires the application of some form of smoothing process to provide a consistent estimator. This counters the problem that as lag length k increases towards series length T, the precision of the sample autocovariance coefficients $\tilde{\gamma}_k$ decreases, because they are calculated on fewer and fewer terms. The smoothing process tackles this problem in two ways: first, by weighting the autocovariance coefficients with a set of weights υ_k, termed the *lag window*, which decrease as lag length k increases; second, by restricting the summation range for the coefficients to a maximum lag M (<T), termed the *truncation point*. This modifies equation (A.37) to become:

$$\tilde{f}(\omega_j) = 1/\pi[\upsilon_0\tilde{\gamma}_0 + 2\sum_1^M \upsilon_k\tilde{\gamma}_k \cos(\omega_j k)] \qquad (A.38)$$

With the estimated spectrum truncated in this manner, it is normal to restrict the number of harmonic frequencies at which it is estimated to $\omega_j = \pi j/M$, j = 1,...,M.

A variety of lag windows have been proposed for smoothing the periodogram (Chatfield, 2004: 131–4), and the one that has been chosen for this analysis is the *Tukey window*:

$$\upsilon_k = \tfrac{1}{2}[1 + \cos(\pi k/M)] \qquad\qquad k = 0, 1,...,M. \qquad (A.39)$$

As the value of truncation point M increases, so does the number of harmonic frequencies over which the periodogram is estimated. In other words, the bandwidth of the spectral window narrows, which means that the variance of the estimated spectrum increases and thus the degree of smoothing decreases. The choice of bandwidth needs to balance 'resolution' against 'variance': if M is too small, and the bandwidth therefore too wide, important variations in the spectrum are lost through over-smoothing; if M is too large, and the bandwidth too narrow, there is insufficient smoothing to remove erratic fluctuations from the periodogram. A favoured compromise is to set $M = 2\sqrt{T}$. As far as the number of observations T is concerned, Granger and Hatanaka (1964: 17) propose that series should be at least 7 times as long as the longest cycle being investigated, while Chatfield (2004: 152) suggests that between 100 and 200 observations are required to obtain a satisfactory estimate of the spectrum.

A.4.2 Estimated spectra for the detrended building series

Estimated spectra have been derived for the seven alternative versions of the detrended London building series discussed in Section A.3; the spectra of the series derived by fitting smooth trends are plotted in Figure A.10, while those for the series derived from fluctuating trends are shown in Figure A.11. The statistical package used to estimate these spectra was Microfit 4.0 (Pesaran and Pesaran, 1997), which offers estimates based on alternative lag windows and the ability to vary the truncation point, with a default setting of $M = 2\sqrt{T} = 28$ with T = 187 observations. By experimentation, the best balance between resolution and variance for the smooth trend residuals was achieved using the Tukey window and a truncation point of M = 50. This gives better resolution than the default setting without introducing excessive fluctuations into the spectra, although it increases the standard error from 0.34 to 0.45 times each spectrum value. For the fluctuating trend residuals, the Tukey window was used at the default setting of M = 28, since in these cases, any higher value does cause excessive fluctuation in the spectra.

The cyclical components identified by these alternative spectra can be summarized as follows:

• The spectrum of the series derived from the deterministic linear growth trend is dominated by frequencies at and close to zero, indicating that it is insufficiently detrended and that the residual trend swamps the higher frequency

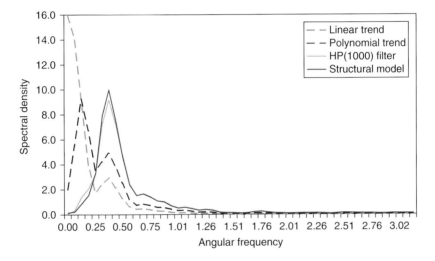

Figure A.10 Spectral density functions for cycles around smooth trends in London building. *Source*: Sheppard et al. (1979).

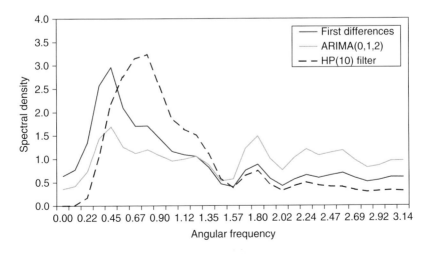

Figure A.11 Spectral density functions for residuals around fluctuating trends in London building. *Source*: Sheppard et al. (1979).

components. Nevertheless, even with this series, the spectrum reveals a modest secondary peak at harmonic frequency 0.377, equivalent to a cycle period of 16.7 years – which is close to the long cycle frequency already identified by fitting the structural model (see Section A.2.7) and by observation of the autocorrelation functions (Section A.3.1).

- The series derived from the polynomial trend also shows a secondary peak at the 16.7-year long cycle period, while having a much lower spectrum value at zero frequency. This confirms that the polynomial is a better detrending procedure than the single linear trend, because it captures some structural change in the trend rate of growth. However, there is a strong spectrum peak at a frequency of 0.126, equivalent to a long wave period of around 50 years, suggesting that the deterministic polynomial cannot capture the variation in trend as well as the structural model, which incorporates the long wave into the stochastic trend slope (Section A.2.7).

- The spectra of the two stochastic cycles produced by the structural model (Model 2) and the HP(1000) filter are dominated by strong peaks at the harmonic period of 16.7 years. As already noted, this spectral frequency is close to the 15.9-year long cycle period identified by the structural modelling exercise, while the sharpness of the spectrum peak is consistent with a cycle having a high damping factor. The values of these two spectra at the lower frequencies are much smaller than those derived from the deterministic trends, once again confirming the superior performance of stochastic procedures for detrending a time series and isolating its main cyclical components.

- The estimated spectrum for the first differenced series does show a peak in the frequency range corresponding to the identified long cycle, though it is less pronounced than the equivalent spectra peaks derived using the smooth stochastic trends. This indicates that, despite appearances, the simple first differencing procedure does not entirely subsume the trend-reverting long cycle frequencies within its fluctuating trend, which implies that the building series is not a random walk with drift – confirming the observations made with respect to its correlogram.

- The long cycle frequencies are much less obvious in the spectra of the residuals derived from the other fluctuating trend procedures – the ARIMA(0,1,2) model and the HP(10) filter – confirming that these procedures have largely absorbed the long cycle into their fluctuating trends. The spectrum for the ARIMA(0,1,2) model shows a weak residual peak around the long cycle frequencies, but also marked peaks at higher frequencies. The spectrum for the HP(10) filter is dominated by a higher frequency peak in the range 0.67–0.79, equivalent to a major cycle with a period of 8–9 years. A weak secondary building cycle at these frequencies was also identified using the structural model (Table A.2).

A.5 Turning points

A.5.1 Cycle dating

Real-world economic phenomena do not, of course, exhibit cycles of constant frequency or amplitude; rather they are subject to cyclical tendencies which are continuously modified by the influence of exogenous events and endogenous market conditions. Therefore, while formal statistical procedures for time series detrending and cycle identification are invaluable tools of analysis, they should be complemented by more informal methods of cycle dating, which rely upon the identification of peak and trough turning points. As was discussed in Chapter 2, this was the approach first adopted by the pioneers of business cycle analysis, particularly those who established the rich empirical tradition of the US National Bureau of Economic Research (NBER), as embodied in the classic works of Mitchell (1927) and Burns and Mitchell (1946).

It is worth noting here that the relatively mild short cycle fluctuations explored in business cycle analysis often consist of no more than variations in the economic growth rate around an average trend. Under these conditions, the identification of precise cycle turning points can be quite difficult, especially when monthly data are used. To deal with this problem, analytical procedures have been devised to systematize turning point identification as far as possible. A widely used approach devised by Bry and Boschan (1971) eliminates extreme outlier observations from a time series, then applies various smoothing procedures to the data in order to identify the neighbourhoods of potential cycle turning points, which are then located precisely using the raw data. Typically, each of the chosen turning points marks a change in direction in the values of the series that is sustained for some minimum period of time and creates fluctuations that exceed some minimum amplitude. Periods of expansion start with the observation following a trough and run up to the subsequent peak, while periods of contraction run from the observation following a peak down to the next trough. For example applications of this approach, see King and Plosser (1994) and Watson (1994).

For the reasons discussed in Chapter 3, long cycles in building activity tend to exhibit much more pronounced fluctuations than those of the shorter business cycle. Building cycle turning points are therefore generally easier to identify as strong peaks and troughs separated by marked upswings and downswings in activity. As a result, it is usually possible to identify cycle turning points even when the building series has not been detrended. Nevertheless, there remains an important element of subjective judgement in the dating of building cycles, just as there is with any other type of economic cycle. With building cycles, a particular issue that requires judgement is distinguishing between major and minor turning points, which may indicate the superimposed effects of two or more cycles of different frequency.

A.5.2 Identified turning points in the London building series

The clearest identification of cycle turning points for the London building series can be obtained from Figure A.6, which shows the cyclical components derived from three alternative smooth detrending procedures – the deterministic polynomial trend, the stochastic HP filter with a high smoothing parameter and the stochastic structural model. It has already been observed in Section A.2.7 that these three cyclical components exhibit very similar peak and trough turning points: the timing of the two stochastic cycles is identical, while the turning points derived from the polynomial trend deviate from those of the stochastic cycles on only 6 out of 26 occasions, and for 4 of these, the difference is only one year. There are more noticeable differences between the identified cycles in terms of the relative amplitude of their fluctuations. In particular, the fluctuations derived from the fitted polynomial trend tend to have larger amplitude than those of the other two cycles, because the deterministic function is less able to capture major changes in the slope of the trend than the stochastic functions.

The peak and trough dates identified from the stochastic cycle defined by the structural model are marked in Figure A.6 and listed in Table 5.10, together with the duration and extreme amplitude of each cycle. These amplitudes are measured as the proportionate deviation of each turning point from the fitted structural trend (the amplitudes derived from the HP(1000) filter are similar). The 26 identified building cycle turning points mark out 12 complete cycles with an average duration of 14.3 years (trough to trough) and an average deviation at the turning points of 0.246. These cycle dating statistics compare with the fitted stochastic cycle period of 15.9 years and amplitude of 0.280 derived from the structural model (see Table A.2).

Examination of the individual cycles shows that 9 out of 12 of them have trough-to-trough periods in the range 15–17 years – the same cycle frequency as identified by the structural model, the autocorrelation functions and the spectral analysis. The exceptions result from two shorter period cycles, Cycle 5 (trough to trough) and Cycle 9 (peak to peak), superimposed respectively on the downswing and upswing of longer cycles. If they are removed from the calculation, the average cycle duration increases to 17.2 years and the average deviation to 0.262 – closer to the values obtained from the structural model. The identification of these two shorter cycles, and their impact upon average cycle frequency and amplitude, illustrates the importance of combining an informal dating procedure with the more formal techniques of cycle analysis.

A.6   Multivariate analysis

So far we have concentrated on the univariate analysis of the example London building series, exploring alternative methods for detrending and cycle identification over the period 1714–1900. The final step is to move to a multivariate analysis, designed to identify exogenous variables that may have influenced the trend and/or cycle in building activity, and then estimate the relationships between these explanatory variables and the building series.

A.6.1   Explanatory variables

Four available long-run data series may offer some explanation for the trend and cycle in London building activity between 1714 and 1900:

• The growth of population offers one simple measure of domestic demand for urban building. While there is no available series covering annual population growth in London over the full period, Wrigley and Schofield have constructed annual estimates of *population growth in England* as a whole spanning the period 1541–1871, which they consider to be 'tolerably reliable' (Wrigley and Schofield, 1989: 483). Annual data on England and Wales population are available from 1801

(Mitchell, 1988: 11–4), and have been used for illustrative purposes to scale the English population series forward to 1900. This national population series has been used as a crude proxy for the general trend in population growth in eighteenth and nineteenth century London.

- Some measure of economic growth is needed to provide a complementary indicator of industrial and commercial demand for urban building. Again, there is no aggregate economic index for the growth of the London economy, but a national index of *UK industrial production* covering the period 1700–1913 (the 'revised best guess') has been compiled by Crafts and Harley (1992). An earlier version of this index was tested for trend and cycle using a structural modelling approach similar to that being adopted for this building analysis (Crafts et al., 1989).
- Although there is no aggregate index of London's economic growth over the sample period, there is a series that measures *coal imports to London* by sea and rail between 1700 and 1879 (Ashton and Sykes, 1964: 249–51; Mitchell, 1988: 244–5). This provides a useful proxy indicator of the growth of both the industrial and domestic economies of the city during the eighteenth and nineteenth centuries, insofar as it is reflected in their fuel consumption.
- The compilers of our illustrative London building series note a strong relationship between levels of building activity and the cost of capital as measured by the *price of Consols* (Sheppard et al., 1979). An annual yield series is available on 3% Consols from their inception in 1753 up to 1888, and on an estimated 2.75% Consol between 1888 and 1903. This series has been extended further back to 1729 using the yield on equivalent 3% annuities (Homer and Sylla, 2005: 157–8, 192–4).

Indices of the three growth series – English population, UK industrial production and coal imports to London – are illustrated in Figure A.12, alongside the London

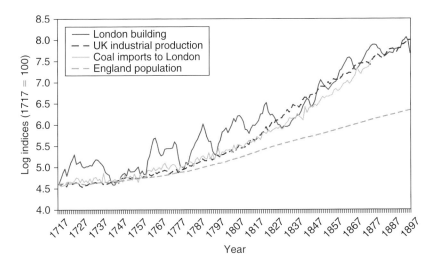

Figure A.12 Growth in the UK economy and London building 1717–1900.
Source: Feinstein (1976), Sheppard et al. (1979), Mitchell (1988), Wrigley and Schofield (1989), Crafts and Harley (1992), Homer and Sylla (2005) and ONS.

building series, all expressed in logarithmic form and indexed from 1717, an approximate building cycle midpoint. Though much more volatile than the other series, the growth in London building activity (averaging 1.9% per annum) matched that of UK industrial production (1.8%) and coal imports to London (1.7%) between the cycle midpoints of 1717 and 1876, while all three grew at around double the average rate of population growth in England (0.9%) over the period.

A.6.2 Cointegrated growth trends

The theory of cointegration (Granger, 1981; Engle and Granger, 1987) provides a formal technique for investigating the long-run relationships between trended time series such as those plotted in Figure A.12. Two economic time series x_t and y_t that are I(1), i.e. they are stationary in their first differences, are said to be cointegrated if there exists a non-zero value of parameter β such that the long-run relationship:

$$y_t = \alpha + \beta x_t + u_t \tag{A.40}$$

yields residuals u_t that are I(0), i.e. they are stationary and therefore integrated of order zero. What this essentially means is that the two series are linked by a linear equilibrium relationship that is stable through time.

The basic test for cointegration between two economic series is thus to use a unit root test to check if they are I(1), then estimate equation (A.40) by OLS regression and test the stationarity of the residuals $\tilde{u}_t$ derived from the cointegrating regression by another unit root test (see Section A.3.2). The t-ratio from this test no longer has the Dickey–Fuller distribution, but has a different distribution tabulated in MacKinnon (1996).

A more general approach to cointegration builds the unit root test into the model, which is expressed in a vector autoregressive (VAR) form that can be generalized to cover n variables with up to k lags, between which there may be as many as r cointegrating relationships, where r is the order of cointegration. Johansen (1988) has devised a widely used procedure for determining the cointegrating vectors in a general VAR model of this form, by calculating the characteristic roots of the coefficient matrix and testing whether they are unit roots or not. The methodology does rely on the original time series being I(1) and is sensitive to the specification of the lag length assumed for the model. Furthermore, the approach can be criticized for being 'a-theoretical'; it is a purely statistical construct that can generate multiple cointegrating relationships between the variables which are difficult to interpret in economic terms. For an introductory review of the methodology and its strengths and weaknesses, see Maddala (2001: 556–66).

Granger (1969) offers a particular definition of causality between two variables, which is a natural extension of the concept of cointegration, since in a later paper (Granger, 1986: 218) he points out that if a pair of time series are cointegrated, then there must be Granger causality between them in at least one direction. The basic concept of Granger causality is simple: if changes in x are a cause of changes in y, then changes in x should precede changes in y. Furthermore, if x causes y, then y should not cause x, since this means it is likely that one or more other variables are in fact causing the observed changes in both x and y (Pindyck and Rubinfeld, 1998: 243).

The test of Granger causality is to regress y against lagged values of itself and lagged values of the hypothesized explanatory variable x (the unrestricted equation), and compare the results with those from a regression of y against only lagged values of itself (the restricted equation), i.e. compare

$$y_t = \alpha_0 + \sum_1^k \alpha_i y_{t-i} + \sum_1^k \beta_i x_{t-i} + u_t \qquad (A.41a)$$

with

$$y_t = \alpha_0 + \sum_1^k \alpha_i y_{t-i} + u_t \qquad (A.41b)$$

where k is the chosen number of lags. An F-statistic calculated on the unrestricted and restricted residual sum of squares can be used to determine whether the lagged values of x contribute significantly to the explanatory power of the unrestricted equation: if the test shows the effect of including x to be significant, then the null hypothesis that x does not cause y can be rejected. The reverse hypothesis can be tested in the same manner.

Unit root tests on the log indices of London building and the three possible explanatory growth variables (English population, UK industrial production and coal imports to London) show each to be I(1), with the probability of their first differences having a unit root being very close to zero. Regression equations between London building and each of the other three series establish strong cointegrating relationships in all cases, with the residuals from each cointegrating regression proving to be stationary; these cointegrating relationships are also confirmed by the Johansen test. Finally, Granger causality between each explanatory series and London building is also demonstrated strongly, using the F-test to reject the null hypothesis. Furthermore, in no case does any evidence of reverse causality exist to indicate that London building influences the other series (Table A.4).

A.6.3 Co-movement of cycles

The preceding analysis of cointegrated growth trends was conducted using the original data series. If cyclical components in the explanatory variables can be isolated, as already achieved with the London building series, then the extent of the co-movement between the building cycle and cycles in the explanatory economic variables can also be explored. Granger causality tests can be applied to the cycle components in the same way that the original data series have been tested. This causality analysis is a natural extension of the use of cross-correlation functions as a basic tool for measuring the interrelationship between two data series in the time domain, separated by different time lags. Equivalent cross-spectral density functions can also be defined to explore these interrelationships in the frequency domain; however, the specification and interpretation of cross-spectra are complicated, and it seems to be accepted that the technique is more suited to applications in engineering and the physical sciences than to the analysis of economic data (Chatfield, 2004: 162).

Table A.4   Cointegration and causality between London building and the explanatory growth variables.

Test statistics	Building	Industrial production	Coal imports	Population
Stationarity[a]				
t-statistic	−9.308	−14.72	−14.49	−4.320
Probability	0.000	0.000	0.000	0.001
Cointegration[b]				
t-statistic		−4.459	−4.402	−4.607
Probability		0.000	0.000	0.000
Causality[c]				
F-statistic		4.423	6.859	4.991
Probability		0.002	0.000	0.001
Reverse causality[d]				
F-statistic		0.453	0.473	0.493
Probability		0.770	0.756	0.741

Notes:
[a] The stationarity of the first differences of each series is expressed in terms of the t-statistic and associated probability of there being a unit root as derived from an ADF test with the number of lags chosen to maximize the Schwarz Bayesian information criterion.
[b] Cointegration between the London building series and each of the other three growth series is tested by estimating an OLS regression equation between each pair of variables and applying an ADF test to establish whether or not the residuals are stationary.
[c] The Granger causality test is applied to OLS regression equations estimating the extent to which changes in London building were separately caused by each of the other three series, using four lags on the dependent and independent variables.
[d] The reverse causality tests check whether London building may have influenced the other series.

The structural modelling procedure outlined in Section A.2.7 has been applied to each of the possible explanatory variables, including the Consols yield, in order to estimate their stochastic trend and isolate any stochastic cycles that may be present in the series. The coal imports series exhibits no significant stochastic cycle. The population series generates a significant long cycle with a period of 15.1 years, but its fluctuations are so mild that they have little impact on the building cycle. However, both the Consols yield and industrial production series exhibit significant cyclical fluctuations that do show some relationship with the building cycle. For the consols yield, over the period 1729–1900, a long cycle of 19.2 years duration is identified; for industrial production between 1714 and 1900, there is a major cycle with a period of 9.9 years. In Figure A.13, these two cycles are compared with the 15.9-year long cycle in London building that was derived by structural modelling in Section A.2.7. Cross-correlation and causality tests of the interrelationships between the long building cycle and the cycles in the two explanatory variables are presented in Table A.5.

The relationships between the cycles in the explanatory variables and the London building cycle can be summarized as follows:

- The cross-correlations demonstrate a strong negative relationship between the interest rate cycle and the long building cycle. Furthermore, there is a significant causal relationship from yield cycle to building cycle, but no evidence of reverse causality. Figure A.13 shows that the yield cycle was particularly volatile during the eighteenth and early nineteenth centuries, with strong peaks in building coinciding with interest rate troughs, and vice versa.

Table A.5 Interrelationships between the cycles in London building and the explanatory variables.

	Consols yield (1729–1900)	Industrial production (1714–1900)
Cross-correlations		
Lag 0	−0.668	0.238
Lag 1	−0.664	0.223
Lag 2	−0.526	0.112
Lag 3	−0.300	0.009
Lag 4	−0.054	−0.055
Granger causality[a]		
F-statistic	3.051	0.681
Probability	0.019	0.606
Reverse causality[b]		
F-statistic	1.223	0.936
Probability	0.303	0.444

Notes:
[a] The Granger causality test is applied to OLS regression equations estimating the extent to which changes in London building were separately caused by each of the other three series, using four lags on the dependent and independent variables.
[b] The reverse causality tests check whether London building may have influenced the other series.

- The cross-correlations between the major cycle in industrial production and the long cycle in building are weaker, and there is no evidence of a causal relationship. Figure A.13 shows that the industrial cycle is much less volatile than the building cycle, and the correspondence between their turning points is less obvious than that between the yield cycle and the building cycle.

A.6.4 *Structural model with explanatory variables*

The univariate structural time series model specified in Section A.2.7 can be expanded to accommodate exogenous explanatory variables alongside the unobserved stochastic components (Durbin and Koopman, 2001: 43). To this end, the basic components equation (A.1) can be expanded to include lagged explanatory variables $x_{i,t-\tau}$, for $i = 1,...,k$ variables, each with $\tau = 0,...,m$ lags:

$$y_t = g_t + c_t + \sum_1^k \sum_0^m \varsigma_{i\tau} x_{i,t-\tau} + \varepsilon_t \qquad t = 1,......,T \qquad (A.42)$$

where $\varsigma_{i\tau}$ are regression coefficients on the explanatory variables.

Multivariate equation (A.42) has been estimated for the London building series in log form over the shortened period 1730–1900, using the unlagged Consols yield as the explanatory variable, since this has emerged as the single strongest influence on the building cycle. In Table A.6 the results for this long cycle model with the explanatory variable (Model 6) are compared with the parameters of an equivalent long cycle model without the explanatory variable (Model 5); this latter model

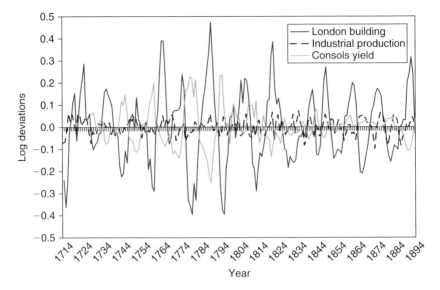

Figure A.13   Cycles in London building and explanatory variables.
Source: Feinstein (1976), Sheppard et al. (1979), Crafts and Harley (1992), Homer and Sylla (2005) and ONS.

Table A.6   Parameter estimates and diagnostic results for structural models of London building with and without explanatory variable (1730–1900).

	Model 5	Model 6	5% value
Explanatory variable	–	Consols yield	
Number of parameters	6	7	
Number of restrictions	1	1	
Cycle parameters			
Period	16.1 years	15.2 years	
Damping factor	0.913	0.900	
Amplitude	0.289	0.242	
Variance	0.0325	0.0216	
Disturbance variances ($\times 10^{-3}$)			
Level (σ_η^2)	0.000	0.000	
Slope (σ_ζ^2)	0.061	0.084	
Cycle (σ_χ^2)	5.425	4.095	
Irregular (σ_ε^2)	0.000	0.000	
Log-likelihood	396.54	412.26	
Likelihood ratio[a]	41.65	31.45	7.81/3.84
Goodness of fit R_d^2	0.1550	0.3351	
Standard error	0.0943	0.0839	
Normality	6.44	4.21	5.99
Heteroscedasticity (h = 56)	0.491	0.565	0.641
Durbin–Watson	1.840	1.808	1.78
Box–Ljung statistic	14.42	12.08	21.03/19.68

Notes:
See Tables A.1 and A.2.
[a] Likelihood ratio statistics compare Model 5 to equivalent model without long cycle, and Model 6 to Model 5.

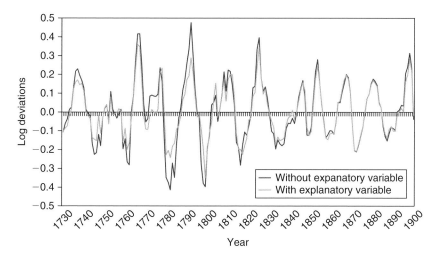

Figure A.14 London building cycle modelled with and without the explanatory variable. *Source*: Sheppard et al. (1979), Homer and Sylla (2005) and ONS.

is equivalent to Model 2 in Section A.2.7 estimated over the shortened period. Figure A.14 compares the building cycles derived from the models with and without the explanatory variable.

The estimated model incorporating the unlagged Consols yield as explanatory variable is as follows:

$$y_t = \tilde{g}_t + \tilde{c}_t - 0.154x_{ct} + \tilde{\varepsilon}_t, \qquad T = 171,$$
$$(-6.81) \tag{A.43}$$

where x_{ct} is the Consols yield and $\tilde{g}_t$, $\tilde{c}_t$ and $\tilde{\varepsilon}_t$ are the estimates of the trend, cycle and irregular components, respectively. The coefficient on the explanatory variable is significant at the 1% level, and the model residuals satisfy the normality and serial correlation tests at the 5% level; however, the significant heteroscedasticity noted with the univariate model remains. The inclusion of the single explanatory variable increases the first difference goodness of fit measure from 0.155 to 0.335 when compared to the univariate model, and the likelihood ratio test indicates that the restriction of there being no explanatory variable can be rejected at the 1% level. Compared to the univariate model, the period of the building cycle decreases slightly, from 16.1 to 15.2 years, and there is also a reduction in the amplitude and variance of the cycle. This indicates that some of the variation attributed to the stochastic cycle in the univariate model has been accounted for by the Consols yield cycle (see Figure A.14).

A similar modelling exercise was undertaken using industrial production as the explanatory variable over the full period 1714–1900. However, although its estimated coefficient (0.411) is significant at the 5% level (t-value 2.54), its inclusion does not produce a significant improvement in overall model performance (likelihood ratio statistic 1.75).

A.7 Conclusions

The following conclusions can be drawn from this exploratory analysis of the example London building series:

- Different detrending methods can produce very different cyclical components.
- Detrending methods that assume a stochastic, rather than deterministic, trend tend to produce more stationary cyclical components.
- Stochastic methods such as the HP filter and structural modelling, which generate a smoothly varying rather than fluctuating trend, produce components that are theoretically more plausible and do not absorb long-period cycles into the trend.
- Structural modelling of unobserved components has the additional benefit of allowing one or more stochastic cycles to be specified simultaneously with the stochastic trend.
- A variety of complementary methods (turning points, autocorrelation, spectral analysis) can, and should, be used to identify cycles within detrended series.
- Similarly, the interrelationships between cycles can be investigated by a variety of methods, including cross-correlation, causality testing and structural modelling.

The empirical analysis of the London building data in the eighteenth and nineteenth centuries shows building activity to have been trend-reverting when a smoothly varying growth trend is fitted to the data. On this basis, a strong and persistent long cycle in building is identified, with an average period of around 16 years; there is also evidence that the long cycle can be decomposed into a long wave and a major cycle. Multivariate analysis reveals the cost of money to have been a strong influence on the London building cycle, particularly during the eighteenth century, but the major cycle in national industrial production seems to have had only a weak influence on the building cycle.

Appendix B

The Building Cycle Model

The model of the building cycle described in Chapter 7 was first presented in Barras (2005), and is reproduced in this appendix. The model is formulated as a series of difference equations, in which the dynamic change in market variables occurs over discrete time periods. Flow variables such as output, take-up and development starts are defined as a cumulative total during each period, while the levels of stock variables such as building capital, vacancy and rents are defined at the end of one period and the start of the next. The model is applicable either to building investment in aggregate, or alternatively to investment in particular building types such as offices, shops, factories or dwellings. For a general introduction to difference equations, see Elaydi (1996); for the application of difference equation models in business cycle theory, see Gabisch and Lorenz (1989).

B.1 The model

B.1.1 Demand for building stock

Assume an economy with a level of aggregate output Y_t during time period t, expanding along an equilibrium growth path at constant rate ε:

$$Y_t = (1 + \varepsilon)Y_{t-1} \tag{B.1}$$

where $\varepsilon = \omega + \varphi$ is the constant rate of output growth, comprising the sum of the labour force growth rate ω and the rate of labour augmenting technical progress φ.

The quantity of occupied building stock B_t required at the end of the period to sustain the economy operating at level of output Y_t can be expressed as a function of a building capital–output ratio or occupancy rate α_t:

$$B_t = \alpha_t Y_t \tag{B.2}$$

For the basic version of the model, we shall assume a constant *natural occupancy rate* that is rent inelastic, i.e. $\alpha_t = \alpha^*$; a rent elastic version is introduced later. Here stock B_t is assumed to represent the aggregate volume of buildings in all uses. If the model is formulated in terms of separate uses, the economic activity variable Y_t will represent an appropriate measure of sectoral output in the case of non-residential building, or household income in the case of residential building.

The desired level of total building stock K_t^* at the end of the period consists of the occupied stock B_t plus an additional component of natural vacancy V_t^* required as a buffer stock to accommodate both the expansion of occupier demand as the economy grows, and the regular turnover of occupiers moving between buildings as their requirements change:

$$K_t^* = B_t + V_t^* \tag{B.3}$$

The required level of vacant space can be expressed in terms of a constant *natural vacancy rate* v^* applied to scale up the occupied stock, sufficient to ensure the efficient functioning of the market:

$$V_t^* = v^* B_t \tag{B.4}$$

giving

$$K_t^* = (1 + v^*)B_t \tag{B.5}$$

If output growth equation (B.1) is applied to equations (B.2) and (B.5), it can be seen that, as long as the occupancy rate is constant, both the occupied building stock B_t and the desired total stock K_t^* increase by the constant rate of output growth ε:

$$B_t = (1 + \varepsilon)B_{t-1} \tag{B.6}$$

and

$$K_t^* = (1 + \varepsilon)K_{t-1}^* \tag{B.7}$$

B.1.2   Occupier take-up

During each time period t, a quantum of building stock U_t is taken up by occupiers, consisting of two components – the net absorption of occupied stock N_t resulting from the additional demand created by the growth of the economy, and the turnover T_t, resulting from existing occupiers moving between buildings to satisfy their changing requirements. Take-up is thus given by:

$$U_t = N_t + T_t \tag{B.8}$$

with its two components defined as:

$$N_t = B_t - B_{t-1} \tag{B.9}$$

and

$$T_t = \tau B_{t-1} \tag{B.10}$$

where net absorption comprises the increase in occupied space between one period and the next, and turnover is expressed as a constant turnover rate τ applied to the level of occupied stock at the beginning of the period.

Combining equations (B.8)–(B.10) and dividing through by B_{t-1} produces an equation in the rate of take-up $u_t = U_t/B_{t-1}$ expressed in terms of the levels of occupied stock at the beginning and end of the period:

$$u_t = (B_t/B_{t-1}) - (1 - \tau)$$

Substituting from equation (B.2), the rate of take-up becomes a function of the output growth rate, the occupancy rate and the turnover rate:

$$u_t = (\alpha_t Y_t/\alpha_{t-1} Y_{t-1}) - (1 - \tau) \tag{B.11}$$

With steady-state output growth, as expressed by equation (B.1), plus a constant occupancy rate $\alpha_t = \alpha^\star$, equation (B.11) simplifies to:

$$u^\star = \varepsilon + \tau \tag{B.12}$$

where $u^\star$ is the *natural take-up rate* under conditions of steady-state growth, consisting of the sum of the constant turnover and growth rates.

B.1.3   Development starts

The required level of building investment I_t over time period t, is a function of two components of demand for new space – induced investment I_t^n and replacement investment I_t^r :

$$I_t = I_t^n + I_t^r \tag{B.13}$$

Induced investment is a response to the demand for additional space generated by economic growth. This can be expressed as the difference between the desired level of building stock at the end of the period $K_t^\star$ and the actual stock available at the end of the previous period K_{t-1}:

$$I_t^n = K_t^\star - K_{t-1} \tag{B.14}$$

Replacement investment is a response to the loss of building stock over the period, comprising stock that is either demolished or retired because it is no longer functional or profitable in use due to its age or poor condition. This can be expressed as the product of a constant depreciation rate δ applied to the level of building stock inherited from the previous period:

$$I_t^r = \delta K_{t-1} \tag{B.15}$$

Combining equations (B.14) and (B.15),

$$I_t = K_t^\star - (1 - \delta)K_{t-1} \tag{B.16}$$

Adapting the concept of the flexible accelerator introduced in Chapter 2, the planned level of building starts S_t during the period consists of the required level of investment I_t adjusted by a *direct development reaction coefficient* γ that allows for investor uncertainty about the future demand for space, given the lags inherent in the building process:

$$S_t = \gamma[K_t^\star - (1 - \delta)K_{t-1}] \tag{B.17}$$

If the economy is following a steady-state growth path, then the actual stock at the start of the period equals the desired stock, i.e. $K_{t-1} = K_{t-1}^\star$; this means that the stock is expanding at the equilibrium growth rate ε, as given by equation (B.7), given the simplifying assumption of a constant occupancy rate. Under these conditions, equation (B.17) can be simplified to express the natural level of starts $S_t^\star$ required to maintain steady-state growth as a function of the desired stock at the start of the period:

$$S_t^\star = \gamma(\varepsilon + \delta)K_{t-1}^\star \tag{B.18}$$

with the natural level of starts also growing at the equilibrium rate:

$$S_t^\star = (1 + \varepsilon)S_{t-1}^\star \tag{B.19}$$

Using equation (B.5) to convert total desired stock $K_{t-1}^\star$ to occupied stock B_{t-1}, equation (B.18) can be transformed to define the *natural rate of starts* $s^\star$ supporting steady-state growth as a constant ratio applied to the level of occupied stock:

$$s^\star = \gamma(1 + v^\star)(\varepsilon + \delta) \tag{B.20}$$

where $s^\star = S_t^\star/B_{t-1}$ is given by the sum of the induced and replacement components of investment demand, as represented by the output growth rate and the depreciation rate, moderated by the reaction coefficient and boosted by the natural vacancy rate.

B.1.4   Deviation from equilibrium

Planned building starts can be translated directly into actual building orders according to equation (B.17) in an owner–occupier market in which occupiers undertake their own building investment. However, in reality, most building is undertaken by a separate development sector which cannot know at first hand the investment intentions of occupiers. Under these conditions, developers must respond indirectly to investment demand as it is mediated through the market signals of vacancy and rents or prices.

Assume that at the end of the previous time period, the market deviated from its equilibrium trajectory such that the actual level of building stock K_{t-1} relative to occupied stock B_{t-1} did not match the desired level K_{t-1}^*, i.e. $K_{t-1} \neq K_{t-1}^*$. Adapting equation (B.3), this implies a similar disparity between the actual and required or natural level of vacant space at the end of $t-1$, i.e. $V_{t-1} \neq V_{t-1}^*$, where:

$$V_{t-1} = K_{t-1} - B_{t-1} \qquad (B.21)$$

The required level of starts S_t over the current period can then be broken down into two components: the natural level of starts S_t^* required to increase the stock from the previous desired level K_{t-1}^* to new desired level K_t^*, as defined by equation (B.18), and a correction $S_t - S_t^*$ required to compensate for the previous deviation in stock $K_{t-1}^* - K_{t-1}$. Equation (B.17) can be expanded to make these two components explicit, using equation (B.18) to make the substitution in S_t^*:

$$S_t = S_t^* + \gamma(1 - \delta)(K_{t-1}^* - K_{t-1}) \qquad (B.22)$$

It follows from equations (B.3) and (B.21) that the deviation in stock $K_{t-1}^* - K_{t-1}$ can be replaced by the deviation in vacant space $V_{t-1}^* - V_{t-1}$, so that:

$$S_t - S_t^* = \gamma(1 - \delta)(V_{t-1}^* - V_{t-1}) \qquad (B.23)$$

This yields an equation expressing the required level of starts relative to their natural level during the current period as a function of the actual level of vacancy relative to its natural level at the start of the period.

Dividing through by the level of occupied stock B_{t-1} transforms equation (B.23) into a relationship between the relative rates of starts and vacancy such that:

$$s_t - s^* = \gamma(1 - \delta)(v^* - v_{t-1}) \qquad (B.24)$$

where $s_t = S_t/B_{t-1}$ is the required rate of starts expressed in terms of the level of occupied stock at the start of the period, s^* is the natural rate of starts required to maintain the natural vacancy rate v^*, and $v_{t-1} = V_{t-1}/B_{t-1}$ is the actual vacancy rate at the start of the period.

B.1.5   Rent adjustment

While the observed vacancy rate v_{t-1} at the start of the current period provides a partial signal to developers, it is not sufficient to enable them to judge the required rate of starts without direct knowledge about the natural vacancy and start rates in the market. For this they need the further, indirect signal provided by property rents or prices. The following analysis is expressed in terms of rents; an identical formulation can be derived using prices or capital values. Myopic pricing is assumed, that is developers are forming price expectations on the basis of current real rents at the start of construction, rather than a correct forecast of their value at completion; however, current rental change as well as the current rent level is allowed to influence developer behaviour, introducing some expectations effect by signalling improving or deteriorating market conditions.

Assume that in equilibrium the market establishes a real level of *natural rent* r^* (or prices p^*) that on the demand side provides a cost of capital affordable enough compared with other factor costs for occupiers to utilize the total stock of space up to its natural vacancy rate v^*, and on the supply side maintains a rate of profit sufficient for developers to undertake the natural rate of building starts s^* when set against the prevailing level of development costs and property yields. This means that when actual vacancy equals its natural rate at the beginning of a period, rents remain constant in real terms at their natural level during the period, so maintaining starts at their natural rate:

$$\Delta r_t / r_{t-1} = 0 \text{ and } r_t = r_{t-1} = r^* \text{ when } v_{t-1} = v^* \text{ and } s_t = s^* \tag{B.25}$$

where $\Delta r_t = r_t - r_{t-1}$. These equilibrium conditions differ from those proposed for many rent adjustment models, in that when rents and vacancy equal their natural rates, development can be undertaken profitably at a natural rate determined by the rates of economic growth and depreciation, rather than dropping to zero. In other words, the equilibrium trajectory of the model incorporates a steady-state growth path.

Now if the vacancy rate at the start of a period is less than its natural rate, then according to equation (B.24), the rate of starts over that period should exceed its natural rate. The signal for this to happen depends upon the responsiveness of real rents to shifts in vacancy. If there is *full adjustment* of rents, then by the end of the period, they will have moved to a new level just sufficiently higher than their natural level to have allowed profitable development of the additional starts necessary to compensate for the relative shortage of space. Alternatively, with only *partial adjustment*, a positive rate of rental growth moves rents towards the level necessary to sustain the required increase in starts:

$$r_t > r^* \text{ or } \Delta r_t / r_{t-1} > 0, \text{ when } v_{t-1} < v^* \text{ and } s_t > s^* \tag{B.26}$$

Conversely, depending on whether there is full or partial rent adjustment, a rent level correspondingly lower than the natural rate, or rental decline, signify a relative excess of space that triggers a reduction in the rate of starts below its natural rate:

$$r_t < r^* \text{ or } \Delta r_t / r_{t-1} < 0, \text{ when } v_{t-1} > v^* \text{ and } s_t < s^* \tag{B.27}$$

B.1.6 Transmission process

Equations (B.25)–(B.27) define two stages of a transmission process, acting from vacancy to building starts through rents, which translate the demand for new building into a market signal to which developers can respond. The transmission mechanism can incorporate either full or partial adjustment of rents to relative vacancy:

$$r_t - r^* = \rho(v^* - v_{t-1})$$ (B.28a)

or

$$\Delta r_t/r_{t-1} = \rho(v^* - v_{t-1})$$ (B.28b)

where ρ is a *rent adjustment coefficient*, acting like an inverse elasticity to determine the extent of the proportionate rental response to a given gap between the actual and natural vacancy rates. Note an important difference between these two formulations: full adjustment incorporates a unique equilibrium relationship between the level of vacancy and the level of rent; partial adjustment incorporates a hysteresis relationship, in which the current level of rent also depends on its own previous value (for a similar partial adjustment model of the relationship between inflation and unemployment, see Gordon, 1989).

If full adjustment is assumed to operate instantaneously, rather than over one time period, then an intermediate, *composite adjustment* process can be constructed as a normalized weighted sum of full and partial adjustment:

$$(1 - \beta)(\Delta r_t/r_{t-1}) + \beta(r_{t-1} - r^*) = \rho(v^* - v_{t-1})$$ (B.28c)

where β is a feedback coefficient expressing the extent to which the rent gap, as well as the vacancy gap, at the start of the period influences rental growth during the period.

The response of building starts to rents can similarly be expressed in terms of a full, partial or composite adjustment process:

$$s_t - s^* = \mu(r_t - r^*)$$ (B.29a)

or

$$s_t - s^* = \mu(\Delta r_t/r_{t-1})$$ (B.29b)

or

$$s_t - s^* = \mu[(1 - \beta)(\Delta r_t/r_{t-1}) + \beta(r_{t-1} - r^*)]$$ (B.29c)

Here parameter μ is an *indirect development reaction coefficient*, acting as a form of supply elasticity that determines the extent of the developer response to a given rent signal, rather than the direct investor response to a shortfall in building stock as represented by accelerator coefficient γ in equation (B.24).

In whichever form, equations (B.28) and (B.29) can be combined to reproduce the equation linking the relative rate of starts to the relative vacancy rate:

$$s_t - s^* = \mu\rho(v^* - v_{t-1})\qquad\qquad(B.30)$$

where the combined *transmission coefficient* $\mu\rho$ encapsulates the rent adjustment process. This corresponds to equation (B.24) under the condition that the direct and indirect development reaction coefficients γ and μ conform to the relationship:

$$\mu\rho = \gamma(1 - \delta)\qquad\qquad(B.31)$$

B.1.7 Changes to stock and vacancy

If the average *construction lag* from the start to completion of building is q time periods, then the level of completions C_t during period t is equivalent to the level of starts during period $t-q$:

$$C_t = S_{t-q}\qquad\qquad(B.32)$$

This determines the stock adjustment process such that stock K_t at the end of each period is given by the stock available at the beginning of the period K_{t-1} augmented by newly completed buildings C_t and reduced by the stock that is demolished or retired at rate δ according to equation (B.15):

$$K_t = (1 - \delta)K_{t-1} + C_t\qquad\qquad(B.33)$$

To close the circuit of market relationships, completions acting together with take-up, feed back to determine changes in vacancy. The change in vacancy over each period is a function of the change in total stock and the change in occupied space, or net absorption. Thus from equation (B.21):

$$V_t - V_{t-1} = (K_t - K_{t-1}) - (B_t - B_{t-1})$$

Equation (B.33) can be used to express the change in stock as the difference between completions and retirements, and equations (B.8)–(B.10) used to express net absorption as the difference between take-up and turnover, giving:

$$V_t - V_{t-1} = (C_t - \delta K_{t-1}) - (U_t - \tau B_{t-1})$$

Total stock K_{t-1} can be restated in terms of occupied stock and the vacancy rate, and the equation reordered so that vacancy change is expressed as a function of completions, take-up and occupied stock to give:

$$V_t - V_{t-1} = C_t - U_t + [\tau - \delta(1 + v_{t-1})]B_{t-1} \tag{B.34}$$

Dividing through by occupied stock at $t-1$, this equation can be transformed into a relationship between rates of vacancy change, completions and take-up:

$$\Delta v_t = c_t - u_t - \delta v_{t-1} + (\tau - \delta) \tag{B.35}$$

where $\Delta v_t = (V_t - V_{t-1})/B_{t-1}$ is the rate of change in vacancy between the beginning and end of the period, $c_t = C_t/B_{t-1}$ is the rate of completions, and $u_t = U_t/B_{t-1}$ is the rate of take-up, all expressed in terms of the level of occupied stock at the beginning of the period.

B.1.8 Development floor and ceiling

The level of development can be constrained to operate between a floor and a ceiling. However adverse are market conditions, an absolute floor is imposed by the constraint that the level of starts in any period cannot be less than zero:

$$S_t \geq 0 \tag{B.36}$$

This constraint plays a crucial role in the behaviour of the model, as demonstrated in Chapter 7.

Perhaps more realistically, the floor can be set to a minimum level of starts S_t^a, corresponding to some volume of autonomous development which tends to be undertaken irrespective of current market conditions:

$$S_t \geq S_t^a \tag{B.37}$$

For convenience, this minimum level of autonomous starts can be expressed as a proportion ζ^f of the occupied stock at the start of the period:

$$S_t^a = \zeta^f B_{t-1} \tag{B.38}$$

A ceiling is set by the constraint that the level of development underway in any period D_t, equal to the sum of the uncompleted starts from the current and previous periods, does not exceed the capacity of the development industry D_t^c:

$$D_t = \sum_{q-1}^{0} S_{t-x} \leq D_t^c \tag{B.39}$$

It can also be assumed for convenience that the capacity of the development industry is a proportion ζ^c of the occupied stock at the start of the period:

$$D_t^c = \zeta^c B_{t-1} \tag{B.40}$$

B.1.9 Rent elastic demand and depreciation

If the initial assumption of inelastic occupier demand is relaxed, the building occupancy rate α_t employed in equation (B.2) can be assumed to be an inverse function of rents. The assumption is that if real rents are above their natural level, or if they are increasing, then occupiers will choose, where possible, to decrease the amount of space they inhabit, leading to a lower occupancy ratio. Assuming either a full or partial adjustment process, as with the rent elastic supply equations (B.29), a simple linear formulation of the rent elastic occupancy relationship can be expressed as either:

$$\alpha_t = \alpha^\star [1 - e^\alpha (r_t - r^\star)] \tag{B.41a}$$

or

$$\alpha_t = \alpha^\star (1 - e^\alpha \Delta r_t / r_{t-1}) \tag{B.41b}$$

where $\alpha^\star$ is the natural occupancy rate when rents are at their natural level $r^\star$, and e^α is an elasticity of change in occupancy relative to rental change.

Like the occupancy rate, the depreciation rate δ_t can also be made to vary around its natural rate $\delta^\star$ according to whether rents are rising or falling – the higher rents go, the more slowly do building owners retire their least profitable space. The way in which elastic demand and depreciation interact with elastic supply to modify the building cycle is illustrated in Chapter 7.

B.1.10 Variable natural rates

Because the emphasis in the model is upon reproducing cyclical fluctuations around an equilibrium growth path, the natural rates defining that equilibrium path have been assumed to be constant. However, these rates are themselves a function of conditions in other factor and product markets, and as conditions in those markets change, so will the natural rates defining the property market growth trajectory.

To illustrate this, let us concentrate on the central supply–demand relationship for new building starts which links the user, development and investment markets in determining the natural rent level. First, a time-dependent natural occupancy rate $\alpha_t^\star$, expressing the level of occupier demand for building stock per unit of output or income, can be defined by a demand relationship that is a function of the time-dependent natural rent $r_t^\star$ acting as the user cost of building capital, plus the exogenously determined prices of the other inputs, represented by vector $\mathbf{p}_t^d$:

$$\alpha_t^\star = f(r_t^\star, \mathbf{p}_t^d) \tag{B.42}$$

For non-residential buildings, the other inputs are factors of production; for dwellings, the other inputs are consumer goods. This formulation allows for non-residential occupiers to substitute equipment for building capital over time, as equipment cheapens more rapidly (see the argument outlined in Chapter 4), and for residential occupiers to substitute between housing and other consumer goods as relative prices change.

The natural rate of starts can also be defined as a time-dependent demand variable s_t^d if the natural occupancy rate is allowed to vary. Equation (B.20) defines the natural rate of starts as a constant on the assumption of fixed natural occupancy and vacancy rates, together with constant rates of output growth and depreciation. If these are all allowed to vary, then so does the natural rate of starts according to the general relationship:

$$s_t^d = f(\alpha_t^\star, v_t^\star, \varepsilon_t, \delta_t) \qquad\qquad (B.43)$$

The natural occupancy rate $\alpha_t^\star$ has already been defined as a function of the natural rent according to equation (B.42); if other market parameters such as the natural vacancy rate and depreciation rate are also assumed to be endogenous functions of the natural rent, then equation (B.43) can be simplified to give:

$$s_t^d = f(r_t^\star, \varepsilon_t, \mathbf{p}_t^d) \qquad\qquad (B.44)$$

A corresponding supply function for the natural rate of starts s_t^s can be defined in terms of the profitability of development expressed as the capital value of new buildings (determined by the natural rent $r_t^\star$ and natural property yield $w_t^\star$) less the costs of development represented by price vector $\mathbf{p}_t^s$ (determined by construction, land and capital costs):

$$s_t^s = f(r_t^\star, w_t^\star, \mathbf{p}_t^s) \qquad\qquad (B.45)$$

The market clearing equilibrium defined by demand and supply equations (B.44) and (B.45) determines unique values for the natural rate of starts $s_t^\star$ and natural rent $r_t^\star$ for any combination of exogenously determined values of the property yield (partly dependent on conditions in other investment markets), the output growth rate and the vectors of other input and development costs:

$$s_t^\star = f(r_t^\star, w_t^\star, \varepsilon_t, \mathbf{p}_t^d, \mathbf{p}_t^s) \qquad\qquad (B.46)$$

Changes in any of the exogenous variables will shift the natural values of rents and starts rate to a new equilibrium. Thus, for example, if the rate of output growth increases due to enhanced technical change, or an increase in the labour force growth rate, then the natural rate of starts will tend to rise because of higher demand growth; this will induce an increase in the natural rent level sufficient to support the increased level of development activity; however, to an extent determined by relative supply and demand elasticities, these shifts will be offset by a decrease in the natural occupancy rate as the natural rent level rises.

B.2   Cycle generation

Even when model relationships are formulated as linear difference equations, the introduction of boundary constraints and time-variant parameters means that the overall structure of the model becomes non-linear. However, under the simplifying assumptions of fixed parameters and no boundary constraints, the model can be reduced to a set of second-order linear difference equations that are amenable to analytical solution for a market characterized by inelastic demand and elastic development supply. For this basic version of the model, we can now derive the conditions under which cycles will be generated, whether they will be damped or explosive, and the determinants of the period of the cycle. The behaviour of more complex versions of the model, involving longer lags, floor and ceiling constraints, elastic demand and alternative rent transmission processes, is demonstrated in Chapter 7 using numerical simulation.

B.2.1   The basic model

Let us return to equation (B.22), describing how the level of actual building starts S_t during time period t deviate from their equilibrium or natural level $S_t^\star$ when actual stock K_{t-1} deviates from its desired level $K_{t-1}^\star$ at the start of the period:

$$S_t = S_t^\star + \gamma(1 - \delta)(K_{t-1}^\star - K_{t-1})$$

This equation can be simplified by eliminating $K_{t-1}^\star$, using the equilibrium relationship (B.18) between the natural level of starts $S_t^\star$ and desired level of stock $K_{t-1}^\star$, and replacing direct accelerator term $\gamma(1 - \delta)$ with indirect transmission coefficient $\mu\rho$ according to equation (B.31) to give:

$$S_t = \Omega S_t^\star - \mu\rho K_{t-1} \tag{B.47}$$

where

$$\Omega = (1 + \varepsilon)/(\varepsilon + \delta) \tag{B.48}$$

Now, from equations (B.32) and (B.33), the adjustment process for total stock is given by:

$$K_t = (1 - \delta)K_{t-1} + S_{t-q} \tag{B.49}$$

The starts and stock equations (B.47) and (B.49) can be restated in terms of their equivalent lagged levels S_{t-1} and K_{t-1}:

$$S_{t-1} = \Omega S_{t-1}^\star - \mu\rho K_{t-2}$$

and

$$K_{t-1} = (1 - \delta)K_{t-2} + S_{t-q-1}$$

Using these expressions for K_{t-1} and S_{t-1}, starts equation (B.47) can now be expanded and reorganized to give a $(q+1)$th order linear difference equation for actual starts as a function of natural starts:

$$S_t - (1 - \delta)S_{t-1} + \mu\rho S_{t-q-1} = \Omega[S_t^{\star} - (1 - \delta)S_{t-1}^{\star}]$$

This equation can be simplified, by substituting for Ω from equation (B.48) and allowing for the constant rate of growth of natural starts according to equation (B.19), to yield the basic $(q+1)$th order starts equation:

$$S_t - (1 - \delta)S_{t-1} + \mu\rho S_{t-q-1} = S_t^{\star} \qquad (B.50)$$

For higher order linear difference equations of this type, analytical solution is difficult, and simulation may be the only feasible solution method. However, if the simplifying assumption is made that the unit time period of the model corresponds to the average construction delay between building starts and completions (i.e. $q = 1$), then the equation in starts is reduced to a second-order linear form that is amenable to analytical solution:

$$S_t - (1 - \delta)S_{t-1} + \mu\rho S_{t-2} = S_t^{\star} \qquad (B.51)$$

Dividing through by occupied stock B_{t-1}, and assuming a constant rate of growth in demand ε, an equivalent second-order difference equation in the rate of starts can be derived as:

$$s_t - [(1 - \delta)/(1 + \varepsilon)]s_{t-1} + [\mu\rho/(1 + \varepsilon)^2]s_{t-2} = s^{\star} \qquad (B.52)$$

Similar equations can be derived for the rates of completions, vacancy and rents.

Second-order linear difference equations of this type can be solved as a combination of a *particular solution*, representing the equilibrium path of development starts with respect to the growth trajectory of economic activity, plus a *complementary solution* describing the cyclical fluctuations which may be generated around this path following some displacement from equilibrium.

B.2.2   The equilibrium path

The particular solution describing the equilibrium path for development starts is defined by the condition that by the end of each time period, the actual building stock K_t always matches desired stock $K_t^{\star}$, and therefore that the actual level and rate of starts S_t and s_t during each period always correspond to their natural levels $S_t^{\star}$ and $s^{\star}$. Similarly, the vacancy rate v_t at the end of each period always equals its natural rate $v^{\star}$, and the real rent level r_t stays constant at its natural level $r^{\star}$.

Under these conditions, the second-order starts equations (B.51) and (B.52) reduce to identities that constitute their particular solution:

$$S_t^\star - (1 - \delta)S_{t-1}^\star + \mu\rho S_{t-2}^\star \equiv S_t^\star \tag{B.53}$$

and

$$s^\star - [(1 - \delta)/(1 + \varepsilon)]s^\star + [\mu\rho/(1 + \varepsilon)^2]s^\star \equiv s^\star \tag{B.54}$$

Equilibrium condition (B.54) reduces to the equality:

$$\mu\rho = (1 - \delta)(1 + \varepsilon)$$

and using equation (B.31), relating the direct and indirect development reaction coefficients, this condition further reduces to a definition of the direct reaction rate necessary to maintain the equilibrium trajectory of total stock and development activity:

$$\gamma = 1 + \varepsilon \tag{B.55}$$

This shows that to deliver the desired amount of completed stock with a one period delay, developers must boost starts by an expectations increment ε to anticipate the growth in demand during the development period. By substituting for γ in equation (B.20), the value of the natural rate of starts which maintains the equilibrium trajectory is redefined as:

$$s^\star = (1 + \varepsilon)(1 + v^\star)(\varepsilon + \delta) \tag{B.56}$$

The natural rate of starts, defined relative to occupied stock, is thus shown to comprise three components:

- The sum of the induced and replacement components of demand for new space $(\varepsilon + \delta)$.
- A vacancy increment to maintain the inventory of vacant space at its natural rate $(1 + v^\star)$.
- An expectations increment to anticipate the growth in demand during the construction period $(1 + \varepsilon)$.

These equilibrium conditions can be generalized to the case of a q period construction lag using equation (B.50). To maintain the equilibrium trajectory, the reaction rate must boost starts by an expectations increment:

$$\gamma = (1 + \varepsilon)^q \tag{B.57}$$

defining the equilibrium rate of starts as:

$$s^\star = (1 + \varepsilon)^q(1 + v^\star)(\varepsilon + \delta) \tag{B.58}$$

B.2.3 Cyclical fluctuations

The complementary solution, describing the cyclical fluctuations in building starts which follow a displacement from the equilibrium path, can be derived either in terms of the level or rate of starts. For the purposes of simulation, it is more convenient to derive the cycle equation in terms of the rate of starts. Let the variation in the rate of starts s_t around their equilibrium path s^* be expressed in terms of deviations z_t, where:

$$z_t = s_t - s^* \tag{B.59}$$

Subtracting particular solution (B.54) from equation (B.52), a homogenous second-order difference equation is derived for the deviations around the equilibrium path:

$$z_t - [(1 - \delta)/(1 + \varepsilon)]z_{t-1} + [\mu\rho/(1 + \varepsilon)^2]z_{t-2} = 0 \tag{B.60}$$

By setting,

$$z_t = z_0\psi^t$$

difference equation (B.60) can be transformed into a quadratic characteristic equation of the form:

$$\psi^2 - [(1 - \delta)/(1 + \varepsilon)]\psi + \mu\rho/(1 + \varepsilon)^2 = 0 \tag{B.61}$$

which will generate cyclical fluctuations if its roots are complex, that is if:

$$[(1 - \delta)/(1 + \varepsilon)]^2 < 4\mu\rho/(1 + \varepsilon)^2$$

This condition can be reordered to give the *critical value* of the combined transmission coefficient $\mu\rho$ above which the rent adjustment process, from vacancy to starts, will generate cyclical fluctuations:

$$\mu\rho > (1 - \delta)^2/4 \tag{B.62}$$

Following Elaydi (1996: 69–70) and Gabisch and Lorenz (1989: 45–8), the cyclical solution of the characteristic equation can be derived in terms of polar coordinates and simplified by DeMoivre's theorem to give:

$$z_t = \lambda^t(A_1\cos\theta t + A_2\sin\theta t) \tag{B.63}$$

where the modulus of the cycle λ is given by:

$$\lambda^2 = \mu\rho/(1 + \varepsilon)^2 \qquad (B.64)$$

Equation (B.63) describes the cyclical fluctuation in the rate of development starts around their equilibrium path which are generated by an initial displacement, assuming the condition given by equation (B.62) holds. Constants A_1 and A_2 depend upon the extent of the initial disturbance, while modulus λ determines the subsequent behaviour of the cycle. The combination of the initial disturbance and modulus determines the *amplitude* of the cycle oscillations. The cycle *period* is given by:

$$\upsilon = 2\pi/\theta \qquad (B.65)$$

where frequency parameter θ is measured in radians, and defined by:

$$\cos\theta = (1 - \delta)/2(\mu\rho)^{1/2} \qquad (B.66)$$

Since the amplitude of successive oscillations of the cycle depend on λ^t, the building cycle is explosive if $\lambda>1$, and damped if $\lambda<1$. From equation (B.64), the *crossover point* generating a stable cycle of harmonic oscillations is thus defined by the condition:

$$\mu\rho = (1 + \varepsilon)^2 \qquad (B.67)$$

If the building cycle equation is derived in terms of the level rather than the rate of starts, it can be shown that the critical value of the transmission coefficient above which cycles are generated is the same as given by equation (B.62), and so is the period of the cycle as given by equations (B.65) and (B.66). However, the modulus of the cycle and thus the crossover point from damped to explosive cycles differ from those given by equations (B.64) and (B.67) for the rates cycle; the equivalent conditions for the levels cycle are:

$$\lambda^2 = \mu\rho \qquad (B.68)$$

and

$$\mu\rho = 1 \qquad (B.69)$$

B.2.4   A simplified version

A simplified version of the model can be derived in a form which corresponds to the widely used error correction model of short-term dynamic adjustment around an equilibrium growth path (see Chapter 8). Reverting to the second-order rate of starts equation (B.52):

$$s_t - [(1 - \delta)/(1 + \varepsilon)]s_{t-1} + [\mu\rho/(1 + \varepsilon)^2]s_{t-2} = s^\star$$

assume that the coefficient on s_{t-1} is approximately unity, i.e. $[(1 - \delta)/(1 + \varepsilon)] \approx 1$. The equation can then be re-expressed in difference form:

$$\Delta s_t = \lambda^2 \Delta s_{t-1} - \lambda^2 z_{t-1} + (1 - \lambda^2)s^\star \qquad (B.70)$$

where $\lambda^2 = \mu\rho/(1 + \varepsilon)^2$ defines the modulus of the cycle λ according to equation (B.64), $\Delta s_t = s_t - s_{t-1}$ is the first difference in the rate of starts and $z_{t-1} = s_{t-1} - s^\star$ is the lagged deviation in the actual rate of starts around its natural rate $s^\star$ as defined by equation (B.59).

Two opposing forces are at work in this version of the model equation. The positive first difference term $\lambda^2 \Delta s_{t-1}$ reinforces the deviation in starts away from equilibrium, while the negative feedback term $\lambda^2 z_{t-1}$ restores starts back towards equilibrium. When starts are close to their equilibrium trajectory, the reinforcement term predominates; as they move further away, the damping force of the error correction term takes over. Following equations (B.62) and (B.67), the size of the transmission coefficient $\mu\rho$ determines the cyclical behaviour of the model – the larger the coefficient, the stronger the cyclical fluctuations. Again, similar equations can be derived for vacancy and rents; that for rents takes the form:

$$\Delta r_t = \lambda^2 \Delta r_{t-1} - \lambda^2 q_{t-1} + (1 - \lambda^2)r^\star \qquad (B.71)$$

where $q_{t-1} = r_{t-1} - r^\star$ is the lagged deviation in the actual level of rents around their natural level $r^\star$.

B.2.5   Cyclical behaviour of the model

Four parameters determine the cyclical behaviour of the model: the length of the delay q between building starts and completions, the size of the combined transmission coefficient $\mu\rho$, the rate of output growth ε and the rate of depreciation δ. The following initial observations can be made about each parameter, while more precise estimates are derived in Chapter 7, which reports the results of fitting the model to data on the City of London office market.

- For the purpose of analytical solution, the *construction lag* q has automatically been set to the unit time period of the model, so that q = 1. In practice, the length of this period varies widely according to the type of building and the size and complexity of the development scheme; it typically ranges between 1 and 3 years.
- The *transmission coefficient* $\mu\rho$, measuring the effect of the market adjustment of rents to relative vacancy combined with the developer reaction to rent signals, is difficult to measure directly. However, it is reasonable to assume that there is a cautious response to demand signals in a market such as real estate which operates with excess capacity under conditions of considerable uncertainty (see

Chapter 2). This implies a value for the transmission coefficient lying somewhere in the range 0–1.

- The trend *rate of output growth* ε depends upon economic conditions such as the rates of technical progress and labour force growth; in a mature industrialized economy such as the United Kingdom, the trend rate may typically lie in the range 2%–3% per annum.
- As for any type of capital goods, the *rate of depreciation* δ for buildings can be estimated approximately from the age distribution of the existing stock. Most estimates for buildings suggest values in the range 1%–3% per annum.

Using these assumptions, three questions about the building cycle can be answered by the model:

Under what conditions will cycles be generated?

The critical value of the transmission coefficient $\mu\rho$ above which cyclical behaviour is generated by the model is given by equation (B.62). With depreciation rate δ set in the range 0.01–0.03, then cyclical fluctuations are generated if the transmission rate exceeds 0.23–0.25. This low threshold suggests that plausible response rates by the development industry to market demand signals are likely to generate building cycles.

Under what conditions will cycles be damped or explosive?

For the levels cycle, the crossover point between damped and explosive cycles is shown in equation (B.69) to be reached when the transmission coefficient reaches 1, whereas for the rates cycle, equation (B.67) shows it to be reached at the slightly higher value of $(1 + \varepsilon)^2$, equivalent to 1.04–1.06 with output growth in the range 2%–3%. It seems intuitively reasonable that the crossover point for the level of starts is reached when the transmission rate is unity – below it, the development industry is moderating its response to a relative shortage or excess of space; above it, the supply response amplifies the demand signal. The slightly higher crossover point for the rate of starts allows the amplitude of the levels cycle to increase in line with the volume of stock.

   These conditions only hold under the simplifying assumption that the average construction lag is set to the unit time period of the model. If the delay is greater than one period (q > 1), generating a higher order difference model, then the crossover point will be reached with a lower transmission rate. This is because, the longer the delay, the greater the total supply response to a given demand signal, as successive periods of development starts accumulate. The manner in which the crossover value of the transmission coefficient decreases, as the construction lag increases, is illustrated by simulation modelling in Chapter 7.

What will be the typical period of the cycle?

The period of the building cycle is given by equations (B.65) and (B.66). At the crossover point for the rates cycle ($\mu\rho$ = 1.04–1.06), and with δ in the range 0.01–0.03, these equations yield values of the cycle parameter θ of 1.06–1.08 in radians, producing a cycle period of 5.8–5.9 time periods. As the transmission coefficient decreases, so the cycle period increases; thus, if $\mu\rho$ halves from 1.05 to 0.525, the cycle period increases from 5.9 to 7.6 time periods. Another way of putting this is that as the transmission rate increases, so does the frequency of the cycle. Again, these numerical results only apply to the simplifying case in which the average construction lag is set to the unit time period of the model. It is demonstrated in Chapter 7 that as the construction lag increases, so does the period of the cycle for any given value of the transmission coefficient.

References

Abbott, C. (1987) Urban America in the Modern Age, Arlington Heights, IL, Harlan Davidson.

Abernathy, F. H., Dunlop, J. T., Hammond, J. H. and Weil, D. (1999) A Stitch in Time, New York, Oxford University Press.

Abraham, J. M. and Hendershott, P. H. (1996) 'Bubbles in metropolitan housing markets', Journal of Housing Research, 7(2): 191–207.

Abramovitz, M. (1961) 'The nature and significance of Kuznets cycles', Economic Development and Cultural Change, 9: 225–248.

Abramovitz, M. (1964) Evidences of Long Swings in Aggregate Construction Since the Civil War, New York, National Bureau of Economic Research.

Abramovitz, M. (1968) 'The passing of the Kuznets cycle', Economica, 35: 349–367.

Abramovitz, M. and David, P. A. (2000) 'American macroeconomic growth in the era of knowledge-based progress: the long-run perspective', in S. L. Engerman and R. E. Gallman eds., The Cambridge Economic History of the United States, volume III, Cambridge, Cambridge University Press, 1–92.

Adams, J. S. (1970) 'Residential structure of Midwestern cities', Annals of the Association of American Geographers, 60: 37–62.

Adelman, I. (1965) 'Long cycles – fact or artifact', American Economic Review, 55: 444–463.

Aftalion, A. (1927) 'The theory of economic cycles based on the capitalistic technique of production', Review of Economic Statistics, 9: 165–170.

Aghion P. and Banerjee, A. (2005) Volatility and Growth, Oxford, Oxford University Press.

Aghion P. and Howitt, P. (1992) 'A model of growth through creative destruction', Econometrica, 60(2): 323–351.

Aghion P. and Howitt, P. (1998) Endogenous Growth Theory, Cambridge, MA, MIT Press.

Akerlof, G. A. and Yellen, J. L. (1985) 'A near-rational model of the business cycle, with wage and price inertia', Quarterly Journal of Economics, 100: 823–838.

Aldcroft, D. H. and Fearon, P. eds. (1972) British Economic Fluctuations 1790–1939, London, Macmillan.

Allen, F. and Gale, D. (2000) 'Bubbles and crises', Economic Journal, 110: 236–255.

Allinson, K. (2003) London's Contemporary Architecture, third edition, Oxford, Architectural Press.

Alonso, W. (1964) Location and Land Use, Cambridge, MA, Harvard University Press.

Amin, A. and Thrift, N. (1992) 'Neo-Marshallian nodes in global networks', International Journal of Urban and Regional Research, 16: 571–587.

Anas, A., Arnott, R. and Small, K. A. (1998) 'Urban spatial structure', Journal of Economic Literature, 36: 1426–1464.

Antwi, A. and Henneberry, J. (1995) 'Developers, non-linearity and asymmetry in the development cycle', Journal of Property Research, 12(3): 217–239.

Aoki, K., Proudman, J. and Vlieghe, G. (2002) 'House prices, consumption, and monetary policy: a financial accelerator approach', London, Bank of England Working Paper No. 169.

Arestis, P. ed. (2007) Is There a New Consensus in Macroeconomics? Basingstoke, Palgrave Macmillan.

Arnold, L. G. (2002) Business Cycle Theory, Oxford, Oxford University Press.

Arrow, K. J. (1962) 'The economic implications of learning by doing', Review of Economic Studies, 29: 155–173.

Arthur, W. B. (1989) 'Competing technologies, increasing returns and lock-in by historical events', Economic Journal, 99: 116–131.

Arthur, W. B. (1994) Increasing Returns and Path Dependence in the Economy, Ann Arbor, MI, University of Michigan Press.

Aschauer, D. A. (1989) 'Is public expenditure productive?' Journal of Monetary Economics, 23: 177–200.

Ashton, T. S. (1959) Economic Fluctuations in England 1700–1800, Oxford, Oxford University Press.

Ashton, T. S. and Sykes, J. (1964) The Coal Industry of the Eighteenth Century, second edition, Manchester, Manchester University Press.

Ashworth, W. (1960) An Economic History of England 1870–1939, London, Methuen.

Atack, J. and Margo, R. A. (1998) '"Location, location, location!" The price gradient for vacant urban land: New York, 1835 to 1900', Journal of Real Estate Finance and Economics, 16(2): 151–172.

Attanasio, O. P. and Weber, G. (1994) 'The UK consumption boom of the late 1980s: aggregate implications of microeconomic evidence', Economic Journal, 104: 1269–1302.

Augar, P. (2009) Chasing Alpha, London, Bodley Head.

Backus, D. K. and Kehoe, P. J. (1992) 'International evidence on the historical properties of business cycles', American Economic Review, 82(4): 864–888.

Bagwell, P. S. (1988) The Transport Revolution 1770–1985, London, Routledge.

Bairoch, P. (1982) 'International Industrialization levels from 1750 to 1980', Journal of European Economic History, 11: 269–333.

Bairoch, P. (1988) Cities and Economic Development, Chicago, IL, University of Chicago Press.

Ball, M. (1994) 'The 1980s property boom', Environment and Planning A, 26: 671–695.

Ball, M. (2003) 'Is there an office replacement cycle?' Journal of Property Research, 20(2): 173–189.

Ball, M. and Sunderland, D. (2001) An Economic History of London 1800–1914, London, Routledge.

Ball, M. and Wood, A. (1996a) 'Does building investment affect economic growth?' Journal of Property Research, 13: 99–114.

Ball, M. and Wood, A. (1996b) 'Trend growth in post-1850 British economic history: the Kalman filter and historical judgement', The Statistician, 45(2): 143–152.

Ball, M., Lizieri, C. and MacGregor, B. D. (1998) The Economics of Commercial Property Markets, London, Routledge.

Ball, M., Morrison, T. and Wood, A. (1996) 'Structures investment and economic growth: a long-term international comparison', Urban Studies, 33(9): 1687–1706.

Banham, R. (1971) Los Angeles, London, Penguin Books.

Barker, T. C. (1980) 'Towards a historical classification of urban transport development since the later eighteenth century', Journal of Transport History, 1: 75–90.

Barker, T. C. (1988) 'Urban transport', in M. J. Freeman and D. H. Aldcroft eds., Transport in Victorian Britain, Manchester, Manchester University Press, 134–170.

Barker, T. C. and Robbins, M. (1963) A History of London Transport, volume 1, The Nineteenth Century, London, Allen and Unwin.

Barker, T. C. and Robbins, M. (1974) A History of London Transport, volume 2, The Twentieth Century to 1970, London, Allen and Unwin.

Barker, T. C. and Savage, C. I. (1974) An Economic History of Transport in Britain, third edition, London, Hutchinson.

Barras, R. (1983) 'A simple theoretical model of the office development cycle', Environment and Planning A, 15: 1381–1394.

Barras, R. (1984) 'The office development cycle in London', Land Development Studies, 1: 35–50.

Barras, R. (1986) 'A comparison of embodied technical change in services and manufacturing industry', Applied Economics, 18: 941–958.

Barras, R. (1987) 'Technical change and the urban development cycle', Urban Studies, 24: 5–30.

Barras, R. (1990) 'Interactive innovation in financial and business services: the vanguard of the service revolution', Research Policy, 19: 215–237.

Barras, R. (1994) 'Property and the economic cycle: building cycles revisited', Journal of Property Research, 11: 183–197.

Barras, R. (2001) 'Building investment is a diminishing source of economic growth', Journal of Property Research, 18(4): 279–308.

Barras, R. (2005) 'A building cycle model for an imperfect world', Journal of Property Research, 22(2–3): 63–96.

Barras, R. and Clark, P. (1996) 'Obsolescence and performance in the Central London office market', Journal of Property Valuation and Investment, 14(4): 63–78.

Barras, R. and Ferguson, D. (1985) 'A spectral analysis of building cycles in Britain', Environment and Planning A, 17: 1369–1391.

Barras, R. and Ferguson, D. (1987a) 'Dynamic modelling of the building cycle: 1 Theoretical framework', Environment and Planning A, 19: 353–367.

Barras, R. and Ferguson, D. (1987b) 'Dynamic modelling of the building cycle: 2 Empirical results', Environment and Planning A, 19: 493–520.

Barro, R. J. (1976) 'Rational expectations and the role of monetary policy', Journal of Monetary Economics, 2: 1–32.

Barro, R. J. (1981) Money, Expectations and Business Cycles, New York, Academic Press.

Barro, R. J. ed. (1989) Modern Business Cycle Theory, Cambridge, MA, Harvard University Press.

Barron, C. M. (2000) 'London 1300–1540', in D. M. Palliser ed., The Cambridge Urban History of Britain, volume I, 600–1540, Cambridge, Cambridge University Press, 395–440.

Basalla, G. (1988) The Evolution of Technology, Cambridge, Cambridge University Press.

Bascomb, N. (2003) Higher, New York, Doubleday.

Basker, E. (2007) 'The causes and consequences of Wal-Mart's growth', Journal of Economic Perspectives, 21(3): 177–198.

Batten, D. (1995), 'Network cities: creative urban agglomerations for the 21st century', Urban Studies, 32(2): 313–327.

Baum, A. (1991) Property Investment Depreciation and Obsolescence, London, Routledge.

Baum, A. and Lizieri, C. (1999) 'Who owns the City? Office ownership and overseas investment in the City of London', Real Estate Finance, Spring, 87–100.

Baumol, W. J. (1967) 'Macroeconomics of unbalanced growth: the anatomy of urban crisis', American Economic Review, 57(3): 415–426.

Baxter, M. and King, R. G. (1999) 'Measuring business cycles: approximate band-pass filters for economic time series', Review of Economics and Statistics, 81(4): 575–593.

Beauregard, R. A. (1994) 'Capital switching and the built environment: United States 1970–89', Environment and Planning A, 26: 715–732.

Bernardini, O. and Galli, R. (1993), 'Dematerialization: long term trends in the intensity of use of materials and energy', Futures, May: 431–448.

Bernanke, B., Gertler, M. and Gilchrist, S. (1996) 'The financial accelerator and the flight to quality', Review of Economics and Statistics, 78(1): 1–15.

Berry, B. J. L. (1964) 'Cities as systems within systems of cities', Papers of the Regional Science Association, 13: 147–163.

Berry, B. J. L. (1991) Long-Wave Rhythms in Economic Development and Political Behaviour, Baltimore, MD, John Hopkins University Press.

Berry, J. and McGreal, S., eds. (1995) European Cities, Planning Systems and Property Markets, London, Spon.

Bertaud, A. (2003) 'Clearing the air in Atlanta: transit and smart growth or conventional economics?' Journal of Urban Economics, 54: 379–400.

Beveridge, S. and Nelson, C. R. (1981) 'A new approach to decomposition of economic time series into permanent and transitory components with particular attention to measurement of the "business cycle"', Journal of Monetary Economics, 7: 151–174.

Bischoff, C. W. (1970) 'A model of nonresidential construction in the United States', American Economic Review: Papers and Proceedings, 60(2): 10–17.

Bird, R. C., Desai, M. J., Enzler, J. J. and Taubman, P. J. (1965) ' "Kuznets cycles" in growth rates: the meaning', International Economic Review, 6(2): 229–239.

Björklund, K. and Söderberg, B. (1999) 'Property cycles, speculative bubbles and the gross income multiplier', Journal of Real Estate Research, 18(1): 151–174.

Black, D. and Henderson, J. V. (1999) 'A theory of urban growth', Journal of Political Economy, 107(2): 252–284.

Black, D. and Henderson, J. V. (2003) 'Urban evolution in the USA', Journal of Economic Geography, 3: 343–372.

Blackaby, F. ed. (1978) De-industrialisation, London, Heinemann.

Blackburn, K. and Ravn, M. O. (1992) 'Business cycles in the United Kingdom: facts and fictions', Economica, 59: 383–401.

Blank, D. M. and Winnick, L. (1953) 'The structure of the housing market', Quarterly Journal of Economics, 67: 181–208.

Blinder, A. S. (1987) 'Keynes, Lucas and scientific progress', American Economic Association Papers and Proceedings, 77(2): 130–136.

Blinder, A. S. and Fischer, S. (1981) 'Inventories, rational expectations and the business cycle', Journal of Monetary Economics, 8: 277–304.

Borchert, J. R. (1967) 'American Metropolitan Evolution', Geographical Review, 57: 301–332.

Boulton, J. (2000) 'London 1540–1700', in P. Clark ed., The Cambridge Urban History of Britain, volume II, 1540–1840, Cambridge, Cambridge University Press, 315–346.

Bowman, A. K., Garnsey, P. and Rathbone, D. (2000) The High Empire A.D. 70–192, second edition, Cambridge Ancient History volume XI, Cambridge, Cambridge University Press.

Bowley, M. (1937) 'Fluctuations in house-building and the trade cycle', Review of Economic Studies, 4: 167–181.

Bowley, M. (1966) The British Building Industry, Cambridge, Cambridge University Press.

Bradley, S. and Pevsner, N. (1997) The Buildings of England: The City of London, London, Penguin Books.

Bramley, G., Munro, M. and Pawson, H. (2004) Key Issues in Housing, Basingstoke, Palgrave Macmillan.

Braudel, F. (1980) On History, Chicago, IL, University of Chicago Press.

Breheny, M.J., ed. (1992), Sustainable Development and Urban Form, London, Pion.

Bresnahan, T. F. and Trajtenberg, M. (1995) 'General purpose technologies 'Engines of growth?'' Journal of Econometrics, 65: 83–108.

Brezis, E. S. and Krugman, P. (1997) 'Technology and the life cycle of cities', Journal of Economic Growth, 2: 369–383.

Briggs, A. (1968) Victorian Cities, London, Penguin Books.

Broadberry, S. N. (1987) 'Cheap money and the housing boom in interwar Britain: an econometric appraisal', Manchester School, 87: 378–391.

Broadberry, S. N. (1997) The Productivity Race: British Manufacturing in International Perspective 1850–1990, Cambridge, Cambridge University Press.

Broadberry, S. N. (2006) Market Services and the Productivity Race, 1850–2000, Cambridge, Cambridge University Press.

Broadberry, S. N. and Ghosal, S. (2002) 'From the counting house to the modern office: explaining Anglo-American productivity differences in services, 1870–1990', Journal of Economic History, 62(4): 967–998.

Bronfenbrenner, M. ed. (1969) Is the Business Cycle Obsolete? New York, Wiley.

Brotchie, J., Batty, M., Blakely, E., Hall. P. and Newton, P., eds. (1995) Cities in Competition, Melbourne, Longman Australia.

Brown, S. J. and Liu, C. H. eds. (2001) A Global Perspective on Real Estate Cycles, Boston, MA, Kluwer.

Brueckner, J. K. (1980) 'A vintage model of urban growth', Journal of Urban Economics, 8: 389–402.

Bruegmann, R. (2005) Sprawl, Chicago, IL, University of Chicago Press.

Bry, G. and Boschan, C. (1971) Cyclical Analysis of Time Series: Selected Procedures and Computer Programs, Technical Paper 20, New York, National Bureau of Economic Research.

Brynjolfsson, E. and Hitt, L. M. (2000) 'Beyond computation: information technology, organizational transformation and business performance', Journal of Economic Perspectives, 14(4): 23–48.

Buckley, K. A. H. (1952) 'Urban building and real estate fluctuations in Canada', Canadian Journal of Economics and Political Science, 18(1): 41–62.

Burns, A. F. (1934) Production Trends in the United States Since 1870, New York, National Bureau of Economic Research.

Burns, A. F. (1935) 'Long cycles in residential construction', in Economic Essays in Honor of Wesley Clair Mitchell, New York, Columbia University Press.

Burns, A. F. and Mitchell, W. C. (1946) Measuring Business Cycles, New York, National Bureau of Economic Research.

Burnside, C. and Eichenbaum, M. (1996) 'Factor hoarding and the propagation of business cycle shocks', American Economic Review, 86(5): 1154–1174.

Cadman, D. and Topping, R. (1995) Property Development, fourth edition, London, Spon.

Cairncross, A. K. (1934) 'The Glasgow building industry (1870–1914)', Review of Economic Statistics, 2: 1–17.

Cairncross, A. K. (1953) Home and Foreign Investment 1870–1913, Cambridge, Cambridge University Press.

Cairncross, A. K. and Weber, B. (1956) 'Fluctuations in building in Great Britain, 1785–1849', Economic History Review, 9(2): 1–17.

Campbell-Kelly, M. (1992) 'Large-scale data processing in the Prudential, 1850–1930', Accounting Business and Financial History, 2(2): 117–139.

Canova, F. (1998) 'Detrending and business cycle facts', Journal of Monetary Economics, 41: 475–512.

Cargill, T. F. (1971) 'Construction activity and secular change in the United States', Applied Economics, 3: 85–97.

Carter, S. B., Gartner, S. S., Haines, M. R., Olmstead, A. L., Sutch, R. and Wright, G. eds. (2006) The Historical Statistics of the United States, five volume Millennial Edition, Cambridge, Cambridge University Press.

Case, K. E. (1992) 'The real estate cycle and the economy: consequences of the Massachusetts boom of 1984–87', Urban Studies, 29(2): 171–183.

Case, K. E and Shiller, R. J. (1989) 'The efficiency of the market for single-family homes', American Economic Review, 79(1): 125–137.

Cassis, Y. (2006) Capitals of Capital: A History of International Financial Centres, 1780–2005, Cambridge, Cambridge University Press.

Castells, M. (1989) The Informational City, Oxford, Blackwell.

Castells, M. (2000) The Rise of the Network Society, second edition, Oxford, Blackwell.

Castells, M. and Hall, P. (1994) Technopoles of the World, London, Routledge.

Chandler, A. D. (1965) The Railroads: The Nation's First Big Business, New York, Harcourt Brace.

Chandler, T. and Fox, G. (1974) 3000 Years of Urban Growth, New York, Academic Press.

Chang, W. W. and Smyth, D. J. (1971) 'The existence and persistence of cycles in a non-linear model: Kaldor's 1940 model re-examined', Review of Economic Studies, 38: 37–44.

Chatfield, C. (2004) The Analysis of Time Series: An Introduction, sixth edition, London, Chapman and Hall.

Cheape, C. W. (1980) Moving the Masses, Cambridge, MA, Harvard University Press.

Checkoway, B. (1980) 'Large builders, federal housing programmes, and postwar suburbanization', International Journal of Urban and Regional Research, 4: 21–45.

Chenery, H. B. (1952) 'Overcapacity and the acceleration principle', Econometrica, 20(1): 1–28.

Chiaromonte, F. and Dosi, G. (1993) 'The micro-foundations of competitiveness and their macroeconomic implications', in D. Foray and C. Freeman eds., Technology and the Wealth of Nations, London, Frances Pinter, 107–134.

Chinloy, P. (1996) 'Real estate cycles: theory and empirical evidence', Journal of Housing Research, 7(2): 173–190.

Cho, M. (1996) 'House price dynamics: a survey of theoretical and empirical issues', Journal of Housing Research, 7(2): 145–172.

Chow, G. C. (1960) 'Tests of equality between sets of coefficients in two linear regressions', Econometrica, 28(3): 591–605.

Christiano, L. J. and Fitzgerald, T. J. (2003) 'The band pass filter', International Economic Review, 44(2): 435–465.

Church, R. A. (1975) The Great Victorian Boom 1850–73, London, Macmillan.

Clapp, J. M. (1993) Dynamics of Office Markets, AREUEA Monograph Series 1, Washington, DC, Urban Institute Press.

Clark, C. (1967) Population Growth and Land Use, London, Macmillan.

Clark, G. L. (2002) 'London in the European financial services industry: locational advantages and product complementarities', Journal of Economic Geography, 2: 433–453.

Clark, J. M. (1917) 'Business acceleration and the law of demand: a technical factor in economic cycles', Journal of Political Economy, 25(1): 217–235.

Clark, P. ed. (2000) The Cambridge Urban History of Britain, volume II, 1540–1840, Cambridge, Cambridge University Press.

Clayton, J. (1996) 'Rational expectations, market fundamentals and housing price volatility', Real Estate Economics, 24(4): 441–470.

Coakley, J. (1994) 'The integration of property and financial markets', Environment and Planning A, 26: 697–713.

Coakley, J. and Harris, L. (1983) The City of Capital: London's Role as a Financial Centre, Oxford, Blackwell.

Cogley, T. and Nason, J. M. (1995a) 'Output dynamics in real-business-cycle models', American Economic Review, 85(3): 492–511.

Cogley, T. and Nason, J. M. (1995b) 'Effects of the Hodrick–Prescott filter on trend and difference stationary time series', Journal of Economic Dynamics and Control, 19: 253–278.

Cohen, J.-L. (1996) Mies van der Rohe, London, Spon.

Colean, M. L. and Newcomb, R. (1952) Stabilizing Construction, New York, McGraw-Hill.

Collyns, C. and Senhadji, A. (2003) 'Lending booms, real estate bubbles, and the Asian crisis', in W. C. Hunter, G. G. Kaufman and M. Pomerleano eds., Asset Price Bubbles, Cambridge, MA, MIT Press, 101–125.

Committee on Invisible Exports (1974) Office Rents in the City of London and Their Effect on Invisible Earnings, London.

Condit, C. W. (1964) The Chicago School of Architecture, Chicago, IL, University of Chicago Press.

Cook, G. A. S., Pandit, N. R., Beaverstock, J. V., Taylor, P. J. and Pain, K. (2007) 'The role of location in knowledge creation and diffusion: evidence of centripetal and centrifugal forces in the City of London financial services agglomeration', Environment and Planning A, 39: 1325–1345.

Cooney, E. W. (1960) 'Long waves in building in the British economy of the nineteenth century', Economic History Review, 13: 257–269.

Coppock, J. T. and Prince, H. C. eds. (1964) Greater London, London, Faber.

Corporation of London (1984) Continuity and Change: Building in the City of London 1834–1984, London.

Corporation of London (2005) The City's Importance to the EU Economy, London.

Corporation of London (2006) Core Strategy: Issues and Options, London.

Cowan, P., Fine, D., Ireland, J., Jordan, C., Mercer, D. and Sears, A. (1969) The Office: A Facet of Urban Growth, London, Heinemann.

Crafts, N. F. R. (1985) British Economic Growth During the Industrial Revolution, Oxford, Clarendon Press.

Crafts, N. F. R. (1992) 'Productivity growth reconsidered', Economic Policy, 15: 388–426.

Crafts, N. F. R. (2004) 'Long-run growth', in R. Floud and P. Johnson eds., The Cambridge Economic History of Modern Britain, volume II, Cambridge, Cambridge University Press, 1–24.

Crafts, N. F. R. and Harley, C. K. (1992) 'Output growth and the British Industrial Revolution: a restatement of the Crafts–Harley view', Economic History Review, 45(4): 703–730.

Crafts, N. F. R. and Woodward N. eds. (1991) The British Economy Since 1945, Oxford, Clarendon Press.

Crafts, N. F. R., Leybourne, S. J. and Mills, T. C. (1989) 'Trends and cycles in British industrial production 1700–1913', Journal of the Royal Statistical Society A, 152(1): 43–60.

Crampton, G. and Evans, A. W. (1992) 'The economy of an agglomeration: the case of London', Urban Studies, 29(2): 259–271.

Cronon, W. (1991) Nature's Metropolis, New York, Norton.

Cross, R. (1993) 'On the foundations of hysteresis in economic systems', Economics and Philosophy, 9: 53–74.

Crouzet, F. (1972) Capital Formation in the Industrial Revolution, London, Methuen.

CSO (1985) United Kingdom National Accounts: Sources and Methods, third edition, London, Central Statistical Office.

Daniels, P. W. and Bobe, J. M. (1993) 'Extending the boundary of the City of London? The development of Canary Wharf', Environment and Planning A, 25: 539–552.

D'Arcy, E. and Keogh, G. (1997) 'Towards a property market paradigm of urban change', Environment and Planning A, 29: 685–706.

D'Arcy, E., McGough, T. and Tsolacos, S. (1997) 'National economic trends, market size and city growth effects on European office rents', Journal of Property Research, 14(4): 297–308.

Daunton, M. J. (1983) House and Home in the Victorian City, London, Edward Arnold.

Daunton, M. J. ed. (2000) The Cambridge Urban History of Britain, volume III, 1840–1950, Cambridge, Cambridge University Press.

David, P. A. (1975) Technical Choice Innovation and Economic Growth, Cambridge, Cambridge University Press.

Davis, J. H. (2004) 'An annual index of U.S. industrial production, 1790–1915', Quarterly Journal of Economics, 119(4): 1177–1215.

Deane, P. and Cole, W. A. (1962) British Economic Growth 1688–1959, Cambridge, Cambridge University Press.

Defoe, D. (1929) 'A Tour Thro' London About the Year 1725, edition edited by M. M. Beeton and E. B. Chancellor, London, Batsford.

De Long, J. B. (1992) 'Productivity growth and machinery investment: a long-run look, 1870–1980', Journal of Economic History, 52(2): 307–324.

De Long, J. B. and Summers, L. H. (1991) 'Equipment investment and economic growth', Quarterly Journal of Economics, 106(2): 445–502.

Denison, E. F. (1967) Why Growth Rates Differ, Washington, DC, Brookings Institution.

Dennis, R. (1984) English Industrial Cities of the Nineteenth Century, Cambridge, Cambridge University Press.

Derksen, J. B. D. (1940) 'Long cycles in residential building: an explanation', Econometrica, 8(2): 97–116.

Diamond, D. R. (1991) 'The City, the "Big Bang" and office development', in K. Hoggart and D. R. Green eds., London: A New Metropolitan Geography, London, Edward Arnold, 79–94.

Dickey, D. A. and Fuller, W. A. (1981) 'Likelihood ratio statistics for autoregressive time-series with a unit root', Econometrica, 49: 1057–1072.

DiPasquale, D. and Wheaton, W. C. (1992) 'The markets for real estate assets and space: a conceptual framework', Journal of the American Real Estate and Urban Economics Association, 20(2): 181–197.

DiPasquale, D. and Wheaton, W. C. (1994) 'Housing market dynamics and the future of housing prices', Journal of Urban Economics, 35: 1–27.

DiPasquale, D. and Wheaton, W. C. (1996) Urban Economics and Real Estate Markets, Englewood Cliffs, NJ, Prentice Hall.

Dixon, T. J., Crosby, N. and Law, V. K. (1999) 'A critical review of methodologies for measuring rental depreciation applied to UK commercial real estate', Journal of Property Research, 16(2): 153–180.

Domar, E. (1946) 'Capital expansion, rate of growth and employment', Econometrica, 14(2): 137–147.

Domosh, M. (1988) 'The symbolism of the skyscraper', Journal of Urban History, 14(3): 321–345.

Dore, M. H. I. (1993) The Macrodynamics of Business Cycles, Oxford, Blackwell.

Dosi. G., Freeman, C., Nelson, R., Silverberg, G. and Soete, L. (1988) Technical Change and Economic Theory, London, Frances Pinter.

Dosi, G., Teece, D. J. and Chytry, J. eds. (2005) Understanding Industrial and Corporate Change, Oxford, Oxford University Press.

Dow, C. (1998) Major Recessions: Britain and the World, 1920–1995, Oxford, Oxford University Press.

Driver, C. and Moreton, D. (1992) Investment, Expectations and Uncertainty, Oxford, Blackwell.

DTZ (2008) Money into Property, London, DTZ Research.

Duffy, F. (1997) The New Office, London, Conran Octopus.

Duncan, B. and Lieberson, S. (1970) Metropolis and Region in Transition, Beverly Hills, CA, Sage.

Dunning, J. H. and Morgan, E. V. (1971) An Economic Study of the City of London, London, Allen and Unwin.

Duranton, G. (1999) 'Distance, land and proximity: economic analysis and the evolution of cities', Environment and Planning A, 31: 2169–2188.

Duranton, G. and Puga, D. (2000) 'Diversity and specialisation in cities: why, where and when does it matter?' Urban Studies, 37(3): 533–555.

Duranton, G. and Puga, D. (2004) 'Micro-foundations of urban agglomeration economies', in J. V. Henderson and J.-F. Thisse eds., Handbook of Regional and Urban Economics, volume 4, Cities and Geography, Amsterdam, Elsevier, 2063–2117.

Durbin, J. and Koopman, S. J. (2001) Time Series Analysis by State Space Methods, Oxford, Oxford University Press.

Dynan, K. E., Elmendorf, D. W. and Sichel, D. E. (2006) 'Can financial innovation help to explain the reduced volatility of economic activity?' Journal of Monetary Economics, 53: 123–150.

Dyos, H. J. (1961) Victorian Suburb, Leicester, Leicester University Press.

Dyos, H. J. (1968) 'The speculative builders and developers of Victorian London', Victorian Studies, 11: 641–690.

Eaton, J. and Eckstein, Z. (1997) 'Cities and growth: theory and evidence from France and Japan', Regional Science and Urban Economics, 27: 443–474.

Edel, M. and Sclar, E. (1975) 'The distribution of real estate value changes: Metropolitan Boston, 1870–1970', Journal of Urban Economics, 2: 366–387.

Edgington, D. W. (1995) 'The search for paradise: Japanese property investments in North America', Journal of Property Research, 12: 240–261.

Eichler, N. (1989) The Thrift Debacle, Berkeley, CA, University of California Press.

Elaydi, S. N. (1996) An Introduction to Difference Equations, New York, Springer-Verlag.

Ellin, N. (1996) Postmodern Urbanism, Oxford, Blackwell.

Engerman, S. L. and Gallman, R. E. eds. (2000) The Cambridge Economic History of the United States, three volumes, Cambridge, Cambridge University Press.

Engle, R. F. and Granger, C. W. J. (1987) 'Cointegration and error correction: representation, estimation and testing', Econometrica, 55(2): 251–276.

Engle, R. F. and Granger, C. W. J. (1991) Long-run Economic Relationships: Readings in Cointegration, Oxford, Oxford University Press.

Englund, P. (1999) 'The Swedish banking crisis: roots and consequences', Oxford Review of Economic Policy, 15(3): 80–97.

Englund, P. and Ioannides, Y. M. (1997) 'House price dynamics: an international empirical perspective', Journal of Housing Economics, 6: 119–136.

Ermisch, J. ed. (1990) Housing and the National Economy, Aldershot, Avebury.

Evans, A. W. (1991) '"Rabbit hutches on postage stamps": planning, development and political economy', Urban Studies, 28(6): 853–870.

Evans, A. W. (1995) 'The property market: ninety per cent efficient?' Urban Studies, 32(1): 5–29.

Evans, G. W., Honkapohja, S. and Romer, P. (1998) 'Growth cycles', American Economic Review, 88(3): 495–515.

Fainstein, S. S. (2001) The City Builders, second edition, Lawrence, KS, University Press of Kansas.

Fama, E. F. (1970) 'Efficient capital markets, a review of theory and empirical work', Journal of Finance, 25: 383–420.

Farrelly, K. and Sanderson, B. (2005) 'Modelling regime shifts in the City of London office rental cycle', Journal of Property Research, 22(4): 325–344.

Feinstein, C. H. (1976) Statistical Tables of National Income, Expenditure and Output of the U.K. 1855–1965, Cambridge, Cambridge University Press.

Feinstein, C. H. and Pollard, S. (1988) Studies in Capital Formation in the United Kingdom 1750–1920, Oxford, Clarendon Press.

Fergus, J. T. and Goodman, J. L. (1994) 'The 1989–92 credit crunch for real estate: a retrospective', Journal of the American Real Estate and Urban Economics Association, 22(1): 5–32.

Field, A. J. (1985) 'On the unimportance of machinery', Explorations in Economic History, 22: 378–401.

Field, A. J. (1992) 'Uncontrolled land development and the duration of the Depression in the United States', Journal of Economic History, 52(4): 785–805.

Fischer, D. H. (1996) The Great Wave: Price Revolutions and the Rhythm of History, Oxford, Oxford University Press.

Fishlow, A. (2000) 'Internal transportation in the nineteenth and early twentieth centuries', in S. L. Engerman and R. E. Gallman eds., The Cambridge Economic History of the United States, volume II, Cambridge, Cambridge University Press, 543–642.

Flaus, L. (1949) 'Les fluctuations de la construction d'habitations urbaines', Journal de la Société der Statistique de Paris, 90: 185–221.

Flink, J. J. (1988) The Automobile Age, Cambridge, MA, MIT Press.

Floud, R. and Johnson, P. eds. (2004) The Cambridge Economic History of Modern Britain, three volumes, Cambridge, Cambridge University Press.

Fogel, R. W. (1964) Railroads and American Economic Growth, Baltimore, MD, John Hopkins Press.

Foray, D. (2004) The Economics of Knowledge, Cambridge, MA, MIT Press.

Foray, D. and Freeman, C. eds. (1993) Technology and the Wealth of Nations, London, Frances Pinter.

Foster, L., Haltiwanger, J. and Krizan, C. J. (2006) 'Market selection, reallocation, and restructuring in the U.S. retail trade sector in the 1990s', Review of Economics and Statistics, 88(4): 748–758.

Frankel, M. (1955) 'Obsolescence and technological change in a maturing economy', American Economic Review, 45: 296–319.

Freeman, C. and Louca, F. (2001) As Time Goes By: From the Industrial Revolutions to the Information Revolution, Oxford, Oxford University Press.

Freeman, C., Clark, J. and Soete, L. (1982) Unemployment and Technical Innovation, London, Frances Pinter.

Freeman, M. J. and Aldcroft, D. H. eds. (1988) Transport in Victorian Britain, Manchester, Manchester University Press.

Frickey, E. (1934) 'The problem of secular trend', Review of Economics and Statistics, 16: 199–206.

Friedman, M. (1957) A Theory of the Consumption Function, Princeton, NJ, Princeton University Press.

Friedman, M. (1968) 'The role of monetary policy', American Economic Review, 58(1): 1–17.

Friedmann, J. (1986) 'The world city hypothesis', Development and Change, 17: 69–83.

Frisch, R. (1933) 'Propagation problems and impulse problems in dynamic economics', in Economic Essays in Honour of Gustav Cassel, London, Allen and Unwin.

Frost, M. and Spence, N. (1993) 'Global city characteristics and Central London's employment', Urban Studies, 30(3): 547–558.

Fujita, M. (1989) Urban Economic Theory, Cambridge, Cambridge University Press.

Fujita, M. and Thisse, J.-F. (2002) Economics of Agglomeration, Cambridge, Cambridge University Press.

Fujita, M., Krugman, P. and Venables, A. J. (1999) The Spatial Economy, Cambridge, MA, MIT Press.

Gabisch, G. and Lorenz, H-W. (1989) Business Cycle Theory, Berlin, Springer-Verlag.

Galbraith, J. K. (1975) The Great Crash 1929, second edition, London, Penguin Books.

Gallman, R. E. (2000) 'Economic growth and structural change in the long nineteenth century', in S. L. Engerman and R. E. Gallman eds., The Cambridge Economic History of the United States, volume II, Cambridge, Cambridge University Press, 1–55.

Gann, D. M. (2000) Building Innovation, London, Thomas Telford.

Garbade, K. D. and Silber, W. L. (1978) 'Technology, communication and the performance of financial markets: 1840–1975' Journal of Finance, 33(3): 819–832.

Gardiner, C. and Henneberry, J. (1991) 'Predicting regional office rents using habit-persistence theories', Journal of Property Valuation and Investment, 9: 215–226.

Garreau, J. (1991) Edge City, New York, Doubleday.

Garvy, G. (1943) 'Kondratieff's theory of long cycles', Review of Economic Statistics, 25(4): 203–220.

Gaspar, J. and Glaeser, E. L. (1998) 'Information technology and the future of cities', Journal of Urban Economics, 43: 136–156.

Gatzlaff, D. H. and Tirtiroglu, D. (1995) 'Real estate market efficiency: issues and evidence', Journal of Real Estate Literature, 3: 157–189.

Gayer, A. D., Rostow, W. W. and Schwartz, A. J. (1953) The Growth and Fluctuation of the British Economy 1790–1850, two volumes, Oxford, Clarendon Press.

Gershuny, J. and Miles, I. (1983) The New Service Economy, London, Frances Pinter.

Ghosh, C., Guttery, R. S. and Sirmans, C. F. (1994) 'The Olympia and York crisis: effects on the financial performance of US and foreign banks', Journal of Property Finance, 5(2): 5–46.

Gibbs, A. (1987) 'Retail innovation and planning', Progress in Planning, 27(1): 1–67.

Gieve, J. (2007) 'The City's growth: the crest of a wave or swimming with the stream?' Bank of England Quarterly Bulletin, Q2: 286–290.

Giussani, B. and Tsolacos, S. (1994) 'Investment in industrial buildings: modelling the determinants of new orders', Journal of Property Research, 11: 1–16.

Glaab, C. N. and Brown, A. T. (1967) A History of Urban America, New York, Macmillan.

Glaeser, E. L. (1998) 'Are cities dying?' Journal of Economic Perspectives, 12(2): 139–160.

Glaeser, E. L. (1999) 'Learning in cities', Journal of Urban Economics, 46: 254–277.

Glaeser, E. L., Kallal, H. D., Scheinkman, J. A. and Schleifer, A. (1992) 'Growth in cities', Journal of Political Economy, 100(6): 1126–1152.

Goddard, J. B. (1968) 'Multivariate analysis of office location patterns in the city centre: a London example', Regional Studies, 2: 69–85.

Goddard, J. B. (1975) Office Location in Urban and Regional Development, London, Oxford University Press.

Goetzmann, W. N. and Wachter, S. M. (2001) 'The global real estate crash: evidence from an international database', in S. J. Brown and C. H. Liu eds., A Global Perspective on Real Estate Cycles, Boston, MA, Kluwer, 5–23.

Gomez, V. (2001) 'The use of Butterworth filters for trend and cycle estimation in economic time series', Journal of Business and Economic Statistics, 19(3): 365–373.

Goobey, A. Ross (1992) Bricks and Mortals, London, Century Business.

Goodrich, C. ed. (1961) Canals and American Economic Development, New York, Columbia University Press.

Goodwin, R. M. (1948) 'Secular and cyclical aspects of the multiplier and the accelerator', in L. A. Metzler ed., Income, Employment and Public Policy: Essays in Honor of Alvin H. Hansen, New York, Norton, 108–132.

Goodwin, R. M. (1951) 'The nonlinear accelerator and the persistence of business cycles', Econometrica, 19(1): 1–17.

Goodwin, R. M. (1955) 'A model of cyclical growth', in E. Lundberg ed., The Business Cycle in the Post-war World, London, Macmillan.

Goodwin, R. M. (1967) 'A growth cycle', in C. H. Feinstein ed., Socialism, Capitalism and Economic Growth, Cambridge, Cambridge University Press.

Goodwin, R. M., Kruger, M. and Vercelli, A. (1984) Nonlinear Models of Fluctuating Growth, Berlin, Springer-Verlag.

Gordon, R. J. ed. (1986) The American Business Cycle: Continuity and Change, Chicago, IL, University of Chicago Press.

Gordon, R. J. (1989) 'Hysteresis in history: was there ever a Phillips curve?' American Economic Review, 79(2): 220–225.

Gottlieb, M. (1965) 'New measures of value of nonfarm building for the United States, annually 1850–1939', Review of Economics and Statistics, 47: 412–419.

Gottlieb, M. (1976) Long Swings in Urban Development, New York, National Bureau of Economic Research.

Gourvish, T. R. (1988) 'Railways 1830–70: The formative years', in M. J. Freeman and D. H. Aldcroft eds., Transport in Victorian Britain, Manchester, Manchester University Press, 57–91.

Graham, S. and Marvin, S. (1996) Telecommunications and the City, London, Routledge.

Granger, C. W. J. (1969) 'Investigating causal relations by econometric models and cross-spectral methods', Econometrica, 37(3): 424–438.

Granger, C. W. J. (1981) 'Some properties of time series data and their use in econometric model specification', Journal of Econometrics, 16: 121–130.

Granger, C. W. J. (1986) 'Developments in the study of cointegrated economic variables', Oxford Bulletin of Economics and Statistics, 48(3): 213–228.

Granger, C. W. J. and Hatanaka, M. (1964) Spectral Analysis of Economic Time Series, Princeton, NJ, Princeton University Press.

Grebler, L. and Burns, L. S. (1982) 'Construction cycles in the United States since World War II', Journal of the American Real Estate and Urban Economics Association, 10(2): 123–151.

Grebler, L., Blank, D. M. and Winnick, L. (1956) Capital Formation in Residential Real Estate, Princeton, NJ, Princeton University Press.

Grenadier, S. R. (1995) 'The persistence of real estate cycles', Journal of Real Estate Finance and Economics, 10: 95–119.

Griffin, T. (1976) 'The stock of fixed assets in the United Kingdom: how to make best use of the statistics', Economic Trends, 276: 130–143.

Grimaud, A. (1989) 'Agglomeration economies and building height', Journal of Urban Economics, 25: 17–31.

Groak, S. and Ive, G. (1986) 'Economics and technological change: some implications for the study of the building industry', Habitat International, 10(4): 115–132.

Grossman, G. M. and Helpman, E. (1991) 'Quality ladders and product cycles', Quarterly Journal of Economics, 106: 557–586.

Grübler, A. (1990) The Rise and Fall of Infrastructures, Heidelberg, Physica-Verlag.

Guthrie, W. K. C. (1962) A History of Greek Philosophy, volume 1, Cambridge, Cambridge University Press.

Guttentag, J. M. (1961) 'The short cycle in residential construction, 1946–59', American Economic Review, 51(3): 275–298.

Guy, C. (1994) The Retail Development Process, London, Routledge.

Guy, S. and Henneberry, J. eds. (2002) Development and Developers: Perspectives on Property, Oxford, Blackwell.

Habakkuk, H. J. (1962a) American and British Technology in the Nineteenth Century: The Search for Labour-Saving Inventions, Cambridge, Cambridge University Press.

Habakkuk, H. J. (1962b) 'Fluctuations in house-building in Britain and the United States in the nineteenth century', Journal of Economic History, 22: 198–230.

Haberler, G. von (1937) Prosperity and Depression, Geneva, League of Nations.

Hadfield, C. (1974) British Canals, fifth edition, Newton Abbot, David and Charles.

Hägerstrand, T. (1967) Innovation Diffusion as a Spatial Process, Chicago, IL, University of Chicago Press.

Hall, P. (1998) Cities in Civilization, London, Weidenfeld and Nicholson.

Hall, P. (2000) 'Creative cities and economic development', Urban Studies, 37(4): 639–649.

Hall, P. and Preston, P. (1988) The Carrier Wave, London, Unwin Hyman.

Hall, P., Gracey, H., Drewett, R. and Thomas, R. (1973) The Containment of Urban England, two volumes, London, Allen and Unwin.

Hamnett, C. (1999) Winners and Losers: Home Ownership in Modern Britain, London, Routledge.

Hansen, A. H. (1941) Fiscal Policy and Business Cycles, New York, Norton.

Hansen, A. H. (1951) Business Cycles and National Income, New York, Norton.

Harkness, J. P. (1968) 'A spectral-analytic test of the long-swing hypothesis in Canada', Review of Economics and Statistics, 50: 429–436.

Harris, R. (2005) Property and the Office Economy, London, Estates Gazette Books.

Harrison, A., Wheeler, P. and Whitehead, C. (2004) The Distributed Workplace, Abingdon, Spon.

Harrison, D. and Kain, J. F. (1974) 'Cumulative urban growth and urban density functions', Journal of Urban Economics, 1: 61–98.

Harrison, F. (2005) Boom Bust, London, Shepheard-Walwyn.

Harrod, R. F. (1936) The Trade Cycle, Oxford, Clarendon Press.

Harrod, R. F. (1939) 'An essay in dynamic theory', Economic Journal, 49: 14–33.

Harrod, R. F. (1948) Towards a Dynamic Economics, London, Macmillan.

Hartman, R. S. and Wheeler, D. R. (1979) 'Schumpeterian waves of innovation and infrastructure development in Great Britain and the United States: the Kondratieff cycle revisited', Research in Economic History, 4: 37–85.

Harvey, A. C. (1975) 'Spectral analysis in economics', The Statistician, 24(1): 1–36.

Harvey, A. C. (1985) 'Trends and cycles in macroeconomic time series', Journal of Business and Economic Statistics, 3(3): 216–227.

Harvey, A. C. (1989) Forecasting, Structural Time Series Models and the Kalman Filter, Cambridge, Cambridge University Press.

Harvey, A. C. (2004) 'Tests for cycles', in A. C. Harvey, S. J. Koopman and N. Shephard eds., 102–119.

Harvey, A. C. and Jaeger, A. (1993) 'Detrending, stylized facts and the business cycle', Journal of Applied Econometrics, 8: 231–247.

Harvey, A. C. and Proietti, T. (2005) Readings in Unobserved Components Models, Oxford, Oxford University Press.

Harvey, A. C. and Trimbur, T. (2003) 'Generalised model-based filters for extracting trends and cycles in economic time series', Review of Economics and Statistics, 85(2): 244–255.

Harvey, A. C., Koopman, S. J. and Shephard, N. eds. (2004) State Space and Unobserved Components Models, Cambridge, Cambridge University Press.

Harvey, D. (1978) 'The urban process under capitalism: a framework for analysis', International Journal of Urban and Regional Research, 2: 101–131.

Harvey, D. (1985) The Urbanization of Capital, Oxford, Blackwell.

Hawke, G. R. (1970) Railways and Economic Growth in England and Wales 1840–1870, Oxford, Clarendon Press.

Healey, P. (1991) 'Models of the development process: a review', Journal of Property Research, 8: 219–238.

Healey, P., Davoudi, S., Tavsanoglu, S., O'Toole, M. and Usher, D. (1992) Rebuilding the City, London, Spon.

Heim, C. E. (2000) 'Structural changes: regional and urban', in S. L. Engerman and R. E. Gallman eds., The Cambridge Economic History of the United States, volume III, Cambridge, Cambridge University Press, 93–190.

Hekman, J. S. (1985) 'Rental price adjustment and investment in the office market', Journal of the American Real Estate and Urban Economics Association, 13(1): 32–47.

Helpman, E. ed. (1998) General Purpose Technologies and Economic Growth, Cambridge, MA, MIT Press.

Helsley, R. W. and Strange, W. C. (2008) 'A game-theoretic analysis of skyscrapers', Journal of Urban Economics, 64: 49–64.

Hendershott, P. H. (1995) 'Real effective rent determination: evidence from the Sydney office market', Journal of Property Research, 12(2): 127–135.

Hendershott, P. H. and Kane, E. J. (1992) 'Causes and consequences of the 1980s commercial construction boom', Journal of Applied Corporate Finance, 5: 61–70.

Hendershott, P. H. and MacGregor, B. D. (2005) 'Investor rationality: an analysis of NCREIF commercial property data', Journal of Real Estate Research, 27(4): 445–475.

Hendershott, P. H., Hendershott, R. J. and Ward, C. R. W. (2003) 'Corporate equity and commercial property market "bubbles"', Urban Studies, 40(5/6): 993–1009.

Hendershott, P. H., Lizieri, C. M. and Matysiak, G. A. (1999) 'The workings of the London office market', Real Estate Economics, 27(2): 365–387.

Hendershott, P. H., MacGregor, B. D. and Tse, R. Y. C. (2002a) 'Estimation of the rental adjustment process', Real Estate Economics, 30(2): 165–183.

Hendershott, P. H., MacGregor, B. D. and White, M. (2002b) 'Explaining real commercial rents using an error correction model with panel data', Journal of Real Estate Finance and Economics, 24(1/2): 59–87.

Henderson, J. V. (1974) 'The size and types of cities', American Economic Review, 64: 640–656.

Henderson, J. V. (1988) Urban Development, Oxford, Oxford University Press.

Henderson, J. V. and Mitra, A. (1996) 'The new urban landscape: developers and edge cities', Regional Science and Urban Economics, 26: 613–643.

Henderson, J. V. and Thisse, J.-F. eds. (2004) Handbook of Regional and Urban Economics, volume 4, Cities and Geography, Amsterdam, Elsevier.

Henneberry, J. (1999) 'Convergence and difference in regional office development cycles', Urban Studies, 36(9): 1439–1465.

Hercowitz, Z. (1998) 'The "embodiment" controversy: a review essay', Journal of Monetary Economics, 41: 217–224.

Herring, R. and Wachter, S. (2003) 'Bubbles in real estate markets', in W. C. Hunter, G. G. Kaufman and M. Pomerleano eds., Asset Price Bubbles, Cambridge, MA, MIT Press, 217–229.

Hickman, B. G. (1963) 'Postwar growth in the United States in the light of the long-swing hypothesis', American Economic Review, 53: 490–507.

Hicks, J. R. (1950) A Contribution to the Theory of the Trade Cycle, Oxford, Clarendon Press.

Higgins, M. and Osler, C. (1997) 'Asset market hangovers and economic growth: the OECD during 1984–93', Oxford Review of Economic Policy, 13(3): 110–134.

Hodrick, R. J. and Prescott, E. C. (1997) 'Postwar U.S. business cycles: an empirical investigation', Journal of Money, Credit and Banking, 29(1): 1–16.

Hoesli, M. and MacGregor, B. D. (2000) Property Investment, Harlow, Longman.

Hohenberg, P. M. and Lees, L. H. (1995) The Making of Urban Europe, 1000–1994, second edition, Cambridge, MA, Harvard University Press.

Holden, C. H. and Holford, W. G. (1951) The City of London: A Record of Destruction and Survival, London, Architectural Press.

Holmans, A. E. (2005) Historical Statistics of Housing in Britain, Cambridge, Department of Land Economy University of Cambridge.

Homer, S. and Sylla, R. (2005) A History of Interest Rates, fourth edition, New York, Wiley.

Hoover, E. M. (1948) The Location of Economic Activity, New York, McGraw-Hill.

Howitt, P. and McAfee, R. P. (1992) 'Animal spirits', American Economic Review, 82(3): 493–507.

Howrey, E. P. (1968) 'A spectrum analysis of the long-swing hypothesis', International Economic Review, 9(2): 228–252.

Hoyt, H. (1933) One Hundred Years of Land Values in Chicago, Chicago, IL, University of Chicago Press.

Hudson, P. (1992) The Industrial Revolution, London, Edward Arnold.

Hunter, W. C., Kaufman, G. G. and Pomerleano, M. eds. (2003) Asset Price Bubbles, Cambridge, MA, MIT Press.

Iacoviello, M. (2005) 'House prices, borrowing constraints and monetary policy in the business cycle', American Economic Review, 95(3): 739–764.

IATA (2000) Global Airport Connectivity Monitor, London, International Air Transport Association.

IMF (2008) World Economic Outlook April 2008: Housing and the Business Cycle, Washington, DC, International Monetary Fund.

IPF (2005) The Size and Structure of the UK Property Market, London, Investment Property Forum.

Inwood, S. (1998) A History of London, London, Macmillan.

Inwood, S. (2005) City of Cities: The Birth of Modern London, London, Macmillan.

Ireland, P. N. (2004) 'Technology shocks in the New Keynesian model', Review of Economics and Statistics, 86(4): 923–936.

Isard, W. (1942) 'A neglected cycle: the transport-building cycle', Review of Economic Statistics, 24(4): 149–158.

Isard, W. (1949) 'The general theory of location and space-economy', Quarterly Journal of Economics, 63: 476–506.

Jackson, A. A. (1973) Semi-Detached London, London, Allen and Unwin.

Jackson, K. T. (1985) Crabgrass Frontier: The Suburbanization of the United States, New York, Oxford University Press.

Jackson, R. V. (1992) 'Rates of industrial growth during the industrial revolution', Economic History Review, 45(1): 1–23.

Jacobs, J. (1969) The Economy of Cities, New York, Random House.

Jahn, M. (1982) 'Suburban development in outer west London, 1850–1900', in F. M. L. Thompson ed., The Rise of Suburbia, Leicester, Leicester University Press, 94–156.

Jenkins, S. (1975) Landlords to London, London, Constable.

Jefferys, J. B. (1954) Retail Trading in Britain 1850–1950, Cambridge, Cambridge University Press.

Jenks, M., Burton, E. and Williams, K., eds. (1996), The Compact City: A Sustainable Urban Form? London, Spon.

Johansen, S. (1988) 'Statistical analysis of cointegration vectors', Journal of Economic Dynamics and Control, 12: 231–254.

Jones, C. I. (1995) 'R&D-based models of economic growth', Journal of Political Economy, 103: 759–784.

Jorgenson, D. W. (1963) 'Capital theory and investment behaviour', American Economic Review, 53(2): 247–259.

Jorgenson, D. W. (2001) 'Information technology and the US economy', American Economic Review, 91(1): 1–32.

Jorgenson, D. W., Ho, M. S. and Stiroh, K. J. (2005) Information Technology and the American Growth Resurgence, Cambridge, MA, MIT Press.

Jorgenson, D. W., Ho, M. S. and Stiroh, K. J. (2008) 'A retrospective look at the U.S. productivity growth resurgence', Journal of Economic Perspectives, 22(1): 3–24.

Kaiser, R. W. (1997) 'The long cycle in real estate', Journal of Real Estate Research, 14(3): 233–257.

Kaldor, N. (1934) 'A classificatory note on the determinateness of equilibrium', Review of Economic Studies, 2: 122–136.

Kaldor, N. (1940) 'A model of the trade cycle', Economic Journal, 50: 78–92.

Kaldor, N. (1954) 'The relation of economic growth and cyclical fluctuations', Economic Journal, 64: 53–71.

Kaldor, N. (1957) 'A model of economic growth', Economic Journal, 67: 591–624.

Kaldor, N. (1961) 'Capital accumulation and economic growth', in F. A. Lutz and D.C. Hague eds., The Theory of Capital, London, Macmillan, 177–222.

Kaldor, N. (1972) 'The irrelevance of equilibrium economics', Economic Journal, 82: 1237–1255.

Kalecki, M. (1935) 'A macrodynamic theory of business cycles', Econometrica, 3: 327–344.

Kalecki, M. (1937) 'A theory of the business cycle', Review of Economic Studies, 4: 77–97.

Kanaya, A. and Woo, D. (2000) The Japanese Banking Crisis of the 1990s: Sources and Lessons, Washington, DC, International Monetary Fund, Working Paper WP/00/7.

Kellett, J. R. (1969) The Impact of Railways on Victorian Cities, London, Routledge.

Kennedy, C. (1964) 'Induced bias in innovation and the theory of distribution', Economic Journal, 74: 541–547.

Kennedy C. and Thirlwall, A. P. (1972) 'Surveys in applied economics: technical progress', Economic Journal, 82: 11–72.

Kenworthy, J. R. and Laube, F. B. (1999) An International Sourcebook of Automobile Dependence in Cities, 1960–1990, Boulder, CO, University Press of Colorado.

Keogh, G. (1994) 'Use and investment markets in British real estate', Journal of Property Valuation and Investment, 12(4): 58–72.

Keogh, G. and D'Arcy, E. (1994) 'Market maturity and property market behaviour: a European comparison of mature and emergent markets', Journal of Property Research, 11: 215–235.

Key, T., Zarkesh, F. and Haq, N. (1999) The UK Property Cycle – A History from 1921 to 1997, London, Royal Institution of Chartered Surveyors.

Key, T., Zarkesh, F., MacGregor, B. D. and Nanthakumaran, N. (1994) Understanding the Property Cycle: Economic Cycles and Property Cycles, London, Royal Institution of Chartered Surveyors.

Keynes, J. M. (1936) The General Theory of Employment, Interest and Money, London, Macmillan.

Keynes, J. M. (1939) 'Professor Tinbergen's method', Economic Journal, 49: 558–568.

Kindleberger, C. P. and Aliber, R. Z. (2005) Manias, Panics and Crashes: A History of Financial Crises, fifth edition, Basingstoke, Palgrave Macmillan.

King, A. D. (1990) Global Cities, London, Routledge.

King, R. G. and Plosser, C. I. (1994) 'Real business cycles and the test of the Adelmans', Journal of Monetary Economics, 33: 405–438.

King, R. G. and Rebelo, S. T. (1993) 'Low frequency filtering and real business cycles', Journal of Economic Dynamics and Control, 17: 207–231.

King, R. G., Plosser, C. I. and Rebelo, S. T. (1988a) 'Production, growth and business cycles: I. The basic neoclassical model', Journal of Monetary Economics, 21: 195–232.

King, R. G., Plosser, C. I. and Rebelo, S. T. (1988b) 'Production, growth and business cycles: II. New directions', Journal of Monetary Economics, 21: 309–341.

Kitchen, J. (1923) 'Cycles and trends in economic factors', Review of Economic Statistics, 5: 10–16.

Kitson, M. (2004) 'Failure followed by success or success followed by failure? A re-examination of British economic growth since 1949', in R. Floud and P. Johnson eds., The Cambridge Economic History of Modern Britain, volume III, Cambridge, Cambridge University Press, 27–56.

Kiyotaki, N. and Moore, J. (1997) 'Credit cycles', Journal of Political Economy, 105(2): 211–248.

Kleinknecht, A. (1987) Innovation Patterns in Crisis and Prosperity, Basingstoke, Macmillan.

Kleinknecht, A., Mandel, E. and Wallerstein, I. eds. (1992) New Findings in Long Wave Research, New York, St Martin's Press.

Kling, J. L. and McCue, T. E. (1987) 'Office building investment and the macroeconomy: empirical evidence, 1973–1985', Journal of the American Real Estate and Urban Economics Association, 15(3): 234–255.

Knox, A. D. (1952) 'The acceleration principle and the theory of investment: a survey', Economica, 19: 269–297.

Kondratieff, N. D. (1935) 'The long waves in economic life', Review of Economic Statistics, 17: 105–115.

Koopman, S. J., Harvey, A. C., Doornik, J. A. and Shephard, N. (2006) STAMP: Structural Time Series Analyser, Modeller and Predictor, London, Timberlake Consultants.

Koopmans, T. C. (1947) 'Measurement without theory', Review of Economic Statistics, 29(3): 161–172.

Krugman, P. (1991a) Geography and Trade, Cambridge, MA, MIT Press.

Krugman, P. (1991b) 'Increasing returns and economic geography', Journal of Political Economy, 99(3): 483–499.

Krugman, P. (1993) 'First nature, second nature, and metropolitan location', Journal of Regional Science, 33(2): 129–144.

Krugman, P. (1996) The Self-Organizing Economy, Oxford, Blackwell.

Krugman, P. (2009) The Return of Depression Economics and the Crisis of 2008, New York, Norton.

Kummerow, M. (1999) 'A system dynamics model of cyclical office oversupply', Journal of Real Estate Research, 18(1): 233–255.

Kuznets, S. (1930) Secular Movements in Production and Prices, Boston, MA, Houghton Mifflin.

Kuznets, S. (1940) 'Schumpeter's Business Cycles', American Economic Review, 30(2): 257–271.

Kuznets, S. (1958) 'Long swings in population growth and related economic variables', Proceedings of the American Philosophical Society, 102(1): 25–52.

Kuznets, S. (1961) Capital in the American Economy: Its Formation and Financing, Princeton, NJ, Princeton University Press.

Kydland, F. E. and Prescott, E. C. (1982) 'Time to build and aggregate fluctuations', Econometrica, 50(6): 1345–1370.

Kynaston, D. (1994) The City of London: A World of its Own 1815–90, London, Chatto and Windus.

Kynaston, D. (1995) The City of London: Golden Years 1890–1914, London, Chatto and Windus.

Kynaston, D. (1999) The City of London: Illusions of Gold 1914–45, London, Chatto and Windus.

Kynaston, D. (2001) The City of London: Club No More 1945–2000, London, Chatto and Windus.

Landau, S. B. and Condit, C. W. (1996) Rise of the New York Skyscraper 1865–1913, New Haven, CT, Yale University Press.

Landes, D. S. (1969) The Unbound Prometheus, Cambridge, Cambridge University Press.

Landes, D. S. (1994) 'What room for accident in history? Explaining big changes by small events', Economic History Review, 47(4): 637–656.

Lang, R. E. (2003) Edgeless Cities, Washington, DC, Brookings Institution.

Langton, J. (2000) 'Urban growth and economic change: from the late seventeenth century to 1841', in P. Clark ed., The Cambridge Urban History of Britain, volume II, 1540–1840, Cambridge, Cambridge University Press, 453–490.

Lawton, R. ed. (1989), The Rise and Fall of Great Cities, London, Belhaven Press.

Leitner, H. (1994) 'Capital markets, the development industry and urban office market dynamics: rethinking building cycles', Environment and Planning A, 26: 779–802.

Lever, W. F. (2002) 'The knowledge base and the competitive city', in I. Begg ed., Urban Competitiveness, Bristol, Policy Press, 11–31.

Lizieri, C. and Finlay, L. (1995) 'International property portfolio strategies', Journal of Property Valuation and Investment, 13(1): 6–21.

Lizieri, C. and Satchell, S. (1997) 'Interactions between property and equity markets: an investigation of linkages in the United Kingdom 1972–1992', Journal of Real Estate Finance and Economics, 15(1): 11–26.

Lizieri, C., Baum, A. and Scott, P. (2000) 'Ownership, occupation and risk: a view of the City of London office market', Urban Studies, 37(7): 1109–1129.

Lloyd-Jones, R. and Lewis, M. J. (1998) British Industrial Capitalism Since the Industrial Revolution, London, Routledge.

Lombard Street Research (2003) Growth Prospects of City Industries, London, Corporation of London.

London Chamber of Commerce and Industry (1998) London: A Foreign Banking Perspective, London, LCCI.

Long, C. D. (1936) 'Seventy years of building cycles in Manhattan', Review of Economic Statistics, 18: 183–193.

Long, C. D. (1939) 'Long cycles in the building industry', Quarterly Journal of Economics, 53: 371–403.

Long, C. D. (1940) Building Cycles and the Theory of Investment, Princeton, NJ, Princeton University Press.

Lösch, A. (1954) The Economics of Location, English translation of revised German second edition 1944, New Haven, Yale University Press.

Lucas, R. E. (1975) 'An equilibrium model of the business cycle', Journal of Political Economy, 83: 1113–1144.

Lucas, R. E. (1981) Studies in Business Cycle Theory, Oxford, Blackwell.

Lucas, R. E. (1988) 'On the mechanics of economic development', Journal of Monetary Economics, 22: 3–42.

Lucas, R. E. (2001) 'Externalities and cities', Review of Economic Dynamics, 4: 245–274.

MacGregor, B. D. and Schwann, G. M. (2003) 'Common features in UK commercial real estate returns', Journal of Property Research, 20(1): 23–48.

MacKinnon, J. G. (1996) 'Numerical distribution functions of likelihood ratio tests for cointegration', Journal of Applied Econometrics, 11: 601–618.

Maddala, G. S. (2001) Introduction to Econometrics, third edition, Chichester, Wiley.

Maddison, A. (1991) Dynamic Forces in Capitalist Development: A Long-Run Comparative View, Oxford, Oxford University Press.

Maiwald, K. (1954) 'An index of building costs in the United Kingdom, 1845–1938', Economic History Review, 7: 187–203.

Maisel, S. J. (1963) 'A theory of fluctuations in residential construction starts', American Economic Review, 53(3): 359–383.

Mandel, E. (1995) Long Waves of Capitalist Development: A Marxist Interpretation, second edition, London, Verso.

Mangoldt, K. von (1907) Die Städtische Bodenfrage: Eine Untersuchung über Tatsachen, Ursachen, und Abhilfe, Göttingen, Vandenhoeck und Ruprecht.

Mankiw, N. G. (1985) 'Small menu costs and large business cycles: a macroeconomic model of monopoly', Quarterly Journal of Economics, 100(2): 529–539.

Mankiw, N. G. (1989) 'Real business cycles: a New Keynesian perspective', Journal of Economic Perspectives, 3(3): 79–90.

Mankiw, N. G. and Romer, D. eds. (1991) New Keynesian Economics, two volumes, Cambridge, MA, MIT Press.

Mankiw, N. G. and Weil, D. N. (1989) 'The baby boom, the baby bust, and the housing market', Regional Science and Urban Economics, 19: 235–258.

Mankiw, N. G., Romer, D. and Weil, D. N. (1992) 'A contribution to the empirics of economic growth', Quarterly Journal of Economics, 107(2): 407–437.

Mankiw, N. G., Rotemberg, J. J. and Summers, L. H. (1985) 'Intertemporal substitution in macroeconomics', Quarterly Journal of Economics, 100: 225–251.

Mansfield, E. (1961) 'Technical change and the rate of imitation', Econometrica, 29(4): 741–766.

Margo, R. A. (1992) 'Explaining the postwar suburbanization of population in the United States: the role of income', Journal of Urban Economics, 31: 301–310.

Marriott, O. (1967) The Property Boom, London, Hamish Hamilton.

Marshall, A. (1920) Principles of Economics, eighth edition, London, Macmillan.

Martin, P. and Ottaviano, G. I. P. (2001) 'Growth and agglomeration', International Economic Review, 42(4): 947–968.

Massey, D. and Catalano, A. (1978) Capital and Land, London, Edward Arnold.

Mathias, P. (1983) The First Industrial Nation, second edition, London, Methuen.

Matthews, R. C. O. (1959) The Trade Cycle, Cambridge, Cambridge University Press.

Matthews, R. C. O. (1972) 'The trade cycle in Britain 1790–1850', in D. H. Aldcroft and P. Fearon eds., British Economic Fluctuations 1790–1939, London, Macmillan, 97–130.

Matthews, R. C. O., Feinstein, C. H. and Odling-Smee, J. C. (1982) British Economic Growth 1856–1973, Oxford, Oxford University Press.

McCallum, B. T. (1986) 'On "real" and "sticky-price" theories of the business cycle', Journal of Money, Credit and Banking, 18(4): 397–414.

McDonald, J. F. (2002) 'A survey of econometric models of office markets', Journal of Real Estate Literature, 10(2): 223–242.

McGough, A. J. and Tsolacos, S. (1997) 'The stylised facts of the UK commercial building cycles', Environment and Planning A, 29: 485–500.

McWilliams, D. (1992) Commercial Property and Company Borrowing, London, Royal Institution of Chartered Surveyors, Research Paper 22.

Meen, G. (1996) 'Ten propositions in UK housing macroeconomics: an overview of the 1980s and early 1990s', Urban Studies, 33(3): 425–444.

Meen, G. (2000) 'Housing cycles and efficiency', Scottish Journal of Political Economy, 47(2): 114–140.

Mensch, G. O. (1979) Stalemate in Technology: Innovations Overcome the Depression, Cambridge, MA, Ballinger.

Mera, K. and Renaud, B., eds. (2000) Asia's Financial Crisis and the Role of Real Estate, Armonk, NY, M. E. Sharpe.

Metcalfe, J. S. (1981) 'Impulse and diffusion in the study of technical change', Futures, 5: 347–359.

Metcalfe, J. S. (1998) Evolutionary Economics and Creative Destruction, Abingdon, Routledge.

Metzler, L. A. (1941) 'The nature and stability of inventory cycles', Review of Economic Statistics, 23(3): 113–129.

Michie, R. C. (1992) The City of London: Continuity and Change, 1850–1990, London, Macmillan.

Miles, D. (1992) 'Housing markets, consumption and financial liberalization in the major economies', European Economic Review, 36: 1093–1136.

Mills, E. S. (1967) 'An aggregative model of resource allocation in a metropolitan area', American Economic Review, 57: 197–210.

Mills, E. S. (1972) Studies in the Structure of the Urban Economy, Baltimore, MD, John Hopkins Press.

Mills, E. S. (1992) 'Office rent determinants in the Chicago area', Journal of the American Real Estate and Urban Economics Association, 20(2): 273–287.

Mills, E. S. (1995) 'Crisis and recovery in office markets', Journal of Real Estate Finance and Economics, 10: 49–62.

Mills, T. C. (2003) Modelling Trends and Cycles in Economic Time Series, Basingstoke, Palgrave Macmillan.

Mills, T. C. and Crafts, N. F. R. (1996) 'Trend growth in British industrial output, 1700–1913: a reappraisal', Explorations in Economic History, 33: 277–295.

Minsky, H. P. (1964) 'Longer waves in financial relations: financial factors in the more severe depressions', American Economic Review, 54: 324–335.

Mitchell, B. R. (1988) British Historical Statistics, Cambridge, Cambridge University Press.

Mitchell, W. C. (1913) Business Cycles, Berkeley, CA, University of California Press.

Mitchell, W. C. (1927) Business Cycles: The Problem and its Setting, New York, National Bureau of Economic Research.

Mokhtarian, P. L. (1990), 'A typology of relationships between telecommunications and transportation', Transportation Research, 24A(3): 231–242.

Mokyr, J. (1990) The Lever of Riches: Technological Creativity and Economic Progress, Oxford, Oxford University Press.

Mokyr, J. ed. (1999) The British Industrial Revolution, second edition, Boulder, CO, Westview Press.

Monkkonen, E. H. (1988) America Becomes Urban, Berkeley, CA, University of California Press.

Mosekilde, E., Larsen, E. R., Sterman, J. D. and Thomsen, J. S. (1992) 'Nonlinear mode-interaction in the macroeconomy', Annals of Operations Research, 37: 185–215.

Mouzakis, F. and Richards, D. (2007) 'Panel data modelling of prime office rents: a study of 12 major European markets', Journal of Property Research, 24(1): 31–53.

Muellbauer, J. and Murphy, A. (1990) 'Is the UK balance of payments sustainable?' Economic Policy, 11: 347–395.

Muellbauer, J. and Murphy, A. (1997) 'Booms and busts in the UK housing market', Economic Journal, 107: 1701–1727.

Mumford, L. (1961) The City in History, London, Secker and Warburg.

Munro, M. and Tu, Y. (1996) 'The dynamics of UK national and regional house prices', Review of Urban and Regional Development Studies, 8: 186–201.

Muth, J. F. (1961) 'Rational expectations and the theory of price movements', Econometrica, 29: 315–335.

Muth, R. F. (1969) Cities and Housing, Chicago, IL, University of Chicago Press.

Needleman, L. (1965) The Economics of Housing, London, Staples Press.

Nelson, C. R. and Kang, H. (1981) 'Spurious periodicity in inappropriately detrended time series', Econometrica, 49(3): 741–751.

Nelson, C. R. and Plosser, C. I. (1982) 'Trends and random walks in macroeconomic time series', Journal of Monetary Economics, 10: 139–162.

Nelson, R. R. (2005) Technology, Institutions and Economic Growth, Cambridge, MA, Harvard University Press.

Nelson, R. R. and Winter S. G. (1982) An Evolutionary Theory of Economic Change, Cambridge, MA, Harvard University Press.

Nerlove, M. (1958) 'Adaptive expectations and cobweb phenomena', Quarterly Journal of Economics, 72: 227–240.

Newbold, P. and Agiakloglou, C. (1991) 'Looking for evolving growth rates and cycles in British industrial production, 1700–1913', Journal of the Royal Statistical Society A, 154(2): 341–348.

Newman, P. and Kenworthy, J. (1999) Sustainability and Cities, Washington, DC, Island Press.

Newman, W. H. (1935) The Building Industry and Business Cycles, Studies in Business Administration V.4, Chicago, IL, University of Chicago Press.

OECD (2001) Measuring Capital: A Manual on the Measurement of Capital Stocks, Consumption of Fixed Capital and Capital Services, Paris, Organisation for Economic Co-operation and Development.

Oizumi, E. (1994) 'Property finance in Japan: expansion and collapse of the bubble economy', Environment and Planning A, 26: 199–213.

Okun, A. M. (1980) 'Rational-expectations-with-misperceptions as a theory of the business cycle', Journal of Money, Credit and Banking, 12(4): 817–825.

O'Leary, P. J. and Lewis, W. A. (1955) 'Secular swings in production and trade 1870–1913', Manchester School of Economic and Social Studies, 23(2): 113–152.

Olsen, D. J. (1976) The Growth of Victorian London, London, Batsford.

ONS (2007) Capital Stocks, Capital Consumption and Non-Financial Balance Sheets, London, Office for National Statistics.

Osborn, D. R. (1995) 'Moving average detrending and the analysis of business cycles', Oxford Bulletin of Economics and Statistics, 57(4): 547–558.

Palliser, D. M. ed. (2000) The Cambridge Urban History of Britain, volume I, 600–1540, Cambridge, Cambridge University Press.

Parry Lewis, J. (1964) 'Growth and inverse cycles: a two-country model', Economic Journal, 74: 109–118.

Parry Lewis, J. (1965) Building Cycles and Britain's Growth, London, Macmillan.

Perez, C. (1983) 'Structural change and assimilation of new technologies in the economic and social systems', Futures, 15: 357–375.

Perez, C. (2002) Technological Revolutions and Financial Capital, Cheltenham, Edward Elgar.

Perron, P. (1989) 'The Great Crash, the Oil Price Shock, and the unit root hypothesis', Econometrica, 57(6): 1361–1401.

Pesaran, M. H. and Pesaran B. (1997) Working with Microfit 4.0, Oxford, Oxford University Press.

Pevsner, N. (1970) An Outline of European Architecture, new impression edition, London, Penguin Books.

Phelps, E. S. (1990) Seven Schools of Macroeconomic Thought, Oxford, Clarendon Press.

Phillips, P. C. B. and Loretan, M. (1991) 'Estimating long-run economic equilibria', Review of Economic Studies, 58: 407–436.

Pigou, A. C. (1927) Industrial Fluctuations, London, Macmillan.

Pikovsky, A., Rosenblum, M. and Kurths, J. (2001) Synchronization: A universal concept in nonlinear sciences, Cambridge, Cambridge University Press.

Pindyck, R. S. and Rubinfeld, D. L. (1998) Econometric Models and Economic Forecasts, fourth edition, New York, McGraw-Hill.

Pollakowski, H. O., Wachter, S. M. and Lynford, L. (1992) 'Did office market size matter in the 1980s? A time-series cross-sectional analysis of metropolitan office markets', Journal of the American Real Estate and Urban Economics Association, 20(2): 303–324.

Pollard. S. (1983) The Development of the British Economy, 1914–1980, third edition, London, Edward Arnold.

Pollard, S. (1989) Britain's Prime and Britain's Decline: The British Economy 1870–1914, London, Edward Arnold.

Porter, R. (1994) London: A Social History, London, Hamish Hamilton.

Poterba, J. M. (1984) 'Tax subsidies to owner-occupied housing: an asset-market approach', Quarterly Journal of Economics, 99(4): 729–752.

Powell, C. G. (1980) An Economic History of the British Building Industry 1815–1979, London, Architectural Press.

Pred, A. R. (1966) The Spatial Dynamics of U.S. Urban-Industrial Growth, 1800–1914, Cambridge, MA, MIT Press.

Pred, A. R. (1977) City-Systems in Advanced Economies, London, Hutchinson.

Priestley, M. B. (1981) Spectral Analysis and Time Series, London, Academic Press.

Pryke, M. (1994) 'Looking back on the space of a boom: (re)developing spatial matrices in the City of London', Environment and Planning A, 26: 235–264.

Randall, F. A. (1999) History of the Development of Building Construction in Chicago, second edition, Urbana, IL, University of Illinois Press.

Rasmussen, S. E. (1982) London: The Unique City, revised edition, Cambridge, MA, MIT Press.

Rauch, J. E. (1993) 'Does history matter only when it matters little? The case of city-industry location', Quarterly Journal of Economics, 108: 843–867.

Reddaway, T. F. (1940) The Rebuilding of London after the Great Fire, London, Cape.

Reeder, D. and Rodger, R. (2000) 'Industrialisation and the city economy', in M. J. Daunton ed., The Cambridge Urban History of Britain, volume III, 1840–1950, Cambridge, Cambridge University Press, 553–592.

Reich, E. (1912) Der Wohnungsmarkt in Berlin von 1840–1910, Munich, Duncker und Humblot.

Reid, M. (1982) The Secondary Banking Crisis 1973–75, London, Macmillan.

Renaud, B. (1997) 'The 1985 to 1994 global real estate cycle: an overview', Journal of Real Estate Literature, 5: 13–44.

Renaud, B., Zhang, M. and Koeberle, S. (2001) 'Real estate and the Asian crisis: lessons of the Thailand experience', in S. J. Brown and C. H. Liu eds., A Global Perspective on Real Estate Cycles, Boston, MA, Kluwer, 25–61.

Renfrew, C. and Bahn, P. (1991), Archaeology: Theories, Methods and Practice, London, Thames and Hudson.

Revell, J. (1967) The Wealth of the Nation, Cambridge, Cambridge University Press.

Richardson, H. W. and Aldcroft, D. H. (1968) Building in the British Economy between the Wars, London, Allen and Unwin.

RICS (2000) Forecasting Office Supply and Demand, London, Royal Institution of Chartered Surveyors.

Riggleman, J. R. (1933) 'Building cycles in the United States, 1875–1932', Journal of the American Statistical Association, 28: 174–183.

Roberts, R. (2004) The City, London, The Economist.

Robertson, D. H. (1915) A Study of Industrial Fluctuation, London, King and Son.

Robson, B. T. (1973) Urban Growth, London, Methuen.

Rodger, R. (1989) Housing in Urban Britain, 1780–1914, Cambridge, Cambridge University Press.

Rogers, E. M. (2003) Diffusion of Innovations, fifth edition, New York, Free Press.

Roll, E. (1992) A History of Economic Thought, fifth edition, London, Faber.

Romer, P. M. (1986) 'Increasing returns and long-run growth', Journal of Political Economy, 94(5): 1002–1037.

Romer, P. M. (1990) 'Endogenous technological change', Journal of Political Economy, 98(5): S71–S102.

Rosen, K. T. (1984) 'Toward a model of the office building sector', Journal of the American Real Estate and Urban Economics Association, 12(3): 261–269.

Rosen, K. T. and Smith, L. B. (1983) 'The price-adjustment process for rental housing and the natural vacancy rate', American Economic Review, 73(4): 779–786.

Rosenberg, N. (1982) Inside the Black Box: Technology and Economics, Cambridge, Cambridge University Press.

Rosenberg, N. and Frischtak, C. R. (1983) 'Long waves and economic growth: a critical appraisal', American Economic Review, 73(2): 146–151.

Rosenthal, S. S. and Strange, W. C. (2004) 'Evidence on the nature and sources of agglomeration economies', in J. V. Henderson and J.-F. Thisse eds., Handbook of Regional and Urban Economics, volume 4, Cities and Geography, Amsterdam, Elsevier, 2119–2171.

Rostow, W. W. (1948) British Economy of the Nineteenth Century, Oxford, Clarendon Press.

Rostow, W. W. (1971) The Stages of Economic Growth, second edition, Cambridge, Cambridge University Press.

Rostow, W. W. (1975) 'Kondratieff, Schumpeter and Kuznets: trend periods revisited', Journal of Economic History, 35: 719–753.

Rostow, W. W. (1990) Theories of Economic Growth from David Hume to the Present, New York, Oxford University Press.

Rouwenhorst, K. G. (1991) 'Time to build and aggregate fluctuations: a reconsideration', Journal of Monetary Economics, 27: 241–254.

Sahlman, W. A. and Stevenson, H. H. (1985) 'Capital market myopia', Journal of Business Venturing, 1: 7–30.

Sakolski, A. M. (1932) The Great American Land Bubble, New York, Harper.

Salter, W. E. G. (1966) Productivity and Technical Change, second edition, Cambridge, Cambridge University Press.

Salway, F. W. (1986) Depreciation of Commercial Property, Reading, College of Estate Management.

Samuelson, P. A. (1939) 'Interactions between the multiplier analysis and the principle of acceleration', Review of Economic Statistics, 21: 75–78.

Sanderson, B., Farrelly, K. and Thoday, C. (2006) 'Natural vacancy rates in global office markets', Journal of Property Investment & Finance, 24(6): 490–520.

Sargent, T. J. and Wallace, N. (1976) 'Rational expectations and the theory of economic policy', Journal of Monetary Economics, 2: 169–183.

Sassen, S. (2001) The Global City, second edition, Princeton, NJ, Princeton University Press.

Sassen, S. (2006) Cities in a World Economy, third edition, Thousand Oaks CA, Pine Forge Press.

Saul, S. B. (1962) 'House building in England 1890–1914', Economic History Review, 15: 119–137.

Saul, S. B. (1985) The Myth of the Great Depression 1873–1896, second edition, Basingstoke, Macmillan.

Saunders, P. (1978) 'Domestic property and social class', International Journal of Urban and Regional Research, 2: 233–251.

Schabas, M. (1995) 'Parmenides and the cliometricians', in D. Little ed., On the Reliability of Economic Models: Essays in the Philosophy of Economics, Boston, MA, Kluwer, 183–202.

Scheidel, W., Morris, I. and Saller, R. eds. (2007) The Cambridge Economic History of the Greco-Roman World, Cambridge, Cambridge University Press.

Schmookler, J. (1966) Invention and Economic Growth, Cambridge, MA, Harvard University Press.

Schumpeter, J. A. (1927) 'The explanation of the business cycle', Economica, 21: 286–311.

Schumpeter, J. A. (1934) The Theory of Economic Development, Cambridge, MA, Harvard University Press.

Schumpeter, J. A. (1939) Business Cycles, two volumes, New York, McGraw-Hill.

Schumpeter, J. A. (1943) Capitalism, Socialism and Democracy, London, Allen and Unwin.

Scott, A. J. (1988) New Industrial Spaces, London, Pion.

Scott, P. (1994) 'Learning to multiply: the property market and the growth of multiple retailing in Britain, 1919–39', Business History, 36(3): 1–28.

Scott, P. (1996) The Property Masters, London, Spon.

Scott, P. (2000) 'The evolution of Britain's urban built environment', in M. J. Daunton ed., The Cambridge Urban History of Britain, volume III, 1840–1950, Cambridge, Cambridge University Press, 495–523.

Scott, P. (2001) 'Industrial estates and British industrial development, 1897–1939', Business History, 43(2): 73–98.

Scott, P. and Judge, G. (2000) 'Cycles and steps in British commercial property values', Applied Economics, 32: 1287–1297.

Setterfield, M. (1997) Rapid Growth and Relative Decline, Basingstoke, Macmillan.

Shackle, G. L. S. (1970) Expectation, Enterprise and Profit, London, Allen and Unwin.

Shannon, H. A. (1934) 'Bricks – A trade index 1785–1849', Economica, 3: 300–318.

Sheppard, F., Belcher, V. and Cottrell, P. (1979) 'The Middlesex and Yorkshire deeds registries and the study of building fluctuations', London Journal, 5: 176–217.

Sherman, H. J. (1991) The Business Cycle: Growth and Crisis under Capitalism, Princeton, NJ, Princeton University Press.

Shiller, R. J. (2005) Irrational Exuberance, second edition, Princeton, NJ, Princeton University Press.

Shilling, J. D., Sirmans, C. F. and Corgel, J. B. (1987) 'Price adjustment process for rental office space', Journal of Urban Economics, 22: 90–100.

Shleifer, A. (1986) 'Implementation cycles', Journal of Political Economy, 94: 1163–1190.

Short, J. R. (1982) Housing in Britain, London, Methuen.

Siegel, D. R. ed. (1990) Innovation and Technology in the Markets, Chicago, IL, Probus.

Silverberg, G., Dosi, G. and Orsenigo, L. (1988) 'Innovation, diversity and diffusion: a self-organisation model', Economic Journal, 98: 1032–1054.

Simmons, J. (1986) The Railway in Town and Country 1830–1914, Newton Abbot, David and Charles.

Simmons, P. A., ed. (2001) Housing Statistics of the United States, fourth edition, Lanham, MD, Bernan.

Simon, C. J. and Nardinelli, C. (1996) 'The talk of the town: human capital, information, and the growth of English cities, 1861 to 1961', Explorations in Economic History, 33: 384–413.

Simon, H. A. (1979) 'Rational decision making in business organizations', American Economic Review, 69(4): 493–513.

Simon, H. A. (1992) Economics, Bounded Rationality and the Cognitive Revolution, Aldershot, Edward Elgar.

Simpson, M. (1972) 'Urban transport and the development of Glasgow's West End, 1830–1914', Journal of Transport History, 1: 146–160.

Sivitanides, P. S. (1997) 'The rent adjustment process and the structural vacancy rate in the commercial real estate market', Journal of Real Estate Research, 13(2): 195–209.

Skinner, D. (2007) 'A move towards European retail', Journal of Property Investment and Finance, 25(2): 166–178.

Skinner, J. (1989) 'Housing wealth and aggregate saving', Regional Science and Urban Economics, 19: 305–324.

Skott, P. and Auerbach, P. (1995) 'Cumulative causation and the "new" theories of economic growth', Journal of Post Keynesian Economics, 17(3): 381–402.

Slutzky, E. (1937) 'The summation of random causes as the source of cyclical processes', Econometrica, 5: 105–146.

Smith, L. B. (1969) 'A model of the Canadian housing and mortgage markets', Journal of Political Economy, 77(5): 795–816.

Smith, L. B. (1974) 'A note on the rent adjustment mechanism for rental housing', American Economic Review, 64(3): 478–481.

Smith, M. R. and Marx, L. eds. (1994) Does Technology Drive History? Cambridge, MA, MIT Press.

Smithies, A. (1957) 'Economic fluctuations and growth', Econometrica, 25: 1–52.

Smyth, H. (1985) Property Companies and the Construction Industry in Britain, Cambridge, Cambridge University Press.

Sokoloff, K. L. (1988) 'Inventive activity in early industrial America: evidence from patent records, 1790–1846', Journal of Economic History, 48(4): 813–850.

Solomou, S. (1988) Phases of Economic Growth 1850–1973, Cambridge, Cambridge University Press.

Solomou, S. (1998) Economic Cycles, Manchester, Manchester University Press.

Solow, R. M. (1956) 'A contribution to the theory of economic growth', Quarterly Journal of Economics, 70(1): 65–94.

Solow, R. M. (1957) 'Technical change and the aggregate production function', Review of Economics and Statistics, 39: 312–320.

Solow, R. M. (1962) 'Technical progress, capital formation and economic growth', American Economic Review, 52: 76–86.

Solow, R. M. (2000) Growth Theory: An Exposition, second edition, New York, Oxford University Press.

Solow, R. M., Tobin, J., von Weizsacker, C. C, and Yaari, M. (1966) 'Neoclassical growth with fixed factor proportions', Review of Economic Studies, 33: 79–115.

Soper, J. C. (1975) 'Myth and reality in economic time series: the long swing revisited', Southern Economic Journal, 41: 570–579.

Sorensen, P. B. and Whitta-Jacobsen, H. J. (2005) Introducing Advanced Macroeconomics: Growth and Business Cycles, Maidenhead, McGraw-Hill.

Spensley, J. C. (1918) 'Urban housing problems', Journal of the Royal Statistical Society, 81(2): 161–210.

Stadler, G. W. (1994) 'Real business cycles', Journal of Economic Literature, 32: 1750–1783.

Starrett, W. A. (1928) Skyscrapers and the Men Who Build Them, New York, Charles Scribner.

Sterman, J. D. (1985) 'A behavioural model of the economic long wave', Journal of Economic Behaviour and Organization, 6: 17–53.

Stock, J. H. and Watson, M. W. (1988) 'Variable trends in economic time series', Journal of Economic Perspectives, 2(3): 147–174.

Stoneman, P. (1983) The Economic Analysis of Technological Change, Oxford, Oxford University Press.

Strogatz, S. H. (1994) Nonlinear Dynamics and Chaos, Cambridge, MA, Perseus Books.

Summerson, J. (1973) The London Building World of the Eighteen-Sixties, London, Thames and Hudson.

Summerson, J. (1977) 'The Victorian rebuilding of the City of London', London Journal, 3(2): 163–185.

Summerson, J. (1978) Georgian London, London, Penguin Books.

Sutcliffe, A. (2006) London: An Architectural History, London, Yale University Press.

Swan T. W. (1956) 'Economic growth and capital accumulation', Economic Record, 32: 334–361.

Syz, J. M. (2008) Property Derivatives, Chichester, Wiley.

Szostak, R. (1991) The Role of Transportation in the Industrial Revolution, Montreal, McGill-Queen's University Press.

Taylor, L. (2004) Reconstructing Macroeconomics, Cambridge, MA, Harvard University Press.

Taylor, P. J. (2004) World City Network, London, Routledge.

Taylor, W. R. (1992) In Pursuit of Gotham, New York, Oxford University Press.

Thomas, B. (1973) Migration and Economic Growth, second edition, Cambridge, Cambridge University Press.

Thompson, B. and Tsolacos, S. (1999) 'Rent adjustments and forecasts in the industrial market', Journal of Real Estate Research, 17(1/2): 151–167.

Thompson, F. M. L. ed. (1982) The Rise of Suburbia, Leicester, Leicester University Press.

Tinbergen, J. (1939) Statistical Testing of Business Cycle Theories, two volumes, Geneva, League of Nations.

Tinbergen, J. (1940) 'On a method of statistical business-cycle research. A reply', Economic Journal, 50: 141–154.

Tobin, J. (1980) 'Are new classical models plausible enough to guide policy?' Journal of Money, Credit and Banking, 12(4): 788–799.

Trollope, A. (1972) Phineas Finn, Penguin English Library, London, Penguin Books.

Tsolacos, S. (1995) 'Industrial property development in the UK: a regional analysis of new orders', Journal of Property Research, 12: 95–125.

Tsolacos, S. (1998) 'Econometric modelling and forecasting of new retail development', Journal of Property Research, 15(4): 265–283.

Tsolacos, S. and McGough, T. (1999) 'Rational expectations, uncertainty and cyclical activity in the British office market', Urban Studies, 36(7): 1137–1149.

Tsolacos, S., Keogh, G. and McGough, T. (1998) 'Modelling use, investment, and development in the British office market', Environment and Planning A, 30: 1409–1427.

Turnbull, G. (1987) 'Canals, coal and regional growth during the industrial revolution', Economic History Review, 40(4): 537–560.

Turvey, R. (1998) 'Office rents in the City of London 1867–1910', London Journal, 23(2): 53–67.

Tylecote, A. (1991) The Long Wave in the World Economy, London, Routledge.

Underhill, P. (2004) Call of the Mall, New York, Simon and Schuster.

United Nations (2007) World Urbanization Prospects, New York, Population Division.

Vaggi, G. and Groenewegen, P. (2003) A Concise History of Economic Thought, Basingstoke, Palgrave Macmillan.

van Ark, B., O'Mahony, M. and Timmer, M. P. (2008) 'The productivity gap between Europe and the United States: trends and causes', Journal of Economic Perspectives, 22(1): 25–44.

van Duijn, J. J. (1983) The Long Wave in Economic Life, London, Allen and Unwin.

Veblen, T. (1904) The Theory of Business Enterprise, New York, Charles Scribner.

Velupillai, K. ed. (1990) Nonlinear and Multisectoral Macrodynamics: Essays in Honour of Richard Goodwin, London, Macmillan.

Verspagen, B. (1992) Endogenous innovation in neo-classical growth models: a survey, Journal of Macroeconomics, 14(4): 631–662.

Vigier, F. (1970) Change and Apathy: Liverpool and Manchester During the Industrial Revolution, Cambridge, MA, MIT Press.

Vipond, M. J. (1969) 'Fluctuations in private housebuilding in Great Britain 1950–66', Scottish Journal of Political Economy, 16: 196–211.

von Thünen J. H. (1826) Der Isolierte Staat in Beziehung auf Landschaft und Nationalökonomie, Hamburg, translated by C. M. Wartenberg (1966) von Thünen's Isolated State, Oxford, Pergamon.

Waller, P. J. (1983) Town, City and Nation, Oxford, Clarendon Press.

Ward, D. (1964) 'A comparative historical geography of streetcar suburbs in Boston, Massachusetts and Leeds, England: 1850–1920', Annals of the Association of American Geographers, 54: 477–489.

Ward-Perkins, J. B. (1981) Roman Imperial Architecture, second edition, London, Penguin Books.

Warner, S. B. (1962) Streetcar Suburbs, Cambridge, MA, Harvard University Press.

Warner, S. B. (1972) The Urban Wilderness, New York, Harper and Row.

Warren, G. F. and Pearson, F. A. (1937) World Prices and the Building Industry, New York, John Wiley.

Watson, M. W. (1986) 'Univariate detrending methods with stochastic trends', Journal of Monetary Economics, 18: 49–75.

Watson, M. W. (1994) 'Business-cycle durations and postwar stabilization of the US economy', American Economic Review, 84(1): 24–46.

Weber, B. (1955) 'A new index of residential construction and long cycles in house-building in Great Britain, 1838–1950', Scottish Journal of Political Economy, 2(2): 104–132.

Weber, B. (1960) 'A new index of house rents for Great Britain, 1874–1913', Scottish Journal of Political Economy, 7: 232–237.

Weintraub, E. R. (1979) Microfoundations: The Compatibility of Microeconomics and Macroeconomics, Cambridge, Cambridge University Press.

Weiss, M. A. (1987) The Rise of the Community Builders, New York, Columbia University Press.

Wheaton, W. C. (1987) 'The cyclic behavior of the national office market', Journal of the American Real Estate and Urban Economics Association, 15(4): 281–299.

Wheaton, W. C. (1999) 'Real estate "cycles": some fundamentals', Real Estate Economics, 27(2): 209–230.

Wheaton, W. C. and Torto, R. G. (1988) 'Vacancy rates and the future of office rents', Journal of the American Real Estate and Urban Economics Association, 16(4): 430–436.

Wheaton, W. C. and Torto, R. G. (1990) 'An investment model of the demand and supply for industrial real estate', Journal of the American Real Estate and Urban Economics Association, 18(4): 530–547.

Wheaton, W. C. and Torto, R. G. (1994) 'Office rent indices and their behaviour over time', Journal of Urban Economics, 35: 121–139.

Wheaton, W. C., Torto, R. G. and Evans, P. (1997) 'The cyclic behaviour of the Greater London office market', Journal of Real Estate Finance and Economics, 15(1): 77–92.

Whitehand, J. W. R. (1987) The Changing Face of Cities, Oxford, Blackwell.

Williams, K., Burton, E. and Jenks, M., eds. (2000), Achieving Sustainable Urban Form, London, Spon.

Williamson, J. (1984) 'Why was British growth so slow during the industrial revolution?' Journal of Economic History, 44(3): 687–712.

Willis, C. (1995) Form Follows Finance, New York, Princeton Architectural Press.

Witkiewicz, W. (2002) 'The use of the HP-filter in constructing real estate cycle indicators', Journal of Real Estate Research, 23(1/2): 65–87.

Wrigley, E. A. (1987) People, Cities and Wealth, Oxford, Blackwell.

Wrigley, E. A. (2004) 'British population during the "long" eighteenth century 1680–1840', in R. Floud and P. Johnson eds., The Cambridge Economic History of Modern Britain, volume I, Cambridge, Cambridge University Press, 57–95.

Wrigley, E. A. and Schofield, R. S. (1989) The Population History of England 1541–1871, Cambridge, Cambridge University Press.

Yeates, M. H. (1965) 'Some factors affecting the spatial distribution of Chicago land values, 1910–1960', Economic Geography, 41: 57–70.

Young, A. (1928) 'Increasing returns and economic progress', Economic Journal, 38: 527–542.

Young, A. (1993) 'Invention and bounded learning by doing', Journal of Political Economy, 101(3): 443–472.

Youngson Brown, A. J. (1951) The American Economy 1860–1940, London, Allen and Unwin.

Zarnowitz, V. (1992) Business Cycles: Theory, History, Indicators and Forecasting, Chicago, IL, University of Chicago Press.

Zarnowitz, V. (1998) 'Has the business cycle been abolished?' Business Economics, 33(4): 39–45.

Zook, M. A. (2005) The Geography of the Internet Industry, Oxford, Blackwell.

Index